The
FILM EDITING ROOM
Handbook

Third Edition

HOW TO MANAGE THE NEAR CHAOS OF THE CUTTING ROOM

by Norman Hollyn

lone eagle™
PUBLISHING COMPANY

Los Angeles, CA

THE FILM EDITING ROOM HANDBOOK
Or, How To Manage The Near Chaos of the Cutting Room

LONE EAGLE PUBLISHING COMPANY™
1024 North Orange Avenue
Hollywood, CA 90038-2318
Tel: 800-345-6257; 310-471-8066
www.loneeagle.com & www.eaglei.com

Printed in the United States of America

First Lone Eagle Printing—April 1990
Cover design by Lindsay Albert
Book design by Carla Green
Edited by Lauren Rossini
Photo of author by Janet Conn

Library of Congress Cataloging-in-Publication Data

Hollyn, Norman
    The film editing room handbook : how to avoid the near-chaos of the cutting
    room / by Norman Hollyn. — 3rd ed.
        p.   cm.
    Includes bibliographical references and index.
    ISBN 0-580-65000-6 (alk. paper)
    1. Motion pictures—Editing—Handbooks, manuals, etc.   I. Title.
    TR899.H64 1998   98-30708
    778.5'35–dc21   CIP

Distributed to the trade by National Book Network, 800-462-6420

Lone Eagle Publishing Company is a registered trademark.

CONTENTS

iv

ACKNOWLEDGMENTS

The editing process has changed drastically since the second edition of this book was written over eight years ago. And as the filmmaking world around me has transformed, so have I. Yet one thing remains the same. As I wrote in both earlier editions of this book: "I have yet to have an editing room job in which I did not learn something about editing, filmmaking, or people." Not all of the jobs that I have worked on nor all the people I've worked with have been fun. Still, I maintain that it is possible, no—necessary, to learn with every job. When that stops happening, it's time to start selling real estate.

In this spirit of learning, I dedicate this latest edition to all of those people that *I've* learned from, with the hope that this text will be able to teach.

I would like to thank the rooting section for this book, in both its original and later editions—Bob, for kind words and sage advice (he's still getting sager all the time), Lou, who was there at the beginning but, sadly, will never get to see this latest edition, Joan, for getting behind me this third time (book publishers put up with as much nonsense as film editors do), Bethann for all of her support and prodding, Lauren for plowing through the book in record time, Alan Bell for fact checking, Nancy and Joe and their family for moral and emotional support, and David Fechtor and others (you know who you are), for suggesting corrections. My Mom and Dad deserve a special award for their continued support and love. Thanks for being there.

Every job has its continuous ups and downs; life is no exception. There is no way I can express enough love, admiration and thanks to my wife, Janet, for being my steady co-captain during both the rocky and smooth portions of our voyage. Words are inadequate to describe my emotions. I will always be in her loving debt.

When I wrote the first edition of this book, my daughter Elizabeth wasn't even around. When I wrote the second edition, she wasn't old enough to know what it was that I was doing hunched over the keyboard late at night. Now she is old enough to read the book and give criticism. She has changed more than the editing world has, taking me along on a wonderful, joyous ride. My life is much richer for it. Thank you. I love you.

And a final thank you to Jasper. He's been by my side during much of the writing of this book, silently supporting me through thick and thin.

Believe me, the result of all of these people's help is a better and richer book than I could ever had written if I had been without them. Thank you everyone.

INTRODUCTION TO THE THIRD EDITION

Eight years ago, in the introduction to the last edition of this book, I wrote: "...it is now possible to see the day when editors and directors will be able to make the choice as to whether they would like to cut on film or video." The reality today, at the begining of the twenty-first century, is that there is almost no choice to be made. Unless budget dictates otherwise, almost all film and television is now cut on digital electronic editing machines (and I now use *that* term, rather than "video").

Once the digital editing transition hit the industry, the changes happened fast. Sound editing transformed first, quickly followed by television post-production. Now, feature films have moved almost completely over to electronic editing. Almost no part of the editing world has remained untouched by technology. Editors have had to learn new technology, adapt to new job demands, and grapple with reduced staffs. Assistant editors have had to learn new techniques to go with this technology. But, just as I wrote in the introduction to the last edition, the basic skills needed to make an assistant editor a *good* assistant editor have changed very little. There is still the need for organization, planning and a pleasant personality.

The changes have been so wide-ranging that the second edition of this book seemed increasingly, hopelessly, out of date. Not only had editing changed, but *electronic* editing was changing nearly monthly.

Still, feature films are shot on film and made to be released on film. Many of the tasks a good assistant needed to know remain the same, there is just a lot more to learn and know in addition to all the old skills. Now, it is just as important to know a computer operating system as it is to know how an optical is created.

As a result, parts of this book were required to remain the same as its second edition. There are additions and changes, of course, but like the job description of the assistant editor, this book hasn't completely changed so much as it has grown more complex. Not only are the old film skills important and documented here, but computer editing skills also need to be developed and written about. As I said in the last edition, at its core film editing is still film editing. All of the skills and systems developed over many decades to make the putting together of thousands of little pieces of celluloid go smoothly, are just as applicable today as they were eight years ago. On second thought, make that "twenty-five years ago." On third thought, make that "when assistant editors first started assistant editing."

INTRODUCTION

At the end of my first week working on my first feature film I rushed out to the producer's bank to cash my very first paycheck. Though I saw long lines, I was not dismayed. I had in my hands a check from United Artists/Marvin Worth Productions proclaiming in bold letters: *Lenny*. I was working on a film with Dustin Hoffman! Surely the bank officers would usher me to the front of the line and give me my money without so much as a glance at my identification.

Of course, it didn't work out that way. Not only did I have to wait in line with everyone else, but when it finally was my turn, the teller refused to give me any money because I didn't have an account with the bank.

Thus I learned my first and perhaps most valuable lesson about working in the film business: film editing is a job—make no mistake about that. After all of the mumbo-jumbo we read about the movies and their glamour, it is a bit of a shock to learn that people working in moviemaking are judged by the same criteria as the rest of the world: how well they get the job done. Your standing in the business comes from how well you do the job, not just from the fact that you are doing it.

The second lesson to be learned about film editing is that there are a lot of ways to get the job done. Line up twenty different editors or assistant editors and you'll probably get twenty different systems of organizing a cutting room. Many work, some do not, but the worst thing you can do is attempt to impose the system that worked on film 'A' onto the very different film 'B'. One of the tests of a good editing crew member is flexibility. And with the arrival of computer and digital editing, organizational tasks change seemingly every month.

That leads to lesson number three—it takes a certain type of person to be comfortable in the field of editing. Flexible working habits are just the first necessity. You have to be able to work long days, long weeks, and long months in a small, dark, crowded room with the same small group of people. You have to be able to concentrate on the tiniest detail and never give up until it is right. Editing can be an obsession, good editing almost certainly is. The editing of any film usually requires large amounts of energy, not all of it well or gratifyingly spent. To work under these conditions takes real dedication.

Anyone interested in film editing as a career would be well advised to internalize these rules before setting foot into a cutting room. For, while I try to talk in this book about film editing rooms and the nuts-and-bolts techniques used in running them, I could never write about how to *be* an assistant film editor. You either are or you're not—or you learn how to be, by living in an editing room day after long day, month after long month.

If you are interested in editing as a way to meet people and become a director or a producer, forget about working there. Some editors eventually do make those transitions, but only after years of editing and being good at it. And the only way to do both of those things is to love what you are doing.

If you are a person easily bored by details and constant repetition, you can also forget editing as a profession. Eventually, editors get past the most mundane details, but until they reach that point these details are their life, and it helps to be able to deal with that.

If you are a person who needs a complete, separate, private life—you might as well forget most forms of editing. Fourteen–hour days and six– or seven–day weeks leave very little time for life as others know it. Unless friends and loved ones are as flexible as you are, film editing's hours will leave you (and them) very unhappy.

But, all of that having been said, I can tell you this—once you do it, it is all worth it.

And let that be lesson number four.

This book is written primarily for those who have an active interest in how a professional cutting room operates. To help those who are thinking of making it their career, I will often be quite detailed, though this may give more information than the normal film student would like. There is an additional purpose to this. Editing room procedures have been developed over many years to expedite the editing process. Therefore many of the techniques could be of help to *all* filmmakers, regardless of their budget or the type of film they are doing. However, since few film teachers or professors are also professional film editors, these techniques are rarely taught. This book will, I hope, give film students, independent filmmakers, and others enough knowledge about editing room procedures that they can decide for themselves just how they can best organize *their* editing process to conserve the time and money usually in such short supply. It won't be necessary to completely ape every system I explain in the book, but the discussion should help them choose which things are important in their own editing rooms.

Film buffs will probably be both fascinated and overwhelmed by the sheer mass of technical data here. To them, my apologies. But I believe that to truly understand the art of film, the *modus operandi* of the film editor must be understood as well. In the years to come, as increasing sophistication opens the film audience up to an awareness of film editing, those film buffs who know *how* it is done will be in a much better position to say *why* it is done.

A friend of mine describes the assistant's job as "primarily grunt work."

An assistant editor is defined, under the IATSE Local 771 (East Coast) contract as "a person who is directly assigned to assist the Editor(s) and a person who, among other duties, may be engaged in: synchronizing dailies, taking notes at screenings, obtaining cutting room facilities, breaking down daily takes, pulling out and assembling selected takes, making trims, ordering opticals, and performing other preparatory work in editing rooms."

The IATSE Local 776 (West Coast) contract defines the assistant as "...a person who is assigned to assist an Editor. His duties shall be such as are assigned to him and performed under the immediate direction, supervision and responsibility of the editor to who he is assigned to assist."

Frankly, though I dislike all of these definitions, I much prefer the last one (despite its innate sexism). The assistant's main task, as I see it, is to make sure the cutting room runs smoothly for the editor. Period.

The implications of that statement are what this book is all about. Assistant editing always seems to boil down to this one question: "How can I make this run better?"

Keeping the editing room functioning depends upon many things. One of the most important is controlling the film. An average film prints about twenty miles of 35mm film. That footage might be transferred onto approximately forty or more videotapes and matching computer disks. Additionally, many of today's films use a large amount of special effects work—film is digitally manipulated to add spaceships, remove wires, and a host of other visuals. Vast amounts of film and video are created.

A good assistant should be able to locate, almost immediately, pieces as short as one–sixteenth of an inch long (one frame in 35mm). To this end, editing staffs have, over the years, developed a number of methods for logging, storing, and retrieving footage. As anyone who has ever looked for editing room work and been denied it can tell you, this is what is called "the system." I, and almost every other editor I know, would rather hire someone who knows this system over someone who doesn't, all other things being equal. As we shall soon see, however, there is no real mystery to this system; it is all rather logical and straightforward.

So why would people rather hire someone who knows the system? Simply put, the real test of an assistant editor comes when the editor is cutting fast and furiously. There is rarely time for the assistant to step back and think about how to handle new situations. The more you have internalized this system (and the more you have internalized the exceptions to the system) the more efficiently you will be able to serve the editor during these constant crisis situations. This is where the experienced (and good) editing staff earns its salary.

Network, for example, was nearly a textbook case in proper editing room procedure. Everything seemed so easy to me. It was a dialogue film, for starters. The director, Sidney Lumet, shot in a straightforward style using only a single camera (except in some of the television studio/control room scenes). There were no complicated effects or opticals. Lumet shot very little footage; usually no more than 3000 feet (about twenty-seven minutes) were printed per day. The script supervisor, Kay Chapin, was a model of efficiency; her notes were explicit, fast, and accurate. I cannot remember a day when the picture and sound crews forgot to get slates for synching purposes, or when their reports were inaccurate or misleading. There was only one editor on the film, Alan Heim, and he was wonderfully efficient. He worked on an upright Moviola, cutting primarily in the order that the scenes had been shot. Dailies were shown every evening after the day's shoot, so we had plenty of time to prepare for them and still go about the business of cutting the picture.

Less than one week after the completion of shooting, a first cut of the film was ready for Lumet to see. And no wonder. The wheels of the entire process had worked exceedingly smoothly, helping us in the editing room do our jobs very fast and just as effortlessly.

But *Network* was a rarity. Other films, with equally fine crews, can be very problematic.

Hair, for instance, was an organizational task of immense proportions. First, it was a musical, and that complicated the task. Then, the director, Milos Forman, was shooting with multiple cameras (most often with two, but on some days there were as many as seven) and shooting a lot of footage. Days when we had to sync 10,000 feet of film were very common; there were several days when we had 25,000 feet. Because of the subject matter of the film as well as Forman's personal style, much of the footage was neither as predictable nor as easily categorized as that from *Network*. Despite a superb script supervisor, keeping up with the film was a Herculean task. Not surprisingly, there were days when her notes, the camera and sound reports, and the processed footage and sound transfers, bore little resemblance to each other. There was one, then were two, and then three editors on the film, all working on KEM flatbeds. Flatbeds, as we shall see, are more difficult to organize in general, but the fact that three editors were cutting at once added to the assistant's tasks. Dailies were often shown in the mid-afternoon on the set, and when the film was shooting out on location, the footage would not arrive in the cutting room until the afternoon. Both of these cases gave the editing staff no more than a few hours to sync the dailies.

In short, *Hair* tested the organization of its editing crew to the utmost. The fact that we kept everything moving, accessible, and pleasant is a testament to what good, experienced crews can do with a good, workable system.

Today, with the advent of computer editing systems much of the most boring cataloguing work is handled by the editing system. However, computers being what they are, they can only process the information given them, so it is up to the assistant to verify the accuracy of every piece of information put into the computer. At various times during the editing of the film, the assistant will need to take data out of the computer. If the information is entered incorrectly (either manually or automatically), it will be just as bad for the production as if there were three feet of film missing from a trim bin.

But organizing and accessing footage is only one part of an assistant's mandate to "keep things moving." He or she must be the editing crew's link to the outside world, interacting with the suppliers, laboratories, job seekers, and the general chaos arriving at the editing room door every day.

Much of the assistant's day is spent on the phone making things happen. Equipment always seems to be breaking down; labs never seem to give you exactly what you've asked for; supplies always seem to be used up too fast; job seekers always seem to show up with their resumés just as the director walks in the door; and the editor always seems to need you just when you are in the middle of solving another crisis. The assistant editor must be able to cope with all of this, sort it out, and make it all work. As we say in the business: "That's what they pay us the teeny–tiny bucks for."

The task of organizing an editing room is generally assigned to an assistant editor. For that reason, we will examine editing from the assistant's point of view in this book. There are three types of editors in feature filmmaking: picture, sound, and music. Each of the assistants to these various editors perform some tasks that are similar to the others', and some that are particular to their specific department. Because the first assistant picture editor is usually on the film before any other assistant, it is he or she who often has the information and experience with the film that the other assistants need. Therefore, an unwritten chain of command exists in the editing room. Both the sound and music departments maintain their own semi–autonomous crews, with apprentices taking direction from assistants who take direction from editors. The picture department has a similar chain of command, but it is the responsibility of the picture department to provide the sound and music people with all the help and information that they can give and, in exchange, the sound and music departments report to the picture department. Thus, the supervising picture editor is regarded as the ultimate editorial arbiter (though, of course, that editor is responsible to higher powers, like the producer and director) and the first assistant editor is the ultimate editorial organization arbiter.

In recent years, with the advent of digital editing rooms, a fourth type of assistant has also evolved: the digital assistant. On smaller films and most television shows, the first assistant editor performs this job. On larger films this person is responsible for all of the tasks involving the digital editing machines. This digital assistant (who will often have the title of "Avid Assistant" or "Lightworks Assistant") usually reports to the first assistant editor, who remains the nexus for most of the crucial information in the editing process.

Regardless of what kind of film you work on, you will find that the tasks of these three departments have to get done one way or another. In many documentaries and low–budget films, one person does the work of all three departments. In still other situations, the editor functions as his or her own assistant. But, no matter who is doing the work, those tasks always exist in roughly the same chronological order as in the feature film.

You will find this book organized, more or less, in this chronological order—the order that the assistant will normally have to deal with the problems. As you read about how to make a cutting room work, therefore, you will also get a tour of the filmmaking process itself, as seen through the editor's eyes.

Because of the importance of both film procedures and the newer digital editing systems I have chosen to break the book up into sets of dual chapters. In the first chapter of every pair (which I've numbered normally, Chapter 1, 2, 3, 4, etc.) I discuss the various facets of editing in a film-based editing room, that is, a cutting room using 35mm or 16mm film. In the second chapter of every pair (which I've indicated with the letter "A," Chapter 1A, 2A, 3A, 4A, etc.) I discuss the same portion of the editorial process from the point of view of a film that is being cut digitally. On many features it is important to know both parts of each set of chapters.

What you will not find in this book is a discussion of the aesthetics of film editing except as they influence the assistant's job. There are already several books and articles covering that subject (for a list of some of these works, see the Bibliography). What I hope becomes apparent from this book is that there is also an "aesthetics of assistant editing." There are good and bad ways to organize, there are smart and stupid ways to try to keep things moving. And when everything is working properly, the organization has a beauty all its own.

N.H.

CAST OF CHARACTERS

Throughout this book, I refer to a core group of people working in the editing rooms of our fictional film, *Silent Night, Silent Cowboy*. For your convenience, here is a list of who they are and what their functions on the film are.

Director .... Adam Free
Editor .... Wendy Libre
Assistant Editor .... You
Apprentice Editor .... Philip Spring
Composer .... Lester von Beethoven
Music Editor .... Nate High
Assistant Music Editor .... Betty Bound
Supervising Sound Editor .... Charles "Chuck" Lone
Assistant Sound Editor.. Liz Clear
Looping Editor .... Glynis Lowe

EDITING WITHIN
THE FILMMAKING PROCESS

Making a movie is often compared to running a war. It is a huge, complicated process, involving hundreds of people who must all be in the right place at the right time. They are all involved in their own chains of command with one or two leaders at the very top who determine, for right or for wrong, the course of their work. It is an exhausting process that is not often very fulfilling until the film is complete and viewable.

1

Editing is just one part of the movie–making battlefield but it is for me one of the most important parts, since it is where all the disparate elements come together. Whoever controls the editing process (and this can be the director, the producer, the distributor, or, in a few cases, the editor) controls how the film is presented to the public. That person can, with the changes that can be made through editing, save or ruin a film. If the shooting process is one of creating, the editing process is one of *re*creating.

The overall filmmaking process is divided into three handy categories—preproduction, production, and post-production. Much has been written about the general process and I won't attempt to delve very deeply into it, but here is a brief description of the tortuous road that a film must take to get to your neighborhood theatre.

Preproduction

The very earliest stage of moviemaking begins with an idea. Either a writer, producer, director or studio executive gets an idea for a film that is then sold to a movie company. As soon as the money is exchanged, the writer begins writing and the other facets of the production begin to come together. A director must be chosen, if none is already involved. A cast and crew are hired. Chief among these is the production manager, who will supervise the day-to-day operations for the producer. This production manager (sometimes called the line producer) determines the actual budget and shooting schedule, supervises the obtaining of locations and equipment, makes most of the deals with the crew members (cast salaries and some heads of departments are handled by the producer) and, in general, makes sure that everything will be in place for the first day of shooting.

Production

When that day arrives, a battery of people descend on the set. On *Four Friends*, there were days when over 120 cast and crew were working. On *Cotton Club* there were often days when we had that many crew members alone (not to mention the dozens of cast, extras, and dancers; for a total over 250). Even on the low-budget film *Heathers* the average day saw nearly 70 people involved in making the movie. There are departments to handle every conceivable job—from lighting the set to providing the cigarette lighters the actors will use, from supplying bushes and shrubs to training the cats, dogs, sheep and cattle that may be used, and from driving the cars that transport the crew members to managing the special effects that will make it seem to rain or snow on cue.

2

While all of this chaos is occurring on the set, the editor and staff are quietly working away in another location, perhaps even another city. They are organizing it so that the people on the set can see the results of the previous day's work (called the *rushes* or *dailies*). At the same time, they are beginning to cut the film.

Requests flood in from the set. "We need to reshoot part of a scene, how was the lead character wearing his tie?" or "The sound on one take last night wasn't very good, do we need to get a wild line?" Each question is important and the answer can't come too soon. And, all the while, the film is being edited together.

Post-Production

When the film is finished shooting, most of the production crew goes off to find other work, the director takes a short vacation and, after a week or so, he or she and the editing crew meet in the editing room or a small theatre to screen the cut that the editor has been working on during the shooting. Afterwards, they begin recutting the film, attempting to bring out what is good in the film and trying to minimize what is not. There are several screenings, after each version (or *cut*) is completed and, slowly, a film emerges from the mass of raw material shot on the set.

The movie is periodically taken into a screening room or movie theatre and previewed for the general public. After each preview you ask the audience questions. Generally, studios like to have a more finished soundtrack and cleaner looking picture for these previews so often sound and music editors are brought on for this series of previews.

Marketing people from the distributor begin to make plans for the publicity campaign—posters, trailers (those "coming attractions" you see in movie theatres), television spots, promotions, etc.

Sound editors are hired to begin work on the sound effects and dialogue where the soundtrack needs to be cleaned up. If some of the lines need to be redone for clarity, members of the cast are brought into a recording studio to rerecord the lines. A composer is hired and a music editor assists in creating a score for the film.

Finally the film's sound is mixed together into one soundtrack for the film's release. The original negative is cut to match the editor's cuts and the color is corrected on every shot used. The picture and the soundtrack are then *married* onto one piece of film and the first full screening of the movie can take place!

After that, the film opens and (everyone hopes) is very successful. All of the editing crew members can then go off of some badly needed vacations or onto other work on other films.

EDITING IN A DIGITAL WORLD

4

As anyone who has spent any time in the editing world in the last five years can tell you, non-linear editing systems have taken over the film editing process. It is now as essential for the assistant editor to know how to work on computer/digital non-linear systems as it is for them to know the difference between KEM and Moviola systems. As a result we will cover both film and computer systems in this book.

People use many different terms to talk about computer editing. Some call it just that—"computer editing." Others call it "non-linear editing." Still others call it "digital editing" or "electronic editing." Each of these terms has its own values. Sure, this style of editing is done with a computer, but computers are used in other non-editing functions in the editing room. Sure, this style of editing is non-linear (we'll define this term in a minute), but so is traditional film editing. Sure, when this editing is done with computers it uses digital imagery, but there are many times when videotape (a non-digital, as well as a linear, medium) is necessary in the editing process. And, as for "electronic editing"—that term is very broad and takes into account many forms of editing not within the scope of this book. For the purposes of this book I will use all four terms, often interchangeably. The term that I prefer, however, is "digital editing" since I think *this* is what differentiates the new editing and assistant processes from their earlier counterparts.

A Brief History of Linear Editing

Years ago, when videotape first became popular for television storage and viewing, shows were edited on film in the old-fashioned way and transferred to videotape for airing. Editing of the video-tape was not usually necessary using this method, but eventually some producers (especially of live and news shows) wanted to cut the expense of finishing on film by physically editing the videotape. At first, tape was edited just like film—a razor blade was used to slice the tape into small pieces. These individual strips of videotape were then taped (or *spliced*) together.

There were countless problems with this method. First, be-cause it is impossible to see an image on tape, it was difficult to make edits exactly on the "frame line." Second, if the editor wanted to change a cut it was hard to splice consecutive frames back to-gether again without getting some unwanted interference. It was a lot like the old days when film was cut with a razor blade and then cemented back together, losing frames in the process.

To solve these editing problems, clever engineers came up with another way of editing videotape. With this new system you never actually cut the dailies of your film. Instead, you played the dailies tapes back while simultaneously making a videotape copy (this pro-cess is called making a *transfer*; the video copy is called either a *transfer* or a *dub*) of exactly the section you wanted. Then you found the piece of the next shot you wanted and transferred *that* to the end of the first transferred piece. This way, you were able to as-semble an entire show without destroying the original tapes.

5

Of course, there were problems with this method. It was just as difficult to find the exact frame lines on which to start and stop transferring the tapes as it had been in making physical slices with a razor. Eventually, the engineers were able to solve this problem when they discovered it was much easier for a *machine* to find the frame lines than for a human to do so (though it is more expensive for a machine). Technicians invented a machine that could find frames and start and stop the copying process so precisely there was no visible interference at the point where one shot was cut to another.

A second problem with this method arose because one piece of videotape looked very much like any other part to these editing machines, unlike celluloid, where there were all sorts of identifying numbers put on the film. This made it more difficult to recognize and locate particular frames on tape than on film.

This problem was solved when the Society of Motion Picture and Television Engineers (SMPTE, pronounced "simptee") came up with a standard for a special series of numbers that could be elec-tronically recorded on the tape. It was called SMPTE Time Code. In theory, a SMPTE code number could be used very much like a film code number except, rather than calling a particular frame

"106A2034," as you might with an edge code number in film (don't worry about these terms, we'll cover them in more detail in Chapter 4), you would name a particular video frame 3:07:36:19, for instance. Now, before we get to wrapped up in how SMPTE saved the day, let's take a brief break from our history of non-linear editing to talk about SMPTE codes.

A Short Course in SMPTE Time Code

The entire basis for videotape and digital editing is based on the ability of a computer to identify each individual frame instantaneously and accurately. The ability to do this is based on the SMPTE Time Code. But, like everything else in this world of electronic editing, SMPTE is not as simple as it may seem.

SMPTE numbers are electronic signals, standardized to include a lot of information is used to identify the particular frame the code number is associated with, say 3:07:36:19. This number is the sequential hour, minute, second and frame from an assigned starting point. Thus, if we assign the start mark for reel number three the SMPTE code three hours (3:00:00:00), the first frame of the picture (which would be at twelve 35mm feet, or eight seconds) would be called 3:00:08:00 and the frame with code number 3:07:36:19 would probably run seven minutes, 36 seconds and 19 frames after that start mark.

Now, let me explain that word "probably."

Video footages run a little different than film footages. For one thing, there are 30 frames to each second, rather than 24. Thus, a SMPTE number of 3:07:36:29 would be followed by 3:07:37:00. Also, because of the way SMPTE code and video work, each second of video time will not really be precisely one second of real time. Thus, a reel that started at 3:00:00:00 and was nine minutes and 35 seconds long would not end at 3:09:35:00. This became confusing to people who needed to know real-time lengths. As a result, another type of SMPTE code standard was developed. In it, periodic frame numbers were dropped, so at the end of nine minutes and 35 seconds the SMPTE Code numbers would read, properly, 3:09:35:00. This type of SMPTE code became known as *drop frame* code. The original type of code became known as *non-drop frame*. Both types of code are still in use today and many recording studios and computer composing programs are able to use either type of code. The code of choice, however, seems to be non-drop frame.

Whichever time code you use, editing systems count on the fact that, using SMPTE Code, every frame of videotaped dailies can be assigned a unique code number, just like film. The computer running the editing machine can store this number and use it to find the exact frames the editor needs to use for his or her cut points.

Back to Our History Lesson

With the invention of the electronic editing machine and SMPTE code many of the barriers to effective editing on tape began to disappear. But there was still one giant problem: the linearity of the tape medium.

Just what do I mean by "linearity"? Well, let me give an example.

Let's say you made a series of one hundred and fifty edits (this is a normal number of edits in about ten minutes of film), one after another on the transferred ("recorded") videotape. Now let's say your director wanted you to make the fifth cut ten frames longer. On film you could simply find and insert those ten frames at the end of shot number five (before shot number six). Using our tape editing/transferring process, however, there would be no way to physically insert ten frames of video into the already copied videotape. Remember, we would not be physically cutting the videotape, merely transferring the image from the original tapes to the recorded tape (the "*dub*"). If you retransferred shot number five onto the videotape and extended it ten frames you would have recorded on top of the first ten frames of shot number six. Videotape editing, in which shots must be laid down one after another in a linear fashion, is therefore called *linear editing*. And it is this linearity that creates the difficulty in editing videotape.

7

The work-around solution to this problem was for the editor to record a completely new videotape with all of the same cuts, adding the additional ten frames at the end of shot number five. Even with an automated editing machine remaking the edits, redoing an entire ten minute sequence simply because you had to make a change in the first minute was an incredible waste of time, not to mention downright tedious.

Editors got around this problem by making a new videotape of the first portion of the film (with the additional ten frames at the end of the fifth shot) and simply re-recording the remainder of the tape that had been unchanged from the first tape onto the new tape. There were, however, two problems with this approach. First, it meant that when the editor remade the edit in the first minute, he or she had to sit and watch the unchanged nine minutes of the film, wasting a lot of valuable time. Second, as anyone who has ever copied tapes at home can tell you, a copy of a videotape never looks as good as the first tape (called the *source tape*). In an editing room, where a film might be re-edited ten or fifteen times, making a new copy of each version using parts of the previous version would degrade the image ten or fifteen times. The resulting copies would be very fuzzy, making it impossible to judge whether an edit was working or not.

Obviously, most people were not about to move from editing on film to videotape editing while that situation remained.

Then Along Came Non-Linear

A solution was eventually found (you guessed that, didn't you?) by some clever technicians who thought the way to get around the problem of the linearity of the edited videotape was never to edit a tape at all. Instead, they proposed faking the editing, allowing you to see the edits without actually making them.

Good trick, eh? This is how they did it.

Most of these systems (they had names like Ediflex, Montage, Touchvision, EditDroid, E-Pix and Laser Edit) worked by making numerous copies of the dailies tapes, either on videotape or videodisk. These copies were then put into several videotape or disk playing machines and a computer was attached to them all.

To make an edit, the editor told the computer which frames he or she wanted to edit, say from shot one to shot two (*see* Figure 1A.1). The computer then would tell one of the video machines to play back (without transferring or recording to another tape machine) its copy of shot one until it reached the SMPTE code that was the number of the last frame that the editor wanted, in this case 15:26:13:18. At the exact instant the machine reached that frame the computer told another video machine to begin playing from the SMPTE code number of the first frame the editor wanted in shot two (in this case, 07:53:27:07). This process continued on a shot by shot basis until there were no more edits to play back.

No tape was recorded until everybody was happy with the sequence. If the director wanted to add ten more frames to the end of shot five, the editor would give the computer that instruction. The computer would then tell the machine playing back shot number five to keep playing for ten more frames before switching over to playing back from the machine with shot six in it. All it needed to do was add ten frames to the SMPTE code number that it was sending to the machine playing back shot five.

The key to making this all work was having enough machines playing enough copies of the dailies. That way the computer could think far enough ahead so it could have those machines wound up to the exact point where the footage would be needed in four or five

```
        15:26:13:13              07:53:27:07

    ┌─────────────────┐      ┌─────────────────┐
    │  Video Source #1 │      │  Video Source #2 │
    └─────────────────┘      └─────────────────┘

    ┌──┬──┬──┬──┬──┬──┐┃┌──┬──┬──┬──┬──┬──┐
    │ 1│ 1│ 1│ 1│ 1│ 1│┃│ 2│ 2│ 2│ 2│ 2│ 2│
    └──┴──┴──┴──┴──┴──┘┃└──┴──┴──┴──┴──┴──┘

        01:00:00:00              01:00:00:06
```

FIGURE 1A.1 *Diagram of non-linear tape-based editing machine making cut from shot one to shot two. In this example the image in video player #1 begins at SMPTE Code 15:26:13:13 and plays for six frames (the last frame of which would be 15:26:13:18). Then, at the exact moment that it would have played the next frame from shot one, the computer switches and begins playing machine #2 from the SMPTE code 07:53:27:07. This creates the appearance of a cut between the sixth and seventh frames of the edit.*

or six or seven more edits.

This style of editing is called *non-linear editing* because the film didn't have to be edited in a linear fashion, from the beginning through to the end, in order to view it. It could be cut and viewed in any order at all.

Obviously, there were problems with this approach as well, though it made the editing process much more flexible than ever before. For one thing, if you didn't have enough playback machines, the computer couldn't line them up far enough ahead to make a whole string of edits. The machine getting ready to play back shot number six would not have finished rewinding or fast forwarding to get to the necessary SMPTE code number (that is, a particular frame) when shot number five had finished playing on another machine. As a result, the playback of the edit would stop until all the machines had cued themselves to the right positions and the editor pressed the "Go" button again. Machines like the Ediflex originally tried to get by with eight tape machines, but twelve proved to be more workable. Other systems used up to seventeen machines but even that proved not to be enough for sequences with a lot of sound and picture cuts (remember, whenever picture and sound were cut at different frames another machine was required).

Another problem was that the software that ran the computer

was written by computer programmers—not editors. As a result, it was often hard to make the system do the types of things any good editor would want it to do. "The interface is not user-friendly" was what everyone said. (Actually they said a lot more unprintable things.) It was enough to make editors furious, and a lot of rented machines were returned at the end of the job with dented sides where they had been kicked by irate editors in frustration. Editors working these editing machines often felt they had to be computer operators first and editors second.

A third problem was the time constraint. Although an editor had access to an entire videotape or videodisk worth of dailies at one time, no more than an hour's worth of material could usually fit on each set of videotapes. This meant the complete film had to be broken up into sections short enough that the combined total of all of the dailies shot for each section wouldn't exceed sixty minutes in length. Though there were cumbersome workarounds devised, this made it much more difficult to take a scene shot for one part of the picture and move it to another part of the film. The dailies for that moved scene simply wouldn't be on the same set of videotapes or discs as the section it was being moved into.

So, once again, the technical geniuses went to work.

10

Enter Digital

Since the late 1980s, the trend in non-linear editing machines has been to avoid using videotapes and videodisks entirely. Instead, the picture image on each frame of film is converted into digital numbers computers can read (zeroes and ones) and it is this *digitized* image and sound (stored on computer hard drives) that is played back, rather than a video image from tape or videodisk. The computer thinking process is still the same as it was in the tape or disk form of non-linear editing, but now the computer is bossing around locations on its own hard drives, rather than locations on videotapes.

Because computer hard drives are much faster than videotape or videodisk machines, the editor no longer has to wait until all of the videotapes are cued up in their proper places for play back. Access to any frame became virtually instantaneous.

In addition to the advantages of immediate access to material these new systems (with names like Lightworks, Avid, D/Vision, Media 100 and TurboCube) have also pioneered software making these machines work more like editing machines than computers. In computer language we say they have a better "user interface." The interface is easier to use because it is more visually-oriented than number-oriented. The editor looks at picture frames just like on film. He or she makes splices, overlaps, and edits more like a film editor than a computer operator.

Really, the only weak points of the new machines are their expense and image quality. Because each frame is turned into thousands of tiny zeroes and ones for the computer, and because there are usually 24 frames in each second of film, the amount of stored information needed for even the average television movie or low-budget feature is enormous. As a result, many expensive computer hard drives are needed to store all of this information.

One way to minimize the amount of space needed to store each frame is to compromise in terms of image quality. Less information is needed for images that are slightly degraded. Put another way, the better the quality of the images, the more hard drive space needed to store the images. For example, on some hard drives, about one hour of dailies can be stored with average picture quality, but only ten minutes can be stored at their best quality.

At the present time, in order to get image quality close to the equivalent of tape you need so many disk drives you exceed the capacity of the editing machine to handle them swiftly or the ability of the film company to pay for them.

Once again, the computer engineers are leaping into the fray to try to solve these problems, introducing new ways of compressing the information as it is put into the computer, and expanding the capacity of the hard drives and the editing computers handling that information.

The day when an entire feature's worth of information can be stored at videotape picture and sound quality may be in the future, but that future isn't very far away.

Non-Linear Digital Editing in the Process

Trying to describe how the new technology fits into the film-making process is like trying to teach a frisky puppy to obey the command to sit. Everything is moving too fast; nothing stays the same from month to month. As new technology is invented, new editing room techniques must be invented to accommodate them.

As a result, though the general outlines of digital editing can be discussed here, many of the specifics about what the editing machines can do and what they look like will, of necessity, be outdated within a year, if not sooner. It will be the assistant editor's responsibility to continue to ask the questions: "Is there a better way of doing this job?", "Is there a better tool for this job?" and "What did I learn last month that might be outdated this month?" The assistant who continually challenges himself or herself to keep up with the escalating technology will be in the best position to use it, as opposed to being used.

One more detail needs to be mentioned. The growth of digital editing has widened the gulf between small and large budget films terms of in terms of what kind of equipment each can afford. In the old days, a higher budget film was distinguished by the amount of footage shot and the length of the editing schedule. If an additional editor was brought on to help meet a schedule, the cost of additional equipment was minimal—an extra flatbed, an additional editing bench setup, and some more bins.

Today, on a digitally edited film, a larger budget buys all sorts of different toys. Not only is additional digital editing equipment far more expensive than its 35mm equivalent, but there are a host of options available to those films with the most expensive tastes. Mass storage of huge quantities of dailies, networking multiple editing machines, integration with CGI, etc. are all expensive but valuable options.

As a result, I will be approaching the digital chapters in this book in a slightly different manner than the film chapters. In the latter case, I will describe the procedures for a normal medium to high budgeted feature. All of the details that I talk about will still be applicable to lower budget films.

When I discuss digitally edited films, I will talk about a typical medium or lower budgeted film, encompassing the vast majority of films and television made today. Nearly all of these procedures will apply to high budget films as well, though I will not be focusing on techniques that apply solely to high budget projects.

PRELIMINARIES

The first time I ever entered a feature film cutting room I was looking for work. I had heard of a film called *The Taking of Pelham One Two Three* that needed an apprentice film editor. I had gone over the few film books I could find, trying to gather enough information so I wouldn't seem like a complete dunce when I went up for an interview. I called the editor, Jerry Greenberg, made an appointment, got reasonably well dressed—but not *too* dressed (mustn't look too green, I thought), and arrived about five minutes early on the appointed day.

I took only two steps into the cutting room before I realized just how useless all of my reading preparation had been. I had walked into another world. Ceiling to floor, several walls of the room were stacked hundreds of white boxes, each labeled with one of three or four colors of tape. Some boxes had red writing on them, some had black. Each of the editing tables was stacked with an array of equipment and supplies that none of the books had mentioned. A stack of looseleaf notebooks lay open on a table and though I couldn't read anything in them, I suspected that even if I could I wouldn't be able to understand a thing.

No one had prepared me for the sheer awesome complexity of the thing.

I still think of that day when I see job seekers visit the cutting rooms where I work. What now seems simple and logical to me must look frighteningly complicated to anyone seeing it for the first time.

How does a professional cutting room look? Depending on the film's budget the cutting room may actually be several rooms. Or it may be the back of someone's home or office. Whatever the

FIGURE 2.1 *A typical editing room using an upright Moviola, albeit cleaner than most and minus the usual cutter Moviola. The editor has attached a large velvet cloth below the picture gate, on the right side of the Moviola, to protect the film from rubbing against the machine and scratching.*

14

situation, every cutting room has many things in common—they all have a place to store the film, they all have a place to work on the film, and they all must have the equipment to do both adequately. Figure 2.1 shows a typical editing room.

An average cutting room on a medium budget feature film begins with a place for the editor to work. The editor needs an editing machine or two, an editing table complete with all of his or her favorite supplies, the film logbooks, a series of trim barrels, and as much room as possible. Sometimes a computer or a fax machine is part of the editing room equipment.

Let's examine each of these in turn.

An Editing Machine or Two

There are two types of editing machines common in today's film cutting rooms: *uprights*, usually called *Moviolas*; and *flatbeds*, called variously, KEMs, *Steenbecks*, *Moviola flatbeds*, or by any number of other manufacturers' names.

The Moviola has been *the* editing machine for many years in the film business and, at least in 35mm, is still a popular, if fast disappearing, choice. It retains this loyalty for two main reasons: (1) it is much cheaper to buy and rent Moviolas than flatbeds, making them the preferred choice for some college and low-budget films; and (2) they make certain kinds of editing easier. Though most of sound and music editing has moved over to digital systems, if a movie is to cut its sound or music on film, it is, in my experience, easier on uprights—they are easier to thread with short pieces and they stop on a dime. In addition, as we shall see later, setting up a movie's logging system is easier for an upright than for a flatbed and therefore preferable when on a low budget or abbreviated time frame.

Basically, a Moviola is an instrument that pulls the separate rolls of picture and soundtrack from reels on the bottom of the machine to the top, either independently or in synchronization. One of the first things an apprentice editor usually learns is how to thread a Moviola for the editor, and it's no wonder—next to his or her hands, the Moviola is the editor's most important physical tool. In fact, with the best editors, their hands actually become part of their Moviolas.

There are several types of Moviolas. Picture editors use two of them. The first is the kind you see in Figure 2.2, sometimes called a *takeup Moviola*. The second is often called a *cutter Moviola* or, simply, a *cutter* (*see* Figure 2.3). It is much the same as the first except is designed to be softer on the film and faster to thread. Gentleness is a serious concern if you're going to be cutting a movie for six months or more—making, unmaking, and remaking splices all the while. The cutter has no take–up arms and no threading wheels above and below the picture gate and sound head. This means it is simplicity itself to thread the machine—simply drop the picture in at the picture gate, the sound at the sound head and "let 'er rip" (figuratively, of course). This speed is of great help to the editor during the cutting process—the fewer physical encumbrances placed between the editor and the process of editing, the happier the editor will be.

15

Many editors like to cut with two Moviolas. This enables them to make their selections for good cutting points on one machine (usually the cutter) and add them to the roll of already cut material on the other (either another cutter or a takeup Moviola). We'll see more about this later, for now, it is only important to remember that these editors work best with two machines—one to keep the cut film on and one to select the next cut from.

The other type of machine commonly found in film cutting rooms is the *flatbed*. A flatbed is a machine that pulls the separate rolls of picture and soundtrack from left to right, either independently or in synchronization (*see* Figure 2.4). The flatbed has a few advantages over the upright. First, it is extremely gentle on film. As a result, it is my only choice for 16mm film—the upright can be so

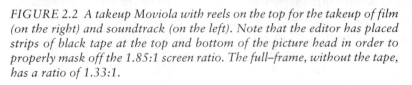

FIGURE 2.2 *A takeup Moviola with reels on the top for the takeup of film (on the right) and soundtrack (on the left). Note that the editor has placed strips of black tape at the top and bottom of the picture head in order to properly mask off the 1.85:1 screen ratio. The full–frame, without the tape, has a ratio of 1.33:1.*

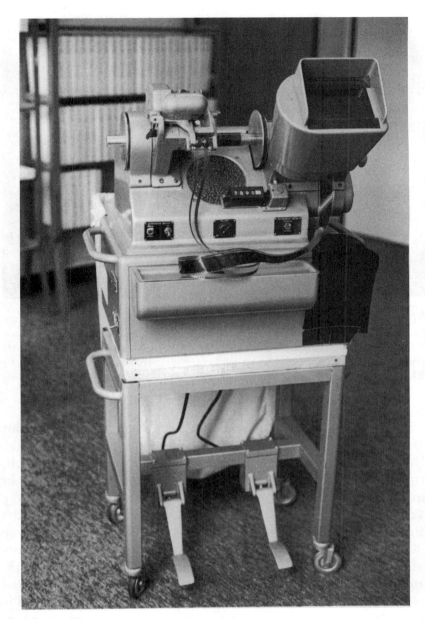

FIGURE 2.3 *A cutter Moviola has no gates or reels above or below the picture head. This makes it softer on the film. The film and track are hand–held on a small roll and fed through their proper heads.*

FIGURE 2.4 *A flatbed editing machine, in this case a Steenbeck. The machine functions as the editor's editing table as well, with the editor making his or her cuts at the machine rather than on a separate editing bench. Note the splicer and grease pencils on the front of the flatbed. A small rack for cores (and small rolls of film or fill on cores) is attached to the machine at the far left. (Photograph by the author)*

18

brutal that is a rare editor who can cut a complete film without damaging some footage. Second, it has several fast-forward speeds. This makes it very easy to find one take or scene on a large roll, rapidly compare two similar takes, or make fine–cut corrections in an already cut film. A third advantage of the flatbed is its large screen size. Directors love this feature as it allows them to view the film without hunching over the editor's shoulder. Therefore, some editors find this to be a bit of an encumbrance. Even these editors will admit a larger screen does help see things in a frame more clearly (though I find the focus sharper on an upright, precisely because of its smaller screen). Finally, compared to the upright, the flatbed is also very quiet, making it much nicer for screening. An editing room with more than one upright running can leave you wondering when the man with earplugs will be coming around.

Some editors, myself included, like to cut with a combination of uprights and a flatbed, either doing the first cut on uprights and changing to flatbeds for fine cutting or doing most of the cutting on the uprights and viewing and making fine trims on the flatbed.

The large flatbeds can run up to four separate rolls of film at one time, usually two picture/two sound, or, alternatively, three picture/one sound, or one picture/three sound. This enables the editor, on one machine, to run the equivalent of two uprights—leaving the cut footage on one pair of *gangs* (as each path is called) and the selecting of cut points on the other pair. In addition, more than one flatbed can be electronically linked together, giving the editor an almost overwhelming number of picture/track combinations. On *The Sign*, a film meant to be projected on nine screens simultaneously, I linked up three flatbeds, each of which had three picture heads and one track gang. This allowed us to run nine pictures in sync all with the push of one button (on any of the three flatbeds).

Both of these types of editing machines have their own pluses and minuses and, therefore, their own set of supporters and detractors. The editor will make his or her own decision about what type of machine to cut on. The assistant editor is expected to be able to set up a system for any of them.

I have my own preferences, of course. When I edit on film, I like to cut sound and music on upright Moviolas. I like to cut 16mm film and complicated 35mm films (musicals, action pictures, documentary-style films) on a flatbed. Dialogue pictures are no easier on one machine than on the other, so I let the demands of the individual film's schedule and budget, as well as the preference of the director, dictate what machine to use.

19

Regardless of what machine I do the bulk of my editing on, I like to have a small flatbed (usually a six-plate machine) so the assistant and I can look at the dailies after they have been sunk up.

There are times when these uses overlap. What, you may ask, do you do then? Do the best you can.

An Editing Table with Supplies

In the United States, a normal editing table (or *editing bench*, the two terms are interchangeable) looks very much like the one shown in Figure 2.5. (For a fairly thorough discussion of how an English editing table is set up, see Ernest Walter's *The Technique of the Cutting Room*.) The essentials on it are as follows:

Synchronizer: In much the same way that the Moviola or flatbed can pull the film and soundtrack along together in sync with each other, editors need to have a way of doing that on an editing table. The synchronizer (*see* Figure 2.6) does this so well, it is regarded as the ultimate sync setup (in fact, it is called a *sync block* by some). It is a passive mechanical device that usually has four identical wheels (called *gangs*), welded together so they spin with each other. Film locked into one of the four gangs will

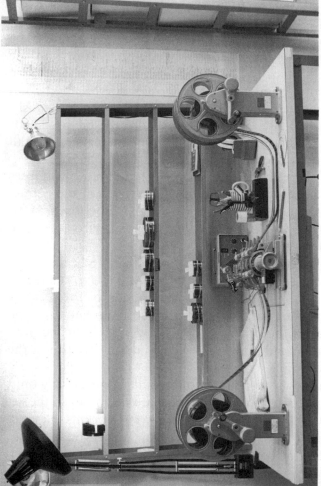

FIGURE 2.5 *An editing bench. The film and soundtrack are fed from the reels on the left rewind (picture first, and soundtrack behind it), through the synchronizer, and are taken up on the right rewind. Trims and outs for the scene which the editor is working on are sitting on the back rack. Note the other supplies and equipment on the table with the synchronizer: the sound amplifier (also called the sound box or squawk box) behind it, and the splicer and tape dispenser (with two rolls of white paper tape in it) to the right. Stacked on a pin at the read of the splicer are two rolls of splicing tape. Next to the splicer is a hole punch and at the front of the table, sitting next to the right rewind, is a Reddy-Eddy, a time-to-footage converter.*

travel at exactly the same speed as film locked into any of the other gangs. Moviola and flatbed synchronization has been known to slip, but there is no way film locked into the synchronizer can slip. Everyone in the editing room will have their own synchronizer, though flatbed editors will have less need of one than their upright Moviola counterparts. When I edit on a flatbed, I often have a small two gang synchronizer fastened to the front of the flatbed (there is actually a space built-in for one to the left of the seating hole on most KEMs). I use this synchronizer to measure the film. I can also use its sound head to slowly play back a piece of track to find individual modulations at the beginning or middle of words.

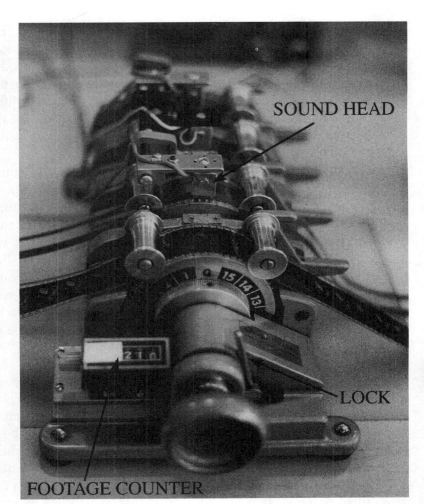

SOUND HEAD

LOCK

FOOTAGE COUNTER

FIGURE 2.6 A synchronizer. It is made up of (usually) four wheels called gangs which are all locked together. Each wheel has sprockets on it so that it can transport film or track. In this case, the first gang is running picture and the second gang is running sound. On the front of the first wheel is the frame counter which is marked from zero to fifteen frames. The frame counter on the synchronizer indicates that the frame of picture on the white zero frame mark is at 210 feet and zero frames exactly (210'00). The lock on the right side of the synchronizer can be engaged to freeze the wheels at a particular frame. Normally, the wheels turn freely.

Sound Reader: Some way of hearing the soundtrack as it runs through the synchronizer is required. This is accomplished by placing a little sound head on at least one of the gangs (the first gang is usually not used, being reserved for picture) and connecting that to an amplifier with a built-in speaker. This amplifier/speaker combination is known variously as the *sound reader*, *squawk box*, or "that damned box." Sound reproduction is *never* as good as it should be through a system like this, which is the reason many sound editors rent better amplifiers and separate speakers. On *Hair,* we rented a good speaker and installed a good amplifier in our KEM flatbed as well.

Rewinds: These are the two stands at either end of the editing bench. The reels containing the picture and sound film are slipped onto the protruding shafts of the rewinds. Clamped together, they can all be moved in forward or reverse by turning the handles. These handles can be pulled out part way from the rewind stand, disengaging the handle from the shaft. This does not mean, as I thought back in college, that you've broken the rewind. It is a particularly helpful way to wind film very fast. You turn the rewinds faster and faster and when you've gotten up to a good speed simply pull the handle out and let the film coast along, virtually winding itself up.

22

Splicer: There are a few types of splicers. The two most popular are the Rivas (*see* Figure 2.7) and the Guillotine (*see* Figure 2.8). Both do the same things: provide an edge for cutting the film evenly on a frame line, and a setup block on which two pieces of cut film can be aligned and taped together. This is the extent of the "cutting" part of film editing. Cut piece number one, cut piece number two, lay them side by side, and tape them together. It is ridiculously simple, which is why many editors (myself included) get touchy about being called "cutters." Cutting and splicing is easy, it's the editing that's difficult.

Both of these splicers use tape to fasten the pieces of film together. There is virtually no use for cement splicers in a film editing room today unless you intend to cut your own camera original. If you don't, stick with the tape splicers.

There is one other type of splicer—the diagonal splicer. It is used only for soundtrack and cuts on an angle, rather than straight up and down. This splicer is used primarily to finesse sound or music edits. A diagonal splice will more gently smooth a sound transition than a straight cut. A Guillotine splicer has a diagonal cutting surface mounted onto the splicer in addition to the straight edged one.

FIGURE 2.7   *A Rivas splicer. The film is placed across the base of the splicer so that its sprocket holes fit into the pins. The tapper (A) is brought down lightly onto the film to smooth it out. The cutting blade (B) is then brought down to cut the film at the metal wedges (C). Soundtrack splices are made by placing each piece of track base up (oxide side down) on the pins so that the two butt up at the metal wedges. White splicing tape is then put on the base side of the track covering two sprockets on either side of the cut. The tapper is then brought down to smooth the tape over the cut and the tape is split using the blade built onto the side of the tapper. Picture is spliced differently. One piece of film is placed so that two sprockets overlap past the pins on the left. The other piece of film is then butted up against it so no sprockets overlap. Clear tape is then placed over the cut, covering one sprocket on either side of the cut. These two sprocket splices will barely be seen when projected in the 1.85 screen ratio. The same two sprockets are then spliced on the back of the film as well since film running through a Moviola needs to be spliced on both sides (double–spliced) in order to go through smoothly. Film run on a flatbed need only be spliced on one side, with the second side being spliced before screenings only.*

23

FIGURE 2.8 *A Guillotine splicer. The film is placed on the base of the splicer and cut with the lever-like blades at its right side (there are two - one is for a straight cut and the other is a diagonal blade for some sound edits). The cut portions are then moved to the center of the splicer, the sprocketless tape is pulled up over the cut and the top of the splicer is brought down on top of the film. This smoothes the tape down as well as perforating the sprocket holes in the tape. Once again, the tape should be applied on both sides of the film. (Photograph by the author)*

24

Supplies: First, the list, then the explanations.
> Splicing tape — clear and white
> Leader — white, yellow, black, and clear (some assistants also use other colors—blue is common)
> Fill leader (also called slug film)
> "Scene Missing" and "Shot Missing" leader
> Academy leader
> Stationery supplies
> Spring clamp
> Differential
> Loupe
> Rulers
> Architect's tape
> Reddy-Eddy and/or calculator
> Trim tabs (also called cinetabs)
> Beep tone roll and virgin stock
> Spare take-up reels, split reels and cores
> Gloves

Velvets
Webril wipes
Cleaner (such as Ecco)
White boxes
Differential
Q-Tips

Splicing tape—This is the tape you use to splice the film together. Clear tape is used for picture splices, white tape is used for sound. On a guillotine splicer, many editors use clear tape for both picture and sound since it is awkward to change tape rolls in between each cut.

Leader—Solid white, yellow or black film, as well as clear. Its uses are myriad and we'll discuss each of them as we come on them in the text. For now, let's say that on the average feature you can expect to under-order this leader. Except for the black leader, which is pricier than gold jewelry around a producer's neck, order accordingly.

Fill Leader—Fill is waste film. It is usually old movies or rejected lab prints that have been discarded. It is spliced into the cut soundtrack when a length of silence is needed.

"Scene Missing" and "Shot Missing" Leader—As cut scenes are put together on reels for projection, scenes that belong in between two cut scenes but have not yet been shot or edited are indicated with a short length (often, three feet) of leader with the words "Scene Missing" printed on it. In addition, as the editor is cutting a scene missing some shots (usually an insert, that is, a close-up of some action, say a person's hand sliding a key into a lock), he or she will want to indicate where the shots should go and approximate lengths for them. They will cut in some leader with the words "Shot Missing" on it. Both types of leader can be purchased from a film supply house. When you do, buy very little. In television, it is also necessary to get a number of "Insert Commercial Here" leaders.

Academy Leader—The numbers you sometimes see at the beginning of a film (you know, 8-7-6-5, etc.) are part of a standard designed by the Academy of Motion Picture Arts and Sciences (AMPAS), the same Academy that gives out the Oscars every year. The leaders count down in seconds from eight to two and then go to black before the picture begins (an alternate standard counts down in feet, from twelve to three, which is the same thing). Also imprinted on these standard leaders are all kinds of helpful information. There is a field for the projectionist to focus on, there are sometimes markings showing the borderline of the screen area since, normally, only part of the full frame is meant to be projected and the rest has to be covered up by a plate in the projector. There are also marks that the lab uses to position the film negative properly on its printing machines. One Academy leader should be placed at the head of everything to be projected, so order a lot of it, either from your lab or a supply house.

On many films that I've worked on (*Heathers*, *Four Friends*, *Cotton Club*), the cinematographers shot their own framing leader, which they felt more accurately gave them a sense of what their cameras were looking at as they screened dailies. The editing crew should cut this leader onto the head of every dailies reel. I find no real value in this after the first several days of shooting, but it does suggest an alternate, and cheaper, way of getting the scene and shot missing leaders—having the camera crew shoot them. A word of warning about using these alternate framing leaders at the head of your picture. Industry standard is to have *exactly* twelve feet from a "picture start" mark to the end of leader (four feet and thirty-two frames in 16mm). You must keep this length constant in every head leader you make. (More on this in Chapter 4)

26

Stationery Supplies—Editors use grease pencils (also called "china markers") to write on film because the marks are easy to see and equally easy to erase. In addition, a healthy supply of regular pencils, pens, markers, various sizes of notepaper, rubber bands, and paper clips will keep the editing room humming along happily. It is the assistant's job to make sure the editor never runs out of anything that he or she needs. Often, this job is delegated to an apprentice if there is one on the job.

Spring clamp—Something has to hold the multiple reels on the rewind shafts together or they won't take up at the same rate. A clamp will do it. Make sure you get one with the table setup when you rent it.

Differential—A thick wheel-like gizmo which, when hooked up between a reel of picture and a reel of sound, forces them to take up at the same speed on your rewinds. Because picture and sound film are of different thicknesses they tend to take up at different rates. Without a differential, one of the two will tend to spill out all over the table, making it dangerous (to the film) to wind. A cheap and less effective fix for this is to separate the reels on your rewinds with 16mm cores and apply a little wrist action while winding the reels to make the soundtrack take up faster than the picture.

Loupe—This is a little magnifying glass you can set on top of the film when you need to examine a single frame on the editing bench or flatbed. In the center of most editing tables there is a lamp set into the table and covered, at table level, with a sheet of frosted glass or plastic. You can turn on the light to provide back illumination for the film. Assistant editors will need to see a lot of single frames as they sync up the dailies.

Rulers—There are a few times when it will be necessary to draw straight lines onto the film (to indicate fade, dissolves, or other types of opticals, for instance). A two-foot ruler will take care of most of these needs. I find it helpful to have rulers in half, one, two, and three-foot lengths.

Architect's Tape—Instead of drawing lines on the film, a niftier way of creating them is to set a length of thin architect's tape (usually 1/16") onto the film.

Reddy-Eddy—This is a little wheel that converts footage to time. Calculators can do the same thing. In the appendix of this book there are a set of conversion charts. You might want to hang a copy of them around the editing room (then again, you may not).

27

Trim tabs (also called *cinetabs*)—These are small pieces of cardboard onto which everything from code numbers to personal notes can be written. There are two main types of trim tabs in the United States (*see* Figure 2.9).

Beep tone—This is a roll of 35mm or 16mm soundtrack, depending on what gauge film you're cutting with, onto which a continuous tone (usually 1000 cycles, or Hertz) has been recorded. This has a lot of uses, that we will discuss later, the primary one is that you can cut single frames off of the roll and cut them into your leaders for the little beep (or "pop") occurring six seconds after the start mark, which is nine feet in 35mm (three feet, 24 frames in 16mm). Some editors like to use little pieces of 1/4" tape with the tone recorded onto it with glue put on the back so they can be stuck directly onto the leader. I find this less accurate than cutting in exactly one frame of track. Also, it's cheaper and easier to have someone in the transfer house knock off one minute of 1000 cycle tone than to be taping those messy pieces of tape onto the film.

Along with this beep tone roll, a small roll of track that has never been recorded onto (called *virgin stock* for all too

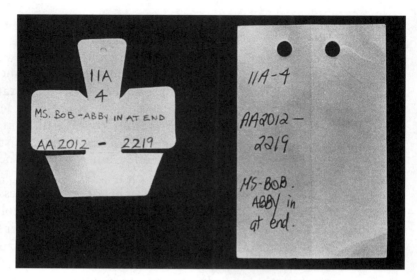

FIGURE 2.9 *Two types of trim tabs (also called cinetabs). Both are made of stiff cardboard. The version on the left is used primarily in New York. The one on the right is used largely on the West Coast (it is folded lengthwise down the center and inserted in between layers of the rolled–up film). Both types of tabs give the same information. In England, usually no trim tabs are used. A piece of tape is placed on the top of the rolled–up film instead.*

obvious reasons) is useful. You can use it to check out the fidelity of all of the sound equipment.

Spare take-up reels, split reels and cores—On a Moviola, film is wound on reels, and a healthy supply of them is essential. Alternately, film can be wound on 3" plastic cores (also called *spools*) and placed into split reels (which are nothing more than take–up reels which can be split, or unscrewed, in two). A number of these reels (eight for each person in the editing room is not too few) along with a huge quantity of cores should be ordered. On flatbeds, film is always wound on cores, which are slotted onto the flatbed.

Other editing supplies—White editing gloves, film cleaner (like Ecco), sound track cleaner, two-piece white boxes for storage, a few film cans for shipping, Q-Tips for cleaning the machines, and whatever other effluvia the editor likes to have surrounding him or her. Some small black velvet cloths (usually sewn across the side) will work well for cleaning film without any danger of scratching it. Also, a phone list, placed prominently by the editing room phone, will save everyone a lot of time looking for the numbers of suppliers and contacts.

None of these supplies magically appear when you sign onto

your job. It is the job of the assistant to rent what can be rented and to purchase the rest. In some situations, you can rent a cutting room complete with an editing machine, a table, synchronizer, sound reader, rewinds, splicer, and take-up reels for one flat price (on a daily, weekly, or monthly basis). More often, the room comes equipped with nothing other than a door and (rarely) a window or two. You will have to rent all of the equipment from a separate supply house. Sometimes the editor or assistant has some of the equipment and rents it to the production. No matter where you get it from, it is wise to order the equipment as far ahead of time as possible, since this equipment can get booked weeks in advance and you'll end up spending days of your time trying to find equipment for your editor. Supplies, of course, can be purchased almost any time, so long as you've got the money.

If you are working on a studio lot, some of the equipment and supplies may be provided for you by the post-production department or facilities manager of the studio. Let them know what you need and make sure your editor's needs are taken care of.

The Film Logbooks

We will discuss the nature of the logbooks in Chapter 5 but you should know there will be a few types of logs. Some will be on clipboards hung on the walls and some will be in looseleaf notebooks near the editor or assistant. A small table will be helpful for these items. Editing tables get crowded almost immediately. They're no place for logbooks.

A Series of Trim Barrels

These are also usually rented as part of the editing room equipment package. There are two main types of barrels (or *bins*). One kind, popular on the East Coast, is a rectangular barrel, almost waist-high, lined with soft cotton material topped with either one or two metal parallel bars (*see* Figure 2.10). The other kind (more popular on the West Coast) is a knee-high barrel, with a metal bar rising from the back, elevated above it (*see* Figure 2.11). In either case, out of these bars stick either a series of tiny pins or metal loops which fit neatly through the sprocket holes in the film. As the editor is cutting, he or she will hang anything not used in the cut on one or another of these pins. This keeps the film hanging in an orderly manner near the Moviola. When the editor is done, it also keeps the pieces hanging in an orderly manner near the apprentice who spends hours splicing and wrapping them all back together.

FIGURE 2.10 *A tall trim bin of the kind normally used in New York. Film is hung beneath its trim tab so that the trims can be easily located by looking at the take and code numbers (see FIGURE 6.1 for a closer view). Note that very large trims are flanged up and hung by a rubber band run through the trim's center. In this photograph, rubber bands have been stretched across the pins over the tops of the trims to prevent them from falling off when the barrel is rolled from place to place.*

FIGURE 2.11 *A shorter trim bin, common on the West Coast. Film is hung on the looped pins. The trim tabs are inserted into paper clips which have been taped on top of the single cross bar. (Photo by the author).*

Sometimes a Computer or a Fax Machine

Whether a film is being edited on a computer system or on film, computers have become a fact of life in the editing room. On every film I edit, I bring my own computer into the editing room (or the production rents one for me). Over the course of many years I have developed a large number of templates that help me or my assistant make continuities, faxes, schedules and the large amount of paperwork any editing room generates.

I am often able to get a separate phone line attached to the computer that permits me to fax these things directly from my computer. It also allows me to connect to the Internet to do research and e-mail from my computer. Over the course of the last several years more and more crew members have e-mail addresses. I have communicated with directors, producers, script supervisors and suppliers over the phone line using a computer modem. I have even heard of an editing room that received their daily computer files over a phone line from their telecine house, hours before they would receive the disk and videotape. This let them prepare for their digitizing (we will discuss this in Chapter 4A) quite a bit before the editor walked in the door in the morning.

Obviously, if you are going to have a computer in the editing room an extra desk will be needed for it and its printer.

Another machine that is increasingly useful in an editing room is the fax machine. Today, it is much more efficient for the production office to send you some of the script supervisor's daily notes via fax than it is to copy them and rush them over to you by messenger or p.a. It is also extremely useful in sending and receiving purchase orders, optical count sheets, title lists and galley proofs, and lab and telecine orders for immediate attention.

32

Plenty of Room

Actually, this is the one thing editors get all too little of. Editing rooms are usually small and dimly lit, with barely enough electricity to plug in the editing machines without blowing a fuse. These are the conditions you'll find in most New York editing rooms as well as many independent houses in Los Angeles. Editing rooms at the major studios in Hollywood, range from the luxurious to the ludicrously closet-sized.

Because of the temperature and cleanliness needs of the new computer editing machines at least editing rooms have gotten cooler and less dirty than they were even ten years ago.

The assistant editor must play the part of interior designer and come up with a comfortable and efficient layout for the room, whatever its size and wherever it is. Remember, you'll be living in it for the duration of the film.

For example, let's say you have one editor, two Moviolas, one assistant, and one apprentice to fit into one room. Your first questions should always center around the editor's comfort. Does he or she like to work facing the windows or away from them? Near the door or far away from it? Near a phone or isolated from it? Some editors like to be insulated from the outside world; others like to be part of it.

Figure 2.12 shows one typically cramped arrangement that I've had to work with in the past. This layout is a good compromise between many bad elements. It insulates the editor somewhat from traffic, provides easy access for the assistant to the phone and the door (remember that an assistant spends much of his or her time dealing with the outside world), and it provides working space for the editor as well as some nearby rack space.

An alternative arrangement (for an editor preferring more isolation) would be to place him or her where the apprentice's table is. Note also this revised arrangement works if the editor is right-handed and prefers to work with the Moviolas on the right side.

If the editor wishes to work on a flatbed, I might arrange the room as shown in Figure 2.13. Some flatbed editors don't feel the need to have their own editing bench, as the space on the flatbed is designed to provide them with a cutting surface. A small table next to the flatbed would contain the logs and perhaps a small synchronizer (with no sound heads) for making precise footage counts. If the editor needs an editing bench, a small one might be set up nearby, out of the way. Often, a smaller flatbed is rented in addition to the larger one. This would be set up next to the first machine.

33

Frequently, on a feature film, you are able to rent two rooms, or one room with a smaller anteroom. In this case, I prefer to put the apprentice and the film library in the smaller room, and leave the editor and the assistant in the other. This is always preferable since apprentice work, by its very nature, is noisy and can often be distracting. Once again, it is the assistant's job to think of the editor's comfort. The fewer distractions, the faster and better the film can be edited. And, in the hierarchy of editing room personnel, if the assistant or the apprentice must be a little less comfortable in order to make the editor more so—so be it.

There are, of course, many other possible situations in editing rooms. Most non–features don't have apprentices at all. Some low-budget films can't even afford an assistant, leaving the editor to perform all of these tasks. Some high–budget films have more film than can fit in the same room with the editors. On *Hair* we had one room stacked ceiling to floor with film. But the principle always remains the same—make sure everyone can get their work done as efficiently and humanely as possible. If that can happen, the job of making the best film out of the available material seems that much easier.

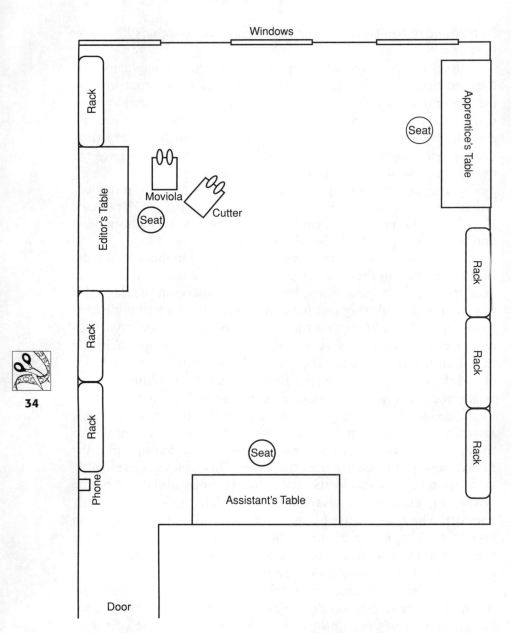

34

FIGURE 2.12 *Floor plan for a Moviola editing situation. This editing room will be home for three people and four racks of film. If additional racks are needed they can be lined up against the windows. Note that in this position the editor works to his or her right and that the Moviola picture screens face away from the windows, avoiding glare.*

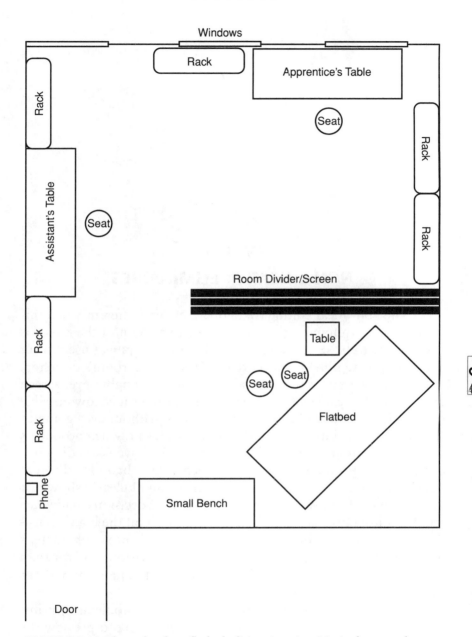

Windows

Rack

Apprentice's Table

Seat

Rack

Rack

Rack

Assistant's Table

Seat

Room Divider/Screen

Table

Seat

Seat

Rack

Flatbed

Rack

Phone

Small Bench

Door

35

FIGURE 2.13 *Floor plan for a flatbed editing situation. Notice how much more room is needed here. There is no room for additional racks.*

NON-LINEAR PRELIMINARIES

The non-linear editing room operates very differently in terms of space and equipment than the film editing room. If the movie is never going to be screened on film, all of the equipment used to cut and manipulate film will never darken the editing room's doorstep.

First, let's answer the question of why you might never screen on film. With the advent of digital editing systems it is now possible to completely edit a film or television show without ever going to the expense of printing film and sound. As a result, when producers want to save money, one of the first ideas they have is to edit without the work print and track. This is generally a bad idea. Even at the best resolution, digital editing systems cannot clearly show just what is on the film. As a result, certain creative decisions made during the editing process might not show up well on the big screen—dialogue lines from one take which are edited into a character's mouth in another might look better on the television monitor than on the big screen, for instance. It is also difficult to judge how sharp the focus really is on a piece of film.

On *Mad Dog Time* we solved some of these problems by printing the picture only. Since we knew we were going to preview the movie in a film theatre we knew we were going to have to print film anyway. During production, this tactic allowed both the director of photography and me to view silent dailies and to accurately select takes on the basis on what they *really* looked like rather than on what appeared on the videotape of dailies. Quite often, these were two different things.

Almost no television shows will print film today since the final format is for television, rather than for the theatre. Most television companies want to cut the film negative (so they are prepared when high definition video is broadcast into homes), but there is no need to see the footage on film.

The rule of thumb that I like to use is this: if the movie is eventually going to be shown on film, then it is a good idea to see the dailies on film.

However, because of the expense, many low budget films will not print film. In these cases, as well as in all television shows, you won't need to have most of the film editing equipment that we've seen in Chapter 2.

On most medium and higher budget films, both film and non-linear equipment are needed. We will get into the specifics of combined film and non-linear films in Chapter 4 but, for now, we will concentrate solely on the computer equipment and supplies needed for these types of jobs.

If you were to look into a working computer digital editing room (*see* Figure 2 A.1) you would see an editor or assistant sitting at a large desk. Either under the desk or near to it would be a series of large metal boxes. On top of the desk you would see two or three television monitors. A keyboard would be sitting in front of him or her and placed nearby would sit a rack of electronic equipment—one or two videotape machines, an audio cassette deck and/ or a CD player, and a mixing board to blend sounds from several different sources into one. Off to one side might be a microphone, sitting either on the table or on a tall stand.

37

Somewhere in this or another room you would see a large bookcase filled with videotapes and a stack of supplies. Sometimes a large bank of computer hard drives are put in this other room as well. You would also find a number of log books and printed manuals.

You might also notice that, in general, the room seemed quieter, cleaner and more comfortable than film editing rooms you may have been in. Some editors like digital editing because it is faster, some like it because gives them the opportunity to experiment more, but many like it because it is inherently a saner way of working than with dirty, loud Moviolas and KEMs.

Some Large Metal Boxes

An electronic editing machine looks more like a combination of a television and a computer than it does a flatbed or a Moviola. In fact, these editing machines look a lot like the home computer you might have at home or at school. The Avid editing machine as well as the Media 100 and TurboCube systems, are, at present, basically Macintosh computers. The difference is in the amount of

FIGURE 2A.1 A typical computer editing room. The editing machine, in this case an Avid, occupies the center of the editor's table. To the left of the two Avid graphics monitors is a mixing board, connected to a microphone for recording wild lines. On the left, below the main table, is a stack of machines. The 3/4" tape machine is on the bottom, sitting underneath a VHS deck, a CD player, and a patch bay. Under the table, on the right, is the main computer with a Zip drive. To the right of the main table is the NTSC monitor for playing back edits and dailies. On the floor below that monitor is the tower which contains the six hard drives containing all of the digitized footage. To the left of the main table is a DAT machine. Underneath that table are a number of looseleaf books containing the editor's dailies notes and other paperwork. Not shown is a table or music stand on which the editor will often put the lined script. The map of Paris on the wall isn't essential editing equipment, it is used more for late night travel fantasies. (Photo by the author)

equipment added onto that computer. The storage demands of digital editing mean that every computer must be accompanied by numerous hard drives or a similar means of storing the digitized images.

Hard drives are finicky beasts and if you ever had a chance to look inside them you would quickly figure out why. Essentially, they are a series of small metal platters that spin very fast. Above them sits a series of magnetic heads (not completely unlike the sound reader on a synchronizer) that dive on and off the metal platters. If anything gets in the way of that magnetic head as it touches the metal platter, data can't be read off of the hard drive.

The alignment of these heads is very particular, so hard drives react very badly to being dropped even as little as three or four inches. In addition, the trickiest part of normal operation is when

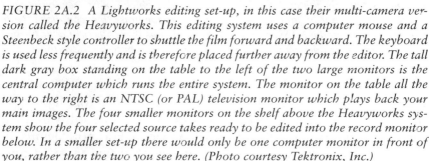

FIGURE 2A.2 *A Lightworks editing set-up, in this case their multi-camera version called the Heavyworks. This editing system uses a computer mouse and a Steenbeck style controller to shuttle the film forward and backward. The keyboard is used less frequently and is therefore placed further away from the editor. The tall dark gray box standing on the table to the left of the two large monitors is the central computer which runs the entire system. The monitor on the table all the way to the right is an NTSC (or PAL) television monitor which plays back your main images. The four smaller monitors on the shelf above the Heavyworks system show the four selected source takes ready to be edited into the record monitor below. In a smaller set-up there would only be one computer monitor in front of you, rather than the two you see here. (Photo courtesy Tektronix, Inc.)*

the drives are turned on or off. As a result, some assistants never turn off their hard drives, preferring to leave them on all night.

On the Lightworks (*see* Figure 2A.2) both the computer and these hard drives come in towers about two feet tall, usually placed under or to the side of the table where the editor is working. On the Avid (*see* Figure 2A.3) the main brains of the Macintosh computer are kept in the same place. A number of removable disk drives of some sort sit nearby. Other machines operate with different storage media (Magneto-Optical disks, called MOs, for instance). All of them require some place to record and play back the digitized images, just as you need a cassette machine to record and play back audio tapes at home.

FIGURE 2A.3 An Avid editing set-up. This editing system makes extensive use of both the mouse and the keyboard so both are placed within easy reach of the editor. Right-handed editors usually prefer to work with the keyboard on the left and the mouse on the right. Left-handed editors often work the other way around. In some systems the material hard drives (the top of which can be seen to the right of the table) are put in another room to minimize the noise they can make. Note that the picture on the NTSC monitor on the right has three pieces of code burned in the letterboxing above and below the picture area. (Photo by the author)

40

There are actually two types of Avids, which differ only in their software—the Film Composer is the Avid used for all projects that will end up on film, the Media Composer is the software used for most projects that will only finish on video. For more details on this difference, check out the section on 24 frame vs. 30 frame projects in Chapter 4A.

As I've mentioned, there are a number of other digital editing systems, some of which can be used for film and television projects and some of which are designed for shorter projects like commercials or corporate videos. There are two significant differences between these machines and the Avid and Lightworks. The first is their ability to handle film-based 24 frame projects. Programs like the Media 100 and TurboCube are not designed with film in mind. The second major difference is the quality of the image. Machines designed to handle large amounts of footage (like the Avid, the Lightworks and the D-Vision) sacrifice image quality to store massive amounts of dailies. As a result, the image on these machines is not good enough to be used for the final version of the project. These machines are called *off-line* machines. This expression comes from the days when video programs were pre-cut and then brought to an *on-line* editing bay where the cuts were remade using the better quality images on the original tapes. This is still the practice on most television shows. However, as the quality of the image on many digital editing systems has improved it is becoming increasingly rare for corporate videos, music videos and many reality based television shows to go through a separate on-line session.

Both Avid and Lightworks are capable of quality on-line editing, much like the Media 100, TurboCube and other 30 frame machines. However, for nearly all features and most television, they are still used as off-line machines.

What sits on the desk in front of the editor as he or she cuts will, therefore, depend upon what type of end product is needed.

On top of that desk sit a pair (or more) of television monitors. At least one of these is actually a computer monitor. The other is a regular, though high-end, television set.

Somewhere else on the desk sits a way of telling the computer how to move your digitized images around, much like the motor controls on a Moviola or a KEM. Usually this is a computer keyboard and a mouse. Some machines also provide a console which operates almost exactly like a flatbed controller. The Lightworks and Avid controllers feel remarkably like Steenbeck motion control dials, with a large knob which is pushed to the right for forward motion and to the left for backward motion. The computer updates the visual image to move it forward or backward at a variable speed depending upon how far the editor has pushed the knob.

Some editing systems, like the Avid, use the keyboard to do most of their image movement. The Lightworks uses the keyboard less frequently, relying primarily on its Steenbeck-style controller. The Lightworks also comes with a small black and white computer monitor (they call it a "debug monitor") which is normally put out of the way. Its major use is to give you more information when something goes wrong with the computer system.

Somewhere slightly off to the side of the editor, on the table top, will sit a *mixing board*. This machine, used for sound, takes a number of sound signals and funnels them through separate volume controls (or *sliders*) into one pair of signals, one for each speaker you are going to be listening on. The most common configuration is a board with eight individual sliders and several master sliders that control the overall sound.

You should also have a small box attached to everything, tucked away somewhere on the floor. This box (or, often, a series of boxes) is called a *Uninterruptible Power Supply*, abbreviated as UPS.

This box is essentially a giant battery designed to begin operating your system should the building's power supply ever fail. In that case, the UPS will beep regularly to warn you that your power has disappeared. The box will then provides power on its own for anywhere from three to five minutes, giving you enough time to back up all of your work and safely shut down your computer. This way, you can protect your information during those infrequent, but still annoying, power outages.

A Rack of Electronic Equipment

Having all of this computer equipment is all well and good, but you need machines to help get all of the picture and sound into and out of the computer. To that end, you will usually have a stack of machines placed just off to the side of the editor's table. The better editing rental houses put all of this equipment into a big metal shelf, called a *rack mount*, which permitting access to all the equipment easily and safely.

The equipment sitting in this rack mount will vary depending upon the editing system you use and the needs of your production. In general, however, it will usually contain the following items:

An Input Videotape Machine: As we will see in the next chapter, the dailies shot each day usually arrive in the editing room for input into your computer editing system on some sort of videotape format. The types of tapes vary but they usually are one of the following:

> *3/4"*—This is by far the most common tape format since it is the cheapest. These large tapes (see Figure 2A.4) have better picture image than VHS tapes. A slightly better quality 3/4" format is the 3/4"-SP. Its case looks exactly the same as a regular 3/4" tape but the picture and sound are quite a bit better. It normally costs just a bit more to create tapes for this format than for normal 3/4". Interestingly, it often will cost no more to rent the tape decks.
>
> *Super-VHS (S-VHS)*—This is a rather good VHS format though the cassette looks just like a regular home VHS tape. Many telecine houses cannot transfer directly to this format, so it is often appreciably more expensive to create tapes. In general, the quality of both the picture

FIGURE 2A.4 *Four common videotape formats in use in computer editing rooms. On the bottom left is the 3/4" tape format. On the top left is a VHS tape, the type you probably use in your home VCR (Super-VHS, S-VHS, looks exactly like this; the difference is in the recording machine). On the right are two different sizes of the Beta-SP format. The top cassette is one hour in length, the bottom cassette comes in a number of shorter lengths. (Photo by the author)*

and sound is superior to 3/4" tape. Also, it can sometimes be played on home decks. One editor who compared S-VHS to 3/4"-SP, found the S-VHS was equal in sound quality and superior in picture, with some substantial cost savings in equipment rental and tape stock purchase. The only disadvantage to S-VHS seems to be that it is slightly more temperamental than a 3/4" tape deck about accepting commands from your editing machine.

Beta-SP-This tape (see Figure 2A.4) offers very high picture and sound quality. Its disadvantages are completely cost related, with both its tapes and its tape machines costing appreciably more than the 3/4" format. However, because it looks so much better, the digitized image inside the computer also looks that much better.

There are much higher end video formats, such as D-1 or D-2, but they are almost never used in the editing room.

A VHS videotape machine: This videotape machine is exactly the same kind of player you have at home. Though you will rarely digitize material from this VHS machine you will often find yourself outputting to it. In the course of the editing process you will frequently find yourself making tapes for the director, producers, composers and other people. This VHS machine is very convenient for that. In addition, on *Mad Dog Time* we got sample reels of stock footage on VHS tape and were able to digitize those images and test them within the context of the film.

A CD player: During the course of the editing process the editor will often want to brighten up the edit with some music or sound effects. Something is needed to play back these sounds into the editing computer. Usually this is a CD player, often the same type as you would have in a decent sound system at home.

An audio tape machine or two: In addition to the CD player, music and sound effects might also be transferred from tape formats. The most common are the home audio cassette and a *DAT* (Digital Audio Tape) player. The DAT machine (*see* Figure 2A.5) records a digital sound (like CDs) and, therefore, has much better sound quality. On many films, the recordist on set records the sound onto DATs. These tapes, or copies of them, are given to the assistant in the editing room who will input them into the computer editing machine and sync up the dailies. A time-coded DAT machine is usually used in these cases.

A rarer tape machine is called the DA-88. This uses the same tape cassette found in Hi-8 videotape cameras. Used for professional sound recording, it can record up to eight tracks of digital audio. On *Mad Dog Time* we used this format to output our sound for the hand over to the sound department at the end of the editing process.

A patch bay system/router: With all of the various video and audio formats in use you will often be switching among them. You *could* get behind your machines and switch the cables between each machine and your computer every time you needed to switch your format. This would quickly get to be a colossal bore. Most good equipment rental houses now provide an easy switching system called a *patch bay*, a *router* or a *switcher*. If you want to record from your 3/4" deck into your

FIGURE 2A.5 *Two professional audio tape formats and two computer disk formats. On the top left is a Zip disk which is being used for the afternoon back-up of the editing system. The disk on the top right is the normal 3-1/2" computer disk. The cassette on the bottom left is a two-track DAT (Digital Audio Tape). The cassette on the right is an eight track DA-88. (Photo by the author)*

editing machine, for instance, all you need to do is press a few buttons or flip a switch. Every rental house has a different set-up and it will take you a little while to familiarize yourself with the differing configurations. It is often helpful to post a diagram next to the switcher listing what buttons to press for each variation.

A mixing board: The typical patch bay or router sends video signals from one designated machine to another. A mixing board does the same for sound. Additionally, it controls the audio levels and equalization (the relative amount of treble, medium and bass frequency sounds). Often the mixing board works along with a patch bay or router, sometimes it takes the place of one. However, almost no digital editing set-up is complete without one. These days, when digital systems can provide eight tracks of output, and accept input from a variety of different machines, a mixing board helps the editor to sort out just where the audio is coming from, where it is going to, and what it sounds like.

A backup disk drive: Because computers can be finicky beasts, it is a good idea to back up all of the editor's work at regular intervals, usually twice a day. Every system works differently, but the basic idea is always the same. You take your editing information (what footage is on the system, what and where every version of every edit was made, etc.) and copy it onto a disk that can be removed from the computer and placed in a safe area. Backups are made to regular 3-1/2" computer disks, to removable drives (like Zip, Jaz, or Syquest) or to magneto-optical disks (often called MO disks). The least satisfactory is the 3-1/2" disk because very little information can be stored on it and it will often take many disks and a lot of time to make the backup. An external removable drive like a Zip or a Jaz drive is often put into the rack mount. The Lightworks machine comes with a built-in MO drive.

A UPS (Uninterruptible Power Supply): Even the best outfitted editing room can have accidents. The power might go out for the building or someone trips over the electric cord running to the computer. Much of what your editor and you will be doing on your computer editing system is stored in the computer's memory and that memory disappears whenever the machine is shut off. You can see the danger of losing power to your system. Most systems periodically back up crucial data automatically to their own hard drives but you could still lose everything done since the last automatic save. Uninterruptible Power Supplies do exactly what their names suggest. They keep a certain amount of power running to the machine even if the main power to the machine is cut off. You then have enough time to save whatever you've been working on before shutting the computer off.

A Microphone

One of the advantages of a computer editing system is how easy they make trying out different editing scenarios. Often a piece of dialogue or voice over that was not scripted or recorded on the set is necessary to make a point. With a microphone, it is very easy to temporarily record these lines onto a roll of tape (either video-tape or audio tape will work) for inputting into the system, or directly into the editing machine. The editor can then try out these ideas and then easily make editing choices.

46

Microphone controls are usually located on the sound mixer where you can control the level of the spoken line as well as its switching.

A Bookcase, Supplies and Books

Just as you need to have someplace to store all of the 35mm film on a normal film show, you will need to store all of the video-tape reels created during the course of the production and post-production process. In addition, if you are synching film you will need to have a complete film library.

You will be receiving tapes of your dailies during the course of production, at least one for each day (each tape is usually no more than 60 minutes long; if you get more dailies than that you will usually receive more than one tape). Each tape will be numbered sequentially from the first day of shooting until the end. That number will appear on all of your computer disks for the day as well as the front label of the tape and any paperwork you receive from the telecine house (Once again, don't worry. We will cover all of this in more detail in the next chapter.) I find it helpful to put a piece of white tape on the bottom of the spine of the tape box and write its tape number with large numeral right onto it. That way when the tapes are standing up on the bookcase it will be easy to locate any necessary tape.

47

In general, you will rarely need to go back into these tapes once they have been digitized (occasionally, you might need to redigitize certain takes due to computer problems). Your editor will almost definitely not need to access them. As a result, they can be put in a more out of the way place than film dailies, which need to be accessed on an continuous basis.

During the course of editing you will also be receiving additional tapes—of music, of sound effects, of stock footage, of opticals, and of *B-negative* takes. You should leave room for them on your shelves.

In addition to the paperwork you will have from a film show you will be receiving paperwork from the telecine house that you also need to have available. Keep them on clipboards hung on the wall or in large binders placed on bookshelves.

Unless you and your editor are computer geniuses, you will often need the reference books that come with your computer editing system. I like to keep them on a shelf above my machine in the editor's room. Other editors like their assistants to keep them.

You will also need room for all of the supplies you would normally need in an office—including a supply of computer disks, both the 3-1/2" variety and whatever backup format you are using (Zip or Jaz disks, MO disks, et al). It is a good idea to pre-format a number of them so they can be used whenever you need them. You should also lay in a supply of tape labels in all of the sizes you will need: VHS, 3/4", Beta-SP (if you expect to output in this format). You should get the labels for the cassettes and the boxes you will be packing them in.

I have a series of templates in my word processing program that will print out labels onto 8-1/2" by 11" label paper. The assistant can then cut out the labels and put them on the cassettes and boxes. Pre-cut labels in many of the cassette formats are also available.

Other Supplies and Equipment

Depending upon the budget of your movie you may be lucky enough to have an extra computer editing machine. Often they will be *networked* together. This means that both machines can use the same dailies material without having to make additional copies for each machine.

There will also probably be at least one other computer in the editing room. This is useful for a number of reasons, from creation of logs down to the more mundane tasks of writing memos and creating tape labels.

If you are also dealing with film there will probably also be at least one film editing machine, usually a flatbed, sitting in the main editing room as well.

Computers often get sick and usually this happens at the most difficult times—like at ten o'clock on the evening right before a major screening. You will need to know something about how to fix them and a list of numbers to call if you cannot. Each computer editing system has its own help line numbers, most of which aren't worth very much. You should also get the help line numbers of the rental house that you are getting the editing machines from, as well as a few home numbers in case no one is available when you need them. Many rental houses advertise what are called "24/7 help lines," that claim to offer help 24 hours a day, seven days a week. Often these numbers are no more than pagers which, as you can imagine, are sometimes left behind when the technical support people go to the theatre, or to their mother's house for dinner. It is always a good idea to be as prepared as possible for disaster.

One way you can be prepared is to have a set of useful tools with you. Unlike 35mm film toolboxes, which are mostly a collection of screwdrivers and pliers, your digital editing toolbox should also contain some computer floppy disks filled with programs that can help you diagnose and attempt to repair some elementary computer problems. Often these programs will be on the main computer systems. However if your entire computer system is down (that's computer talk for "not working at all"), then separate disks with programs like Norton Disk Doctor, a virus detection program, and a number of other diagnostic aids, can come in very handy.

Floor Plans

Obviously, the type of floor plan your editor will want for a digital show will vary depending upon the show's requirements. If you are printing film as well as editing digitally you will obviously need a lot more room than you would if you were just using one of the two. You will want to figure out some arrangement that will place the flatbed editing machine nearby your editor, without cramping him or her too much. Often, it will be necessary to compare images from the flatbed against your digital system. Make sure your editor can see both screens from his or her seat.

In the example in Figure 2A.6 on the next page, we are using the same room that we set up for film in Chapter 2, except we are adding a digital editing machine. Notice that the computer screens are facing the window in this layout, so we've introduced a divider to block out the ambient light that will make the images hard to see on the monitors. Another alternative would be to place the editing machine where the couch is located have the editor face the divider.

In actuality, this room would be too small for a movie with film, an assistant and an apprentice. You would probably need a second room for the apprentice and the film racks. Unlike a film show, where access to the trims is very important for the editor, digital editing does not require that the film be housed in the same room with the editor.

49

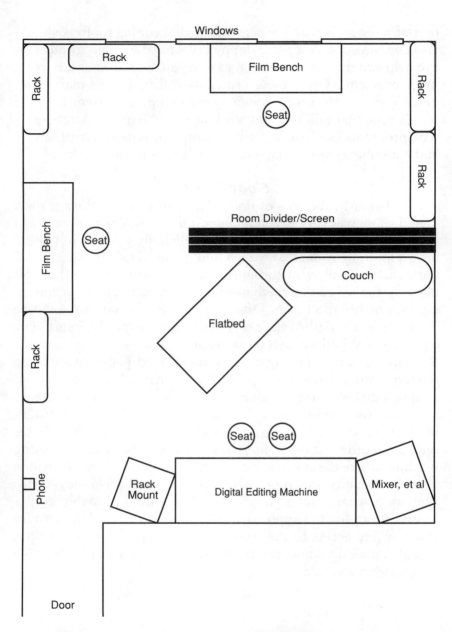

FIGURE 2A.6 *A sample floor plan for the same room as shown in Figure 2.12 and 2.13. This arrangement is for use with a digital editing machine, a flatbed for 35mm film, and film racks for storage. This room is actually too cramped for confortable work.*

BEFORE THE FILM BEGINS

Before the Moviolas and the flatbeds or the digital editing machines move into the editing room there are things that an assistant editor must do. The first, of course, is to get hired on the job, but let's assume you've already managed that (for an exploration of that topic, see Chapter 19, "The Hardest Job of All—Finding a Job").

Let's say you've just been hired onto the director Adam Free's new picture, entitled *Silent Night, Silent Cowboy*. Your editor is a woman named Wendy Libre (editing has traditionally had more women in it than almost any other film trade).

The first thing to do after Wendy hires you is to determine your salary, if this hasn't already been determined for you by Wendy or the film's production manager. Though many editors have agents or lawyers to talk money with the production, assistants almost never do. Be aware, if you negotiate your own salary, people get paid in more ways than money. Working on a good film with good people, learning a lot about your craft, and making more contacts are all legitimate forms of payment on film. And while your landlord probably won't want to get paid with that kind of currency, all of these points should be taken into account when you are deciding how much you need in salary.

As soon as you've taken the job on *Silent Night* you should get a copy of the script. The script will tell you a lot about how you should set up the film. A musical will be organized differently than a straight dialogue film. On an action film, you will get different kinds of footage than on either of the above. You will see if much special effects work is planned (*opticals, matte shots, stock footage, on-set projection*, et al). You will see if there are many short scenes or if the film is made up primarily of longer scenes. For the sake of complicating this example, let us assume the following about the movie you are about to do.

Silent Night, Silent Cowboy is a film about the shooting of a Western movie. It focuses on the scriptwriter's life, which is (naturally) falling apart just as the film is being made. There are going to be three weeks of shooting in a desertlike location (for the Western film-within-a-film), one week on various locations in the city, and four weeks in a studio. Because of the nature of the film, there will be scenes of people watching projected film, some opticals and some on-set music. Though there might be one or two scenes in the Western with fast action, most of the film appears to be dialogue oriented, with a lot of long scenes intercut with the Western.

This may be all that you can tell from a few readings of the script (and you should read it a few times so you know what everyone is talking about as they discuss the script with you), but this has already given you quite a bit of information. As you learn more and more of what different kinds of film demand of you in the editing room, you will be able to read scripts quite easily for these types of clues.

After you've read the script, you will discuss the job with Wendy. She will tell you how she wants things set up. Some editors have more demands than others, but all of them have *some*. Most of their requests are reasonable ones that they have learned help them do their job better. In this case, Wendy wants to work on a Moviola. She tells you she is not going to be on the location during the weeks when the company is shooting in the desert; instead, she will be cutting back in the city. She will also be able to tell you the results of any conversations she has had with the director—how much coverage he intends to shoot, any special requirements *he* has, what kind of cutting he wants done without him, when he wants to see the first cut, etc. etc.

The production manager will also be able to give you some valuable information. You'll want to know approximately how much printed footage he has budgeted for since you will have to organize the cutting room differently for 80,000 feet of film than for 500,000. He will probably also have decided what laboratory will be processing the dailies, what sound house will be transferring the sound dailies, and where you will be cutting. The production manager or the production office coordinator (often called the p.o.c.) can also give you some idea of where and how to obtain supplies, how you can obtain a supply of petty cash, and a current crew list. Get your name and Wendy's on the crew list immediately (as well as your apprentice's name, if you have one). Often, you will be working with people you already know. This can help you to see the strengths and weaknesses you will be faced with during the filmmaking process.

The people you will need to know most directly are the director (of course), the sound recordist and whoever is taking the sound notes, the second assistant camera (this person takes the camera notes) and, most importantly, the script supervisor. The script supervisor's paperwork will be your most direct link with the set. If you have a good rapport with him or her, everything will run that much more smoothly.

Finally, you should do something that seems so obvious to me that I am always shocked by how many people never bother to do it. I make a point of meeting the people with whom I'll be dealing. I drop by the laboratory to introduce myself to the customer contact person and the shipping clerks. I say hello to the dailies projectionist (often this is at the lab where you'll be processing your dailies). I go by to see the person doing the sound transfers and the shipping clerks at the sound transfer house. In fact, I introduce myself to as many people as I can—at the editing rental house, in the production office, on the set. At each stop I'll try and iron out procedures. What time will I be getting my dailies? Should I pick them up or will you deliver? Who will get the paperwork from the office every day during the shoot? When do you need the *negative* and *1/4" tapes*? Where can I reach you after–hours if there is an emergency (though editing staffs often work late and on weekends, many of your contacts will not)? I tell the projectionist all the details about the film (*aspect ratio*, whether the dailies will come on reel or cores, Moviola or flatbed wind, et al). I work out a system for the delivery of all paperwork to the editing room. I find out how to submit time cards and get paychecks.

The assistant's job is to keep things moving smoothly during the editing process. A little bit of advance work here will ease your path later in countless ways.

If you are lucky, the production manager will hire you early enough to do all of these things (two or three days is plenty). But one is rarely that lucky. On most films, you will probably find yourself put on the payroll on the first day of shooting. The dailies will start arriving early the next morning and you will have your hands full making sure all of the equipment and supplies arrive in the cutting on time and in one piece. With the general lethargy of suppliers you will find that one day isn't enough time to get all of this done properly. In that case, I usually spend a day or so during the preceding week making those contacts and ordering the supplies. This is not, of course, a completely satisfactory solution. There are always a thousand things you must do in your personal life the week before you start a film (that dentist appointment really won't wait another ten months) but production managers seem to expect that you will give them this free time and, in order to avoid hassles later in the film, you should oblige them if there is no other alternative.

Meeting people before the film begins really *is* that important.

Another major task at this point is hiring the crew. On some films it is obvious at the outset that the complexity of the film will exceed the crew's capacity to get it done effectively, and the hiring of an extra assistant (or an additional apprentice) is permitted. In any case, if the crew of *Silent Night* is to exceed you and Wendy, the two of you will have to decide who to hire.

From reading the script, you and Wendy have decided that no additional assistant will be necessary on this film. This is often a budgetary constraint put on you rather than a well-thought out decision on your part. The crew will consist of the two of you and an apprentice. There are many ways of finding qualified editing crews. After having worked in the business for a while, you will probably know people with whom you're comfortable working. Actually, this is one of the assets that you bring to the editing crew—your contacts with potential apprentices. It is possible that Wendy might have someone she wants to hire. You may have worked with an apprentice before who already knows how you work and could handle the job with a minimum of learning your own system. The unions also keep lists of qualified people and you can call them for this "availability list" (though I have often found these lists to be quite out of date). In many cutting rooms, job seekers come by in a seemingly never-ending stream, leaving their resumes behind. I have sometimes hired from among these people after talking with them.

54

One word of warning on this last method. For union jobs on either coast, there is a rule that you must first give all out-of-work and qualified union members a chance at the job before hiring outside of the union. In practice, this means interviewing the people on the availability list first. In some cases it may be helpful to involve the production manager in your decision.

However you've chosen to find additional crew, the one guiding factor in making that decision is to realize that this person must help to move things smoothly during the editing process. Many people prefer to hire someone they've already worked with and with whom they feel comfortable for this very reason.

Let's say that Wendy and you have decided to hire Philip Spring, a young man who worked with the two of you on your last film.

You've all settled on your salaries and read the script, you have already set up the cutting room with the Moviolas and supplies. Maybe you've even met the director to say hello.

The first day's shooting has been completed. It is now Tuesday morning. Your real work is about to begin.

WORKING DIGITALLY BEFORE SHOOTING

Since most of what the assistant editor does before shooting deals with organization and getting acquainted, most of the processes we talked about in Chapter 3 apply equally to working on a film to be cut digitally. One of the major differences you will find in the preparation for a digitally cut film has to do with the capricious nature of computers. You will certainly need more than one day to make sure your systems are set up properly.

Computers are testy by nature. Cabling that worked fine on one film malfunctions on the next. Additional programs on the computer may conflict with the editing programs. I have had machines delivered without the proper set-up, machines that edited fine but were not be able to control tape machines or input footage from them properly. All of these things need to be ironed out before the first dailies tape comes through the editing room door.

Both the Lightworks and Avid machines enable anyone who works on them to create a large number of special settings, specific to the way they like to work. One editor may prefer to have information set up very differently than another. Luckily, these settings can be saved on a computer disk and carried from job to job. One of your jobs will be to get Wendy's settings disk from her and set it up on the machine so she will be working with familiar settings.

If possible, you should try and save one day's worth of dailies from a previous film on whatever tape format is to be used on your new film, along with the computer disk file for that day's dailies. That way, when your computer editing system is set up, it will be a simple matter to test the entire process from beginning to end—

digitizing in the dailies, organizing it in the machine, attempting a trial edited sequence and outputting it to video. You can also try and generate some cut lists and EDLs as well (Don't worry about any of these terms right now; we will get to all of them in future chapters. Your patience will be rewarded—or you can look them up in the Glossary at the back of the book.)

You also have at least one more stop to make along your get-acquainted tour of your suppliers—the telecine house. This is where your negative or work print dailies will go every day, along with your sound, to be transferred to the videotape you will use to input into your editing machine.

Telecine machines are large and expensive so the telecine house usually makes sure that the machines are booked in advance. It wouldn't do to have any of their machines laying idle—the interest on the purchase loans is way too high. You will need to book a certain amount of time on a regular basis (just how much time may have already been determined by the production manager, if not, you should discuss it with him or her first), letting them know what shooting days will be night shoots, what days you will not have dailies and the like. Like any supplier, the better the relationship you have with them (which means the more abreast you keep them of information affecting them) the more flexible you will find them to be when you need changes. Keeping them informed works to *everyone's* advantage.

57

You should also find out from the sound recordist what format of sound they will be working with. Some location recordists use 1/4" tape, recorded on Nagra machines. These machines can be mono or stereo. Some recordists use DAT (Digital Audio Tape). Each format will require that the telecine house have a different piece of equipment.

You can also help things move smoothly by making sure everyone on the set knows exactly what the telecine house needs to do its job properly. The second assistant camera person may need to mark the camera report or the purchase order "PREPARE FOR TELECINE" so the negative preparers at the lab know to punch a hole at the top of each selected roll of negative. The sound recordist will probably need to make sure there are at least five or ten seconds of *pre-roll* before the recording of any sync sound (including the slate). This means the recordist will need to roll his or her tape machine for at least five or ten seconds before the slate is clapped. This allows the telecine house enough time to make sure the original DAT (or 1/4" tape) is in perfect sync with their master videotape before they start recording.

If you are going to telecine from negative you need to schedule its transport from the lab after processing. If there is to be print made you need to schedule whether it is done before or after a negative telecine. On *Mad Dog Time* we telecined from the negative but still made prints of all of the selected takes so the director of photography and I could look at it each day for quality. We used a lab that did both printing and telecine, but we had them do the negative telecine first because that was done with sound, the picture film dailies were done silent.

If you are going to telecine from the print after it has been sunk up, you need to schedule the telecine so as to leave enough time for dailies synching and projections. This will need to be worked out with the production manager as well as the projection facility.

Everything is about proper communication. Without it, something will surely go wrong. And it is one of the major jobs of an assistant editor to anticipate every potential problem so nothing goes wrong that could have been avoided.

Determining Storage Needs

Digital editing systems work by converting the film picture image into a series of bits saved onto the computer's hard drives. The computer then plays back the images by very rapidly reading this data and converting it into video information on the computer screen. Each frame takes up an enormous amount of room on those hard drives; it is not uncommon to need many drives for an average film. One of your jobs will be to make sure the producers rent an adequate amount of storage for the amount of footage to be shot.

As we discussed in Chapter One, the better the picture quality, the more space will be needed for storage of those bits of picture information. The degree of picture quality is referred to as *resolution*. Different computer systems use different terms to refer to resolution settings. Avid labels each resolution with an arbitrary AVR (Avid Video Resolution) number. AVR 1 is the worst picture quality, AVR 77 is one of the best (it is also a two field image as opposed to the usual where only one of each frame's fields are digitized; that makes it an ideal resolution for videotape quality projects). Because of the huge amounts of hard drive space needed to digitize at AVR 77, no feature can digitize dailies at that rate. The typical resolution is either AVR 4 or AVR 6 (there is no longer an AVR 5). Lightworks labels its resolutions by the approximate amount of footage a one gigabyte hard drive will hold. The lowest resolution (worst picture quality) is 90 minutes. Presently, the best on your average machine is 30 minutes (though there are resolutions up to five minutes available on the high end machines). Once again, no one cuts at the best resolution. The typical feature will cut at the 40 minute resolution.

Wendy (perhaps in concert with Adam or with you) will need to balance the need to conserve storage space with the need for a high enough picture quality to make good editing decisions and decent quality viewing tapes. Once the resolution is determined, it is a simple matter to determine how much hard drive space is needed. Avid provides a chart to help make the computation. Since Lightworks' resolutions refer to time and hard drive space all that is needed is a calculator to do the math.

As an example, on Lightworks systems, a film printing one hour of footage a day for a shoot of 60 days will need 60 hours of space for dailies alone. I like to leave an additional 20 percent for opticals, sound effects and music, B-negative prints and the like. That means you should make sure there is enough room for 72 hours of material. At a resolution of 45 minutes (that is, 45 minutes for each gigabyte of hard drive storage) you would need 96 gigabytes of storage. If this is too much storage, you would need to edit at a lower resolution (you'd need 86 gigs to cut at the 50 minute resolu- tion). Both Avid and Lightworks now allow you to edit material digitized at different resolutions. You may find that you can digitize most of your footage at AVR 4 (or 50 minutes on the Lightworks) but that the darker material needs to be digitized at a better resolution.

You will also need to determine at what sample rate the sound will be digitized. Various editing systems have different options but the general rule of thumb is that the better the resolution, the more space the sound will eat up. Possible sample rates are 16, 22.05, 24, 32, 44.1 or 48 Khz. If you are intending to use the sound from your machine for previews and large screenings it makes sense to digitize at the higher sample rates. In addition, if you are going to hand your media files over to your sound editing house at the end of your editing process (using a standard format such as OMF, the Open Media Framework) you might want to digitize at the most professional quality available. You will also want to decide if you will be inputting from an analog source (such as 3/4" or Beta-SP tape) or a digital source (such as DigiBeta). Unlike picture resolutions, you cannot mix sound sample rates on a project.

Storage comes in different formats—towers enclosing stacks of several drives, bricks holding either four or nine gig drives (these sizes are constantly changing), or R-mag drives which are removable blocks that slide into a case moving the hard drives. It all amounts to the same thing and you'll have to determine just how much storage the production will need.

You don't need to start off with the full amount of storage at the beginning of your shoot. You can begin with far less and add more in chunks as you come close to filling up each drive.

Special Television Needs

On shows that are not finishing on film there are a few more things that may be helpful for you to work out before the dailies start coming in. They all fall under the category of preventing errors in the distant future.

Unlike 35mm film finishing, television shows are finished on some high end tape format like *D-1*, *D-2*, or *Digital Beta*. We will examine the process in more detail in Chapter 16A but, as you can imagine, you will need to create all kinds of lists so your *on-line* editor, who will be matching the show (not unlike a negative cutter), can properly put together an edit on that high end tape matching the edit you did inside your computer editing machine.

At the heart of that group of lists is something called the *Edit Decision List*, often abbreviated *EDL*. This is, in a nutshell, a list showing all the cuts (called *events*), titles and transitions, the type of cut (e.g. picture only, track only, both), and all of the pertinent time code information from the footage. It also lists the original videotape rolls the footage can be found in. This way, the on-line editor can easily (with the aid of a computer) and quickly find the exact tape you used to make every cut in the film and match it frame-to-frame, in its exact length, copying every fade and dissolve.

Obviously, the information on this list better be completely accurate. In the next chapter we will discuss the ways that you can make sure the data going into these lists is correct. However, there is another factor you can verify right now, before a single frame has been shot.

Like everything else in this world of computer editing, there are a host of standards for EDLs. The most popular formats are called CMX and GVG (named for two of the original manufacturers of linear tape editing machines). A third, less popular version, is the Sony format. Additionally, there are three existent CMX formats (called CMX 340, CMX 3400 and CMX 3600). At the end of your editing process you will create an EDL in one of these formats and save it on a computer disk that you will take to the on-line house. The computer the on-line editor works with will read this EDL and magically match the original video footage to your cut, using the list. Though many on-line editing bays can accept disks written in any of these formats, not all of them can. It would be a good idea if you check with your final on-line post house to find out what types of formats they can read. You should also find out what type of disks they need since, once again, there are several standards. The most common is a disk format called RT-11. You still use normal floppy disks (though you should make sure that they are marked "Double Sided, Double Density" (DD2D) rather than the normally formatted floppy disks which are "Double Sided, High Density" (DDHD). Sony EDLs use normal DOS (IBM-PC style) computer disks.

Get all of the pertinent information including permissible reel, disk and file names. Some computer editing systems will create names that are illegal to the EDL reading computer at your on-line house. Make sure any decisions you make at this stage will not create problems for you later.

This would also be a good time to request that your telecine house send over a videotape in your format containing your *banners*. These are short lengths of titling, the equivalent of the "Scene Missing" leaders which are used in film. If you have made a tape for a previous show with all your banners you should bring this in to the editing room.

Your banner reel should include the following titles, set against a black background:

- Scene Missing
- Shot Missing
- Optical Missing
- CGI Shot Missing
- Insert Commercial Here

Some assistants joke that they should make a banner saying "Plot Missing."

Many of the digital editing systems allow you to create your own title cards quite easily. Rather than going to the expense and trouble of having your telecine house create the banners you should spend a few minutes when your machine arrives in the editing room making them yourself.

61

SHOOTING

Dailies Preparation

If everything is moving smoothly, on Tuesday morning you will either pick up or receive three different packages from three different locations. From the film laboratory, you will get the picture dailies and their accompanying paperwork. The sound transfer house will give you the track dailies and their accompanying paperwork. And, from the production office, you will receive a copy of the script supervisor's notes (some supervisors supply you with a rough copy now and follow up a few days later with a typed-up final version). If you are lucky enough to be working at a studio in Los Angeles where everything is done on the lot (with the exception of the lab work) your apprentice can pick everything up in five minutes. On films with tight deadlines I often have the dailies picked up very early in the morning so the synching can be finished early. Every assistant starts at different times depending upon when the film and track comes to them but, during dailies, you can count on starting anywhere between 7:00 and 8:30 a.m.

The paperwork you get with the picture dailies should include the *laboratory report* and the *camera report* (sometimes the camera reports come from the production office rather than the lab). You should also get at least a verbal report (a *negative report*) from the customer contact person at the lab if there is anything wrong *whatsoever* with the printed dailies. Often they will have already notified the director of photography and, perhaps, the producer if there is something drastically wrong with the footage. However, if there are some scratches, some dirt (either on the negative or on the print) or some other more minor problem, you may be the only one to know at this point. You should also determine whether the problem is correctable.

Sometimes, in the case of problems existing only on the dailies print, the lab will reprint the piece for you in time for you to include the corrected take in the dailies screening later in the day. Sometimes that isn't possible or preferable. However, by the time you walk into that dailies screening, you should know everything there is to know about the footage everyone else is going to look at for the first time. If something looks wrong, people will want to know immediately whether it is a problem with the print or on the camera original, and whether or not it is correctable. You, as the assistant, will probably be the only one who can know the answer and you'd better know it (it's also a good idea to tell the editor about it as soon as you find out; that way he or she can determine just how serious the problem is with regards to the rest of the coverage).

In many cases you will receive dailies not from the lab but from a telecine house which will have already sunk up the material for you, with greater or lesser accuracy depending upon how many cups of coffee the telecine operator had in the evening while doing the transfer. We will discuss all of these options in Chapter 4A.

One note about lab contact people. I have only twice met anyone in this position who did not think that part of their job description was to protect their lab—even by lying, if necessary. This is why a good rapport with them is absolutely essential. You'll find out fast if you can trust them or not.

The camera report you receive is written up by the second assistant cameraperson on the set (*see* Figure 4.1). It lists a lot of information helpful to the lab and a few useful tidbits for you. For starters, it shows you everything that was shot the day before.

In the normal American system of shooting, each successive camera set-up (that is, each time the camera or lens is reset to a different position) is given a different and unique letter. In Scene 11, for instance, the first set-up would be called Scene 11. The next set-up would be Scene 11A, followed by 11B, 11C, etc. etc. Each time the camera is rolled on a set-up the set-up letter is followed by a sequential take number. Therefore, the first take of Scene 11A is called Scene 11A-1, followed by 11A-2, 11A-3, etc. After the last take of 11A is shot, the next take would be Scene 11B-1, followed by 11B-2, 11B-3, etc.

There are other methods of slating takes and I will cover them in Chapter 7, "Special Cases."

Takes your director, Adam Free, wanted printed for editing

CAMERA REPORT

			Roll #	Sheet #
			/	/

Film: Silent Night	Director Adam Free	Cam# 2	Mag# A
Job #	D.P. M. Carne		
Date 9·13·99	Asst.		

Scene	TK	SD	Ftge	Remarks	Scene	TK	SD	Ftge	Remarks
10	1		70						
	2		105						
	3		178						
	4		250						
	⑤		320						
	⑥		390						
10A	1		410	MOS					
	②		435	"					
10B	1		485						
	②		535						
10C	①		585						
10D	1		625						
	⑥		675						
	⑧		755						
10E	1		775	TS					
	②		800	TS					

INSTRUCTIONS: **PRINT CIRCLED TAKES ONLY**

PRINT NORMAL
DAY - INT
PREP FOR TELECINE

TYPE of NEG	5247

FIGURE 4.1 *A camera report. As this is the first roll shot on the first day of filming it is labeled "Roll #1". Often camera rolls are preceded by letters indicating if it was shot by an A or a B camera (e.g., "Roll B32"). Note that both takes on setup 10A are MOS and that both takes on setup 10E were tail slated ("TS"). Only the circled takes will be printed. The processed takes from the rest of the negative (called the "B-negative") will be stored at the lab. The cameraperson has instructed the lab to print the circled takes normally for a day interior scene. If the negative is to be telecined directly to videotape for editing on a digital editing system the designation "PREP FOR TELECINE" is written in the instructions.*

are circled. Each camera roll is usually 1000 feet in 35mm or 400 feet in 16mm (approximately 11 minutes). As each take is shot, the second assistant marks the approximate ending footage of each take on the sheet. This continues until the camera roll is used up, or is used up enough so that the second assistant does not want to take a chance it will roll out before the end of the next take.

On top of the camera report are two pieces of information that are also important—the shooting date (in this case September 13, 1999) and the camera roll number (the cumulative count of rolls shot over the entire movie shoot; since this is the first roll shot on the first day it is called camera roll number one). Each camera roll takes up one or two sheets, depending upon how many takes were shot on that roll. In no case does any camera report include data for more than one camera roll.

With the camera report and the picture dailies, it is common for most labs to send a *lab report* (*see* Figure 4.2). After processing the original negative, a *negative assembly* person at the lab pulls out the negative for the selected (circled) takes and strings them all together. The lab then prints only these selects (the remaining non-printed takes—called *B-negative*—are stored for possible later use). Since a lot of negative has been removed from the camera rolls, selected takes from several camera rolls usually end up on a single lab roll. The lab report is a list of all takes on that lab roll. Also listed will be the color timing lights (the amount of red, blue and green used in the printing process to get the color image you see in the print; these numbers are sometimes given for their complementary colors—yellow, cyan and magenta, the numbers are therefore sometimes known as *Y-C-M numbers*) for the takes on the lab roll, the date, and a few other bits of information. In 16mm it is common practice to print all takes on every camera roll, since most labs won't take the chance of damaging the smaller negative by handling it to remove takes.

65

At some point, your sound dailies will arrive (often, this occurs before the picture dailies). And, like almost everything else involved in your job, they come with some paperwork. The *sound report* is analogous to the camera report—it lists all takes recorded and indicates (by circling the take number) which are the selected ones. It also lists the sound roll number (the cumulative roll number for the original quarter-inch tape reel the sound has been recorded on), the date of recording, and any special transfer instructions (*see* Figure 4.3). In addition, a report similar to the lab report sometimes comes from the transfer house. This *transfer report* lists everything actually transferred along with any special procedures done to the sound dailies.

You can get your sound dailies on any number of formats—35mm single-stripe, three-stripe or full coat are the most common. This 35mm sound film is called *mag*, referring to the magnetic oxide onto which the sound is transferred. We will discuss single-stripe primarily, but you should know that there are some advantages and

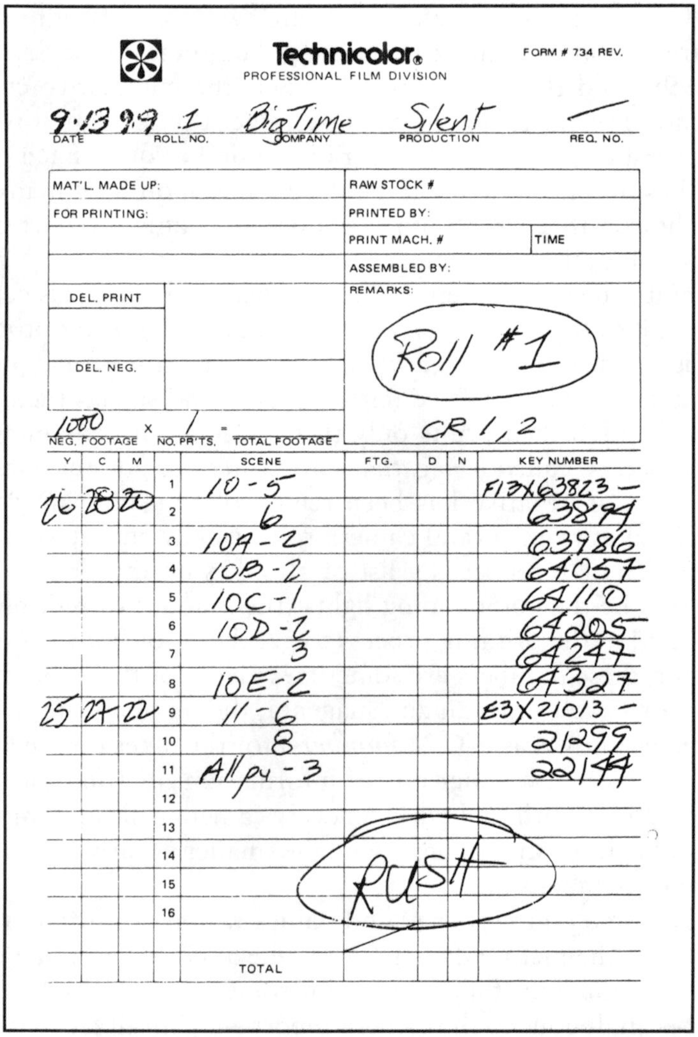

Technicolor®
PROFESSIONAL FILM DIVISION
FORM # 734 REV.

DATE: 9·13·99 ROLL NO.: 1 COMPANY: BigTime PRODUCTION: Silent REQ. NO.: —

MAT'L. MADE UP:	RAW STOCK #
FOR PRINTING:	PRINTED BY:
	PRINT MACH. # / TIME
	ASSEMBLED BY:
DEL. PRINT	REMARKS: Roll #1
DEL. NEG.	CR 1, 2

NEG. FOOTAGE 1000 × NO. PR'TS. 1 = TOTAL FOOTAGE

Y	C	M		SCENE	FTG.	D	N	KEY NUMBER
			1	10-5				F13X63823 –
26	28	20	2	6				63894
			3	10A-2				63986
			4	10B-2				64057
			5	10C-1				64110
			6	10D-2				64205
			7	3				64247
			8	10E-2				64327
25	27	22	9	11-6				E3X21013 –
			10	8				21299
			11	All py-3				22144
			12					
			13					
			14					
			15					
			16					
				TOTAL				

RUSH

FIGURE 4.2 The lab report. Only the circled takes from the camera reports have been printed. This single lab roll contains takes from camera rolls one and two. The numbers listed on the left are the amounts of yellow, cyan, and magenta used in color balancing (timing) the dailies. When you get one-light dailies all takes will be printed at the same timing lights. The numbers at the right are the initial key numbers for each take. (Courtesy Technicolor, Inc.)

disadvantages to transferring to 35mm full-coat or three-stripe. The disadvantages are simple; it is more expensive to buy full-coat and it is often harder to code and cut it. However, if your production sound recordist has recorded the tracks using a time-coded DAT or Nagra, then there are strong advantages to using this more

4 Film Forms

SOUND REPORT

COMPANY _Big Time Films, Inc._   Roll # _1_   Sheet # _1_ of _1_

TITLE _Silent Night_

Date	_9.13.99_			Mic		
Job #		Recordist	_T.A. Edison_			
Director	_Adam Free_			Speed	_30 NDF_	

Scene	TK	Remarks	Scene	TK	Remarks
		1 K TONE	WT 001		Room Tone
10	1	Bad num	11	1	
	2	″		2	Print for sound
	3	OK		3	
	4			4	
	5	Best for sound		5	
	6			6	
10B	1			7	
	2			8	
10C	1		Allpu	1	
10D	1			2	
	2			3	
10E	1				
	2				

INSTRUCTIONS FOR TRANSFER:
Transfer left channel only
Head tones: left ch   -20 db
         right ch   -30 db

FIGURE 4.3 A sound report. Since setup 10A was shot MOS there is no sound listed for those takes. Note the wild track taken and the printed take marked "Print for sound only." No picture will be printed for this take. Note its presence in the lined script and the log, then file this extra print along with the wild track. The instructions at the bottom of the sound report are for the transfer house. In this case they note that the sound has been recorded in mono with the same track being laid onto both tracks of the stereo DAT at two different levels. The person doing the transfer should transfer only the left channel. The second channel is used in case the first track has some distortion in it. Since the second channel was recorded at a lower level it will often not have that distortion. Note that the recordist notes that the DAT was recorded at 30 NDF. This means that the tape is running at 30 frames per second with non-drop frame time code. In order for the telecine or sound transfer house to transfer the tape in perfect sync, they will have to play it back at exactly 30 fps.

pg 1 of 2

EDITOR'S DAILY LOG

COMPANY Big Time Films Inc.

TITLE Silent Night

SCRIPT SUPERVISOR
Ashley Ligne

Date	9·13·99			
Job #				
Director	Adam Free			
Scene	TK	CR	SR	Remarks
10	5	1	1	Master – ABBY
	6			
10A	2		MOS	ABBY's pov of room
10B	2		1	MS – ABBY at cabinet
10C	1			CU – ABBY at cabinet
10D	2			MCU – ABBY thru room
	3			M.S. TK 4
10E	2			MCU – ABBY thru hallway
WT 1001	—			Sc 10 Roomtone
11	3	2		WS – master ABBY + BOB
	6			
	8			
A-1 pu	3		2	pu master
11A	2			MS – BOB
	3	3		
	6			Best!
11B	2			CU – BOB
	3			
11C	1		4	MS – ABBY
	3			
	4			

EDITOR'S DAILY LOG

68

FIGURE 4.4 *The Editor's Daily Log as prepared by the script supervisor. It lists, in a nutshell, every piece of picture and sound which was printed for the day's shooting, along with descriptions of each take. This log is the ultimate guide for what takes should be arriving on the assistant's bench for synching.*

expensive format. It is very easy to transfer that code onto channel three of the mag. In addition, one sound transfer house in Los Angeles has patented a way of encoding scene, roll and take information onto the three-stripe mag stock. After the film is edited, it is then possible, using a special reader, to decode all the information from the cut work tracks and create an Edit Decision List (EDL, of which we will talk more about in Chapter 11A). This EDL will save a lot of time and mistakes at the beginning stage of sound editing, as the sound house begins to retransfer and rebuild all of the dialog tracks.

Another common piece of paperwork is the *Editor's Daily Log*, though it is often called by other names depending on the jargon your script supervisor uses. This log (*see* Figure 4.4) lists every picture and sound take Adam wanted printed in the order that they were shot, which is the order you will normally be receiving them. It also lists camera and sound rolls as well as short descriptions of each set-up. This information can be your guide as to exactly which picture and sound takes you should have delivered to you. If there is anything missing you can quickly order it up so you can get it in time for the dailies screening.

A final, but crucial, piece of paperwork you will receive are the *script supervisor's notes* , made up of two pieces of paper, the *script notes* (see Figure 4.5) and the *lined script,* so called because they are script pages the supervisor has drawn lines on, denoting just what lines are covered by which takes (*see* Figure 4.6). This paperwork, along with Editor's Daily Log, is the only real link you have with the director. You will soon find that there are as many systems for script supervisors as there are for assistant editors. Every person seems to have his or her own paperwork form. Often you will get more paperwork than listed here, some of which will be useful and some of it completely superfluous to your job (script supervisors have to create a lot of paperwork for departments other than editorial). It is a good idea to familiarize yourself with the type of notes the script supervisor will be sending to you *before* shooting begins since they are all interesting, but you won't have a lot of time to peruse them during the busy synching period

With the advent of fax machines it is now possible to get the camera, sound and script reports from the production office *before* the actual film and sound comes to you. In that case, you can do all of your organizing early, with just the paperwork in hand.

The first thing you'll want to do is to compare all the paperwork to make sure everything that was supposed to be printed was actually printed. You may be surprised to find out how often things

PICTURE <u>Silent Night, Silent Cowboy</u>   DIRECTOR <u>Adam Free</u>
                                              DATE <u>9·13·99</u>

Sc.	Tk	SR	CR	Comments	Description
10	1	1	1	0:40 "Horrid"	40MM - ABBY enters room screen r.,
	2			0:20 INC	x's to desk and throws mss.
	3			0:41	onto table. He reaches for
	4			0:38 "Rushed"	cabinet, gets shocked, then
	⑤			0:45 "Good"	pulls out liquor. He drinks,
	⑥			0:45 "Best"	hears typewriter, then exits
					cam. r.
10A	1	MOS		0:10	40MM - ABBY's P.O.V. of the room.
	②			0:12	
10B	1	1		0:35	60MM - ABBY reaches for cabinet,
	②			0:37	gets shocked, hears noise, and
					exits cam. r.
10C	①			0:29	90MM - Closer of 10B
10D	1			0:21 "NG"	75MM - ABBY walks in from S.R.
	②			0:20 "Good"	and throws mss. on table.
	③			0:30 "Best"	He exits S.R.
				(slated TK4)	
10E	1 TS			0:15	75MM - ABBY enters O.S.L., goes
	② TS			0:10 "Good"	into bedroom hall, and exits.

FIGURE 4.5 The script supervisor's notes. See the caption for FIGURE 4.6.

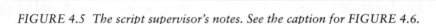

go wrong, either because the second assistant camera or assistant sound didn't circle the proper takes, or because the lab or sound house made an error. If there is any discrepancy, you should call the lab or sound house and get it corrected immediately. If the dailies screening is not scheduled until the end of the day it is often possible to get an unprinted take sent to you in the afternoon, in time to get into the screening. Sound transfers are usually easier to get than picture reprints.

The ability to phone in for a quick print is why I prefer to have the original negative and sound tapes stored at the lab and sound transfer house, respectively. On some documentaries or low-budget films the sound tapes and sometimes even the negative are stored in the editing room. I don't like this idea because labs and transfer houses are better equipped to store and handle this material than an editing staff. All you need is one friend stopping by to say hello carrying a big radio (or any other item with a large magnet in it) and stepping too close to the sound tapes and—presto!—instant blank tape. There is a scene in Brian DePalma's *Blow-Out* in which sound editor John Travolta returns to his editing room to find all of his sound tapes demagnetized. He plays roll after roll and hears no more than tape hiss on any of them. It is a sound editor's ultimate nightmare.

After you've checked all of the paperwork you can plan the dailies rolls. Based on the camera and lab reports you should know how long each printed take is. Based on the other paperwork you can now make a plan for how to lay out the dailies rolls.

Using the footage on camera reports you can determine approximately how long each printed take is. The footage on the camera report is sequential, listing the footage on the camera roll when the camera stopped after the take. On our sample camera report in Figure 4.1 we can see that take 10-5 began at 250 feet (this is where the end of take four was) and ended at 320 feet. Take 10-5, therefore, will be about 70 feet when you receive it from the lab.

You should make a copy of the Editor's Daily Log and write the footages of each take next to every printed number listed. Then you can plan how to build up your dailies screening rolls. Generally, it is a good idea to keep the rolls in the 800- to 900-foot range (not too big but also big enough to give the projectionist time to thread up the next reel). It is sometimes possible to leave the takes on the dailies rolls in the same order as the lab rolls. That way you can save yourself the time of cutting apart and rearranging the dailies. This is very helpful if you are pressed for time. What this means, though, is that the crew will see the film projected in the order it was shot. Many directors and editors, myself included, prefer to see the dailies in the order that it will appear in the final film (that is, in scene number order).

There are other times when the lab rolls will have to be cut apart and respliced. When a director is shooting with more than one camera, he or she will usually want to see both cameras for each camera set-up (or take) one right after another. Since the takes will come in different camera rolls (since they've come from different cameras) they will almost never end up in the proper sequence in the lab rolls. You will then have to cut the takes apart and resplice them into the proper order.

8   INT   BARROOM SET   DAY

On the right we can see JAMES sitting next to the
cameraman as COWBOY and PETE are fighting. They aren't
really hitting each other, of course, and the absence
of the smacking sounds is highlighted by the absence
of most of the other sounds normally associated with a
bar brawl: cheering people, smashing chairs, etc. etc.
There is a complete silence, broken occasionally by
the grunts of the actors and a command or two from
JAMES. COWBOY falls to the ground and is immediately
set upon by the four other EXTRAS. He has his money
bag and gun taken from him. All of the extras back off
the set, guns drawn, until they are out of camera
range, where they break character and sometimes watch
the remainder of the take. Finally, James stands up
from his director's chair.

                    JAMES
        Cut!

There is an immediate roar of noise.

                    JAMES
              (to the cameraman)
        Did the zoom look okay?

                    CAMERMAN
        Fine, James, fine.

ABBY enters and leans on part of the set in the right
of the frame.

                                     CUT TO:

9   EXT   LOT   TWILIGHT

It is twilight as a number of people exit the studio.
Several technicians who we recognize are walking to
the parking lot. In the back of the crowd is ABBY,
walking slowly, in a bit of a fog. He crosses the
parking lot as several cars whiz by him. By the time
he has rached his car and gotten inside the car,
almost all of the other cars have left the lot. ABBY
starts his engine and watches as all the cars leave,
their noise dying out, only their taillights visible.
He revs the engine once and then slams the door shut.

                                     CUT TO:

10   INT   ABBY'S   APARTMENT   NIGHT

ABBY's apartment is a fairly modest one with a few
extravagances and concessions to life in a world of
fads and fashions. He enters and crosses over to a
large plastic rocking chair, sitting on a huge white

72

FIGURE 4.6 *The lined script. The script notes (see FIGURE 4.5) and the
lined script are your best links with the set. Every take made is listed along
with comments on them. By looking at any given line of dialogue or action on
this lined script you can easily see the shots that were taken that cover that
line. For instance, for the last line on the second page of the script you can see
that there were eight shots made: a master and its pickup, three shots of BOB
(including a pickup) and three shots of ABBY. The squiggly lines denote action or dialogue that is not performed on camera in that particular setup.*

10   10B   10C

shag rug. Throwing his script down on a glass coffee
table, he reaches for a small metal filing cabinet. He
touches it and receives an electric shock.

                    ABBY
        Damn!

He reaches inside the file for a bottle of whiskey,
and is pouring himself a drink when he hears a   10E
typewriter start up in the next room. He follows the   MS-A
sound around the corner and into his bedroom.

11   INT ABBY'S BEDROOM   NIGHT
11-WS   11B MS-BOB   11 CU-B

As ABBY enters he sees a man sitting at a small desk
by the window. He is hunched over a typewriter making
yet another correction. As soon as ABBY sees him his
face relaxes a bit — he knows this man. It is BOB, his
next-door neighbor.   MCU-A

                    ABBY
        Evening Mister Hemingway.

Bob, startled, turns around.

                    BOB
        Why don't you move into the twentieth
        century and get a word processor already?

                    ABBY
        How'd you get into my apartment?
                dolly →
                    BOB
        I told the landlady I needed some
        typewriter ribbon. How'd the filming go Mr.
        DeMille?
                                11D   11E
                    ABBY   MS-A   CU-A
        Perfectly shitty. I don't even recognize
        what he's filming.

                    BOB
        He didn't switch movies on you, did he?

                    ABBY
        No, I still recognize some of the plot
He stops, at a loss for words, then sits on the bed.

                    ABBY
        How's the Great American Novel coming?
                AllBob
                    BOB
        Fine, except for the part where I have to
        pay the rent. Speaking of which … your
        agent called.

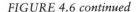
Dolly to →
M2/S

73

FIGURE 4.6 continued

Once you have determined the content and order of each dailies
roll, make up one list for each reel. Tape them somewhere prominent.

Up until now you've done a lot of paper pushing and haven't
even touched the film. Now you can do that (about time, huh?).
Assuming that the last of the paperwork arrived by 8:30 a.m. (this
almost never happens, but let's make believe), by 9:15 you should

have had your morning coffee, chatted with the crew of the film down the hall, checked out all the paperwork and are now ready to proceed.

So, let's sync the dailies already.

Philip, your apprentice, should by this time have made up a complete set of head and tail leaders for each reel you're going to sync up today. I usually have the apprentice make up plenty of leaders before the job begins—-about 20 is usually enough for a film edited on a Moviola. For a flatbed film you will need many more. These leaders will be spliced onto the beginning and end of each roll of picture and soundtrack and provide identification as to what is on the roll. Leaders also protect the first and last takes from the normal abuse anything on the outside of film reels usually suffers.

Use white leader for both the picture and track leaders. Then put a long piece of 1" white tape on one end of the leader and write on it with black felt-tip pen (*all* picture labeling should be in black) as shown in Figure 4.7. The soundtrack leader should be written in red as in Figure 4.8. All soundtrack labeling should be in red marker; this will help you to easily differentiate between reels of picture and track.

Before you even stick the white tape onto the leader make sure you are taping it onto the correct side of the leader. Leader, like film, has two sides to it—a shiny side called the *base* and a slightly duller side called the *emulsion*. When 35mm picture is projected it reads correctly if the emulsion if "up," meaning up as it spins off the reel (16mm reversal film, on the other hand, reads correctly "base-up"). This emulsion can scrape off fairly easily when dragged across sound heads. For that reason, the soundtrack leader (as well as any *fill* you are going to insert into the sound rolls) should *never* be emulsion-up; it must always be base-up.

74

You can usually tell which side of a piece of film or leader is which by holding it near a light and moving it around. The emulsion side will appear more matte than the base side, which will seem quite shiny. If it is a piece of film, you might even be able to see some raised edges within the frame on the emulsion side (this is actually a colored layer of the picture image). If you still can't tell, a surefire test is to touch the film with your lips. If you've just "kissed" the base side, the moisture left will wipe off very easily. One of the two disadvantages to this method is, if you've just "kissed" the emulsion side of the film, it will leave little marks there. Try to test a portion of the film that won't be needed (like the leader on the head or tail of the lab roll). The other disadvantage to this method is that you can look awfully silly kissing a piece of film at 9:00 in the morning.

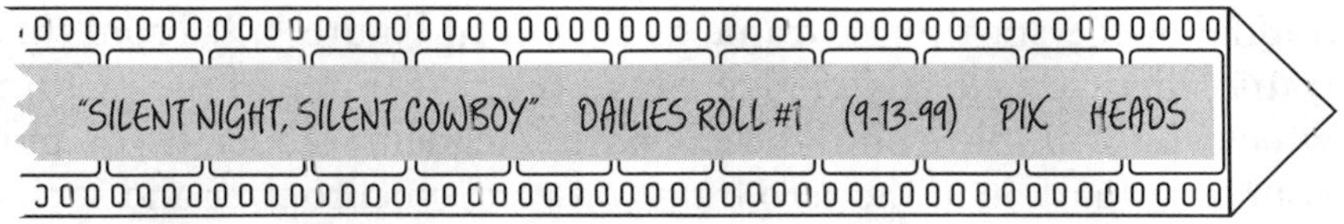

"SILENT NIGHT, SILENT COWBOY" DAILIES ROLL #1 (9-13-99) PIX HEADS

FIGURE 4.7 *Picture head leader (to be written in black). A small wedge is cut on the top of the head leader and reinforced with splicing tape. This prevents the end of the leader from becoming frayed with use.*

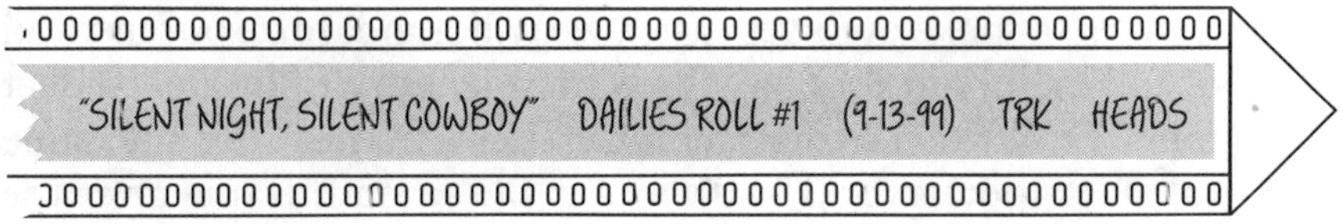

"SILENT NIGHT, SILENT COWBOY" DAILIES ROLL #1 (9-13-99) TRK HEADS

FIGURE 4.8 *Soundtrack head leader (to be written in red).*

So, when you begin to prepare your leaders, make sure the *picture* leaders have their tape stuck onto the emulsion side (since that is how you will wind them on the reels) and the *track* leaders have their tape stuck onto the base side (since you don't want the sound head to be running over the emulsion side of the leader).

A word about track wind, or, the manner in which the soundtrack is wound up onto the reels. Most projectors and 35mm soundtrack playback machines (called *dubbers* or *dummies*) are capable of running with the sound part of the reel facing up or down, either out from the center of the reel or facing in towards the center. You should make sure you are consistent winding the track onto your reels and let the projectionist know how you've wound them. There are various terms to describe the winds. Reels with the sound pointing away from the center of the reel are called "Mag up" or "Moviola wind" (since that is the way sound needs to be wound in order to run through the Moviola properly). Sound facing towards the center of the reel is called "Mag down" or "KEM wind" (since that is the way sound used to have to be threaded in order to go through KEM flatbeds). Some assistants like to put a piece of tape onto the soundtrack head leader telling the projectionist which wind the reel is.

After ten 35mm feet or so (this extra length is necessary so the projectionist has some footage to thread up on his projector before the start mark), splice the picture leader onto an Academy leader about one foot before the picture start mark. Punch a hole in the middle of the start mark frame as shown in Figure 4.9. From this frame, there are exactly twelve feet to the first frame of the picture which you will splice onto the end of the Academy leader. If you put your start mark in at the zero frame on your synchronizer and set its counter to zero, you should cut your Academy leader off at the frame line between the fifteenth frame after the eleven-foot mark and the exact zero frame of the twelve-foot mark. You'll be happy to know that actually *doing* this is much simpler than reading about it.

> [NOTE: To make our lives easier, we will standardize our method of talking about footage. If I want a length of film twelve feet long, I'll write 12'0 feet (12 feet, zero frames). By the same token, a footage of 370'07 means the seventh frame after the 370 foot and zero frame mark. On a synchronizer, you would always place your first frame (which we will call the zero frame) on the white zero mark. 370'07 would therefore fall on the frame marked "seven." However, when I want to mark the frame that I am cutting on, I'll write 370'07/08, which means to cut on the frame line between 370'07 and 370'08. So, an Academy leader begins at 0'00 and cuts to footage at 11'15/00.]

76

The length of the soundtrack leader should be the same, but it will be made entirely out of white leader. After ten or so 35mm feet on the track leader, put a piece of white tape on the leader and mark it as shown in Figure 4.10. Mark it in red, of course (DO NOT write in the bottom half of the leader; this passes over the sound head and may leave some residue that will degrade the sound quality). Once again, punch a hole in the start mark frame. Now, put that frame in the second gang of your synchronizer (your picture is in the first) at the 0'00 mark (the "zero frame") and spin down to the 12 foot mark. Mark the leader at 11'15/00 and make a cut there. Your picture and track leaders will now be the same length *from the start marks* (which is where it counts). All your leaders should be made this length since it is the standard head leader length and will guarantee that when you mix-and-match picture and sound leaders from different reels, they will all be the same length.

Tail leaders are much less complicated to set up. They are about ten feet long and end with the inscription shown in Figure 4.11 written on a piece of 1" tape. The example shown is for a picture tail leader only; track tail leaders look the same except they are written in red and say "TRK" instead of "PIX."

At the tips of both the head and tail leaders I like to cover four to six sprockets with splicing tape cut into a wedge as shown in

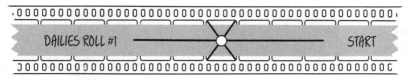

FIGURE 4.9 *Picture start mark.*

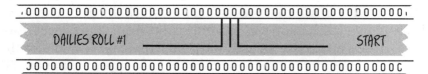

FIGURE 4.10 *Soundtrack start mark. Note that the mark does not extend down into the bottom of the track area since that is where the sound head will be running.*

FIGURE 4.11 *Picture tail leader (to be written in black). The soundtrack tail leader would say "TRK" instead of "PIX" and would be written in red.*

Figure 4.11. This wedge helps you to thread the film onto a reel and prevents the ends from being slowly shredded away by the constant wear and tear they will suffer.

Dailies Synching

You've already decided what is going into each dailies roll. You even have little pieces of paper listing them. For today's dailies you have decided to make the lab rolls the dailies rolls. You will notice that this means one of the dailies rolls will be a little large (since lab roll one is 980 feet long), but this is not inordinately large (1025 feet or more is too large). I prefer to keep the rolls smaller, but in this case, it just isn't worth the extra work to begin splitting everything up into smaller rolls. This would involve splitting take 11pu-3 (the pick-up of set-up 11) off of lab roll number one and putting it onto the head of lab roll number two; then splitting take 11D-5 off the end of lab roll number two and putting that onto the head of lab roll number three.

This illustrates one of the conflicts you will be getting into nearly every day on a film. No matter how many sensible rules you may have set up, they won't help the editing room run smoothly if you don't know when to bend them a little. You must have a sense of priorities. When there is time to do everything you want to do (and this will happen once every ten years or so), you can do them the way you want to do them. When things are moving more slowly than you would like, it is wise to sacrifice some things in order to make sure there is a complete set of dailies for the crew to watch. You will have to use your judgment as to which things can be sacrificed and which cannot; this can only come from experience.

About now, the producer, the production manager and/or the director of photography will probably be calling you to find out "if everything looks all right." Naturally, everyone is nervous. Can the camera operator follow focus? Is the lighting too dark? Did the lab do the job they were supposed to do? If you have to tell them, "Hey, I'm not finished synching yet. I'm still moving the takes around on the lab rolls so I can have all the reels be under 900 feet" they're not going to be very happy or secure with you. So, let's bend the rules about reels being about 900 feet for now.

You now have several rolls of film and several rolls of soundtrack. Things move much faster if the film is already marked. Let's do that.

78

Take the first roll of film. The chances are that it is wound with the tail out, called *tails out.* (If it isn't, don't worry; this system works just as well from the head of the roll as from the tail.) Attach a tail leader to the end of the roll, cutting off anything that is truly garbage. Generally, you will not want to remove anything from the picture roll in case someone needs to see it, but some things are plainly not needed. Cut off portions of the picture before or after the takes that are completely clear or black. Cut off long pieces at the end of takes where the assistant cameraperson has put his or her hand over the lens. Do not cut out, unless asked, *color cards, grey scales,* or pauses at the end of takes where the actors are still visible. On *Fame,* one take was going badly for one of the actresses. She stopped in the middle of the take and waved for the director to cut. Later on, the editor, Gerry Hambling, was able to utilize that wave to make another story point altogether. Had I thrown away this "obviously bad" part of the take, he never would have known it existed on the negative and he would have lost the solution to the problem with this scene.

So, take the tail leader for the first dailies roll, attach it (on the frame line please) emulsion-up to the end of lab roll number one (also emulsion-up), and begin to rewind it until the beginning of the last take on the roll (take 11-8). Between takes there are usually one

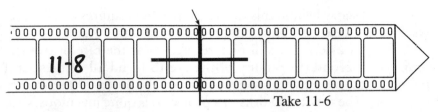

FIGURE 4.12 *The head picture ID is written in grease pencil on the film near the top of each take. Note the cross which is marked at the flash frame between takes 11-6 and 11-8.*

FIGURE 4.13 *The exact frame where the slate is closed (no light can be seen coming through the clapper and the slate itself) is marked with an X and the take is marked with its ID. An arrow points to the frame where the slate is closed.*

79

FIGURE 4.14 *In some cases there is one frame where the clapper is visible both as a blurred image moving towards the slate and already closed. In these cases you should marked the next frame (that is, the one in which it is fully closed and clear) with the "X" and the frame with the blurred slate image with an "O".*

or two completely clear frames called *flash frames*. Even if you are rewinding quite fast, you should be able to see these easily. This gets quite simple to do with practice.

At the point where take 11-6 is cut together with 11-8, put a cross on the frame line and, just to the left of this cross (at the beginning of 11-8) write the take number very large in yellow or white grease pencil (*see* Figure 4.12). Then, using your loupe if you have to, find the first frame where the slate is completely closed. While you're looking at this frame, check the setup and take number to make sure this really is 11-8. If it is, mark that frame as indicated in Figure 4.13—large and in grease pencil. On some takes you will see a frame where there is a completely closed slate but also a blurry trail showing the top of the slate closing on the bottom of the slate (*see* Figure 4.14). If this is the case, mark that frame with a big zero and mark the next frame with the "X".

The theory behind this is very simple, but requires a little side-track, while I explain how film projection works.

Film is a series of still pictures shown at the rate of twenty-four every second (the ability of the eye to blend all of these still pictures into one moving image is based on the thoery of *persistence of vision*). The way this works in a projector is quite ingenious. One frame is shown for one forty-eighth of a second. A plate then drops down in front of the film, blacking out the image for another one forty-eighth of a second. Meanwhile, the next frame is pulled down in front of the lens. The plate moves out of the way and this next frame is projected for one forty-eighth of a second before the plate drops down in front of the film again. If that plate were not dropping down we would actually see the image of the film being pulled down into view. But because the projector is synchronized so the film is only pulled down while the image is blacked out, we never see that happen.

A similar thing happens when the film is shot. But, instead of the light going out to the screen from the projector, the light is coming from the set *into* the camera. The film is exposed for one forty-eighth of a second, during the time the film is steady in the camera. The plate drops down in front of the lens and the film is moved down one frame. This means every forty-eighth of second the film is not recording anything. (This also means that during one–half of the time we watch a film, we are watching a blank screen. This could account for the quality of some of what gets distributed today.)

So...back to marking up the picture frames. Normally, you can look at the frames and see the slate open in one frame and see it closed in the next. We can assume that the slate closed during the one forty-eighth of a second when the plate was in front of the lens. In other words, it happened between the two frames—on the frame line. But in the case where there is a blurred slate, we know that the actual moment when the slate made contact was during the frame that is blurred as well as closed. To be precise in synching dailies, I like to note the difference. Thus, the big circles on the blurred frame. We will get back to them in a few pages.

After marking 11-8, move back to the next take in the reel—11-6. Mark this in the same way. Then do 11-3. Normally, you would continue along the roll after this, doing 10E-2, and so on until you'd finished the roll. But 10E-2 is marked "T.S." (short for *tail slate*) on the reports. This means, for one reason or another, the slate comes at the end of the take, rather than at the head. So, you should not spin back to the top of take 10E-2, but you find the slate and mark it in the same way as just described at the tail of the take.

Every time you write the take number (at the identification at the top of the take as well as on your paperwork) list this take as 10E-2ts.

After you've marked this slate, go to the head of the take and make your cross dividing 10E-2ts from 10D-3. Mark the head identification. Often, there is a closed slate held in front of the camera before the actual synching slate. This is used for identification purposes. You should put your dividing cross *before* this i.d. slate. Continue on with the process until you get to the top of the roll.

When you get there, and have finished with 10-5, attach (at a frame line, please) the end of your head leader onto the head of the roll, leaving out any of the garbage before take 10-5. When this is done, the very first frame of the roll will begin at 12'00, if the head leader is inserted into the synchronizer in our standard way—at 0'00. You have now completed marking up your first roll of picture dailies. When you complete the other two rolls you will have three rolls of picture dailies, all marked up, and all heads out. If the picture came to you heads out, and you marked it from the head rather than from the tail, you would have ended up tails out. In this case, all three rolls should be rewound so they are heads out and ready for synching

Often the lab rolls will come to you not in the order you want to screen them at dailies. In this case, you will need to rearrange them. The fastest way to do that is to separate the takes where you know they are out of order. If all of the takes for Scene 11 came before Scene 10, for instance, you could proceed as normal until you got to the break between the two scenes. You could then separate the rolls at that point.

The other place where I like to break picture takes is when I reach the point where I know the dailies rolls will break. As an example, let us say that I have determined that one of my dailies reels will end at 12B-6 and the next reel will begin with 12C-1. I would be sure to separate the rolls of picture at that point when I am marking them up.

I like to write the contents of each roll of picture on a piece of paper and attach it to the outside of each roll of takes so I can easily see what each roll contains when they are sitting in a row on the film rack.

Dailies rolls should be numbered sequentially from the first day of shooting through to the last. If there are six rolls of dailies on the first day, the second day's dailies rolls will begin with Dailies Roll Seven. All you need to do is put a piece of tape over the roll number and date on the leaders and you can reuse one day's dailies roll leaders on another day.

Before you are completely ready for synching you must similarly mark up the soundtrack dailies, a process known as "popping the tracks." The track will also, in all likelihood, come to you tails out, but very rarely will they come to arranged in rolls in the same manner as the picture dailies. To help you out of this, it is best to begin marking them up from the tail. That way, you can build them into the rolls that you've already determined as you go along (you can now see the advantage of figuring out the dailies reel breakdown ahead of time). An alternate method of breaking down the track is to separate each set-up into its own roll (spun onto cores or their own hand-rolls). All of the takes in set-up 12A would be rolled up together and all of the takes in set-up 12B would be rolled up together in their own separate roll. I normally set these in a sequential row on one or two shelves on the back rack on the editing bench.

There is a slightly different procedure for marking the track dailies. Before I start talking about that, however, I should mention a recent improvement to sound transfers that has been appearing with increasing frequency. Most of the sound recorded on movies today is recorded with a machine that records a SMPTE Time Code as well as the sound being taped. This time code will make it much easier for your sound editors to find each take and line of dialogue from within the original production 1/4" or DAT tapes when they begin their dialogue editing process near the end of the editing process.

82

But they will need to have some way of telling, by looking at any given piece of mag soundtrack, just what time code it represents. The way this is now done is to record the dailies onto three-stripe stock, rather than a piece of single stripe. The production dialogue and other sound is still transferred onto the first (bottom) stripe of oxide but, in addition, the synchronous SMPTE Time Code is transferred onto the center (middle) stripe. This way, the sound editors will be able to easily find the time code for any given piece of film by simply running the center stripe through a time code reader (either on a synchronizer or on a sound dummy).

This time code stripe need not have any bearing on how you sync up your footage so it is not important to do anything with it at this time. What you need to concentrate on now is the marking up of the sound dailies reels.

For now, don't put any leaders on the rolls. Just spin them onto cores or reels in the order you want them. Run them through the synchronizer on the gang with the sound head, so you can listen to them. At the beginning of every take the sound recordist will probably have put a beep on the track. At the end of the take they usually beep several times. Just as you look for the flash frames

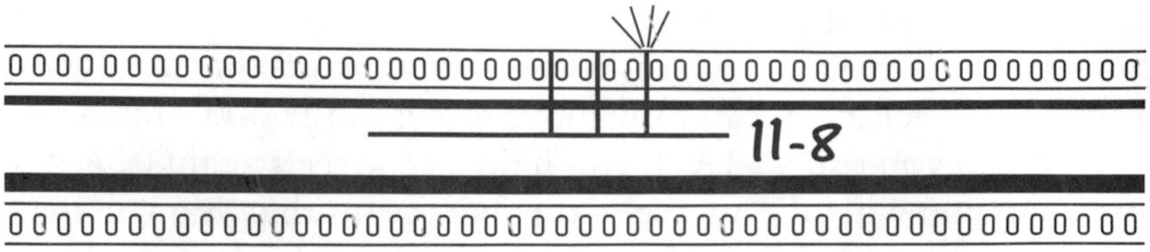

11-8

FIGURE 4.15 *The sprocket where the first sound of the slate occurs (called the "first modulation") is marked as the beginning of the slate frame.*

when you mark up the picture, you will be listening for these beeps as you pop the tracks. As you rewind and hear the beeps (which should be quite evident, even at high speed), stop and roll forward, listening to the track. You should hear the assistant cameraperson call out the take number (for 11F-7, for instance, it would sound something like "Scene 11, Frank. Take Seven. Marker!"). Continue to roll forward until you hear the sticks of the slate close. Listen carefully, there are often noises on the set you might confuse with the sticks.

For some reason, many crews are abandoning the idea of identifying the scene and take number before the slate is clapped. In these cases the assistant cameraperson simply yells "Marker!." In cases like this it is a good idea to see if you can convince the first assistant director to speak to the camera department and ask them to slate the takes with i.d. (you can see the advantage of getting to know the crew). Many hours can be wasted in editing rooms trying to identify which sound transfer goes with which take and if at all possible, it is wonderful to be able to avoid those unnecessary delays.

When you have found the area with the sound of the sticks hitting, rock the track slowly back and forth under the sound head until you find the exact point where the sound begins (this is called the *first modulation*). Slate boards are designed to have very sharp sound attacks so there should little problem with this. Mark this with grease pencil as the first sprocket of your slate frame (*see* Figure 4.15), then mark the entire frame much as you did the track start mark. Once again, be careful not to extend your mark down into the area where the sound is, as the grease pencil will rub off on the sound head if you do.

After you've marked and identified the slate, move back to the next one, continuing in this fashion until you reach 11E-4. At the point between the double beep signifying the end of the preceding take (11D-5) and the beep signifying the beginning of 11E-4, make a straight cut on your splicer. This will be, as you've already determined, the beginning of Dailies Roll Three. Put this up on the shelf next to the already marked picture reel for dailies roll three. Tape the little piece of paper listing the takes on that reel to the front of the reels. You can now move along to the other takes.

When you reach 11A-4, you'll break the reels again (this does not mean you will take an axe to them; it means that you will make a cut between 11A-4 and 11pu-3), and continue back to the beginning of the roll.

A few words of warning. There are times when the sound recordist will take some wild sound (that is, sound for which there is no picture). These *wild tracks*, along with any sync sound takes without matching picture (either because of the director's request or because the recordist thought that there would be something valuable in them), should be saved on a separate roll. There is often a need for them in the editing process and it will be good for the editor to have them available. There are also times when a take is shot *MOS*, without sound, take 10A-2 for instance. We will see how to deal with this in a few pages.

We now have three rolls of marked picture and three rolls of matching marked track. If there have been no terrible problems with paperwork or slating, it is probably about 10:00 am. We are now ready to sync everything up.

84

Put the matching picture and track rolls up on your bench. Thread them up on the synchronizer so the picture is in the first gang and the track is on the second, where the sound head is (these are the positions you will use most often to load the film up on your synchronizer). With this arrangement, you will find that the track will not wind up (or "take up") at the same rate as the picture. This is what the *differential* is for. You put the differential in between the picture and sound reels on the right (take–up) side, after making sure that you've put the little washer that comes with it between the picture reel and the rewind. The two reels will now take up at the same rate. If you don't have a differential you can use 16mm cores to space the reels out (or use actual, rented, spacers) you might want to reverse the order of the picture and track by putting the track in gang two where there is a sound head and putting the picture in gang three where there is not (if there is a sound head hanging there, you will obviously want to be *very* careful not to let the head slip onto the film as it will put an embarrassingly long colored gouge into the film).

Put the reels into the synchronizer so the picture start mark is at 0'00 on the counter. Since you have no head leader yet on the track, put the track in randomly. Then wind the two of them down until you see the first picture slate—for take 10-5. The chances are infinitesimal that the sound slate will line up exactly with it. In fact, it's quite likely that your sound slate is many feet away. To correct this, remove the track from the synchronizer and, by hand and without running the synchronizer, pull the sound out of the feed reel (the left one) until you get to the marked-up slate. Put this slate into the second gang so it lines up exactly with the picture slate. The picture and sound are now locked in sync with each other. Now, using your left hand, slowly roll the film backwards (you might want to rotate the wheel of the synchronizer with your right thumb) until you see the cut point on the picture, which in this case is where the top of take 10-5 is cut to the head leader. Make a little mark on the track. Cut the track at this point and attach the head track leader to it (you'll probably want to put your splicer on the right side of the synchronizer to do this; one of the only times that you'll be making your cuts on that side of the synchronizer). When you run backwards to the picture start mark, the track start mark should line up perfectly with it, at the 0'00 mark. If this has happened, congratulations, you've just sunk up your first take ("sunk up" functions as the past tense for sync up; I know it looks silly, but that's what everybody says).

At the head of the take on the track you can now write 10-5 (the scene and take number) in the position corresponding to the identification mark on the picture. Hang the excess track that you've chopped off on a pin in a trim bin you've cleverly placed next to you, and you're ready to move onto the next take.

But before we do, let's take a step back and examine what we've just done. The theory behind synching dailies is quite simple. Because the recording of sound and picture is done on two different machines you will end up with materials of differing lengths. In order to sync the two, you leave the picture as it comes to you and adjust the length of the track to match the picture by adding or, more often, removing pieces of track as necessary.

Now, move down to the end of take 10-5. Where you have made the cross dividing the two picture takes, make a cross on the corresponding point on the track (once again, making sure not to write in the lower stripe where the sound is). This cross will be a sync point for you.

Roll down until you reach the next picture slate (10-6), lock in the synchronizer at that point, then pull out the track from the feed reel by hand until you get to the track slate. At this point there are two schools of thought on how to sync the rest of reel. Some assistants prefer to continue as they did for the first take on the reel, removing the track from synchronizer and pulling out the track so the track slate lines up with the picture slate. Other assistants prefer never to remove the track from the synchronizer (thereby minimizing the danger of losing sync). The second method is the one I'll describe here.

After finding the track slate for 10-6, put it into the *third* gang on the synchronizer so the slate lines up exactly with the picture slate. Slowly roll back until you reach the cross between the two takes, marking the corresponding point on the track in the third gang (as well as on the second gang, if you haven't already done so—some assistants using this method prefer to make both of the marks at the same time). You have just marked the beginning of take 10-6 on the track in the third gang as well as the end of take 10-5 on the track in the second gang. All you have to do now is remove everything between these two marks. To do this you can roll backwards a bit and make cuts at both of these marks with your splicer on the left side of the synchronizer (Some assistants like to roll the film forward and make the cuts on the right side of the synchronizer, but it is too easy to get yourself out of sync that way. If you make *all* of your cuts to the left of the synchronizer then you always know everything on the right side is in perfect sync). You will then have a long piece you can remove from the splicer (this is the footage between the end of 10-5 and the start of 10-6). Hang the piece you've just removed on top of the other piece of track in your bin, splice the pieces that are still in the synchronizer together and roll forward. You will now have sunk up 10-6, leaving the picture in the first gang and the track in the second. You should have nothing running in the third gang.

What you have done, essentially, is find the end of 10-5 and the beginning of 10-6, removed the excess between them, and then butted the two takes together so the end of 10-5 comes at the same point as the beginning of 10-6—at the cross.

If there had not been enough track at the end of 10-5 before 10-6 began you would have found the beginning of 10-6 and added as much fill onto the end of 10-5 as was necessary to butt it up against 10-6.

You can now move onto the next take. Spin down to the end of 10-6, and mark the cross on the track. However, you can see that the next take, 10A-2, was shot MOS, that is, without sound (this is why I write MOS after the take number on all of the identifications; i.e. 10A-2MOS). The next take on the sound roll will, therefore, be 10B-2, not 10A-2 (since no sound was recorded during 10A-2). Make your track cut at the end of 10-6, at the cross as usual, but splice fill leader onto the end of the take. Then spin down to the end of 10A-2 and mark the cut point as you normally would, except you will put it on the fill. You can then proceed as normal, finding the slate for 10B-2, putting that in the third gang, rolling backwards, lining up the cross marks and splicing the fill to the head of 10B-2.

To simplify it, you do everything you would normally do except you obviously don't have to listen for the sound slate on the MOS take and line it up.

Continue until the end of the roll. When you've finished, cut the track tail leader on at the last cut point and you are finished with your first roll of dailies. Continue onto the next two rolls and, by 11:00 a.m. or noon, you should be done with the day's dailies.

A word about those pieces of track you've been accumulating in your trim bin (one dailies reel per pin). After you've sunk all of the dailies you or Wendy will be checking them for proper sync. This is why it is good to have an extra upright Moviola or a small flatbed for the assistant's use. If you find that you've made any mistakes in synching up a roll of dailies, it will be relatively easy to go back to the pin where the excess track for that reel is hanging, find the piece of track for that take, and re–sync it. If everything is all right (and it most often will be) you can throw all of those pieces away.

One final note. Remember those takes with blurred slates? Remember how I asked you to put a big circle on the blurred frame? Now I'll tell you why, and it involves a slight adaptation to your synching method. For these takes, we can assume that the actual first modulation occurs not in between two frames but while the camera shutter was open. Generally, this is two sprockets before a normal slate. That is, instead of it happening on the frame line before the frame you've marked with an "X", it is happening somewhere in the middle of the preceding frame. So, as you sync a take like this (and you'll know which takes they are because they'll be the ones with the circles on them), instead of making the first modulation fall on the first sprocket of the "X" frame, you make it come two sprockets before that frame line, in the middle of the frame with "O" on it. When you put the track in the synchronizer, you put it in two sprockets earlier than normal. You then erase the old track slate mark and correct it (*see* Figure 4.16). This enables you to get to within two sprockets of what the correct sync must be, as that is one forty-eighth of a second, that should be close enough for everyone. Of course, in 16mm you won't have the option of sliding it a fraction of frame as there is only sprocket per frame. This is an inaccuracy you'll have to live with. In this case, I usually put the "X" of the slate on the first fully closed frame.

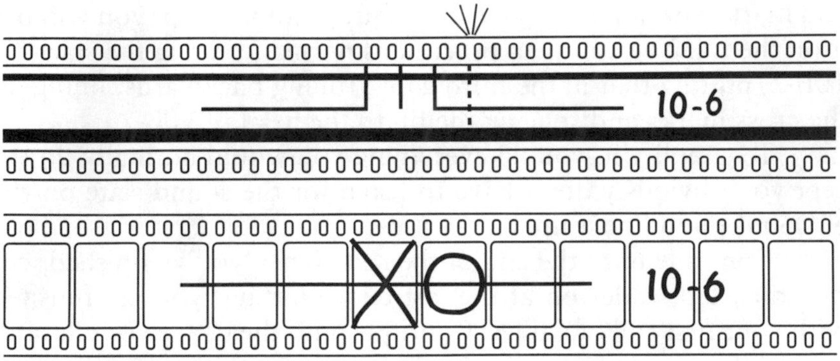

10-6

10-6

FIGURE 4.16 Synching takes with blurred frames requires making the marked slate on the track fall two sprockets earlier than it normally would, so that the actual sound of the slate falls in the middle of the blurred frame (where, presumably, the slate actually struck). The dashed line on the track indicates where the first sprocket of the marked slate, the first modulation, used to be before it was moved to accommodate the blurred slate.

88

Now comes the time to check your work. It is essential for the assistant (with or without Wendy) to look at the dailies before the dailies screening, unless there is absolutely no time to do so. Not only can you check the sync, but you can prepare all the paperwork that will help the editor take notes at dailies. It also gives you the first real look at any problems inherent in the footage. If there is anything serious that hasn't come to your attention by now, a viewing (and, let us not forget, a listening) will bring it to your attention.

Thread the Moviola (*see* Figure 4.17). There is a special way to accurately thread the film at the picture and sound gates and it is tied to how you've marked the slates. You've sunk the film up so the sound of the slate hitting occurs in between two frames; you should line them up in the Moviola that way.

To do that, place the start marks for the reels in their gates. Then disengage the two heads so you can move the picture independently of the track. First, frame up the picture so it is positioned correctly in the gate (use the Academy leader for this, to make sure that the full frame can be seen in the Moviola, with no frame lines visible at either the top or bottom of the frame), then go back to the start mark and, rocking it with the connecting bar, position it so that with one more little turn of the bar it would begin to bring the picture into the frame. Then, position the track so the first sprocket of the start mark line is under the sound head. Now you can lock the two of them together knowing that they are in as close a sync as the machines can give you.

FIGURE 4.17 *The picture is threaded up from the feed reel (A), around two sets of rollers (B), through a gate (C), under the picture head (D), through another gate (E), a roller (F), and onto the take–up reel (G). Care must be taken to leave adequately sized loops above and below the picture head, between each of the gates.*

At this point, you should also set the *footage counter* on the Moviola to 000'00. It is a good idea to get in the habit of *zeroing out* the counter before running any roll on the Moviola.

Hopefully, you will have access to a flatbed for screening dailies. The threading of these machines varies, depending on their make, but I find it nearly impossible to get as accurate a line–up as I can on a Moviola. There is a point on most flatbeds where, by rocking the picture back and forth, you will be able to see two frames superimposed on one another. This is as close to the frameline position as you will be able to get. Line that up with the first sprocket of the start mark of the track, lock the two together, and you'll be in sync.

Now you can run the dailies. Try to listen with headphones, especially if you are using a noisy stand–up Moviola. As you watch the dailies you should have the script supervisor's notes to refer to as well as your own lists of what is on each dailies roll.

You are now going to make the *Editor's Dailies Notes Sheets* for Wendy (*see* Figure 4.18). Some editors like these notes on looseleaf paper, some in spiral notebooks. Whatever their preference, the basic concept remains the same. At the top of the page is the *dailies roll number* and the *date of shooting*. Following each take on the roll is a short description of the shot. Leave some room for any notes that Wendy or Adam will want to make during the dailies screening. Your description should be fairly short and standardized. List the size of the shot (WS for wide shot, CU for close–up, etc.) and a description to help identify it for the editor (master, dolly to CU of ABBY, etc.). You can decide what to write as you watch the shot (using the script supervisor's notes if necessary). As you watch the dailies, check that everything is in perfect sync.

90

Many editors like to have their assistants break to a new page of Dailies Notes whenever a new scene starts. That way, when they are finished watching dailies, the sheets can be separated and placed into a large three ring binder along with the Dailies Notes from earlier days, in scene order. It will be easier for Wendy to find her notes if they are in scene order than if they are kept in the order of the dailies reel number.

When you've finished checking the dailies, the picture and track should be cleaned with a velvet while your apprentice, Philip, rewinds (make sure that no scratches are put on the film during this cleaning), packed into some transporting device (the most common are fiber cases that hold six reels comfortably with a handle on top of the case, making them easy to carry) along with notes and a little penlight for Wendy to see and write with in the darkened screening room.

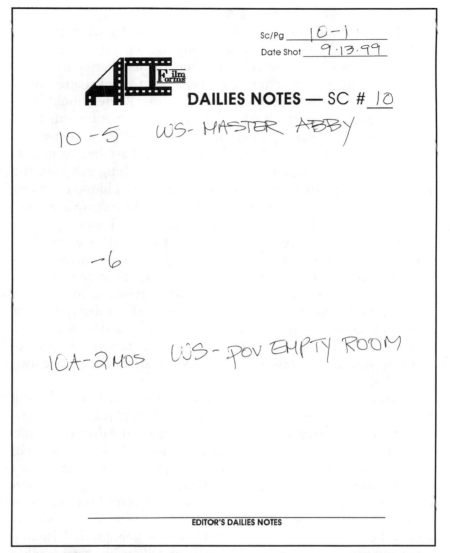

Sc/Pg ___10-1___
Date Shot ___9·13·99___

DAILIES NOTES — SC # _10_

10-5   WS- MASTER ABBY

-6

10A-2 MOS   WS - POV EMPTY ROOM

91

EDITOR'S DAILIES NOTES

FIGURE 4.18 *The first page from the Editor's Dailies Notes. Enough room is left so that the editor can write his or her (along with the director's) comments during dailies and cutting. Note also that when more than one take from a set-up is printed only the take number of the second is listed, not the scene number. This provides a good visual clue to anyone looking at the list that the takes are from the same set-up. Subsequent pages from this scene wouldn't have the large scene number written in it, the pages would be labeled in the upper right hand corner 10-2, 10-3, etc.*

When you're done with all of this, you're done synching the dailies.

Dailies Screening

Later that day, your film, Wendy, Philip, and much of the production crew will march into a screening room ready to watch the first day's dailies. Actually, you and your film had better arrive ten or fifteen minutes before the scheduled time to make sure everything is going to flow as smoothly as it can. Philip should have rewound and cleaned each reel of dailies so the picture and track are both wound correctly for projection (remember what we discussed about KEM versus Moviola winds?) and are free from dirt. Give Wendy all of your notes and check everything out with the projectionist (I usually tell him—it still usually is a him—what reel numbers he is showing that day, what format the picture is in, and what wind the track is), then take your seat in the room.

Seating preferences vary from film to film. I've worked on movies where the director has opened the dailies to anyone who wanted to come, and I've worked on some where attendance was very restricted. Some directors prefer that everyone sit in the same places every day; some don't really give a hoot. The most important thing for you, as the assistant, is to be near the sound level controls (if you're going to be working them) and the intercom to the projectionist so you can relay the seemingly endless stream of instructions up to him.

Some directors like the assistant or the editor to call out the number of prints of each setup as they are screened (e.g., "Scene ten master, two takes"), some don't. Ask Wendy what Adam will want.

Once everyone has arrived and the doors have been closed, someone (guess who?) will signal the projectionist to begin. Then you will notice several things happening. For one thing, every person in the room is going to be looking at the film for his or her own reasons. The camera crew is going to want to be sure the film was shot and printed correctly. The sound crew is going to be listening for sound problems. Costume and makeup will dislike certain takes because the star had his hair messed or his handkerchief wasn't folded properly. In fact, about the only people who will be looking at the film as a whole are the three people whose jobs depend on it—the director, the producer, and the editor.

This is going to put you in a very interesting spot. For one thing, you are going to have to be noticing *all* the things that the other people are noticing individually. It *is* important that the star's handkerchief matches from shot to shot. It will also be important to remember just which shots have lousy sound or focus problems (these things are usually difficult to tell on the editing machine and, if you will be cutting on a digital editing system, they will be impossible to see). It is also important to note which shots have the best performances in them, and which are the most consistent with each other.

All of these things are important to the editing of a film and Wendy should be taking careful note of all of them. Yet, very often, it is the assistant who must take note of things like technical problems so he or she can mark it down on all of the paperwork as necessary. You will often need to pass along comments to the lab for Wendy (reprinting takes that are too dark, checking for dirt that was only visible when projected on the big screen). There's also a good chance that at some point during the editing, Wendy will turn to you and say, "Remember the shot that had the bump in the middle of the dolly?" It helps if you take your own notes during dailies screenings so you can remember all of these things. And since you'll never write it down if you don't notice it first, pay attention at dailies.

At the same time that you will be taking some of your notes, Wendy will probably be taking hers. She will most likely be seated next to Adam, who will be giving her feedback on what things he likes best and least in the dailies. Some directors prefer that their editor do no first cutting until they are there with them, but the normal practice is for the editor to be cutting day by day as the crew shoots. Adam's notes on what takes he liked and didn't like (and why) will be very helpful to Wendy as she cuts the footage.

93

As a result of these notes, Wendy may ask you for certain things. For instance, she may ask you to print up an unrequested take (the *B-negative*), or to reprint a take with a different color balance. Or she may ask that you listen to the original sound tape of a particular take to see if some annoying sounds can be gotten rid of. Write all of these requests down (it helps to buy a nice supply of flashlight pens or little flashlights) and act on them immediately after the screening or the first thing the following day.

After the screening is over, collect all of the paperwork and film and arrange to get it back to the editing room. Your footage is too important to risk being misplaced by screening room personnel who don't really care about your troubles (they have three more films coming in after you anyway). Unless you feel 100 percent sure that your film will return to you safely, always move it yourself.

One final word about dailies screenings. Many production managers, in their desire to be thrifty, think that banning editorial assistants and apprentices from dailies (if they are in the evening overtime hours) is a good way to save money. The truth, however, is exactly the opposite. The more you and Philip know the film, the more help you will be to Wendy in the editing. This will, in the long run, save a lot of time and money. There is no better way to examine the film than to see it on a large screen. In addition, there is the very human side of things. Philip will be working with you for many more months (possibly a year or more) and there is no faster way to alienate people than to ban them from a screening of a project they are working on. Besides, Philip can help you get all of the film back to the cutting room after the screening.

So, we will assume that you and Philip have gathered up Wendy's notes after the dailies. You have dutifully written down all of the instructions you have been given. Wendy is going back to the production office with Adam to discuss the footage or the next day's coverage with him (and, presumably, a dozen other department heads, all of whom need to know some crucial information in order to plan for the future). The two of you, therefore, bring the film back to the editing room, rewind it (many projectionists will not rewind your film for you unless they're given something extra—like money), clean it, and set it out on the film racks, ready for tomorrow's work.

Most frequently today, studio executives, producers and directors like to have a videotape copy made of the day's dailies for their reference. If this is the case, you wouldn't set out the reels on a film rack but pack up the reels of picture and track, making sure they are heads out, and ship the lot of them off to a video transfer house. Here the film will go through a *telecine* process which will take the film images and put them onto a set of videotapes. Telecine rooms are busy places, especially in the evenings, since this is when they do most of their dailies work. If you are going to have to make videotapes of your dailies you should make sure you have discussed scheduling with your video transfer house. Many assistants like to make a standard booking for a certain amount of time every night. Be aware that it will take more minutes to transfer your dailies than you have in footage. Depending on how much footage you have, you should allow at least 50 percent to 75 percent additional time for transfer. One hour of dailies might take approximately 90 to 105 minutes to transfer. Check with your transfer house. You should also keep them up to date with changes in your shooting schedule. If Tuesday's shoot was at night, chances are good that you will have no dailies on Wednesday. If you let the video house know about this ahead of time they will be able to let go of your scheduled time and book it with someone else, something they will be grateful for. It will also guarantee you don't get billed for time you cannot use. You should also give them a call on days when you receive much less or much more footage than usual.

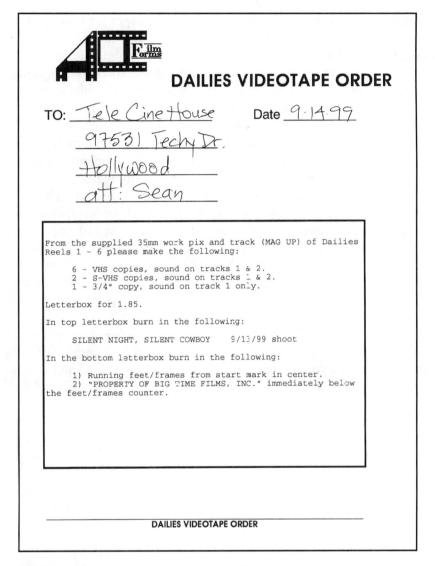

DAILIES VIDEOTAPE ORDER

TO: _Tele Cine House_   Date _9·14·99_

97531 Techy Dr.

Hollywood

att: Sean

From the supplied 35mm work pix and track (MAG UP) of Dailies
Reels 1 - 6 please make the following:

    6 - VHS copies, sound on tracks 1 & 2.
    2 - S-VHS copies, sound on tracks 1 & 2.
    1 - 3/4" copy, sound on track 1 only.

Letterbox for 1.85.

In top letterbox burn in the following:

    SILENT NIGHT, SILENT COWBOY   9/13/99 shoot

In the bottom letterbox burn in the following:

    1) Running feet/frames from start mark in center.
    2) "PROPERTY OF BIG TIME FILMS, INC." immediately below
the feet/frames counter.

DAILIES VIDEOTAPE ORDER

95

FIGURE 4.19 *Videotape Transfer Work Order. This work order is usually attached to a purchase order listing the billing and shipping addresses.*

You should always enclose a work order (or a purchase order if your production manager wants the billing to go through the editorial department) listing exactly how many reels of film you are supplying, what formats you want the tape transferred to, and what writing you want put on the screen. Most studios are justifiably worried about someone making copies of the tapes for their films so you often will be asked to *burn in* some writing either over or just under the picture area.

In the work order in Figure 4.19, the assistant has requested that the videotape house create letterboxing bars to black out any picture above or below the 1.85 film size ratio that most films are projected in. He or she has also instructed the telecine house to burn in the name and date of the film shoot above the picture. The legend "Property of Big Time Film, Inc." will be burned in below the picture, immediately below the running footage count of each reel. This footage gives Adam a reference point to use when he gives Wendy notes, if he chooses to do so. The work order also gives a detailed breakdown of how many videotape copies of the film to make, as well as what format to transfer them on to. This work order will usually come attached to a purchase order giving the telecine house the shipping and billing addresses, as well as a purchase order number allowing your accounting department to track expenditures.

Since we have been to an evening dailies screening, it is probably about 8:00 or 9:00 p.m. before you've finished with all of your work. What do you do now? If you ask me, you should go home to your other life already.

4A/DIGITAL
· · · · · ·
SHOOTING THE DIGITALLY EDITED FILM

A digital editing room looks very different from a traditional film editing room, but the differences only *begin* there. When you start to handle the footage coming into your editing room, you will find there are differences within differences within differences.

There are many paths to creating the tapes that will need to be input into your editing system but they all pretty much break down into two distinct categories. For the first path, you print film just as you would in an all film job. For the second, you don't print film at all during the editorial phase. There is a third possibility which involves printing up film at a point later in post-production that we will discuss briefly now and in more detail in Chapter 9A.

First Film, Then All Film
The all-film editing process we discussed in Chapter 4 takes a path similar to the road map in Figure 4A.1. Separate picture and sound are delivered to the editing room where they are sunk up by you and Philip. As we will see in later chapters, Wendy will cut the dailies, everyone will preview with this cut film and, after *locking* the picture (that is, completing the editing), the film is separated back into its film and sound components. Finally, the negative is sent to a negative cutter who matches all of Wendy's workprint edits using the original camera negative. The picture and sound are then worked on and polished until they are finally combined, or *married*, for the lab process resulting in the release prints made for theatres around the country.

Voila! Your film is done.

Editing Process - Printing Film, Editing On Film

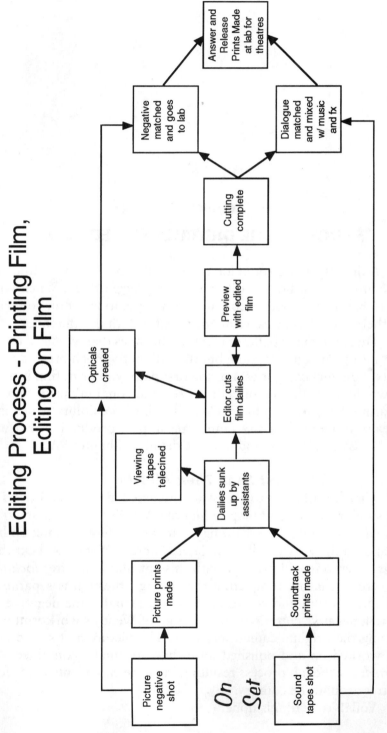

FIGURE 4A.1 The editing process when a movie is edited completely on film.

This all-film path has one major advantage over digital systems—cost. Though the expense of printing film and sound, synching it up and doing all of the intermediate work on film is high, the cost of renting a computer editing system is so much greater than a Moviola or a flatbed that the all-film path is still attractive to producers of low budget films. In fact, about the only path lower in cost than the all-film path is an all-videotape path because linear videotape editing systems are appreciably lower in rental costs than non-linear digital editing systems. However, the problems inherent to editing on tape (particularly with a film release) are so enormous that the all-video path is not practical for a feature film.

For extremely cost conscious producers, the all-film path is probably the lowest priced available. But with lower priced systems like the Media 100 quickly taking on more of the capabilities of the heavy-duty systems like the Avid and Lightworks, the day will come relatively soon when almost no filmmaker, save the dedicated film lovers, will be editing primarily on film.

Still, the beauty of having a film print to screen is so overwhelming to many filmmakers that, given the budget, most films prefer to work with both.

Film, Then Film and Tape, Then Film Again

This process, outlined with rather more arrows than I would like in Figure 4A.2, starts the same way as the all-film path does. Film and sound are processed and sent to the editing room where you and Philip sync them up for your dailies screenings. After the reels are edge coded (a process we will discuss in Chapter 5) the film dailies are sent to a telecine house for the creation of viewing and editing tapes. It is this editing tape (typically a 3/4" or a S-VHS tape) that is input into your digital editing machine.

Wendy then cuts digitally until it is necessary to screen the 35mm film for an audience. This is often for an audience preview or a studio screening, where you want the best possible visual image. It will then be necessary to recreate on film every cut that Wendy has made digitally. Luckily, the digital machines can create *Film Cut Lists* that refer back to the inked edge code numbers. Some of your assistants, or a service specializing in film matching, will methodically cut your dailies prints to match every one of Wendy's digital cuts using a videotape and the Film Cut List. The sound for the screening is output to tape (usually a DAT or a DA-88) directly from the Lightworks or Avid. It is then either additionally worked on by sound editors or is transferred to 35mm film and screened from that mag.

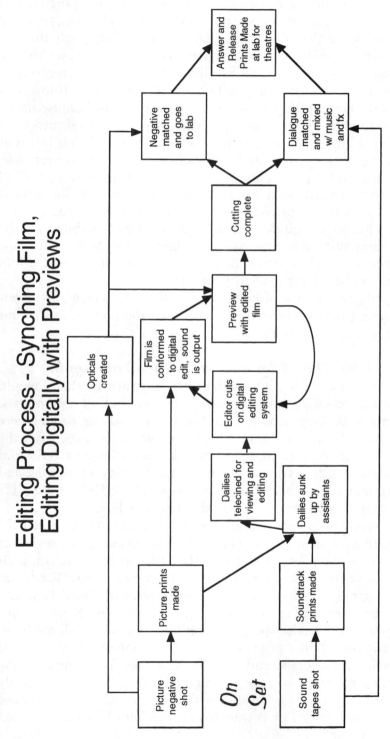

Editing Process - Synching Film, Editing Digitally with Previews

FIGURE 4A.2 *The editing process when film dailies are sunk but the picture is edited digitally.*

After the screening, Wendy and Adam will make their changes digitally. For the second screening you will be able to get a *Change List* from the computer, comparing the first and second cuts and printing out a list of the changes you will need to make in the cut work picture (which has been left in its first screening form). This process goes on and on until you have finished cutting the film.

At this point, the computer will be able to print out a set of final change lists for the picture. It will also generate a sound Cut List so the magnetic soundtrack can be matched just like the picture. Alternatively, the sound can be rebuilt digitally from the original source tapes using an *Edit Decision List*, or an *EDL*. The final cut workprint can then go to the negative matcher, just as in the all-film path. The sound is polished separately. From here, the path is exactly the same as the all-film path.

Voila! Your film is done.

Tape, Then Tape, Then Film

The third possibility is the path chosen by virtually all television shows and the majority of low budget films being made today. It involves working exclusively in the video and digital realms during the editorial process. No film or sound dailies are ever printed.

In this path (*see* Figure 4A.3) the picture negative and sound tapes are sent directly to the telecine house where they are sunk up and put onto a videotape master. Tape copies are made from this master for viewing and for editing. On television shows where the final format will exist on tape rather than film, this video master is on a high quality videotape, usually on D-1, D-2 or Digital Beta (DigiBeta) tape, with a series of SMPTE Time Code numbers. The viewing and editing tapes made from this master tape have the same time code numbers as on the master, making it easy to match back to this high quality tape at the end of the editorial process.

This editorial tape is input into the digital editing system. Screenings are usually done with a direct output from the editing system, though occasionally an *EDL (Edit Decision List)* is made of the cut that Wendy has done. This EDL is then used to recreate the cut using the Master Tapes (instead of the editing tapes).

After every screening, and there can be many, changes are made on the digital system.

If you are working on a feature to be released on film, a *Film Cut List* and a separate Sound *EDL* are created once the editing is complete, just as in the previous path. The negative is matched directly from this list and the sound is re-created using the sound EDL. From here on, the path is similar to the previous two paths—

Editing Process - No Film, Editing Digitally with no Previews

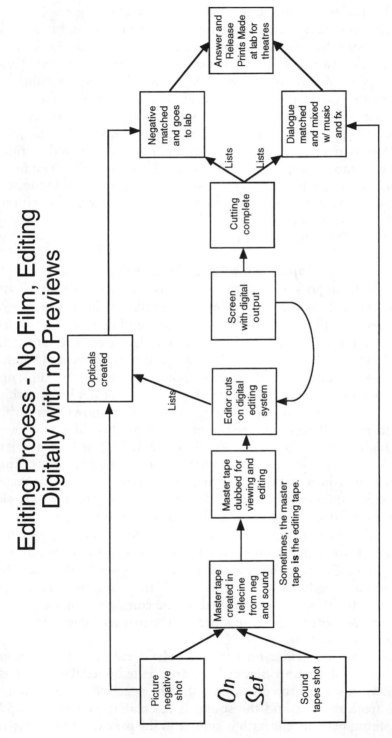

FIGURE 4A.3   The editing process when there is no film printed at any time during the editorial stage.

the picture and sound are worked on and improved until they are finally married into the release prints.

If you are working on a television show or a film that does not need a film finish (such as a direct to video movie), a Picture EDL is generated instead of a film cut list. This EDL is used to recreate Wendy's edits using the Master Tapes. This Edited Master is color corrected and the polished sound is laid onto it.

Voila! Your film is done.

Tape, Then Tape, Then Film, Then Film Again

There is one final pathway (*see* Figure 4A.4), a combination of the second and third methods. In it, no film or sound dailies are made and the film is cut entirely in the digital world until it is time to have an important screening. A *Film Cut List* is created from Wendy's digital cut. One part of this list is a section listing every take used in the film, complete with key numbers and lab and camera rolls. After checking it for accuracy, this list is sent to the lab which prints up just these takes. That film is then used to match, cut for cut, the digital edit.

From here on out, this path resembles the second path (*see* Figure 4A.2) with a matching workprint eventually being delivered to the negative matcher for completion, when it will be married to the finessed soundtrack.

Voila! Your film is done.

Going Into More Detail

Whether you are receiving tapes made from printed dailies or sunk negative, certain details are important to remember if you are editing on a digital system. Any 24 frame editing system, whether it be Avid, Lightworks or a 30 frame per second system using some software conversion program like Slingshot or OSC/R, works on the same principle: every frame of film is converted into video which is then input into your editing system in a pre-arranged manner. Along with this video, a certain amount of computer information is also input into the computer controlling the editing system. This information contains a link between each frame of video and its matching frames of film and sound. The computer will maintain a record of this link throughout the editing process; when you need to convert your digitally edited sequence back into film it will be a simple matter for it to convert the time code numbers into the proper film and sound numbers for matching.

To explain just how this is done I need to take a detour into discussing the *3:2 pulldown* (also called the *2:3 pulldown*). In the

Editing Process - No Film, Editing Digitally with Film Previews

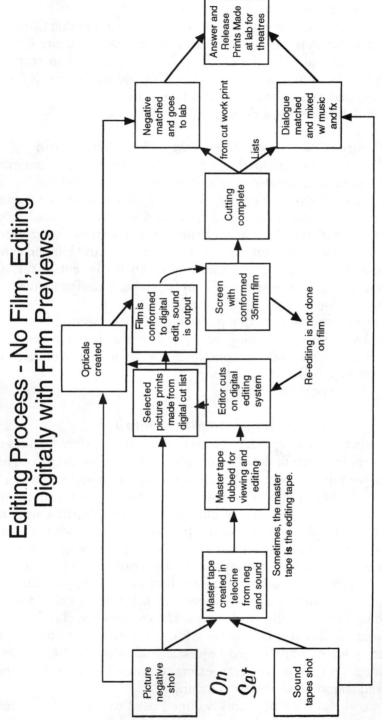

FIGURE 4A.4 The editing process when no dailies are printed but it is still necessary to preview with film.

United States, film is projected at 24 frames per second while video is projected at about 30 frames per second. Additionally, every frame of video is actually made up of two matching frames of video called *fields*. When film is run through the telecine chain to be converted into videotape some compensation must be made for these differing frame rates.

To do this, every other film frame must be converted into *three* video fields rather than the usual two. One extra field is *pulled down* into the frame. As a result, this conversion is called a *3:2 Pulldown* or a *2:3 Pulldown*.

You can see from Figure 4A.5 how this is accomplished. The first film frame out of every set of four (called the *A-frame*) is converted into two fields—the first video frame. The second film frame, the *B-frame*, is converted into three fields—the full second video frame and the first field of the third video frame. The third film frame, the *C-frame*, is converted into two fields - the second field of the third video frame and the first field of the fourth video frame. The fourth film frame, the *D-frame*, is converted into three fields— the second field of the fourth video frame and the entire fifth video frame.

The sequence is then repeated for the next set of four film frames—two fields, three fields, two fields and three fields. This alternating sequence of two and three fields is what gives this conversion process its name—the 3:2 pulldown, though it should more accurately be called the 2:3 pulldown.

The problem with this conversion process arises when Wendy is making cuts in the 30 frame per second video world. If she happens to cut from the third video frame in the 3:2 sequence to the fourth frame in another 3:2 sequence, her cut actually occurs between two video frames which are made up of a combination of *two* film frame images. Where, pray tell, should you make the film cut when you attempt to match the film back to Wendy's video edit? Cutting in the 30 frame per second mode makes matching back to the film (shot at 24 frames per second) very difficult.

The solution is to take the 30 frames per second video and convert it back into 24 frames per second inside the digital editing machine. As long as we can accurately determine which video frames are the A-frames of any 3:2 sequence the computer will easily be able to re-convert the images back to the proper film sequence— four frames, with the proper fields. In fact, nearly all off-line editing systems digitize only one of the two video fields to save space on their hard drive drives.

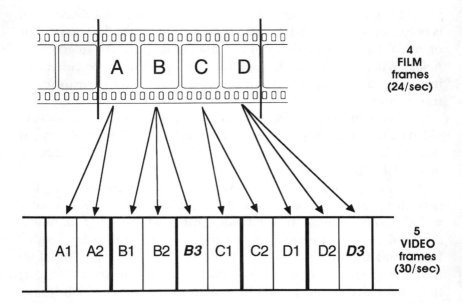

FIGURE 4A.5 *The 3:2 Pulldown sequence explained. In order to convert from film's projection rate of 24 frames per second to video's 30 frames per second, every four film frame sequence is converted into a five frame video sequence by making every other film frame convert to three, rather than the normal two, fields. The digital editing machine needs to know which video frame is made from the A-frame of film in order to properly remove the extra fields when it converts the 30 frame video back into a 24 frame project for editing.*

In order to do this, however, the computer needs to know just which frames are A-frames, which are B-frames and so on. Actually, it only needs to know the orientation of one of the five video frames for it to deduce the proper order of all of them (aren't computers smart?). Traditionally, the frame used is the A-frame.

When your telecine house transfers the film to videotape, normally you will request that they make their cuts on A-frames and that they put their A-frames on the zeroes and fives. This means every time they make an edit in their videotape transfer (and this will happen whenever they stop and then restart the recording process, usually at each new take), they should make sure the A-frame falls on the time codes ending in either a zero or a five. In other words, if the video frame at time code 1:13:23:05 is an A-frame then the next A-frame will fall at 1:13:23:10.

Recent advances have made some of the A-frame issues less crucial. If you have your telecine house put all of the time code and key number information into the *Vertical Interval* (we will discuss this in a few pages) portion of your tape, some editing machines can automatically compute which frame to throw out when digitizing at 24 frames.

If your telecine house has not put the A-frame on a zero or five, you can still tell which frame is the A-frame by examining the time code burn-in on the videotape. As you rock the videotape forward field by field, the A-frame should have no timecode change between the fields. The B-frame, which is made up of three fields, will have no timecode change between the first two fields but will have a change between fields two and three. The C-frame will have two fields with a timecode change between them. The D-frame, made of three fields, will have a change in between fields one and two but not between fields two and three.

Now we can discuss what sort of information the telecine house will give you that you will need to input into your digital editing computer.

Whether you are receiving video dailies created from your already sunk film dailies (method number two from above), or from negative the telecine house has sunk up (methods three or four from above) you should also receive some paperwork and a computer disk. The paperwork consists of a *Telecine Log* and, occasionally, a report of any problems occurring in the telecine (sound is too loud, a take is out of focus, etc.). The computer disk contains a file with all the information from the telecine log along with some information telling the computer how to read the file.

A typical telecine log from a session where the telecine house has sunk up the negative will contain a set of information for every take on the tape. That information will include the name of the take (the scene and take number, e.g. 10-5), the starting time code numbers, the Keycode of the first frame of the take (this is the key number for the take and it is automatically read by a machine at the telecine session), the time code of the first frame of the sound used if the on-set sound recordist used a time coded machine (and, if they didn't, it will make synching at the telecine house an expensive nightmare), the camera roll, the sound roll, which tracks of the videotape the sound was recorded onto (none, if the shot was MOS), the date the take was shot and some other assorted information you may or may not need.

There are several standard formats for these files—FLEx, Evertz, Keyscope, ALE and ODB. The last two files are proprietary formats developed by Avid and Lightworks, respectively, for their own machines. Some telecine houses can now create logs directly in those two formats. Otherwise, you will have to translate the file you get into the format appropriate for your machine. When you examine the files on the disk from the telecine house they will have names like SN001.FLX for the first FLEx file created for *Silent Night, Silent Cowboy*, SN002.FTL for the second Evertz file, SN010.KSL for the tenth Keyscope file, SN034.ALE for the thirty-fourth Avid file, or SN056.ODB for the fifty-sixth Lightworks file. You will typically get one file for every videotape you receive. Since each videotape will normally hold up to sixty minutes of footage, you may get several files if you have a lot of dailies. The files are quite small so you will probably receive several files on one disk, a new disk delivered every day with your editing tape. An example of a FLEx file is shown in Figure 4A.6.

If you have already sunk your dailies on film your files will look a little different. When you send your film to the telecine house you will attach a piece of tape at the start mark showing what code number you will eventually start edge coding at that point, 010-1000 for the tenth dailies roll, for instance. (Don't be put off by this discussion of edge numbers; we will get into them in detail in Chapter 5.) The telecine house will use that ink number rather than the key code in the telecine and you will receive a Telecine Log listing each dailies reel as one edit, rather than breaking them down into individual takes. The file will not contain the starting key code numbers of each take. Instead, it will contain the starting edge code number of each dailies roll. The files will contain camera and sound roll numbers as well as the original sound time code numbers since the telecine will not be coming from the original picture and sound rolls.

Recently, some editing machines have made it possible to put both the code and the key numbers into this database. Telecine houses need to adapt their hardware and software to accommodate the additional information, and that day will probably come in the not-too-distant future.

When you assign inked code numbers, make sure the format of your numbers conforms to what your editing software expects. Some systems, for instance, expect the prefixes to be eight digits. In that case you will need to make sure your telecine house labels reel ten as 010_____0000+00 (those are five underlines after the reel number).

This will give you enough information to trace back each cut from the video time code to the inked code numbers.

In addition to putting this information onto the telecine file, there are two ways much of it is also put onto the videotape. First,

```
000 Manufacturer da Vinci    No. 022 Equip TLC2      Version 633      FLEx 1004

010 Title                              SILENT NIGHT
011 Client BIG TIME FILMS.                   Facility TELECINE HOUSE
012 Shoot Date 10-04-99  Transfer Date 10-05-99  Opr SM   Asst      Bay 6


100 Edit 0001 to V1234       Field A1 NTSC Split             Delay
110 Scene CHART     Take 1         Cam Roll A15        Sound
120 Scrpt COLOR CHART
200 IMAGE 35 23.98 A15       005209+00 000015+00 Key EASTM KI296989 005209+00 P4
300 VTR-A INSERT     SN0027     At 03:00:00:00.0 For 00:00:10:00.0 Using LTC
300 VTR-B INSERT     SN0027     At 03:00:00:00.0 For 00:00:10:00.0 Using LTC
500         Cut             to A15      Fx       Rate       Delay

100 Edit 0002 to V1234       Field A1 NTSC Split             Delay
110 Scene A77       Take 2         Cam Roll A15      Sound 5        12:27:16:00.0
200 IMAGE 35 23.98 A15       005265+00 000050+12 Key EASTM KI296989 005265+00 P4
300 VTR-A ASSEMBLE   SN0027     At 03:00:10:00.0 For 00:00:33:25.0 Using LTC
300 VTR-B ASSEMBLE   SN0027     At 03:00:10:00.0 For 00:00:33:25.0 Using LTC
400 SOUND 29.97 fps 5         At 12:27:16:00.0 For 00:00:33:20.0 Using LTC
500         Cut             to 5        Fx       Rate       Delay

100 Edit 0003 to V1234       Field A1 NTSC Split             Delay
110 Scene 77A       Take 3         Cam Roll A15      Sound 5        14:17:28:08.0
200 IMAGE 35 23.98 A15       005475+00 000045+04 Key EASTM KI296989 005475+00 P4
300 VTR-A ASSEMBLE   SN0027     At 03:00:43:25.0 For 00:00:30:05.0 Using LTC
300 VTR-B ASSEMBLE   SN0027     At 03:00:43:25.0 For 00:00:30:05.0 Using LTC
400 SOUND 29.97 fps 5         At 14:17:28:08.0 For 00:00:30:05.0 Using LTC
500         Cut             to 5        Fx       Rate       Delay

100 Edit 0004 to V1234       Field A1 NTSC Split             Delay
110 Scene 77B       Take 1         Cam Roll A15      Sound 5        14:31:29:11.0
200 IMAGE 35 23.98 A15       005524+00 000046+00 Key EASTM KI296989 005524+00 P4
300 VTR-A ASSEMBLE   SN0027     At 03:01:14:00.0 For 00:00:30:20.0 Using LTC
300 VTR-B ASSEMBLE   SN0027     At 03:01:14:00.0 For 00:00:30:20.0 Using LTC
400 SOUND 29.97 fps 5         At 14:31:29:11.0 For 00:00:30:20.0 Using LTC
500         Cut             to 5        Fx       Rate       Delay

100 Edit 0005 to V1234       Field A1 NTSC Split             Delay
110 Scene 77B       Take 2         Cam Roll A15      Sound 5        14:32:41:11.0
200 IMAGE 35 23.98 A15       005572+00 000041+04 Key EASTM KI296989 005572+00 P4
300 VTR-A ASSEMBLE   SN0027     At 03:01:44:20.0 For 00:00:27:15.0 Using LTC
300 VTR-B ASSEMBLE   SN0027     At 03:01:44:20.0 For 00:00:27:15.0 Using LTC
400 SOUND 29.97 fps 5         At 14:32:41:11.0 For 00:00:27:15.0 Using LTC
500         Cut             to 5        Fx       Rate       Delay

100 Edit 0006 to V1234       Field A1 NTSC Split             Delay
110 Scene 77B       Take 3         Cam Roll A15      Sound 5        14:34:03:00.0
200 IMAGE 35 23.98 A15       005615+00 000043+00 Key EASTM KI296989 005615+00 P4
300 VTR-A ASSEMBLE   SN0027     At 03:02:12:05.0 For 00:00:28:20.0 Using LTC
300 VTR-B ASSEMBLE   SN0027     At 03:02:12:05.0 For 00:00:28:20.0 Using LTC
400 SOUND 29.97 fps 5         At 14:34:03:00.0 For 00:00:28:20.0 Using LTC
500         Cut             to 5        Fx       Rate       Delay

100 Edit 0007 to V1234       Field A1 NTSC Split             Delay
110 Scene 77       Take 3         Cam Roll B10      Sound 5        13:53:29:23.0
200 IMAGE 35 23.98 B10       000584+00 000117+08 Key EASTM KI307897 000584+00 P4
300 VTR-A ASSEMBLE   SN0027     At 03:02:40:25.0 For 00:01:18:10.0 Using LTC
300 VTR-B ASSEMBLE   SN0027     At 03:02:40:25.0 For 00:01:18:10.0 Using LTC
400 SOUND 29.97 fps 5         At 13:53:29:23.0 For 00:01:18:10.0 Using LTC
500         Cut             to 5        Fx       Rate       Delay
```

FIGURE 4A.6 *An example of a FLEx file as it comes from the telecine house. You will notice that the first piece of footage on your editor's cassette is a color chart (that information is listed after the identification block from lines 010 through 012). Each take is listed as a separate block of information. The line 100 information shows that the cut was made to the video as well as all four channels of sound (V1234) and the cut was made on the first field of the A frame. The next line (110) gives the identification for each take—scene and take number, camera and sound roll numbers, and the audio time code from the on-set recording. The 200 line gives picture information—speed of transfer (this will normally be 23.98 frames per second for film projects), as well as key code information. The next lines (300) give the video time code information followed by the sound time code information (400).*

the data is put onto spare tracks of the videotape in areas your editing room videotape machine will be able to read. There are two locations where this information is usually placed: on the *Longitudinal Time Code* (LTC) area, sometimes called the *address track*, and in the *Vertical Interval* area (VITC), which is a number of scan lines that are not used for the picture.

Another place to put longitudinal time code is on the second audio channel, though this leaves no room for stereo sound on a 3/4" or S-VHS tape since the time code can not live in the same place as audio and these tapes have only two sound channels. You'll need to be careful where you put this information, however, because some older tape machines cannot read information off of the VITC. You should check with your telecine and equipment rental houses to make sure the equipment you rent will be able to read your tapes.

The second way in which some of the information will be placed is visually—on the picture you will be inputting into the computer for Wendy to cut. This is called a *burn-in* because the numbers will be burned on top of the picture, obliterating the image underneath. Typically you will need no more than three pieces of information: the video time code, the original key numbers (or inked edge numbers), and the original sound time code if you are having the telecine house sync the dailies. These burn-ins should be small enough to avoid blocking out too much of the picture, but large enough to be read. You will normally have a choice of where to place the information. Some editors like to place all of the information on two lines across the bottom or top of the picture. Others like to split it between one line at the top of the picture and one at the bottom. However Wendy likes it, be sure the telecine house is clear about the details before they make the first day's transfers. It is better to have every day's dailies be consistent.

110

On feature films, it is common practice to have the picture *letterboxed* to simulate the 1.85:1 aspect ratio that the film will be projected at in the theatres. This is akin to taping off the picture heads on a Moviola or flatbed. Black bars are put at the top and bottom of the video frame, precisely where the theatre projector will cut off the film image. This way, Wendy will be able to get a good sense of just what the audience will be seeing. If there is a microphone hanging at the top of the frame she will only see it if the audience will see it too. This does create some difficulty if Wendy needs to see the picture out of the 1.85 area, but this happens so rarely that the advantages of letterboxing normally outweigh the disadvantages.

Obviously television shows using the entire picture frame area would not letterbox their dailies.

It is important to make sure that the letterboxing is done precisely to the proper 1.85:1 aspect ratio. It is a good idea to put some leader at the head of every roll of dailies clearly marking off where the top and bottom borders of that ratio are. That way the telecine operator can properly align the letterboxing to fit those lines. The leader can be a framing chart shot for you on the set, or it can be the standard lab focus and framing leader.

If you are telecining directly from your camera negative, you can (at some added cost) have your lab splice some leader onto the head of each processed roll of negative when they are prepping it for telecine. A less satisfactory, but workable, solution is to send over some leader (preferably on negative stock) on its own roll. The telecine house can use that to pre-set their letterboxing matte.

When I letterbox my dailies I like to burn-in all of my numbers into the black bar far enough away from the picture so they are evident on the editing monitors but will disappear when shown on a normal home television. That way they are visible but will not block any of my picture.

You and your production manager will also need to decide just what kind of tape your dailies will be transferred to. The choice will be dependent on two things: budget and the number of copies needed each day. The least expensive alternative is to telecine the dailies directly to a 3/4" tape for the editing room and make no copies for anyone else. That option is rarely acceptable for most films because nearly everyone wants a tape of the day's dailies—from the director and all the producers, to a host of studio executives.

The normal procedure is to make one master tape and the editing room tape directly from the negative and make all of the copies from that master after the telecine session is over. Since your tape will be made simultaneously with the master tape, it is often called a *simo cassette*. The advantage of making a simo cassette is that your editing tape can get to the editing room several hours earlier than it would if everyone's viewing tapes were made from your tape.

On television shows and direct-to-video films there is another factor to consider. The quality of the tape you use to input into Wendy's editing machine will probably not be good enough to make the edited master that will be shown on television. A high quality videotape must be made for airing. It would make no sense to go back to the original negative at the end of editing and remake the videotape transfer onto this high quality tape (usually a D-1 or Digital Beta—or "DigiBeta" tape format). Shows that will be completed on videotape always create the high quality tape at the original telecine session.

For films that will not be finished on tape you will probably have very little need for a high quality master tape so the master tape can be done in a lower quality format.

Editing cassettes are generally made in 3/4", Super-VHS (S-VHS), or Beta-SP formats. Sound quality is better on S-VHS and Beta-SP. Another 3/4" format with better sound is the 3/4"-SP tape. It requires special 3/4"-SP video decks in both the telecine house and editing rooms but if you are planning on having large screenings using sound taken directly from your editing machine, you will need the superior sound quality either the SP or S-VHS formats will give you.

Editors who have compared the S-VHS and 3/4"-SP formats report that the S-VHS tapes have sound quality equal to the 3/4"-SP format. The S-VHS tapes, however, have superior picture quality. If it is possible to make S-VHS editor's tapes (not all telecine house can make them easily), that is definitely the better way to go. The best choice, of course, is the most expensive—BetaSP.

112

Your production office will determine just how many viewing tapes need to be created and in which tape formats. It is not uncommon for a dozen tapes to be struck every day on an average feature film, in two or three different formats, with differing sound specifications. When you make your initial contact with the telecine house you should make sure they have all of this tape dubbing information. A sample Telecine Spec Sheet is shown in Figure 4A.7. It is usually made up by the production office or your Post-Production Supervisor, and you should make sure that the telecine house has a copy of it or a tape order listing all the same information. Inevitably, your needs will change as the production period goes on and some people who feel left out demand their own videotapes. Always let your telecine house know, preferably on the Spec Sheet, how many tapes of each format you need.

You will then need to make arrangements with the production office so they can pick up and distribute the tapes to everyone that is supposed to get them. Make sure you receive *your* editing room tape as early as possible—even if you or Philip need to go get it yourselves.

Some productions insist that each individual viewing cassette is labeled and burned-in with the name of the person who is receiving it. This is to protect against illegal duplication of tapes.

BIG TIME FILMS, INC.
3265 Hollywood Blvd., Hollywood, CA 90048
Feature Film - **"SILENT NIGHT, SILENT COWBOY"**

Contact: Assistant Editor - You R. Assistant   123-456-7890 (editing room)
                                          123-098-7654 (home)
         Production Coordinator - Ruth Hochberg   123-444-5678 (office)
                                          123-975-8642 (home)

SHOW DETAILS
- Production will be in Los Angeles and some desert locations.
- Production is shooting 48 days beginning Monday, September 13, 1999 and ending November 18, 1999.
- Production will shoot five day weeks, Monday through Friday, with one Saturday shoot on October 16, 1999.
- There will be approximately 9,000 feet of processed film per day. We anticipate shooting with two cameras throughout most of our schedule. There are presently three days where more than two cameras will be used. Production will notify telecine house of those shooting days.
- 35mm negative (24fps/4 perf) will be processed and prepped for telecine at Favorite Film Labs and telecined at Tele Cine House.
- Favorite Film will punch each camera roll.
- Production will shoot a smart slate and recording DAT with 30 fps non-drop frame time code (left channel = 20db headtone, right channel = 30db headtone). We have notified the sound recordist and assistant directors to provide at least ten second of audio pre-roll prior to the slate clap.

TELECINE DETAILS
- DATs will be delived to Tele Cine House each night. TCH will pick up processed and prepped negative at 2am each morning. Camera reports and purchase order will travel with the negative.
- Dailies will be transferred each day from 2:30am until 8:30 in Room 6 with Jonathan DeCarlo. All grey scales and color charts should be transferred.
- Dailies will be transferred to ONE Beta-SP editors' cassette and ONE Beta-SP production master viewing cassette simultaneously. Editorial will be editing on Avid and will need FLEx files and printouts with their Beta-SP cassette.
- Transfer with non-drop frame time code.
- Each take shall be edited with A frame edits.
- The first take on each roll should have at least ten seconds of pre-roll.
- Transfer will be made with 1.85 letterboxing using the leader edited onto each lab roll at Favorite as reference.
- The following information needs to be burned in:
    - Visual Time Code in lower left.
    - Negative Keycode in lower right.
    - Original DAT Sound Code in top left.
    - Tape Roll Number in top right.
- Time code, keycode, camera, sound and lab roll numbers shall be transferred into VITC.
- All wild tracks should be transferred last in a given session.
- Dailies Reels should be coded beginning with Reel One equals 1:00:00:00. Time code should be rolled over back to one hour after each **twenty** dailies reels (i.e., Reels 21, 41, 61 should start the cycle with 1:00:00:00 over again).

DUB DETAILS
- All dailies viewing dubs should be made from the Beta-SP master as follows:
    - ONE 3/4" with address track time code
    - TEN VHS copies
    - TWO S-VHS copies.
- All tapes should include the following information on the slate and on labels:
    - BIG TIME FILMS INC.
    - "Silent Night, Silent Cowboy"
    - Transfer Date
    - Shooting Date(s)
    - Dailies Reel Number
    - Time Code Hour Number
    - Total Running Time
    - "NDFTC"
- All dubs should have the following legend burned in:
    - "PROPERTY OF BIG TIME FILMS, INC." in the center upper letterbox
    - Video time code in the center of the lower picture area.

SHIPPING DETAILS
- Editor's Beta-SP cassette will be picked up by client at 9:00am each weekday. Call the asssitant editor at any of the numbers listed at top of sheet if there will be a delay.
- Dubs will be picked up by client at 11:30am each weekday. Call production office coordinator at numbers listed at top of sheet if there will be a delay.

VAULTING DETAILS
- The Beta-SP production viewing master, film negative and DAT sound rolls will be vaulted at Tele Cine House.

01:02:13:00
01:02:18:05
01:02:21:10
01:02:24:15
01:02:27:20
01:02:30:25
01:02:33:00
01:02:36:05
01:02:39:10

FIGURE 4A.7 A Telecine Spec Sheet. Though many sheets are not this detailed this list includes nearly every conceivable question that the telecine house might have about how to process your film. For those questions that it doesn't answer it also gives the contact numbers for both the production coordinator and the assistant editor.

Also on the Spec Sheet should be an indication of what your daily shooting schedule is. Shooting days that create more dailies will need more telecine time and since telecine time is very tightly booked you may need to book extra time at the telecine house or be caught with an incomplete set of dailies. If you are shooting on Saturday or Sunday, for instance, in addition to your normal Friday shoot, your lab will probably not process that weekend's negative until the same Sunday night bath normally used to process your Friday negative. As a result, you will have extra dailies on Monday morning for your telecine house to transfer. Make sure they expect them. Days on which you will be shooting with more cameras than usual (like heavy stunt or crowd scene days) will also create a need for extra telecine time.

By the same token, let your telecine house know if there are days the crew will not be shooting (if they are traveling or have the day off, for instance). The telecine house will then be able to fill up your time slot with another client and you won't be charged for the time. It is always a good idea to keep the telecine house informed of any shooting schedule changes affecting them as well.

114

An Alternate Telecine Route

There is an alternate, though slightly more time consuming, way of proceeding to telecine if you are synching film dailies and transferring them to film. Under the assumption that no one cares about your footage and the accuracy of the data attached to it as much as you do, a recent program called Logmill (developed by an assistant editor who needed the program himself) allows you, as the assistant editor, to prepare the telecine file yourself. Since telecine operators or their assistants need to hand enter all the information about key numbers, scene and take numbers, camera and sound rolls, etc., there is always a chance they will introduce errors. Also, they never enter description information that you will need in the system anyway.

Logmill works something like this: either as you are synching the dailies or immediately afterwards, you (or Philip) will type in all of the information that you have available about the dailies rolls and each take on them. The program figures out what time code numbers will be assigned to each take and prepares a telecine log that can be given on disk to the telecine house (as well as creating ODB or ALE files). This eliminates most chances for database errors in the telecine process, as well as speeding up the transfer from film quite a bit. The program also generates the editor's screening note sheets, and the editing room logbooks. It's not a system every editing room can use (it won't work, for instance, if you aren't print-ing film) and it does require an investment in at least one laptop computer to sit on the assistant's editing bench as he or she syncs the dailies. Still, it is one solution to the perennial problem of get-ting reliable data into the editing machine.

24 vs. 30 Frame Projects

Before you begin digitizing your first day's worth of dailies you will need to make one irrevocable decision—what frame rate to input your footage. Earlier in this chapter we learned about the 3:2 pulldown. You should remember that in the United States, film is projected at 24 frames per second (fps) and video is projected at approximately 30 fps. This creates certain problems in converting from one frame rate to another as you digitize the 30 frames per second video dailies.

If your project is going to end up back on film, you will have to digitize and edit the film at 24 fps. On the Lightworks, you will need to inform the machine that you are cutting in a 24 frame project. On the Avid you will usually be editing with the Film Composer soft-ware, rather than the Media Composer, which works at 30 frames.

With television shows the issue is a little trickier. Normally, it would make sense to edit the film in 30 fps since that is how the project will be shown. This way, there would only be one conversion necessary—when the original film was digitized. Your 30 fps digi-tized material would directly match your 30 fps final edited master.

However, most television production companies insist that you deliver either a cut negative to them or a *Film Cut List* that they can eventually use to cut the negative. There is rarely an immediate need for this cut negative except perhaps in delivery to some inter-national markets. Production companies still insist on this film delivery requirement for another reason: they are preparing for the future day when *HDTV* (high definition television) will require the resolution and quality that only film negative can deliver. For HDTV, they will need to make high resolution masters from the negative and to do that, they need to have a properly edited film negative.

This leaves you with two choices. You can cut the project at 30 fps, making the video finish easier and more accurate, but also making the potential film finish a bit more difficult and less accu-rate. Alternatively, you can cut the project at 24 frames, making the film finish accurate but creating a few problems in your video fin-ish. Many editors will gladly cut the project at 30 FPS and deal with the conversion problems at a later time.

Actually, this is a decision rarely left to the assistant. Usually the production company will make the decision, with or without the editor's input. In either case, you will need to know this decision before you start to digitize anything on the film.

Once You Have the Tape in Hand

At some point, early in the morning if things go well, you should receive the editor's tape, the Telecine Log and your computer disk. You will already have gotten the paperwork we discussed in Chapter 4 from the production office. Your task is to look at all of the paperwork and make sure everything was transferred that was supposed to be put on tape.

Telecine operators have an unenviable task. They are usually working in the middle of the night with very little paperwork, under the influence of far too many caffeinated beverages. All of the production paperwork mistakes that you have to deal with when *you* sync the dailies on film are magnified for them because they can't call the production office coordinator and ask for missing paperwork, errant sound rolls, or more legible notes from the set. Takes with no slates or misslated identifications have to be decoded in the expensive telecine bay, working against an overly tight time frame.

116

If your production has booked the proper amount of time, the operators are usually able to get all of your dailies done in time, but not always done perfectly. It will be your job to make sure everything is correct before you digitize it into your editing machine. The operative phrase that computer programmers use is "Garbage In, Garbage Out" (GIGO). If you expect to match film or a Master Tape to your digital edit, you'd better make sure that every bit of information your editing system is using to identify frames of film is correct, or else there will be many problems later on down the line.

If your telecine house synched your dailies, you need to make sure they transferred everything that the script supervisor's notes (in particular the Editor's Log) and the camera and sound reports say should have been transferred. Since much of the information appearing in the Telecine Log and computer files is input by hand, you need to check it for accuracy. You should make sure that the information for every take is correct. If multiple cameras were used on the set, you will probably have to include the designations for A and B cameras that are added to the end of the scene and take number (e.g., 34-2a or 34-2b). Most telecine operators don't bother to write the camera designations in the name portion of the file.

Make sure your video burn-ins are placed properly on the screen and that every A-frame is on a zero or a five frame if your editing machine requires that.

You should also compare the visual burn-in codes at the start and the end of every take against the database to make sure they match. It is one further verification of the integrity of the Telecine Log. If you are going to be cutting your negative, you might want to check one more number and that is the end key number for each take. Though it is a mammoth job, there have been numerous complaints in the past about inaccurate burn-ins, transfers where the key code numbers skip a frame and the like. This is very dangerous to your film conformations (we will discuss all of this in both Chapters 8A and 14A), so you will want to make sure they have been done correctly. Some assistants do this after the footage has been digitized.

If you have sunk the film and had your dailies rolls transferred to tape there will be some different work to do. Since there will be no stops and starts between takes you need only check that the very first cut is on an A frame. You should verify that the code numbers burned into the video match your inked numbers. The easiest way to do this is to check that the code number at your tail sync mark is the same as the burn-in time code at the same point on the video (check the section on logging in Chapter 5 for information on how to put that code number onto your film).

If your dailies were transferred to three-stripe with the sound roll time code on the center stripe, as we discussed in Chapter 4, your telecine house should be able to burn-in the sound code information onto the picture. They might also be able to input it into your database, greatly simplifying the procedure of handing the film over to your sound department after you *lock* your picture. Not every telecine house can deal with the changes in the time code that will occur every time you cut two takes together, so you should check with them before you make any plans.

117

We will cover this in more detail in Chapter 11A.

There is one final note on telecine that I should mention. Occasionally, in order to get a cheap reverse action, the production camera department will shoot a scene upside down or in reverse. It is important that the negative key numbers run in ascending order for most computer editing machines to track them properly. As a result, you should make sure that if a piece of film was shot upside down with the intention of flipping it over and running it backwards, the telecine house transfer it in its original shooting order (I also prefer to flip it in the editing machine, if possible) so the key numbers run in the proper order. If a piece of negative was run in reverse in the camera, it should be telecined *backwards to the way it was shot*. That is, it should be transferred so the key numbers run in ascending order.

There is a simple reason for this. Virtually all of the editing machines keep track of key numbers by noting the key number of the first frame of each take and extrapolating it to the end of the take. They all make the assumption that the key numbers are running in ascending order. If the key numbers run backwards from that first key number, the machine won't know to adjust the calculations, and will figure that a frame ten feet later than the first frame will have a key number ten numbers larger, rather than ten numbers smaller.

Paperwork and More

As each day's dailies come in you will start accumulating a large amount of paperwork. Much of it will look exactly the same as the paper we described in Chapter 4—script notes, camera and sound reports, lab reports, etc. All of this needs to be filed in an easily accessible manner. Get yourself a number of archboards (these are clipboards with two metal arches at the top instead of the clip). Punch two holes in the top of each piece of paperwork you might need to quickly access and put it on an archboard—one each for your lab, sound, camera, and telecine reports. When the next day's camera reports come in, put them on top of yesterday's in reverse numeric order (that is, the lowest number on the bottom).

You will also need to store the computer disks arriving every day from the telecine house. Get yourself a large disk storage case and keep those disks in order by tape number. You will also be creating disks of your own, or receiving disks from other people, during the course of the film—either EDLs or files with graphics. If you get a disk holder with two columns you can store these other disks separate from your dailies disks. Keep everything as orderly as your paperwork because you can be sure that if you've misfiled a disk, Wendy will need something that can only be taken from that disk.

Put this disk box in a safe place, far away from anything that might have a magnet in it. Radios, sound amplifiers and speakers are all things that may demagnetize your disks. Assistants working with their own computers often make *backup* copies of the files from the telecine disks onto their own computer's hard drive. Anything lost from the original disks can easily be recreated from their backups.

Synching in the Editing Machine

On some films it is becoming common to have the assistants sync up the dailies directly in the editing machine from the DATs shot on-set (or a copy of that DAT). If this is the case in your film, you need to make sure your editing set-up includes a time-coded DAT machine properly hooked up to your editing machine. You will need to be able to input the sound with its own time code.

Each digital editing machine works differently, but the general procedure is the same. You will receive the DATs from the set and the picture-only videotape from the telecine house. You will input each of these separately (which will effectively double your digitizing time), then edit the soundtrack onto the picture for each take, synching up the clappers just as described in Chapter 4. This synching process will take less time than it would to synch 35mm dailies but, between the double digitizing and the synching, you will be on the editing machine for most of the day. This method can only be used by films that have invested in an editing machine for the assistant as well as for the editor or those who have the assistant working late at night.

An important consideration to remember when digitizing these DAT tapes is the issue of the 3:2 pulldown in relation to the telecine process. When the picture was telecined, frames of video were added to make the videotape run at 30 fps. As you digitize it into your editing machine, these frames are removed to bring the picture back to the original 24 fps. This changes the speed of the videotape, speeding it up slightly. However, since the sound recorded on the set was not telecined at the 3:2 pulldown, it cannot be digitized in the same way as the picture. If frames were removed from the sound, the way they are from the picture, the sound would no longer run at the same speed as the picture.

Sound needs to be digitized at a different setting than the picture. On the Avid, for instance, there is a 0.9999 setting, which corrects for picture pulldown. The sound, however, needs to be digitized at another setting—1.000—that does not remove any frames. Other systems use similar settings.

An additional problem you may run into when you sync dailies in your machine is that you will probably need to create videotapes for distribution to the production and studio personnel. This is handled in several ways but all of them require additional time and work from you.

The easiest way to create this tape is to create a sunk-up soundtrack precisely matching the picture on your editing cassette. There are two ways to do this, each with its own positives and negatives. First, you can telecine each videotape in as one take, then sync up every take within an edit. This leaves you with one long reel of sunk picture and sound matching the original editor's tape frame-by-frame. The second method is to digitize each take on the reel separately (as we have already discussed), sync each take up individually, then edit all of the takes back into one edit, making sure there are no time code gaps or overlaps. When you are done you have one long edit, made up of a number of takes, that should match the original editor's tape precisely, frame-by-frame. Some editing machines have commands to simplify this process.

The disadvantage of this second method is, unless you build the long edit with care, it will be all too easy to create a reel not exactly matching the original tape. The disadvantage of the first method is, you will lose much of the convenience of the logging process and will have to carefully separate out your long sunk-up reel into individual takes so Wendy can have her dailies delivered by takes.

Whichever process you choose, you will end up with one long edit that should match your editor's tape exactly. You can then *playout* the sound channels of only this edit (see Chapter 8) back onto the editor's tape. This way you create a tape with the original telecined picture, sunk up with the digitized sound.

At this point, you will send this new editor's tape out to a tape house (often your telecine house) to have the necessary number of copies made for the production and the studio.

Since telecine houses often sync their dailies with less precision than you will, this method provides your dailies with the best sync possible.

In many cases, the production crew and studio personnel will want to see their dailies on film rather than solely on videotape. This creates a large problem if you are synching dailies in your editing machine. A 35mm print of all selected takes will need to be struck. You will need to organize all of the takes into dailies rolls, just as you did in Chapter 4. You will need to make sure the dailies rolls are no larger than 1000 feet.

You will then need to create a synchronous roll of 35mm soundtrack to match the 35mm picture on the editor's videotape. You can create this 35mm track either from the editor's master tape or from an audio tape (usually a DAT) you create in a playout (either separately or simultaneously with the playout to the editor's master tape). Whichever way you generate this dailies sound tape, you should make sure both the picture and sound rolls have leaders on them and that there is a sync pop on the soundtrack at a easily found and referenced to the picture. The normal place is opposite the last number on the Academy Leader. If there is no Academy

Leader on the picture you receive from the telecine house, then you can choose another frame. One possible point is the frame immediately before the first frame of picture.

You should then send the dailies sound tape to a transfer house to be put onto 35mm stripe full-coat or three-stripe. Because of the varying transfer speeds involved in a videotape process you should make sure the sound transfer house references the proper speed. If your dailies sound tape is a videotape, they will need to transfer it at a slightly different speed than if you supply them with a DAT (this will also depend on how you created the DAT). Make sure all the technical details are discussed and ironed out before your first day of dailies so everything goes smoothly in the crunch of that first day.

When you get the dailies reels back in the editing room you will need to sync each reel up with its matching 35mm picture. If you have intelligently selected the sync point for your pop, it will be a simple matter. First, spin down on each sound transfer reel until you reach the pop at the head of the reel (in many cases you will receive them tails out). Find the pop and mark the frame on the mag with an indelible marker. Then put each picture reel up in the front gang of your synchronizer and spin down until you reach that sync point on the reel. Set the counter at 9'00.

Put the mag in the second gang with the marked frame opposite it at the same 9'00 mark and roll backwards until the counter reads 0'00. You should see the Academy Start mark on the picture at that point. Mark that frame on the mag in much the same way you marked it in Chapter 4, punching out a hole to give an obvious indication that it is the start mark.

In most cases it is not necessary to put attractive leaders on the head and tail of each reel of picture and sound. Because these dailies reels will be shelved until it is necessary to *conform* the picture, these leaders will be used only once. You only need to spin back about another ten feet and tape on some reel identification tapes just as you did on the sunk reels in Chapter 4. Then spin down until you get to the end of the reel, stopping every now and then at random slates to listen and check that the track is running in sync with the picture. To do this, mark the mag at the first modulation of the stick's closing sound, mark the matching frame on the picture, and then check that frame with a loupe over the lightbox to make sure it is the frame where the slate closes. Don't be alarmed if successive slates are off by a few sprockets in one direction or another. The realities of the telecine, synching and playout processes introduce some slight variations.

At the end of the reel, mark the frame of sound opposite the last frame of the picture (called either the *Last Frame of Action, LFOA,* or the *End of Reel, EOR*), attach leaders if necessary, and make sure each reel has proper tail leader identification on it. You can then rewind and clean each reel and pack it up for screening.

Though it is certainly cheaper to sync dailies within the editing machine if you've already got an extra machine assigned to the assistant editor (if you don't, the cost of renting an additional machine may be too expensive), you will find that the added time of creating the sound dailies tape, transferring it to mag, and synching that mag up with the picture creates problems in terms of having the dailies ready for a seven o'clock dailies screening (lunch time dailies screenings are simply out of the question using this system).

Digital Telecine

Recently, a few productions have tried a different procedure. They have allowed their telecine houses to sync *and* digitize the dailies. This saves the assistant the time digitizing them from a tape in the editing room and will often result in a superior picture since the digitized image will be coming directly from the picture negative without going through a videotape intermediary. There are, of course, some minuses in this approach, not the least of which is the amount of control which you give up. Quality can be sacrificed and information can be lost in this process.

If your production decides to go this route, you will need to discuss with your telecine house at just what specifications you need the material digitized. You might want to spend the first few days of dailies at the telecine house to make sure that everything is being done as requested.

In this case, you would add some description to your Telecine Spec Sheet, detailing at what resolution or resolutions you want your dailies transferred. If you don't need your wild track digitized at as high a resolution as your picture, you should state that specifically on the Spec Sheet.

The dailies are usually digitized either to an *R-mag* (a removable hard drive) or a portable hard drive, either of which can easily be transported from the telecine house to the editing room. Once you've received the digitized dailies you need only transfer the information over to Wendy's hard drives, organize it for her, and your dailies are done. The drive is returned to the telecine house for the next day's dailies.

In reality, schedules being what they are, there are usually two traveling R-mags or drives. While drive number one is in your editing room, you should have already sent the second drive back to the telecine house for their use. The next day you will get the dailies on drive two and you return drive number one.

Oh yes, it is a more expensive process as well.

After the Telecine Is Done

After your telecine house has finished telecining your footage you will receive the tape. Your original sound and picture will still be sitting there, however, ready to go wherever you bid.

If you have created your dailies tape directly from your original camera negative and sound tapes, you should have the OCN sent either to your lab or to your negative cutter. Your sound tapes should be kept in storage at the telecine house or at your sound editorial house if your film has already made a deal with one. The idea is to store all of your material in the safest, yet most accessible, place. There will be times during the editing of the film that you might need to go back and telecine something again or telecine something that wasn't done in the first pass. It is important that the material be available so this can be done as quickly as possible.

If you made your telecine from your sunk dailies then you will probably want the footage returned to your editing room. There you will file it away in dailies roll order, with the code numbers written on the outside of the box.

123

Some assistant editors use a separate computer database program, like FileMaker Pro, to create their log books. On a recent film with a lot of CGI effects, the assistant was able to export frames from the Avid into FileMaker Pro. This picture (in a computer file called a PICT file) became part of the database and could be printed out and sent to the special effects department to simplify phone discussions.

In addition, some assistants like to use this database to keep track of the negative as it is being shipped from negative cutter to lab to optical house, etc.

For *Trigger Happy* I wrote a program that took information from both the FLEx and ODB files, combined them, and created a FileMaker Pro database which in turn generated the logbooks we handed over to the sound department at the end of the film.

The point of this discussion is that one of your tasks, as an assistant editor in the world of computer editing, is manipulating data. When you think of it, this isn't much different than in the all-film days. You needed to keep track of where every frame of film was in the editing room, now you need to keep track of where every frame is in the editing machine. You needed to keep track of where every roll of film was between lab and editing room, now you need to keep track of where the negative or print is between the lab, the telecine house, and every hard drive on the editing machine.

You'll need to know a bit more about computers in general, and your computer editing machine in particular. The main thrust of your job remains the same—keep it organized!

PREPARING FOR EDITING

Coding and Logging

One of the greatest tasks of an assistant editor is assuring the editor will always have any piece of film whenever it is needed. It is this vast librarian-like task that makes good assistants so valuable. If Wendy cannot find the three frame addition to a shot she knows she needs to make an edit work, she's not going to be able to edit the film, is she? There are assistant editors who always seem to work in a chaotic state of near-hysteria, in which the three frames are always misplaced, always madly searched for, and always belatedly found. A good system will enable anyone—be it the editor, assistant, or apprentice—to find anything within seconds. If Wendy wants to see a piece of film, it should take no longer to get it than it takes to walk over to a box, lift it out, and bring it back to her. If I seem rather insistent on this point, it is only because it is one I see as the cornerstone of good assistant work. Unless everyone, including the director, editor, apprentice, and producer, works better in the midst of chaos, I see no reason to have chaos in the editing room. Relaxed but tightly run editorial situations make for better filmmaking.

This is why it is important that every assistant get serious about setting up the system for a film. There are virtually as many systems as there are assistants organizing them. Yet nearly all are based on certain principles that make life easier for their editor(s).

The cornerstone of any film editing system is the code number. With anywhere from 100,000 to one million feet of film printed on most features, finding individual frames can get very complicated without a way to identify each frame. How, pray tell, does one differentiate between one take of a close-up of our hero, Abby, and another take from the same camera angle? There is no way to tell by looking at the picture. And how does one identify a piece from the soundtrack? There is nothing on it to see.

One thing you definitely DO NOT do with unidentifiable pieces is throw them out. That tiny little piece of film that you need today is almost always the one you threw away two weeks ago. *Nothing should ever be thrown away.* That's rule number one for a system.

So, how will you identify the film and track? Luckily, this problem was solved long ago. Before any film goes to be edited you should have it *edge coded* (sometimes called *edge numbered*).

This means your film (both picture and track) will be run through a machine that will print inked numbers on one edge of the film (*see* Figure 5.1). One number will be printed for every foot in 35mm. The coding machine printing the numbers automatically increases the printed number by one every time it prints a new number. This way every foot of the film will have a different code number assigned to it. In practice, this is just as good as if you had coded every frame of the film. In fact, it is better, since it would be hard to read film with code numbers on every frame.

In many editing rooms, the apprentice editor will be the one coding the dailies on a rented coding machine. Some films send their film out to coding services to have it edge numbered, but this is very rare and usually doesn't save enough money to make it worthwhile. In some cases, when you are printing up single takes after production is over, it is actually more expensive to send the rolls out to a service.

The numbers printed on the film are almost completely up to you, within the limits of the printing blocks on the coding machines. One setup is to have seven or eight digits, of which only the last four need be numbers (e.g., 123C5678 or 1234567 or 1BCD5678, etc.). Another common arrangement is to have two letters followed by four numbers (such as AB3456). These machines have many different brand names, the two most common are Acmade and Moy coding machines.

While code numbers for identification are very important for the assistant editor, the editor has an even more important use for it. If matching rolls of sunk-up picture and track (such as the pix and track rolls for a dailies roll) are coded in the same way, each code number will also serve as a point where the picture and track sync up in much the same way that the slate does. This way, the editor can

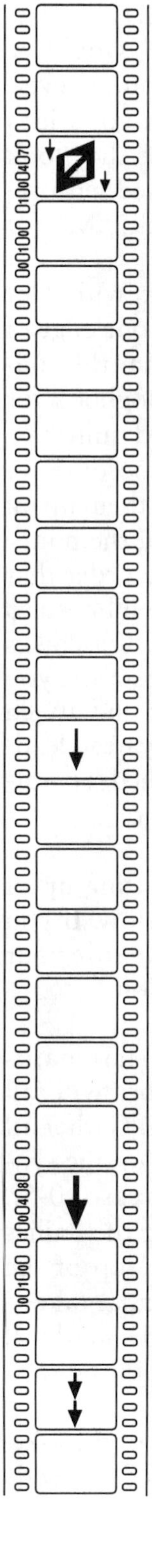

FIGURE 5.1 Coded film. The frame with the design in it is coded 010-1047. The frame with the single large arrow is 010-1048. Thus, the frame with only the two small arrows is called 010-1048⁺³. Note that the frame with the single small arrow in it can be called either 010-1047⁺⁹ or 010-1048⁻⁷. The arrows all point towards the tail of the film.

instantaneously line up picture and track, and run them in sync.

Don't worry if this sounds a little confusing. It is actually much easier in practice, as we shall now see.

After the dailies have been returned from the dailies screening you can have them coded. For our system we will use the common eight digit coding system and code the rolls by scene numbers. This way, all of the dailies on the first roll for scene ten will be assigned the code number 010 1000 at its start mark (note the space after the first "010"). At the start mark, fasten a piece of paper tape saying exactly that ("Start Code 010 1000") on both the picture and the track reels. The second roll for scene ten will be coded 010 2000, if there is a third roll it will be 010 3000, up to roll 10 which will be 010 0000. There are rarely more than ten thousand feet of dailies on one scene but if there are, it is common practice to put a letter reserved for this purpose in the fourth position. In other systems, the fourth position is often reserved for letters which denote A, B, or C cameras, or letters for music ("M"), effects ("E"), or wild track ("W").

Occasionally, an assistant will use the first three numbers to denote the dailies reel, rather than the scene number. This means you don't have to rearrange the reels for coding since dailies reels with multiple scenes on them won't need to be separated.

A common, but disappearing, system, using six digit code numbers, is to code the first ten dailies rolls AA1000, AA2000, AA3000, through

127

AA0000. The next ten dailies rolls would begin with BB1000. The next ten dailies reels (that is, numbers 31 through 40) would be CC1000 through CC0000. After you run out of letters you can cycle back to AB1000, AC1000, and so on. Generally it is a good idea not to use both EE and FF, or both VV and WW (since they look alike) or the letter OO codes (since they can get confused with zeroes). I also like to reserve the letters "W" for wild track, "M" for music, and "F" for sound effects.

After the footage has been coded it will be tails out, with a lot of funny white, yellow or black numbers running down one edge of the film. Two things need to be done now—checking that the coding was done properly, and logging the numbers into a logbook for easy reference. Both of these things can be accomplished quite easily if we make one small adjustment to the synching procedure we discussed in Chapter 4. Before you code your dailies put them up on your table, run them through your synchronizer and log them in.

First, you need to rearrange the dailies rolls in the order that you want to code them. In most cases, that means you will need to make sure each roll contains takes from only one scene. If a dailies roll contains takes from both scenes ten and eleven, for instance, you would separate the reel at that point in the synchronizer and attach short tail leaders to the end of scene ten's footage and new head leaders to the beginning of scene eleven's. After you have finished separating all of the reels you can begin to log all of your footage.

[NOTE: Many assistants actually combine this splitting up of the reels with the logging process as described below. If you choose this method, you need to be careful to make sure your numbering is correct on both sides of the separation.]

Run the film through the synchronizer and put the start marks in at 0000'00. This is where the 010-1000 code number will fall after the reel is coded. Take out a blank code book sheet. Gather all of your paperwork around you and begin rolling down on the synchronizer until you reach the first take on the roll (in this case 10-5). Begin to fill out the sheets as shown in Figure 5.2. Enter the dailies roll number and the date the footage was shot at the top of the page. Then enter the information pertinent to this particular take—the lab roll number, scene and take number, camera and sound roll numbers, and the short description you gave the take in the editor's dailies notes.

Now, look at the footage counter at the first frame of the take. It should read "0012." This means, when this roll is coded, the code

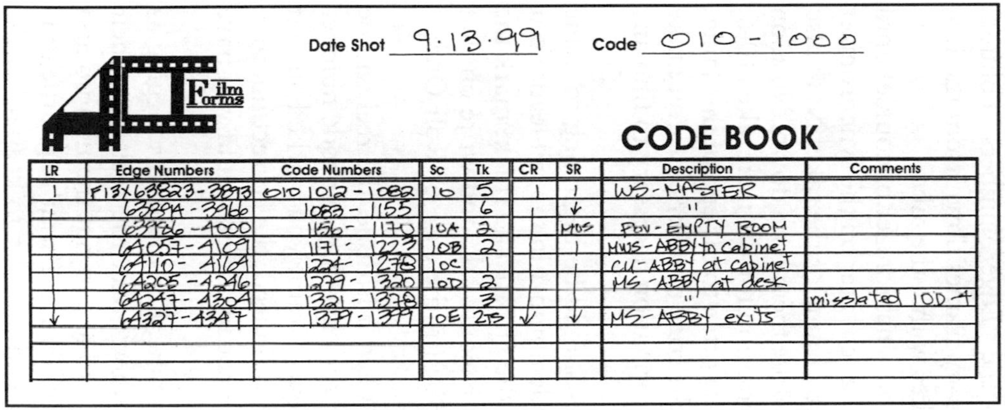

Film Forms

CODE BOOK

Date Shot 9.13.99 Code 010-1000

LR	Edge Numbers	Code Numbers	Sc	Tk	CR	SR	Description	Comments
1	F13X63823-3893	010 1012-1082	10	5	1	1	WS-MASTER	
	63894-3966	1083-1155		6		↓	"	
	63986-4000	1156-1170	10A	2		MOS	POV-EMPTY ROOM	
	64057-4109	1171-1223	10B	2			MWS-ABBY to cabinet	
	64110-4164	1224-1278	10C	1			CU-ABBY at cabinet	
	64205-4246	1279-1320	10D	2			MS-ABBY at desk	
	64247-4304	1321-1378		3			"	misslated 10D-4
↓	64327-4347	1379-1399	10E	2TS	↓	↓	MS-ABBY exits	

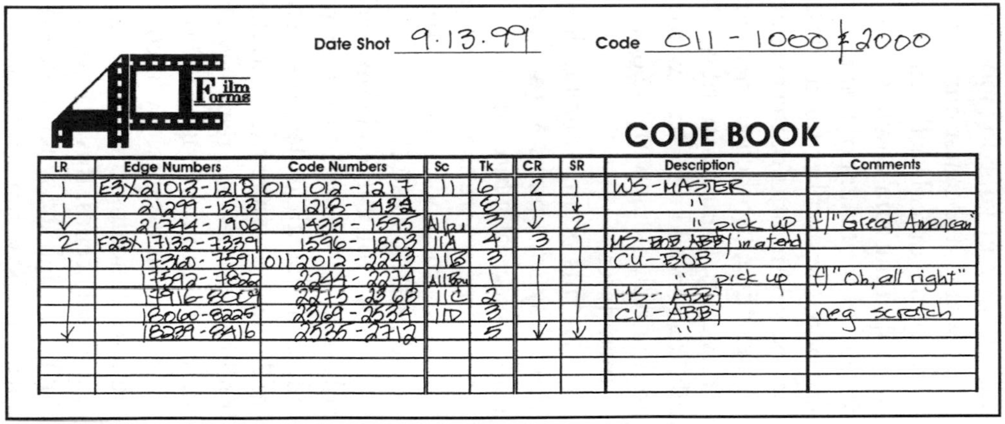

Film Forms

CODE BOOK

Date Shot 9.13.99 Code 011-1000 & 2000

LR	Edge Numbers	Code Numbers	Sc	Tk	CR	SR	Description	Comments
1	E3X21013-1218	011 1012-1217	11	6	2	1	WS-MASTER	
	21299-1513	1218-1432		8		↓	"	
↓	21744-1906	1433-1595	All[illegible]	3	↓	2	" pick up	f) "Great American"
2	F23X17132-7339	1596-1803	11A	4	3		MS-BOB, ABBY in a tent	
	17360-7591	011 2012-2243	11B	3			CU-BOB	
	17592-7822	2244-2274	All[illegible]	1			" pick up	f) "Oh, all right"
	17916-8009	2275-2368	11C	2			MS-ABBY	
	18060-8225	2369-2534	11D	3			CU-ABBY	neg scratch
↓	18239-8416	2535-2712		5	↓	↓	"	

FIGURE 5.2 Two pages from a code book (also called a logbook). Note that this assistant is using a new page for each scene number code number prefix (one page for 010-1000 and another for 011-2000). This makes codes and scenes easier to find than the alternative, which is to put as many dailies reels on one page as will fit. The comments column is for notations of misslates, negative damage, etc.

number 010-1012 will be on that frame. Enter that number under the column "Code Numbers." Now look at the edge of the film with a color band on it. Every 16 frames there is a number imprinted within that blue or black band. For 35mm film the number will usually look something like KI3212345. In 16mm the numbers are much smaller and less visible. This is called the *latent edge number* or the *key number*. This is a number Kodak (or whatever company manufactured the raw stock that your movie is being shot on) imprinted into the original negative. These numbers become visible after processing and printing. These are the *only* numbers on the original negative and therefore the only numbers your laboratory will know about. Enter this number in your logbook under the "Edge Numbers" column. Don't worry if the first number is many frames down from the first frame of the take. Use the first number within the take.

Spin the film down (through the synchronizer of course) until the end of the take. Look at the footage counter on the synchronizer and note the number for the last zero frame of the take. Note also the last key number of the take and write them both down. Now, on the next line, list the pertinent information for the next take (10-6, in this case). Continue until you have gotten to the end of the dailies roll. You should now have written the code numbers for every take on that roll, along with the other information necessary to find any of them later.

130

At this point, your tail leaders should be beginning to come into the synchronizer. At the first code number in the tail leader put a small piece of white tape on both the picture and track, mark the exact frame where that code number would fall, and write on that tape what the code number would be (in the case of Roll One, it would be 010-1380).

Now you can code this reel. When it is done, the reel will be tails out. All you need to do is to check that the first code number falling on the tail leader falls on the exact frame you marked on that small piece of white tape and that it is, indeed, the correct number. If all is well then the reels have been coded correctly and you have entered them in the logbook correctly.

Some assistants, given enough time, like to do this logging as they are synching the dailies or as they break the reels into their individual scenes, this way they won't have to put the film up and run it through the synchronizer a second time. If you've got the time during the synching process as well as the ability to keep all of the synching and logging tasks straight in your head at one time, then by all means go ahead and do this. Just be extra careful about watching for mistakes.

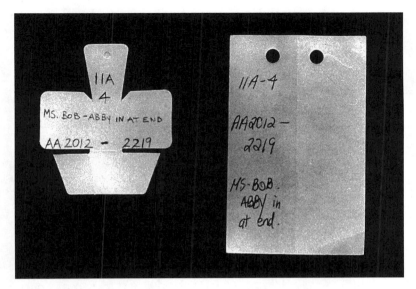

FIGURE 5.3 Note that the descriptions used on these tabs (the East Coast tab on the left, the West Coast tab on the right) are the ones used in both the dailies log and the code book.

Breaking Down the Footage

131

By now, you've got an awful lot of paperwork and some coded footage sitting tails out on your film rack. Wendy is probably dying to start editing and to do this she needs the footage. After all, at this point in the film, there is nothing else for her to cut. Once you are further along into the film, chances are good she will be cutting more slowly than the film crew is shooting and there will be slightly less pressure to provide her with footage.

So, can you just give her the footage and paperwork and let her cut? Of course not. There are still more things to do, depending upon whether you are cutting on an upright Moviola or on a flatbed.

If you are working on an upright, one of the next things you will do is to create the *trim tabs* I mentioned back in the list of supplies. These tabs will always be stored with the film—one tab for each take (*see* Figure 5.3). Listed on them will be the shot (10-5, in this example), the code numbers (10 1012—1082), and the short description you gave the take (WS—MASTER). Now you can see why I encouraged you to be concise in these descriptions; there just isn't much room on these damned things. These trim tabs can be made up as soon as the logbook has been done since it contains all of the necessary information.

The final bit of necessary paperwork to be done is filling in

FIGURE 5.4 *Marked-up script notes. The editor can find takes using the lined script and these notes without ever referring to the log book.*

the code numbers in the lined script. On the notes pages you should fill in, next to each printed take, its proper code numbers (*see* Figure 5.4). The script pages should then be put in a three-ring binder. Every day, as the new script pages come in, you will add these new script pages to the binder in their proper scene number order.

Writing the codes into the script can save Wendy a lot of time when she's looking for takes. All she has to do is look at the script, find the setup she needs, and she can see the code number.

Once these things have been done, the individual takes can be flanged off and made ready for Wendy if she is cutting on an

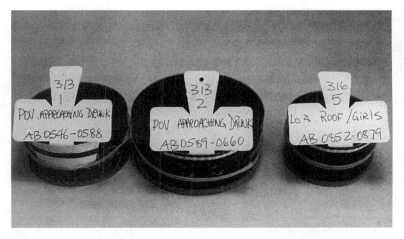

FIGURE 5.5 *These three takes have been flanged up and wrapped up with a rubber band. With their trim tabs slipped between the first and second layers of film, they can now be given to the editor for cutting.*

upright. (If she is cutting on a flatbed you should look ahead to Chapter 7 for more details.) To do this, place the picture and track rolls on the rewind on the right side of your bench, tails out (this is how they ended up after they were coded anyway). Put them into the synchronizer, in sync. Take off the tail leaders and hang them up in a trim bin (you can reuse them by simply taping a different dailies roll number and date over the old information). Now, wind the take onto your flange (this is a piece of equipment which looks like half of a take-up reel with a one-inch hub at its center) until you get to the head of that take. Wind it *through* the synchronizer so it is on the left side of the table, and cut the two takes apart at the grease pencil mark you used to divide the takes when you were synching them up. This will leave the single take by itself on the flange, heads out.

Remove this take from the flange by giving the flange a little quick turn in the opposite direction from the way you were winding it. Wrap a rubber hand around the take so it won't flap loose, tuck the trim tab between the first and second layers of film, and set it up on your table. It's now ready for the editor. Of course, one take isn't going to do too much good, so continue this process until you've got all of the footage for one scene broken down (*see* Figure 5.5).

If you are using the rectangular trim tabs, you won't need rubber bands. When folded in half, you can slip them around the outside of the film, leaving about one extra turn of film above the tab. This excess can be tucked inside the tab and tightened gently.

This will hold the trim roll together.

Now, and only now, can Wendy actually cut the scene.

Odds and Ends

You will notice that you've got some track left over from the synching of the dailies that you never used. This *wild track* or *wild sound* was sound taken on the set with no picture rolling. This is often done to get the ambiance of the room (helpful for the sound effects editors later on), specific effects peculiar to the location, or readings of lines that the director wanted to do on the set (off-camera lines, other ends of telephone conversations, voice-over speeches and the like) are often done this way. Though they are often redone in a looping stage near the end of the editing process (see Chapter 13 for more details on this), having temporary lines here can help the editor pace out the scene properly.

This soundtrack material may be very helpful to Wendy as she cuts. Then again, it may be of no use to her whatsoever, but let her make that decision. For this reason, it should also be coded and logged.

If you are coding using scene numbers, separate each scene's wild track onto separate rolls for easy coding and mark each roll for coding with the prefix "W." Thus the first reel of wild track for scene 10 would be coded 010W1000. In the six or seven digit system most assistants will code this wild track with the prefixes WS, WT, and WV; so make sure not to use these codes for any of your dailies. When you or Philip write up the trim tabs, do them all in red (to indicate soundtrack only takes).

Make a note in your log of the last code number for each roll of the wild track so if you ever have more wild track from this scene (either because more is shot on the set or because you are printing up extra copies of the original wild track) you can start the coding of the new material at a later code number. You don't want to duplicate any code numbers.

The way you divide the work between yourself and Philip depends entirely upon your work load and your confidence in him. At the beginning of any film the assistant normally syncs the dailies. As the shooting progresses it is not uncommon to hand this task over to the apprentice. It is a good way for your apprentice to learn, as well as a good way to free you up for other tasks, especially if Wendy is the type of editor that wants you standing next to her as she edits.

However, you should always be the one to screen the footage before dailies and prepare the editor's logs. This way you will get familiar with the film. Also remember, ultimately, it is your job to make sure that every task in the editing room (regardless of who does it) is done correctly.

Different editors will ask for their film in different ways. I generally like to put all the takes for any given scene in order into a series of white two-piece boxes. The assistant marks the outside of the box with the scene number. Never put takes from different scenes in the same box. The box can then be put on a shelf reserved for material the editor has not yet begun to cut.

Thus, when Wendy asks you for the footage to Scene 10, you can go to the boxes marked Scene 10 on the shelf (which includes all takes and wild tracks) and either give them to her in the boxes or set them out for her, as she wishes. Some editors like them lined up in set-up order on a shelf on the rack on their bench. Others like them lined up in large plastic colored racks (like egg cartons for film). These are portable and can be easily set down wherever he or she likes them.

When Wendy asks you for Scene 11 it should be ready for her. As you get more and more footage in, always check with her to see if she has a priority as to which scenes she would like to cut next. That way, if you have four scenes to prepare you can know the order you should code and log them. Most of the time, you will be able to keep up with the dailies on a day-to-day basis, so you will never be more than a day behind getting footage ready for Wendy. Sometimes, however, you will fall behind. On *Hair*, one scene took two and a half weeks to shoot and ran through nearly 80,000 feet of film. It took us nearly a week to get it all prepared. The bottom line, though, is to ensure that Wendy has the film she wants to cut when she wants to cut it.

135

One final task you should perform is creating a list of all of the scenes in the film, with their scene numbers. This list, called a Continuity (*see* Figure 5.6), can be posted on the walls near Wendy's, yours and Philip's benches. The descriptions for each scene should be short but should indicate exactly which scene it is. Wendy can use it to check off the status of every scene during production (shot, screened, edited, etc.)

Silent Night, Silent Cowboy
Pink Script
September 3, 1999

1	Credit montage
2	On the set
4	Backstage
5	Driving home
6	Abby's empty room
7	Driving to work the next day
8	"Did the zoom look okay?"
9	Alone in the parking lot
10	Abby arrives home and gets shocked
11	"Evening, Mr. DeMille"
12	The hot dog stand
17	Abby meets Sean
18	Abby and Sean back at Abby's
19	"Jimmy the Baby"
20	Cowboy and James fight
22	Lunch with Genie
23	"The rushes are a disaster"
24	Parking lot rewrites
25	Phone call from Genie
26	"Have it out with him"
27	Abby and James have it out.
28-30	Abby wanders about
31	Dream montage
32-33	Abby in the hills/L.A. at night

"Silent Night, Silent Cowboy"   September 3, 1999 Pink Script
Page 1

FIGURE 5.6 *A Continuity. This is a list of all of the sequences in the film, in script order. As Wendy watches each scene in dailies, she might put a mark next to the number to indicate that she can edit the scene. After she cuts the scene she can check if off so she can keep a record of everything that has already been edited. Later, as you begin to balance the film onto reels you can turn this continuity into the Reel Continuity (see Figure 8.5).*

. . . . . .

PREPARING FOR DIGITAL EDITING

Once you have all of your dailies in your editing room and have verified all of the information on your files and Telecine Log, it is probably time to input all of that footage into Wendy's editing system so she can being cutting. The reason I use the word "probably" in that sentence is because you will have an additional factor to deal with that you never had in an all-film editing room—traffic.

Most films don't have the budget for an extra Avid or Lightworks for the assistant so you will constantly be competing with the editor for the use of the one system you do have. You will not be able to digitize your dailies until Wendy can give up her machine for the necessary amount of time. And how long is that necessary amount of time? It will depend on the number of takes you have and the condition of the telecine logs. In general, you can count on using up to about 50% more time than there are dailies. For instance, if you have 60 minutes of dailies you can count on spending up to about 90 minutes digitizing them in, more if there are many short takes.

Digitizing

Every digital editing system works a little differently, but they all operate on the same general idea. You need to take your telecine file and convert it into one the editing machine can read. All systems, and third-party programs like Slingshot, come with conversion programs to do this. Every machine has its own internal file format. Examples are ALE files, for the Avid, ODB files, for the Lightworks, PowerLog files, for the Media 100, ImMIX logs, for the TurboCube, and Adobe Premiere files for(wonder of wonders) Adobe Premiere.

To be sure this process works, you should examine the database the telecine house has prepared for you, if you haven't already done so. I described how to do this in Chapter 4A. After you have made sure that all of the numbers are correct, you can begin to digitize your footage.

Once your FLEx (or whatever) file is converted, you can begin the process that will help you to *digitize* your dailies (this is what the process of inputting the videotaped dailies into your computer system is called). In the old days you would have to sit at the machine, marking the time codes where every take began and ended. However, the files you have received from the telecine house now allow you to automate most of this process. This automation is called *batch digitizing* because it permits you to digitize everything in one batch rather than take by take.

In both the Avid and Lightworks systems you can also override some of the batch digitizing defaults. Normally, you will digitize the picture and either one or both soundtracks that you get on the editorial cassette. However, for wild track or MOS takes you can edit the database to supersede these settings. This is generally done by adding the designation V (for picture only, that is—MOS) or A12 or A1A2 (for soundtracks one and two only, that is—wild track) to the database. On some machines it is also possible to edit with footage digitized at varied resolutions. Some editors (especially documentary editors) conserve hard drive space by digitizing close-up shots at lower resolutions than the rest of the footage. That change can also be made in the database at this time.

In most systems you can add, either now or later, information to the database that will be the equivalent of the Cinetab or trim tab on your 35mm film. You will be able to enter the characters' names in each shot as well as the size of each shot (WS, MCU, etc.). Some systems have space for notes (out of focus, pick-up shot, etc.), scene number, and blank categories for information of your own choosing. You might enter some of this information as the material is being digitized. In other systems you need to do it immediately afterwards. You can get the description either from your viewing of the tape as you digitized it or you can use the script supervisor's descriptions.

Another check you need to make, especially if you are going to on-line your show at a later date, is an inspection of the video reel number. Every day's dailies will come on a tape labeled with an increasing reel number. If the production shot 90 minutes of material on the first day of shooting, you would normally receive two dailies tapes (each 3/4" or Beta-SP tape fits one hour of footage), numbered something like SN001 and SN002. Some on-line editing systems have very specific reel naming conventions. You will need to make sure that the reel numbers going into your machine from the database will be readable months later at the on-line. Check with your on-line facility.

A safe convention is to use numbers only and make sure there are three digits in each tape number. Tape reel number one would be 001, reel 23 would be 023, and reel 156 would be 156. This system ensures that the numbers sort in the proper order, even with a computer that thinks all numbers beginning with one (reel one and 156) belong before all reels beginning with two (reel 23). All computers think that way.

The important byword here is accuracy. The database you will be digitizing from will contain all the information affecting how the 35mm or 16mm OCN (original camera negative) is later conformed to Wendy's picture edit. It contains all of the numbers that guide either the on-line editor or your negative cutter to match her cut. It has all the details telling your optical house and your sound editors how to do their jobs properly. If there are any mistakes here you may never get a chance to find them until it is too late to correct them. As I've already mentioned, the computer term for this is GIGO—"garbage in, garbage out." If your information is wrong, then all of the lists using that information will be wrong.

So you'd better check those numbers well.

Before you can actually begin to digitize the footage make sure the sound and video will be input at standard levels. At the top of every dailies tape you should see at least thirty seconds of *bars and tone*. These are a number of vertical lines of different colors conforming to a set standard for video color. Simultaneously with the color bars you should hear a steady sound tone. This is a 1 KiloHertz tone, the universal standard for aligning sound machines.

The Lightworks allows you to set only the level of the sound coming into your machine. The Avid allows you to set both the picture and sound levels. To set the sound, run the tape and raise or lower the level of the sound (usually at your mixer, though some set-ups may require you to change it on the output controls of your tape machine) until it is just a tad below the red. If both the sound recordist and the colorist/editor at the telecine house have done their jobs correctly, this will assure that the sound going into your editing machine is high enough to get clean dialogue but not so high as to distort the sound.

To set the color levels you will need to send the color bars signal through an oscilloscope of some sort (Avid has their own built-in scope tool) and set the signals so the peaks of the colors reach the proper settings. Every system is a little different. On some machines you won't be able to set the color levels at all.

On the Avid you can save the color settings for each day's dailies by its own name, usually the tape number. That way, if you ever need to redigitize a take from that day, it is a simple matter to call up the old settings and use them, rather than going through the alignment process one more time.

You should also make sure that your sound settings are correct—tracks properly switched on, pulldown settings correctly chosen, levels set through your sound mixer.

Once you have corrected, added to, checked every item in the logging database, and set your levels, you can simply click an on-screen button with your mouse to start the digitizing process. The machine will take control of your videotape deck if you've set all of its switches properly. Make sure that the "Remote/Local" switch on the videotape deck is set to "Remote" and that the "Line/Dub" switch is set to "Dub." Other settings should be discussed with your equipment rental house since video switchers and patch bay settings vary from set-up to set-up.

The videotape will automatically roll to the beginning of the first take to be digitized, roll far enough back to make sure that it is up to speed on the first frame that it needs to input (this is called the *pre-roll*), and then roll forward. When it gets to the exact frame listed in the Telecine Log, the computer will automatically start digitizing the footage into one or more of its disk drives. It will continue to input the take until it reaches the time code that the Telecine Log says is the end of the take. It will then automatically stop digitizing, roll a short distance more to insure that everything is properly recorded (this is called the *post-roll*), and stop the tape.

The computer will then send the tape to the next take and go through the same process again and again until all the takes listed in the database have been digitized. If you've done your job right, this list will include all of the takes on the dailies tape.

Some editors, myself included, like to view the dailies during the digitizing process, taking the same notes that I would if I were watching the dailies for the first time on film. I like to have my assistant make up my dailies notes before the digitizing for this reason. These dailies notes look exactly the same as I described in Chapter 4.

Because the tools you will be using to digitize and organize the dailies are so different than the ones Wendy will use for cutting, it is helpful to keep your assistant's work separate from hers. On the Lightworks many assistants like to set up a separate project to digitize material, put it into a gallery devoted solely to that day's dailies, and then move or copy it over to a room devoted just to assistant's work within the editor's project. The Avid works analogously. You should digitize the material into a bin devoted solely to dailies and rearrange it later for Wendy. We will discuss some of these strategies in the next chapter, but the general rule of thumb is to make the digitizing and organizing process completely invisible to the editor. Just as Wendy shouldn't have to get involved with the way you are ink coding the edge numbers of 35mm film, she should have to know nothing about the organizational details of your work before she sees it.

Many assistants like to note on their Telecine Logs just what hard drives the day's dailies were digitized on to. If there is ever any disaster making that drive unusable, it will be quite easy for them to figure out just what material needs to be re-digitized.

There are many different strategies for how you might want to apportion your material on the hard drives. Some assistants like to digitize dailies on different drives than the music and sound effects. Others like to nearly fill up one drive with dailies before moving onto another. A third strategy is to spread the dailies evenly around all of the drives. About the only rule of thumb is that you should never completely fill up a drive. I usually like to leave at least 5 percent empty.

Some assistant editors use a separate computer, sometimes accompanied by a separate videotape machine (often attached to their computer with a special cable, called an RS-422 cable, enabling the computer to control the deck), to pre-log all the information. Using this system, they receive the Telecine Log file and, in their own computer, make all of the corrections and additions they need to. As a result they don't need to take any of their editor's time on the Avid or Lightworks. They can look at the dailies on their own videotape machine and make all of the notes and descriptions directly into the database. They can use this corrected and hopefully, complete database to batch digitize their dailies. This way, the only time they require on their editors' machine is to actually digitize the dailies, rather than prepare *and* digitize.

Re-Synching the Dailies

The sad truth is that almost no one will care about your film in the way that you do. Telecine houses may have great looking reception areas and catered lunches, but the accuracy of their synching (either on tape or direct to R-mag) often leaves much to be desired.

Partially, this is a result of the inherent inaccuracy of the time coded smart-slates used on sets today. There is often a two or three frame difference between the code appearing on the front of the smart slate and the actual time code on the original production sound tapes. It is also a result of lax standards in which sync can be off by as much as one and one-half frames and still be considered acceptable. A third factor is the inherent inaccuracy of both the on-line (telecine) and off-line (editing room) equipment. Finally, to some degree this is a result of general tiredness and sloppiness on the part of telecine operators who know that sound problems are much cheaper to fix later than color and other visual problems.

Whatever the reason, you will probably find that at least some of your dailies are sunk up inaccurately. Once you have digitized your material, you will want to go through every take and its sync. You should re-sync takes that are not up to your specifications and replace the old take with the new one. It is a good idea to rename one of the takes so the two can be differentiated. Some assistants like to rename the new take (25A-3 would become 25A-3* or 25A-3 (resync)), others like to rename the old one (25A-3 would become 25A-3* or 25A-3 (badsync)).

142

Organizing the Material

Once the dailies have been digitized, you should organize all of the material so Wendy can begin working with it. If you have film in the editing room, you should make sure it is properly edge coded and filed in an accessible manner. Eventually, you will need to cut your 35mm film to match the digital cut. The computer editing machine will spit out lists organized either by key number (if your film was telecined from the negative), or edge code number (if your film was telecined from the sunk dailies). You should organize your film footage so that any frame can be easily found using these numbers.

Your digitized footage will also need to be organized in a sensible order.

First, you should make one final check that the time and key code (or edge code) burn-ins are the same as the codes on the VITC and the telecine log. Often, the lab will have prepared the negative for the telecine by placing a hole punch at the head of each take, and you can check the footage at that point. Otherwise, I usually check each take at the slate. Compare the number on the burn-in with the number on the telecine log and in your machine. On nearly all of the digital systems allowing film footage numbers there are settings that enable you to see what key code has been loaded into the machine for any frame of digitized picture. It is a simple matter to compare it against the burn-in and the telecine log.

If your editing tapes were made from sunk 35mm footage, your digitized footage will probably not yet be broken down into individual takes. If you've used a program like LogMill to create the internal databases ahead of time, your computer will automatically break the footage at the breaks between takes where you've assigned a code number to end a take. If you haven't then you will need to break it down yourself.

Every digital editing system has different terminology for this but, in general, you must divide the long roll of dailies into its separate takes. You can split the takes at the flash frames, much as you did during the film synching process. It is not crucial that you make the splits without duplicating frames from take to take, but it certainly wouldn't hurt. You want to be sure that any material Wendy might need to use from take 25A-3 exists only in the clip that you've labeled 25A-3. If you don't do that then your Film Cut Lists might have confusing take numbers on them.

Once you have checked that the information in the log and on screen is correct then you can begin to rearrange the footage in whatever order Wendy likes. This order will differ from machine to machine as well as from editor to editor. There are, however, some guidelines.

143

It is sometimes necessary to go back to the dailies and either check certain information or redigitize takes. For this reason, it is usually helpful to keep the original order of dailies some place in the machine. Luckily, the very nature of digital editing makes this extremely easy. As I explained earlier, when Wendy edits she is not really creating any new footage. She is merely writing a set of computer instructions pointing to the frames she is editing into the film. By the same token, this means you can create any number of arrangements for dailies without creating any actual new footage.

This means you can easily have one gallery or bin (to use the Lightworks and Avid terms) with the dailies arranged by tape number and another one arranged by scene number without creating any new footage to gobble up space on the hard drive. This way, you can leave one gallery or bin arranged in the order in which you digitized and then create any number of other galleries or bins for Wendy.

How does this work in practice, you ask? In both the Avid and the Lightworks systems you can create areas that Wendy will never see. You can then create the galleries and bins from which Wendy will be editing. I like to have a gallery or bin for each sequence in the film, much like the continuity. To assure that the scenes are alphabetized in the proper order by the computer you should number them all with three digits. Scene one would be labeled "Scene 001," scene 23 would be "Scene 023" and scene 123 would be "Scene 123." You also need to do this for another reason. When you search for scene five, for instance, if you simply typed the number five you would get all of the takes with the number five in them. This would include scene 5, scene 15, scene 25, scenes 51, 51, 52, 53, etc. If you search, instead, for 005, you force the computer to ignore every gallery other than 005, giving you only Scene 5.

After doing this, you would then copy over all of the shots, including wild track, from the dailies bins into the bins for each scene. It is important that you copy *every* shot, even shots done on separate days, or Wendy will not have the complete set of dailies to work from.

It's as if you broke down all of your 35mm dailies into little rolls, one shot apiece, and moved them into a separate box for each scene. The differences are that it is easier to do it digitally, and you can place the same shot in an unlimited number of different bins if necessary. One film I worked on, used the same establishing shot for two scenes in the film. It was easy for my assistant to make an additional copy of the establishing shot and put one in each of the galleries for the two scenes.

On the Lightworks, it is very easy to search for all of the takes containing the number "023" (for scene 23). On the Avid it is a bit harder—you need to use the Media Tool. Once you have all of scene 23's material in front of you, it is a simple matter in both systems to store it all in one bin and put that within Wendy's reach.

Some editors like to start the name of the gallery or bin for each uncut scene with an asterisk sign. As Wendy cuts each scene she would remove the asterisk from the front of the bin or gallery name. This would indicate that she had cut the scene. This system requires you to make special note of takes for scene 23 coming in from telecine *after* the editor has already cut the scene. In that case, you would retype in the asterisk (or other character) to let Wendy know that new material has been added to an already cut scene within the bin—such as "*Scene 023."

For a recent film I cut on the Avid, my assistants created bins for each uncut scene and called them "Scene 1," "Scene 12," etc. As I cut each, I retitled them "zScene 1" and "zScene 12." This forced each scene's bin to fall to the bottom of the alphabetized Project

144

Window, making it easy for me to see the scenes I still needed to cut at the top of the list.

In the Lightworks, galleries can be arranged into groups called "racks." Similarly, on the latest Avids, bins can be put inside of folders. Using these capabilities, Wendy might want you to make a rack or a folder called "To Be Cut" containing the galleries or bins of the scenes still needing to be cut. In this case there would probably be no need for the asterisk or the "z" in front of the gallery name.

You should also create a number of other bins or galleries for material either coming in from telecine or to be created elsewhere. You can create a place for leaders (Academy, Scene Missing, Shot Missing, and the like), another one for music (I like to keep source and score music separate), another one for sound effects (you might want to keep ambient and specific sound effects separate), and other bins or galleries for opticals, CGI effects and cut sequences. You might also want to create a bin or gallery for copies of all of the wild track on the film.

Not every editor likes to see all of this information and not every editor likes it all arranged this way. It is your responsibility as the assistant to present Wendy with a system that not only allows you to do your job perfectly, but one she is completely comfortable with.

When you've done that, you've really done your job.

Odds and Ends

Much of the paperwork you needed to create for a film job will also be necessary in a digital, especially if you've sunk dailies before telecine and are doing a film finish. If you've coded your dailies, make sure those code numbers are entered into the Script Supervisor's Lined Script and Notes Pages, just as described in Chapter 5.

The division of your work will vary from film to film, depending on their budget and their work path. On higher budget films it has been traditional to have a normal size film crew—at least one assistant and at least one apprentice—supplemented by another assistant responsible for the digital editing machine. On lower budget movies the film is not sunk up, so there is no need for a full film crew in addition to the digital crew. In this case, both the first assistant and the apprentice function in all phases—film and digital. In many television shows and very low budget movies there is no apprentice at all, the editing room functions with only one assistant editor. If both you and Wendy need to use the one digital editing machine you've got, you will be forced to work at completely differ-ent hours. On *Cherry Pink* I cut from 9 a.m. to 7 p.m. and my first assistant worked from 7 p.m. to 5 a.m. Our Avid got only four hours of rest each day during production!

This raises an interesting side issue. If you and Wendy are working different hours or, God forbid, not at all, how will you learn how to edit? How will Philip ever learn how to assist?

This is a topic of much discussion among editors at meetings and parties (Hey, no one ever said editors were loads of *fun!*). It is getting increasingly difficult for an assistant to have the time and contact with the editor to learn both editing and the political as-pects to the job of picture editor. It will fall on you to create those opportunities. When you aren't working on another task, ask if it's okay to sit in the back of the room and eavesdrop on the editing process. Listen carefully to how Wendy and Adam come to their decisions, what they try and how the two of them work out differ-ences.

Go to all dailies screenings and listen. Attend as many meet-ings as you are allowed to (tell Wendy that you'll take notes). Stay late if you can and cut scenes on your own that you can show Wendy for her critiques.

146

Don't wait for something to come to you. Move out and create opportunities.

· · · ·

THE EDITOR EDITS

Eventually, Wendy is going to need to start editing. On some films, the producer or director will be in a mad rush to get the first few scenes cut to see whether a particular actor or actress can really act, if the director is getting the proper coverage, or if the editor can edit. Even if there is no rush to see edited scenes, the schedule of most films will still require that Wendy begin editing while the film is still being shot, normally as soon as the dailies have been broken down and given to her.

Wendy's first step will probably be to re-screen all of the footage shot for the scene she is about to edit. In general, most directors like to shoot a *master shot* of all or most of each scene from the widest possible angle (so it shows as much of the action as possible). They will then go in to shoot *coverage*, the myriad of other camera set–ups making up the film—close-ups, two-shots, panning shots, etc. etc. Anything providing an alternate view of the action from the master is called coverage. Wendy will examine all of it.

If she has already cut the scene immediately preceding or following the one she is working on, she may screen those scenes as well to remind her where the new scene should start or end. All the while she will probably be taking notes as to what her preferences are and what the problems are with each take. She will integrate these notes with those she took at the dailies screenings so she has a thorough idea of what both she and Adam want to do with the scene. She will then make a little plan (either in her head or on paper) as to how she wants to cut the scene. She will decide what take she wants to begin the scene with. Placing that take in her Moviola she will run it until she gets to the point where she wants to cut to her second take. She will mark this frame with a grease pencil. Leaving the first take in the Moviola she will screen other takes on her cutter to remind herself of her options. When she finally decides on the correct take to cut to, she will find the frame she wants to cut into on the second take. She will mark this frame as well. She will then rewind the edited film (the piece she is cutting away from) back out of the Moviola until she has the frame she marked over her splicer on the editing table. Then she will make the cut. She will then remove the picture and track of the second take from the cutter, find that marked frame, and cut it. Some editors will immediately cut the sound as well, lining up the matching picture and sound code numbers in the synchronizer to maintain sync. Other editors run the picture cut first to verify that they have chosen the correct cut points and, if they decide they have, then cut the soundtrack. Often she will make her sound cuts at different frames than her picture cuts.

If you think about it, this will leave several things around the editor's table. There will be the first part of the first take (from its very beginning, including the slate) cut onto the second part of the second take (all the way until its very end, including the flash frames) together on the Moviola. This piece, because it contains the cut (or cuts) that Wendy has already made, is known as the *cut* or the *edit*. There will be no film on the cutter. There will be two loose rolls— one of them will be the remainder of the first take and the other will be the first part of the second take. Pieces left over after a cut has been made are called *trims*. A trim coming after a piece in the cut is called *tail trim*, and a trim that comes before a piece in the cut is called a *head trim*.

Let's assume Wendy was cutting Scene 10. She has decided to start with the master shot and to use take 6 (i.e., Scene 10-6) for the opening of the scene. She wants to cut out of it after ABBY enters and stops to look around the room; then she will cut to a shot of ABBY looking (she will use 10D-3 for this).

After she has made this cut, you will have the following:

a) Cut-together pieces of 10-6 onto 10D-3 (the cut)
b) Head trim on 10D-3
c) Tail trim on 10-6

You will also have the master shot, take 5, which she did not use. Completely unused takes are called *outs*. So, unless Wendy uses 10-5 later on in the scene, you will have 10-5 as an out.

Some editors will leave the slate and excess material on the head of the take with which they started the scene (scene 10-6, in this case) until they have the preceding scene to cut it onto. Others do not. Let's assume Wendy does not want to keep the head piece on. She makes a decision as to where she wants the scene to begin and removes the head piece. You will now have two trims from 10-6—a head trim and a tail trim.

Well, what do you do with these trims? If Wendy is the kind of editor who works by herself, you will have to do nothing at this point—she will do it all. Some editors like to have their assistants standing by them, doing all of their filing work. In that case, you would have a trim bin right next to you. When Wendy goes to use a take you (or she) would take the trim tab from the take she is using and hang it (and the rubber band around it) onto the top row of pins. If you are using a low bin you would place it onto the rack above the curled pins. You and she will then be able to see the code numbers, scene/take numbers, and description quite clearly.

When Wendy hands you the two pieces of 10-6 you hang them on the pin on the rack immediately below the matching trim tab. It is all right to spool off the film from a short roll so it is all unwound in the barrel. If the trim is too big you can take the rubber band, thread it through the center of the roll, loop it back onto itself to make a sort of rubber band hook, hanging the trim (as a roll) from the proper pin. This way, all trims from any particular take are located immediately below their identifying trim tab and will be easy to find (see Figure 6.1).

149

As Wendy gets further into Scene 10 you will have more takes to hang up and, undoubtedly more individual trims from any particular take. If you are standing right by Wendy and the barrel, it would be very helpful to you to be sure the trims are hung in numerical order (I like to hang them with the highest numbers on the top). When Philip puts the trims away they need to be put away in numerical order; this will save time later on, as well as making finding individual trims just a little bit faster while you are working with Wendy.

Often Wendy will need to use a piece from a take that she has already cut into. If you've hung up all the trims in reverse order on the pin, then chances are good that the piece she wants will be in the top trim or trim roll. All you will need to do is remove the piece from the pin and hand it to her.

Sometimes there are so many big and little trims, the pin becomes overloaded. Nearly all assistants use a rubber band, stretched tight over a number of adjacent pins, to trap the film down and keep it from falling off the pin. In fact, when you are finished

FIGURE 6.1 These trims are hung underneath their respective trim tabs. Note that very small trims which might get lost hanging with the long ones on the lower rack are hung underneath the trim tab on the top rack. This insures that they won't accidentally be dropped into the bin while the editor is looking through the trims on the lower rack.

150

working on a scene it is always a good idea to rubber band all of the takes down so nothing will shake loose as you roll the bin away from Wendy's bench and into Philip's room.

So, Wendy is going to have a cut on her Moviola. When she is finished cutting the scene, it would be nice if she could look at it from the very beginning, but since she has cut it from the very first frame she (or you) won't be able to thread it up on her Moviola or flatbed (many editors like to view cut material on a flatbed, even if they've cut it on uprights). You deal with this problem by having Philip prepare a number of leaders that can be used for thread-up purposes. He can make them just like the dailies reel leaders, except he should leave the identification section blank (the leader will list just the name of the film followed by a blank space, then the designation "Cut Pix" or "Cut TRK," and finally the word "Heads"). Tail leaders can also be made for this purpose. The cut scene number with a description will be inserted into the blank section as she splices it onto the cut material (Sc. 10—ABBY arrives home).

Some editors, myself included, don't like to have so much leader before their cut film. They prefer just four or five feet of blank white leader onto which they can write the scene number. They will use the first frame of picture and track to sync the footage up rather than a start mark.

You will find it extremely helpful to make a list of all the scene numbers in the film followed by a short four- or five-word description of the scene. This list is called a *continuity* (*see* Figures 6.2 and 6.3). As you get further into the editing of the film it will be easier to identify scenes by this description rather than by their scene numbers. If you post the scene list everyone can get to know them faster. These descriptions can be merely a few words of memorable dialogue from the scene (Scene 11 might be called, "How'd the filming go Mister DeMille?" or just "Mr. DeMille"), a reminder of a particular shot in the scene, or a piece of scenery from the scene in question (on *Hair* we titled three musical numbers shot together in a Central Park tunnel as "The Tunnel Suite").

The idea of these descriptions is to give everyone in the editing room a handy set of short cuts to describe and remember any of the scenes in a film.

To return to the scene of the editing...Wendy is now cutting away. As she looks at the cut again, she realizes that she would like to add three more frames of the master shot 10-6 before she cuts to 10D-3. Those three frames are on the tail trim hanging in the barrel. She will look at the code numbers on the cut film, see that last code number before the cut is 10-1032, and ask you for "the tail trim of 10-1032" or for "the tail trim, 10-1033." You can look across at the trim tabs and see, at a glance, in which take 10-1033 falls, go to the take immediately underneath the tab and find the piece she's asking for almost at once (since you've put the trims in numerical order on their proper pin). This additional piece that she is going to cut in (called an *extension*) will normally be called for by code number since she has the code number of the piece staring at her on her cut. Sometimes she may ask for the extension by its description—"the trim on that big wide master shot," for instance. You can determine which take she wants from the description on the cinetab or, if there are several "big wide master shots," you can ask her which one she means.

151

There is an alternative to asking Wendy for the code number and, as you get better at being an assistant, you will get better at this method. If you are paying attention while she is editing, you will be following her progress as she cuts. By the time she asks you for a trim, you should know the footage and the cut points almost as well as she does. All you have to do then is look at the point she is examining on her Moviola and you can know what take she will need. This is the kind of shorthand that make an observant

"Silent Night, Silent Cowboy"

August 25, 1999 script

Scene	Description		Scene	Description
1	Credit montage		49	Abby's still empty room
2	On the set		50	Sean and Bob talk
3	Abby and James		51	Sean and Bob pick up Bob
4	Backstage		52	The three musketeers party
5	Driving home		54	Driving to work happy
6	Abby's empty room		55	Redo the bar fight
7	Driving to work the next day		56	James is happy
8	"Did the zoom look okay?"		57	The happy parking lot
9	Alone in the parking lot		58	Bob and Abby at "La Bar"
10	Abby arrives home and gets shocked		59	"La Bar" backstage
11	"Evening, Mr. DeMille"		60-61	Abby writes, day into night
12	The hot dog stand		62	Abby, Michael, Uri talk
13	Abby talks about Claire		63	"Great dailies!!"
14-16	Pinball hall montage		64	Abby & Sean's eat Mexican
17	Abby meets Sean		65	Abby writes/Sean writes
18	Abby and Sean back at Abby's		66	Sean tries to sleep
19	"Jimmy the Baby"		67	Drive to the baseball game
20	Cowboy and James fight		68	Outside Dodger Stadium
22	Lunch with Genie		69	"Those Dodgers!"
23	"The rushes are a disaster"		70	In the stands
24	Parking lot rewrites		71	In the Dodger bathroom
25	Phone call from Genie		72	Return from the ballgame
26	"Have it out with him"		73	They watch the sports channel
27	Abby and James have it out.		74-75	Abby and Sean on the roof
28-30	Abby wanders about		76	"No dailies today"
31	Dream montage		77	"I've got a bad feeling"
32-33	Abby in the hills/L.A. at night		78	"We've got a problem"
34	"Can I make a nuisance of myself?"		79	Abby rewriting
35ptI	Abby/Sean at Sean's		80	Abby at Pink's
36	"I can't get out of bed"		81	Abby at Musso's
37	Phone call home		82	Abby at City
39-42	Going home		83	Abby writes into the dawn
44	Abby sits in front of his home		84	Abby and J.B. - "A two base hit"
45	The family inside		85	"Fuck him, it was a home run"
46	Abby Returns		86	Abby with Sean at Griffith
47	Birthday party		87	Abby rewrites for a homer
48	Abby flies back to L.A.		88	Abby & J.B. - "You try harder."
A49	"The yellow zone is for loading"		90	Champagne corks don't pop

"Silent Night, Silent Cowboy" Continuity
August 25, 1999 script
Page 1

FIGURE 6.2 *It is helpful to have some sort of list which shows all of the scripted scenes. Later on, as you build reels and drop scenes you can adapt this list to your changing cut film.*

"Silent Night, Silent Cowboy"

August 25, 1999 script

1	Credit montage
2	On the set
3	Abby and James
4	Backstage
5	Driving home
6	Abby's empty room
7	Driving to work the next day
8	"Did the zoom look okay?"
9	Alone in the parking lot
10	Abby arrives home/shocked
11	"Evening, Mr. DeMille"
12	The hot dog stand
13	Abby talks about Claire
14-16	Pinball hall montage
17	Abby meets Sean
18	Abby & Sean back at Abby's
19	"Jimmy the Baby"

153

FIGURE 6.3 *This is an alternate version of the continuity which has the advantage of having large enough print so that it can be posted on the editing room wall and read from the editor's seat. Note that some of the scene names have been shortened to allow them to fit on one line of the continuity.*

assistant editor so valuable. There were times, when I was working on *Hair* or *Fame* where I would try to guess ahead as to what my editors' needs were going to be and have the piece ready for them before they even asked for it. When they did, it was fun to have it ready for them.

Assistants get their kicks from strange things, don't they?

After the Editor Edits

When Wendy is finished with Scene 10 she will want two things to happen. First, she will want to go on to Scene 11 (assuming the footage for that scene has already been shot). You should have everything prepared so she can begin cutting the next scene as soon as she is ready for it. Try to stay at least two or three scenes ahead of Wendy, whenever possible. Once again, being ready means that all footage, wild sound, and paperwork are complete and ready for the editor's use.

The second thing Wendy will want is to have the trims from Scene 10 taken away and to be given an empty trim bin for Scene 11.

Once she is working on Scene 11, you should have Philip put away the trims from Scene 10. Trims must be put away in an orderly manner so they may be retrieved rapidly, upon demand.

There are a number of ways to file the trims and outs. I personally prefer to file all of the footage, identified by scene number/ code number (these will be the same if you've coded the footage with the scene number as its prefix) into a series of boxes. In this system the wild track is put in the last of the boxes for its scene.

The trims should be organized in the trim bin in numerical order with particular attention to two problems. The first is, in many cases, Wendy may have cut pieces apart that actually belong together. She may have decided to remove frames from one end of a cut she'd already made, or she might have cut apart take three of a particular set-up, then switched to take two. In any case, you will end up with several pieces of film that need to be attached back to each other. Splice them together, checking to be sure that the sequential code numbers are sixteen frames apart.

The second problem occurs when Wendy has attached pieces of film from different takes. These pieces must be separated and hung on their own pins.

Once all of the trims have been set in order, remove them from the pin while still holding them together in the proper order. Wrap a rubber band around the top of all of the trims about an inch or so down from their ends (*see* Figure 6.4). Spin the rubber band around them two or three times until the pieces hold together, then

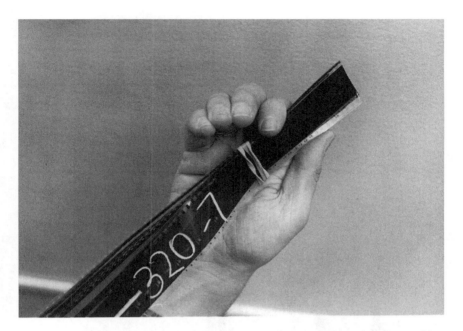

FIGURE 6.4 *After the trims have been put together in numerical order a rubber band is wrapped around them at the head (top). They are then flanged up from their head.*

flange the trims up starting from the end with the rubber band. When you get to the other end the trims will be tails out. Wrap a rubber band around the entire roll, slip the trim tab back in as you did originally and go on to the next trim (*see* Figure 6.5). If you are using California trim tabs, you don't need the second rubber band. If you wrap the trim tab about one loop down from the end of the trim and wind the last loop of film around the roll (through the inside of the trim tab) you will find that the tab will hold everything in place. Take my word on this—it's easier to do then it is to describe in words.

If Wendy has cut into the wild track, splice the roll back together in order even where pieces have been removed. Differentiate these splices from continuous ones with a red grease-penciled "X" across the cut.

When you are done, you should have a set of trims wound tails out, a number of outs wound heads out, and the wild track. Now you should box them up for easy access.

To do this, take a white box, run a strip of white tape horizontally down one of its sides, and write on it as shown in Figure 6.6. Then put all of the footage pertaining to those code numbers in the

FIGURE 6.5 After the take has been flanged up, a rubber band is put around it and its tab is removed from the trim bin and put into the trim. Note that this tab has been put into the center hole rather than slid between a few wraps of the film at the trim's edge. This has been done to show you the rubber band in the center. Normally you would wind trims as shown in FIGURE 5.5.

box. At times you may find that you will need more than one box for a scene (this often happens when there are long takes). After you are done, you should have at least one box for Scene 10, another for scene 11 and so on. Wild track for Scene 10 would be filed in the last box for that scene and listed in red on the side.

As scene after scene is completed and the trims and outs are done, you will find yourself building up quite a number of shelves of trims and outs. You will also start getting additional material that needs to be filed (opticals, dupes, scratch mixes, temp music transfers, temp sound effects, etc.). I generally file each of these categories on different shelves, always trying to leave room for the material that you know will come in as the show continues shooting. It doesn't make much sense to put Scene 10 next to Scene 36 if

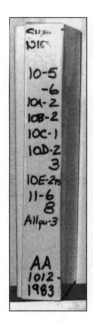

FIGURE 6.6 A trim box where trims and outs are filed together. All of the takes included in the box are listed on the side, with the code numbers included in the box printed large at the bottom of the box. Often there are several boxes needed for each code prefix (whether it be AA1000, in this case, or 010-1000). (Photograph by the author).

you know you will get material for Scenes 11 through 35 later.

Some assistants prefer to keep all of the wild track together, rather than with its scene.

If you have not coded the dailies by scene number, there is an alternate way to file the trims. Some assistants like filing trims separately from the outs since they find that their editors ask for them differently. If Wendy needs an extension to a shot she's already cut, she will generally call for the needed trim by its code number (since she will have the adjacent code number on the film in the cut, sitting right in front of her). If she wants an out, she will normally ask for it by scene number or description (e.g., "Do we have alternate on 106A?").

In this case, you would write the code numbers for the trims on the side of the box as shown in Figure 6.7. If there were too many AA1000 trims to fit in one box you would create a second box, label the first one with the highest number contained in it (AA1000-1605) and label the second one with the lowest number contained in it (AA1606). In this system it is especially important to leave extra room in the box. Often in the re-editing of the film, takes that were outtakes at one point are used and, therefore, become trims.

The outs will be handled differently. I like to write vertically on the box, rather than horizontally (*see* Figure 6.8). Each take inside the box should be listed on the outside. That way, when Wendy asks if there is an out for a particular setup you can look at the outside of the box and tell her the answer. When you remove the take from the box, cover over its number with a piece of white tape; that way if she decides not to use the trim you can just peel the tape off, exposing the number again.

Wild track is filed, as I've already said, wound up in individual takes and stored by code number.

In order to keep the boxes organized, I store the boxes for

FIGURE 6.7 *A trim box used in a system where trims and outs are filed separately. If there were too many AA1000 trims to fit into one box, this box would also list the last code number inside (such ass AA1000—1654) and a second box would begin with the first code number of the next trim (AA1655).*

158

FIGURE 6.8 *An outs box used in a system where trims and outs are filed separately. Note that one take, which had been an out, has been removed from the box and, presumably, used in the film. Its number has been covered over with tape. If it is ever returned as an out it is a simple matter to remove the tape from the box.*

trims on a separate rack from the outs leaving one or two shelves for the wild track (you rarely need more than this). You should mark the front of the shelf crossbar with a long length of tape. You can write on the tape what kind of footage is on that rack (trims, outs, etc.). Right now, when all you have are trims, outs, and wild track this may seem like a silly idea. But remember, you will be receiving other types of footage later on, and these categories may be helpful to those trying to locate material in the cutting room.

All at the Same Time?

You may have noticed that a lot of things happen simultaneously during shooting. Dailies have to be sunk and screened, logs must be maintained, footage needs to be readied for the editor, scenes to be cut, and trims and outs to be stored. All of this happens *right now* and that can be a problem. An assistant editor must be a good office manager in order to accomplish everything without forgetting anything.

Quite often there will be special requests from the producer, director, or other people on the set. On *Fame*, which was shot in New York City, one rented lens was out of focus ruining a day's shoot for us. To claim the insurance money due us, we had to ship the takes in question to Panavision out on the West Coast, as well as screen them for our insurance company. This meant separating them out from the dailies (I got them coded first so the coding process could go on uninterrupted) and shipping them from one place to another. It was my responsibility to make sure that I knew where the footage was at all times and that it got back to me safely.

On the same film we had to send selected takes to Hollywood every week or so for screening by M-G-M executives. You can appreciate how this disrupted the normal flow of the film from screening to cutting. I had to keep logs of exactly what the executives had seen and what they hadn't. I had to keep a record of the status of the footage at every moment (some of the footage had been coded and some, unfortunately, couldn't be). I had to keep Gerry Hambling, the editor, informed of exactly what scenes were completely ready for him to cut and what scenes were partially in Los Angeles.

On *Hair* we were always sending clips of previous scenes out to the set so they could check matches on hair, makeup, lighting, and set.

An additional burden is the shipping of videotapes out of the editing room to whoever needs them. Often, the dailies will be videotaped and copies sent to the director, producers, studio executives and more. Though this is usually organized and handled by the production office it will often fall to you to smooth out any of the kinks that inevitably crop up along the way. It will be your responsibility to arrange for the filmed dailies to be telecined. You will obviously need to slot that in before your break it all down for Wendy. Usually, you can schedule some unsupervised telecine time overnight, after you have screened your dailies. Sometimes you can send the reels out even before the dailies screening. It is a good idea to get all of the logging and trim tab work completed before sending it out for telecine. That way, when the film returns, you can simply break it down and pop on the trim tabs.

There will also be occasional requests for videotape copies of edited scenes or shots which someone needs to see for some technical reason. If you are not editing on a digital non-linear machine, you will need to find the footage, separate it out onto its own separate picture and sound reel (with leaders and start marks to help match and sync), and expedite its shipment to and from the videotape telecine house. You will, no doubt, also be responsible for making sure that the needed tape was of good quality and actually got to its destination in the required time.

160

In short, there are always too many disruptions and never enough time. But, if the editing room system is set up efficiently, everything can flow very smoothly anyway. Gerry never lacked scenes from *Fame* to cut, the *Hair* set people always got their clips, the M-G-M executives always got their takes to screen, and everyone seemed happy. Everything depends on creating a system that can function so smoothly that even a kink in the works doesn't stop the work.

Checking the Cut

When Wendy is finished with each scene she should let you have it so you can check her sync and the sound cuts.

To do this you should *zero out* your synchronizer and put the cut scene in it, making sure that the picture and sound track start on the zero frame. You should then wind slowly through the cut, checking that every picture and sound splice is smooth and continuous. If the film on one side of a splice doesn't line up properly with the film on the other, it will either jump in the gate of a projector or the editing machine, or get stuck there. When this happens the film piles up like an accordion, shredding sprockets and scratching film. It's not a pretty sight.

You will also check to make sure that the picture and sound are in perfect sync after every edit. Sometimes Wendy will have deliberately thrown a piece of track out of sync with the picture. When she does, she should make some indication of that on the track. I

10-0649

00 1 00   00 6 5 4 0

FIGURE 6.9 *The track sync has been adjusted, intentionally throwing the picture and track out of their original sync. The actual code number (10-0654) is indicated in the sprockets of the track where it would be inked. The slipped sync number (10-0649) is written on the soundtrack, usually in grease pencil.*

generally write a picture code number onto the soundtrack, indicating where the picture and sound frames should line up (see Figure 6.9). In this example, the soundtrack that would normally line up with the picture at 10-0654 has been moved to earlier in the shot. The picture code number it is now lined up with, 10-0649, is written on the track with grease pencil.

If there is no indication that the sync has been slipped, you need to determine if the change was intentional or an error. After you've worked with Wendy enough, you will probably be able to look at the footage and guess whether she intentionally slipped the sync. If there is any doubt at all, however, you should check with her. You don't want to undo something she went to a lot of trouble to create.

If the sync slippage was a mistake, you should adjust the track (never the picture) to bring it back into sync. This will usually require removing the necessary number of frames from one side of the track edit and adding the required number to the other side. To do this, you need to go into Wendy's trims for the scene. For that reason, you should try and check sync on the scene before Philip files the trims away in their boxes. If there is time, or if you have enough apprentices, you will first want him to go through the trim bin and organize all of the trims, making sure everything is on its proper pins and that nothing has fallen to the bottom of the bin. It will then be an easy task for you to find the necessary frames to adjust the sync.

If the adjusted sync is intentional, you should add the slipped sync picture numbers on the track as indicated in Figure 6.9.

As Wendy edits each scene, she will often need to remove pieces of sound from her edited sound track. At times there will be unwanted voices—a director's cue, an animal trainer calling to a dog, or off-screen actors giving lines to an actor. In order to keep her soundtrack in sync with her picture after she removes an offending piece of soundtrack, she will usually simply slug out the gap with a piece of *fill leader*, also called *slug*, exactly the same length as the piece of soundtrack she removed. Sometimes she will be able to replace these slugs with other sounds to fill in those gaps. In most cases, it is too time-consuming and tedious for Wendy to do this herself, and she will ask you to replace the slugs with sound that blends in with the adjacent soundtrack.

You will do this while you are spinning down on the synchronizer checking sync and cuts. It is best to listen to the track with a pair of headphones on, since many finer details of the sound are hard to hear through the little speakers on your bench, though they will become quite obvious when you listen to the track later on in the screening room in front of Wendy and Adam.

This process of filling in the holes is known as *toning out* the tracks, as you will be inserting pieces of tone into the mag track to put some neutral sound where Wendy had put fill. The most important thing to keep in mind when looking for proper tone is that it must match the adjacent pieces of sound as closely as possible in both sound quality and volume level.

Sometimes you can find matching tone in room tone that may have been recorded as a wild track at the time of the shoot. You should wind down a little bit into the roll of sound and put it into the third gang of your synchronizer opposite the piece of fill. After making sure that the volume knobs on your sound box are set at the same level, you can rock back and forth over the area where the fill is cut in. If the sound feels like it might work, you can make a cut in the tone roll and splice it onto the tail of the outgoing piece of track on the left side of the synchronizer. For now, it is not necessary to cut in the proper length. As you do this, make sure that you do not let your track fall out of the second gang since you want to keep sync with the picture in gang one.

Listen to the cut, rocking it back and forth in the synchronizer. There will, of course, be some difference in the quality of the sound from the take to the room tone, but if the two are of close enough quality then you can place the edited cut track on the third gang of the synchronizer, lining the first frame of the fill up with the first frame of the tone you've just cut in. Roll down until the end of the piece of fill and mark the frame line on the tone roll where you will need to make the cut out of the tone.

Roll the footage out to the left of the synchronizer, make a cut on the tone at your mark, remove the piece of fill from the edited track, and splice the cut piece of tone to the head of the remainder of the cut track. If you've done everything correctly, when you wind your cut picture and track through the synchronizer now, you should hear the track cut almost seamlessly to the tone and then back out again to the worktrack.

Often you will find that the recorded room tone won't really be a good match for the cut work track. This is not the fault of the recordist but of the nature of wild track. Room tone is generally recorded from a fixed position without the camera running. However, the soundtrack takes you have in the cut work track were recorded with the camera running and in all sorts of mic positions— pointing to different actors, close to their mouths or far away from them depending on how wide the image size was. In fact, you'd be pretty lucky to get a perfect match with all of those variables.

In that case, the best place to get similar tone is from the actual takes the cut work track came from. As a rule, I like to use the sound from the outgoing take but either take will do. You will wind down the track from the take and listen to it until you find a piece of track as long as the piece of fill you are replacing and has no voice or noise on it.

163

The trick here is to choose the piece of tone from someplace that Wendy won't need later. The best places to look are right before and after Adam has yelled "Action!" near the beginning of the take. Sometimes you can find tone pieces around his yelling "Cut!" at the end of the take.

The other thing you should be listening for as you roll through the cut scene (with your headphones on, of course), are for pieces of dialogue with their opening or closing words chopped off. Words that have been cut too short are said to be *upcut*. Sometimes Wendy has done this intentionally because there was another sound (like a different actor's voice) she didn't want to hear. However, sometimes she will have upcut the words by accident because she couldn't hear the exact start or finish of the word with her Moviola running. You will need to go back into the trims and add the necessary frame (sometimes it is just a matter of a few sprockets) making the upcut word complete. Obviously, you will need to remove exactly the same amount of track (in exactly the same place) that you are adding in order to keep everything in sync. It is always a good idea to make these edits on the left side of the synchronizer so you are sure that everything is being taken up on the right rewinds is in perfect sync.

Other Bits to Remember

There are a few other tasks to keep you occupied during the editing process (as if you didn't already have enough to do). At least twice a week or so you or Philip should maintain Wendy's editing machines. Often you will need to do this every day.

Running film through Moviolas or flatbed editing machines tends to get them dirty. Celluloid picks up a static charge as it is run and that, in turn, picks up dust. That dust is easily transferred to the Moviolas. Wendy will also constantly be making grease pencil marks on the film. As she does, she will also be inadvertently marking up the editing machines around the picture and track heads. The grease pencil marks also tend to come off around the gates. Finally, editing machines are big mechanical beasts. They tend to get oily and will break down on an all-too-frequent basis.

It is essential then, that you or Philip keep the machines in as fine a running order as possible. Check the equipment every morning and clean them at least twice a week, or when you see they are getting even the slightest bit dirty. To do this, take a Q-Tip, dip it in some alcohol or film cleaner and rub it along any surface the film comes in contact with. Clean around the sprocket wheels. Clean the sound heads. Clean around the picture gate. Take a Webril and put a batch of film cleaner on *it*. Clean up any stray grease pencil marks on Wendy's Moviola and/or flatbed.

Keep a stock of extra Moviola or flatbed bulbs handy (there's a small well in the front of the Moviola with a removable cover; inside is a perfect place to store a few extra Moviola bulbs) since I can assure you that, machines being what they are, they will certainly blow bulbs late at night or on weekends when you can't easily get a fresh supply.

If Wendy is cutting on a English style bench, dig into the bags hanging in it and fish out any loose pieces of fill, picture or track as she is finishing each scene. And always, no matter what type of system or bench Wendy is using, check all over her bench and in the bottom of every trim bin for trims that may have been dropped or misplaced, as well as for pieces of fill or leader that can be thrown away.

In short, no matter how sloppy Wendy is, try and keep her working area as clean as she will allow you.

Finally, you will want to keep a calendar hanging in the cutting room. Periodically, you will receive memos from the producer giving his or her latest version of the post-production schedule. Keep your calendar updated to reflect these changes. Write down on the calendar the date and time for any screenings, mixes, meetings, or shoots that need to be remembered. (The wall calendar is also a handy place to put people's birthdays.)

On some films that I've worked on, the assistant actually made a calendar on a large sheet of thick, clear plastic. Information was written in with grease pencil, making it easy to write down those inevitable changes. A dry-erase board is another alternative.

You can also use a computer program to print out the calendars. They are very flexible and there is no muss and fuss when dates are changed for the tenth time. The only problem is that you really need to have the computer in the editing room or changes are very inconvenient to make.

Whatever system you come up with, the calendar should be big, hung in a prominent place, and easily changed. Flexibility is, after all, the hallmark of a good editing system, isn't it?

THE EDITOR EDITS DIGITALLY

The work flow in a digital editing room is far less complicated than in a film editing room. The major difference you will notice is that since Wendy is not actually editing the 35mm film there will be no trims or outs to file. All the muss and fuss of a cutting room based only on 35mm film nearly disappears when you move to a digital editing room. Things should be a lot easier. And they are. But that's not the whole story.

166

You knew that, didn't you?

The Footage Arrives

We've already discussed in Chapter 5A how the footage gets from the set to the telecine house to you and, ultimately, to Wendy. Now we need to discuss how she will start working on the footage.

As I mentioned in Chapter 5A, some editing systems (like the Lightworks) work on a "file card" metaphor, into which you enter descriptions of every digitized take. The FLEx, Keylog or Evertz files that you receive from the telecine house will, if they have sunk up the footage, contain a some of this information—camera roll, sound roll, date created, etc. You will need to add shot descriptions and, in a special category, the character names of all the characters covered in the shot. You need not write the complete names, a unique abbreviation for each character will do. You should post a list of these abbreviations within Wendy's sight. You should let her know how you are labeling wide, medium and close shots (is it WS or w/s?). You should be just as clear and unambiguous as you would be in a film system—in your log books, trim tabs, etc.

This way, Wendy will be able to search for all of the close-ups of ABBY in scene 21 by typing CU in the description field of the file card, AB in the "who" field, and 21 (or 021, depending upon how you entered the information; if a movie has more than 100 scenes it is best to add the leading zero in the scene number otherwise typing in 21 will give you scenes 121, 210, 211 etc. as well) in the "scene" field.

Avid systems don't work on the same metaphor but you can add comment headings to the bins allowing you to enter all of the same information.

Wendy's first step will probably be to screen all of the footage shot for the scene, just as she would as if she was working on film. In fact, if you're working on a movie in which you've sunk up film dailies (even if you're going to be editing electronically), Wendy might want to sit down at the flatbed and look at all the footage there, instead of on the Avid or Lightworks.

The reason to watch the dailies on film is simple: film images look better than digitized images. A lot better. It will be easier for Wendy to see nuances in performance, areas of questionable focus, details in production design and a lot more, if she examines the footage on 35mm film rather than on her computer editing machine.

Of course, she will have probably already seen the dailies projected in a screening room and, if you and she have taken copious notes, you will have almost all of the technical information you need. However, there is something to be said for repetition; each time you look at footage you see different things. During the first screening you may notice the way an actor moves his body, on the next you may notice an extra making a face in the background at the same moment.

167

Obviously, if you are working on a film or television show that is not printing film dailies, there will be only one choice—Wendy will have to examine her dailies from the editing cassette coming from the telecine house. This is preferable to watching the digitized image in the editing machine.

Ultimately, she will need to start editing the footage. She will go the gallery or bin labeled with the new scene number, open it, and proceed to examine each take inside, checking them against her notes. If you've organized each bin so it contains every shot she will need to cut the scene, Wendy will be able to find everything she needs.

If she has already cut the scene immediately before or after the one she is working on, she may want to screen those scenes as well. Every editor works a little differently, I like to file all of my edited first cut scenes in one gallery or bin. Each one will have a name listing the scene numbers included in the edit and a version number.

If I've cut scenes 10, 11 and 12 for the first time I will call the edit "010-012 v100." Some editors put their first cuts into the same bins or galleries as the scene's dailies, but this fast becomes useless as you string consecutive scenes together.

Let me take a side trip to explain the version numbering system. Throughout the course of editing there will be a number of screenings, each one of which will require a complete version of the film, ready for viewing. I give each separate full screening version a new number in the hundreds. Thus, my first cut (the editor's cut) is called version 100. The first director's cut is called version 200, the second director's cut (often the first version shown to the studio or to the public) is called version 300 and so on. Between each version of the film, however, there might be several different versions. For instance, there might be two different ways of editing scene 10 that Wendy wants to try out on Adam before he sees the entire film. I would call the first version "010 v100" and second one "010 v101." When he has chosen the version he wants, and Wendy has combined it with scenes 11 and 12, you could call the edit "010-012 v102."

You end up having a number of versions of the editor's cut in its bin or gallery when it comes time to assemble them all into the screening version for Adam. It should be a simple matter to find the highest version number of each section or reel to construct the complete film.

As Wendy puts together more of her cut scenes she will find herself with a bin full of several versions of various scenes, many of which will duplicate each other. I don't mind having all of these different edits in the same bin but some editors prefer to remove the original cuts that have been combined with other scenes to make longer sequences. In that case, you might want to move these edits into a bin marked "Out Of Date Edits" or to lose them altogether. Deleting them from a particular bin or gallery will not delete them from the computer, so you can always find them again if you need to.

By putting all of the cuts into one bin Wendy will easily be able to find scenes surrounding the scenes she is about to edit. "010-012 v103" will be in the same gallery or bin as "014-015 v102." If Wendy is about to cut Scene 13 she can examine both of these bracketing edits before she begins editing the scene so she can see where she is coming from and where she is going to. She may decide to cut Scene 13 onto the tail of the edit named "010-012 v103." When she is done with her cutting of the scene, you will want to rename the edit "010-013 v103." If you then combine it with "014-015 v102," you would rename the edit "010-015 v103."

Editing digitally is a lot like editing on film without the grease pencil to mark up frames. Though every editor will work differently, the process will be very similar to the process described in Chapter 6 for editing on film. Wendy will determine which take she wants to start the scene with and mark the opening frame electronically. She will then watch the take until she finds the frame she wants to use to cut out. After marking this frame, she will determine the take she wants to cut to, and which frame in that take she will cut to. All she needs to do to complete the process is press a button and the edit is made. When she presses the "play" button she will be able to see the cut she wanted.

There is one thing non-linear digital editing enables Wendy to do that is much more difficult in the film world. Now, it is much easier to begin editing a scene in its middle than at its beginning. It is no more difficult to add footage onto the head of a take than it is to add it to its tail.

Some editors are perfectly capable of setting up their computers to edit new scenes; others like their assistants to do it for them. Some prefer their assistants name and label every edit; others can easily create their own and stay within their assistant's conventions. Whichever way your editor likes to work, it is important that you establish the systems you can both work with and make it clear to them just what those systems are. Wendy will often need to find a take or an edit that has not been filed within easy sight. Your system should be clear enough that she should be able to find anything, even when you are not there to help them.

During the Editing

Once Wendy begins editing you will have a number of tasks of your own to perform. Some of these jobs will need to wait until you can get onto her editing machine and some can be done away from the machine. In some of the higher budget films you will have your own editing machine "networked" together with Wendy's (See Chapter 17A for more details). This will enable you to do all of your electronic housekeeping chores while your editors are working. Otherwise, you will need to wait until lunch time, or before or after Wendy's work schedule to do them.

One of the most crucial tasks you need to perform will be to *backup* Wendy's work. The computer is saving the edit list instructions, along with all of the computer data needed to locate and playback every frame of film in the show. As you digitize new footage (whether it is dailies or music and opticals) and as Wendy continues to edit, new computer data is created. If that information is damaged or lost it will be a tragic job recreating all of the work you both have performed so far, if it can be recreated at all.

For this reason, it is essential that you make copies of all of the computer data on some sort of disk that can be stored separately from the data on your machine's hard drive. This copy is called a *backup*. On the Avid, most rental companies will now supply you with an external drive, like a Zip or Jaz drive. These machines use disks that look like large floppy disks, but are capable of storing several times the information found on a floppy. To make the backup you simply take the project file and drag it onto the icon for the Zip or Jaz disk on the Macintosh's desktop. This creates the backup copy without disturbing the original. You should retitle the backup with the date and time of the backup (09-16-99 a.m., for instance). The Lightworks comes with a magneto-optical (MO) disk drive built into the system. Backups are made onto alternating sides of these large, rectangular, disks using the backup tool within the Lightworks.

It is a good idea to make backups at least twice a day. Generally, you can make the first one at the lunch break, and the second one at the end of the day. On the Lightworks I usually reserve one side of the MO disk for morning backups and the other for evening backups. On the Avid (or similar, Macintosh based systems) I keep filling up the Zip or Jaz drive until I run out of room. I then trash the earliest backups.

The advantage of having at least two backups is to prevent loss of work in the unlikely event that one of the backups is no good.

There are also some housekeeping chores to keep up with. As you edit, your hard drives get a lot of use. Not only is the visual and audio material constantly pulled off of the disks for playback, but the editing instructions (the Edit Lists) are updated every time Wendy makes another cut. Additionally, your computer will store information on every piece of film, every optical created and every edit that Wendy puts together. Eventually, the hard drive will start to run more slowly, as more and more information is stored and deleted

This delay is caused by something called *fragmentation* occurring when information from a single computer file is stored on different, non-contiguous, areas of the hard drive. There are programs designed to go through the hard drive, find broken files, and pull together all the parts of the file into one piece, as well as arrange them on the hard drive in a sensible way. The most common program is called Norton Disk Doctor and it is a good idea to run

NDD (as it is called) frequently. Some assistants run NDD once a week, others run it every night. On systems with more than one editing station it is a good idea to run NDD once a day.

One of the components of NDD is a program called Speedisk. This is the piece of software that is intended to defragment your hard drive files and speed up access time. There is one large caveat to running this program and that is that it is only good to run it on the hard drive with your EDLs on it. For DOS or Windows based systems this will usually be your C: drive. On Macintosh systems, this will usually be your startup drive. You should never run Speedisk on any of your media files. These picture and sound files are arranged in very special ways on your hard drives and running Speedisk will rearrange them in ways that may completely confuse your computer. This is not a good example of housekeeping.

Before you run Speedisk, you should run the Doctor portion of Norton Disk Doctor. This section, and compatible parts of other programs, goes through every file on every hard drive in your system, looking for technical errors that may cause problems now or down the road. You can run these portions of NDD on *all* your drives, including the media files.

Generally, you can simply start to run NDD, then just turn off the monitors and go home. If you've set NDD's parameters correctly, the program will run by itself and there will rarely be a problem it cannot automatically detect and repair. When you come in early the next morning, you can check what the program found. If there were any problems it will probably say a problem was fixed (these problems often occur in the Master Directory Block).

On a Macintosh based system like the Avid and the Media 100 there is an additional tool you can use to improve performance—"rebuilding the desktop." The desktop is an invisible file keeping track of all of the files and icons associated with them. After a while, this desktop gets so cluttered it begins to slow down the Macintosh. You should check with your rental house to see how they recommend rebuilding.

On Avids you may also need to remove any unused optical effects (called *precomputes*) that have accumulated over the course of the editing.

Another piece of software you should periodically run is a virus checking utility. Computer viruses are small programs written by malicious people that can, like a human virus, spread throughout the system. As it moves over all the hard drives on your computer, it can damage performance. They may even prevent your computer from working.

171

There are a number of programs to combat these viruses, which normally enter your computer through files given to you, either on a disk or via the Internet. Because you are putting foreign disks into your computer every time you take a telecine file and read it in, or whenever you move a CGI file off of a Zip disk into your system, you would do well to run a virus check program every week or so (more often during dailies). Your equipment rental house will probably be able to supply you with a copy of their preferred virus utility.

Adding Sound and Music

During the course of the editing Wendy will often need to add sound and music to the edit as well as insert stock footage and temp ADR. Each of these items needs to be put into your machine in different ways.

Many of the music cues and sound effects she will need will come from CDs. I bring a large collection of movie soundtrack and sound effect CDs with me to every film I edit. If you have already contracted with a sound editorial house, you will often be able to get sound effects from them (ask them to provide the sound effects to you on a time coded tape, of whatever sort you used during dailies—3/4", Beta-SP, or DAT). My assistant has also collected a series of time coded videotapes with sound effects created for previous films.

Temporary ADR can usually be recorded directly into your editing machine using a microphone hooked into your mixing board. Sound effects can also be recorded this way (on one film, my assistant recorded a fantastic chair squeak by micing my own editing chair). Some assistants, time permitting, like to record the ADR onto a time-coded DAT, Beta or 3/4" tape first, then digitize it into the editing machine. Without a tape backup (or a computer copy of the media files of the non-time coded material) there is no way to recover the files if they are corrupted or lost within the editing machine. If something gets lost from your dailies (a time-coded source), it is a simple matter to redigitize the material and tell your machine to replace all the bad footage with the redigitized footage. Without that time code it is much harder to replace the material.

All of the material without time code will need to be digitized using the machine's settings for non-time coded material (often called "Free-running"). Whether or not you are digitizing with time codes, you should assign reel numbers to each category of additional material. This will enable you to easily identify the material you need. One system would be to assign the reel number 999 to all sound effects digitized from CDs, 888 to all music from CDs, 777 to all temp ADR, etc. Label every stock footage reel with its own unique reel number (use numbers all in a single hundreds series; e.g. 600, 601, 602, 603, etc.) and digitize it using the appropriate reel number. If you are digitizing sound effects from a time coded tape, give each tape its own unique number in the 900 series.

This way it will be very easy to tell, from an EDL or cut list, just what type of material is being used. A number with all repeating digits (like 999 or 888) comes from a non time-coded source. Any other number in the 900 series is a time coded sound effect, any number in the 800 series is a time-coded music cue, etc.

Be sure to title each digitized piece with a sensible name. Sound effects should be identified with a concise description ("BMW start and away," "Elevator bell," "Phone rings," etc.). Music cues can be identified by their source ("Braveheart 3" for the third cue on that film's soundtrack, "Mahler 6" for the sixth cue on the demo CD that Gustav Mahler's agent submitted, etc.). Stock footage should be identified by its description ("Star cluster," or "F-15 take-off"). Temp ADR can be named with the scene number and character name. Remember to make a note of the source of the material (which sound effect CD or tape, for instance) in the database somehow so any effect Adam falls in love with can be easily reused in the final mix.

Make a number of galleries or bins for each category of sound, sound effects, music, stock footage, etc...If you have a large number of individual pieces, you will probably want to divide them up in a logical manner. On a recent film of mine I divided the music into separate galleries for score and source cues, with the score being divided further into temp cues submitted by the composer and cues from other composers' CDs. I called them "Music—Score," "Music—Source" and "Music—Scott." This way the names for all of the galleries or bins appeared next to each other in an alphabetized list, but none of the galleries were too crowded.

I then divided the sound effects up into bins for phone effects, car effects, backgrounds, body effects (punches, falls, and the like) and a miscellaneous category. I labeled them with names like "FX—Phone," "FX—Car," etc. for the same reason. Some sound effects fit in several categories (a car phone, for instance), so I put the effect in each appropriate bin. Remember that copies of material take up almost no additional room on your hard drives so you can make as many as you need to sensibly catalog them.

When every additional digitized piece is filed, it will be as easy for Wendy to find and cut it in as it is working with a piece of original dailies.

After the Edit

As Wendy completes each scene, you need to clean up her computer desktop, just as you would have to clean up her film bench if she were editing on film. Once again, some editors are able to perform this task themselves, others will want you to do it.

In either case, as soon as you can get onto her machine, you should check that Wendy has removed any loose takes she will not need for her next scene from the desktop.

If you have time you should also go through the edit and make sure everything is in sync. You should also fill any sound track holes. Since it is so easy to fill holes on computer editing machines, many editors do it themselves. Even when they do, you should check their work because you may find, in their rush to move onto the next picture edit, the tone they have chosen is not very good. You may also find places where words of dialogue have been chopped off (this is often called *upcut*).

Filling tone holes is a trivial matter on these systems since it is only necessary to find a piece of silence near the area with the hole (it is better to use tone from the outgoing sound take), copy it and cut it into the hole. Unlike finding tone on 35mm film, you can re-use a piece of tone as many times as you want and you don't have to worry about using a piece that Wendy might need.

Another thing you will want to check is reuse of frames. Because Wendy will not be cutting with actual film footage, it is very easy for her to use the same frame in more than one place. Though this is not a problem in the video and sound worlds, it is not possible to reuse the same piece of 35mm negative. In order to do that, you would need to make a duplicate negative of the original frames optically (see Chapter 10), then cut in this copy for the second usage of that footage.

Sometimes this reuse is exactly what Wendy wants. In most cases, it is simply a case of accidentally extending a piece of picture too much. It is all too easy to do this when you are cutting electronically. Your job is to make sure it doesn't happen accidentally.

Both the Avid and Lightworks editing systems, as well as add-on software programs like Slingshot, have modes allowing you to check for duplicate or re-used frames. You should run these checks on an edit every time Wendy has cut or recut it.

After you have cleaned-up and verified the edit, you can put it into the bin or gallery for edited scenes. Make sure it is named using your version number system. Some assistants like to include the date in the name of the edit. After you do this, you can check with Wendy to see what scene she wishes to cut next and bring it out onto the computer's desktop.

Testing Your Work

As soon as you have some scenes cut together, it is a good idea to check the system that you will be following at the end of the editorial process. You should make Film Cut Lists and Edit Lists (sound and video, if you are going to do an on-line). First, you should call your negative editors, your sound house and your video facility to get their specifications for these lists. Then you can create all of them.

You may not know your negative cutters at this point, but if you do, you should send a copy of your negative cut list to them so they can tell you whether the format is what they need. You can also send them a videotape in the format they will eventually need (We will get into this in more detail in Chapter 16A, so don't worry too much if you don't get it all right now).

Copies of your sound EDLs can go to your sound effects house, both in printed format and saved on disk if you are working on a project finishing on tape. Video EDLs can go to your video on-line house. Have them make a thorough check of your work so you know there will be no problems with your delivery when you give it to them in the much more rushed atmosphere at the end of the editing process.

175

Outputs

As Wendy completes scenes she will probably want to have Adam watch them. Perhaps she will want to take them home herself so she can watch them in a more relaxed atmosphere than the editing room. She will then ask you to *output* a tape. This is also called a *playout* or a *Digital Cut*.

There are several types of outputting, the two main ones being outputting to a time-coded tape, and a free-running output. For the first kind you use a tape that has been *pre-blacked*, in which time code has been pre-recorded onto the tape. In most cases, you will only pre-black 3/4" or Beta tapes. VHS (1/2") tapes almost never are run with time code. Each editing system has a different method for this type of outputting, but they all require you to go into a separate mode and set up your edit to match the time code on the tape you are using to output. You then press a button and the tape syncs up to the edit as it plays out.

The advantage of this type of output is that it is very controllable. If, for some reason, you don't like one part of the playout (let's say that your sound mix was not good, for instance), it is very easy to go back and re-do just that small section. This type of playout also assures that the 3 to 2 pulldown is correctly created on the output tape.

For casual VHS viewing copies, it is not necessary to be so meticulous. In these cases, you need to make sure the VHS machine is running and in record mode, then simply press the play button on your editing machine.

Before you do either of these outputs you should quickly run through the edit to make sure it doesn't need any sound adjustment. Most editing machines allow you pre-set sound levels and fades on a shot-by-shot basis, making it easy to wrap music around dialogue and mix sound effects in the proper relationship to the rest of the soundtrack. The Avid also allows you to set different equalizations, making it possible to fix dialogue problems and create much more interesting sound mixes (you can change the dialogue, for instance, to make it sound like it's coming from a television or a telephone). Most editors cut with up to four channels of sound—two dialogue, one effects and one music track. Advances in computer technology are already enabling some editors to work with more tracks; this will only increase the amount of planning you need to perform before making outputs.

In any case, you will want to check out how Wendy has cut her tracks so you can make an output that is properly balanced. Wendy will be able to give you details on what she wants.

Some editors, myself included, like to operate the sound mixing board during the output. Others want nothing to do with it. In the latter, you will sit by the mixing board as the edit is playing out, adjusting the levels of all of the tracks and watching the screen to be sure all of the images are being recorded properly. You should also check the sound level meters on the video deck to ensure you are not recording the sound too loudly.

When the output is complete, you should spot check the tape you've created by playing it in several selected spots. Make sure the volume is neither too soft or too loud and check the visuals to be sure there were no problems. Early versions of editing machine software often had problems generating smooth flowing pictures. In some cases today, where there are a number of complicated opticals or a series of short cuts, it is possible that the picture will seem to *stutter*—it will freeze for a moment and then pick up a number of frames later.

Once you have made sure that the tape is correct, you or Philip should label both the tape and its box with the film name, output date, a short description of the material ("Second Version of Sc. 21 for Adam"), your name and the editing room phone number.

I use a computer to print out tape labels onto Avery or compatible label stock. It is then a simple matter to cut out the labels and paste them on the tape and box for delivery.

Other Bits (Pun Intended) to Remember

Though editing with computers cuts down on the dirt associated with 35mm film, these machines still tend to get dirty. And when they get dirty they get more cantankerous than the old Moviolas and Steenbecks ever did. This is why it is important you keep the editing area as free of smoke (including cigarette smoke—sorry all you puffers out there) and dirt as possible.

You should have some computer monitor cleaning fluids and cloths (don't use Windex, it may eat away at the protective coating some computer screens have on their surfaces) and wipe down every monitor at least twice a week. Make sure the area around the editing machine is vacuumed several times a week. Take a can of compressed air and blow out all of the dirt, dust and loose crumbs that have accumulated in the keyboard. You should also open up the mouse (the ring around the little ball unscrews easily) and give the ball and the works inside a thorough cleaning once a week. Using tweezers, pry out any dust and string that has wrapped itself around the internal rollers.

177

Make sure that all of your videotape machines are clean (you can buy a VHS cleaning tape). When you are not using them, make sure no tapes are parked inside them. You might even want to shut off all of the machines when they are not being used. You can also buy computer disk cleaning kits, made for your floppy drives.

If you are working in an editing room with printed film, make sure all of your filmed dailies are filed away properly in boxes. Since you will not need this material until your first film *conform*, all that is necessary is that it be easily accessible. Put the picture (and track, if you have it) in two-piece white boxes with the starting and ending matching code numbers that were printed onto the picture window burn displayed on the outside of the box. If you have printed picture only, and have not ink coded the footage you will need to write the camera and lab rolls, as well as the starting and ending key numbers of all of the footage in the box. If you have sunk up footage and telecined *that*, then you would list the dailies roll number and the starting and ending inked code numbers. It will not be necessary to break the footage down into takes.

There are some similarities between an electronic editing room and a film one that are worth mentioning. A calendar should be prominently posted and updated daily. Phone lists should be kept up-to-date and correct. And, most importantly, you will need to continue to keep up thorough and accurate communication between the editing room and the production office as well as between all of your suppliers.

Needs from the Set

Just because you are cutting on a digital machine doesn't mean the requests from the set are going to diminish. In fact, the tendency is for them to increase. You will continue to get requests for match clips, for instance. If you are working on a film that is also printing 35mm it may still be better to supply the set with clips from the 35mm. The director of photography will be able to see the lighting better, the script supervisor will be able to find matches more easily, and the production designer will be able to see the set design more clearly.

If you've got a color printer attached to your editing machine you can print out a match frame onto a piece of paper and send that to the set. This way, they have a color still reference for the shot. Depending upon the quality it may work better for them than a frame clip.

178

However, there are many cases where an output from the Avid or Lightworks or a copy of the original taped dailies will be acceptable or better than the 35mm film. In fact, if you aren't printing film you will have no choice at all. In any case, since the video or digital image is a moving one, it will be much easier to match movements than with a film frame clip. This is one of the advantages of editing electronically.

. . . .

SPECIAL CASES

The procedures I've already outlined apply primarily to straight dialogue movies being cut on an upright Moviola in the United States. There are many more types of movies and many more ways to edit them. We'll consider a few of them now.

Musical Systems

I mentioned earlier that *Silent Night, Silent Cowboy* had a few musical scenes in it. One of them takes place on a saloon set where the lead in our movie-within-a-movie, COWBOY, enters the town saloon for the first time and gets involved in a fixed poker game. As he enters, he walks around the room, amazed at the newness of everything. One of the things he sees is two cowboys singing together, one of whom is playing a guitar.

This scene could be shot in several ways. One way would be to hire actors who could sing and have them play and sing live on the set. This, however, would create two problems. First, since the performers would rarely be singing at the exact same rhythm and pitch from take to take and from angle to angle, it would be impossible for the editor to cut performances from different takes together and have them make musical sense. In addition, music recorded on the set is rarely as clean as music recorded in a music studio.

Many songs are recorded this way, however, to the chagrin of the director and editor when they see (and hear) it later in the editing room.

A better way, from the standpoint of lip sync, is to record to *playback*. One clean track is obtained, either through a recording in a music studio (this is the way musicals are done) or by recording a wild track on the set before the shooting of the scene. This sound track is then played back over loudspeakers (or through tiny ear pieces, called *earwigs*) to the actors on the set who sing and play back to it, attempting to copy it exactly. This way there is only one musical track, and each take is shot at the same rhythm and pitch. During the picture editing and in the music editing variations in the lip sync can be corrected and any sync mistakes the actor or actress made during the shooting can be modified or eliminated.

The way a playback sequence is handled on the set of a major feature is to have two recording machines, such as Nagras or DATs. One of them is used to play back the master tape of the song to the actors. The output of this machine is also fed to the second machine, which records it as well as the synching slate and any other sounds the recordist is able to isolate from the din of the played-back song. If earwigs are used to cue the actors, no music will be broadcast out loud on the set and a clean, live production track can be recorded. This tactic is often used when the director wants to get a live singing voice.

If this method is used, you can sync the dailies as you normally would. Each take will have a slate as recorded live on the set. The soundtrack will then segue into the direct feed of the song from the playback sound machine.

180

However, on lower-budget films, it often is not possible to rent two tape machines. As a result, the tape machine is used for playback only and no live recording is done on it. This creates many extra steps in the synching. Since no sound was taken during the playback takes, the dailies will either have to be looked at in silence or the sync tracks will have to be created by you in the editing room. To do this, you need a copy of the original playback tape (you need this tape anyway, even if you are supplied with dailies soundtrack from two recorders; you should make sure your music editor or sound recordist gets you a copy).

From this tape, make as many mag transfers of the song as there were takes printed on the set using the song (you will need to have the script supervisor's daily notes to determine this). On a Moviola or flatbed, you must then match up by eye every take to its own transfer of the music. Be aware that the singers or guitar picker will rarely be exactly in sync for the entire length of the song. You should choose the sync position that puts most of the song in comfortable sync. Then mark a fake slate mark near the top of each take. This will help you to sync and Wendy to line up the takes on her Moviola later on. Then you can prepare the dailies rolls just as you normally would. Now, regardless of whether one or two sound machines were used, you will have sync dailies with sound for all takes.

No matter how the takes are sunk up, when these dailies rolls come back to you after the dailies screening your complications will begin, for coding musical footage is a much different process than coding normal dailies. Once again, the problem stems from the fact that all the sound has been generated from only one source—the original DAT or 1/4" tape. When Wendy cuts the picture it will be much easier for her to cut all of her picture takes to only one soundtrack. This way, she will end up with a cut picture that will run in frame-to-frame sync with the original recording.

For Wendy to cut take after take to one soundtrack she must have *all* her picture takes coded in sync to that one master music track. Therefore, you must *spot code* each of the takes individually. You will need a synchronizer with sound heads in both the second and third gangs to do this.

You should double code your music dailies so they have their normal dailies coding on one edge of the film and the special music coding on the opposite edge, usually in a different color. You would start the process by logging each roll normally

To start the special music coding, you must have one copy of the complete song on 35mm sound film (called the *playback master*). Before you code any of your dailies, this track must be coded. My suggestion for coding it is to assign each musical number its own prefix code. For instance, let's say there are three musical numbers in our film. For convenience's sake we shall code the playback for our first song, "Jimmy the Baby" (*see* Figure 7.1, script pages for this scene), 019M0000, since it appears in scene 19 in the film. The "M" stands for "Music."

After the playback master is coded you will be ready to music code each of the takes. Let's say there were four set–ups involving our singers. They are as follows:

> 19, takes 4,6,8—Master shot of the entire scene
> 19E, takes 2,4,7—MWS of the two singers
> 19F, takes 2,3—MCU of the singer/guitarist
> 19G, take 2—MCU of the singer

All the other setups involve portions of the scene where the musicians are not visible. These set–ups were, therefore, not shot to playback. Let us also assume that Adam, knowing he would not begin the scene with the medium close–ups of the singers, only shot them singing from the second verse until the end, as shown in the line script.

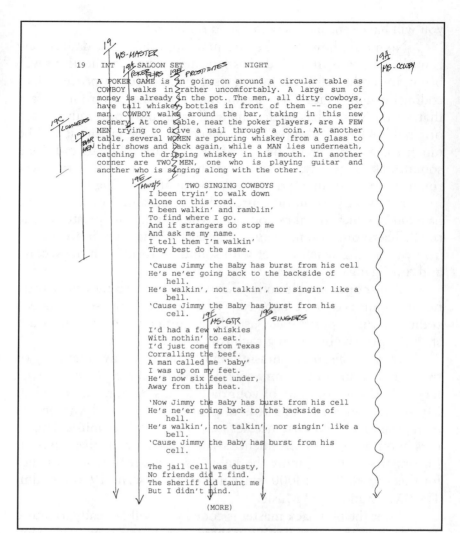

FIGURE 7.1 Script pages for a musical scene.

Take the playback master and run it down on your synchronizer until you can hear the song from your soundbox. Now, choose a word in the song with a definite *hit* to it. This means a sound as sharp and identifiable as the slate. Good choices for this are words beginning with the letters b, a hard c, d, g, k, p, or t. In this song, a few good hits would be the beginnings of the words "been," "tryin'," or "down" in the first line. Listen to your playback master on your synchronizer and locate a few of these easily identifiable hits. You can find them by sliding the track back and forth under the sound head exactly as you did to find the sound slates when you were

19 CONTINUED 19F

> I been around many
> Of men like his kind.
> But I was fixin' on leavin'
> That jail cell behind.
>
> 'Now Jimmy the Baby has burst from his cell
> He's ne'er going back to the backside of
> hell.
> He's walkin', not talkin', nor singin' like a
> bell.
> 'Cause Jimmy the Baby has burst from his
> cell.

Eventually COWBOY finds his way to the outside of the poker table. A hand has just been completed.

                    JIM
        That's it for me.

                    SAM
        Chrissakes Jim!

                    JIM
        Naw, that's it. I gotta save something for my
        other pleasures.

Laughing, he gets up and exits through the crowd, past Cowboy who is watching nervously. Unfortunately, at that minute Sam notices him.

                    SAM
        Well, lookit. A new face! How'd you like to
        get your official welcome to this friendly
        town. My name's Sam Robson.

He holds out his hand to Cowboy who, startled, takes it. He is quite confused about the offer. He is being tested, he feels.

                    COWBOY
        Sure.

He sits down and look about nervously.

                    SAM
        The kitty son.

It is a few seconds before Cowboy catches Sam's meaning. After a pause he hurriedly pushes some money into the pot. Sam deals out the cards and a short game ensues in which Cowboy plays stupidly and loses. During this game, we see the SHERIFF enter and watch from a distance. He is just about the only person in the bar who is watching the game, including some of the players in it. There are

                    (MORE)

FIGURE 7.1 continued

synching the dailies. As you find each word, mark the exact sprocket on the track and note the word that you've found as shown in Figure 7.2. Since you know that some of the takes don't begin until the second verse, mark some sync points down there as well (the second syllable in the word "whiskey" might be a good choice as well as the word "Texas.")

Then temporarily take your playback master out of your synchronizer (you don't have to rewind it past the beginning of the song), and put the dailies roll with the playback takes up. Any takes without playback in them should be separated so all playback takes *tryin'   *been

FIGURE 7.2 A section of a musical playback master track with three sync points marked on it. Each point is marked at its first modulation. In a real situation, the two points would be much further apart on the mag.

are on one reel and all non-playback reels on another (note that they will still all be entered in the logbook as from the same dailies rolls; they are being separated here for music coding purposes only.) Run them down until you get to the first take (19–4). Run down even further until you get to the first word you have chosen as your sync point ("been" in this case). When you find the first modulation of the word, mark it on your dailies track with a grease pencil. In the third gang place your playback master at the same point so the two sync points line up sprocket for sprocket. If you roll down to the next word you have marked on the playback master you should find that it lines up exactly with the same word on the dailies take. Do this for a few more sync points so you know the two tracks are running exactly in sync.

There is another way of verifying sync on these two music tracks, though it is very difficult to describe in words. If you listen to both tracks at the same time (with both at the same volume level) you should hear the two sounds *phasing* with each other. This phasing sounds like a very slight echo; I often describe it as a "tunnel" effect. If the tracks are one or two sprockets out of sync there wouldn't be any phasing; instead you would hear a very fast echo. The further out of sync they are, the longer the echo delay will be. If this happens, move the playback master one sprocket at a time and listen. When you no longer hear this echo, but hear the sound take on an eerie, hollow quality, you know the tracks are phasing and are therefore in as close a sync as possible.

It is sometimes difficult to hear this phasing, especially with poor quality sound equipment. Phasing occurs more easily on instruments like strings or on solo vocals than it does on drums or brass instruments. As a result, don't count on using phasing as the only measure for whether you're in sync. Always use the individual sync point technique first, and use phasing as a final verification.

After you are sure the tracks are in sync with each other, roll backwards to the beginning of the music. Notice the code number

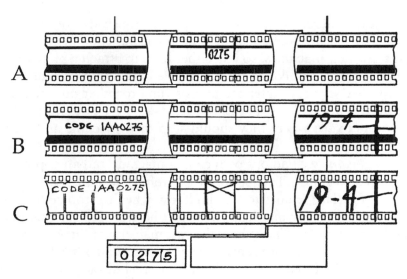

FIGURE 7.3 *The playback master (A) is lined up in the synchronizer with the dailies track (B) and picture (C). The code number 0275 on the playback on the playback master would actually be edge coded on the side of the film. It is shown in the center here for legibility only.*

of the playback master and mark the synchronous frame of picture with this number (019M0275, in the example in Figure 7.3).

Often, there will be some time when the camera is running *before* the men began to sing the song, perhaps because the characters had some dialogue before they started singing. All of the picture *before* the beginning of the song will have only one set of numbers and all of the picture *after* the beginning of the song will have two. The only time Wendy will need to have music code numbers is, obviously, when the music is playing.

Continue marking up every take of picture. In some cases, such as 19F and 19G, the take will begin in the middle of the song. In that case, the first code number you mark onto the picture will come later than 019M0000.

When you are done, you will be able to code each take with its music code. You should make sure that this second set of code numbers is placed on the opposite edge from the first set of the dailies codes. That way, both will be read easily. You will also want to use a different color code number for these music codes.

If you are sending the film out to a coding service, you should check with them first to see how they would like the reels to be prepared. Every coding machine or service has different requirements for spot-coding reels. Some want each take wound on its own individual reel (most coding services charge by the reel for their coding services). Others use electronic sensing equipment to stop and start their machines, so you either have to attach a piece of foil to the end of each take or cut out a little notch on one edge of the film. Other services prefer the takes strung together on one set of reels but with leader connecting each take so it is easy for their operators to see where they should stop their machine and set up for a new take.

On *Fame* we had our own coding machine and an apprentice was hired to run it. This apprentice carefully watched the picture footage for flash frames to let him know when to stop coding one take and set up for another. For track, he watched for the white tape between takes. This is how the vast majority of films are coded today. Nearly all feature films rent their own coding machines.

After the footage is coded you can break down the dailies as you normally would, into little hand rolls. If there is no dialogue on the dailies track, Wendy might ask you to wind the picture up separately from the sound, since she will never need to cut the sound. Put the dailies code numbers, not the musical code numbers, on the trim tab.

186

Unslated Takes

Sometimes, through problems on the set or some other exigency, you will get a take with no visible slate to mark for synching purposes. On *Hair*, several shots during the song "Good Morning Starshine" were shot from a helicopter too far away from the action to have slates. Sometimes, the camera operator will miss the slate either by being out of focus by being pointed just slightly too far up or down. Other times the lab will cut off the head of the shot, losing the slate with it.

In these cases you will have some tricky eye-matching to do, using the same techniques I described earlier in this chapter for musicals where sound was taken with only one Nagra. Once again, the trick is to find something with a definite hit to it. In many cases you can use door slams, an actor pounding on a table, or any number of other sharp sound effects to sync things up (you can usually find the exact frame where these effects happen). Always be sure to check the footage in the Moviola or on your flatbed to make sure you really do have the proper sync.

Sometimes there are no visual clues (this often happens on actor's close-ups) and you must use dialogue to eye-sync. Look for the letters b, c, d, k, p, or t. These usually have fairly definite sounds as well as being reasonably identifiable by lip movements. If you need to, say the words of dialogue while you hold your fingers over your lips to feel them move to see what shape the lips of the actor on your Moviola should be making. As always, check your sync on the Moviola or flatbed before moving along to the next take.

KEM and Other Flatbed Systems

Until now we have discussed only upright Moviola systems. In these systems, takes are individually broken down before being given to the editor. Each take is treated as a separate entity.

But one of the advantages of a flatbed is its ability to high-speed from one take to another. This advantage would be lost if all the takes were broken down individually as we do for a Moviola. Therefore, a flatbed system is set up with completely different parameters than a Moviola system.

To examine the basic reasoning behind a flatbed system, let me remind you of the procedure for editing on a Moviola. On *Silent Night*, Wendy is cutting with two Moviolas—one to examine potential cutting points and another on which to make the cuts. On a flatbed she would do much the same thing. Let us say that she was using an eight-plate KEM. On four of these plates (this would be one reel of picture and one of track, since each reel has both a feed and a take-up plate) she would have her picture and track for the cut and on the other four she would have the picture and track for takes she is going to examine.

187

One of the problems of a flatbed is that it is more difficult to thread and re-thread each roll of film than on an upright. One of the tasks of an efficient flatbed system, therefore, should be to minimize such setup time.

One way to do this is to put as many takes on the same roll as are sensible. These cutting rolls are called *KEM rolls*. A KEM roll has no equivalent in the Moviola world because, in that system, all takes are broken down individually before they are cut. On a flatbed system, individual takes are not broken down but are rearranged into more orderly cutting rolls.

You will have to put some intelligence into the organization of these KEM rolls, of course, otherwise Wendy will spend more time finding takes within a roll or changing KEM rolls than she would save by using the flatbed.

To give a bad example, let's say that you decided to take the dailies rolls from the first day's dailies and use them as the KEM rolls for these scenes. You would then have all the setups for Scene 10 on one roll. If Wendy needed to cut take 10A–2 onto take 10–6 she would have a problem. First she would roll down on the KEM roll until she found the frame on 10–6 that she would like to use to cut out. Then she would have to roll further down on the same roll (losing her place on 10–6) to find the frame of 10A–2 she wanted to cut into.

This is far more difficult for an editor to do than having both frames visible simultaneously and it doesn't take advantage of the flatbed's second picture head.

An obvious solution, therefore, would be to make sure that shots 10–6 and 10A–2 were on different KEM rolls.

This, in fact, is the basis of the flatbed system. Any shot the editor might want to cut *to* should be on a different KEM roll than the shot the editor would be cutting away *from*.

There are times when it won't be possible to know this in advance. In the music playback scene I described earlier in this chapter, you would probably never know ahead of time in just what order all the cutaway shots at the beginning of the scene (19A through 19D) would be used. In general, however, there are some rules that will work for your planning. First, keep all shots of the same person (no matter what their size—wide, medium, or close) on the same roll. In the scene in Abby's bedroom (Scene 11, Figure 4.5) I would keep all the shots of Bob separate from Abby's shots. Next, keep the *master shots* on the same roll with the *insert shots*. Inserts are very close up shots of an action. An extreme close-up of Bob's fingers making a correction at the typewriter, for example, would be inserted into a medium shot of him. Master shots will very rarely be intercut with insert shots, as the cut from very wide to very tight shot is usually not attractive. Insert shots are usually cut to medium close-ups or close-up shots. Similarly, wide shots are usually cut to medium-wide or medium shots. This rule obviously depends upon the footage you get, so it is imperative that you use your brains and your experience in making these kinds of choices.

Lastly, in a montage-like sequence (which may be as complex as a car chase or as easy as all of those atmosphere shots at the beginning of our music playback scene) almost anything can be cut to anything else. In this case, it is helpful to have all the montage elements on the same KEM roll, as close to each other as possible. I would put all takes of scenes 19A through 19D one right after another on a KEM roll (though not the same KEM roll as the master shot). This way, Wendy could roll down past each one rather rapidly and decide which one she wanted to cut into the master shot on the other roll. She would then make the cut and roll down to the final frame that she wants in the insert. After cutting the take at that frame she could either hang the insert in a bin or cut it onto the edited roll. She would then resplice the head and tail trims of the cutaway together using white soundtrack tape (which will be much easier for Philip to find later as he puts away the trims), then continue to roll down on the cutaway KEM roll to find another cutaway if she wanted one immediately afterwards. This is not a perfect solution, but it is an acceptable one.

Obviously, for this method of cutting to make any sense, all takes of any given camera setup should be on the same KEM roll. It would do the editor no good to have to put up two different KEM rolls to see two takes of the same setup. So, unless the lengths of the individual takes are too long to permit it, put all takes of the same setup together.

KEM rolls should be neither too short nor too long. If the rolls are too long (over 800 feet), it will take more time to fast-forward or rewind between setups than it would to put up a new roll. If they are too short (this minimum size will vary depending on the lengths of the takes involved but let us say, for an example only, less than 400 feet), the assistant will spend more time threading up the KEM rolls than the editor will spend looking at them.

Some editors, especially those with shorter arms, prefer to put as many takes on each roll as possible. This minimizes the constant rethreading that is a normal part of editing on a flatbed. Other editors prefer to keep shots split onto different rolls to make it easier to see the cuttable shots on separate picture heads. This is a matter of personal preference and one you should discuss with your editor before the first frame of dailies comes in the door. Remember, one of your jobs is to keep the editing room moving smoothly and part of this task is setting things up in a way that makes it as easy as possible for the editor to work.

189

Working with editors, you will find out how they like to cut. If you pay attention to this you will learn better ways to organize KEM rolls for them. It is not an easy task to think ahead and try to figure out how the editor will probably cut, but it is an important one, and it is one at which you will get better as you get more opportunity to observe how Wendy cuts.

What changes will this new system cause you to make in your paperwork and work-style? As you might expect, there will be many. The most obvious one is, rather than breaking the dailies rolls down into individual takes, you will be breaking them apart only to have to build them back again into the KEM rolls. This means, if you coded the film when it was still in dailies roll form, all the numbers would get jumbled up once the takes were rebuilt into the usually very different order of the KEM rolls.

This is why it would be wise to wait until after the KEM rolls are built before you code and log them. This will, inevitably, slow down the process of getting the film to the editor, but it is an unavoidable side effect of using a flatbed.

As the film is being shot, this KEM system also creates more work in the editing room, resulting in a slightly different work flow for everyone involved. In an average feature editing room the assistant editor would supervise the synching of dailies, determine the KEM roll breakdown, and supervise the building of the KEM rolls. Philip would have to help to sync the dailies (or do them completely himself), build KEM rolls, and put away trims. Unless there is going to be very little footage every day, it would be wise to think about putting on a second assistant to sync the dailies, freeing the first assistant to work with the editor and organize the editing room, and allowing the apprentice to do the work of trims and help in building KEM rolls (which is a very laborious task).

Building KEM rolls involves pulling the takes for each KEM roll from all the dailies rolls that are involved. The best way to do this is to organize the paperwork first. You should determine exactly what takes would go on what KEM roll while, at the same time, noting from which dailies roll each take came.

You or Philip would then take all of those dailies rolls and spin down each one on a synchronizer until you found the necessary take that you would then build into your KEM roll on another synchronizer. In actuality, this process is far more time consuming than it would appear from this description, very often involving two synchronizers (and/or KEMs) and much running around with splicers and pieces of paper. While you are building the KEM rolls, you should also be logging in the footage and setting it up for coding.

On some films, KEM roll building resembles a Three Stooges film and requires at least one person's complete attention. It is an unfortunate fact of life, however, that most production managers do not realize the necessity of an extra assistant (or even an extra apprentice) and insist that everything be handled by an assistant and an apprentice. This works on easy dialogue films but is usually a disaster on larger projects. Editors should insist on a fourth person but they often can't get one. This means that you and Philip will be putting in a lot of overtime hours and your editor will be getting less of your time and, ultimately, less work done.

Another adjustment you'll have to make in your system is dealing with trims and outs. As Wendy removes varying amounts of picture and track from her KEM rolls she will generally be throwing these reels out of sync. When she is done cutting, Philip's major tasks will be to put all the trims hanging in her barrel back into these reels and fill out either the picture (with white leader) or the track (with fill) so that the footage will always run in sync. That way, when Wendy next puts up her KEM rolls to search for a piece of film she will see everything in sync—the way it was meant to be seen.

To do this, Philip will organize all the trims in the barrel by KEM roll, most often one pin for each roll. He can easily determine which KEM roll a trim is on since each roll will have its own unique code number prefix, 019 1000 is a different roll than 019 3000. He will also organize the trims so they are in numerical order on the pin, with the lowest on the top. He will then put up a KEM roll in his synchronizer, line the picture and track up at the start marks, and roll down until he gets to the number of the first trim that he has to put away or until he notices that the picture has gotten out of sync with the track (whichever comes first). He will then insert the trim that he has in his barrel, if necessary, and add leader or fill to the picture or track to bring everything back into sync. He will then roll down to the next place where a trim belongs, or that is out of sync, and do the same thing.

This, you may notice, is a much more time consuming process than filing Moviola trims, which is one reason I prefer to work with the Moviola system on low-budget films with short schedules.

191

You can see that KEM systems, in general, create much more work for the assistant than a Moviola system does. For the editor, however, there are distinct advantages to working on flatbeds. You will learn about these as you do more films with them. Until then I can only reassure you that all the extra work you will have to do is worth it.

On low budget films, 16mm films, and features with very short post-production schedules, it is often impossible to organize KEM rolls in the way that I've been describing. It would be impossible, for instance, to do all the work necessary to organize and sync dailies, organize and build KEM rolls, put trims away, work with the editor *and* do all the other assistant tasks, if there were only one assistant on the film. But sometimes the film's budget only allows for one assistant. In these cases, dailies rolls often become KEM rolls, much logging is skipped, and the assistant never works directly with the editor. Your job on a film like this is much akin to surviving a guerrilla war. It is only your experience that can guide you in deciding which parts of your system you can afford to omit and which you cannot.

Stock Footage

Often, during the editing of the film, Wendy and Adam might have need for a shot that was either too expensive or not possible to get during principal photography. They'll need a helicopter shot of the North Pole. They'll want to see three New York City police cars pull up outside an apartment building. They'll want a shot of a bear looking away from the camera (reacting to a piece of film they have already shot on location). On *Trigger Happy* we needed shots of stars and galaxies to show our conception of the Big Bang at the beginning of the universe. It is possible to get shots of most of these things from people and companies who have already shot the material and made it available for use by others. This type of material is called *stock footage* and the places that make it available for reuse are called *stock footage houses.*

The amount and types of footage available for purchase from stock footage houses around the world is staggering. Many houses specialize in old news footage, others deal in time lapse photography, still others have medical footage of operations. You can buy footage of old cars driving down streets, airplanes in flight, film of the Earth from outer space and more. If you can think about it, the chances are good that some stock house somewhere will have it.

Finding this footage, however, is another thing entirely.

There are lists of stock footage houses in most of the film directories, in the back of many of the technical magazines listed in the Bibliography at the back of this book, and on the Internet (there are some large sites which have sample pictures and movies from a large number of stock houses). In fact, there are so many sources and so much footage that some films hire stock footage researchers to find and obtain the footage they are looking for. On many other films, it will be left to you to do most of the research.

Your search should begin with a thorough understanding of exactly what shots Wendy and Adam are looking for. If they ask for a shot of the outside of a saloon, you should know if they want it deserted or busy, day or night, in a city or a small town, what color scheme they are looking for, and a host of other specifics. The footage you obtain will have to fit seamlessly into the material shot by your own crew so it should have much the same look and feel in terms of lighting, production design and period.

The next requirement that you will need to research is the original format of the stock footage. The material in stock houses across the world varies considerably in quality. Some of it was originally shot on 35mm film, but some might have originated on 16mm film or on various formats of videotape. If you are working on a film to be released on 35mm, it is necessary that you get material originally shot on 35mm. If the footage was shot on any other format, it will look appreciably different in quality from the images surrounding it in the final film. Unless the quality of the image is not an issue (as may be the case if the footage is supposed to be something a character is looking at under a microscope, through a telescope, or in a dream sequence) you should look only for 35mm material.

If your project will be released only on videotape, the originating format makes much less of a difference.

Once you know what you are looking for, you can begin to search for it. You should call every stock footage house likely to have the material you are looking for. Some of them will send over rolls of 35mm film for you to screen, others will send over videocassettes (usually 3/4 ' or 1/2") of the selected material. Many of these houses will want a small fee for the research time and tape duplication costs. Others will provide the tape to you for free.

Every stock shot should have a number on it, either scratched onto the piece of film at its start or burned into the videotape along with a time code. The numbers will probably also be listed on a log sheet with the stock footage. Those numbers, and the time code, will be very important to you later on, so you should log every stock shot that Wendy and Adam think they might need into a separate section of your log book, along with the name of the stock footage house where you got the footage.

If you have been provided with the footage on film, it will be a simple matter to select those shots that you think are potentially useful and make a color dupe of them, making sure any key numbers on the original footage are printed through on the dupe. You should then edge code the dupe, making sure to log the number and source of every shot just as you would log your original footage. If one of those shots ends up in the final film you will be able to use the code numbers and the logs to find out just which shot you need to obtain and who to pay.

If you've received the stock footage on video, things get a little more complicated. You will either need to select the shots that you want to use without seeing them edited into the film, or you will need to do a *transform* of the videotape. A transform, also called a *kinescope*, is the process of taking a videotape and making a 35mm negative and print from it. This is not a cheap process, though it is cheaper than ordering the actual stock shot, and you will want to do it sparingly.

A third alternative is to make a videotape copy of the sequences in *Silent Night* that require the stock footage and edit the stock material into the film using videotape.

There is a problem with the stock footage, however. Even though you now have a print (or a temporary print) of the footage you want cut into your workprint, there is no negative to match the print. In order to get that negative you will need to order some from the stock footage house.

Once the film has been locked you will need to go through it and identify every stock shot that you've used. Your logbook should identify the stock footage house and the shot's identification number. That information, along with the key numbers on the edge of the film (or burned into the image visually if you've done a transform from video), will accurately identify the piece of stock used in your movie.

You should then give those numbers to the stock footage house that originally sent you the material, along with a check to pay for the shot you are purchasing. They will usually make an interpositive (IP) and, sometimes, an internegative (IN) from their original negative. Rarely will a stock footage house send their original for you to make the IP. That footage is how they make their money, and it is the rare house that will want to give up control of it.

194

Don't be surprised if it takes several weeks for the stock house to send you the IP. Often, many of them don't actually have possession of the footage themselves. Instead, they have the rights to make copies of it for sale. In those cases, the stock footage house may not even be in the same city as the lab storing the footage. On *Trigger Happy* one of our stock shots had to be ordered from England.

Once you get the IP, you should get an IN and a print made and then get the IN over to your negative cutter. If the stock house sent you an IN but no print, then you will need to strike a print for yourself. Make sure there are clear key numbers on the print that will match back to the IN. You can then eye match the new shot into your workprint in the same way you cut in reprints (as we will discuss later in Chapter 9). Once this is complete, you can send the marked up workprint to your negative cutter so he or she can complete the job of matching the film.

Location Shooting

Two weeks of the shooting of *Silent Night* involve location shooting in a desert-like area. As mentioned, Wendy will not be going on location but will be staying back in town, continuing to cut as the footage comes in. Adam and the rest of the crew will still need to see the film every day. This will inevitably complicate your life but it is necessary.

The first major change you will have to deal with will be the delivery of the negative and production sound to the lab and sound house every day. Depending on how far away the location is from you, the shot footage may be coming in anywhere from a half day to a week late. On some foreign locations, the footage may come in to you once a week.

Obviously, this will affect your schedule. The best thing you can do in these cases is work closely with your production manager and production office coordinator to make sure that the footage is transported where and when it is supposed to be.

In order for the crew to see the film on location they will need three things—a projection system, a projectionist, and the sunk film. The first two should be arranged for by the production manager who will have already scouted the location. In a few cases a local movie theatre can be outfitted with a *double–system projector* (a projector that can run separate film and soundtrack units in sync with each other, much as a Moviola or KEM can) so the crew can see the dailies there. In most cases, however, a portable projector must be brought in to the location. In either case, it will be important for you to find out the projectionist's requirements before the first day of location dailies. Some projectors will not accept film on cores so the film must be shipped on reels. Some projectors can handle reels built over 1000 feet, others cannot. If there are any special requirements that you must meet, you need to know about them *before* you send the first day's footage or the dailies might not be able to be screened.

You, or the production office coordinator (the person who supervises the day-to-day details of the film), should determine the best way to ship the film to the location. Prompt delivery must be assured, for this reason the film's production assistants are often utilized, rather than messenger services doing runs for many other clients at the same time. Film can be shipped by air, train, or bus. If delivery is to be made out of the country, a customs broker should be hired to prepare all the shipping papers that the various governments will require at the airports, both to get the film to the set as well as to get it back to you. In any case, the fastest, most reliable method should be chosen. A side note—some editors are afraid of the security machines at airports, fearing that they will *degauss* (erase) the film's soundtrack; I have done several experiments with these machines and have never had a track damaged.

The major change in your dailies schedule will obviously be one of time. If the dailies screening on location is at 7:00 p.m. and the film takes six hours to reach the location, you will obviously have to be finished synching and checking the dailies in time for the film to make it to the airport by 1:00 p.m. If possible, try to leave yourself an hour or two of spare time for the inevitable delays.

A copy of the editor's notes should be sent out to the set so someone can take down Adam's notes for the selected takes just as you or Wendy would if the dailies were in town.

Of course, arrangements should also be made to get the film back to you as fast as possible so you can proceed with the coding, logging, and cutting. Often it is possible to ship the sunk dailies back with the unprocessed film and sound tapes. When film is shipped to location it is not uncommon to expect at least a one day delay in being able to code and log everything.

There are times that the editor will be asked to come onto location. In this case, it will be up to the assistant to create a completely functioning editing room there. Editing rooms have been set up in such diverse locations as Bora Bora, Morocco, and Norway. On location, you can't just get on the phone one morning to order a roll of splicing tape or a Moviola bulb and expect to have it that afternoon, so you will have to bring enough supplies to last you the entire time you will be on location.

I should also warn you that being in an editing room in Bora Bora is not as much fun as it sounds.

196

Film-Within-Film

Several scenes in *Silent Night* involve people watching projected film, dailies for instance. To set this up, you will have to provide the film for the shooting.

An example was the *Rocky Horror Show* sequence in *Fame*. In it, several of our characters were in a large audience watching the famous midnight show film. I had to prepare the film for that showing.

Several segments of the film were used. Each was cut from a new print of the movie supplied to us by Twentieth Century-Fox. Each segment was placed on its own reel (along with a backup copy on another reel in case the first one was damaged), each with its own Academy Leader so both the projectionist and the cameraman could quickly focus. Since the film already had a sound track on it, the actual sound of the movie was used for playback to the extras acting as the audience (in other cases, an interlocking 35mm magnetic soundtrack might have been used).

Along with the married film, I supplied the soundman, Chris Newman, with playback tapes of the soundtrack of the sections we were using. I did this so that when the camera was shooting at the audience (and the screen was not visible) only the playback tape needed to be run to give the audience the soundtrack to the movie to shout back to. This saved a lot of time and confusion on the set.

There are frequently times when characters in a film are shown watching television monitors. Supplying the footage that they are looking at is often the editor's job. Once the footage has been selected, it needs to be put onto 3/4" videotape for playback. In addition, to avoid the annoying roll-bar effect, common when shooting directly off a TV set, you should have this tape made at 24 frames per second, rather than the usual video rate of approximately 30 frames per second. This allows the camera operator and the video playback person to synchronize their two machines perfectly. Check with the camera department to verify their requirements.

Often, the company doing the video playback on the set will supervise the creation of the playback tapes. In these cases, all you need to do is provide the vendor with the film and track that needs to be transferred (making sure that it is spliced and cleaned very well). Each roll should be properly leadered and identified.

If you are going to be expediting the transfer, you should be sure that the telecine house doing the transfer can provide you with tapes that have the proper specifications. Then you will carefully splice and clean the material and send it to the telecine transfer house. You should include instructions to transfer at 24 frames per second. The video house will first make a 30 frames per second videotape and then copy it to another tape at the slower speed. If you can, try to view the 30 frames per second tape to make sure it is of acceptable quality in terms of color balance, sync and image quality. Then you can okay the final transfer.

Normally you would have the material transferred to a 3/4" tape but, occasionally, there is need for a different format. Super-VHS (S-VHS) and Beta are two common formats providing high enough quality for on-set playback. Remember that once the television image is played back and captured on film it will be very expensive to go back and correct the video image, so it is imperative that you get it right before it goes to the set for playback.

Foreign Systems

If you have been reading this book in sequential order, you will have noticed that there are many times when the organization will be up to the assistant. This results in almost every assistant having a slightly different way of organizing an editing room. It should come as no surprise to you then that editing systems in other countries vary from those I've described. If you are ever called upon to assist an editor from a foreign country (as I did with Gerry

Hambling on *Fame*) you will have to quickly learn the differences. Always keep in mind, however, that film is film and editing is editing. Though there are differences between the countries, they are mostly on the surface. Film is still spliced together by a person concerned with the aesthetics of editing.

That said, I will also add that an editor from England works in a slightly different manner than an editor in the United States. First, their table setup looks different. Rather than working with a pair of rewinds on their table they have a rewind only on the right side of the table. On the left they have something called a *horse*, a rack onto which the editor can slip many rolls of film that can then feed into the synchronizer. On either side of the synchronizer large holes have been cut in the table into which bags (exactly like those in a trim barrel) are hung. The English editor does a lot more of his or her work at the synchronizer and, as a result, needs to have receptacles for the film on either side. As an assistant, you will find yourself continually searching the bottom of these bags for lost trims or rolls of film. Often, you will find something there.

198

Trims and outs are stored together, by code numbers. This is made easier by the eight-digit coding system used there. As I mentioned briefly in the section of coding systems in Chapter 5, English editors use an eight-digit coding block on a *Moy* coding machine, not unlike the Acmade machines used in the United States. The numbers look something like 123D5678. This is a particularly good coding system because of the way takes are slated in England. Instead of using scene numbers and setup letters (such as Scene 12A, take 3), the English system begins with slate number one on the first day of shooting and continues sequentially each time a new set-up is done. Thus, if a film shoots twenty set-ups on the first day of shooting, they would be Slates 1 through 20 (such as Slate 15, take 2). The next day, they would pick up with Slate 21. In this system there is no relationship between the slate number and the scene number, but that is always evident from the lined script.

Each take is spot coded, as are the musical playbacks. For Slate 35, take 3, A camera, the slate mark would be coded 035A3000. If the next printed take is Slate 36, take 1, A camera, the slate mark would be coded 036A1000. If there was also a second camera printed on that take (or a B camera, as it is called) it would be coded 036B1000. This requires special attention during the coding process since each take must be coded by itself. As I've mentioned, on *Fame*, we hired an apprentice who did very little other than code the dailies and put away trims.

There is one big advantage to this process. Since the code number and the slate number are the same, one will immediately lead you to the other. If the editor wants to see another take on Slate 34, all you do is march to the place Slate 34 is kept and you will immediately see what is there. There is no need to look in a log for a code number first. That is another reason you do not store the trims and the outs separately, since the editor will be calling for both of them in the same way—by the slate number.

On the cinetab for a film shot in this manner I usually put the scene number that the scene is for (I also enter this information in the logbook). I put it up in the top part of the tab.

There are other differences in the English system. Trims and outs are not often stored in white two-piece boxes but in 1000-foot film cans. A notation as to what is inside is put onto the outside of the can using paper tape. Often, there are no cinetabs. Instead, a square piece of tape is placed on top of the roll of film as it sits in the can. This tape contains the information normally found on the cinetab. On *Fame*, I found this method to be less helpful to me than a cinetab so I decided to use tabs anyway. Again, everyone adapts the systems to his or her own use.

DIGITAL SPECIAL CASES

Other Editing Systems

As you might imagine, there are as many digital editing systems as there are film editing systems. Every month seems to bring new announcements of the latest, the cheapest, the most advanced, or the most complete computer editing system. Many of these systems will never see the light of day. A number of them *do* come out but are so riddled with computer bugs that they never catch on.

There are still other systems that have become popular outside of the world of feature films and Movies of the Week because of their flexibility and low cost. Eventually, these systems may become feasible for film work but for now, there are major problems using them on a project that will end up cutting negative.

Systems like the Media 100, TurboCube, D-Vision, and Adobe Premiere specialize in creating programs with very high image quality or requiring numerous special effects. Images can be layered on top of one another, creating an almost endless number of visual possibilities. In many cases, the output from these systems is so good it is possible to record it directly to a high quality tape (like Digital Beta) and send it straight to the television networks for airing.

There are, however, two major problems with these systems if you want to use them for film work. First, they work exclusively in the 30 frame per second world of video. They usually can't create the film cut lists necessary in order to cut negative, and they don't carry all the sound and picture information that a typical FLEx or Keylog file (for instance) contains. The second problem is the amount of storage needed to digitize images of this quality makes both the performance and the price of the storage prohibitive for features.

Still, price and image quality make these systems particularly attractive to a certain group of editors and producers.

Recently, a few outside programs have been developed to take on the task of translating the 30 frame pictures into usable 24 frame lists. Programs like Slingshot or Avid's Matchback require inputting all of the data from your original source material (any normal telecine file will do). When you have finished editing, you can create the film cut lists, opticals lists and a host of other paperwork using this outside program, with almost as little hassle as the Avid and Lightworks 24 frame programs.

Though these programs have been used on some television and low-budget shows, their usefulness has not been fully tested. There are also questions about whether it is ever advisable to edit a film show in a 30 frame environment, even if you can translate it back to 24 frames per second at the end. When you are editing in a 24 frame project you can actually *see* the precise frames of your cuts. Because of the 3:2 pulldown issue (as we discussed in Chapter 4A) a conversion from the EDLs in a 30 frames per second project to the cut list needed in a 24 frames per second project on film can never be exactly correct. There is just no way that the conversion can be made precisely on a frame line every time. Still, when they are able to work in a 24 frame per second world, it will probably be only a matter of time before the use of these systems becomes technically and financially feasible for larger projects.

201

Shooting on Digital Tape

In recent years, digital video cameras of very high quality, such as Panasonic's DVC-PRO or JVC's Digital-S, have been used to shoot material that doesn't have to look exactly like film, but needs to look better than standard videotape. The small size and weight of the camera is also an asset, making it possible to shoot in places a 35mm camera can't access. The quality of the digital image, when transformed to 35mm film, looks much better than a standard video image.

The Panasonic DVC-PRO system also has a laptop editing system some people are using as a final editing station, or as source decks to transfer the images into Avids or Lightworks.

For some films, the digital video format makes transferring material into high-end digital effects systems like the Inferno, Henry or the Flame extremely easy.

Using Outside Programs

One of the advantages to editing in the computer world is that there are a host of other programs, not included in your digital editing system, able to enhance the look and sound of your film. Many of these programs create special effects, others generate 3-D animation, while others can create sound effects that are not possible on the normal picture editing computer.

Programs like Adobe After Effects, Boris Effects, ICEfx, Elastic Reality, Morph and Final Effects can change the moving image over time. I've used these programs to pan a close-up still shot of a moon to match a camera pan in the original photography. I was then able to combine the two in my editing machine creating a shot where the camera panned down from the moon in the sky to reveal a movie theatre on the ground. Many editing houses use these programs to create much more complex special effects with budgets lower than ever before. Some of the special effects in "Babylon 5" and the other Star Trek spin-off television series are created this way.

There are a class of programs that allow you to paint or change an image. Adobe Photoshop, KPT Bryce, StrataStudio and Ray Dream all accept images exported from your editing machine. You can then manipulate them and import them back into your film. Be aware that these programs work on still frames only.

Finally, there are programs like Deck II, CyberSound, Digitrax, SoundEdit and Sound Designer able to take sounds you have in your system and distort them in ways that you might need for temporary mixes—echo, strong equalization, reversing sounds, etc. There are various computer file formats that can encode sounds (AIFF, WAV and Sound Designer II, are a few). Not all computer editing programs can import all of these formats but most sound programs can create most of them. Make sure you create the files in the format your editing machine uses.

All of these programs are vastly more complex than the sound and visual effects portions of the typical Lightworks or Avid. Some of them are so complex that very few picture editors will be able to learn them (as well as knowing their own machines) with enough proficiency to make them worthwhile. In fact, many of these programs are used by CGI and sound professionals who then give you the final files for import into your machine (for more details on this, look ahead to Chapter 10A). Still, as an assistant editor, it pays to have some familiarity with a few of these programs. Occasionally one of them may be useful in the editing room. At the very least, this knowledge will be one more way differentiate yourself from the rest of the pack of job-seeking assistants.

Stock Footage

Stock footage is another area where editing on a digital machine can help the process tremendously. Because a 35mm print is not needed initially, it is very easy and cheap to try out new material within the cut. All you need to do is digitize whatever shots Wendy thinks might be useful from the sample tapes the stock house will send you. She will then be able to experiment with every one without incurring any costs at all.

One or two annoying little problems may crop up when you digitize stock footage into your machine. First, since the material is not being batch digitized from a FLEx or similar file, no film information will be digitized with the image. No key numbers will go into your database, and no film reel numbers. In fact, there is a good chance that the videotape you receive from the stock house won't even have time code on the LTC or VITC it to input into the system. Unless you put time code on track two of their videotape before you digitize it, you won't have any time code to put into your machine. This will make redigitizing impossible. There will probably be a visual time code burned into the image but this code is only a reference number for the stock house, used to locate the exact footage you wish to purchase from them to be put on film.

In addition, there won't be a notation as to which frame of the tape is the A-frame, so your footage will probably appear jittery. Every time a new stock shot appears on the stock house's tape it is likely that the A-frame will change. You can choose to fix this, if it annoys you. To do this, you will need to find the A-frame on each digitized stock shot. If you've digitized a number of them together, you will not be able to fix each one individually, so you might want to consider digitizing each shot separately.

We discussed finding the A-frame back in Chapter 4A. You will do it the same way here. As you rock the source videotape forward field by field, the A-frame should have no timecode change between its two fields. The B-frame, made up of three fields, will have no timecode change between the first two fields but will have a change between fields two and three. The C-frame will have two fields with a timecode change between them. The D-frame, made of three fields, will have a change in between fields one and two but not between fields two and three.

Once you've identified the A-frame you can digitize the material that way. Lightworks allows you to reset the frame that is considered the A-frame after you've already digitized the material, a great time-saving device.

You can choose to name the digitized shots anything you want,

I find it useful to label them with a name which that identifies the shot and the stock house you've received it from (you should also put the information about the stock house within the database that will be created when you digitize the shot, as well as the tape number it was digitized from). A shot of a galaxy exploding that you received from The Stock House could be called "GalaxyExplo1 (TSH)."

You should keep a record of where all of the stock shots came from, within the editing software and in a separate log.

Once Wendy and Adam have finished editing the film you will need to order an IP of the stock shot just as we discussed in Chapter 7. You will need to supply them with the same information—shot number and time code used. The shot number and source will come from the information you entered while digitizing. The time code will come from the visual burn-in on the shot itself.

Musicals

In Chapter 7 we discussed how to set up musical playback takes using 35mm film. It should come as no surprise to you, by this point, that setting up for musicals on a digital system is both easier and harder.

Let me briefly reiterate the film process. A playback master is created, which is a copy of the music on its own 35mm mag. This master is coded. Every picture take with playback sync is then match coded, usually on the opposite edge of the film, with the same code found on the playback master. This way, every frame of picture with lip or instrument sync can easily be lined up against the matching frame of the song on the playback master.

The biggest problem when working on a digital system is that, unlike 35mm film, there is no way you can drop a second set of code numbers onto the picture. There are, however, a few other ways of determining sync. The method you choose will depend on how many takes of playback have been shot and in what formats.

On a concert film, for instance, there are usually multiple cameras shooting the action simultaneously. When the dailies come back from telecine, there will be no common coding between them (unless you've sunk dailies on film and instructed the telecine house to burn in inked code numbers that you've lined up to be in sync). Many of the top editing systems allow Wendy to lock together up to four takes and run them in sync with each other. Avid has a Group Clips option and Lightworks has the Heavyworks machine. Using these systems, it is easy to lock all the multiple cameras up at a common sync point and have them run in sync throughout the rest of take, whether you are viewing at sound speed or in fast motion.

Typically, you can use the slate at the head of each take to line up all of the takes, provided a common slate has been clapped among all of the takes. Sometimes, however, the cameras are located too far apart to have common slates. In that case, you will probably be able to use the time code from the source sound tapes for your line-up. As we discussed in Chapter 7, each camera is sunk up to the same track. As a result, all the sunk-up tracks will have the same time code numbers.

Once you have found the sync points, some assistants like to create a new edit of each take. The first one or two channels of sound will be the same as the original take, but the playback master will be cut into the second or third audio sound track. Each of these edits will be then treated the way we discussed in Chapter 5A about handling takes you've re-sunk. You assign each of these takes a new take number. 19-4 would become 19-4* or "19-4resync," 19G-2 would become 19G-2* or "19G-2resync." This new take replaces the original take in Scene 19's bin or gallery. Wendy then edits using these new takes.

When Wendy goes to cut in take 19-4* she will be able to determine each frame's musical sync point by looking at the time code on the channel containing the copy of the playback master (either audio channel two or three) and lining it up against the play-back master itself, which she will have placed on an open audio channel in her edit.

When you think about it, this procedure is very analogous to what you do on film—create a way of organizing the picture takes so they have the playback master code numbers attached to them. In fact, a good film assistant will always be able to adapt (though not copy, of course) the systems they have developed for film, to the digital world.

Location Shooting

As I've mentioned, Wendy and you will not be going on location for *Silent Night*. If you are printing film dailies for screening on location, you can handle these location screenings just as we discussed in Chapter 7. Some productions will decide not to set up a screening room on location even if you are printing film dailies. Instead, they will watch the videotaped dailies during those two weeks.

Obviously, if you are not printing any film, nothing will change except the traffic flow of negative and production sound to the lab and telecine house, and the delivery of the dailies tapes to the location.

. . . .

On some productions, the editor is asked to be on location so the director can work with him or her during the shooting process. Just as we discussed in Chapter 7, it will be up to you to create a completely functioning editing room there. Many rental houses can pack their digital editing machines into large wheeled carrying cases, such as Anvil cases, for easy transport. Someone from the rental house will usually come and set up the system on location for you, but the portability of digital editing machines makes setting up an editing room in Bora Bora much less stressful than in the days when you needed to ship crates of Moviolas, editing benches and KEMs.

You still need to make sure you have everything you always need in a functioning editing room. Supplies like 3 1/2" computer disks may be easy to get in many places in the world, but your Zip or Magneto-Optical disks may not. Make sure you are fully prepared for the duration of the location shoot.

```
01:02:15:00
01:02:18:05
01:02:21:10
01:02:24:15
01:02:27:20
01:02:30:25
01:02:33:00
01:02:36:05
01:02:38:10
```

CUTTING AWAY

At some point, usually just as you think that you won't be able to handle any more dailies, the shooting will stop. The producers will have a wrap party, the requests from the set for frame clips or special screenings will end, the early morning laboratory delivery problems will cease and the focus of the film will shift to the editing room—right where you are.

It's a rather strange feeling to suddenly be in the spotlight. During the shooting you find that the editing room people are often the last to know about many things—adjustments in the shooting schedule, changes in dailies screenings times, and many other things. The director is, if not exactly a stranger, seen very rarely. It's just been you, Wendy, and Philip.

Now, everything is going to be different. Adam will be coming to the editing room a lot more often (some directors, like Milos Forman, are in the editing room all the time; others, like Alan Parker, visit it much less frequently—it depends upon the relationship between the editor and the director) and this will change your routine. Dailies will stop and this will change your routine. The editing will get more intense and this will really change your routine.

Balancing the Cut Reels

As Wendy has been cutting *Silent Night, Silent Cowboy*, she has been accumulating individual cut scenes. After a while she will have put together enough consecutive scenes to build them together into a reel. Very often she will build these reels as she cuts. Sometimes you will notice, because of the order in which she has had to cut the scenes, there are now several consecutive cut scenes not yet

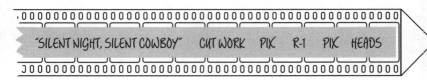

FIGURE 8.1 *Head leader for cut picture (to be written in black). The usual adjustments would be made for track leader.*

been put together. She may want to cut them together herself or she may ask you to do it. As the scenes are put together onto projection reels there are several things to keep in mind.

As usual, the head and the tail of each reel should be leadered. The head leader should look something like Figure 8.1 (the example given here is for picture only). Again, use black ink for picture and red for track.

I like to have my assistants splice five or six feet of clear leader at the beginning of all of the head leaders. This provides some protection for the leaders, which tend to take quite a beating during projection and rewinding. On the end of the clear leader, attach a short bit of white tape. On this tape you can write the scene numbers included in this reel. As the reels change in length and content it will be easy to take this tape off and replace with an up-to-date one.

208

The next thing to remember is a limitation on reel length. They should not exceed 1000 feet by much more than 25 feet or so. However, they should be larger than 700 feet to give the projectionist enough time to thread up the next reel. I like to leave the reels between 800 and 900 feet. As the film is recut, scenes may be rearranged or lengthened, building your reels between 800 and 900 feet gives you up to 200 feet on each reel to add footage later without totally reordering them.

This determination of reel length and content is called *balancing the reels* and it will become quite important later on in the editing process. For now, however, it is most important to balance the film in a way to help expedite the handling of it in the editing and projection rooms.

Another thing to know about when you balance the reels is something called a *changeover*. These are the cues for the projectionist letting him or her know exactly when to make the changeover from the reel on one projector to the reel on the other (projection rooms have two projectors). There are two sets of circles you will see on the screen. On screen each set of circles actually appears as a single circle, but to make each visible to the human eye, each circle is actually a series of circles appearing in the same spot on four succeeding frames. The first set cues the projectionist to begin running the other projector, though not to turn on its light and sound. It is called the *motor cue* because it cues the starting of the second projector's motor. The second set is called the *changeover cue* and signals the projectionist to turn the picture and sound off on the first projector at the exact moment that he turns the picture and sound on the second one—the projector containing the new reel.

Human reflexes being what they are, it would be impossible for the projectionist to make the changeover exactly from the last frame of one reel to the very first frame of the next. The adopted standard is to give the projectionist one second from the changeover cue to the end of the reel "just in case he misses it." Reaction time is supposed to be approximately two-thirds of a second; the extra time is "just in case."

In reality, you will rarely have a screening with perfect changeovers, so it is wise to plan for these eventualities. I try to put changeovers in places where a missed half second will not be so crucial. As a result, I usually put my reel changes in between scenes. In addition, I try to choose a place where the outgoing scene has a pause at its end, and the incoming scene has no dialogue in its first second.

209

Some editors accomplish this by adding *changeover tails* to the end of each reel. These are 24 additional frames (some editors prefer to add 16 frames) beyond the last frame where you would normally make the picture cut to the next scene. Often, the assistant editor will add these tails and be responsible for removing them from the scene if the reel balance should change so the scene no longer comes at the end of the reel. If you have to put the changeover tails on, you should make sure that the piece of footage you add does not contain any movement of actors that would be distracting, and that the matching length of track you add is composed completely of tone. Sometimes it will be impossible to add 24 (or even 16) frames. In these cases you should add as many frames as you can.

Then, after the reel balance has been decided, you can mark the changeovers. Since the balance will be changing a lot before the reels are *locked* (finished, with no more cutting to be done) it is important that these changeover marks be very...well...changeable. Some assistants use grease pencil to make a slash mark extending from the upper right-hand corner of the frame a short way into the frame itself (*see* Figure 8.2). Others like to use a hand hole-puncher and punch out little dots from a roll of paper tape. These dots can then be stuck onto the frame, but easily removed when necessary.

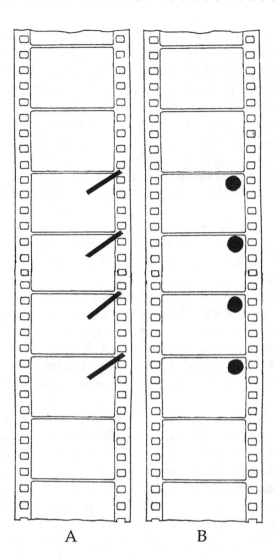

A   B

FIGURE 8.2 *Two types of changeovers. In method A a grease pencil slash mark is drawn. In method B a small stick-on dot (often made from a piece of punched-out paper tape) is placed on the film. In either case you must make sure that the mark extends well past the 1.85 cutoff so that the projectionist will be able to see it during projection.*

This method looks the neatest and has the advantage of looking more like the standard changeover marks (hollow circles scratched into the film). If you ever go into a screening room with a projectionist only used to projecting finished films these circular changeovers will be more recognizable to him. This will lower the possibility of an embarrassing mistake during a screening. Always make sure that your marks extend far enough into the frame to be seen, even if you are projecting in a 1.85 screen ratio.

There is a standard for where the changeover marks (whatever kind you use) go on the film (*see* Figure 8.3).

You need only mark your picture for changeovers. Visible cue marks would make little sense on the track.

As more and more reels are built up, Wendy and Adam will want to screen the film more often in a screening room than on an editing machine. It will usually be up to you, as the assistant, to book these screenings. It is very helpful if you know as many screening rooms in town as possible and the relative merits and demerits of each. Notice, for instance, which rooms have sharper focus, and check out the sound quality of each room (some rooms have more treble than others, some have more bass). All of this will be important as you analyze your movie.

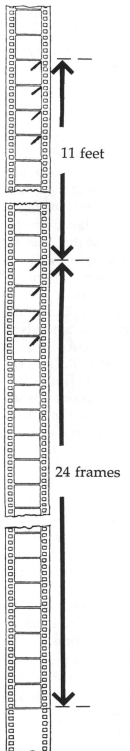

11 feet

24 frames

FIGURE 8.3 The placement of changeover cues. The motor cue begins 12'08 before the LFOA. The changeover cue comes 1'08 (one second) before it.

211

In a studio situation on a Hollywood lot, you will usually be assigned an available screening screen. Often you will have no choice in the matter. However, even here it is helpful to know which rooms and which projectionists are better than others.

Keeping Track

As the film begins to take shape you will want to keep a list of just what scenes are included on each screening reel. This list is called the reel *breakdown* or reel *continuity* (*see* Figure 8.4). On it you will list the sequential reel numbers, the scene numbers included on that reel, and the LFOA. These initials stand for "Last frame of action," which is the footage (from the 0'00 start mark) up to and including the last frame of picture before the tail leader begins. At the bottom of the sheet the total length of the film in both length and time is given. Note that, since the LFOA includes the Academy leader, you must subtract 11'15 from each reel in order to find out the running length of each of the reels. Sometimes, the LFOA is called the EOR (End Of Reel) or the LFOP (Last Frame Of Picture).

212

Some assistants also like to make a slightly more complicated reel continuity. An example of one is shown in Figure 8.5 and you can see that it includes the short scene descriptions as well as the scene numbers. This makes the list rather difficult to refer to quickly but its comprehensiveness will come in very handy.

On recent films, I've used a continuity like the one in Figure 8.6, printing it out on my computer. Scenes removed from the film during the recutting are listed in italics. Reel breaks are noted by drawing thick lines between the scenes where the reel changes.

Once you've determined the footages of each reel you should determine the length of the complete film in minutes and seconds. Add up the lengths of all the reels (remember, the picture length is 11'15 shorter than the LFOA), then use a footage/time chart (*see* Appendix I), a Reddy-Eddy, or a calculator to convert to time. There are specialized calculators for film and video that can easily convert 16mm or 35mm footage to time. They also include time code and a host of other video and film options. Some editors, myself included, have automated this conversion on an editing room computer. There are also small computer programs that can do the same thing.

One of the uses for this kind of continuity comes after rough-cut screenings. After the film has been assembled into its first full cut, it is customary (nay, it is necessary) to take it into a screening room and see just how well it plays "on the big silver" (as one director I've worked with used to call it). This first cut will often

CONTINUITY   1·7·00
Date

Reel	Scenes	LFOA	Time
1	1 - 26	930 + 07	10:12.3
2	27 - 35 PT	944 + 05	10:21.6
3	35 PT - 52	904 + 03	9:54.8
4	54 - 72	994 + 02	10:54.8
5	73 - 85	934 + 15	10:15.3
6	86 - 102 PT	993 + 09	10:54.4
7	102 PT - 113	955 + 11	10:29.2
8	114 - 130	973 + 07	10:41.0
9	132 - 156	943 + 04	10:20.9
10	160 - 181	978 + 03	10:44.2
11			
12			
13			
14			
15			

Total Length   9432 + 12
Total Time   1:44:48.5

FIGURE 8.4 A reel breakdown. The length of each reel is often substituted for the LFOA (the length is 11'15 less than the LFOA). The time is exclusive of the Academy leaders.

"Silent Night, Silent Cowboy"

Director's Cut
January 7, 2000

Reel One

1	Credit montage
2	On the set
4	Backstage
5	Driving home
6	Abby's empty room
7	Driving to work the next day
8	"Did the zoom look okay?"
9	Alone in the parking lot
10	Abby arrives home and gets shocked
11	"Evening, Mr. DeMille"
12	The hot dog stand
17	Abby meets Sean
18	Abby and Sean back at Abby's
19	"Jimmy the Baby"
20	Cowboy and James fight
22	Lunch with Genie
23	"The rushes are a disaster"
24	Parking lot rewrites
25	Phone call from Genie
26	"Have it out with him"

Reel Two

27	Abby and James have it out.
28-30	Abby wanders about
31	Dream montage
32-33	Abby in the hills/L.A. at night
34	"Can I make a nuisance of myself?"
35pt1	Abby/Sean at Sean's — pt I

Reel Three

35pt2	Abby/Sean at Sean's — pt II
36	"I can't get out of bed"
37	Phone call home
39-42	Going home
44	Abby sits in front of his home
45	The family inside
46	Abby Returns
47	Birthday party
48	Abby flies back to L.A.
A49	"The yellow zone is for load- ing"
49	Abby's still empty room
50	Sean and Bob talk
52	The three musketeers party

Reel Four

54	Driving to work happy
55	Redo the bar fight
56	James is happy
57	The happy parking lot
58	Bob and Abby at "La Bar"
59	"La Bar" backstage
60-61	Abby writes, day into night
62	Abby, Michael, Uri talk
63	"Great dailies!!"
64	Abby & Sean's eat Mexican
65	Abby writes/Sean writes
66	Sean tries to sleep
67	Drive to the baseball game

Reel Five

68	Outside Dodger Stadium
69	"Those Dodgers!"
70	In the stands
72	Return from the ballgame
73	They watch the sports channel
74-75	Abby and Sean on the roof
76	"No dailies today"
78	"We've got a problem"
79	Abby rewriting
80	Abby at Pink's
81	Abby at Musso's
82	Abby at City
83	Abby writes into the dawn

Reel Six

84	Abby and J.B. - "A two base hit"
85	"Fuck him, it was a home run"
86	Abby with Sean at observatory
87	Abby rewrites for a homer
88	Abby & J.B. - "You try harder."
90	Champagne corks don't pop

Reel Seven

91	Coke cans pile up
92	Abby sees old movies
93	Studio Meeting success
94	"It's just like it was!"
95	Back On The Set
97	Dailies look good.

"Silent Night, Silent Cowboy"   January 7, 2000 Director's Cut

Page 1

214

FIGURE 8.5 A Reel Continuity (breakdown). Those scene numbers missing from the list were either not shot or cut from the film during editing. Note how scenes which bridge two reels (such as scene 35) are handled.

	25	Phone call from Genie
	26	"Have it out with him"
R-2	27	Abby and James have it out.
	28-30	Abby wanders about
	31	Dream montage
	32-33	Abby in the hills/L.A. at night
	34	"Can I make a nuisance of myself?"
R-3	35	Abby/Sean at Sean's ————————
	36	"I can't get out of bed"
	37	Phone call home
	38	*Mom goes for the liquor*
	39-42	Going home
	43	*Traffic on the 405*
	44	Abby sits in front of his home
	45	The family inside
	46	Abby Returns
	47	Birthday party
	48	Abby flies back to L.A.
	A49	"The yellow zone is for loading"
	49	Abby's still empty room
	50	Sean and Bob talk
	52	The three musketeers party
R-4	54	Driving to work happy

"Silent Night" Continuity   January 7, 2000   Page 2
Scenes in italics have been lifted from the film

215

FIGURE 8.6 *One page from an expanded reel continuity. Though this version of a continuity will take up more pages than the one in FIGURE 8.5 if it is taped to the wall, it is easier to read from your editing bench. It also lists every scene shot, whether in the current version of the film or not, making it easier to discuss lifts which are listed in italics. Note that some directors and studio executives don't like to see lifted scenes at all so you might want to make a second list with no lifts. Notice how reel breaks are shown, as well as scenes which bridge reels (such as Scene 35). On the last page of the continuity I always list the running time.*

include everything that was shot and so it will normally seem too long and quite boring.

First-cut screenings are always very tense moments for everyone involved in the film editing process. Directors often get very insecure or irritable. Editors begin to worry about minutiae (like the number of people coming to the screening and whether the film has been rewound properly). Usually, no one wants the producer around because this is where the film's worst faults will be all too visible. Studio personnel are almost never invited to these screenings (they usually see the film only after the director has completed his contractually guaranteed cut).

As an assistant you can minimize some of the craziness by making sure the film is in proper shape for projection. Be sure the changeovers are on every reel (except, obviously, the last one) and in the proper places. Make sure the head and tail leaders are properly labeled so that the reels are projected in their proper order.

Before the screening you should check for sync. You should also check both the film and the track for splices. To check a reel for sync, put it up in the synchronizer (some assistants like to do this while they are balancing, or rebalancing, the reels) in sync at the start mark. As you roll through the footage, check that the picture codes are in sync with their matching track codes (using the ink numbers). Often Wendy will have pre-lapped, post-lapped, or cheated the track. *Pre-laps* are places where the track precedes the picture cut, *post-laps* are places where the track run past the picture cut. *Cheated track* is sound that has been cut in opposite to a completely different piece of picture. Every time the sound code number is out of sync with the picture code you should check and see whether it is a mistake on Wendy's part. In my experience, it is much easier to be out of sync by a frame or two on films cut on a flatbed than on an upright Moviola. In cases where Wendy has deliberately slid a piece of track she should mark the correct sync code number on the track. This will give you a clue that the cheated track is not a mistake. It will also give you a proper sync point for the piece of film.

To check splices on the reels you should run the picture or track (do not do them together) slowly on your rewinds *without* going through the synchronizer. With your free hand, gently pinch the edges of the film so it bows slightly as it goes through your hand. You will be able to feel whether a splice extends beyond the edges of the film (such splices will have to be shaved level with the film) or whether there are any broken sprocket holes that need to be repaired. As you are running the reel through your fingers, make a visual inspection of the splices to be sure there is not a gap between

216

the incoming and outgoing pieces of film or track. Remake any splices that might jump or break during projection.

In addition, if the film was cut on a flatbed, chances are good that Wendy has only spliced the film on one side. Projectors, being the tough machines they are, will chew up film that isn't spliced on both sides. So, along with everything else that you and Philip will have to do to prepare for the screening, you will have to splice the second side of the film. This process is called *back-splicing*. In some cases, film that has been spliced across eight sprockets will go through well-maintained studio projectors without back-splicing. Don't risk this on screenings in other places, though. It's not worth the small chance of an interrupted screening.

After you have checked the splices and changeovers, you should thoroughly clean the film with a film cleaner like *Ecco*, being careful not to wipe off any of Wendy's marks for optical effects (we will learn about these marks in Chapter 10). This is a rather painstaking and disagreeable task that involves soaking a Webril wipe with Ecco and running the film through it v-e-r-r-r-y slowly. Cleaning it slowly allows the Ecco enough time to evaporate off the film before you wind it up on the right rewind. If it is wound up too fast the Ecco will leave streak marks on the film that are almost worse than the dirt it removed. When you are finished cleaning the film with Ecco, rewind it back to the head through a velvet to buff it up. Clean the track with a velvet (no Ecco, please, as it will dissolve the track).

217

You will probably find it helpful to have a screening check list (*see* Figure 8.7) posted near the assistant's table to keep you apprised of just what still needs to be done in preparation.

Then, pack up all of the reels in order into some sort of packing cartons and get them to the screening room. Bring along several copies of your reel breakdown with you, as well as a paper listing the running time of the film (everyone will want to know the length of the picture).

After the screening there is bound to be a meeting between Adam and Wendy. During the meeting you should be listening to what everyone feels are the film's major strengths and weaknesses. Take careful notes as to the proposed changes. These will include what scenes should be dropped from the film, what alternate takes need to be used, what scenes need to be moved to different places in the film, what sequences need to have major recutting done on them, and a host of other suggestions. All of these points require work from you to prepare for the director and editor. Be sure you know what it is they want done, and when they want it.

At this point it is wise, if the film has the budget to do so, to

SCREENING CHECKLIST

Date __1-7-00__

Reel Number	Pix & Splices	Trk & Splices	COs	Clean Pix	Clean Track	Footage (f/ 1st frame)
1	✓	✓	✓	✓	✓	918+08
2	✓	✓	✓	✓	✓	932+06
3	✓	✓	✓	✓	✓	892+04
4	✓	✓	✓	✓	✓	982+03
5	✓			✓	✓	923+00
6		✓			✓	981+10
7						943+12
8	✓	✓	✓	✓	✓	961+08
9	✓	✓	✓	✓	✓	931+05
10	✓	✓	✓	✓	✓	966+04
11						
12						
13						

Total Length __9432+12__

Total Time __1:44:48.5__

FIGURE 8.7 *A checklist is very handy to make sure that everything that needs to be prepared before a screening is done. Note that in this example all of the reels have been completely prepared except for reel five (picture only has been prepared), six (track only has been prepared), seven (nothing has been prepared).*

make a copy of the entire film. In the past, this was done by striking what is called a *slop print* or *dupe* of the entire film. This is a copy of the picture and a 1:1 track copy of the soundtrack to be stored as a reference. Sometimes, in recutting, a scene will get worse rather than better. It is helpful to have a record of the way the scene was before it was recut so it will be easier to reconstruct properly.

You will make these copies at a lab (for the picture), normally different from your dailies processing lab, and your sound transfer house (for the track). When you send the work picture reels to the lab for duping, you should note on your purchase order that you want the dupe to print through the edges. This means the dupe will contain both the filmed images as well as all of the key and code numbers on the edges of the film. If you ever need to reconstruct a cut, as we will discuss in Chapter 9, you will need these numbers.

When you order your sound dupe, you will ask for it at a 1:1 (read "one to one") level. This means the sound house won't add any equalization or change any volume levels in the transfer. Put a one frame-long beep at 9'00 in the track leader. When the track dupe comes from the sound house, you will be able to hear this beep (also called a *pop*), mark the frame, put it in the synchronizer at 9'00, then roll back to 0'00. You should put a start mark at that frame so it can be properly threaded up should you ever need to screen it.

More recently, productions have avoided the expense of dup-ing a film and track by making videocassettes of the film instead. This also makes it easy to strike extra copies of the film for people who need to see it (to take notes, to prepare publicity, etc.). Though it is not easy to take the videocassette and check exact cuts, it does preserve a record of the general approach to the cut scenes. If Adam or Wendy ever need to answer a question like "How was that scene cut back when I liked it more?" it will be easy enough to pop the tape in and check how the older cut went.

It has become common practice in recent years for videotaped copies of the film to be struck after almost every screening. Produc-ers, writers, the director, and studio executives (when they finally see the film) will need a copy of the film to refer to when they make their notes. There is always the fear that someone will take one of these videotapes and make copies of it for the public. You should keep track of where all of the tapes are going. You can use a form similar to the Tape Request Log I will describe later in Chapter 9A (*see* Figure 9A.2), or make up a simpler one. Needless to say, since the film is still a work in progress (without proper music or sound effects and with the editing still in a state of flux), it is important that the tapes be accounted for.

To this end, some studios require the assistant or apprentice to sit at the telecine house while the video transfer is being made. In addition, the videotapes are made with type superimposed over the image (usually identifying the production company and date of the transfer) as well some random time code "burned in" over the picture. The Walt Disney Company requires the initials of all of those receiving the tape to be superimposed as well.

These visual obstructions make the tape less attractive to bootleggers and decrease the chances of copies of the tape showing up for sale in Hollywood or Times Square.

DIGITALLY CUTTING AWAY

Eventually, as the shooting stops and the director's interest starts to veer over to the editing room, you will need to get the film ready for its first, editor's cut, screening. Though Adam may have seen many of the scenes Wendy has sent to the set on videotape, there is no way to really know how the movie plays without screening the film as a whole.

The editor's cut will usually be due for screening anywhere from two days to two weeks after the wrap of shooting. This is all dependent on the budget of the film, as well as the complexity of the footage. If you and Wendy are lucky, the biggest, most complex, scenes in the film will not be the last ones shot. However, all too often, this is the case and you will be inundated with footage in the last week of shooting. Often, there are also numerous *pick-up shots* and *second-unit* photography all coming in during the final days.

Additionally, scenes shot at different locations meant to be cut together (like two sides of a telephone conversation), cannot be cut until all parts are complete. All these factors, as well as the amount of footage Adam has shot, will influence just how long Wendy will take to finish her cut.

At some point, Wendy will need to finish cutting and screen the film for Adam. Some directors will simply sit down at the editing machine and watch the output, section by section. Other directors will not want to watch it with the editor, but will need a taped output of the entire film. Still others will only want to watch the movie projected in 35mm on a screen (though this is getting increasingly rare). Your thorough work preparing the footage before and during digitizing will now pay off, for if you've done all of the preliminary work properly you should be able to meet any of these scenarios easily and without error.

Preparing for the Screening

In Chapter 6A, we saw how you prepared outputs of individual scenes. Preparing for the first screening is no different. If you've organized all of the various edits with the Version 100 system, there should be one bin or gallery with all of Wendy's latest edits. There might be sequences with multiple versions so be careful to select the latest versions (a version 102 will usually supersede version 101, for instance), making sure that *all* of the scenes in the film are included in the order Wendy wants them screened (it is possible that she may have rearranged some of the scenes during the editing process). Check with Wendy if you have any doubts whatsoever about which version to use.

If you are not going to be matching your cut back onto film, you do not have to worry very much about balancing reels at this point. Because creating new edits requires very little work and almost no computer memory, you can leave your sequences in whatever form Wendy has cut them. You will be able to build a new edit made up of a combination of all of her sequences and do the screening and playout from that. In fact, it will probably be better to screen in overly long sections, rather than breaking everything down into 10 minute reels.

222

Ideally, you want to string the entire film together into one long edit so Adam can see the film without a break. Unfortunately, there are a few problems with this approach. The first is a technical one. Computer editing machines store all the instructions for an entire edit in their memory. The longer the edit is, the more memory required for these instructions. This will slow down the playback of the edit. Sometimes, if there are a lot of cuts in a sequence (including both picture and sound edits), the computer's memory will become so overtaxed that it will not be able to play back the scene properly and the image will appear to *stutter*. The picture image will appear to momentarily freeze then pick up playing a second or two later.

If you are going to need to make more than one tape of the film you generally will want to make a master tape and strike copies from that master tape. Since VHS copies from VHS master tapes look terrible, you will usually need to playout onto a better format master tape, usually 3/4" or Beta. Most films will not fit onto one of those tapes. As a result, you will need to break your film down into hour-long segments.

The ideal lengths for your individual reels, at this stage, would be no longer than 56-58 minutes (you'll want to leave some room at the head of each reel). Obviously, if you are going to match 35mm film to your edit, you should balance your reels in the ten minute sections that we discussed in Chapter 8. We will talk about creating these film reels in a minute.

After you have balanced the reels in whatever length you have decided on, you will need to check the picture for duplicate or re-used frames. When the negative is eventually cut, any frames reused in the video edit will not be available on film. This will create a big problem if it isn't caught early.

Most 24 frame editing systems have a command for identifying reused frames. When you click on it, you will be given a visual indication of the takes reusing frames. Another item that these commands check for is for frame *cutbacks*. If Wendy has used a shot and then returns to the same shot at another time, she will need to leave at least one unused frame between the two shots (I prefer to leave two) to account for the frame that will be lost when the negative cutter attaches the shots to their adjacent shots. Since cutting negative requires destroying one frame next to each cut, if Wendy hasn't left room for these cutbacks the negative cutter will be unable to exactly match her edit. So you should always be checking for these cutback and reused frames. When you find them, check with Wendy to see how she wants to recut the picture to correct the problem.

223

Another of your tasks is checking the dialogue tracks for sync and holes, as we discussed in Chapter 7A. Wendy might also give you the task of adding sound effects and music to the edit (I like to cut the music myself, leaving the sound effects work for my assistant, but as I've mentioned many times before, every editor works differently).

Checking dialogue sync on the Avid and Lightworks is very easy; the machine will highlight areas where the sync is incorrect as well as listing the number of frames that the track is ahead or behind the picture. Checking sync on sound effects and music is much more difficult, since these sounds weren't digitized in with the picture. There are, however, some short cuts to help you out. You can add cue points or locators to these tracks and type in the matching picture code number. A slightly more complicated, but more permanent method, is to copy a small piece of the sync dialogue track and cut it onto the head of the sound effect or music cue in sync with its matching picture. You can then adjust the volume of this little piece down to zero. This piece of silent track will be treated as a piece of dialogue, and the machine will note when and how much it is out of sync. If the effect or music cue slips out of sync, you can easily see it, as well as the amount it has slipped, and adjust to correct the sync.

Presently, most editing machines can play back four tracks at one time (you can edit on many more but will only be able to *hear* four at one time). As an editor, I usually cut the sound so the first two tracks are dialogue, leaving the third and the fourth for sound effects and music. I try to keep the music to the last channel but it is often necessary to segue from one piece of music into another, forcing me to also use the third track for music. This makes filling tracks and mixing down the sound on playout a much simpler situation. On the Lightworks and the latest Avids, the timeline will scroll with the output, letting you see just what sounds are on what tracks, acting almost like a cue sheet. This will make the output easier.

As the number of playable tracks increases, we can probably expect to see more complicated mixes as you output the scene. For now, the complexity of your mix will be determined by Wendy's and Adam's needs. A good rule of thumb is that the more people who are going to see the tape (and the less they are familiar with the movie) the more your output will need music and sound effects.

224

In addition to adding sounds and music, you should also be cleaning up the dialogue tracks that Wendy has cut, removing any unwanted sounds and replacing them with proper tone. You should also be listening, under headphones, for places where the cut between two tracks is not smooth. When you find edits like this, you should try and clean up the transition as best as possible.

It is a good idea to work on a copy of the complete sequence so you will always have the back-up to return to in case you mess something up so badly you can't get back to it.

If Adam and Wendy are simply going to watch the playout without needing any tapes, you are done with your work. In most cases, however, Adam is going to want to take a tape home with him, even if he is going to watch the film in the editing room with Wendy. In that case you will need to prepare the edit for a playout.

Playouts are done differently depending upon the machine you have been editing on. There are, however, certain similarities between all of the systems. If copies from your playout are to be made at the same color and sound levels, it is essential that the picture and sound have some sort of reference at the beginning of the tapes. To do that you should attach, to the head of the first reel, approximately one minute of color bars and sound alignment tone (this combination is usually referred to as *bars and tone*). Some editing machines can create these references automatically or they come as digitized material already on the system (Avid supplies bars and tone that they advise using), on others you should use a digitized copy of the bars and tone that should have come on the head of every roll of dailies tapes you have. Digitize in one minute from one day's run and label it "Bars and tone." Then, as you balance your reels, cut a full minute of the bars and tone onto the head of the first reel (you could cut it onto the head of every reel, but it is necessary only to have it on one; by convention, dub houses expect to see it on the first reel), leaving some black at the head and tail. Adjust the time code of the edit so the first frame of picture still begins at the zero hour, 1:00:00:00 for Reel One, 2:00:00:00 for Reel Two, and so on. Then, before you do the output, run the edit and adjust the sound levels at your mixer's output so the tone rides at the ideal level—on most machines this is just below the bar crosses into the red area. This provides all of the necessary references, allowing copies of your master tape to be made at picture and sound levels neither too loud or too quiet.

On the Lightworks it is possible to set up the machine to burn in a time code window as the playout is being made. This is sometimes helpful so Adam can make his notes using the time code as an exact reference. However, it can be a nuisance to view the tape with the time code burned in, especially if it sits on top of the picture. You can adjust the placement of the code, but you should check with Wendy to see if she wants this BITC (Burn-In Time Code).

Another item you might want to add to the top of the playout (usually, after the Bars and Tone) is a *slate*, an identification card. You can create this card relatively easily using the Title Tool in your editing system. If your machine doesn't have a titling tool, you can create the slate in a computer graphics program like Adobe Photoshop as whatever sort of picture file your system can import. Lightworks, for instance, can only import Targa files. PICT, JPEG and TIFF files are also common.

This slate should include the name of the film, the edit title ("First Cut," for instance), the date of the playout, and a designation as to which reel is on the tape ("Reel 1 of 3," for instance). You should also list the Total Running Time (often abbreviated TRT) of the sequence. You can easily get this information from the edit itself. I also like to put the editing room contact information on the bottom of the slate (your name and editing room phone number) so the person viewing the tape can find it easily if they need to contact you. Put about ten seconds of this slate after the black following the bars and tone. Add about fifteen seconds of black between it and the first frame of picture. You can now see why I told you to balance the reels with no more than 58 minutes of footage altogether.

Make sure the tapes you are recording on have been *pre-striped* with the correct time code (if you are editing in Non-Drop Frame, then the tapes should also be in Non-Drop) at the appropriate hour. Once the tape is in the tape machine and the edit is in place all you need to do is press the button that will start the playout.

On the Avid you can choose to have the machine add a countdown leader (like an Academy leader) at the top of each reel. At this stage, unless you are sending the tape out to begin music or sound spotting (we'll discuss what this means in Chapter 12), it is not necessary to have a leader on the playout.

If there is time before Adam's screening, you might want to do the playout before the screening. In most cases, you will wait until after the screening to do your playout and make your dubs.

We will discuss actually making the playout and the dubs in just a few pages.

Consolidation

Occasionally you will need to create a tape with a better quality image than the one Wendy has been using to cut. In all probability, she has not been editing at the highest resolution available on the machine in order to conserve hard drive space. Your machine probably has the ability to go back and redigitize the footage Wendy has used in the edit at a higher resolution.

Undoubtedly, a large amount of material was shot that is not being used in the edit. This includes all the head and tail trims of shots you've used, as well as the outtakes, which Wendy didn't cut into the film. It would be extremely wasteful to digitize *that* footage. To deal with this problem, most digital editing machines have the ability to consolidate footage. In this process, the machine goes through every cut in the film and creates a list of only that material. You have an option to digitize an additional amount of footage on the head and tail of each cut in the event that Wendy wants to adjust a cut. This *handle*, as it is called, can be any length you set, though you probably won't need any more than eight frames, if that much.

After you consolidate the footage, you will create a new digitizing database that you will use to redigitize the material at the higher resolution. This will often be a day-long process if you've got a typical 100 minute film, and involves a lot of swapping of tapes and staring at the computer monitor to check that the footage is being digitized properly. After all of the new material has been redigitized, you need to create a new copy of Wendy's edit, telling the computer to replace all of the footage with the newly digitized material. On the Lightworks the command is "Find Material To Fill Edit," on the Avid it is "Fit To Fill."

When the machine is finished, you have a new edit with the higher quality images inserted in place of the ones Wendy originally edited with.

Because of the higher quality, more data being will be moved back and forth from the hard drives. It is possible that the image may appear jerky in some places with faster cutting. This *stuttering* normally occurs when the computer is trying to shuttle over the hard drive faster than it is capable of moving.

Conforming to Film

Sometimes, your director will not want to screen the first cut with the digital output (it really is a terrible looking image compared to film). In that case, you will need to match the 35mm dailies to the digitally edited picture. This process is called *conforming the work print* and there are several ways to do this.

The first thing you need to do is balance the reels into the typical 1000' reels discussed in Chapter 8. You then add an Academy Leader onto the head of each reel in your editing machine, making sure you adjust the time code so that the even hour (01:00:00:00 for Reel One, 11:00:00:00 for Reel 11, etc.) falls exactly on the frame marked "Picture Start." On most films you can have the telecine house transfer a piece of 35mm Academy Leader. My assistant has a 3/4" tape with this leader already telecined on it from an earlier show. Make sure you cut in one frame of 1000 cycle tone (this is the same tone you hear on the bars and tone) directly opposite the number two on the Academy leader. This is the frame right before it cuts to black.

When you cut this Academy Leader into your edit, you should make sure you take it all the way to the end of the leader. Usually there is a large arrow immediately after the last frame of the leader saying "Cut Here." You should also make sure that the first frame of the picture after this Academy leader comes at exactly twelve feet and zero frames (or eight seconds and zero frames).

As digital editing has developed, some negative cutters have begun to offer their services as conformers for the work picture as well. The process is almost identical to negative cutting so this does make sense, though it is an expense some films will be unable to handle. Regardless of who does the conformation, the process is similar.

At the telecine session, you may remember the colorist/telecine operator created a floppy disk for you containing a file of some sort (usually a FLEx, Evertz or Keylog file) with all the video information as well as whatever film information was available at the time. If you telecined directly from the negative, this would include the camera roll and the latent edge key numbers. If you telecined from your sunk dailies, this would include the dailies roll and the inked code numbers. When you digitized the dailies using this log, this information should have been attached to every take you put into your machine.

Now it is time to use this information.

Any system allowing you to cut in 24 frame mode, should be able to generate a *Film Cut List*. Quite simply, this list takes the digital cut Wendy has been working on and translates the video numbers visible on screen into the matching film numbers. If the time code 04:02:13:12 on Dailies Tape 34 matches up with the code number 034-1625+05, the computer translates any cut occurring at that time code into a cut at that exact key code number. It is a tedious process, but one the 24 frame process was built for. If you have been cutting in 30 frame mode, but still have all of the film information, you can translate (though not to the exact frame on every cut) it into the 24 frame mode.

The exact command to make this translation will vary depending upon the machine you are working on, and there are a number of options available with each command. Check the machine's manual as well as your conformist, to determine which pieces of information you will need. I find that the key (or inked code) number, the camera or lab roll it is coming from, the name of the take (36A-4, for instance), and the length of each cut are the minimum items I need, though I usually get more information.

The first step to conforming the 35mm workprint is making sure you *have* the 35mm workprint. If you have telecined from the workprint, there will be no problem, you should have been storing the 35mm coded dailies roll in your editing room. If you printed all of your dailies but did not sync them, then you should have all of the 35mm uncoded dailies stored in your editing room (you will need to access them using their latent edge key numbers).

If you never printed any film whatsoever (or printed only a few takes), you have to order up from the lab everything you need to cut the workprint together. Your computer editing machine can generate a list, called a *Pull List*, (*see* Figure 8A.1), listing all the takes used in the film, organized by camera roll and key number. This list will usually be quite massive and, for that reason, it is a

```
Avid Cut Lists                    created at 22:18:23 Tues 7 Jan 2000
Project: Silent Night
List Title: R06 v100

R06 v100                          15 entries,      handles = -1
Picture 1                          0 dupes
Pull List
```

	Footage	Duration	First/Last Key	Lab Roll	Cam Roll	Clip Name	Asm #
1.	12+00 23+02	11+03	KI 48 2791-3956+15 3968+01	000051	A52	74-1a	2
2.	25+13 28+03	2+07	KI 48 2791-3970+04 3972+10	000051	A52	74-1a	4
3.	32+01 35+11	3+11	KI 48 2791-3976+06 3980+00	000051	A52	74-1a	6
4.	42+08 49+08	7+01	KI 48 2791-3985+14 3992+14	000051	A52	74-1a	8
5.	56+07 62+05	5+15	KI 48 2791-3999+12 4005+10	000051	A52	74-1a	9
6.	67+04 70+11	3+08	KI 48 2791-4012+06 4015+13	000051	A52	74-1a	12
7.	75+06 82+00	6+11	KI 48 2791-4097+05 4103+15	000051	A52	74-1a	14
8.	87+07 97+08	10+02	KI 48 2791-4215+12 4225+13	000051	A52	74A-1	16
9.	23+03 25+12	2+10	KI 48 2791-4976+00 4978+09	000054	B8	74-1b	3
10.	28+04 32+00	3+13	KI 48 2791-4981+13 4985+09	000054	B8	74-1b	5
11.	35+12 42+07	6+12	KI 48 2791-4987+03 4993+14	000054	B8	74-1b	7
12.	49+09 56+06	6+14	KI 48 2791-5000+14 5007+11	000054	B8	74-1b	9
13.	62+06 67+03	4+14	KI 48 2791-5046+09 5051+06	000054	B8	74-1b	11
14.	70+12 75+05	4+10	KI 48 2791-5054+15 5059+08	000054	B8	74-1b	13
15.	82+01 87+06	5+06	KI 48 2791-5111+08 5116+13	000054	B8	74-1b	15

```
(end of Pull List)
```

FIGURE 8A.1 The first page from a Film Pull List which lists all of the pieces of film that will need to be assembled in the order of their key numbers, to make the complete reel of cut picture of this reel. This makes it easier to pull all of the pieces in the order that they will appear within the camera rolls. In addition to listing the lab and camera rolls, the list also gives you an assembly number, which gives you the order of the particular piece in the final assembly of the cut. You would write this number down in grease pencil at the head of each piece that you remove from the lab rolls.

```
Avid Cut Lists                      created at 22:18:23 Tues 7 Jan 2000
Project: Silent Night
List Title: R06 v100

R06 v100                      16 events      handles = -1
Picture 1                      0 dupes       total footage:  97+10
Assemble List                  1 optical     total time: 00:01:05:01
```

	Footage	Duration	First/Last Key	Lab Roll	Cam Roll	Clip Name
1.	0+00 11+15	12+00	Opt 1-0000+00 0011+15	OPTICAL #1		
2.	12+00 23+02	11+03	KI 48 2791-3956+15 3968+01	000051	A52	74-1a
3.	23+03 25+12	2+10	KI 48 2791-4976+00 4978+09	000054	B8	74-1b
4.	25+13 28+03	2+07	KI 48 2791-3970+04 3972+10	000051	A52	74-1a
5.	28+04 32+00	3+13	KI 48 2791-4981+13 4985+09	000054	B8	74-1b
6.	32+01 35+11	3+11	KI 48 2791-3976+06 3980+00	000051	A52	74-1a
7.	35+12 42+07	6+12	KI 48 2791-4987+03 4993+14	000054	B8	74-1b
8.	42+08 49+08	7+01	KI 48 2791-3985+14 3992+14	000051	A52	74-1a
9.	49+09 56+06	6+14	KI 48 2791-5000+14 5007+11	000054	B8	74-1b
10.	56+07 62+05	5+15	KI 48 2791-3999+12 4005+10	000051	A52	74-1a
11.	62+06 67+03	4+14	KI 48 2791-5046+09 5051+06	000054	B8	74-1b
12.	67+04 70+11	3+08	KI 48 2791-4012+06 4015+13	000051	A52	74-1a
13.	70+12 75+05	4+10	KI 48 2791-5054+15 5059+08	000054	B8	74-1b
14.	75+06 82+00	6+11	KI 48 2791-4097+05 4103+15	000051	A52	74-1a
15.	82+01 87+06	5+06	KI 48 2791-5111+08 5116+13	000054	B8	74-1b
16.	87+07 97+08	10+02	KI 48 2791-4215+12 4225+13	000051	A52	74A-1

(end of Assemble List)

FIGURE 8A.2 *The first page from a Film Cut List, also called an Assembly or Assemble List, for a film which did not have 35mm film printed during dailies. If film dailies had been sunk and telecined then the key numbers would be replaced by inked Code Numbers. In a normal film, the reel would be much longer and have many more edits.*

good idea to start printing up all of this negative weeks before you know that you are going to need to conform your workprint.

After you create this list, you should make a copy of it for your negative cutter (or whoever is storing the negative). Check the list carefully to make sure all the information on it looks correct, remove any takes that may have already been printed during the production period, and send it over so they can start pulling all of the negative that needs to be printed up. You should keep a copy of this list as well.

When the negative cutter has pulled the requested negative, it will be sent to the lab and printed up just like B-negative. When the print is returned to you, make sure you've gotten everything you asked for. On most films, it is a small miracle if everything is printed the way you requested it. It is always better to discover the inevitable errors before you are in the throes of conforming the work print.

If an outside service is conforming the work print, have them do these checks as they receive the film. You will also need to get them a copy of your Film Cut List (*see* Figure 8A.2). In a few cases you can also supply them with an optical list, so they can mark up the workprint for fades and dissolves. Most of the time, they will not want to mark opticals for you, so you will do that when the cut reels are returned to you. Many conformists also want a videotaped copy of the film with a burn-in showing the reel's footage, in feet and frames. If you have created your master tapes properly, it should be a simple matter to have the dub house burn-in the necessary codes as they make the tape copies. The Lightworks BITC Panel also has a setting to create foot and frame burn-ins, though at times I have found these numbers to be inaccurate.

231

Conforming is a time-consuming process to do properly, so you should get a time line from your conformist as to when you can expect your reels back. On a typical twelve-reel film, you can anticipate an average turnaround time of one week or more, depending on how big a crew they have working on your project. You should plan your time accordingly, so you can receive the reels back in time to check them against the sound and prepare them for the screening.

If you and Philip are going to do the conformation yourselves (typically, the work is intensive enough that an additional assistant or two is hired to do the first conformation), you should organize your 35mm footage by the roll order listed in the Pull List. If your lists use only key numbers then you should organize them in key number order instead.

Prepare your head and tail leaders exactly as I described in the all-film chapters. Place the Academy Leader on the head leader into your synchronizer so that the "Picture Start" mark is lined up at 0000'00. Then spin down to the first edit listed on the Cut List after the Academy Leader (listed as event number one). This edit (also called an *event*), edit number two, should be at 12'00, the first frame after the Academy head leader ends. In this Assembly List you can see the first edit with the key number KI 48 2791-3956+15 from Camera Roll 51 (if you had telecined from your sunk dailies this key number would actually be an inked edge code number).

Attach this first piece to the end of the Academy Leader on the left side of the synchronizer (remember to erase the grease pencil number you wrote on it). When you begin to take it up, you should see the listed key number come into the synchronizer at the 12'00 frame. Run carefully down to the end of the piece, then splice the piece you've labeled number two onto the end of the first piece. Run that into the synchronizer and check that the listed key number (KI 48 2791-4976+00) comes in at 23'03 on the synchronizer.

Continue in this fashion until you get to the end of the reel. When you get to the last edit in the reel, you can attach your premade tail leader, add a tail sync mark, and rewind and clean the film. You will want to code this cut reel (after you check it against the sound track) and the tail sync mark will give you a good reference to check your coding.

Be careful that you don't do any damage to the work picture as it is hanging loose in the trim barrel. It is also important to take great care in making the initial pulls. If you have made a mistake, it is time consuming to go back and correct, and you end up with an extra splice in your film if you need to add a frame or two.

Now, let's talk about the sound track.

It is possible, to match the 35mm dailies sound track much as you've matched the picture (if you've sunk up your sound dailies). However, because all of the track work you have done has been in the Avid or Lightworks (including music and sound effects not existing on film, as well as reused pieces of tone), it is actually better to use the sound output from your editing machine for the screening than it is to match the original dailies track.

There are a number of formats for outputting the track. To assure the best quality, make sure your original sound was digitized at 48Khz and output onto a good quality tape, either a DAT, a DA-88 or a Beta tape. In a pinch, 3/4" SP will do, but then you are bound to hear some unwanted hissing and other noises when you listen to this track in a good screening room.

The Playout

Once you have your edit in acceptable shape, you can begin the playout. Whether you do your playout before or after your screening, the idea is the same. Of course, the exact command to do this varies from system to system. If you've done all the set-up properly, all you need to do is start the playout and begin to ride the sound levels. Make sure that the monitor you are looking at shows the output of the recording videotape so you can tell immediately if there are any problems. As you are recording, have Philip monitor the volume levels on the record deck to make sure nothing gets so loud as to cause distortion. I find it useful to listen to the mix while wearing a pair of headphones, though this will depend on how quiet your editing room is and how good your sound system is.

Occasionally, you will find that you are unhappy with something as it was laid down on tape—either the sound mix wasn't clear or the picture stuttered, or any number of other problems. You should note the record time code of the problem. Later on, you will be able to go back and fix just that area.

When the playout is complete, check both the picture and the sound at several points in the reel. Then have Philip label both the tape and the tape box with all of the information on the slate (film name, edit title and date, reel number, total running time and editing room contact information).

233

Most probably, you will need to make copies of this master tape before distributing it. You should send the tape, properly labeled, along with a work order listing the format of your tape (it may be stereo; it may have sound on two, three or four tracks. If it is Dolby encoded, note that as well), and the quantity and format of the dubs that you want.

In addition, you can request the dub house burn in any numbers or words into the visual image. To protect against illegal duplication, you often will need to put a burn in stating the owner of the videotape ("Property of Paramount Pictures," for instance). You may also want to list the name of the cut ("Editor's Fist Cut"), and burn in either the time code or footage to help Adam in identifying frames for his notes. If the original film was transferred in 1.85 format, you will have some nice black space at the top and bottom of the picture (called *letterboxing*) to burn in this information. If your picture is full frame, you have to decide where to place the burn-in to cover up the least important area of the picture. The very bottom of the screen is the best place, though you can place some information at the very top as well.

All this information should be written on the work order. It is also a good idea to talk to someone at the tape dub house to make sure they are aware of all of your needs. The better the communication, the fewer the errors.

If you are planning on screening on film, you will probably do a sound-only playout (unless you are playing out to a high sound-quality videotape like a Beta or Digi-Beta). Whether you are outputting to a DA-88 or a time-coded DAT, the principle is the same as if you are outputting to a videotape.

After you have created your output you will need to have the tape transferred to 35mm mag sound film. Many editors like to transfer to full coat because of its tougher quality in projection.

When the transfer is complete, you will receive it in the editing room. Put it up in the synchronizer and find the one frame tone pop. Mark that frame and then put it in your synchronizer at 9'00. Roll down to 12'00 and mark the frame line at 11'15/12'00. Cut the track on this line and attach your sound head leader to it. Some assistants don't make up leaders for each screening mix, but simply flip the track (if you are working with 35mm, stripe) at this mark and roll it back to the 0'00 frame. They then mark that frame as the Sound Start Mark.

234

In either case, after you have labeled the start mark for the sound, you should roll it down in the synchronizer with the picture until you reach the Last Frame Of Action (also called the End of Reel, EOR). Splice on the sound tail leader after this frame (or flip the track at this point) and mark a tail sync mark.

You will now be able to check that everything was conformed properly. Take the rewound picture and track, thread them up in your flatbed at the start marks and proceed to look at the entire reel at sound speed. Pay careful attention to lip sync. If a piece of picture was conformed incorrectly you will probably notice that it is out of sync. You should also pay attention to pieces that look incorrect for any other reason (bad matches, shots from other scenes, etc.). If there is any question about the accuracy of a cut, visually check the film and its code numbers, against the same piece in your digital editing machine. If something needs to be corrected, you need the original work print rolls to get the trims and outs, so make sure you have every piece of film from the reels you are checking in the editing room, regardless of where the conformation was done.

Once you've verified the picture and sound, and corrected any problems, you should code both the picture and track reels using a preview coding system. In this system you should code each reel with its own reel number (001S0000 at the start mark for reel one,

012S0000 for reel twelve, etc.), making sure to use the same code for the picture and track. This way, if any problem arises during the screening you will easily be able to re-thread the reels, even in the middle, and still find sync.

The Inevitable—Paperwork

The amount of paperwork that you need to create for the screening doesn't decrease just because you are working digitally. You still need to supply a continuity and an LFOA list. Running times will be easier to get, in minutes and seconds, because the editing machines can provide that information for you. Just make sure you take that information from a drop frame number, since non-drop frame counts don't accurately represent real time.

Be sure the continuity lists the scenes in the order they appear in the film, even if Wendy has restructured the film so they are no longer in numerical order.

In addition, I like to add a column onto the LFOA list listing the version number of the edit for each particular reel. Later on, when you are breaking the film down into 1000' reels (if you haven't already done so), this will be a good way of keeping track of all of the versions of the film.

235

The Screening

First cut screenings on a digitally cut movie are almost as nerve-wracking as 35mm cut films. Everyone is nervous, though if Adam has seen a number of the sequences Wendy has cut, everyone may be a bit more relaxed.

After the screening, you will still need to sit with both of them, prepared to take notes and answer questions. If the screening and discussion are held in the editing room, it will be a simple matter to check the lined script or notes if Adam has questions.

When the screening has finished and the meeting is over, you will probably need to make the playouts and dubs, if you haven't already done them. Adam can then take his tape, rewatch the film, and begin to formulate his notes for the next phase of the editing process—recutting.

RECUTTING AWAY

After the first cut is screened, critiqued, and re-critiqued, it will then be time to begin recutting the film. There are some editors and directors that love this part of the film; there are others that despise it. It encapsulates everything that makes editing what it is—attention to the most minute detail while still paying attention to the whole film.

236

On *Heathers* we continually experimented with the order of different scenes. I would re-edit the film for a week and then screen again for the director. Sometimes he would come into the editing room and work on scenes, other times he would go away while I reworked the scenes with his notes. Then we would go back to the screening room for another screening. The process went on for months.

For *Trigger Happy*, on the other hand, the director and producer spent most of their time in the editing room once we passed the first screening. After every screening there would be intense discussions about the relative weight we were attaching to a given character, a given scene, or a given action. "It moved slowly in this part," someone would say, and if there was agreement everyone would then try to figure out why the sequence moved slowly and how we could recut to remedy the situation.

As an assistant editor you have to keep track of all of those suggestions and prepare to carry them out. I like to take my own notes at these sessions as well as having my assistant take notes. Inevitably, the discussion moves so fast and ranges over so many different areas of the film, that one of the two of us will miss or confuse something. In those cases it is helpful to have a second, independent, set of notes to clarify what was really said. You should be prepared to take thorough notes, scene by scene. If you have a copy of the continuity to refer to, it will make your job a lot easier.

You will also find it handy to keep a three-ring binder notebook with a new date on each page, listing everything to be done that day and everything that *was* done on that day (rarely the same). Meeting notes, special addresses, or other pertinent information can be kept there as well. This helps to plan what you need to do to prepare for the editor. It is also helpful to have an erasable calendar posted prominently on the wall.

Lifts

The first type of recut you are liable to face is called a *lift*. A lift is, simply, a scene (or a portion of a scene) being dropped in its entirety from the film. Often a director will want to see how the film will play without a scene. You will then lift the scene from the film.

Lifts are never broken down and returned to the trims unless Wendy specifically requests it (in which case they really wouldn't be lifts at all, merely trims). They are stored and logged as lifts and saved for a time when they might need to be used again. This way, if it is ever decided to put the scene back into the film, you won't have to reconstruct every one of the cuts from scratch.

This system is not as elegant as it may seem on the surface. For one thing, it means there is now one more place where pieces of the picture or track may be found—in the lifts as well as the trims, outs, or in the cut. You will need a way of locating specific code numbers in the lifts, and this requires another log. This log, which we will (predictably enough) call the *lift log*, is not very difficult to maintain. It consists of large index cards upon which all the code numbers (both picture and track) included in the lift are written (*see* Figure 9.1). These numbers (the head and tail codes for each cut in the lift) are taken directly from the film while it is in the synchronizer.

In the example shown for Scene 27, "ABBY and the DIRECTOR have it out" (this has been taken from the scene descriptions on your continuity), we can see that the lift is made up of seven picture cuts and five track cuts (two picture cuts, numbers four and five, have cheated track running under them—that is, track from another shot, in this case the shot used in cut number three of the lift). We can see what the scene is and what each of the picture cuts actually are. We label this lift "Lift #1" or "Lift 19-1" since it is the first lift for Scene 19.

This card should be put in an index file reserved for lifts and filed in scene number order. During the cutting process some large scenes may have as many as three or four sections pulled from them,

FIGURE 9.1 A lift log card. Notice that for shots numbered three to five only one piece of track was used.

238

FIGURE 9.2 A trim tab for a lift.

each filed as its own lift. If you cannot find a particular trim in its proper trim box, you should check the lift log to see if it might be in one of the lifts from that scene.

The lift itself should be put into a box reserved for lifts. You should make up a cinetab (*see* Figure 9.2), then label the outside of the box "LIFTS Sc. 1 - 20" (eventually you will probably need to have several boxes of lifts).

Another, quicker, way to file lifts is to label each by its scene number and a description of the part of the scene the lift is from, if it is not the entire scene ("Scene 27—DIRECTOR and ABBY at desk during fight," for instance). No log is kept and the lift is filed in a lift box labeled with all the scene numbers of the lifts in that box. If there are three lifts from scene 27 in the box, then the number 27 would be written three times on the side of the box. Each number should be written on a small piece of white paper tape and taped to the side of the box. That way, when you give Wendy a lift you can also peel the tape off the side of the box so you will always be able to tell just how many lifts you have for any given scene. When Wendy needs a piece of film, and it is not in the trims, you will have to check the entire lift to see if it is within it, obviously a slower process than checking the lift log index card. However, for films with small crews, you save so much time by not compiling the lift log, it is worth the extra time later.

This is one of those choices you have make depending on your work flow. You need to balance the time spent searching for a trim (with Adam and Wendy waiting for you to find it) with compiling the lift log. Honestly, on all but the most heavily crewed film, I never demand a lift log.

Complete Recuts

In some cases, everyone is so depressed by the way a particular scene is cut that they feel it is better to recut the scene from scratch. In this case, you will do exactly what you did not do in the case of the lifts—completely break down the scene, returning each piece to its virgin state as complete uncut takes (outs).

In situations like this I feel it is very important to have a dupe of the cut you will be destroying. There are always times when, after recutting the scene, someone decides that the old scene was better or a combination of the two approaches would work best. At that stage it would be almost impossible to remember exactly how the original scene was cut. So I like to make a dupe to preserve a record of the cut.

Years ago, the fastest and cheapest way of making dupes was to strike a black and white copy. Now, it is just as cheap and fast to make a color dupe. In a pinch you can always use the color dupe as a temporary replacement for the work picture. It is a vastly inferior copy in quality, but it still looks better than cutting a black and white copy into the color work picture.

When you order the dupe tell the lab to print through both edges. This way your dupe will have the edge and the key numbers copied onto it as well as the picture image.

But how do you match up the track? When you make a track

copy there is no way to print code numbers onto the new track. How can you get back to the old cut on the track?

To do this you need to hand-code the track with the numbers. The easiest way to do this is as follows. Before you send the track in for duping (or re-transferring), put a one-frame long beep tone on its head leader (you will remember to put head and tail leaders on everything you send out of the editing room, won't you?) There is a standard place for this—exactly three feet before the first frame. Then, when the dupe track comes back from the transfer house, you can listen to it, find the beep tone, and from there find the first frame of action. You should also, just as a matter of practice, check the two tracks—original and dupe—against each other to make sure they are the same. You do this by listening for the phasing described in Chapter 7 in the section about lining up playback music tracks.

Now you have the original picture, the original track, and the new dupe track lined up in your synchronizer. Run them down together and every time there is a picture or track cut, mark it as shown in Figure 9.3 using black to mark picture cuts and red to mark track cuts. Where the picture and track are cut at the same spot, mark the cut point with both red and black marks. On either side of each cut, mark the closest code number. Where the picture and track cuts do not come at the same spot mark each of them separately, again marking the code numbers appearing on either side of the cut. If you are in a rush, or if the cuts are coming rather close together, you can leave out the code number preceding the cut. Always mark the one following it.

240

Some people do not mark down the picture code numbers since there is already a picture dupe marking the cuts. I find it helpful to have all the information in the same place. If there is a lot of time pressure, you can do without the picture code numbers.

With this set of dupes it is relatively easy to get back to the original cut picture and track if necessary. Simply put the dupe picture and track in the back two gangs of your synchronizer and match the cuts and code numbers on both the picture and the track in the first two gangs. When you have finished, run the picture against its dupe in the synchronizer to check them, you should also run the two tracks together to check them using phasing.

Normal Recutting

By far the largest part of your recutting work, however, will lie somewhere between the extremes of completely recutting a scene, and completely lifting it out of the picture.

Before Wendy begins recutting each scene you should know

which reel it appears in and give thread it up for her. You should also know the scene number so you can research the outs and let Wendy know, as she asks, just what other choices are available to her. Make yourself aware of any lifts that have already been made on the scene, if any.

Wendy will begin recutting and will almost immediately ask you for footage. She will ask for it in one of two ways. If she wants to extend a shot already in the film, she will look at the take in the cut footage and ask for either the head trim (if she wants to extend the top of the cut) or the tail trim (if she wants to extend the end). In both cases she will look at the number in the cut and ask for "the head (or tail) trim of 042-1695." Since the trims are filed by code number, all you have to do is to walk over to the box with the 042-1000 trims in them, open it, and look through the trim tabs for the take including 042-1695. When you find it, you take it out of the box, remove the tab (and the rubber band from the take if you are using New York style tabs) and hang it on the upper metal bar on the trim barrel. You then unwind the take, remove the rubber band from around the top of the pieces of film (hanging it up with the rubber band already on the bin), and put the trims

241

FIGURE 9.3 Marking up dupe track. Black cut marks (shown with the letter A) are drawn wherever picture cuts were made on the cut work picture. Red cut marks are made where track cuts were made on the work track. Code numbers are listed where helpful. At point A the picture and track cut at the same time. The last code number on the outgoing shot, before the cut, is EE6328. But the incoming shot used track cheated from another take than the picture, so both code numbers are written down (picture codes in black, track codes in red) on the pin directly below the tab. Since the trims are in numerical order, it should take only a matter of seconds to find the proper trim and hand it to her. All of this should take about thirty seconds to accomplish if everything is moving right. In fact, some editors prefer to get their own trims if they know how everything is filed.

Obviously, the importance of having every trim filed properly cannot be stressed enough. Each time a trim is filed with the wrong take, or in the wrong box, or not put away at all (as sometimes happens if it falls into the bottom of a barrel) it takes up time while the editor sits around doing nothing except getting angry. The fewer mistakes the better. No mistakes is the ideal.

The other way Wendy may ask for a piece of film is if she and Adam (or just Adam, to be honest about who is calling the shots) feel that a take she used for a piece of dialogue or a piece of action was not as good as it could have been. She may want to see other takes or angles shot for that part of the scene. In that case, she will ask for "an alternate take to 042-1695." If she's already looked at the lined script and knows what setup she needs she may ask for "an alternate take to 42A-4." If she asks for it in the first way all you have to do is look in the logbook to see what take 042-1695 comes from. "Aha!," you'd say. "Take 42A-4." A look back at the logbook will tell you what other takes were shot for this setup. Write them down on a piece of paper or a piece of paper tape that you can stick to the back of your hand.

242

Then, check the boxes where the shot might be. Written on the outside will be a list of the takes for Scene 42. If you see another 42A there, take it out and give it to Wendy.

If you are filing the trims separately from the outs, the alternate takes will often not be in the out boxes but will be classified as trims because other parts of the take have been used in the film. In that case you will give those entire trims to Wendy so she can find the part she needs (if you've been following her as she edits perhaps you can do it). One of the advantages to filing trims and outs together should be immediately apparent from this example—there is one less place to look for trims.

There are two other places you might find a trim: the lifts and, in a few cases, in the cut itself. Sometimes the editor has used the exact part of a shot she needs in another part of the scene (as a reaction shot, perhaps). What usually happens in this case is that you run around in a small panic for a bit because you can't find the trim in any of the places you've looked and you dread spending time going through all the takes in the movie looking for a misfiled trim. Then you ask Wendy if she could have used it anywhere else in the film. She will either answer an embarrassed "yes" and go on editing or she will say "no," then go and check the footage and give you a doubly embarrassed "yes" a few moments later.

Unfortunately, there are times when the dreaded event does happen: the trim has been misplaced and you have to look in all the takes of the film to find it. Because the editor is going to be pacing around waiting for you to find the missing piece, the time you spend frantically looking for the trim will feel like a short visit to Hell. There are some common mistakes people make that might save you some time in searching.

First, check all the other takes from that setup. Then, if you still haven't found the take, look in takes with similar code numbers. Eights can look like zeroes on inked code numbers, especially after a few months of wear and tear. The letter E looks like the letter F (which is why I never use both in any one coding system). The letter B might be confused with the letter R. Check for reversals of numbers—123-4253 might be filed as 123-4523 or with scene 132, as in 132-4253.

If the entire take is missing, the search becomes a little easier since all you have to do is to check other, nearby, boxes for the errant take. Also be aware that another person (another editor, if you have one, or a sound or music editor if you have one of them on) might also be working on that scene and have the take.

243

Questions! Questions! Questions!

During the re–editing process, you will be faced with questions you have to answer. Many of them will deal with organization—how should we code this print, how should we log in this scratch mix, how should we handle this optical? All these questions will have to be dealt with some degree of foresight. For, in much the same way you have attempted to create a system that will function all the way through the movie, you must learn to deal with those exceptions to the system without ruining it or creating even more work for yourself.

Let's examine these exceptions one at a time.

During the editing, someone will most assuredly rip a piece of film or soundtrack, or put a gouge in the film to such a degree that the piece is no longer acceptable for viewing, either because it would be too distracting to look at or because it won't go through a projector without trouble.

You will need to order another print for that piece of film or track and be able to integrate it into the system. The only way to do this is to reprint the entire take from which the ripped piece came.

In your logbook *(see* Figure 5.2) you can see a list of all the takes on the first dailies roll. Let's say that the piece Wendy ripped had the code number 010-1352. A quick look in the code book tells us that this comes from 10D-3. This will be the only piece with that code number since that's the way the system works (pretty good, isn't it?). The information in the log will also tell us that the take (1) was shot on September 13, 1999; (2) was from lab roll number one; (3) was from camera roll number one; (4) had the code numbers 010-1321-1378; and (5) had the latent edge numbers KJ13X64247 through KJ13X64304.

This gives you all the information you need to reorder the take from the lab. Tell them you want a reprint of take 10D-3, shot 9-13-99, lab roll number one, key numbers KJ13X64247—64304. Tell them you would like it at the same timing lights as before. You can find these numbers on the lab report (*see* Figure 4.2), in this case 26-28-20. That's all you have to do (except to make sure that they deliver it on time). If you were ordering the track reprint (sometimes called the *retransfer*) of this take you would tell the sound transfer house that you wanted a retransfer of take 10D–3, shot 9-13-99, from sound roll number one.

244

When you get the reprint back from the lab, you have to code it exactly as you did the first print. The best way to do this is to get the trims of that take out from the trim box and line up the new and the old prints in the synchronizer. Copy all the marks (slates, identifications, etc.) onto the new take. Find the first code number on the old take (it will be 010-1321) and mark where it would fall on the reprint, just as you set up your dailies reels for coding.

Some assistants like to code reprints a different color from the original take so there will be no confusion between the two. This is good protection but not necessary if you throw away the old print. In addition, this only works with tape coding systems like the Acmade that allow you to take off one color coding tape and replace it with another.

After you code the take you are going to completely replace the old print with the new one. Once again, get the trims from that take down from their box. In the synchronizer, line up the new and old prints. Then roll forward until you get to the first place where there is a piece of film missing on the old print. This is where there is either something in the cut work picture or in a lift. Make a cut in your new print in exactly the same spot and hang the two head trims (old and new) on separate pins in a barrel.

Then find the next trim and line it up against the new print in the synchronizer. Cut the reprint at exactly the same point the old trim begins. The piece you've just cut off will be a piece that is being used (either in the cut work picture or in a lift). For now, hold it aside on its own pin, clearly marked as "New Print—In Cut." This way you won't confuse it with any part of the old print.

Continue on in this manner, replacing all the pieces in the trim with the reprint. When you have finished, you should have three pins of material—the first will be the trims from the old print, the second will be the matching trims from the new print, and the third will be those pieces destined for the cut. Make sure each of the three is clearly marked. If you've coded the reprint with a different color you can check to make sure that you've sorted everything properly.

Now take the cut work picture for the scene you are replacing (in this case, you would take the reel that contained Scene 10) and roll it down in the synchronizer until you get to the first cut that comes from 10D-3 (you will be able to check this with the code numbers but you should have a very good idea of what it looks like and be able to spot it by eye). Choose the proper piece of reprint from the third pin and line it up against the cut work picture. The first frame of that piece of the reprint should exactly coincide with a piece of picture in the work picture (where the old print begins). If it does not, you have made a mistake somewhere along the line and you must go back and figure out where.

If all is well (and there is no reason to think it won't be), you will find that the new reprint will exactly replace the old piece frame to frame. In that case, carefully undo the splice in the cut work picture, remove the old print, and replace it exactly with the new reprint making sure all code and key numbers still line up in exactly the same way they used to.

When this is done, hang the old print up on a fourth pin and continue with the replacement process until all of your new reprint pieces are used up. If you finish your scene without using up all the pieces, check to make sure you haven't skipped a piece in the workprint. If you haven't, check to see if there is a lift from that scene and, if there is, replace the old print in the lift with the new reprint. If you have checked all the trims, all the lifts and still have a piece left over then you have made a mistake somewhere or there is a missing piece of film.

In that case there is only one piece of advice I can give you—find that piece!!

When you have finished replacing all the pieces. you will have ended up with three pins of film. The first holds the old reprint trims, the second the new trims, and the third is the old print that used to be in the cut or in the lifts. Flange up the pieces on the second pin, with the matching track as you normally would, and return it to the trims. Then combine the pieces on the other two pins. You should find that all the pieces of the old print should now go together sequentially, forming one complete take. When you have done this, you know you have found every piece of old print existing.

Then you can throw away the entire old print. Make sure that no bit of the old take is left in the cutting room to be confused with the new print. As I've already mentioned, some assistants like to save the old print in a box marked "Old Prints Replaced By Reprints." If the new print ever gets damaged with no time to make a second reprint they have an emergency back-up. In this case it is essential to code the reprint a different color than the original print.

The reason you go through this long involved process is rather simple, though not immediately apparent. Even though you requested a reprint at the same timing lights as the first print, differences in the temperature of the water at the laboratory, in the amount of time that various parts of the printing process take place, and many other minute differences will make the new reprint look slightly different from the old print. If Wendy ever wanted to extend a shot and cut part of the old print onto a part of the reprint, the color would not match exactly. This would be very distracting. To have a consistent color balance throughout any one take, you must make sure all the pieces of that take are from the same printing of that take.

246

The process for reprinting and replacing track is much the same as that for picture. After retransferring the needed take at your sound house in the same way it was originally transferred, you will code it to match the original track. You will then replace all the trims, then all the pieces in the cut work track.

Scratch Mixes/Temp Dubs

When Wendy and Adam screen the film there may be sections with more than one sound happening at the same time (dialogue between two characters while a scene is being shot in the background, for instance) or places where they would like to hear temporary music under dialogue. Because the work track is only a single strand of track, they won't be able to hear both things at once.

Most sound and music work is left until the end of the movie, when a sound editor will correct everything in preparation for the final film mix (or *dub*). Sometimes there will be things they want done for earlier screenings (either for themselves or for producers, distributors, etc.). Then you will have to *scratch mix* (also called *temp dub*) the movie.

Understanding the process of scratch mixing requires that you understand the process of film mixing, which is too large a subject for this book. But let me give a brief explanation to suffice for now.

When a movie is being shot, the sound behind any given piece of dialogue will almost surely not match the sound behind any other piece of dialogue, even if that second piece is just the reverse angle on the same scene. In a scene of two people talking, if the director has covered it in a wide-shot master, a closer two-shot, and close-ups on each of the people talking, the chance that all of these four camera set-ups will have the same background sound is very slim. This is not the fault of the sound recordist but is a simple function of differing microphone placements as well as (for films shot on location) the uncontrollability of the background sound outside of camera range.

Now, when Wendy cuts these angles together, there is going to be a different background sound every time she cuts one sound to another. Those changes aren't too bothersome when you are cutting a movie, but in a movie theatre a regular audience would be distracted by them, being accustomed to smooth backgrounds. A dialogue editor is brought on to correct these *bumps* (as the points where the background changes are called).

This dialogue editor will *split* the dialogue tracks, which simply means he or she will separate the pieces of dialogue onto two or more synchronously running tracks so each sound can be controlled separately, with a separate volume control and equalizer. This way, when the tracks are combined back into one track at the film mix the dialogue mixer can even out any disagreeable difference.

Now, of course, nothing is as easy as all that. The dialogue editor must do a lot of trickery with these tracks to prepare them properly for the dialogue mixer. But that is much too complicated a subject for us to deal with here and now. That must be left for another book (which, hopefully, someone else will write).

Another task of a sound editor is adding sound effects to the soundtrack. To have the utmost control of the dialogue sections in both the editing and the mixing, dialogue is shot with as few extra noises as possible. Phones ringing, radios playing, guns shooting, etc., are all left out during the shooting, to be added in the final mix. But those are the kind of things that can help a story along. So, before some screenings, Wendy and Adam may want to add those sounds (along with some music) to give them some rough idea about how the film plays.

Sometime there is no sound editor on the film at this time so it will fall to Wendy, you, and Philip to prepare for this mix. Since this will be a mix just to give everyone a general idea of the film, the mix will be done very fast and without much finesse. This is why it is often called a rough, scratch, slop, temp mix or temp dub. Dialogue is almost never split in these mixes. The usual purpose is to add a few sound effects to make the film more intelligible, and try out some sample music.

Music is usually lifted from already recorded albums, or CDs. Sound effects are available at many sound houses or from sound effects CDs. You will usually call up the effects house, or go there for an hour or two and audition some effects. You will tell them, "I need a very loud door slam, two different types of horse hoof beats, a series of gunshots, and a few modern phone rings," and they will be able to give them all to you in a short time, transferred directly onto 35mm film (or 16mm, if that is your need). You should always make a note of the effects numbers of every effect (all reputable sound libraries have their effects catalogued in some manner) so, in the likely event that Adam falls in love with one of the effects, the sound editor will later be able to go back and get additional prints of the same effect if needed.

Then, you should have all the scratch effects and music coded. I like to code the effects with the prefix code FX1000 (or 001F0000) and up, and the music with the code MX1000 (or 001M0000) and up. Any effects that you are going to be using from the wild track will already be coded, so you don't have to worry about coding them.

Start two new sections in your logbook—one for the temp effects and one for the temp music. List each effect by its code numbers, origin (effects house), catalogue number, date transferred, and description of effect. Make up cinetabs listing the code number and description on the front, and origin and catalogue number on the reverse. List each piece of music by its code numbers, origin, date, and title.

You then must do a little sound editing. Many editors like to do this themselves and many do not. In case they do, watch them closely to see how they do it. In case they don't, I can offer this brief explanation.

You will need a three-head Moviola (called a *console*, or a Moviola with an add–a–plate) or a flatbed with two sound heads and one picture head. On eight-plate KEMs you can even get a third sound head by removing the second picture head and replacing it with an extra sound head.

Thread up the picture and sound at the start mark (on the Moviola you should put the cut work track on the outside sound head, leaving the center one free) and zero out the counter. Run down the film until you reach the place that you want to add the effect or music cue. Place the effect in the center sound head (or, on a flatbed, in the other sound head), disengage this head from the other ones, and run the effect or music cue until you get to the place in the sound that you want to line up against the picture point you have sitting in the picture viewer. Engage all three heads and run them together. You will be able to hear both tracks (dialogue and effect, or dialogue and music) at the same time and get some idea of how they line up. If you need to change the relationship between the cut reel and the new piece, move the effect or music cue only. Never move just the picture or just the dialogue track as that will throw them out of sync.

Once you have a relationship you are happy with, go back to the beginning of the effect or music and find a zero frame (if the effect begins at 152'10, go to 153'00). Now, with a grease pencil, mark that frame on the track (*see* Figure 9.4). On a piece of paper you should begin to make a cue sheet (*see* Figure 9.5). This cue sheet will list all the elements for the temp dub for this reel.

If you are editing in 16mm you should convert your numbers to 35mm footages (it is usually best to do this after you have finished with the entire cue sheet). The reason for this is that one foot in 16mm is equivalent to two and one-half feet in 35mm. This means the sound mixer will have two and one-half as many numbers to time his mixing actions.

FIGURE 9.4 This sound effect begins at 152'10. The first whole number is marked on the piece of track. An alternate way would be to write the footage 152'10 at the head of the effect. Some sound editors will put a mark on the picture at 153'00 to match the one on the track.

249

MIXING CUE SHEET

DATE 2-14-00
REEL ONE
PAGE 1 OF 4

FILM "Silent Night"

DIAL	MUSIC	FX-1	FX-2
0 START	0 START	0 START	0 START
9 BP	9 BEEP	9 BEEP	
12+0	12+0		
WORK TRACK	Bach's "Wedding Cantata		
	>	152+10	
	170+0	Horses whinny (A 13-2)	
		196+2	
		215+1 Gunfight (G27-5)	215+1 Gunfight (G36-2)
	217+8 Chopin's "Piano Concerto #1"		
		245+6	245+6
	301+6		
	(MORE)		

FIGURE 9.5 *A cue sheet for a temp dub (also called a scratch mix). Note that the work track runs continuously from the first frame of action. Also note that beeps are put on the track at 9'00 on the first unit of any set of units (i.e. dialogue, music, effects).*

For this example (a portion of the cue sheet for reel one) we can see that we have our work track running during the entire reel. At 152'10 we have the effect we just selected—a horse whinnying. We also have some gunshots later on, as well as two pieces of music. Let's analyze the cue sheet a little bit.

At the top of the cue sheet we have listed much of the same information as you put on the head leaders of reels—the name of the film and the reel number. We have also listed the date of the scratch mix.

Under that, we have listed the mix *units* (also called *elements*). After we cut all the effects they will all have footage numbers on them. We will then have to cut them into reels of fill at those exact numbers so that they can run on mag playback machines (called, in an unfortunate turn of phrase, *dummies*) in perfect sync with the dialogue track. Since only one effect can be on a reel at one time, whenever we have more than one sound going on at a time we will need more than one reel of sound. In this case we are going to need four reels. One of these reels will be your work track reel, containing the dialogue. Another reel contains the music. The remaining two reels contain effects we will need, including the horse whinnies. When all the elements are run in sync, the dialogue, effects, and music will be combined—mixed together into one soundtrack for the screening. For temp dubs you should try to stay on no more than three added tracks though some complex scenes may require a fourth. Anything more than that takes longer to prepare and mix then it is worth.

On the first effects track (called FX-1 or FX-A) we have put a beep at 9'00, the standard place for a beep (this is three feet before the first frame of action). This beep will be transferred into the mix. Later you will be able to use it to line up the mix with the picture. Then, at 12 feet, a piece of music begins, lasting until 170 feet. The carat symbol (>) at the end of the line means that the music should be faded out. This is also noted by the initials F.O.

Apparently the music is fading out into the sound of horses whinnying. The horses come in at 152'10 and last until 196'02 (the dialogue track has still been running the entire time). Since the music, the horses, and the dialogue are all going on at the same time (during the period from 152'10 to 170'00) we need three tracks to hold all the elements.

At 215'01, a gunfight breaks out and, to attain the proper frenzy, two tracks of gunshots will going at the same time. For that we need a second effects track. We might have put the additional sounds on the music track, but it is best to keep them on separate tracks for the mixer's sake. In any case, the music returns again before the end of the gunfight (at 217'08) so we would need all four tracks running at that time to handle every sound we want.

You can see just from this simple explanation that this process can get complicated very, very fast. In fact, for final mixes it is not uncommon to have eighty to ninety tracks running for the same reel. For one film I worked on there were over one hundred tracks on one reel!

When you go to the mix, all of these four tracks will be lined up at their start marks then run together. If everything has been lined up properly, when you get to 9'00 you will hear the beep. At 12'00 your dialogue track will begin. When you get to 152'10 you should hear the horse whinnying while the dialogue and music are going on. The mixer will then set the relative levels of everything and mix them together. This process will continue for all the reels of the film that need to be mixed.

At the completion of the mix, you will want to take a 35mm stripe copy of the mix back to the editing room. This is also called the *mixed mag*. This stripe copy is made up of the type of track that you are used to dealing with—a strip of oxide on 35mm film with a second, smaller stripe, called a balance stripe, on the other edge (*see*

Figure 4.14). Some studios can mix directly onto 35mm stripe, others must mix onto a 35mm four–track (a piece of soundtrack completely covered with oxide and onto which four separate tracks can be recorded; because of this it is often called full–coat), then make a transfer of that mix onto stripe. Regardless, when you are done you should end up with a 35mm stripe that you will code. I like to code it SA1000, or 001S1000, for "scratch mix" of Reel One and then to move through SB1000, SC1000, etc., or 001S2000, 001S3000, etc., as the need arises. Log the reels in a section of your logbook devoted to scratch mixes. The mix can now be used instead of the dialogue/work track.

Some editors, to save money on 35mm stock, like to mix only the portion of the reel that needs mixing, then to cut that portion into the work track before the screening. I have never found this a particularly worthwhile way to save money since the amount of time needed to cut the mixes into the work track reels and remove them later (after the screening, when you will want the reels returned to normal) more than makes up for the increased cost in stock used. I like to mix the entire reel, even those sections that don't need mixing. For those areas, this "mix" amounts to nothing more than a straight transfer. But, after the mix is over, you end up with one complete track for the reel that will completely substitute for the unmixed reel. During subsequent scratch mixes, when you may not need to remix the horse whinny section but want to mix something else in the reel, I would simply use this mix as an element in the new mix.

When the mix is finished, the elements should be saved in their own section of the cutting room, plainly labeled with the date they were used and what reel they come from. If those effects are ever needed again, one look at the filed cue sheets will automatically lead you back to those exact reels. If Adam liked those horse whinnies, the sound editor will be able to use those exact ones for the final mix. To this end, it would be helpful if there was a mark on the horse whinny track listing not only the footage (153'00 as we have already written) but the closest picture code number of the shot around that 153-foot mark. That way you will always be able to find the exact sync point of the effect, even though the reel may have been recut and rebalanced so many times that the footage count may be meaningless. You can put these codes onto the mag as you cut them.

On most larger films today temp dubs (especially for previews) have become quite extensive. It isn't uncommon to temp mix up to five days in stereo, or even in six-track Dolby, mixing dozens of tracks together.

There are many more fine points in the process of scratch mixing that you will only learn by watching and doing. Every editor and assistant has his or her own method, what you have just learned are only the basics.

Alternates to Temp Dubbing

Some films I've worked on screened nearly once a week. On *Mr. Destiny* we must have screened the complete film more than a dozen times by the time we stopped editing, not to mention the countless times we screened individual reels for the studio or producers. Though there were scenes where dialogue ran concurrent to music or effects, it was too expensive and time-consuming to do a temp dub every time we were going to screen.

What we did instead was find a screening room that would allow us to run two tracks at the same time, in sync, and still have changeovers in between reels. Then I, or my assistants, would build the music or effects reels and adjust the volume levels while we were running the movie.

This is, of course, a less precise way of getting the sound mixed and would never do for the first run for the studio executives. Since there were not very many complicated scenes it worked out fine for everybody and, by the final screening, we had music in virtually every scene of the film as well as effects all cut together on the same second track. This method does require that the assistant (or whoever is going to running the volume levels during the screening) go over the film at least once beforehand so he or she knows where all the music and effects are. We made up a rough cue sheet using a continuity list that simply listed the places where music or effects came in by scene.

On many films where the editor cuts on a flatbed he or she will cut two tracks at the same time. In these cases you must screen in a room with two sound heads.

9A/DIGITAL

. . . . . .

RECUTTING DIGITALLY

Before Wendy and Adam reappear in the editing room, ready to begin recutting the film, you will need to prepare a few things for them.

First, you should save the version of the film they've just seen. In every computer editing system you will find an easy way to make a copy of whatever edit you happen to need. Make a copy of the last edit (go back to the individual reels or sequences, not the compiled edit that you prepared for output), then label that copy with the same name as the original, but with a new version number series. "R01v103" will become "R01v200." You've moved onto the 200 series because you are now working on the second version of the film. Wendy may eventually cut a later version (v201 or higher), but you will always know that any version in the 200s is being cut for the second screening of the film.

If you were at the meeting between Wendy and Adam after the screening, you may want to have your notes copied and available for her when she begins recutting.

Editors and directors interact in different ways during the recutting phase. Some directors like to sit in the editing room from the second cut through the completion of the entire editorial process. Others like to give their notes and disappear from the editing room for the day or the week. I worked with one director who would come to the editing room at the end of every day, ready to watch my changes and give new notes.

The greatest advantage of computer digital editing machines is the way it streamlines the process of recutting so thoroughly. Now, it is possible for the director to sit with the editor and go over an entire film in several days, making a large number changes in the process. In film, making one set of changes in a film could take two or three weeks. It is also possible to make many different versions of a scenes allowing the director to compare and contrast different approaches. This has brought the director deeper into the editing process and, I believe, improved its quality.

Lifts and Trims

Here's the good news about lifts and trims—they don't exist in the digital world, at least not until you conform your 35mm film (which we will discuss later in this chapter). Since all the footage is always available, there is no need for you to keep track of footage that has been trimmed out or lifted from the cut. Also, because you are never recutting the old version of the film, but making your changes on a copy of the old version, you always have your old edit available should you lift a scene out the movie and need to reinsert it at a later date. Lifts have become a thing of the past. Missing trims are gone. Life as an assistant is much simpler from a library point of view.

256

Of course, there are some additional wrinkles you now need to keep track of. Because you no longer have a lift log, it is important that you keep a record of which scenes appear in every version of the film and which were removed. I prefer to do this on the continuity putting the lifted scenes in italics so they stand out. Since this makes it a little more difficult to read, I also create a version without out the lifted scenes (if you are doing the continuity on a word processor you can make the lifted scenes appear in hidden text and print out one version with the hidden text and one without it).

One word of warning: because there are no trims, Wendy will always have access to everything that was shot. The down side to this complete access is that it becomes very easy for her to cut in duplicate frames as she adds footage into the cut. You need constant diligence to make sure these inadvertent errors are corrected.

Questions! Questions! Questions!

Just because you no longer have to keep track of two or three frame film clips doesn't mean that the demands of the editing process will lessen. You will still be constantly challenged by requests or special needs that will have to be accommodated within your system.

Though you will not have to worry as much about torn film or soundtrack, there will be the random computer gremlin that will arise to test your patience. On a weekly basis you will probably have to deal with a computer error or cataloging problem that you would never have had to worry about in an all-film world.

One of the most annoying computer glitches is a take or an edit that, all of a sudden, refuses to show up on Wendy's computer. Sometimes this will render the entire edit unusable, causing the machine to choke and stop running (or *bomb out*, as computer techies say). Other times you will find a cut that had been playing fine, will suddenly have black or silent spaces where good picture or sound used to be.

At times these errors are simple to repair. If you see a note that says "Media Offline" or "Material Missing" this means the computer can no longer find the footage you digitized for the take. It knows the material is supposed to be there; it just can't find it. Most of the time, this simply means that one of the hard drives storing the digitized footage isn't turned on or has been disconnected from the main computer. If the drive *is* connected and working properly, you may have lost the ability to play back that take. You must then redigitize it. There are special ways to do this so the computer will recognize that you are replacing the original footage with the identical piece, like a filmed reprint. These methods vary from machine to machine, but it basically involves creating a database of the take or takes needing to be redigitized. You then use this database as you did the database you made from the original FLEx files you got with your dailies—to batch digitize the material again. Once you properly redigitize the footage, there is a command that will automatically slip the new takes into the place of the old, unusable, footage.

257

There will, unfortunately, be a few times when the footage is not recoverable at all. Your machine has completely lost track of the original material. In this case you will need to redigitize the footage from your dailies tapes and cut it into the edit using one of your early output tapes as a guide. You digitize the portion of the output tape that you need, and lock it up with the portion of the edit right before and after the area where you need to find the frame.

Both the Avid and the Lightworks have functions allowing you to lock two pictures together and play them in sync with each other. You should find a good eye-sync point (such as a door opening or closing, two objects touching, etc.) and line up the new take with its older cousin in the edit. Using the two player locking function, it will then be a simple matter to drop the new take in right over the old one (remember to do this with both the picture and the track).

In film, you were able to use objects or people as they entered or exited frames to help find sync points for lining up reprints. In video, this is sometimes not accurate, since it is likely that the entire frame was not telecined or the 1.85 letterboxing may vary slightly from day to day at the telecine house.

Some assistants like to line up the new take with the old take at the slate, then calculate the *offset* between the code numbers. This is, simply, the difference between the two. Once you figure out the offset at the slate, you can simply add or subtract that offset from the cut-in point of the old take every time it appears in the edit and drop in the new take at the corresponding code number. The advantage to this procedure is that you won't have to eye-match the new take every time it appears in the film. However, since this is a process requiring a lot of computation (none of it done within the computer) there is room for error. At the very least, you should lock the two takes together before you cut the new one in to make sure they are in sync.

Occasionally, the director of photography or Adam may so strenuously object to the way a shot was color timed at the telecine house, it will be necessary to retelecine the take directly from the negative or print. In a case like this, you then receive a new piece of videotape with new code numbers for digitizing. You will then have to input the take and eye match the new footage to the old take as we've just discussed.

There will be times when Wendy will ask you for some B-Negative. This is footage that was not originally circled and so never printed or telecined. To get the footage onto a tape you can digitize for Wendy, you need to retrieve the negative and original sound roll (if the take is not MOS) from storage. Your script supervisor's lined script notes pages should have all of the information you need—camera roll, sound roll and date shot.

If you have been telecining from the original negative, you should send the telecine house the negative, sound roll and a work order (with purchase order number if necessary), giving them all of the details for the telecine. Make sure they know which take you want transferred, which camera and sound rolls the take comes from, what tape number to telecine it onto (you might as well attach it to the end of a tape you already have room on; the same tape as the other takes from that same set-up would be ideal, though it is not always possible, nor is it necessary), as well as the telecine specifications you used during production.

If you need to telecine from sunk dailies then you will need to get a print of the take before you telecine. Have the negative and sound roll pulled from storage and sent to your lab and sound transfer house for printing and transferring. After this is completed, you should have the footage sent to your editing room where you will sync it up just as you did during production. Only then can you send it to the telecine house.

Telecine time is very expensive and there is usually a minimum amount of time you have to book, so I try and accumulate a number of B-Negative takes (if Wendy can wait a few days for them) and telecine all of them at one time.

The one exception to this B-Negative procedure comes when you are transferring wild tracks or other sound-only takes. If you are lucky enough to have a time-coded DAT machine as part of your editing equipment, you can have the DAT sent directly to you for digitizing. You will need to make sure the time code that is on the DAT is transferred into the editing machine so your sound edit lists have proper information. You also need to be very careful when you handle these tapes since these are probably the original production DATs, with no backups. Destroying them is equivalent to shredding the picture negative.

On *MacLintock's Peach* we went about the B-Negative process on a slightly different fashion. During the original production dailies transfer, we had the video house telecine *all* of the negative to tape, whether it was a circled take or not. We then had them sync up only the takes the director had circled. This meant we were able to look at the silent dailies for all B-Negative and determine what would be useful to us. If we liked a take (and there was sometimes no way of knowing from a silent take), we would have the audio from that take transferred to tape. Audio only takes were much cheaper to order than takes the video house needed to sync.

259

When the tape with the audio transfer (and the FLEx file) came to the editing room, my assistant would transfer it and sync it up in the Lightworks. In fact, if we had a time coded DAT machine we could have done the audio transfer ourselves and saved the production even more money. On *Cherry Pink*, we sunk up the footage in our Avid, and the process was even easier. All the takes had been telecined; since we had a time-coded DAT in the editing room, we were able to input the B-Negative takes without sending the DAT out to the telecine house.

Scratch Mixes

For most films, you can create any temp mixes you might need for screenings right within your editing machine. On some larger budget films, the requirements for a thorough (if temporary) sound mix may exceed the capabilities of your machine. In that case, you need to get your tracks to a sound editor who will use one of their digital work stations to create a denser sound job. There are a number of ways to turn your tracks over to the sound editors; the method you use depends completely on how compatible your picture editing machine is with the sound editing machine.

In some cases, sound files created in Wendy's Avid or Lightworks can be exported using the OMF (Open Media Framework) standard, which can be read directly by your sound editor's (let's say you've hired a man named Chuck Lone) machines. One advantage to this OMFI file format is that, unlike audio transfers, it is a completely digital format and there is no volume adjustment to be made. This means one less place to potentially introduce sound errors.

A simpler way, however, is to create a playout onto a DA-88 tape. The eight tracks of sound on this audio tape format can then be digitized into Chuck's machines. Though he won't have immediate access to the trims of the footage that was used, Chuck will probably know enough tricks and short cuts to create an excellent temp track for preview screenings. If he needs any trims or outs, you can always supply him with the original production DATs.

Change Notes for Film

260
The most complicated part of re-cutting a film electronically comes when you move out of that digital world and try and match the new version of the film to the already cut 35mm work print. You will need to have your editing machine print out a detailed list of all of the changes you've made since your last conformed version of the film.

This is one reason it is a good idea to list the final version number for each screening print in your continuity. If there are three different versions of a reel from your first cut, it is important that you know which version (v100, v101 or v102) was the one you had conformed for the screening.

All the programs that work in 24 frame editing mode can create *Change Lists* documenting in excruciating detail just what changes were made between any two versions of an edit. None of the programs create perfect or easy-to-follow notes. In fact, change lists are among the most complex pieces of software to write. Let's think about it for a minute. It may be easy for you to know you've removed three cuts and moved them completely down 14'08 in the edit. However, the computer may read this change as three separate moves and create an unnecessarily complex change list. Sound change notes are difficult enough for human assistants to write. For a computer, they are almost too intricate.

That said, I should hasten to add that the software to create these change lists is being improved to address many of these complaints, and change list programs are getting smarter every year.

Once again, the actual procedure for using the change list programs varies from machine to machine. However, they all require you to identify the old edit as well as the new one. You select the channels in which to scan for changes (video, audio or both) and hit a button to start the computer thinking. It will spend a bit of time chugging through the edit lists, then create a series of lists for you to print out. (*see* Figure 9A.1)

Some assistants like to include the date of the edit within its name. That way, it not only shows up at the top of the change list, but it is easier to track which version of the edit is sitting in a bin or a gallery.

When they are printed out, take a moment to scan through each change list to make sure it looks sensible.

The Change List is actually a series of lists giving you all the information required to pull the new footage you need, as well as to make all of the changes and check them. The first list, called a Change Pull List in Figure 9A.1, is a list of every new piece of footage Wendy has cut into this reel (Reel Six in this case, though you will usually find your change lists to be much longer than this example). You will notice that this list is for version 200 of reel six. It applies only to the picture changes (if you had asked for a change list for track you would see the designation "Picture 1, Audio 1, Audio 2" at the top of the list). This pull list then goes on to detail, in camera roll order, every piece of picture you need to remove from the dailies rolls to add to the cut work picture.

261

To do this, you would take camera roll A16 (or the lab roll containing this camera roll; you have the option of printing out the lab rolls as well), put it upon your synchronizer, and spin it down until you get to take E-2mos. You then spin down until you reach the key number KK 32 4557-4241+00. You can then remove four feet and 14 frames of film until the second key number listed. Labeling this piece of film as number 11 (we will soon discuss this Assembly Number, listed in the last column), hang it up in a film bin next to you.

Proceed in order down this list, hanging each piece of removed film in its assembly order in your bin. When you have finished with all ten pieces of film, you can put Reel Six up on your bench.

In most cases you will be screening with a mix output of your editing machine. You will not, therefore, be conforming your sound dailies. If you are matching track, however, you will have asked for

```
Cut Lists                     created at 22:35:58 Wed 5 Jan 2000
Project: Silent Night
List Title: R06 v200

R06 v200                            10 entries,     handles = -1
Picture 1                            0 dupes
Change Pull List                     0 opticals
```

	Duration	First/Last Key	Cam Roll	Clip Name	Asm #
1.	4+14	KK 32 4557-4241+00	A16	E-2mos	11
		KK 32 4557-4245+13			
2.	2+10	KI 48 2791-3968+06	A52	74-1a	1
		KI 48 2791-3970+15			
3.	1+00	KI 48 2791-3972+15	A52	74-1a	4
		KI 48 2791-3973+14			
4.	2+11	KI 48 2791-3980+05	A52	74-1a	6
		KI 48 2791-3982+15			
5.	2+06	KI 48 2791-3997+10	A52	74-1a	9
		KI 48 2791-3999+15			
6.	4+05	KI 48 2791-4154+04	A52	74A-1	3
		KI 48 2791-4158+08			
7.	2+01	KI 48 2791-4225+14	A52	74A-1	15
		KI 48 2791-4227+14			
8.	1+05	KI 48 2791-4993+15	B8	74-1b	8
		KI 48 2791-4995+03			
9.	2+05	KI 48 2791-5059+09	B8	74-1b	12
		KI 48 2791-5061+13			
10.	1+15	KI 48 2791-5109+09	B8	74-1b	14
		KI 48 2791-5111+07			

```
(end of Change Pull List)
```

FIGURE 9A.1 *A set of Change Lists for a show which has not ink coded
the dailies. This particular set of lists (most machines allow you to choose
what forms you print) consists of three parts—(a) the Pull List, which
contains all of the pieces you need to remove from the dailies rolls to be
inserted into the new work print, (b) the Change List, which gives all of
the conformation instructions, and the (c) New Assembly List, which
lists what the new cut should look like, number-speaking. It is also possible to print out an Old Assembly List, a list of opticals, a list of duplicated frames, and a number of other lists. Note that the Pull List is
organized by camera roll number, since that is how you stored your
dailies. If you had sunk dailies, the pull list would be organized by dailies rolls, and the key numbers would be replaced by ink numbers on all
lists. Note also that I have created a very short reel for this example.
Normal reels run between 800 and 1000 feet.*

```
R06 v200                    15 events         Old Duration    85-09
Picture 1                   10 insertions     New Duration    86-10
Change List - Reel           5 deletions      Total Change +   1-01
                             0 moves
All Counts Are Inclusive (inside/inside)
```

At This Footage	Do This	For This Length		First/Last Key	Cam Roll	Clip Name		Total Change
1. 23+03 25+12	Lengthen Tail	+	2+10	KI 48 2791-3968+06 KI 48 2791-3970+15	A52	74-1a	+	2+10
2. 28+07 29+06	Trim Head	-	1+00	KI 48 2791-3970+08 KI 48 2791-3971+07	A52	74-1a	+	1+10
3. 28+07 32+11	Insert Shot	+	4+05	KI 48 2791-4154+04 KI 48 2791-4158+08	A52	74A-1	+	5+15
4. 34+03 35+02	Lengthen Tail	+	1+00	KI 48 2791-3972+15 KI 48 2791-3973+14	A52	74-1a	+	6+15
5. 42+11 45+05	Trim Head	-	2+11	KI 48 2791-4987+03 KI 48 2791-4989+13	B8	74-1b	+	4+04
6. 42+11 45+05	Lengthen Tail	+	2+11	KI 48 2791-3980+05 KI 48 2791-3982+15	A52	74-1a	+	6+15
7. 49+07 63+05	Delete 2 Shots	-	13+15	KI 48 2791-3986+02 KI 48 2791-5007+11	A52 B8	74-1a 74-1b	-	7+00
8. 49+07 50+11	Lengthen Tail	+	1+05	KI 48 2791-4993+15 KI 48 2791-4995+03	B8	74-1b	-	5+11
9. 50+12 53+01	Lengthen Head	+	2+06	KI 48 2791-3997+10 KI 48 2791-3999+15	A52	74-1a	-	3+05
10. 59+01 63+14	Delete Shot	-	4+14	KI 48 2791-5046+09 KI 48 2791-5051+06	B8	74-1b	-	8+03
11. 59+01 63+14	Insert Shot	+	4+14	KK 32 4557-4241+00 KK 32 4557-4245+13	A16	E-2mos	-	3+05
12. 72+01 74+05	Lengthen Tail	+	2+05	KI 48 2791-5059+09 KI 48 2791-5061+13	B8	74-1b	-	1+00
13. 79+02 81+00	Trim Tail	-	1+15	KI 48 2791-4102+05 KI 48 2791-4104+03	A52	74-1a	-	2+15
14. 79+02 81+00	Lengthen Head	+	1+15	KI 48 2791-5109+09 KI 48 2791-5111+07	B8	74-1b	-	1+00
15. 96+09 98+09	Lengthen Tail	+	2+01	KI 48 2791-4225+14 KI 48 2791-4227+14	A52	74A-1	+	1+01

(end of Change List)

263

FIGURE 9A.2 *Change List.*

```
R06 v200                14 events       handles = -1
Picture 1                0 dupes         total footage:   86+10
New Assembly List        0 opticals      total time: 00:00:57:21
```

	Duration	First/Last Key	Lab Roll	Cam Roll	Clip Name
1.	13+13	KI 48 2791-3957+03 KI 48 2791-3970+15	000051	A52	74-1a
2.	2+10	KI 48 2791-4976+00 KI 48 2791-4978+09	000054	B8	74-1b
3.	4+05	KI 48 2791-4154+04 KI 48 2791-4158+08	000051	A52	74A-1
4.	2+07	KI 48 2791-3971+08 KI 48 2791-3973+14	000051	A52	74-1a
5.	3+13	KI 48 2791-4981+13 KI 48 2791-4985+09	000054	B8	74-1b
6.	6+06	KI 48 2791-3976+10 KI 48 2791-3982+15	000051	A52	74-1a
7.	5+06	KI 48 2791-4989+14 KI 48 2791-4995+03	000054	B8	74-1b
8.	8+05	KI 48 2791-3997+10 KI 48 2791-4005+14	000051	A52	74-1a
9.	4+14	KK 32 4557-4241+00 KK 32 4557-4245+13	000011	A16	E-2mos
10.	3+08	KI 48 2791-4012+10 KI 48 2791-4016+01	000051	A52	74-1a
11.	6+15	KI 48 2791-5054+15 KI 48 2791-5061+13	000054	B8	74-1b
12.	4+12	KI 48 2791-4097+09 KI 48 2791-4102+04	000051	A52	74-1a
13.	7+05	KI 48 2791-5109+09 KI 48 2791-5116+13	000054	B8	74-1b
14.	12+03	KI 48 2791-4215+12 KI 48 2791-4227+14	000051	A52	74A-1

```
(end of New Assembly List)
```

FIGURE 9A.3 *New Assembly List*

a picture and sound set of Change Lists and you will put both your picture and sound units for Reel Six up on your synchronizer.

For our example, you only need to put your picture reel up on your synchronizer and zero it out at the start mark. Take the change list (*see* Figure 9A.2) (which, you may notice at the top was created at 10:35 p.m., much of your work will occur late at night), go to your synchronizer and roll down to the first change note, occurring at 23 feet and three frames.

Your instructions in this particular Change List format, based on the Avid Change List, tell you that you need to add 2'10 to the tail of the shot ending at 11'02/03. You should have this piece hanging on the first pin in your trim bin (it was the second piece you pulled using the Change Pull List). Back the cut work picture out of the synchronizer and open the splice on the left side of the bench. Add the 2'10 piece at the cut and splice the tail of the reel onto it. The end of the added piece should come at exactly 25'12 in the reel.

If everything checks out, congratulations! You've made your first change and can put a check mark next to change number one. The list even gives you a little place to make the check mark.

Spin down to 28'07 where you will find another edit. You will be removing exactly one foot of film from the top of this new shot. Roll down to 29'06 and mark the frame line at 29'06/07. Back the film out to the left side of the synchronizer and make a cut on that frame. You can then remove the one foot of film back to the top of this shot. When you've finished, resplice the shots and proudly put a check mark next to change number two.

Continue throughout the reel, checking your film against the change lists after each change. There are other lists you can print out to help you. Some give you lists of duplicated shots (hopefully there are none) or opticals. Another list you may find handy details every cut in the reel *after* you have made all of your changes (*see* Figure 9A.3). You can use this list, called an Assembly List (or an Assemble List) to check the accuracy of each of your changes.

When all the changes have been made, you will end up with a large number of trims that have been removed from the edit. You and Philip will need to cut these back into your dailies rolls (or your lab rolls if you have printed picture but no track during dailies). If you spliced your dailies reels back together with white tape when you removed the pieces that went into the first cut, it will be easier to find the areas to cut these trims back in to the complete reels. When you cut the pieces back in, splice them on both the emulsion and base side to minimize the amount of back splicing you need will need to do if the piece is ever put back into the movie.

It is, after all, an axiom of film editing that the piece you removed last week is the same footage you need back in tomorrow. That's what the experimentation of the recutting process is all about.

Requests from All Over

Just because the production company has finished shooting doesn't mean the requests will stop coming. In fact, you may find your editing room turning into a videotape dubbing facility if you're not careful. You will start receiving requests from publicity departments, special effects houses, trailer companies, music supervisors, et al., for copies of the film. In many cases you may need to playout specific scenes of the film, other times you may need to have the master playout tape from your last screening sent out for additional copies.

Each time a tape is requested, you should be very aware of the needs of the person to whom you are sending the tape. A music supervisor will generally need the picture without the music track. Trailer houses may need to see the latent edge numbers burned in (this is easy on the Lightworks). Some places will need time code burned-in and on an audio channel, others may specifically demand that there be no time code. Some people will be happy with VHS tapes, others may require 3/4" or better. Every tape request will have its own specifications and you should make sure you know exactly what you are expected to deliver. You should create a form (*see* Figure 9A.4) that you fill out for each request which lists every possible variation of time code, burn-ins, tape format, etc. It will then be a simple matter to check off the specifications for each individual order as you talk to the person making the request.

Some studios, producers and directors like to keep a record of who is receiving these tapes. At some point, they will ask to get them back, to make ensure unauthorized copies of the film are not floating around. This log will help you to keep track of where each of the tapes has gone. You will also easily be able to see just which tapes have *not* been returned by checking to see which Tape Request Forms don't have that line at the bottom filled out. You will probably need to adapt the form to your own needs.

TAPE REQUEST LOG

Tape(s) Sent To: _____   Date _____

_____

_____

Name _____

Phone _____

From supplied:

(include Name of Tape and format)

Tape Format (with number of copies):

☐ VHS	☐ 3/4″ SP	**Burn-Ins?** What kind?
☐ Super VHS	☐ BetaSP	
☐ VHS-Hi-Fi	☐ DigiBeta	Where?
☐ 3/4″	☐ DA-88 (sound)	

SOUND: Dolby? ☐ A   ☐ B   ☐ C   ☐ SR

Track 1 _____   Track 5 _____

Track 2 _____   Track 6 _____

Track 3 _____   Track 7 _____

Track 4 _____   Track 8 _____

Tape Returned on _____

TAPE REQUEST LOG

267

FIGURE 9A.4 *With this Tape Order Request sheet you can easily determine what the needs of every tape dub request is and transmit that to the tape dub house.*

OPTICALS

The act of making the impossible possible is one of the things that makes a movie so interesting. Watching the Red Sea part or spaceships fly through space is an experience hard to find anywhere other than in a movie theatre.

268

Creating these fantastic effects, as well as a host of much less spectacular ones, falls under the category of making *opticals*. An optical can be as simple as a scene fading out or as complicated as the title ship in *Titanic* tipping on its side, spilling people off. All opticals, however, involve the manipulation of the film negative to create a new negative with some change in the original's image.

Simple Opticals

The four simplest, and most common, opticals used in film editing are the *fade–in*, *fade–out*, *dissolve*, and *superimposition*. In addition, the creation of titles is an optical effect. In 16mm these effects are not created optically (even though they may still be referred to as "optical effects" or just "opticals"), they are created in the lab through a process called *A and B roll printing* (we will discuss this in more detail in a minute). In 35mm, however, these effects are usually created optically, albeit in a very analogous manner.

Let's say that, at the end of one scene in *Silent Night, Silent Cowboy* we wanted the image to fade to black. This is called a fade–out and is accomplished by darkening the image gradually until we can see nothing but black. One way to accomplish this, of course, would be to do it in the camera, while we were shooting the scene. We would simply close the camera's aperture slowly while the actors performed in front of us, so less and less light would be thrown on the negative. When we saw the dailies we would see the image get darker and darker until all we saw was black.

If we changed our minds later on during the editing process and wanted the fade–out to come two seconds later, or wanted the fade to be a little slower or a little faster, there would be no way to do it since there would be no image on the negative to play around with. By creating optical effects in the camera we force ourselves to accept whatever comes out of the camera, no matter how bad or inappropriate it may be.

One solution, then, would be to wait until we are making our release prints (i.e., the prints shown in theatres) to do these effects. That way we could have the lab *stop down* the printing camera's aperture (stopping down is the process of closing the camera aperture so it throws less light onto the film). We could tell the lab exactly where we wanted the fade–out to start and how long we wanted the fade to go on for before the frame was completely dark. We would preserve our original negative, as well as all of our options until the very end.

In fact, this is exactly what is done in most 16mm films. It is part of the process called *A and B roll printing* because the negative to be printed is made up in two reels (rather than one, which is the norm in 35 mm). After the negative is prepared for the lab (and we will cover how that is done Chapter 16) the lab does all the optical work based upon certain marks that have been put on the workprint. The accepted marking for a fade–out is a long "V" whose length is the length of the desired fade–out; the open end is at the first frame of the fade and the point is at the last frame, as in Figure 10.1 (the open end is for *more* light, the closed end is for *no* light).

269

The marking for a fade–in, in which the image on the screen gradually emerges from complete black, is exactly the opposite—a "V" that grows from a single point.

The optical dissolve is a combination of the fade–in and the fade–out: one image is fading while the other is fading out. The effect on screen is of one image crossing into another, thus we say one image "dissolves into" another (*see* Figure 10.2).

The fourth type of optical—the superimposition—is an extension of the dissolve. In it two images are run together at the same time. If one of the characters in our film is reading a letter from another character and we want to show that he is thinking of that person, we might show a picture of the other person superimposed over a close-up of our first character thinking. We would then run the close-up of him and the shot of the other character, exposing both at the same time. When projected, the result would be that we would

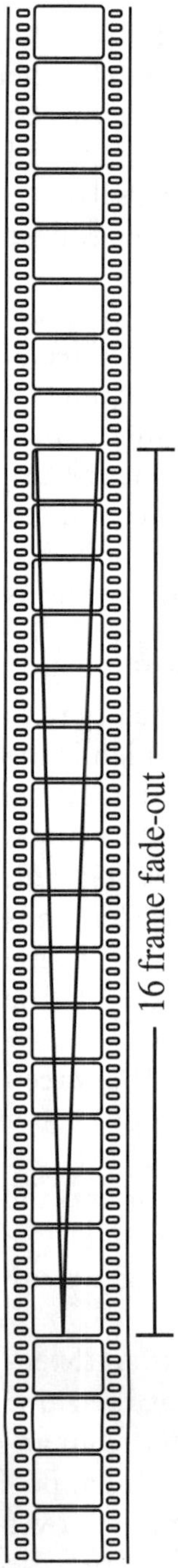

— 16 frame fade-out —

FIGURE 10.1 Fade-out mock–up.

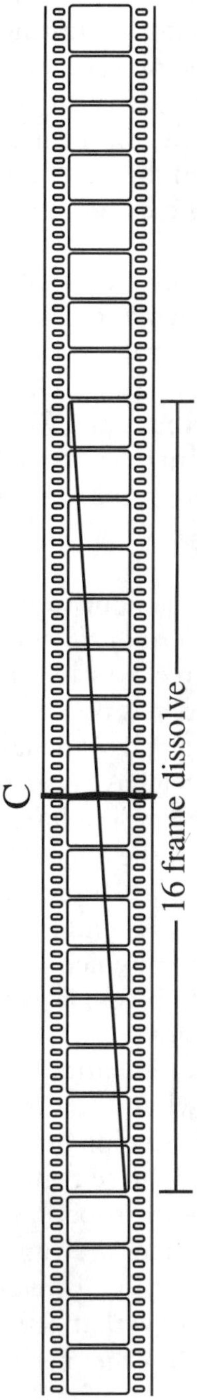

C

— 16 frame dissolve —

FIGURE 10.2 Dissolve mock–up. The mark at C is the center of the dissolve at which point the work picture will cut from the first shot of the dissolve to the second.

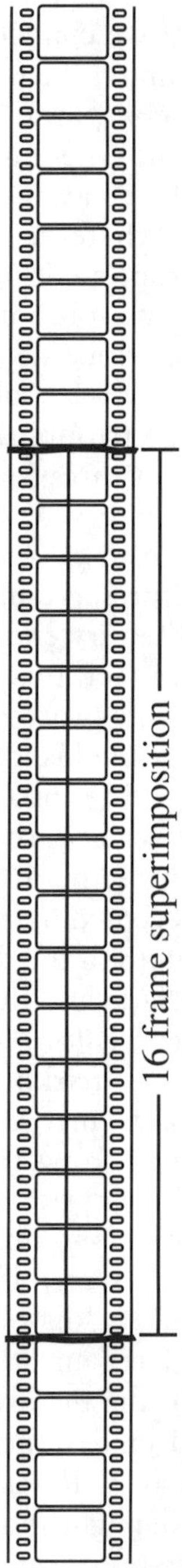

— 16 frame superimposition —

FIGURE 10.3 Superimposition mock–up.

see both images—one right on top of the other (*see* Figure 10.3).

There are two major problems and restrictions in making opticals at the lab. The first is that it is extremely expensive. You may need many prints of your film before you send the movie out to the theatres. If someone from the lab has to turn the printing camera aperture up or down every time you want an optical effect on each print, printing your film will be very expensive.

The second problem is, in the lab, it is necessary to restrict opticals to predetermined lengths, as well as to keep them at certain distances from each other. This places certain limitations on the editing of a film since it will be impossible to make, for instance, several quick dissolves in a row, or to create a fade or dissolve of 27 frames.

You can solve these problems by not doing your opticals in the lab at all but in a place designed to do nothing but opticals—the optical house.

A and B roll printing normally delivers a better quality image than the typical optical because the effects are made directly from the original negative. As we shall see in a minute, effects made in an optical house need to take an extra step and this will, usually, degrade the image a little bit. There are reasons to make this choice, however, most having to do with the extra time and money spent on opticals created in A and B roll printing.

271

Most of your 35mm opticals, therefore, will be done in an optical house, resulting in a piece of completely new negative with the optical effect incorporated into it. It is this negative, rather than the original negative shot on the set, that will be sent to the laboratory for making your answer prints. This way, you end up with one long strand of cut negative with all of your optical effects already incorporated into it. No one from the lab has to stand at the printing machine and create each effect. Each effect can be exactly the length and kind you desire.

Let us follow one short scene from our movie through the optical house to see just how it works. In this scene we are watching a scene from the movie-within-the-movie when it freezes, and turns to black and white. We then discover that this frozen scene is actually a publicity photo the director is looking at.

On the surface it sounds complicated.

In fact, it is complicated.

In this case the editing room staff probably worked with the people on the set during the shooting. When the scene of the director looking at the photo was being prepared, the art director may have asked for a frame clip of the already shot scene to make into the photo. Wendy would have cut that movie-within-the-movie scene and, with Adam, already chosen the frame where the freeze would be. You would have sent a frame or two of that shot to the art director who would have it made into the black and white photo to be used as the prop in the director's scene.

When that scene was shot it began with a close-up of the black and white photo. The photo was then pulled away from the camera and we were able to see that the director had been holding it. The idea, therefore, would be to take the shot of the movie-within-the-movie, freeze the proper frame, and dissolve it into the beginning of the shot of the black and white photo. This complicated optical is really three opticals. The first is the freeze frame. The second is the color turning into black and white, called *color desaturation*. The third is the dissolve into the live shot with the photo.

By the time all the material has been shot and cut, Wendy will have determined the exact frame where the freeze frame begins, the length of time before it starts to desaturate, the length of time it takes to desaturate, the length of time before this image begins dissolving into the black and white photo, and the length of the dissolve. These five items determine how you will lay out the optical.

272

Let's say that these are the details of the optical:

1. freeze frame marked with an X
2. length of time before desaturation—three feet (two seconds)
3. length of desaturation—six feet (four seconds)
4. length before dissolve—four and a half feet (three seconds)
5. length of dissolve—six feet (four seconds)

You should make a list of all the pieces of film involved in the optical. In this case, there are only two—the movie scene and the director's scene. From your logbook, find the information you would normally give to the lab for a reprint order (that is, key and take numbers, lab roll number, date shot). Now, you will order an *interpositive* (or a *registration interpositive*, your optical house will tell you which one is needed; see below for details) from the lab for these two scenes.

To understand just what an interpositive is, let's go over a bit of lab technology (don't worry, it's not too scary). When a copy of a negative is made, the negative is run through a *contact printer*. This means the negative is sandwiched with a new piece of film and some light is shot through it. Any part of the frame that is black will appear white on the copy, and any part that was white will appear black. Colors are reversed in a similar fashion. Therefore, any copy of the negative will be a *positive* image. The work picture that you got every day in dailies was struck in just this manner. If you were to go back and look at the negative for any particular shot in the film you would see that the image's color was reversed (that is why camera original is called "negative") and the actual film stock was an odd orange color.

When your film is completely finished the negative will be cut together to match Wendy's edits (see Chapter 16) and contact printed to make a normal looking film. Any opticals we create for the film must also, therefore, be negative images so that when *they* are contact printed the print will also appear normal. However, if we were to create our optical negative directly from our original negative image, that optical negative would be a positive image (since it would be made by contact printing from a negative image). To remedy this situation we need to make an intermediate print of the original negative. We will then make our optical from this intermediate contact print. Since the intermediate print will be reversed from our original negative, it will be a positive image. Then, when we make our optical negative it will reverse color again, resulting in the negative image we want.

This intermediate print with the positive image is called (oddly enough) an *interpositive*, or an IP. It is a *positive* image printed onto *negative* stock. If you were to look at it, the color would look approximately correct, but the image would have an orange tint to it since it is printed on the orange negative stock.

For certain kinds of optical sequences where it is crucial that the image be rock steady (such as those appearing behind titles) there is a special type of interpositive, called a *registration IP*, that you should order. Your optical house will tell you what kind of IP you will need.

I should note here that some optical houses prefer to make their own interpositives rather than have you make them at your own lab. I've worked both ways, with mixed results. Sometimes, it is better to have the lab responsible for the original processing do the interpositive to maintain consistency. But, if the optical house's lab is very good, it can be better to go with them. That way, they can control the creation of the IP. If anything goes wrong, they will know best how to correct it.

When your optical house wants to strike the IP, you should determine which pieces of negative they will need and have that negative shipped from the lab or negative cutter (wherever it is stored) to the optical house. Call the optical house to verify that the negative has arrived (it is your only negative for those necessary shots, isn't it?)

While the IP is being struck, you will need to create a number of guides for the optical house so they know what pieces of film to freeze and dissolve, where to do those effects, and how to long to do them. Aside from the inevitable paperwork involved in all of this, you should also send them a visual guide that they can put in their synchronizer and run alongside the IPs they will be using.

There are several ways to create this guide. The first is to send them the actual work print that Wendy has marked up for the optical and let them use that to check the paperwork. Another choice is to strike a color dupe of those sections of the film with the opticals in them, and send the dupe to the optical house. A third, and more common way, is to create a template on a piece of white leader listing all of the key numbers involved in the optical as well as all a copy of all of the markings Wendy has put on the workprint.

There are advantages and disadvantages to each of these methods but the reality is, with the fast paced finishing speed of most films today, it is getting increasingly difficult to part with the work print for any length of time, much less the week or so that the optical house will need it. As a result, you will find yourself creating templates more often than not. We will discuss how to do this in a minute or two, but to simplify that discussion, let's talk first about how you would mark up the work picture to send out to the optical house.

The first thing you do is to remove the involved scenes from the cut workprint so you can prepare them for the optical house. Remove the entire piece of the shots involved in the optical. For instance, if the shot in the director's office goes on for twenty-five feet after the dissolve from the black and white photo ends, you would remove the dissolve and the full 25 feet after the dissolve. The same would go for the head piece of the first shot in the optical.

Put head and tail leaders on the removed workprint. In the cut workprint reel where you removed the footage, replace the extracted footage with the same length of white leader so the reel remains in sync with the track. Mark on the white leader exactly who removed the footage, when it was removed, and why (this will help anyone else looking for information about that section of the film). Also mark code numbers of the individual pieces of film used in the optical (as you did when you marked up dupe track) on the leader so you know how the work picture had been cut in.

As we discussed, you can make a color dupe of this section (making sure the key numbers print through) and send it to the optical house. If you are going to go in that direction, this is a good time to make the dupe.

If you are going to create a template, rather than sending the cut work picture or the color dupe; put a roll of white leader in the second gang of the synchronizer, opposite the work picture where Wendy has put her marks. Then, in the leader before the optical starts, write the name of the film, your name and phone number, and the optical number.

Now you will begin rolling down in the synchronizer until you reach the first frame of the optical. Put a long black mark on the white leader opposite the frame line of that frame. Roll slowly down until you get to the first key number. On the white leader, mark the frame where the key number appears. If the number extends over two frames, mark the frame where the big dot appears. Write the key number on the white leader opposite that frame.

This will identify the first piece of negative for the person doing the line-up at the optical house. You would then continue until you reach the "X" Wendy marked on the work picture. Copy that mark onto the template and note "Freeze Frame" on the leader. It is helpful, though not crucial, to mark a frame for the key number immediately preceding this freeze frame.

Continue spinning down for the three feet before you get to Wendy's indication of where the desaturation effect will begin. Mark this frame (in this case you won't have to note the key number since you have frozen the frame) and write "Begin 6 foot desaturation." It is also helpful to put a mark, like a dissolve mark, to indicate the length of the desaturation effect.

275

Continue in this manner, copying over the key numbers and effects onto the template leader until you have completed the entire optical, including the long section after the final dissolve has finished until Wendy cuts away to another shot. This template, rather than the work picture, will be what you send to the optical house.

Once you get good at this method, you will find you can create templates without removing the optical section from the work picture. This will save you a lot of time and splicing.

Some optical houses don't need any picture at all for simple opticals, like dissolves and fades, though I always prefer to send them something they can put in their synchronizer and check. It helps to eliminate communication problems.

One note about sending a duped work print: Wendy's grease pencil marks will not show up particularly well after the dupe process so you need to recreate them in white or yellow grease pencil on the dupe. Line this dupe up with the work picture in the synchronizer, then copy the marks over onto the dupe. Also, make sure that the key numbers have been printed through onto the edge of the dupe are all legible.

You will now need to create some of that paperwork I was telling you about. In the interest of accuracy, I recommend creating the paperwork directly from the work print, rather than from the dupe or template. It will be easier to read the key numbers you will need to write down.

First, take the workprint and put it in the synchronizer. Normally, the optical house will want the first frame of picture to be considered 0'00. Zero out your synchronizer at the first frame of the optical and begin a sheet of paper that will be your optical layout sheet. The purpose of this log will be to communicate directly to the optical house just how you want the optical to look. This paper will supplement the workprint or dupe you will also send to the optical house. Often the optical house has its own optical layout sheets (also called *count sheets*) that you should use. If they are used to their own forms then the communication will be clearer if you use them.

Your optical layout sheet, also called a *count sheet, (see* Figure 10.4) should contain columns for the footage, key number, effect wanted, and comments. I have also included a column at the beginning called "Point Number" counting off the number of instructions I'm giving to the optical house. This makes it easier to talk to the optical house by telephone later on. All you will need to say is, "For point number three I want you to..." instead of, "You know, the point where the desaturation begins."

The information for the first cue point is rather simple. It is point number one, at 0'00. It is described as "Beginning of Optical." The key number can be found by locating the frame with the key number on it (if the number is spread between two frames you should find the large dot following the key number; that is the zero frame) and counting backward to the first frame of the optical. In this case it comes five frames before the key number F32X98534. Since there are sixteen frames to a foot, this frame is also equivalent to being eleven frames after F32X98533. The key number is, therefore, F32X98533^{+11}. Key numbers are usually expressed as positive numbers, that is, frames *after* a given number.

It is also a good practice to ask for extra frames both before and after the optical "just in case." This is called the *handle.* handle lengths differ from optical house to optical house, so make sure you know what it will be. In this case, we've requested "sixteen frame handles" (sometimes you will be given the choice of handle length), one extra foot at the head and tail of the optical.

Then, run down on the synchronizer until you reach the next point of reference. This will be the frame Wendy has marked for the

Date 4/18/00

OPTICAL LAYOUT

Film Silent Night, Silent Cowboy **P.O. #** 1328

Optical Number # 6

Scene # 56/57

Pt #	Footage	Key Number	Effect	Comments
1	0 + 00	F32X98533 +11	Begin optical	
2	15+03	F32X98548 +14	Freeze frame	Marked w/ "X"
3	18+03		Begin 6' desaturation	
4	24+02		End 6' desat.	
5	28+11		Begin 6' diss	Outgoing pix
	"	E26X4,6231 + 04	"	Incoming pix
6	31+11		Center of diss	Work pix cuts
7	34+11		End 6' diss	Outgoing pix
	"	E26X46237 +03	" "	Incoming pix
8	55+05	E26X46259 +14	End optical	

Please provide 16 **frame handles.**

OPTICAL LAYOUT SHEET

277

FIGURE 10.4 An optical layout sheet, or "count sheet," for our sample optical. Note the box below certain of the numbers in the key numbers. This lets the optical layout person know just what part of the key number the zero frame was measured from. The latest key numbers on Kodak stock have a small dot next to the key number which should be used as the zero frame. Note that this assistant has requested one foot (16 frame) handles. Note also that the comment at point six indicates that the work picture cuts from one shot to the other at this point. There are two lines of information given at both ends of the dissolve. That is because there are two pieces of negative involved in this dissolve. The outgoing picture is often called the "A side" and the incoming piece is often referred to as the "B-side."

beginning of the freeze frame. Note the footage and key number. On your layout sheet you will mark down this information for point number two. Also mark that you want a freeze-frame optical. You might also want to note that the frame is marked on the workprint with an X.

Run down until you reach the next point. This will be the beginning of the desaturation. Write down the footage on your layout sheet for point number three. The key number will not have changed, since you've frozen the frame. If this had been a motion optical, you would also write the key number for this frame on the optical count sheet. You should note on the count sheet the length of the optical that you want, in this instance, "Begin six-foot desaturation."

Your next point should be the end of the desaturation optical, not the beginning of the dissolve. All points of reference should be noted, both on the film and on your layout sheet.

When you have finished noting all the optical reference points, you should have the original negative or interpositive sent to the optical house along with your optical count sheet and the template, dupe or cut work picture. If your optical house is striking the IPs you should fax them the paperwork as early as you can, so they can get started on this preparatory work. Then, you should sit down with the person supervising your optical and show him or her exactly what you want. Some opticals are simpler than others. Straight fades or dissolves are such common opticals that your optical house should be able to do them without much consultation. Always, however, explain the more complex opticals such as this one—optical number one.

After you've explained the optical to the supervisor you will leave all your materials at the optical house. Make sure you have copies of all your layout sheets on file at the editing room.

After the Optical Is Shot

When they have completed the optical, which may take as few as two days or as long as a week, depending upon the optical's complexity, you (or Philip) should pick up the materials from the optical house. This will include the marked-up workprint you supplied (if you've sent them a dupe or a template you should have them keep it for future reference) along with an *optical print*. This is a viewable (positive) print of the optical they have just made for you. This print is made from the optical negative, just as your workprint is made from the original camera negative.

If, after you've screened it, the optical turns out to be perfect, you can send the negative to your negative cutter or your lab to be stored with all of the original camera negative. If the optical turns out to need more work, mark it "NG" (for "no good") and file it away in a box for rejected opticals. It would be a good idea to list the number of the NG optical on the viewable side of the box.

The optical negative for all approved opticals should be sent directly from the optical house to your negative cutter (or lab, if you don't have a negative cutter at this stage) for safe storage. If the optical house doesn't need the negative for NG opticals they can send that too. If your optical house struck the IPs for you, make sure the negative that was used to strike those IPs is sent back where it came from as well. The optical house can hold on to the IPs.

Once the completed optical is in the editing room, check to make sure that it looks all right. This involves screening it on the Moviola (and in a screening room) as well as running it through the synchronizer along with the marked–up workprint. Since the optical is shot on its own negative, it will have its own key numbers bearing no relationship to the key numbers on the cut workprint. To give you a reference back to your workprint some optical houses scratch onto the negative, along the edge, a key number so you can easily line up the completed optical with the cut workprint.

Some optical houses, however, do not provide this service. In this case there is no way to line up the optical against the workprint other than by eye matching. This is a tedious and often difficult process that involves finding at least one frame where you can see a precise match between the optical and the cut workprint. Good things to look for are frames where characters enter or exit, frames with two objects hitting one another, frames in which light bulbs go on or off (be careful about these however, since there are usually two or three frames where the light level is gradually increasing), and the like. Find three different sync points, then line one of them up and see if the other two points also line up. If they do, you know you have found proper sync.

Once you have the optical lined up and have marked where the first and last frames are you should code the optical (unless you've coded it before you lined it up). I generally reserve the prefix code "P" or "OP," such as OP1000 or 056P1000 (for an optical designed for scene 56). Naturally, you should enter the complete information about the optical—optical number, codes, key numbers, scenes involved, description of optical, date made, et al., into a new section in your logbook reserved for opticals.

At this point, you should cut the original workprint back into the cut reels if you've pulled it for the optical house's reference.

When the optical is lined up and coded, you can cut it into the cut work picture reel where the original shots were. Then, you, Wendy, Philip, and Adam should screen the film to check for several things. First, you will be checking to see that the optical is correct. It is possible, even though the optical house followed all your instructions correctly, that the optical seems wrong when viewed on the screen. This can happen for several reasons. Wendy may have miscalculated some of the footage. If this is the case you must completely remake the optical. Also, even with the materials available today, it is not always possible to control opticals precisely. Long fades or dissolves suffer most from this, since the degree to which the image will gradually fade in or out is not completely predictable over long lengths. For that reason, a long fade will not always seem gradual. There is virtually nothing to be done about this problem except to keep redoing the optical until you luck into a better result. You could also try the optical digitally where you might have more control. We will discuss this at the end of the chapter.

Another thing you will be looking for, as a further check that you have lined up and cut the optical in correctly, is sync of the picture against the track. This will be the first time you will have seen the optical with a soundtrack.

280

You will also want to check that the color of the optical does not vary too much from the non-optical shots in the same scene. Do not worry too much about minor color shifts. Slight variations in color are always correctable in the laboratory at the end of the film. Major variations may not be correctable. It is also difficult to color correct one part of a dissolve separately from another part of it.

A final word about the quality of opticals. As I've mentioned, an optical print is made from a negative that has been made from an interpositive print that was made from the original negative. As a result, its quality will be slightly worse than the quality of the surrounding non–optical material. You will notice an increase in the graininess of the image and the colors may have a bit more contrast. Some shots degrade worse than other shots. This is an unavoidable by-product of making an optical. Some films, such as *Body Heat*, do their optical dissolves in the lab using A and B rolling rather than in an optical house, just as 16mm films do. If a scene is to contain many opticals intercut with original negative, many editors like to make the entire section (even those parts of the scene that would not normally be opticals) an optical. That way, the entire scene will be of the same quality. Even though it is of a lesser quality than the original negative, it will be less noticeable than intercutting material or varying quality.

The film stock manufacturers, notably Eastman Kodak, are constantly developing better IP stocks to try to minimize this degradation. Recent advances have made optical quality much better for many types of shots. One method that I've used successfully to try to eliminate visible grain is something called *double interpositive* (or double IPs). In this procedure, two IPs are struck of each shot at half the exposure rather than just one at full exposure. When the two are combined in the optical printer the grain will not be the same in each IP and the two have the effect of canceling each other out (to some degree). Obviously this is a more expensive solution, since two IPs need to be printed, but the results are surprisingly good.

If, after screening, the optical is not approved and must be redone, you might need to send the workprint back to the optical house. Obviously, if they have been working from a color dupe (which you had them hold onto) they will already have everything they need. If the layout of the optical is to be changed, you would give it a new optical number (or call it Optical Number 6R, for "revised") and make a new layout sheet for it, then go over to the optical house and talk them through it again. However, if the original optical is approved, you should have Philip bring the optical negative to your negative cutter or the lab so it can be stored with the rest of the original negative.

281

After approval, the original cut workprint that you've replaced with the optical can be stored in a box marked "Workprint Replaced By Opticals." The trims from the optical can be stored in a box for optical trims. I like to use different colored tape on the side of this box so you can easily see which section of the trims is devoted to opticals. In fact, I like to use different colors for lifts, rough mixes, and scratch music as well. This way it is easier to see any one particular box you need and the chance of mis-filing a box in the racks is lessened. One final note about these colors. Some people overdo the color system until it more complicated to remember what each color stands for than it would be to find the materials mixed in with other footage. Usually, a color for trims/outs (white tape), opticals (yellow), scratch mixes (red), and music (blue) are enough for any film.

Titles

A special kind of optical work is the creation of titles (or credits) for the beginning and end of the film. Though credits usually are not done until the very end of the editing process (on some films, the credits are so late in coming that they arrive only days before the opening of the movie) we will consider them here with the other opticals.

Titles come in several forms—on a colored background, supered, or animated. The first kind (such as the kind seen in Woody Allen's films) involves lettering on a plain background. The background may be colored, black, or white, and the lettering may be any color at all. The second kind of titles are those that are superimposed over a scene from the film. There are combinations of the two, such as in *Heathers* where we had the first few titles come up on a plain background, but the bulk of them superimposed over action. Animated titles are an entirely different set of titles, involving someone who draws each frame of the titles, shoots them, and supplies you with a finished piece of negative to be dropped into your workprint.

There are companies that design title sequences for movies. Sometimes they simply design the typestyle (along with the advertising department of the company that is going to distribute the film). Other times they design elaborate title sequences that are almost little movies in themselves.

You should get an approved list of credits from the producer's office (*see* Figure 10.5). These will include a breakdown of all the credits to be seen at the beginning of the film and, on a separate list, the end. It will show which people will share space on the screen (or "share a card" as it is called) and which get "single card" credits. Many directors', writers', or stars' contracts require that their names be no smaller (or the same size) than a certain percentage of the title of the film, so this list should also show the relative sizes of the credits.

Each card will be assigned a number. Thus, the first title would be MT1, meaning Main Title card number one ("An Adam Free Film").

Wendy and Adam, along with the titles designer if there is one, will have determined what the main titles should look like. Often, this will be type that fades in and out over different pieces of picture. Wendy will need to lay out the location of these titles. She will do this by putting grease pencil marks identifying the beginning and the end of each title (they usually run for about four or five seconds apiece) and drawing a grease pencil line down the center of the frame between the start and end marks. She will then be able to look at the film and see how each title times out against the action on screen and the dialogue, if there is any.

After she has completed laying out the main titles, you will need to take this piece of film and create a template (or dupe) just as you did for the optical we discussed earlier in this chapter. You can then create an optical count sheet listing where every background

"Silent Night, Silent Cowboy"

Main Titles
March 28, 2000

MT1	Big Time Pictures presents	100%
MT2	an Adam Free film	100%
MT3	Silent Night, Silent Cowboy	100%
	Starring	
MT4	Carol Lestial	100%
MT5	Enid Gaseous	100%
	and	
MT6	Reed Birney	100%
	as "Doc"	
	with	
MT7	Alice Wannabee	60%
	Philip Striving	
	Bob Robert	
	Sean McKinley	
MT8	Gene Shepherd	60%
	Hut Yabbo	

Silent Night, Silent Cowboy
Main Titles – March 28, 2000
Page 1

FIGURE 10.5 *The first page of the Main Titles list supplied by the producer's office. The cards on the End Titles list (if the end titles used cards rather than a crawl) would be numbered ET1, ET2, ET3, etc. Note the numbers on the right hand side of the page. These refer to the size, expressed as a percentage of the main title ("Silent Night, Silent Cowboy"), that each card must be.*

piece of picture cuts in and out, as well as where each title card (identified by the MT number on the titles list) fades in and out. Once again, the lab or the optical house, will need to make IPs for every background shot in the film. These IPs will be special because there will be type superimposed on them. If the background image wavered in any way (there is often a very slight, normally unnoticed, weave to negative when it is run through an optical printer), the foreground title wouldn't waver with it, and the effect of the superimposition would be quite distracting. To eliminate this wavering, the optical house will need a *registration IP*. In fact, if you have any opticals requiring superimposed type, you will need to have the background image struck as a registration IP. Opticals that may need this treatment would be a card identifying a location or time—"Queens Village, 1955"—or a subtitle card at the bottom of the screen translating what someone is saying in a foreign language. Titles sitting near the bottom of the frame like this are often called *lower third supers.*

Wendy, the director, and the producer will also determine whether they wish the end titles to be a crawl, cards, or a combination of the two. These terms refer to the manner in which the mass of names at the end of the film will be displayed. Some films roll the credits up on the screen slowly (this is called a *crawl*), others present them as cards that fade in and out sequentially. Other films combine the two approaches. Once they have decided, you will be able to determine how the end titles will fall out on the screen. If the names are to be on cards then they will have to be divided logically (usually by job category) without making the individual names too small to be read. Usually no more than seven or eight names are readable on any one card. If the names are to be on a crawl it may be wise to separate job categories with an extra few lines of space to make them easier to read. It also helps to be aware of the legal requirements that various actors and unions have in their contracts. Though the producer's office should have dealt with all of these questions before giving you the list, often someone just plain forgets to check. It is nice, if you are aware enough of what credits normally look like, to spot anything that looks out of the ordinary.

Once all of these questions have been answered you need to have the type prepared for the title cards. A typestyle will have to be selected. Adam should do this, with Wendy (or the title designer) making sure he is selecting a readable typestyle.

Then you, or the title designer, have to go to the typesetter with that titles list to have the type set up for shooting. Someone at the optical house will generally type all of the names into a computer, giving it instructions on placement on the screen, typeface, and size. The computer then prints out the titles in a high quality format that the optical house can shoot directly. Typically, this will take a day or two. While this is being done, there is another piece of title material you will be needing if you haven't already received it. That is the main title logo.

Every distribution company has its own logo. Twentieth Century Fox has the large letters with the meandering klieg lights. M-G-M has Leo the Lion. Columbia has the friendly torch lady. These are all opticals created by the individual company's advertising departments. You should get a print and a negative of that logo (and any soundtrack that should go with it) as early on in the cutting of the film as possible and cut it onto the head of reel one just as it will appear in the film. It is important to cut it on before the sound and music editing departments begin working because it will affect the length of the first reel. When you get this print and negative, treat it as an optical, giving it an optical number and coding it with the proper optical prefix. Then, just as you would with an optical, keep the trims in an optical box and send the negative to the lab to be stored with the rest of your negative.

When the typesetter has finished his or her job you will receive a printed list of all the titles the way they will look when shot. You and the producer should very carefully check each name and title to make sure everything has been spelled correctly and no names have been left out.

If everything is not perfect (and it rarely is on the first try) the typesetter must redo the incorrect parts of the list. If you have any other changes in the titles list, now is the time to bring them up. When everything is perfect, you will have to sign off on the finished titles. Any changes you make from here on will cost you dearly, so make sure everything is correct when you have the producer or director sign off.

Like any other optical, the optical house will need a layout sheet and a workprint mock-up. The most common way of mocking up titles on the workprint is to put a piece of white paper tape on the film (you can also write directly on the film with grease pencil) indicating which title card is going where on the film.

If you are having plain head title cards, you would make the mock-up on a long piece of white leader. If the titles came directly after the distributor's logo you would cut a piece of white leader onto the end of the logo. Then you would roll down a pre-determined length until you reached the point where the first title should begin to fade in. This predetermined length is a purely aesthetic decision and should be made by Wendy and Adam. Let's say that *Silent Night* is going to have three seconds of black before the first title, MT1 (which will say "Big Time Pictures Presents"), fades in. That is the equivalent of four and one-half feet.

If the titles were to be supered onto an existing scene, the process would be very much the same with one exception. Instead of writing with magic marker on white leader you would be making your optical marks with grease pencil on the scene. You would also be making your identification notations with magic marker on a piece of white paper tape that you would attach to the film at the proper place (though some assistants prefer to grease pencil the title card number directly on the film).

Once the type for the titles has been approved, the optical house makes a *hi–con* of the titles. The term hi-con is short for *high contrast*. It is a very sharp black and white negative that will be used in the superimposition of the titles onto the picture (background) negative.

Certain decisions must now be made about how you want the titles to appear. These involve the color of the lettering, the type of lettering (to increase readability most titles are made with a *drop shadow* which is an extension of the letters at the bottom and to the right of each letter), and the color and treatment of the background. In *Four Friends*, when the background scene faded up behind the already running credits, it came in first out of focus and then sharpened up. All of this was created at the optical house. Again, these are artistic decisions Adam and Wendy will make together.

All of these instructions must be communicated to the people at the optical house in as clear a manner as possible. To do this you will create an optical layout (or count) sheet detailing the footage and key numbers of all background scenes, the placement of all titles, as well as the lengths of all fades (whether they are fades of picture or title type). Title creation is a costly process and any mistakes requiring the credits be redone will be very expensive and unwelcome.

Special Opticals

Another kind of optical that is very popular nowadays really deserves an entire book all to itself—the *special effects optical*. These occur quite frequently in films where scenes are recreated in the optical house that would have been far too expensive to shoot live (if they could have been shot at all). The complexity of these types of opticals is so great that it makes the examples that I gave at the beginning of this chapter seem as easy as breathing. Some of the opticals in the *Star Wars* movies combine as many as eight or nine separate pieces of film. In *Titanic* there were almost nine hundred complete opticals. Some films, like *Terminator 2* and *Jurassic Park*, seem almost entirely made up of opticals.

On such jobs the assistant editor rarely supervises opticals. The job is given to an *optical effects supervisor* with their own assistant. You are involved in communicating the editor's needs to the optical people and vice versa.

Computer Opticals

Over the last five years, an increasing number of optical effects are done using a computer. With this method the negative for the shot is electronically scanned. The image is converted into a large number of zeroes and ones that can be stored in a computer. The optical house then manipulates these images inside their computers to attain effects not realistically possible with conventional optical methods.

Complex opticals (like the shots of people changing shape, called *morphing*), and simple ones (like matting a studio shot of a character in a gondola onto a stock shot of the Venice canals) can all be accomplished this way.

It is an expensive process and often a slow one as well. However, the advantages often outweigh the disadvantages.

You, as the assistant, will still need to provide all the same information to the optical house that you do when opticals are shot conventionally. Count sheets, templates or dupes, and some consultation are all necessary. However, since it is the negative that is scanned into the computer system, it is usually not necessary to strike an interpositive.

Computer effects (called *CGI* for Computer Generated Imagery or Images) combining three-dimensional effects with pre-shot backgrounds often need to have those backgrounds input from a videotape telecined using a special *Steady Gate* system. This telecine system will create a much steadier videotape, much like a registration IP. When these backgrounds are combined with the computer generated effects, they will not appear to weave independently of the effects.

CGI is a complex process and shots are continually screened and improved and screened again. Because scanning the optical back out to negative is an extremely time consuming (and expensive) process, some productions will take the temporary videotape output and convert it to film using a process called *conforming* or *kinescoping*. While this gives Wendy and Adam some idea of what the optical will look like, it sacrifices many of the nuances of the final shot. There is also the possibility that the kinescope process will create a film optical that is not frame-to-frame accurate with the final film output version of the optical. You will need to make sure this does not happen because awful consequences to sound and music editing can result if the lengths of an optical were to change late in the schedule.

CGI effects require varying amounts of input from you. Often, you will still need to lay them out, just as though the effects were being done in a traditional film optical house. You will still need to provide key numbers, send the negative to the CGI house, and provide a count sheet. About the only differences you will find are that you will often need to supply a videotape of the edit with some sort of burn-in, and you will not need to create an IP.

Some effects, those that will be created completely from the minds of the CGI artists, will need no more counts from you than a length (though this is often determined by the CGI supervisor) and the key numbers of the background plate.

Once the optical has been completed (and, often, it is possible to be given some intermediate version of the optical to test) the computer converts the ones and zeroes back into an image that is then recorded onto a piece of negative. This process is called *outputting*. This new negative becomes your optical negative and the CGI house will strike a positive print from it for you.

288

The advantage of this method (besides the ability to do opticals that were impossible before) is that there is much less degradation of the image than with conventional opticals. There are often other problems associated with this process to be dealt with and, as with anything, the first try is rarely perfect.

But even with all of those complexities one fact about opticals still remains—optical creation is a process of manipulating the original negative (or negatives) to create a new one. All opticals require laying out of the effects. There is no mystery to the process, though there is great artistry. The idea is not to be intimidated, but to realize it is all "playing with film" and understandable.

OPTICALS IN A NON-LINEAR WORLD

The creation of film opticals in the digital non-linear editing room makes the job of the assistant both easier and harder (just like everything else in this new world of computers). For one thing, the creation of optical count sheets is now more or less automated. However, it is now necessary to do much more work to get opticals into the Avid or Lightworks. Let's take a look at the process.

The Importance of Dailies Preparation

I've mentioned in an earlier chapter the concept of GIGO ("Garbage in, Garbage out."). Quite simply this means the accuracy of your work is based on good record keeping and precision from the very beginning of the film. If the key numbers are not entered properly during dailies, you can not expect to get proper numbers out as you create your optical count sheets.

The advantage of working on a computer non-linear editing system is that Wendy will be able to see many of her opticals in the machine as she is editing. She can view them without having to send any film out to an optical house. With the press of a button or two, users of every editing system on the market today can see their dissolves, fades and in most cases, titles on screen with no more than a minimum of waiting. Many of the higher end systems also allow the editor to create *blue screen* or *green screen* composite shots, a number of *wipes*, a whole range of color changes and a host of other opticals. This way, Wendy and Adam can try out different opticals of differing lengths until they find the optical that is the exact style and length they want.

There are two types of opticals on many digital editing machines: rendered and real-time. For most complicated opticals (in fact, for *all* opticals on many editing machines), the machine cannot handle the intense amount of data needed to play back any opticals requiring more than a simple combination of two images. In order to show Wendy the end result of these opticals, the machine will need to *render* the optical first. All that this means is the machine creates the optical, a frame at a time, making a completely new piece of material. It is this new material, rather than the original dailies, that will be played back on the machine.

There is one advantage to this method and a few disadvantages. The advantage is that the editing machine will be able to play back the optical back without any stuttering or faults. One disadvantage is that it takes some amount of time to render the effect, depending on how complicated it is. Another problem is that the new material won't be any longer at the head or the tail than the optical Wendy has created. If she wants to extend it or change it in any way, she will need to render it all over again.

The reality, however, is that she will rarely have an option. Some effects, such as fades and dissolves, won't have to be rendered. Most others will need to be rendered.

Real-time opticals, on the other hand, are those that don't have to be rendered.

A word of warning about fades and dissolves on these systems. At the present time these machines cannot exactly duplicate the look of a film optical with complete accuracy. As a result there may be slight differences between what Wendy and Adam see on their viewing monitors and what they will see when the 35mm film optical is projected on a screen.

Eventually, there will come a time when the two of them will have decided on several opticals. They will need to see how they look on film. It is usually cheaper to create multiple opticals so, if time permits, you should hold off sending count sheets to the optical house until you have several opticals to make.

Titles

One of the great things about cutting on a digital editing system is their ability to show you the results of many of your opticals before you order them from the optical house. This is especially valuable in the case of titles. Though the choices of type face are more limited than in the optical house, you can create temporary titles that can give everyone a real sense of how the titles will look against picture and dialogue. On many editing systems, you will be able to fade the titles in and out, place them wherever you want within the frame, and even roll them on and off the screen should you want to.

It's a fantastic advantage.

Many of these machines will also be able to generate an optical count sheet listing where these titles come within the sequence as well as how long they are and how long the fades leading in and out of them are. So, let's discuss the count sheets now.

Creating Count Sheets

You will need to provide the optical house with exactly the same data you provided them on a film-only show. It makes no difference to them whether you are cutting on film or on a digital editing system, they still need count sheets and interpositives. They still need to deliver a finished 35mm optical negative and print of each optical to you. The only differences in the process are apparent to *you*.

The real advantage for you, optically speaking, is that your editing machine will provide most of the necessary paperwork for you. In Chapter 8A we saw how most machines with 24 frame software can print out Negative Cut Lists with their matching Pull Lists. They also can print out *Negative Pull Lists* of all the negative that will be needed to create your optical. These pull lists will show every take, with key and lab roll numbers, for which you will need to make interpositives. It will list the key numbers for the entire take, not just for the section used in the optical. In fact, when you are dealing with IPs, this is exactly what the lab or optical house making the IP will need. They usually will not make IPs of sections of the negative since it would potentially damage the negative. Instead, they will go from the beginning flash frame of the take to the ending flash frame. This is called, not surprisingly, *flash to flash* and your Avid or Lightworks digital editing machine can make the list for you. You can then give it to your negative cutter and optical house (or lab, if they are going to print the IP).

Your 24 frame software equipped machine can also print out *Optical Count Sheets.* These are supposed to look very much like your own Optical Count Sheets we saw in the previous chapter.

If you have been conforming work picture along with the digital edit, it is still a good idea to mark up the work picture to match the numbers on the count sheets. You can then either create a *template* or a color dupe, or you can send the marked up work picture to the optical house as we discussed in Chapter 10. Marking up the work picture will also provide you with a way to check the accuracy of the numbers created by your editing machine.

This leads us to the major problem with computer generated count sheets. Try as they might, the count sheet lists generated by even the best digital editing systems are not yet as accurate or well organized as those of a good assistant editor. They are also rarely in the format the optical house is used to seeing. Since that can lead to confusion and errors, I always have my assistant editor rewrite the computer's optical count sheets onto the optical house's preferred forms.

Many assistants using film based logging programs use their digital editing machines as a sort of film synchronizer when making count sheets. Since those systems can show both key numbers and footages, it is easy to stop at the head of the optical and "zero out" the system. The key number will be displayed somewhere on screen. You can then type it into a count sheet on another computer, usually a laptop. Some assistants have created templates in their word processing programs conforming to the count sheets from their optical house. They can then type in this key number (checking carefully to make sure they have entered it correctly) and move onto the next event, which will sometimes be the beginning of a fade or dissolve. It is easy to see the elapsed footage and the correct key number and enter that onto the count sheet. This is a good check on the count sheets automatically generated by the editing machine.

Even if you're not printing any film or conforming your dailies, it is still a good idea to rewrite the count sheets. It is an excellent way for you to understand and double-check the computer's lists. Often there will be minor differences between what the computer generates and what Wendy wanted. Especially tricky are lengths of fades since computers control black differently than optical houses. However, if all of the technical information was input into your machine properly during dailies (this is another reason it is important for you to check *every* take you receive from telecine), these count sheet numbers should be very close or exactly correct.

Once you've generated the proper lists, you can proceed exactly as described in the previous chapter. You take the lists and the marked-up workprint (or mock-up) to the optical house, and sit with your line-up person to discuss the optical if it is at all complex. The optical house makes the optical and sends a print of it to the editing room. Everyone watches it, hopefully on a big screen. Only after the optical has been approved do things get a little more complicated.

Once the Optical Is Finished

To be absolutely strict about it, the ideal path at this point would be to take the negative of the optical and telecine it, just as you telecined every foot of dailies in the film. This way you could match the optical back into your computer cut of the film, complete with all of its key numbers and Acmade numbers, if you are using that system. The final *Cut Lists* the computer will generate for your negative cutter (don't worry, we will discuss these terms in Chapter 16A) will then include all of your opticals with negative cutting information.

To do this you would instruct your optical house to send the optical negative (*not* the original negative you sent to them; that should go back to your negative cutter) over to your telecine house marked "Prep For Telecine." You would then notify your contact at the telecine house that the footage was coming over and needed to be prepped for telecine and transferred as your dailies were (*see* Chapter 4A for more details). A work order, or purchase order, should also be included with all of this information written as specifically as possible, along with the time code you want them to use if you have a specific requirement. Let them know it is a piece of MOS material. Because telecine time is so expensive, and there is usually a minimum, it is nice when you can do several opticals at the same time. If it is possible, within your schedule and Wendy's and Adam's needs, wait to telecine until enough opticals are approved to meet the minimum time. If you are expecting more opticals within a day or two it might be sensible to wait and do all of the material at one time.

Some films don't go through this expensive process. They simply take the approved optical prints and cut them into the conformed workprint, without updating the computer cut. This makes the Avid or Lightworks cut a bit out of date but, since most of the opticals are already shown visually by the machine, the cut is still watchable. In any case, it is the cut work print that will be turned over to the negative cutter, not a Cut List from the computer.

On *Mad Dog Time* this is almost exactly what we did near the end of the film. We telecined most of the opticals but in order to save money on the Lightworks rental, we let go of the machine as soon as we could. There were a few opticals still not completed in time, and we simply cut them into the work print, which was already at the negative cutters by then anyway.

However, this short cut is not really possible on films that have not printed film. In those cases, there is almost no way to expertly cut in opticals except by dropping them into the Avid or

Lightworks edit. Expensive though it may be, there will be little choice except to telecine the optical. The only other alternative (and this is pretty risky so I'd advise against it unless you have a production manager that likes to take chances, or no money left in the film budget) is to have your negative cutter eye-match the optical negative in using a videotape playout of your final edit as a guide.

Cutting Opticals Into the Edit

Once you have telecined the approved opticals, you should input the footage into your editing machine exactly as you digitized your dailies and reprints. I like to have a separate bin or gallery for all of my opticals, as well as having a copy of each optical in with the dailies materials for the scenes in which the optical belongs (remember, this does not require you to digitize the material twice, you are only copying the logs for the material). In the case of our sample optical from Chapter 10, not only would the shot be in an Optical gallery or bin, but you would also put it in the bin or gallery for Scene 56. If there are a lot of opticals on the film, I often create a separate gallery or bin for each day's—or week's—opticals. This is very handy in the case of CGI opticals where there are often several versions of each optical.

294

Just as you would eye match the 35mm print, as described in Chapter 10, you will need to do the same for the video optical. First, make a copy of the edit you are working with. If this optical is going into reel six, and the last version Wendy was working on was Version 900, you should create a Version 901 of the reel (I would call it R06v901-w/opticals). Then use the same procedure as you did for cutting in reprints described in Chapter 9A. When you are sure the optical and its original material are in perfect sync, cut the new footage in, replacing the old footage frame for frame.

When you have completed that, you are sort of done.

If you are working on a film that has been conforming workprint you will be able to check that you have dropped in your optical correctly. Follow the procedures outlined in Chapter 10 for replacing the work picture with your new optical. When you are finished, check the key number on the very first and very last frame of the cut-in optical. These key numbers should exactly match the burned-in key numbers on the first and last frames of the cut-in optical on your Lightworks or Avid. If they don't, then one of the two edits—your work picture reel or your computer edit—is incorrect and you will need to retrace your steps to figure out which one needs to be fixed.

And once you have done that, you are *really* done.

CGI Opticals

In the last several years, the number of films using CGI opticals has dramatically increased. As we discussed in Chapter 10, these opticals are created on computers which then output their computer frames onto film frames. This film output is very expensive and time consuming, and it has gotten very common to have the optical house create an output of intermediate versions of effects onto tape that you can input into your digital editing machine. You must take great care to make sure that this CGI tape gets to you in the proper format. If the CGI house has not pulled down the footage properly in transfer to the 30 FPS world of the videotape, you will have a piece of footage that will not match the 24 FPS pieces you have in your cut. On *Quicksilver Highway*, a television movie I edited based on a Stephen King short story, the special effects created for us tended to run a frame or two out of sync, even when they were pulled down properly. When they weren't...they were too different in length to be cut in reliably. They also looked very odd, since their speed rate (after my Avid removed the pulldown frames) varied from the original material. They had the jerkiness of old movies.

In fact, because these computer opticals use the same computer technology as your editing machine (that is, zeroes and ones arranged in a particular order to create individual frames of picture) many editing rooms have taken to inputting directly from a computer picture format rather than going through a videotaped intermediate stage.

Different editing machines can import different graphics files. Importing is simply the acting of taking a computer file created on a different computer or in a different file format and bringing it into your own editing program on your own computer. Depending on your machine, you may be able to import QuickTime movies, Targa or TIFF files or a host of other formats.

To do this, you would ask your optical house to supply you with the optical in the format you need, on a disk you can use with your editing computer. On one film we had our Special Effects Supervisor put the computer graphics files onto a hard disk that we then hooked up to our Avid. On other films you may ask that your CGI opticals be supplied to you on R-mags or on a Jaz or Zip disk format (Zip disks, however, are usually too small for anything but the shortest files).

A recently popular file format, called OMF (Open Media Framework) allows machines to create visual images that can be read by other editing machines. On some recent films, effects created on high end machines and software programs like Discreet Logic's Flame, SGI's Onyx or Iris, and Alias were imported into Avid Film Composers. On some machines the process is as simple as pressing an OMF button to recreate the effects in the OMFI (Open Media Framework Interchange) format. Other machines you will require you to select the function for exporting a file and select "OMF" in some way. The files that will be created should be saved on some sort of removable hard drive, like an R-Mag or a Jaz cartridge. This drive is what you will receive in the editing room.

When you receive the drive, you will import it as a file and put it into a bin or gallery reserved for opticals. If you've received the optical on a videotape, you will digitize it just as you would a piece of dailies. You can then treat the optical as any other piece of film.

If your CGI house gives you digital output on a Jaz disk or hard drive not in an OMF format, you will need to have them create the files in the proper format and with the proper frame rate. Make sure you discuss your needs with your optical house before they begin making outputs for you.

296

It is also possible, using some of the editing machines or using a separate program, to create your own CGI opticals. The Avid, Media 100, Turbo Cube and computers using Adobe Premiere all allow multiple layers of video, that can be combined using a large number of filters to get many types of opticals. Some of the rock videos you see on television today were created completely in one of these systems then output to digital tape for airing. If you are creating a feature film or even a network television show, it is more likely that you will only be creating templates for the effects, rather than the final optical. However the day is looming when editors will need to know almost as much about creating opticals as on-line editors do today. Certainly, most commercials editors are already in this position. In the future, off-line editing rooms will need to function as optical houses, videotape dubbing facilities, and mixing stages as well as editing room. An assistant comfortable in all these areas will be much more in demand then one without the same technical skills.

Opticals in the 30 FPS World

Opticals created for television shows, or any other release exclusively in the videotape format, can be handled quite differently, since you will not need to create an optical on a piece of film. Instead, most opticals will be created in some sort of video system or in the on-line editing.

Simple effects like fades, dissolves, superimpositions and speed changes are very easily handled in the on-line session after you lock.

As we will see in Chapters 11A and 16A, the video-only project never goes through lab finishing but is, instead, matched in a high end editing bay, using the high-quality set of videotapes (usually D-1 or DigiBeta) made in the telecine bay during dailies.

Using a picture EDL, listing every picture edit and effect made in Wendy's computer editing machine, the on-line editor will painstakingly, though with great assistance from his or her computer, recreate every edit and effect using these high-quality tapes. At this time, many of those effects can be recreated as well.

Fades, dissolves, superimpositions, speed changes, reverse printing, and many more effects are very easy to do in the on-line. Effects that cannot be done there can usually be handled in a separate video suite in the same facility using the numbers from the EDL. They will then be inserted back into the *Video Master* tape created in the on-line session.

For some video-only projects, it is possible that there will be a number of effects that cannot be done on-line or in a separate effects bay. CGI falls into this category. On *Quicksilver Highway* we had a large number of 3-D and 2-D special effects shots that needed to be created at a CGI house. The effects were then dumped out onto tape and sent back to us in the editing room.

As I mentioned back in Chapter 9A, both the Avid and Lightworks have a function allowing you to lock two monitors together and play them at the same time, in sync. When the effects on *Quicksilver* arrived in our editing room, my assistant digitized them and then one of us would look for a sync point between each CGI shot and its matching piece in a copy of the latest edit. After we had determined that one sync point, we locked two monitors together and played them down until we saw another sync point. By stopping on this frame, we could check the optical against the original footage and make sure they were still in sync. If they were, we tried one more sync point that was normally in sync.

If these points weren't in sync, we looked for better sync points and checked three of them again. In the one or two cases where we could find no sync points, we realized there was a problem with the effect. In our case, the problem was the effect was not being converted from the 24 FPS mode they were using to create it back into the 30 FPS mode before our videotape was made.

However, if all sync points checked out, it was an easy matter to edit the completed effect into the copy of the edit. This copy then became the master, from which we made our EDLs for the on-line session.

In the cases where the completed effect arrived after we had already done our on-line session, my assistant kept a record of all of the changes that came in and where they fell in the Video Master tape so we could go back into the on-line bay near the end of the process and drop those CGI shots into the final tape.

PREPARING FOR SOUND

After many months of cutting and recutting the day will come when you are nearly finished editing the film. Now, the movie should be turned over to a sound crew who will prepare the film's soundtrack for the final film mix (or dub).

Things never seem to work out this smoothly, however. Mixing studio time is usually booked many months before the film is ready to be handed over to the sound crew. Often a film has a release date planned well in advance and that date sets the post-production schedule, rather than the needs of the film itself. As a result, it's rare nowadays that a film is really *locked* when it is turned over to the sound crew.

Locking a film means, simply, to finish cutting it. It doesn't mean you've finished working on it, only that the picture edits are not going to change. Unfortunately, I have rarely worked on a movie that did *not* come open again after the lock. That is why I prefer to call this part, *latching the film*.

Preliminaries to Handover

Before you even think of making the dupes and videotapes to give to the sound department, a few things are very important. Not only does the film have to be as close to locked as possible, but the reels have to be balanced in their final form. Because of the mechanics of sound editing (where each reel will normally have at least fifty mix elements with matching cue sheets), it will be far more difficult and time consuming to make changes in the reel balancing *after* the reels have been sound edited than before. In fact, each time you make any kind of change after you've handed the film over, you will need to strike new videotapes of the reels involved, as well as partial sections of dupe. As you can imagine, each change you make after striking the dupes and tapes will complicate your life. We will get to that later on in this chapter.

Balancing for final release is very similar to balancing for your earlier screenings with one welcome exception—films are distributed on 2000-foot reels (often called *double reels*), not on the 1000-foot editorial reels you've been working on. So a reel change from an odd to an even reel (such as reel three to reel four) will not exist in the distributed version. This cuts down the number of problems by about one–half.

This does not mean that you should ignore those odd-to-even reel changeovers. If your film is being mixed in 1000 foot rolls, it is more convenient to put reel changes in places without any continuous sound, such as a police siren or music. The even-to-odd changeovers (such as from reel two to reel three), that *will* be projection changeovers in some theatres, should never come in places you want to have continuous sounds, particularly music. Because of the realities of film projection with changeovers, there is no way a reel change can be made without losing some of the end of the outgoing reel and the beginning of the incoming one. Though this is not usually noticeable in parts of the film without dialogue, it is always noticeable (even to the layman) if it interrupts an active piece of music. Knowing this, composers who are forced to write music bridging reels either bring their music to a stop one second before the end of a reel (and don't begin it again for one second after the start of the second), or they bring it into a sustained hold for those lengths of time. From an aesthetic viewpoint, neither solution is perfectly satisfactory. So, if you can guess where music is going to be, it is advisable to balance your reels so true projection changeovers will come where there will be no music. If Wendy has been cutting with temp music, you can use the placement of these cues as a reliable, but not definitive, guide.

Increasingly, it has become possible to hand over the picture in these 2000 foot reels. Now that virtually every sound and music editor works digitally, they are no longer hampered by the unwieldiness of large film reels and multiple tracks. Labs seem to prefer the film in these larger reels. Negative cutters were the last hold-outs for the 1000 foot editorial reels, but even they have now learned how to handle the larger double reels with no potential negative damage.

For this reason, it is possible that you can hand your picture over in these larger reels. You will then have approximately half the number of reel changes to worry about, though each reel will be approximately twice as large.

There is a problem with doing lab work in 2000 foot reels, but it is not one that influences this decision very much (most labs now insist on mounting your film onto double reels even if your negative cutter matched it in single reels). As we will see in Chapter 16, when you finish the lab work on a film, there may be two or three editorial reels that need more work, either because there are late-arriving opticals, or because the color balancing work is more difficult. If these three editorial reels are spread across three double reels, you will be putting up the cut negative on three *double* reels (the equivalent of six editorial reels) to work on problems only found in three *single* reels. This jeopardizes more of the negative than I would like. It also leads to pressure from the lab to accept lesser work and move forward with the finishing process faster than it should go at times.

Still, 2000 foot double reels are the way most productions now finish.

Ironically, most theatres across the country today don't even show the film in these 2000 foot reels because they no longer use the two-projector system (though there are still plenty of exceptions to this). Instead they use what is called the *platter system* of projection. In this system, the entire film is spliced together and put onto a huge platter that looks like an enormous flange. The film is then run through the air, threaded through the projector and, after exiting the projector, is taken up on another platter on the stack (there are generally three platters on each machine stack, one for feeding, one for taking up and the third for a second feature if the theatre shows two movies). When it is time for the next show, the projectionist (or, in many theatres, the manager of the theatre or an assistant) re-threads the film so it feeds from the second platter, through the projector and back up onto the first platter.

As a result there are no changeovers in platter projection. This leads to an interesting set of choices Wendy and you will have to make when determining your changeovers and adding the changeover tails. Since films are rarely seen with changeovers in theatres (or, for that matter, on television and videotapes), most people will be watching your movie *with* any changeover tails you put on. In fact, the places that still screen with changeovers are primarily professional screening rooms where most critics and industry people will see the film.

You will want to balance the needs of the few (but important) changeover theatres against those platter theatres. You can no longer assume no one will see those extra frames after the second changeover cue. In fact, it is certain many people *will* see them. So choose them wisely.

More and more editors, myself included, prefer not to add changeover tails at all to their reels since the bulk of the audience by far will not need them. This choice should be left to Wendy. I still try to balance the reels without dialogue in the first or last foot of a reel to protect against the industry screening prints.

Another factor to keep in mind as you create your final reel balance, is the lengths of the reels. While it may have been all right to include a few undersized or oversized reels as you were cutting, it is not good form to do so now. I try to keep each reel at about 950 feet. When this is not possible, I make sure that the double reels run about 1900-1950 feet. If it is necessary for one reel to run 1050 feet, for example, I make sure the next one runs no more than 850-900 feet. The reason for this stems from the economics of lab work. Rolls of print film come in multiples of 2000 feet. If a double reel comes in at about that length, there is no problem. If it is too large, however, the lab may need to attach another piece of film to the printing reel. This is not only an extra cost but may sometimes lead to problems in projection. If the double reel is too small, there will be an awful lot of print film wasted which the distributor will have to pay for anyway.

302

Some distributors have special length requirements. On most Disney films, they ask the editor to leave an additional 300 feet of room at the top of the first double reel so they can add their own trailers when they send the film out to the theatres. In the reel balancing you would need to make sure the first double reel combination was around 1600 feet, rather than 1900.

The other major preliminary that you need to do before handing over your film is to clean up your tracks. During the course of the editing process it is probable that you or Wendy will have cut some sound effects or music cues into your work tracks. You don't want these non-dialogue sounds to end up on your dupes and videotapes. As the composer and sound editors create the music and sound effects they will not want to hear the temporary ones the picture department cut in for screenings.

You do need to be aware of one thing as you excise these temp sounds from your work tracks. If you're not lucky you will need, at some point, to screen your movie for somebody and (without a doubt) Adam is going to want to have those temp sounds back in the tracks when you do. As a result, you should remove the effects in such a way that you can easily put them back again if you need to.

There are two ways you can do this. Perhaps the easiest is to split every sound you do not want in your work track or tracks onto a separate roll of fill. To do this you would put your work tracks (if Wendy has been cutting on two tracks) into the first two sound gangs of your synchronizer. You would then put a roll of empty fill on the third sound gang and put a head leader tape directly on the fill. Identify this with the reel number, the date you are creating the reel, and the designation "FX and MX removed from Work Track." Spin down until you get to the start mark on the work tracks and add a fresh start mark on the removed FX reel. Make sure all of your reels are lined up at this start mark and that they all are set into the synchronizer at 0'00.

You would then spin down the reels, listening in your head phones as you go. When you get to a sound you do not want in your work tracks, find the frame line where you want to begin removing it, mark the matching frame line on the empty roll of fill and back everything onto the left side of the synchronizer. Cut the fill on this frame line mark and splice the unwanted sound onto the fill roll at this point. Cut the loose piece of fill onto the end of the last piece of sound on the work track reel. When you roll forward, the two reels will cross over each other so that the reel of fill will roll up onto the take-up reels of the work track.

303

It is a good idea to write (in grease pencil) the first code number for the piece of sound that you removed from the work track onto the piece of fill taking its place.

Continue to listen on your headphones until you come to the end of the piece of unwanted sound (which should be running under the back sound head). On the fill reel (which should be spooling up on one of the work track reels) you should then mark the frame line matching the end of that sound. Then back everything onto the left side of the synchronizer. Cut the fill on this frame line mark and splice it unto the end of the unwanted sound. Cut the remainder of the work track reel onto the end of the piece of fill you just cut into the work track. When you roll forward, the two reels will magically un-cross.

What you have just done is simply transfer the piece of unwanted sound onto the roll of fill so it will run in sync with the work track, replacing it with the exact same amount of fill. Should you ever need to put it back into the work track again, it will be a simple matter to spin down the reels together in the synchronizer, remove the effect from the fill reel, and cut it back into the work track. The code numbers you've written on the small pieces of fill within the work track will help make sure you maintain Wendy's original sync.

The second way you might want to clean up your work track reels is to put the work picture and work track up on the synchronizer, zeroing out at the start marks and roll down until you get to an unwanted sound. You would then write the code number of the first synch picture code on the head of the sound, remove it and replace it with exactly the same amount of fill (you might also want to mark the footage—in feet and frames—of the first frame of the pulled piece and the reel number it comes from). On the piece of fill you've just cut into the work track you would write, in grease pencil, the first code number for the piece of sound you've removed. You should then roll the sound up into a little hand roll and place it into a two-piece white box specifically marked for removed sounds from this reel of the film. That way if you ever need to reinsert the sound back into the work track reel you can easily find the sound in its appropriate box, spin the work track reels down in the synchronizer until you get to the piece of fill which replaced the sound effect, and swap the effect back into the reel.

You should check with your sound house to find out just what sounds they do not want cut into the work track reels. A few houses don't want any pieces of fill or tone, most are much more lenient and will only ask you to remove temp sound effects. Still others don't care what is in the tracks just so long as there are code numbers on everything and a reliable code book so they can track down what they find there.

If you have been scratch mixing your film in complete reels, you will already have a mix to screen with, and you won't need to cut the effects and music back into the work track.

There is one final dialogue note you should be aware of. In some cases Wendy may have cheated non-sync dialogue into characters' mouths as a temporary fix for screenings, knowing full well that the actors were going to need to come into the studio and loop the lines for the final mix. If this is the case, it might be helpful to have the actual sync track on the ADR tape as a guide track during the looping session. Split the cheated dialogue out onto the fill reel (or remove it from the work tracks and roll it up if that is what your system is) and replace it with the actual sync track.

Handing Over Materials

On most films, a color dupe print is made of the film for the sound department. You will not want to give your color picture up to them since there will be many things you will have to do with the color print, as we shall see in later chapters. In fact, with nearly every sound editing house working with computerized, digital, edit-

ing systems like Pro Tools or Waveframe you won't have to give up
your work picture at all, but will have it transferred to a set of
videotapes. These videotapes are then divided between the different
editors doing the various sound editing tasks. These divisions are
sound effects editing, looping editing, dialogue editing and splitting, foley editing, and music editing. On some films these tasks
overlap, so it might not be necessary to get a separate videotape for
each category.

The requirements for each sound house will be different but
in general, you will need to supply them with at least a 3/4" videotape copy of the film with numbers *burned into* the picture area and
striped onto one of the sound tracks.

The numbers used in the video are usually both the film footages and the *SMPTE Code Numbers*. SMPTE (pronounced
"simptee") numbers are the electronic signals that have been standardized to include a lot of information used to identify the particular frame that the code number is associated with. We discussed
them way back in the chapter on dailies.

In theory, a SMPTE code number can be used very much like
a film code number except, rather than calling a particular frame of
the film CC2034 or 102-2034, we can name a particular video frame
3:07:36:19. This number is the sequential hour, minute, second and
frame from the start mark. Thus, if we assign the start mark for reel
number three a SMPTE code of three hours (3:00:00:00), the first
frame of the picture (which would be at twelve feet, or eight seconds) would be called 3:00:08:00.

305

Video footages run a little differently than film footages. For
one thing, there are 30 frames to each second, rather than 24. Thus,
a SMPTE number of 3:07:36:29 would be followed by 3:07:37:00.
Also, because of the way time code works, each second of time code
is not precisely one second of actual time. Thus, a reel that started
at 3:00:00:00 and was nine minutes and 35 seconds long would not
end at a time code of 3:09:35:00. Not surprisingly, this became very
confusing to people needing to know real-time lengths.

As a result, another type of SMPTE code standard was developed. In it, periodic frame numbers were dropped (no actual frames
were dropped, just the numbers) so that at the end of nine minutes
and 35 seconds the SMPTE Code numbers would read, properly,
3:09:35:00. This type of SMPTE code became known as *drop frame*
code. The original type of code became known, therefore, as *non–
drop frame*. Both types of code are still in use today and nearly all
editing systems are able to use both types of code. You should find
out exactly what type of code your sound house wants and where

they would like you to put it. We will discuss this in more detail in Chapter 11A.

In any case, you would send your sound house several copies of the film on video. The 3/4" video format is most common because of its professional quality, but an increasing number of systems can handle 1/2" tape on a Super-VHS (S-VHS) format. Some can even handle ordinary home VHS tapes. A few older systems need Beta tapes but that is becoming a rarity.

On this videotape you would normally have the time code superimposed on the picture (sometimes known as *window code* or *burn-in*) as well as put onto channel two of the audio channels, channel one being used for the production track of the film. Sometimes you will be asked to put this audio time code onto the *address track* of the tape. This frees up both audio channels for your production tracks, which is very handy if Wendy has been cutting with two soundtracks.

Each reel of the film would be transferred with its own time code—the convention is to put each reel's number in the hour position of the time code and to begin the reel at zero minutes, zero seconds, and zero frames at the picture start mark. Thus, reel five's start mark would be coded 5:00:00:00, and reel eleven's would be 11:00:00:00. SMPTE hour codes do not run past 23 hours (giving you 24 possible hours including the zero hour), but you will rarely have a film exceeding 24 reels, which is about four hours, so this is not an issue.

As I've mentioned earlier, it is common to also burn in film footages (feet and frames) in their own window.

Most sound houses prefer to have each reel of film transferred onto a separate roll of video. This makes it easy for them to assign separate reels to different editors. Some don't mind if you gang two or three reels on one tape, so long as you provide the proper amount of *pre-roll* and *post roll* for each film reel. Pre-roll is an extra amount of time code that runs before the zero minute start mark, post roll is an extra amount running after the last frame of picture. It is common for sound houses to need up to two minutes of pre-roll and one minute of post roll. In the case of reel four, then, the pre-roll would begin at 03:58:00:00 and run for two minutes before the start mark began at 04:00:00:00. The post roll would run for an additional one minute after the LFOA.

Once the reels have been properly balanced you can send them out to a lab to be duped and to the telecine house for videotaping.

Sometimes, some reels of the film will be locked and others will not. In that case, if your schedule will allow it, you should only make dupes and videotapes of the locked reels. However, this is not always possible. On *Rollover*, for which I was the music editor, the schedule was so tight that I needed all the reels to give music timings to the composer, Michael Small, so he would have enough time to write his music. He needed to know those timings even though there was a possibility that they might change. Often, looping editors will need to have all the reels as well. However you do it, you should give all the editors the same set of reels (either complete or partial), so they will all be working from the same basic set of dupes. When you don't, it creates confusion later if you need to make changes to the reels. Since different editors would have different versions of the film, conveying the changes to them would quickly become a nightmare. So try to keep every department's dupe and videotapes of the film identical.

Let's say that Adam and Wendy have finished all the reels except one particularly troublesome scene in Reel Six (for some reason, every film has one or two problem scenes that either don't get solved until the very last minute or, even more often, never get solved at all). You could dupe and tape only the remaining eleven reels, or you could dupe everything and let everyone know you are going to make changes on the one scene in reel six. Most often you would choose to take the latter approach, since the sound editors would at least be able to work with the rest of the reel. I would then let them know which scene was liable to be changed so they could work on all of the other scenes in the reel without worry.

While you are duping the picture, you may need to send out the reels of track to be duped. This requirement is becoming increasingly rare as more and more sound editors give up working on 35mm. However, some houses still like to have a guide track to ensure that their work is in sync with yours. If you need to supply this 35mm guide track to your sound editors, you might want to replace any temp music or sound effects with work track, tone or fill. In fact, if you've cut your scratch mixes into your work track, they should be removed and replaced with the appropriate pieces of work track (which should have been filed with the scratch mix elements).

Though you will be removing the scratch mixes from your work track before it is duped for the sound department, you will still want to have a mixed track for any future screenings you may be giving before the final mix is completed. Since you will be giving up your original soundtrack to the dialogue editors, you will need one soundtrack for your own use and this track should be the mixed track.

This is one big advantage to having scratch mixed the film in complete reels rather than in sections cut into the work track. Your latest mixed reels should be fairly current. If not, you can easily construct one from them. If, however, you temp mixed sections of the reels, you should make one complete dupe of the film *before* you remove any of the mixes. This dupe should be marked up with codes as I've explained before in Chapter 9 in the section on "Complete Recuts." The dupes made for the sound editors need not be marked. They will code them using their system if they need to.

In any case, you can send the cleaned-up work track out for a *1:1 dupe*. This means the sound will be transferred at the same level it came in, with no changes in level or equalization made during the transfer process. When the dupe comes back to you, you should mark the start mark 9'00 before the sound of the pop. Even if the sound transfer house has marked it you should still check it, they will sometimes be off by a half-frame or more.

If your editor has been cutting on two tracks, both should be duped and transferred.

After you get the picture and track dupes back they should be coded. This will enable you to keep the picture and track in sync as well as making it easier to do conformations (i.e., changes) later on in the sound editing process. Though the picture dupe will have the printed-through key and code numbers, the sound track will not have any code numbers on it, so this coding is essential.

The easiest way to code this is to choose a prefix—you can use "S" for screening dupe. Reel One would be coded SA1000 or 001S0000. Reel six would be SA6000 or 006S0000. Since *Silent Night*, as well as most movies, runs more than ten reels I would code reel eleven SB1000 (or 011S0000) and reel 12 SB2000 (or 012S0000).

The videotapes would not be coded like this, but would have a time code referring to the reel of the picture. Reel One would start at 1:00:00:00, Reel Twelve's start mark would fall at 12:00:00:00. The feet and frame burn-ins would not have any indication of the reel number.

It is important to label each dupe and video reel with the date of its creation. As things change, this will make it easier to communicate the changes to the sound and music departments.

In fact you, as the assistant picture editor, will be the sound department's point of contact with the picture department. It is your responsibility to keep them informed of every change made—in the film and in the schedule. I cannot stress enough that I consider this one of the assistant editor's most important jobs at this point in the film. It is all too easy for the sound department to be isolated from the picture-making process. But changes in schedule affect them at least as much as they affect you. They should know about any changes and should, in fact, be consulted about them before they are made. Sometimes your requirements will conflict with theirs. You, or Wendy, will have to make a decision as to which to change. Regularly sending them calendar revisions will be most helpful.

Because you will be the point of contact, you should set up some of the systems for that interaction (in consultation, of course, with the supervising sound editor). Code your dupes and tapes in an organized manner and let everyone know what your system is.

The picture dupe will already have an Academy leader on it (duped from the one on your work picture). Cut a picture head leader onto the duped Academy leader a little before the start mark.

You should cut the tail leader onto the dupes at the last frame of action. In addition, mark a tail sync mark on the leader. Some assistants like to put this exactly one foot after the LFOA (Last Frame of Action). Others like to put it on the next zero frame after the last frame of action. If a reel has an LFOA of 930+7, the sync mark would be put at 931+00. The only exceptions to this would be if the LFOA was on the fifteenth or the zero frame. If the LFOA was 930+15, then you would put the tail sync mark at 932. My preference is to always put it exactly one foot after the LFOA. That way, there are no exceptions.

In addition, put a tail beep mark three feet after the LFOA. Some people use this beep as their tail sync mark.

Your goal should be to hand over to the sound and music editors the following elements:

1. a dupe picture and/or videotape (often only the videotape is needed)
2. the cut work track (to the dialogue editor)
3. all the elements used in scratch mixes
4. all appropriate paperwork

When the videotapes return from the telecine house you can give them to the sound department, along with a few other things. Every sound editor should get a complete crew list with home phone numbers. Sound editing often involves a lot of late night work and there will be questions that only you or another member of the picture editing crew can answer. They should know how to reach everyone. You should also submit a complete reel list to them, like the one you saw in Figure 8.4 or like the one in Figure 11.1. This list should contain the reel number, scene numbers contained on the reel, length of reel, and the total running time. You can also put the

REEL CONTINUITY

Date ___3 · 27 · 00___

REEL	Scenes	LFOA	Tail Sync
1	1 - 26	930 + 7	931
2	27 - 35PT	944 + 5	945
3	35PT - 52	904 + 3	905
4	54 - 72	994 + 2	995
5	73 - 85	934 + 15	936
6	86 - 102PT	993 + 9	994
7	102PT - 113	955 + 11	956
8	114 - 130	973 + 7	974
9	132 - 156	943 + 4	944
10	160 - 181	978 + 3	979
11			
12			
13			
14			
		Total Length:	9432 + 12

Does ~~not~~ include Head and Tail credits

FIGURE 11.1 *A reel breakdown for the sound department. Note that for reels with LFOAs on the fourteenth or fifteenth frame (reel five, in this case) the tail sync mark is not the next whole foot but the second whole foot. This is done to leave enough room for the tail sync tape marking to be placed on the tail leaders without overlapping into the picture area. Other ways of placing tail sync marks are to have them one foot after the LFOA (905'03 for reel three, for instance) or at the same point as the tail pop - three feet after the LFOA (946'04 for reel nine, for instance). In today's world of digital sound editing, some picture assistants replace the tail sync column with the final frame expressed in time code.*

tail sync footage on if you want. As with any changeable list that you distribute, date it so any subsequent lists will not be confused with the earlier ones. I've seen some films where reel lengths changed so often that the assistant editor began writing the hour as well as the date on his LFOA lists.

Some sound editors prefer to use their own LFOA list (as shown in Figure 11.2) along with your LFOA list since it gives an easily referenced list of all the changes made in the film since it was first handed over to them.

Each version of each reel is given a suffix number. The two versions of Reel Two would be called 2-1 and 2-2, for instance. Reel Six has three versions—6-1, 6-2 and 6-3. This number is written onto a piece of tape on the videotapes, as well as the boxes they're stored in, along with the date of the changes, making it easy to tell at a glance if the reel is the latest. If you put the number on the spine of the tape box it is visible when the reels are stacked on a shelf.

The sound department should also receive a copy of the lined script (with lined notes) and your logbook. They will need this information as they go back into original production sound tapes for sound retransfers. Make sure all of the original production sound tapes are sent to them. Some sound recordists still record on both 1/4" and DAT tapes. You will probably want to send your sound house the DATs, but you should check with them. They may want both.

More Details About Videotape Handover

As I mentioned earlier in the chapter, very few sound houses require film and mag track in their preparation anymore. With the abundance of Digital Audio Workstations (or *DAWs*), they will work almost exclusively with videotapes. If you have been cutting on film you will still need to hand over your original cut work track so they can identify each piece of track you've used. However, the bulk of their work will come with the videotaped picture and track.

The 35mm work track can still be of value to them, however. Many productions use the method of dailies transfer we discussed in Chapter 4, in which the production sound time code is transferred to either the balance stripe of the 35mm single-stripe mag stock, or the second or third stripe of the three-stripe 35 mag. When you hand over this cut work track, it will be a relatively easy job for their computers to run down through every foot of cut work track and read the time code, making a sound EDL that records where every cut comes.

Every sound house has a different set of requirements for the

LFOA CHANGES

REEL	LFOAs at 1st Lock	LFOAs Change #1	LFOAs Change #2	LFOAs Change #3	LFOAs Change #4	Final Combo Reels
1	930+07 (3.27)	965+06 (4.11)				
2	944+05 (3.27)	870+03 (4.4)				
3	904+03 (3.27)					
4	994+00 (3.27)					
5	934+15 (3.27)					
6	993+09 (3.27)	862+13 (4.7)	875+09 (4.11)			
7	955+11 (3.27)					
8	973+07 (3.27)					
9	943+04 (3.27)					
10	978+03 (3.27)	996+02 (4.14)				
11						
12						
13						
14						
15						
16						
17						
18						

LFOA CHANGES

FIGURE 11.2 *An additional LFOA list which gives all of the LFOAs, from the first lock (on March 27, 2000), through each successive set of conformations. Note that the only reels which have been changed as of April 14 are reels one, two, six, and ten. When the film is finally locked and almost finished mixing, the sound editors will compute the footage for each double reel and list that in the final column. This information is helpful in the creation of optical tracks and 2000-foot printing masters. The listing for total footage and time is used only when one LFOA change column is used for each date's conformations.*

LONE STAR SOUND EDITORIAL

Telecine Specifications for Workprint Delivery

Transfer	One-Light Transfer
Format	(3) 3/4" Videocassette and (2) 1/2" S-VHS.
Pre-Roll	No less than 30 seconds before Picture Start Mark
Post-Roll	No less than 20 seconds after tail pop

Picture Reels

Transfer picture reel to video with full horizontal width of 35mm frame visible and a 1.85:1 letterbox matte. For anamorphic films, transfer stretched and letterboxed for correct formatting. We need to see everything that will be shown in theatres. Include head and tail leaders, including head and tail pops, start marks and tail markers if they exist. No more than three film reels can be placed on one videotape.

Audio

Transfer all dialog only to Channel 1 of the 3/4". **No music or sound effects** should be on the transfer.

Time Code and Feet/Frames

Time code should be 29.97 Non-Drop Frame. LTC should be transferred to Channel 2 and the Address Track. VITC should be placed on lines 10 and 12.

The hour code should align with the picture and sound start marks. The number of the hour should represent the film reel number. The start mark of reel one should be at 1:00:00:00, the 2-pop of reel five should be at 5:00:06:00. Pre-roll should begin no later than at 59:30:00 of the preceding hour.

Code should be burned in the upper right portion of the frame in the letterboxing. Feet/Frames should be burned in the upper left portion of the frame in the letterboxing.

If there is any problem delivering exactly these specs, you should call Lone Star Sound immediately.

In addition to the above tapes, you should deliver all materials described in our contract with you including, but not limited to, all original production tapes (DAT and 1/4" if both were recorded), all reels of cut work tracks fully marked with legible inked code numbers, all sound reports, a copy of the editor's log, a complete film continuity, and a list of all reels and their lengths and their EORs (or LFOAs).

313

FIGURE 11.3 A list of specifications for delivery to your sound house of the proper videotapes that they will need to edit the sound on your film.

videotapes you will need to hand over; a sample technical specification sheet is shown in Figure 11.3. Nearly all will require a set of visual burn-ins as well as the non-visual placement of the reel's time code in one or more locations on the tape. Common places for this code are on the second audio channel, the Hi-Fi channel of VHS-Hi-Fi tapes, and usually two pre-selected VITC lines. VITC, the *Vertical Interval Time Code,* is a time code inserted into scan lines of video that are not visible when the image is shown on a television screen. They will also require a certain length of pre- and post-roll and a set of bars and tone on the head of each reel. You should get all of this information sent to you as early in the process as possible and send a copy of this spec sheet to the video transfer house so they know how to create each tape.

Life being what it is, you will probably find that the videotape specifications your dialogue editor needs are quite different from the ones your composer or music editor needs. The sound effects editors will probably want something different from your mixing stage. Keep a list of what everyone's requirements are and try to get everyone a tape as close as possible to their specifications. In some cases it may not be possible to fill everyone's needs. On *Trigger Happy* the music editor wanted visual burn-ins placed differently than the sound editors specifications. Because of the manner in which the master tape was created, some of the burn-ins already pre-existed on the screen. In this case, we needed to discuss the situation with everybody until we came up with a placement that was the least problematic for everyone.

Conformations/Changes

314

In some cases Wendy and Adam will go back to a scene for recutting after a dupe has been struck. You will then have the unenviable task of telling the sound and music editors that changes have been made in the picture and they must *conform* their dupes. Conformation is the process by which the dupes, videotapes and edited sound tracks are brought into agreement with the color work picture. The process is never a particularly happy one but is made even more depressing when the sound elements for the mix have already been built. If there are seventy tracks for one reel (let us say), making a simple one foot addition or removal in the picture and work track requires making that change on seventy tracks. I've seen directors make changes in the film until the end of a film mix, completely oblivious to the chaos they were causing. It is crazy, but it is done very, very often. With the time crunch that most films have at the end of their schedules, even with digital sound editing, these conformations are rarely welcome. They will create some level of havoc in the sound editing process.

For this reason, some very clear and good systems for communicating these changes must be used. In all cases it is the assistant's job to make sure the correct conformations are transmitted to the sound and music editors as rapidly as possible. You will be very busy in these final weeks making sure that the picture editing moves smoothly. There will be a temptation to regard the sound crew and their needs as a burden. But at this stage of the film editing process, they are the major factor in terms of time, energy, money, and process. Without them the film would not be able to be projected in the theatres. Their schedule is difficult enough without you making it impossible.

Transmitting the conformations should be your first priority after they have been made. At the end of every day of cutting you should tell the supervising sound editor (as well as the music editor) exactly what portions of the film were recut that day, even if the cut has not yet been completed. This way they can plan the disbursement of work for their sound crews.

As soon as a scene has been recut and approved, you should take the new reel and put it up against your dupe in your synchronizer. Comparing the two allows you to see exactly what has been done to the film. By running the two together you will be able to get all the information on the changes, since the color work picture will tell you what Adam and Wendy want with the film, and the dupe will tell you what everyone else thinks they want with the film. There should never be a discrepancy between the two.

In the old days, when every sound editing department got their own dupe, the next step would be to make dupe sections of all of the places with changes. Now that sound houses cut on DAWs, you will only have to make a dupe section for yourself, if at all. You will need to create a series of notes telling the sound editors exactly where they will need to make changes on the DAWs, in every reel where Wendy has made changes.

315

To correctly convey to them just what the changes are, you will have to supply them with two, possibly three, things. The first is a precise list of all the changes. These lists are called either the *Conformation Notes* or the *Change Notes*. The second thing is a new set of videotapes for every reel that has been changed. In this case, you will need to retransfer the entire reel not just the changed sections. The possible third item is your own screening dupe so they may follow it if necessary.

Let's examine these in more detail. The first task you have is determining just which sections you will have to dupe. I usually use two guidelines. First, any new material (picture or track) that has been added and is not already in the dupe must be done. Second, any material that has been recut or rearranged so drastically as to make it too complicated to explain and to recut should be duped. This way, rather than recutting your dupe, all you have to do is remove one part of your dupe and replace it with the new piece. Make sure, however, that the changes are drastic enough to make this tactic worthwhile, as this method doesn't give you any specific information you can pass on to the editors about how to change individual tracks that they may have already edited to the old version.

When you have determined exactly which sections of the picture need to be duped, pull them out of the color work picture. You can put them all on one roll and insert short (one foot) slugs between each one as well as leaders on the head and tail of the combined roll. On the slug, write the reel number and the consecutive change number of the within the reel. In Figure 11.4 you would label the fourth change (the addition of 34'07) 6-4. You would do the same for the track that needs to be duped. Remember to put a pop (beep) on the reel three feet before the first piece of track.

When the dupe comes back you should have it coded. Make no attempt to code each conformation separately or each reel of these conformations separately. Merely code each set of dupes with the proper prefix code for the department it is intended for. Since the last code you used for your dupe was SY2000 (for reel 12, screening dupe) code this conformation SY3000. Note in a conformation log you will begin keeping, that SY3000 is the reel containing the conformations for such and such a date.

With eight-digit coding machines you can come up with a different system. Since the code number you used for the last reel of your color dupe was 012-0000, the code number for these conformations can be 013-000. Some assistants use a very high number, like 100-0000, others use a different color coding tape for all changes.

After the dupe is coded, run it down in the synchronizer and mark where the beginning and end of every conformation is on the track. Then cut them all apart, remembering to keep the conformation number on the head of each change.

Now take your screening dupe and your color picture and line them up in the synchronizer. Run them down together until you get to where your first change will be (whether it is an addition or deletion). Note the footage and exactly what the change is. For instance, in Figure 11.4 we see that at 121'07/08 we need to remove 21'05 of both picture and track. This is conformation number one on this reel. The next conformation is the removal of 2'02 of picture only at 230'10. The next conformation is the removal of the matching amount of track at 231'05 to bring the picture and track back into sync. Conformation number four is an addition. At 356'13 the editors must add the 34'07 of picture and track that you are supplying them. And so on.

At each conformation point make the conformation yourself in your screening dupe. Make sure all your footages are correct. For this, it is helpful to have a second synchronizer to measure lengths

CHANGE SHEET for
REEL 6
Date __4·11·00__

#	At Footage	Add/Delete	Pix or Track	Information
1	121 7/8	− 21 + 5	P + T	
2	230 9/10	− 2 + 2	P	
3	231 4/5	− 2 + 2	T	
4	356 12/13	+ 34 + 7	P + T	
5	620 2/3	+ 1 + 12	P	
6	625 3/4	+ 1 + 12	T	Slug Track

New LFOA __875 + 09__

Old LFOA __862 + 13__

CHANGE SHEET

317

FIGURE 11.4 *A change sheet (also called a conformation sheet). For changes four and five, dupe picture should be supplied to the sound department with the numbers "4" and "5" written on them. Dupe track should be supplied with the number "6" written on it. The term slug track means that one foot and twelve frames of fill leader should be added at 625+3/4. The sound department can cut in their own fill or you can supply them with pieces cut exactly to length.*

that have been added or removed. You should hang up all the pieces you remove, putting all the conformations for any one reel on one pin. Mark, with grease pencil or on a piece of white tape attached to the top of the removals, exactly which conformation number it is.

When you are finished with all the conformations for any one reel, run down to the end of the reel and get the new EOR (End of Reel) or LFOA (Last Frame of Action). Make sure it is the same on your screening dupe as on your color work picture. Do the same for all the reels with conformations in them. The new EOR must be listed on the conformation sheet so the sound editors making their own conformations will be able to check that they have made them all properly.

You can then make copies of all your conformation sheets. Use a different conformation sheet for each reel that has conformations in it, as different sound editors may be editing different reels. Then get the boxes of conformations and the conformation sheets to each editor immediately. Sometimes, all you need to do is to send one copy each to the sound and music editors. They will take care of getting copies to their staff.

318

When this is done, and the inevitable questions are asked by the sound editors and answered by you, you will be ready to clean up after yourself. Have Philip box up all the trims you have deleted from your screening dupe. Have him flange up and cinetab each reel's conformations by themselves and then box up the conformations for that date together. Future conformations can be added to the same box as long as the box doesn't get too crowded and as long as a notation of which date's conformations are in the box is made on the outside of the box.

Then, correct your LFOA list and reel breakdown if you haven't already done so. Keep the conformation sheets in one place. I file them by date and then by reel number within that category. I can guarantee you, at some point during the sound editing, things will get just confused enough for you to want to find out what exactly it was you did on such and such a date. It will be very handy for you to have these sheets filed safely away.

These are the primary tasks that will confront you as a picture assistant working with the sound department. You will also have to answer many questions about where certain material came from, if there are alternates that were not used for picture but might be good for sound, exactly what things Adam liked in the scratch mixes, etc., etc., etc. You are the person who has been on the film for the longest time in an organizational capacity. You can answer all kinds of "where can I get...?" questions. If you are bright, you will also be able to help them on the "why was it done like this?" questions. You will function as the focal point for their questions.

319

11A/DIGITAL
. . . .
DIGITALLY PREPARING FOR SOUND

One of the great advantages of editing on a digital machine is the way it simplifies the task of handing your tracks over to the sound house. Nearly every house in the United States today works digitally, so it makes things quite a bit easier for everyone if you have been working digitally as well. In this chapter we will discuss how you take the sounds and the information in your machine and turn them over to your sound department for their work.

320

Of course, there are some complications with a digital to digital handover, most of which are small and will discussed shortly. The biggest disadvantage in editing your picture digitally is that it is very easy to continue cutting forever. As I mentioned in Chapter 11, films today are never really *locked* (that is, they never reach the point in the editing when the picture editing is completed) but merely "latched." By this we mean the editing of the film is rarely completely finished when it is handed over to the sound department. Once the tracks are given to sound, the director and the editor often return to the picture editing process, unlocking the film and creating havoc in the sound editorial process (as well as to the budget).

Making changes to a picture that has already been handed over to the sound department (called *conformations*) is a very expensive and confusing process, yet films do it all the time. As we will see later on in this chapter, it creates repercussions all the way down the editing chain. The ease with which the computer editing process can accommodate conformations, however, makes it easier to invite these repercussions and havoc.

And that is why I call this the biggest disadvantage to editing your picture digitally.

Preliminaries to Handover

Before you can begin handing over any of your materials to the sound department, you need to make sure your film is properly prepared for the handover. Make sure the reels are balanced for release just as we talked about in Chapter 11.

In addition, you need to add Academy Leaders onto the head of every reel if they are not on them already. You need to reset the counter on your editing machine so the zero frame (either 0000'00 if you are looking at feet and frames, or 1:00:00:00 if you are looking at time code and this is Reel One) is on the "Picture Start" mark. The Avid makes it possible to create your own countdown leader, though I prefer to have standard academy leaders digitized so the playouts of the reels look exactly like film reels for the negative cutter.

You also need to remove any unwanted sounds from your tracks before creating the EDLs and dupes. Check with your sound department to see just what sounds they do not want cut into the work track reels. Temp music and sound effects will often not come from the original production tapes, leaving no usable code for the sound editors to trace when they receive the lists.

As a result, you will need to go through Wendy's cuts on the editing machine and remove these unwanted sounds from the channels onto which she has cut dialogue. This is much more complicated then in the days when editors cut with no more than two 35mm tracks. Today, most editors cut with at least four soundtracks. Some cut with up to eight on the latest versions of editing software.

The way you split unwanted sounds out will depend on the way Wendy has cut her tracks to begin with. When I cut, I usually try to put sync dialogue on the first two channels, temp sound effects on the third and temp music on the fourth. There are times when I need to abridge this system, putting temp music onto the third or second channels, or an effect onto the second or fourth. However, I usually try and maintain this fairly consistent split. If Wendy has cut this way, you will have a much easier time cleaning up her tracks.

The first thing you should do is make a copy of the final version of each reel. If the final version of reel eleven is R11v903 you could call this version "R11v903(handover)" or "R11v903h" or whatever unique name you devise.

You should then add four additional tracks, beyond the four probably already in the edit. On most of today's systems you will not be able to hear more than four tracks at a time, but you won't need to play all of these tracks back together. You are simply creating a number of empty tracks analogous to the fill reels you built for removed sounds in Chapter 11.

You should then play down on each reel in turn, moving the unwanted sounds on each track down to the open bottom four tracks in orderly way. Listen under headphones so you can move these sounds without leaving anything behind.

I like to split the tracks so that all production dialogue is on the first three tracks and all temporary ADR (that you may have recorded through a microphone in the editing room) is on the fourth. If any sound effects were recorded on the set during production, and therefore have sound roll numbers and time codes the sound editors can use, I make sure that these are placed on channel three.

When you reach any temporary sound effects that you either digitized from CDs, non-production tapes or live in the editing room, split them off onto tracks five and six. Finally, any music should be split onto tracks seven and eight.

If Wendy has already been editing on eight channels, make sure all of the sounds are placed on these eight in the same orderly manner we've just described.

The reason for splitting the sounds this way will be obvious in a moment, but let me say now that there may be times when the needs of your various sound departments will vary (the ADR department and the effects editors might want to hear the temp ADR, the dialogue editors might not), and the sound they want on their tapes may differ from what the music department wants. Having your channels split up this way will make it much easier to accommodate everyone's disparate needs.

One final dialogue note to be aware of. In some cases Wendy may have cheated non-sync dialogue into characters' mouths as a temporary fix for screenings, knowing full well the actors were going to need to come into the studio and loop the lines for the final mix. In these situations, it might be helpful to have the actual sync track on the ADR tape as a guide track during the looping session. In this case, you should split the cheated dialogue onto track four of your split and cut in the actual sync dialogue track onto tracks one or two.

Handing Over Materials

Locking and latching aside, the needs of your sound departments will probably be pretty much the same whether you've been editing on 35mm film or electronically. You will need to hand over a set of videotapes and, if you are matching your dailies 35mm track to your edit, the coded work tracks as well. For a list of technical specifications usually required by a sound editorial house, see Figure 11A.1.

LONE STAR SOUND EDITORIAL

Telecine Specifications for Video Master Delivery

EDLs	CMX-3600 in C-Mode, on PC or Macintosh disks.
Format	(3) 3/4" Videocassette and (2) 1/2" S-VHS.
Pre-Roll	No less than 30 seconds before Picture Start Mark
Post-Roll	No less than 20 seconds after tail pop

Picture Reels
The picture should be transferred exactly as it exists on the Video Master, including all bars and tone, and slates. We need to see everything that will be shown in theatres or on television. Include head and tail leaders, including head and tail pops, start marks and tail markers if they exist. No more than three film reels can be placed on one videotape.

Audio
Transfer all DIALOG ONLY. **No music or sound effects** should be on the transfer. Combine Video Master channels one and two onto Channel 1 of the tapes.

Time Code
Time code should be 29.97 Non-Drop Frame. LTC should be transferred to Channel 2 and the Address Track. VITC should be placed on lines 10 and 12. The time code on all video copies delivered to Lone Star Sound must exactly match the time code on the Video Master.

The hour code should align with the picture and sound start marks. The number of the hour should represent the film reel number. The start mark of reel one should be at 1:00:00:00, the 2-pop of reel two should be at 2:00:06:00. Pre-roll should begin no later than at 59:30:00 of the preceding hour.

Code should be burned in the upper right portion of the frame. Feet/Frames, if they exist, should be burned in the upper left portion of the frame in the letterboxing.

If there is any problem delivering exactly these specs, you should call Lone Star Sound immediately.

In addition to the above tapes, you should deliver all materials described in our contract with you including, but not limited to, all original production tapes (DAT and 1/4" if both were recorded), all sound reports, a copy of the editor's log, a complete film continuity, and a list of all reels and their lengths and their EORs (or LFOAs).

FIGURE 11A.1 A list of specifications for delivery to your sound house when the handover tapes are created from a video master. If no Video Master was made and you are handing over a cut work picture you will need to follow the spec sheet in Figure 11.4 with the additional delivery of the EDLs as described above.

As we discussed in Chapter 4, often these work tracks will have been transferred with the sound roll time code transferred to the center stripe of the three-stripe 35mm dailies track. In some cases, this means your sound house will be able to read the edited time code numbers directly from the center stripe.

The fastest and (if you've done all of your preparations properly) most precise way to hand over usable edit lists to your sound house will be to output the *EDLs* directly from your digital editing machine onto a floppy disk. But first, let's back up a bit and discuss just what the sound house does with your tracks once they get them.

In the next chapter, we will discuss in some detail how the sound editing house takes the information that you, as the picture assistant, give them in order to create the final tracks for the film mix. It will help, however, to talk about the general process now.

There are several ways dialogue editors can create the final split dialogue tracks. The most common one, at least right now, is to rebuild every edit Wendy has made in her tracks, by retransferring the original production tapes (usually DATs, but sometimes time-coded 1/4" tapes) into digital editing machines. Some of these machines are ProTools, AudioVision, Synclavier, or Waveframe; they are all known by their general description—*Digital Audio Workstations* (DAWs).

When the necessary portions of every take are in their DAWs the dialogue editors need to reconstruct Wendy's edits, frame by frame. Only then can they begin the work of cleaning up the tracks and splitting them so they can be smoothed out in the final film mix.

What your editors need is a way to know exactly where Wendy has made every dialogue edit so they can recreate them in their DAWs. To do this, they need a list analogous to the Cut List that your machine creates to let the negative cutters or you and Philip match the workprint dailies to Wendy's edit. In fact, what they need from you is a version of an EDL listing only sound edits. Oddly enough, this is called a Sound EDL.

You generate this EDL much the same way you generate a Film Cut List. Each editing machine works slightly differently but the overall process is the same. You will take Wendy's edit and open the EDL menu. You need to tell your machine just what type of EDL to create. EDLs come in many different formats. Some of the most common are CMX, Grass Valley or Sony, and there are variations within each of these categories. You also need to tell your machine which channels of sound to include in the EDL, how to handle track reassignments (often Wendy might have put the second channel of a dailies take onto channel one of her edit), whether to include comments in the EDL (these comments are usually the scene and take number of the piece of sound), and a host of other options.

You should get a list of the EDL requirements from your sound house and be sure your editing machine can handle them. I like to get this list from the sound house as soon as they have been hired and do a test EDL, verifying that our lists will work for them.

Each reel will have its own EDL, though you can put them all onto one floppy disk. You will also need to supply the sound house with a printout of each EDL so their editors have a reference.

No matter what the sound house's requirements, I usually like to create an EDL with comments and a picture channel that I keep for myself (as well as whatever sound only EDL we send them) to refer to when they call me with questions later.

Make sure that the floppy disk you supply to the sound house is in a format they can read. Some DAWs require Macintosh disks, others require PC (either double-density or high-density; you will need to check). Other sound houses will be able to convert whatever disk you give them. One of your responsibilities is to make sure the sound editors receive exactly what they need so they can begin their jobs quickly and efficiently.

Another way that some picture editing rooms are starting to handover their sound is directly on hard drive. The basic theory behind this procedure is quite simple. Since you've already gone to the trouble of digitizing all of the sound, and since Wendy has already gone to the trouble of editing a lot of the dialogue, it seems silly to have your dialogue editors redigitize and re-sync the production audio all over again. If there were some way to simply give them all the sound Wendy has already edited, they would be much further ahead of the game.

325

It's a great idea in theory. Occasionally it even works. Here, though, are some of the problems with it.

First, though audio doesn't take up nearly as much room on hard drives as picture information does, high quality professional audio still uses a lot of hard drive space and bandwidth (that is, it takes a lot to get it off of the hard drive for playback). This is why most picture editors won't usually digitize the production dailies at the highest professional quality. In addition, unless you have sunk the dailies from the original production tapes, you will usually have digitized the sound from 3/4" or Beta-SP tapes. This format is vastly inferior to the original production sound and will not work for the final sound mix.

Second, even if you have input the best quality production sound, the sound files your editing machine creates when you digitize your audio are often not compatible with the file format your editors' DAWs are using. You won't be able to give them your hard drives (or a copy of your hard drives) and have them be able to access it. You will often need to convert it into a file format that their machines can read.

Recently, many digital editing machine manufacturers attempted to agree on some sort of standard for these files. This new standard, called *Open Media Framework* (OMF), is a first step in streamlining the handover process. It is still not perfect. Like any attempted standard, it strongly favors the technical specifications of the company that originally developed it—Avid, in this case. Still, even Lightworks is grudgingly coming aboard the OMF standard, and the day sound files can be exchanged between various editing machines may not be too far away.

Of course, even if you could easily give your edited tracks to your sound editors you would still need to take the time to give them to them. Chances are you will not be able to hand your material drives directly over to your sound editors since you will need them for a host of other duties. You will probably need to make copies of the media files onto some transportable format—either Jaz drives, magneto-optical (MO) disks, or removable hard drives (R-mags).

When you hand these disks over to your sound house you need to provide several things. You editors still need a complete set of EDLs. They will often need to manipulate the tracks Wendy has cut and they will want to go back into the original production tapes to do so. The EDLs will give them all the information they need.

Second, they will want you to supply them tracks with handles on them. Part of the trick to smoothly blending dialogue tracks with different background sounds is providing little extra pieces of this background tone on the tops and bottoms of each of the dialogue pieces so the sound mixer can gradually segue from one cut to another. Many of the digital picture editing machines allow you to set the number of frames in these handles. Some will even automatically checkboard the dialogue tracks for you. This feature takes every other track and splits it for you, so dialogue edits one, three, five, seven, nine, etc. will exist on one sound channel and edits two, four, six, eight, ten, etc. will exist on another. In theory, this will make it easier for the sound mixer to seamlessly blend tracks. In fact, your sound house may not want the material split this way. Check with them before performing any of these operations.

What Do I Hand Over?

Your sound house will have provided you with a sheet of paper (or two or three) listing all of their delivery requirements. In general, you will be asked for the following:

1) Videotapes: You will need to supply a certain number of videotapes of the film, usually one to be used for dialogue editing, one for ADR, one for the foley department and at least one for the sound effects editors. Depending on your

sound schedule and your film's budgets there may be several editors in each category; you may need to deliver more than one videotape for each job. You should check how your sound house likes the tapes to be balanced. In most cases, if your negative cutter can handle it, you can probably balance the movie into 2000 foot projection reels and put each double reel onto its own tape (this way it is easier for the sound house to split the work of, say, dialogue editing between multiple editors). In most cases, this videotape is simply a playout of the Avid or Lightworks edit, pixellated images and all. If this is the case, you will probably be required to deliver a second set of videotapes made from the cut negative or from an answer print struck from this cut negative. The reason for this is simple— if the negative cutter has made a mistake (either because the Cut Lists you supplied them weren't good or because *they* aren't very good), you will be unable to catch the problem before you marry your sound and picture unless you run your nearly completed mix and the proper negative cut picture.

All of the tapes will need to be transferred at certain technical specifications. Time code will usually be non-drop frame (though you should check the spec sheet). The sync reference will usually be at 29.97.

327

It is generally not a good idea to transfer your entire movie onto one or two videotapes. Many of the sound editors' machines will not work well with 120 minute VHS tapes and this also cuts down on their ability to have more than one editor working on it at the same time. In addition, some sound mixing stages have very finicky machines requiring no more than two editorial reels be on a tape at one time.

2) Burn-ins: The videotape will need to have certain information burned into the visual image. Most notably will be a running time code from the picture start mark, as well as a running footage length (in feet and frames) also from the picture start mark. Some editing machines allow you to make burn-ins as you do your playout. I usually avoid doing this because it cannot be removed later if you need to make a clean copy or move the burn-in to another location. It is easy for your video dubbing facility to burn in these codes as they make your dubs.

Most sound houses will also have specific places on the frame where they would like their burn-ins. Because their foley artists need to see the characters feet, they will not want a burn-in over the lower part of the picture.

3) Time-code: You will also need to place your reel's time code onto the videotape. This can be a linear time code (LTC) on one of the audio channels on the tape (S-VHS tapes will have both Hi-Fi and normal tracks available) or a VITC. You need to make sure there is proper amount of pre-roll and post-roll for the DAWs and the machines at the dubbing stage can successfully lock up to your tapes.

4) Dupes: In some cases, you may still be mixing to a 35mm print of the film. If so, you will probably need to strike a color or black and white dupe of the film so it can easily go back and forth through the projector without tearing.

5) EDLs: The Sound EDLs are perhaps the most important piece of information you need to provide. They will need copies of the EDLs on a floppy and a print-out of each list. As I've already mentioned, all of the EDLs can generally be put onto one floppy disk. Before you hand over these EDLs, take a look at the printout copy that you've made for yourself to ensure the lists have been correctly created. On the list of reels used, make sure there are no mislabeled reels. For instance, if numbers like 888 or 999 show up, you know that there is a sound effect or a music cue on the tracks that you have forgotten to split off onto one of the lower eight tracks.

You should also make sure your EDLs are in the format your sound house has asked for. A typical request would be for a CMX3600 list sorted in A-mode. The CMX3600 designation refers to a particular EDL format. Others are Grass Valley (GVG) and Sony formats. The A-mode designation refers to one of several methods used to sort the events in the EDL. A-mode refers to a method in which every event is sorted into the order they appear in the edit. Other sort orders are, not surprisingly, given names like B-mode, C-mode or D-mode.

6) Paperwork: Working digitally does not absolve you of the need to hand over additional paperwork. For most films you still need to hand over a logbook. At the very least, you will need to supply your sound house with a copy of all sound reports, the lined script, and a list of all crew contacts. You should, by the way, be sure to get a contact list from them as well.

You should also supply them with a copy of your continuity and an LFOA list (this should list the version name of the completed edits just in case you are going to be making changes), computed in both feet-frames and time code.

7) Original tapes: Have the original production DAT or 1/4" tapes (or both) sent over to your sound house from wherever they've been stored.

8) Dialogue tracks: If you have been matching your 35mm dailies tracks to your digital cut, then hand these cut work tracks over as well. You should mark them up just as you would have on an all-film job, as described in Chapter 11.

The best way to organize all of your tapes for handover is to output a playout tape with no burn-ins and the maximum amount of track separation. You will generally have only two tracks on your output tape, so I like to split them with dialogue (including temp ADR lines) on one track and effects on the other. You may also need to output a second videotape with music mixed in on the second track as well. You should have pre-striped the tapes with enough pre and post-roll time code (of the proper type—drop or non-drop). When you output the edits, have the code placed in the LTC or VITC if possible.

These tapes will not get sent directly to your sound house. Rather, you will send them out to have dubs made. At that point you will need to instruct your videotape duplication house on the placement of the burn-ins and time code for each tape (some editors may want the time code on the second audio channel, some may want it only in the VITC, still others may want it on one of the Hi-Fi channels of a S-VHS tape). You will also be able to tell them which audio channels should be transferred across.

On *Mad Dog Time* our audio specifications were very complicated and varied. Some of our editors wanted the temp ADR, others didn't. Some wanted music and effects separately from dialogue, others didn't want music at all. We found that there was no combination of two playout tracks that would satisfy everyone. In order to fulfill every requirement, we created an audio playout to a DA-88 with the same separation on its eight tracks as our split tracks. Our videotape house then created the sound editors' dubs by running the DA-88 and playout Beta-SP tape together in sync. They were able to transfer just the tracks that were needed for any one particular set of dubs.

Another way of handling that problem would have been to have created multiple sets of playout tapes, each with its own particular track separation.

When you send your master playout tape (or tapes) to the video house for dubbing you should also send a detailed breakdown of what you want on every set of videotapes. Tell the house to label each tape with the track breakdown as well as the editor for whom it is intended (music editor, ADR editor, effects editor, etc.). These notations should be on the tape labels as well as on the boxes.

When the tape dubs come back from the dub house, first make sure you have a complete set of reels for each editor. Separate them into stacks and box each set up individually. When you send the tapes over to your sound or music editors, ask them to check them immediately so any dubbing errors are caught before it is too late to correct them. It is amazing how often a video dubbing house will have a switch flipped incorrectly, sending the wrong code to your dubs, or putting the burn-in in the wrong spot, or patching the music into the dialogue channel, etc. etc. Since you will rarely have the exact same equipment set-up as all of your individual sound and music editors, it is best to have them check their own tapes, to make sure they are all up to their specifications.

Conformations/Changes

I mentioned at the beginning of this chapter that films today are usually "latched" rather than "locked." This means that at some point after you have handed over to your sound department, Wendy and Adam will make changes in the picture edit affecting what the sound editors are already doing.

It is always a good idea to let the sound department know that changes are coming and which areas of the picture they occur in as soon as you know. If they are in the midst of working on Scene 35 and you know Wendy and Adam are making changes in it, they may want to hold off completing their editing of that scene until they find out just what those changes are. They might not want to stop work, of course, depending on how close they are to the mix and how they have apportioned their work flow. But, if you give them the information about impending changes and where they will probably be, they will be able to make that decision on their own.

You need to be able to tell the sound editors how to conform their work to the new version of the picture. In the process I discussed in Chapter 11, you learned how to create a series of Change Notes detailing every picture and sound change so your sound department could correctly conform their tracks to match up with yours. In an all digital world this is both simpler and more difficult.

Right. Of course.

As we discussed in Chapter 9A, both the Avid and Lightworks, as well as some outside programs like Slingshot and the no-longer-manufactured OSC/R, provide a more or less automatic process of generating change lists.

To create Change Lists in most systems you need to save the Cut Lists or the edit from the previous version. You then create a Cut List from the new version. What you do next will depend on the software you are using, but in general you will tell the computer to take the old version (let's call it R03 v802), take the new version (let's call it R03 v900) and compare the two. The program will then generate a Change List (*see* Figure 11A.2).

Some assistants like to name each version with the date of the cut, such as R03 2/10. This makes it easier to track changes simply by looking at their titles.

Computer generated change lists are not always perfect and their problems show up most frequently in their instructions for sound changes. Often the computer will spit out a set of instructions far more complicated than necessary. Therefore, it is important that you go over the change notes your editing machine generates and rewrite them if necessary, so you can hand over a coherent set of notes to your sound house.

If you are working with film and a set of dupes, things will be a bit clearer, though not easier. You will be able to take the machine's change note lists and perform them yourself on your own dupe. If there are any problems, you will spot them first and correct them before anything ever gets to your sound editors.

This raises the question of just how they will be able to get a correct picture. The answer to that question is that you are going to have to create a new set of videotapes for every reel that has changed. This will require a completely new set of handover elements. New videotapes, new EDLs and printouts, as well as corrected EOR lists will need to be created. Make sure each is properly dated and labeled before you send them over.

In addition to all of this paperwork, you will need to create a new set of EDLs for each reel that has been changed. Some of the track changes will not necessarily be clear from the Change Notes, and any new sounds will need to have their original production sound reel numbers, so Liz can digitize them.

```
Change Lists                              created at 18:38:27 Tue 11 Apr 2000
Project: Silent Night                                Sequence Title: R06v402

R06v402                      29 events            Old Duration    85+09
Picture 1                    14 insertions        New Duration    87+06
Change List - Reel           15 deletions         Total Change +   1+13
                              0 moves
All Counts Are Inclusive (inside/inside)
```

At This Footage	Do This	For This Length	First/Last Key	Lab Roll	CR	Name	Total Change
1.							
0+00 11+02	Delete Shot -	11+03	KI 48 2791-3957+03 KI 48 2791-3968+05	000051	A52	74-1a -	11+03
2.							
0+00 2+09	Delete Shot -	2+10	KI 48 2791-4976+00 KI 48 2791-4978+09	000054	B8	74-1b -	13+13
3.							
0+00 2+06	Delete Shot -	2+07	KI 48 2791-3970+08 KI 48 2791-3972+14	000051	A52	74-1a -	16+04
4.							
0+00 3+12	Delete Shot -	3+13	KI 48 2791-4981+13 KI 48 2791-4985+09	000054	B8	74-1b -	20+01
5.							
0+00 3+10	Delete Shot -	3+11	KI 48 2791-3976+10 KI 48 2791-3980+04	000051	A52	74-1a -	23+12
6.							
0+00 6+11	Delete Shot -	6+12	KI 48 2791-4987+03 KI 48 2791-4993+14	000054	B8	74-1b -	30+08
7.							
0+00 7+00	Delete Shot -	7+01	KI 48 2791-3986+02 KI 48 2791-3993+02	000051	A52	74-1a -	37+09
8.							
0+00 6+13	Delete Shot -	6+14	KI 48 2791-5000+14 KI 48 2791-5007+11	000054	B8	74-1b -	44+07
9.							
0+00 5+14	Delete Shot -	5+15	KI 48 2791-4000+00 KI 48 2791-4005+14	000051	A52	74-1a -	50+06
10.							
0+00 4+13	Delete Shot -	4+14	KI 48 2791-5046+09 KI 48 2791-5051+06	000054	B8	74-1b -	55+04
11.							
0+00 3+07	Delete Shot -	3+08	KI 48 2791-4012+10 KI 48 2791-4016+01	000051	A52	74-1a -	58+12
12.							
0+00 4+09	Delete Shot -	4+10	KI 48 2791-5054+15 KI 48 2791-5059+08	000054	B8	74-1b -	63+06

332

FIGURE 11A.2 A page from a Change List from an Avid.

SOUND EDITING

There are various facets to sound editing—dialogue splitting, sound effects editing, looping, and foleys. I described dialogue splitting in Chapter 9. It is the process of putting pieces of sound that need to be treated differently at the sound mix onto separate tracks. This allows the film mixer to treat each track independently and segue between them to create one seamless dialogue track. Sound effects editing is the process by which the sound editor adds the sounds necessary to make a soundtrack feel real (traffic, backgrounds, and specific noises in a film's soundtrack). Looping (also called *ADR* or *EPS*) is the process of re-recording lines of dialogue to replace or add to lines already in the film. Foley editing is the process of recording and adding specific sound effects that need to be created exactly in sync to the picture. Most body movement falls into this category, such as footsteps or various specific sounds of people's clothes. Many of these types of sound editing are set up with similar systems.

Until the mid 1990's, it was not uncommon to find sound editors still working with 35mm magnetic tracks. Except for a few very low budget films, as well as small independent or college films, no sound editing house that I know of edits on film anymore. Everything has moved into the digital world. Sound editors cut on Digital Audio Workstations (DAWs) with names like ProTools, Audiovision, SADiE or Waveframe. It is almost certain you will be handing over your material to a sound house that will cut on DAWs. It is now possible for even low budget films to edit their sound on souped-up home computers, so even the most ardent of do-it-yourself filmmakers can work digitally from the "comfort" of their own homes. As a result, most of this chapter focuses on creating sound tracks in the digital world. I will occasionally mention mag track editing when it is appropriate.

Similarities to Picture Editing

To a large degree, every sound editor and sound assistant must work within the system that you, as the assistant picture editor, have devised for the picture editing. There are countless ways the two departments overlap. The first and most obvious way concerns your code numbers. The code numbers on your color picture refer to your logbook and, therefore, to your system. The sound department may need the original DAT or 1/4" tapes from these codes and unless you want to spend all of your time finding bits of information for them, your logbook and system had better be coherent enough for them to track down what they need without your help.

On any film with more than one sound editor there will usually be more than one assistant sound editor. If there are multiple assistants, the assistant working directly with the supervising sound editor is normally assigned the job of supervising assistants. It will be this supervising assistant setting up all the sound editing systems to be used by the sound editors and assistants.

Additionally, there may be at least one and possibly two apprentice sound editors. In the old days, when sound was cut on 35mm film, these apprentices filed sound trims, made trim tabs, kept the log books in order and got coffee for everyone else. Today, with a much smaller need for assistants, there are even fewer apprentices and they are often given tasks not much more complex than making messenger runs and getting coffee for everyone else. After a little while they might be given the task of checking time code on tapes delivered to the sound house, transferring audio tapes onto CDs, hard drives or other digital tapes, as well as working as a sort of librarian of sound effects. These apprentices, and many of the assistants, will not be assigned to any particular editor but will be doing work for everyone in the sound department, directed by the supervising assistant.

Another change in the sound editing process is that most features and television are now edited by sound editing houses with a staff of their own and a number of other jobs proceeding at the same time as yours. You may be assigned a supervising sound editor but you will rarely be hiring them yourself. Many of the sound assistants will no longer work exclusively on your film.

Delivery of Materials

One of the jobs of the sound assistant will be to convey to the picture department just what delivery requirements (*see* Figures 11.4 and 11A.1) they need in order to cut the sound. As we discussed in Chapters 11 and 11A, these needs vary from sound editor to sound editor. However, there are some similarities between all formats.

The sound house will need a set of videotapes with proper burnt-in time codes and either LTC or VITC code on the tapes so their DAWs can lock up with the video as they edit their sounds. At present most of the sound editing work stations are designed to work with a videotaped picture, rather than a digitized picture of their own. Some newer systems work with digitized picture, but you still need to deliver a videotape of the film for one of their assistants or apprentices to digitize.

Every reel of video will need to be transferred at a very specific speed. This is usually guaranteed by synching the master videotape to a reference of 59.94 Hz (see the delivery requirements list in Figure 11.4) so the picture runs at 29.97 frames per second. Remember, these are videotapes that will play back at nearly 30 FPS even though they represent film running at 24 FPS. In order for everything in the chain to maintain proper sync with the final 24 FPS cut picture, every videotape dub needs to be transferred at precisely the correct speed. Referencing the 59.94 Hertz signal should ensure accurate sync.

The above discussion of speed only applies to NTSC video for 24 FPS film projects. PAL and European video speeds are normally compatible so no special corrections are necessary. We will discuss this in more detail in Chapter 17.

The sound house is also going to want your 35mm work tracks, complete with codes and grease pencil marks. If you've taken advantage of the three-stripe or full-coat dailies formats that we talked about in Chapter 4, the sound house should be able to read the sound roll time codes that were recorded onto one of the open channels (two or three). If they are using the special format that encoded the sound reel, scene and take number, as well as the time code, they will be able to generate an EDL they can use to auto-assemble a matching sound track within their DAW. This saves a lot of time and lowers the possibility of errors.

Sound Effects Editing Personnel

In many editing situations an individual sound editor is assigned a reel in a film (or, more likely, four or five reels in each film). They will be responsible for all the sound work (except the looping) in that reel.

On larger films, there are separate editors hired for the dialogue editing, the sound effects editing and still another editor (or two or three) hired for foleys. Often another editor supervises all of the ADR. There are various pluses and minuses to doing the job in this way. It is certainly more efficient for one person to be doing only one job. Often, foleys take time away from sound effects editing that can hardly be spared in the rush to get to a mix. This enables an editor who is very good in one facet of sound editing to develop a specialty.

However, there are also some problems with this approach. Assembly-line sound editing can leave the editors feeling uninvolved, and without a sense of teamwork, they are less likely to give that little extra effort. If an editor is doing all the sound work on any given reel, he or she will understand more of the needs of the sound on that reel (and, hopefully, on the film) as a whole. If would be lovely, of course, if one sound editor could do all the work on the entire film, but there is never enough time to do a top–notch professional job with a solitary sound editor, though this is often how a low-budget film works. As a result, more than one editor must be brought on to your film.

336

In most cases, a supervising sound editor is hired to design the sound for the movie and select most of the sound effects. They comb through the picture and select specific sound effects that fit Adam's and his or her vision. At times the editor will physically *pull the effects,* meaning he or she will take the sound effects from the media on which they were stored on (DAT, CD, hard drive) and transfer them to another digital medium so they can be edited using the DAW. Most often, the editor will know the sound effects library so well that his or her assistant will pull the effects based on the list the editor creates.

We will discuss each task individually as if different editors were performing each one, though ultimately it won't really matter to you if one or twenty sound editors are performing the tasks. You should be familiar with *all* the necessary skills.

Beginning the Job

When the supervising editor and assistant first come on the film they will be charged with many tasks, not the least of which will be developing a sound effects library for the film. First, they need to screen the film. They should try to get to know it as well as they can, for only then will be able to get the sense necessary to do an effective and creative sound editing job.

If possible, they should view the film in a screening room so they can hear exactly what the tracks sound like. Normally, they are invited to one of the film's audience previews or another screening. Since every theatre has a different sound, it would be helpful to screen the film in a room the sound editor knows fairly well so they have a reference point while listening. After this, the editor and the assistant should begin to screen the film on a flatbed or on a video-tape machine so they can analyze the film scene by scene. As they screen each reel, they should be taking notes on the specific needs of each scene.

Figure 12.1 is a sample sound editor's note sheet. Some supervising sound editors use these to list everything they will have to do with each scene. At the top is listed the *scene title* (this is taken from the reel breakdown or continuity that, of course, you will have already supplied) and scene number. Each scene gets its own page inserted into a master book in the order it appears in the film. Dividers can be placed between scenes at the reel breaks, making it easy to find scenes on any given reel of the film. If the film is re-edited and the scene continuity changes, it will be a simple matter to rearrange the order of these sheets.

337

Underneath this header are five sections, each corresponding to a separate sound editing task. The first section is called "General Comments" and is for notes that don't fit into one of the other sections on the page. Adjectives, notes on sources for sound, and Adam's preferences should go here. Adam will say he wants the scene to "feel festive." The sound editor should write this down. If Wendy says, "This scene will almost certainly be recut before next month," the editor should write this down along with the date.

In the section marked "ADR/EPS," the editor should list all possible candidates for looping. This list will, of course, not yet be definitive, but it will serve to remind the sound editor of any potential problems as well as help him or her provide the producers with a list of all the characters who might have to be scheduled for looping.

Under "Foley," the editor will list all effects needing to be foleyed. The final two sections are for effects. Here, the editor will list the effects he or she feels are needed for the scene. From experience he or she will know what effects exist in their own effects library, which need to be purchased from a sound effects library, and which will need to be recorded especially for the film. In discussions with Wendy or yourself, the sound editor should be told which temp effects Adam liked and must be kept from those scratch mixes, and which need to be replaced. All of this will be noted here. Effects that the sound editor knows will need to be recorded are listed in the

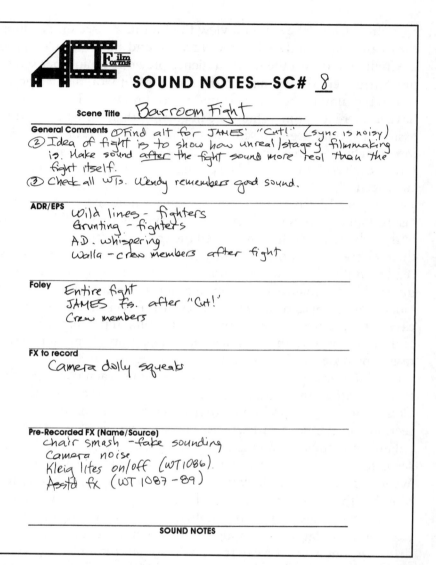

338

FIGURE 12.1 *A sound editor's note sheet. In this case, Charles has listed those items he will need for this scene as well as Adam's and Wendy's comments from the spotting session.*

first section. Effects already cut into the tracks that Adam would like in the final film are listed in the last section ("Pre-Recorded FX") along with their original source, whether that is an original production track (wild tracks, etc.), or from a sound effects library.

The notes on these sheets will grow as the sound editor gets more familiar with the film. Each time the editor looks at the film, he or she may get better ideas for the design of the soundtrack. This will mean changes or additions to these sheets.

As soon as the film is more or less locked (when the dupes and videotapes have been struck), the sound editor should sit down with Adam and Wendy and go through the entire film on a flatbed or on videotape asking detailed questions about what should go into every scene and what is decidedly unnecessary. This screening is called a *spotting session* since they will be spotting exactly where and what type of effects are going to go into the film. The sound assistant should be there taking plenty of notes. Often the spotting session is recorded on a small tape recorder to ensure nothing is missed in the note-taking process.

Sometimes these spotting sessions take place using the videotapes with their SMPTE Time Codes or burned in footages. In all cases, the assistant editor's job is to take notes of the desired effects and mark down the time code or footage where the effect is noted.

It is not uncommon for a director to know very little about sound. Sound editors learn, after a while, to know just which of the director's instructions to pay literal attention to and which to reinterpret. Sometimes a director will say he or she won't need a certain effect that the editor knows damn well will be very helpful. If the editor is smart, he or she will do the effect even though the director has said it isn't necessary.

Let's say you've hired Lone Star Editorial to edit your film. Charles Lone and Liz Clear will be your supervising sound editor and assistant. They've just spotted the film with Adam, Wendy and you. Another spotting session that would be helpful at this stage is one for looping. This session is usually combined with the sound editor's. Every reel is meticulously examined. Any lines the sound or looping editor thinks have to be looped should be discussed at this screening. Possible candidates are lines partially or completely obscured by some unwanted sound (backgrounds, another actor/actress talking, radio interference, etc.), lines for which the director wants to change the performance, lines the sound editor feels may create problems in mixing once the tracks have been split, lines that must be added to help the story line (these lines are usually off–screen lines, that is, coming from a character while they are not seen on screen), or lines needed for a television version of the film. It is best to listen to these lines on a flatbed (and later, using headphones).

At the end of all of these screenings, Charles and Liz will have accumulated enough notes to write a book and enough work to keep them occupied for some time. They can then begin to plan their sound editing tasks.

One of their biggest jobs will be building the effects library. Most editors, after working years on all kinds of movies, will have accumulated a large number of their own sound effects, encompassing everything from "Air Escaping From Balloon" to "Zoo Animals Going Wild." Sounds specific to *Silent Night* that Charles does not have, can be bought from any number of sound effects libraries, each with tens of thousands of effects on tape or CD.

Most sound editing houses have already spent quite a bit of money and time accumulating large numbers of sound effects, both by purchasing CD sound libraries as well as recording their own. It is now very easy to create your own CDs from a computer (this is called "burning a CD"), so Charles may have a large number of sounds recorded on his own CD library.

Charles (but since we're working so closely with him, we'll call him Chuck) will, after going through all the notes Liz and he have been accumulating since they first started working on the film, figure out just what effects they need to purchase for the film, if any. At the same time, he will be listening to the original production tapes, making notes of just what effects can be used from the location recording.

340

In the old days, Chuck would have edited his sound effects on mag stock and Liz would be very busy transferring all of the effects to 35mm or 16mm, coding them and breaking them down into little hand rolls so Chuck could begin working with them. A few films (*very* few) are still done this way. If you are doing it this way, be aware that you may need to transfer a particular sound more than once. You should, regardless of what coding system you come up with, make sure these multiple prints are coded differently.

In most cases today, however, Chuck will be editing on a DAW. Therefore, he will probably go through the film very meticulously, making notes on an Effects Pull List (*see* Figure 12.2) of each effect he wants in the film, with its matching time code within the film. Often Chuck will know his library well enough that he can choose an effect and list the number or its source without auditioning. Other times, either he or Liz will need to screen the film up against the effects to make sure he is getting exactly what he needs. To do this they will need to work at a *Pulling Station*, a computer that is set up to lock to the video. It is usually also connected to a massive CD playback system, storing a hundred or more CDs, each one filled with effects. It will probably also be hooked to a DAT player and, possibly, an analog 1/4" tape machine. It is likely that Chuck will have some sound effects in this analog format as well, though most sound houses have been busy converting their old effects to digital formats.

PULL LIST FOR REEL __1__

FILM NAME __Silent Night__   PAGE __6__ OF __19__

EDITOR'S NAME __Chuck Lone__   DATE __3·31·00__

TC In Reel	FX ID #	Description
06:32	D36-015	Chair squeaks 1
	D36-019	Chair squeaks 2
	D17-032	Wood smash 1
	D17-033	Wood smash 2
06:42	AU02-16	Small bottle break
	AU02-19	Glass shatters
	AU02-25	Plate glass smash
06:58	ED15-142	Camera crane
07:03	HT01-15	1/4" Tape running
07:09	HT01-26	Kleig lite switch
	TH02-136	Kleig lite hums
	TH02-139	Hiss on/off
07:15	TH02-12	Cases open/shut 1
	TH02-13	Cases open/shut 2
	TH01-120	Hammers
	TH01-105	Electric saws
	TH01-06	Alarm bell clang 1
	TH01-07	Alarm bell clang 2

SOUND EFFECTS PULL LIST

FIGURE 12.2 *A Sound Effects Pull List. Charles and Liz together have spotted every effect that he wants for this reel and notes the time code where that effect will be cut in. The time code for this reel is given in minutes and seconds, since the hour will be 01, for Reel One. After Liz or an apprentice pulls the effects (named with the FX ID# on this list), transfers them to a hard drive, and gives them to the sound editor who will be cutting this reel, that editor (Chuck Lone, in this case) will use this list to edit each effect to its proper spot in the reel.*

The procedure for selecting sound effects, whether Chuck is editing on film or on a DAW, is pretty much the same.

In one scene of the film there is a traffic jam. In another, someone is standing alone on the street at night with only one or two cars going by. In several other scenes, Abby is in his apartment which is located near a moderately busy street. All of these effects fall into the category of "Traffic." Each one, however, is a slightly different sound and will require a different effect (in fact, most of these sounds will require a combination of several different effects). On many television shows there are certain standard sounds. A police car appearing in many episodes of a series will have one particular engine sound (along with one particular horn, one particular siren, and a set of car door slams) which will be used every time we see that car. In much the same way, Chuck will want to use similar sounds for traffic at similar locations at the same time of day and weather (don't forget that a car driving on a wet street sounds different from the same car driving on a dry one), but he will try to use different sounds for other cases. It wouldn't do to have every bit of traffic sound the same.

All CD libraries have their effects catalogued, cross-referenced and printed. Most sound houses also have their libraries catalogued on a computer so Liz needs only to type in something like "Distant City Traffic" to generate a list of all the possible sound effects.

Regardless of how the effects are obtained, when Chuck has finished working on one reel he will have a rather extensive list of necessary sound effects. Liz, or an apprentice, will take this list and start to *pull the effects*. This is done at the pulling station I mentioned a page or so back. The pull station will also be connected to a hard drive (often an *R-Mag*) of the same type as the sound editor's. This allows Liz to go down the pull list, transferring the effects appearing on Chuck's list onto the hard drive. When she is done, she will be able to bring the drive to the sound editor working on this reel, who will hook it up to his or her DAW. It will then be possible to edit the effects on the reel.

This system is a logical extension of the days not so long ago, when the supervising sound editor created little boxes (called a *kit*) of rolled up 35mm sound effects for every reel. This box was then given to the sound editor who cut them in at the footage given to him on a small cue sheet or a list, not unlike the pull lists of today.

Some editors like to pull their effects one type at a time (traffic, let's say). Others feel that sitting at a pull station makes the job easy enough so they prefer to pull them reel by reel.

Figure 12.2 shows the first page of the pull list after Liz has made all of her pulls for the second reel of the film. The "FX ID #" column lists Chuck's company's identification number for each pulled effect. Their system gives each sound library disc a specified number. The first effect comes from the thirteenth disk of a library Chuck has called "A2C" (this may be his library or one of a number of commercially available sets). It is the fifth effect on the disk. Sound effects found on DATs are preceded with the letter "D." Every sound house has a different system. Your sound house will use the one that works best for them.

One page of Chuck's list of sound effects for pulling might look like this:

> C13-5   Medium day traffic, no horns
> C11-2   Heavy traffic, many horns, type 1
> C11-2   Heavy traffic, many horns, type 2
> C23-5a   Distant traffic, day—for Abby's room
> C09-1   Light traffic, night, a few horns
> C09-5   Light traffic, night, on wet street
> C15-2   BMW—Single car by
> C15-5   BMW approaches and stops short
> C15-6   BMW slows down and goes by
> C15-9   Revving engine—MG sports car
> C16-23   Rolls-Royce engine idle

This is just a short sample of the kinds of effects Chuck might use for traffic. And, yes, they really do get that specific.

Sometimes effects cannot be obtained from Chuck's sound house or his CD library. These will have to be recorded specifically for the scene. For one film that I worked on, we could not locate a specific sound effect for a modern elevator door closing. We took a Nagra, marched down to the end of the hall where we were cutting the effects, and recorded the sound of the building's elevator. Such occasions are not rare. Almost any film will have effects that need to be recorded specifically. Either a sound recordist or the sound editor takes a professional quality DAT machine and goes out and records them.

Let's say, for *Silent Night*, Chuck cannot find various sound effects of movie making—a film crane rising and lowering, klieg lights coming on, fake-sounding gunshots, a very specific camera's noise and many more. Liz would try to organize a recording session for these things. She might call someone shooting a film and see if she could get permission to record a few effects one day. Or she might arrange with an equipment rental house to do the same thing.

After ascertaining that the booked day was fine with Chuck, she would reserve the sound equipment for Chuck (who probably has a number of DAT machines as part of his company's equipment inventory) or hire an outside sound recordist who often will supply their own recorder.

On the day of the recording, Liz might go to the set with Chuck and take thorough notes of exactly what he is recording. Before each effect is recorded Chuck would announce a voice slate into the microphone, such as "This is sound effect number fifteen, Chapman crane rising slowly." He would then record the effect. Liz should make sure that a proper *sound report* is included with the tape, just as one was submitted with every roll from the dailies shooting.

After the day's session the tape would come back to Lone Star Sound where either Liz or an apprentice would catalog it. It is important that this tape be logged into Lone Star's system just as every other DAT and sound effect CD is. Liz should know the company's logging system well enough to assign the DAT tape a number and enter all of the recorded effects into the company's logs.

There are many systems for logging these new effects into the database but they normally boil down to classifying them into a succession of descriptive words in more or less the following order: Category, Sub-Category, Description One, Description Two. An example might be a car that starts, idles and then takes off. A description might be "Automobile, Ford Taurus, start, smooth idle, away." Every sound house uses different categories, sub-categories, descriptions and abbreviations within them. Whoever is cataloguing the effects will need to be very familiar with the requirements of the sound house they work for.

If Chuck works from CDs, then Liz or an apprentice will need to create (or *burn* as it is called) a CD for the library and catalog that as well.

After that, Chuck will go through the new effects and select the takes he wants to use in *Silent Night*. Liz then needs to pull those individual effects and add them to the various R-Mags or hard drives assigned to the reels that the effects appear in.

Editing Sound Effects on Film

If the sound is being cut on film, Chuck will be editing these sound effects much as described in the section on scratch mixing in Chapter 9. He will run the picture and sound dupes on the two outside gangs of his console Moviola. The middle gang is where he will try out all the sound effects. He will be able to shift the position of the effect he is trying out against the picture to see where the most accu-

SOUND ONE
1619 BROADWAY, NEW YORK, NY 10019 (212) 765-4757

Rerecording Cue Sheet

Production: "Silent Night, Silent Cowboy"

Reel No. SEVEN
Page No. 1 OF 10

FX-1	FX-2	FX-3	FX-4	FX-5	FX-6	FX-7	FX-8	FX-9	FX-10	FX-11	FX-12
0 START											
9 BEEP											
12.00 Car Idle											
	43.02 Car horns (CH-8)										
	52.01										
67.03						67.04 Fire crackle (B7-1)	67.04 Fire crackle (B7-2) ALTERNATE				
103.03 Rain (W3-2)	103.03 Rain off hood (W3-4)	103.03 Windshield Wiper (CIFX-3)	102.03 Car-bys (Z36-2)	103.03 Thunder (N3-24)	103.03 Wind (W6-5)	103 02	103 02				
145 08→	145 08→	145 08→	145 08→	145 08→	145 08→	145.09 Rain (CIFX-1)	145.09 Rain off hood (CIFX-2)	145.09 Windshield wipers (CIFX-3)	145.09 Car-bys (CIFX-4)	145.09 Thunder (CIFX-5)	145.09 Wind (CIFX-6)
172.04 Rain (CIFX-7)	172.04 Rain off hood (CIFX-8)	172.04 Windshield wipers (CIFX-9)	172.04 Car-bys (CIFX-10)	172.04 Thunder (CIFX-11)	172.04 Wind (CIFX-12)	172.03←	172.03←	172.03←	172.03←	172.03←	172.03
						212.11 Knocks X (CIF-5)					
							230.03 Siren (C32-16)				
247.08	247.08	247.08	247.08	247.08	247.08	247.09 PG WALLA (B9-16)	247.09 (FLIP)				

1619 Broadway • New York, N.Y. 10019 • (212) 765-4757

345

FIGURE 12.3 Part of a cue sheet. This cue sheet lists all of the effects for reel seven. Dialogue, looping, foley, music and any other types of effects which may be done separately, like background effects would be listed on separate cue sheets. note the splits at 145'08 and again at 172'03. We are cutting inside and outside of a car during a rainstorm and need to have separate control of the volume and equalization of the effects for the interior and exterior. (Courtesy Sound One Corp.)

rate and pleasing position for the effect should be. When he has chosen the proper placement, he will do two things—the first will be to put a footage on the sound effect he wants cut in, as well as noting which track it is to be put on. The second will be to enter it onto his cue sheets (*see* Figure 12.3). Chuck will then hang the effect on a pin reserved for all the effects for that mix unit (or *element*).

After Chuck has finished cutting the effects for a reel, he will give Liz the barrel with the effects, and the temp cue sheets. Often, if the apprentices are experienced enough, they will end up *building the tracks*. Otherwise, Liz will do it.

Building the tracks means taking all the little pieces of track Chuck has cut and putting them in their proper places in the units.

The basic philosophy of mixing is quite simple. Every sound that has to be separately controlled should be on a different element so from any other sounds that will be played at the same time. This way it will come into the *mixing board* on a separate volume control knob. Its level (as well as its sound quality) can then be controlled without affecting any of the other sounds. This is accomplished by having a large number of reels (called *elements* or *units*) made up of fill. They will all have a start mark and can all be run together, just as you can gang up four tracks at one time in your synchronizer. Every time you want to hear a sound effect you will cut the effect in at precisely the right place into one of these elements. Leading up to it will be fill; leading away from it will also be fill. But at the point where the effect needs to be heard, it will be cut into the units so it can be played back through the mixing board. If five effects need to be heard at the same time (in a thunderstorm, for instance, one might want to hear rain, thunder, wind, cars passing on a wet street, and dripping water) then each must be put on its own element. The more complicated the scene, the more elements will be used.

There are many subtleties Chuck has to take into account in deciding how to apportion the effects on the elements, most of them too complicated to get into here. As an introduction, however, let us say that in the above mentioned rainstorm we cut from inside a car parked in the rain, to outside the car. Every time we cut from inside to outside all the above mentioned effects would get louder. But if the characters inside the car were having a fight, that dialogue would get *softer* when we were outside. Also, the sound of the windshield wipers would change when we went outside the car. This gives us seven elements that must change at precisely the same time and on a single frame. This would be an impossible task if the mixer had to change seven settings at the exact frame. To help the mixer, the sound editor does something called *splitting for perspective*, meaning, at the exact picture frame where we cut from the inside of the car to the outside, the seven effects that were running should be cut and moved onto seven other (usually adjacent) tracks. This way, the mixer can set levels and tone controls separately for the inside–the–car elements (on one set of seven tracks) and the outside–the–car elements (on another set of seven tracks). When we cut back inside the car again the editor would move all the sound effects back to the first set of tracks since the original set of levels and tone controls would still apply. Voila! You've saved everyone a lot of very expensive time at the mix. Since mixing time is now going for upwards of $800 an hour, this is A Good Thing.

When Liz gets these pieces of sound and the temp cue sheet, she will have to build the tracks that will eventually be used in the mix. Everything must be cut into these reels exactly right so an effect that is supposed to come in at 103'03 does come in at exactly 103'03.

All the mixing elements must have proper identification leaders on them since they will be leaving the editing rooms to go to the mixing studio where many other films are working. However, it is not necessary to make up scores of white leaders for every reel on the film. The elements can have head leaders made of fill. Commonly, only the dialogue units are leadered with white leader. In other systems, each sound category (dialogue, looping, effects, etc.) is leadered with a different color.

However they are made, the information on the leaders is usually written in red ink on the color of tape assigned to each particular category of track. In this case, since this is an effects unit, Liz would leader it with green tape.

Looking at the cue sheet in Figure 12.3, we can see the first effect that needs to be cut in is a car idle on element one at 12'00. Liz, or the apprentice, will put the dupe for reel seven in the first gang of her synchronizer and then put three rolls of fill in the next three gangs. She will label these rolls as FX-l, FX-2, and FX-3 (or FX-A, FX-B, FX-C, depending on what system you choose for identifying your elements; some editors use letters for stereo units and numbers for mono units) of reel seven. After about ten feet of blank leader, for the thread-up, she will put start marks on all three elements. Then she will zero out the counter and begin to roll the rolls down through the synchronizer. She will then cut one frame of 1000-cycle tone in at exactly 9'00 on the first element of each category. In our case, this would be on FX–1 (or FX–A).

347

At 12'00 on the first track (which will normally be in the second gang) she will make a cut and put in the car idle effect which Chuck should have hung on the FX–l pin with a footage written on it. She will do this by marking the 12'00 frame line (i.e., at 11'15/00) on the fill then rolling it out to the left of the synchronizer (she will make *all* cuts to the left of the synchronizer). She will cut the fill there and then splice Chuck's already cut effect onto the piece of fill going through the synchronizer. This completes cutting the head of the effect in.

While she is rolling down to the next location for an effect she will listen to the effect she's just cut in. This way she can verify that she has cut in the proper effect. Rolling down to about 43'00 she will stop and look for the car horn effect that should be hanging on the FX–2 pin. This effect, since it does not cut in at exactly 43'00, may be marked in either of two ways (*see* Figure 12.4). The exact footage

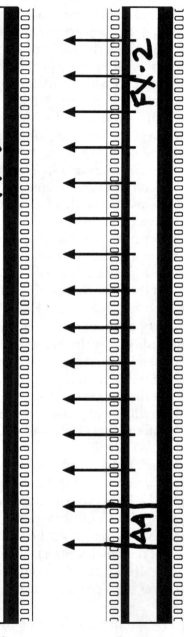

FIGURE 12.4 There are two ways of marking sound effects. In the first, A, the footage of the first frame of the effect as cut (in this case, 43'02) is written on the effect. in the second, B, the next whole number footage (that is, the zero frame of the next foot, in this case 44'00) is marked in grease pencil on the effect. The arrows on B would not be written on the film, they are there simply as a guide for you to count the number of frames from the first frame of the effect, at 43'02, to the 44'00 mark.

(43'02) may be marked on it, or a box may be drawn at the spot where 44'00 will fall. In the first case all Liz would do is make a cut at 43'01/02 and cut in the effect, just as she did with the effect at 12'00 on the FX–1 track. In the second case, she would roll down to 44'00, place the track on top of the fill in gang number two, aligning the track's sprocket holes with the sprockets of the gang, and then carefully roll back to the beginning of the effect while holding the track down against the fill and the gang. She will then mark the fill where the head of the effect is and, after rolling it back to the splicing block, cut the car horn effect into the fill where she has marked it.

Some sound editors like to mark their dupe picture with the footage as well as the track. This means, as Liz builds the tracks, she will have another visual check to make sure she is cutting the effect in at the proper place.

Some editors don't even bother to cut and mark the 35mm sound for general background tones (such as birds or ocean waves). They simply indicate on the cue sheet what effect it is they want and what footages it should begin and end. It will then be up to Liz to find and cut in the proper effect.

If you've been following this explanation so far you will have figured out that Liz will now be running the effects dupe in the first gang of the synchronizer, two pieces of track through the next two gangs, and one complete roll of fill in the back gang. The two effects will not be attached to anything at their tail. The first two rolls of fill will be hanging loose from the left rewind.

As she approaches 52'01, Liz will slow down and stop. The end of the effect on FX–2 is coming up. She can then attach the end of this effect to the second roll of fill that is on the left rewind. At 67'03 she will do the same for the effect on FX–1. As she completes cutting in each effect, she will check it off Chuck's temp cue sheet so she has a record of what she has cut.

The next two effects (at 67'04 on FX–7 and FX–8) cannot be cut in just yet because Liz only has FX–1 through 3 up on the synchronizer now. The next effects that she can cut in are at 103'03 on all of her tracks.

After cutting them in, Liz will notice that they need to be split off for perspective at 145'08/09. Chuck probably did not make the cuts at that point on the effects. Instead, he put them on one roll apiece, running them for the *entire* length that they are needed on both of the split tracks (which, in this case, runs from 103'03, through the perspective split at 145'08, through the next perspective split at 172'03, until the end of the scene at 247'08). It will be up to Liz to make the splits at the proper points.

When Liz makes the cut she will refer to the footage count on the cue sheet as well as the dupe running in gang number one. Considering that so many tracks begin and end at this point, it almost certain that there is a change of location. If the footage count does not come at a point in the picture where she can see a location change, this is a good time for Liz to ask Chuck if the footages are correct. In fact, every time she cuts in an effect she should look to see if it makes sense in reference to the picture. Obviously, there will be many things she won't be able to judge by looking at the picture (and listening to the effect) in the synchronizer. But since she knows the film, there will be many that she can. The best assistants keep a lookout for any oddity and, if they can't figure out an explanation for the oddity, ask their editors for clarification.

After Liz makes the cuts in the long effects (which she will do at 145'08) she should mark the tail trim of the effect with the new footage (145'09) and hang it with the rest of the effects for FX-7, FX-8, and FX-9. She might want to put it in numerical order on those pins to save time when she is building the later reels.

There are three little kinks in the cutting of the tracks listed on this temp cue sheet. The first will come when Liz gets down to 172'04 and is ready to cut in the continuation of the rain effects that are split off FX-7 through FX-12. To do this she needs to find the proper frame in the middle of these effects. She would take the piece from FX-7 at 145'09 (in this case, the tail trim of the piece she cut from the earlier FX-1 piece), put it in another synchronizer at 145'09 and roll down to 172'04. She will mark the track there and cut it at this frame line (172'03/04). She should then mark the tail piece as FX-1 at 172'04. She can do this with the pieces she will need for FX-2 and FX-3 as well. Then, she can hang the head pieces back up in the barrel on their pins (for FX-7 through FX-9) and cut the tail pieces into their proper tracks.

A second little kink occurs on FX-7 at 212'11 where the temp cue sheet lists "Knocks." You may notice that no end footage is listed. Instead, there is a little "X." This is placed there to note that the effect is of very short duration.

The third little kink comes on FX-9 at 230'03 where the cue sheet calls for a siren to begin. Normally this siren would stop at the scene change at 247'08/09. However, Chuck was unsure whether it might not be a good idea to continue the effect for a little bit under the beginning of the next scene (where there is a *crowd walla*—that is, a crowd in the background talking indistinctly). Therefore, at the scene split, he wants Liz to keep the track running but to *flip the track*. The sound effect would be cut at the proper point but instead of attaching the tail of the effect to the fill, it would be attached back to itself with the continuation of the effect flipped over. On playback the sound of this effect would disappear since the playback head would be riding over the back of the track (which has no sound on it). When the track runs out altogether it would be spliced back onto the fill, making sure that the fill would continue to ride with its base side toward the mixer's playback head.

The advantage to flipping this piece of track is, if the director decides at the mix that he *does* want the siren to extend into the crowd walla, it can be flipped back to its proper orientation with only a few minutes' lost time. If Adam does not like the idea, then nothing need be done at all, since a piece of flipped track acts just like a piece of fill—it has no sound on it. I should note that the only type of track that can be flipped is 35mm magnetic stripe. If you tried to flip full–coat stock the top track on the mag (e.g., the fourth track if the mag is four-track) would then come underneath the playback head. Even though the mag is flipped, the head would still be able to hear whatever was on that fourth channel (it would sound muffled, but you would definitely hear it). 16mm sound, since it has sprocket holes on only side, cannot be flipped at all.

After all the effects for these three elements have been cut in and Liz is down at the tail of the reel, she will make sure all the LFOAs match the LFOAs listed in the reel breakdown. I like to physically make a cut in the fill at the LFOA frame line and resplice the pieces back together again. This makes the LFOA very easy to locate later.

After this, the tail sync marks should be marked after the LFOA or EOR (the first unit of every set should also have a tail pop put on at this time, three feet after the EOR) and then the reels wound down for an additional thirty feet beyond these tail sync marks. In addition, about thirty feet of white leader should be added to the end of the dupe (and the same amount of fill added onto the track dupe) so it extends out far beyond the tail sync (try to make all the reels run out around the same time). This extra thirty feet is called the *run-out* and is there because the machines that play back these elements (often called *dummies*) at the film mix take quite a bit of time to slow down to a stop. If the film mixer doesn't hit the stop button until ten feet or so after the LFOA (which is, after all, only about six seconds), it would be likely that the reels would run out past their ends. This extra thirty feet at the end of every reel should be enough to ensure this doesn't happen.

Tail leaders should then be taped on top of the fill at the end of the reels. The dupe can then be rewound and the process re-

peated with FX–4, FX–5, and FX–6. When those units are completed, the next three should be built, then the next three until all
twelve elements have been built.

At some point it would be a wise idea to run these built reels
on a flatbed against the picture to make sure everything is cut together properly. Obviously, you would not be able to do more than
two or three at a time.

There are two additional types of sound effects that Liz may
be dealing with. These are *goodies* and *loops*. Goodies are effects
Chuck has decided *not* to cut in, but that he wants available at the
mix in case he needs to cut them in later. Goodies are placed into
their own white box, marked "GOODIES for Reel 7" (or whatever
reel it is) on one side. On the top of the box, or on a sheet of paper
inside the box, is a list of all the goodies in the box. This list should
contain all the effects, along with the footage where they would
have to be cut in. If there is any conformation at all, these footages
should be changed.

There might also be a separate box for loops. Loops are effects that are so general it does not matter if they repeat after ten
seconds or so. *Room tone* (tone the on-set recordist recorded of the
background neutral sound of the location) is commonly treated as a
loop since it doesn't really matter where it falls in the scene—it should
all sound the same. These loops are filed by number and labeled on
the top of the box or on a separate sheet of paper by scene and
description. Often an editor will make an *analysis loop*. This is a
loop of a particular sound from the original production tracks that
needs to be treated. Some sounds, like hums or air conditioners,
need to be filtered out of the soundtrack where they are buried amidst
the dialogue or they would annoy the audience. Since they appear
only in the background of scenes, usually buried underneath dialogue, it can be very difficult for the mixer to fool around with his
equalizers over the few seconds that the sound is present by itself. In
this case, Chuck would make a loop of just the sound needing to be
filtered out. This could be run continuously until the mixer discov-
ers the proper settings to filter out the unwanted sound. This analysis loop is then filed away. It is not meant to be used in the final
soundtrack. It is only a tool to get a better mix.

Many mixing stages now have equipment that is able to electronically sample a portion of the production track and automatically loop it without creating a 35mm mag for it. This is obviously
a time saver for the sound editor since he or she doesn't have to
create any loops and the mixers can build them from the actual
sounds that they need for the mix.

One other item often brought to the mix is an effects reel. These are full 1000 foot long reels onto which a loop of an effect or tone (ocean, cars, office sounds, etc.) has been transferred from the beginning to the end. These are then put up at the film mix and faded in and out as necessary, saving the editor the job of cutting these tones individually and the assistant the job of building them into the tracks (as well as the expense of having the tone transferred to stripe). Often, these reels are full–coat, with four separate tracks of sound (usually four different, but related, tones).

Editing Sound Effects Digitally

We've just spent a lot of time talking about how a film based sound editing system works, though very few sound editors work that way anymore. Why?, you may ask. The answer is that many of the systems digital sound editors have developed come directly from their experience working with film. When you understand where these systems have come from, it is much easier to see how the DAW systems have evolved.

It is also possible, if you are cutting your own sound on a very low budget or college film, that you may need to work on film.

In any case, you're prepared.

Luckily, most people work in the digital world in the sound editing room, making their job far simpler.

Computerized digital editing first appeared in the arena of sound editing. It combines the sound technology used to create the sound on CDs and the editing technology computer word processors have developed. Common systems are the Macintosh computer based ProTools and the Waveframe.

As we have discussed, sounds are *digitized* into a computer system from any source. In this process, sounds are taken from the original production 1/4" tapes, DATs (the DATs, also being digital, have the most equivalent quality sound to the digitized sound used inside these computer systems), or sound effects CDs and are converted into the zeroes and ones that the computer can understand.

After Liz has pulled all of the sound effects and transferred them to R-Mags or small hard drives, they will be given to the sound editor responsible for the reel, along with the pull list and the videotape of the reel. With the size of hard drives today it is rarely necessary to use more than one drive per reel. The editor then has the equivalent of the picture dupe and sound kit, i.e. everything necessary to put the sound effects to the picture.

Some of the newer sound DAWs give the editor the ability to edit to a digital picture, rather than locking to a videotape running in sync with the workstation. If this is the case, Liz or her apprentice will need to digitize the picture from the videotapes she has received. There are plusses and minuses to working with a digitized picture. One down side is that the image isn't quite as clear as one on a videotape made from the work picture, making it a little harder to see fine details. On the other hand, it makes moving from one part of the reel to another extremely fast, speeding up the editing and playback of effects tremendously.

Going through the reel (usually from the head, though it is possible to go in any order with digital non-linear technology) the sound editor finds every point where an effect is needed and uses the pull list to identify which sound or sounds (often there are several effects at any point on the sound track) Chuck wants there. He or she will then cut the sound in to its best effect.

Most supervising sound editors want their editors to use their own judgments while putting sounds into the picture. Sometimes the individual editors will have additional ideas about what type of sound might be interesting in the picture. In that case, they will add more effects on extra tracks, either from a stash of effects they are carrying on their own hard drives, or from additional effects Liz has pulled from the library. They will often discuss the matter first with Chuck, so he will know exactly what is being put on the tracks before he arrives at the film mix.

A true advantage of editing sound digitally is that it allows the sound editor to create many effects that used to be only possible to make only on the mixing stage, at vastly higher cost. The editor can duplicate, reverse, amplify (make louder), lengthen or shorten, add echo, or move sounds around with ease. This is just a small sample of the types of manipulation that can be accomplished electronically.

The sounds can also be played back mixed with many other effects in a way that could not be accomplished with a Moviola or flatbed, because those film based machines usually could not play more than three or four tracks simultaneously. On electronic systems many more tracks of sound can be laid out and auditioned together.

Simple tasks are even simpler on a DAW. Take, for example, the process of creating tone for a scene. Working on film, the editor would have had to make multiple transfers of a section of the scene with clean tone and edit them together to create one long section of tone. On a DAW it is a very simple matter to copy a piece of tone and add it on to the end of itself. A five second piece of tone can be created from a piece originally half of a second long in no more time than it is taking you to read this sentence. Long sections of ambient tone, like background traffic or birds in a forest, can likewise be effortlessly created.

Foley Editing

Often a scene that has been shot does not have the proper sounds of body movement. A scene in which a person walks across a creaky wooden floor or down a cavernous passageway may have been shot without any sound at all. If sound was taken with the shot, the footsteps might not have the proper spooky sound. In addition, scenes in which the dialogue is being replaced by looping will have absolutely no background sounds at all, since all the original background will be thrown out with the original dialogue. The sound editor cuts in backgrounds and specific effects to help in all of these cases, but there are many cases where a needed effect is too specific to be found in an effects library.

You have already seen that some effects may have to be recorded especially for the scene. In many cases this is done on location. On *Apocalypse Now*, for instance, a sound crew spent weeks recording the sounds of military aircraft. On *Trigger Happy* our sound editors spent an evening in an abandoned warehouse to get the proper large space ambiance and movement. But how would you put in the sounds of those footsteps walking down the cavernous hallway? One choice would be to go to a cavernous hallway and record someone walking down it. But this approach has two problems to it. The first is the uncontrollable nature of the resulting sound. It might have too much echo built into it. While it is always possible to add echo to a sound during the mix it is almost impossible to lessen or remove it. So, if the sound you got by recording the footsteps in a big hallway had too much echo in it for Adam, you would be in a bad fix. The second problem is that, on location, you would have very little way to exactly copy the pace of the actor's or actress' footsteps.

355

Fortunately, there is an easier way (you knew there would be, didn't you?). It's called *foleying*.

Originally, you could define a foley as any kind of body movement effect recorded in a studio while watching the picture. In recent years, sound editors have increasingly been using the process to create all kinds of sound effects requiring specific sync. One film I worked on had several scenes of the two lead characters bicycling. The sound house decided to record the bicycle sounds specifically to picture on a foley stage, rather than find a library effect and edit it to fit the picture. This not only assured that the crucial sound of the bicycles fit the visuals, it also meant that it was easier to accommodate the various starts, stops and motions that the actors made on their bicycles.

A foley stage is a recording studio capable of playing back the picture and sound (usually from a videotape) while someone watches and mimics the action on the screen. In the case of our actor walking down the hallway, the scene would be projected and the *foley walker* (for that is what these people are called, whether they are walking or not) would mimic the way the actor walks on the screen. These footsteps would be recorded. Later on, they would be cut into perfect sync in the editing room (it is almost impossible to get these sounds 100 percent accurate on the foley stage).

Foley stages are interesting places. They are usually large rooms with a number of surfaces to walk on. There may be a section of the floor that is dirt, another that is a polished wooden floor, another that is brick, another that is tile, a fifth that is hollow wood, and so on. Scattered on the floor are dry leaves, stones, and sand. The foley stage gives the sound editor most of the possibilities necessary to recreate footsteps in the studio.

There are tricks that foley walkers use to simulate some sounds. People walking in snow or sand are duplicated by having the walker walk his or her fingers through a bowl of soap flakes. Some sounds can be duplicated without actually recreating the action. For instance, it may be necessary to do the sound effect of someone taking off his pants. This sound is easily gotten by holding the sleeve of a jacket up to the microphone and pulling it inside out. Experienced foley walkers, who know how to get the proper sounds for an effect, can save the production thousands of dollars and create interesting effects that might not be possible in other ways. For this reason, they are often called *foley artists*. In addition, they will often have a wealth of props that they use to record the foley.

Liz will be the point person with the foley walkers. It will be her responsibility to make sure they receive the most current videotape of the film as well as notes describing just what sounds need to be foleyed. Good foley walkers don't need to have everything spelled out for them. They know that when they see two people walking down a hallway, they should record their footsteps. However, there are effects that Chuck may want to get in foley that are not so obvious. On the bicycling film I talked about earlier, I wanted to hear the sounds of the bicycles blend into the sound of a spinning roulette wheel. There is no way the foley walkers would have been able to guess I wanted that effect, since it didn't obviously correspond to anything visual. In a case like this, Liz would supply a list of specific effects to the foley walkers.

Liz should also pass along any notes on things that should not be foleyed. This is a decision that should not be taken lightly. Foleys are not only very time consuming to create (and expensive to record), they can be time consuming to cut into the film and mix later on. If elements in a scene do not really need foleying, by all means don't foley them. Many foleys are eventually not used in the mix anyway. I've seen some editors foley practically everything in a film (including the "sound" of candles flickering in the back of a cave). This seems wasteful to me. But if there is any doubt whether a scene should be foleyed, then it is wiser to take the time to foley it and cut it into units than to show up at the mix without the proper sounds.

There is one additional proviso in determining what should and shouldn't be foleyed in a film. After you have finished doing the English language version of *Silent Night,* the sound editors will have to create a foreign version of the film (see Chapter 15 on mixing). In this version, all the English dialogue in the film will be stripped away so it can be replaced with dialogue in the language of the country buying the film. However, if a particular sound effect is married to the dialogue tracks (for instance, if the sound of someone pulling off his coat is married to his dialogue) then that sound will also be lost when the English dialogue is removed. You will have to foley all the sounds married to the dialogue.

In the old days, when foleys were shot to dupes of the 35mm cut work print (which took forever to rewind back and forth) it was necessary to *streamer* the film. Streamers are three foot long lines that, when projected, appear to cross the screen slowly from left to right. They were made either by scratching a line from the left of the film to the right, or by laying down a piece of architect's tape in the same direction. Streamers were used to warn the person making the foleys that a foley cue was coming up soon. The walker would watch for the streamer to appear. As soon as it hit the right side of the screen he or she would know to begin the foley.

In most cases today, the videotape reels aren't streamered at all. Foleys are shot to videotape with visible time code and the foley walkers use this (or the footages) if they need a precise time cue for their action. In most cases, foley walkers are experienced enough to make streamers and the footage counts unnecessary.

Foleys are often recorded to a piece of 2" tape, giving the foley engineers 23 tracks to record onto (the tape actually has 24 tracks, but the last one is used for the synchronous SMPTE Time Code). If there is a scene with many characters in it, some of them can be done together on one channel of the twenty-four track, more can be done on the second channel during a second recording pass, and so on. This way you can create the effect of an entire crowd using only a few people on the foley stage.

Depending on the budget and time pressures of the film you are working on, there are varying amounts of editorial work performed on these foley tracks. On many television shows and most low budget films, the foley artists record the foley until it is in perfect sync with the picture. Those tracks are sent directly to the mix. Any fine tuning that needs to be done is performed at the mix.

On larger pictures, it is not uncommon to have the foley tapes sent to the editing room, where a foley editor will fine tune the sync before they are sent to the mixing stage. In this case, the foley is digitized into the editor's DAW. He or she will then edit it perfectly into sync with picture.

The person who is recording the foley, or their assistant, should also prepare a detailed cue sheet listing every foley recorded and the track that it appears on. If the foley tape is going directly to the mix, it will be important for the mixers to know just what has been recorded and where it exists on the tape. If a foley editor is going to be fine tuning the foley, he or she should know where everything is as well.

It will be the foley editor's responsibility (or the assistant's) to create the cue sheets for the foley, from the DAW. We will discuss this in a minute.

Preparing for the Mix

If *Silent Night* is like most other films, someone will be building the tracks no more than a day or so before they are to be mixed. After they are built, it is a good idea to check them against the picture.

In fact, it is a good idea to play back the edited effects tracks for Wendy and Adam as soon as they are ready. This will be their last chance before the mix starts to make sure that everything they wanted has shown up in the editorial work, and every effect that has been chosen meets their needs. It will be much cheaper to fix things in the sound house than it will be on the mixing stage at $800 and hour.

This *playback session* is normally held in a room at the sound house, often the sound editor's editing room. Usually, only the most questionable effects will played back for Adam. There is no need to bore him to tears, playing back every footstep foley or traffic background. However, anything that is possibly in doubt should be played back here, e.g. car chases, ambiance, sounds accompanying odd special visual effects, etc. The idea is to make sure that the artistic choices

Chuck has made are in tune with Adam's and Wendy's sensibilities. If not, there will be time to correct them before the mix.

If the sound is being cut on film, then this playback session will probably happen in an editing room on a flatbed. As a result, it will be impossible to play back all of the tracks at the same time, so this session is less productive than a digital playback. In some cases, the tracks are taken into a small mixing stage where they can all be played back together. This is a much more expensive proposition than listening to them on a DAW.

After the tracks have been viewed and approved, then Liz or her apprentice will need to create cue sheets for the tracks and output the digital tracks to the format that will be used in the mix.

As I mentioned above, when sound editors cut on film, they are creating a temporary cue sheet used by their assistants to build the tracks properly. At this point, someone with good handwriting should recopy the cue sheets so they are neat and orderly. All footages within a half foot or so of each other should be lined up on the cue sheets.

Most mixing stages today accept cue sheets written in either feet/frames or time code. It will be important for Liz to make sure that the cue sheets Lone Star is creating are the kind that the mixing stage can use. If time code is to be used, she should check with the stage which type of code they want, drop frame or non-drop frame.

The job is much easier, however, when the editor has been cutting digitally. There are computer programs available able to take the computer session for any reel and convert the computer data into a printed cue sheet that looks like the hand-written sheets mixers have been using for years. It uses the time code data, as well as the effects ID and description the sound editor has been working with all along.

After these cue sheets have been created, Liz should look them over to make sure they are legible and don't contain any errors. Her apprentice should then make at least one copy of each reel's cue sheet so both the mixer and Chuck will have a copy to work from at the mix.

It will also be necessary to output the sound tracks onto a format that will be used in the mix. Format requirements seem to change every year. A few years ago, everybody was mixing using analog 2" tapes, now the format of choice seems to be DA-88 tapes, which have the advantages of being smaller, cheaper, and digital. Other mixing stages use digital hard drives instead, meaning that Liz won't need to output the sound tracks at all. She simply takes Chuck's hard drives to the mix. It's like a miniaturized version of the old days when the sound assistants and apprentices lugged dozens of 35mm reels to the mix.

In any case, it will be necessary for Liz or her apprentice to properly label each output, whether it is on tape or on a hard drive, with the name of film, the reel number, a date of the output (since there are liable to be changes before the film is over), the version of the film that the tracks were cut to, and a list of what tracks are contained on the tape. This information should also appear on the outside box. It is also common to enclose a *track sheet* with the tape, noting what material is on what track and whether it is designed to go to the left, center, right, or surround speakers.

Sometimes, the film mix is done in the same building or on the same studio lot as the sound editing rooms. In this case, it is a simple matter to ship everything over to the mix. But in many cases this is not so—the sound house is far removed from the film mix. If the sound editors are working on film, it will be necessary to set up a little editing room at the mixing stage and to bring all essential trims and outs to the mix with the elements (production tracks as well as looping and effects trims).

Many mixing stages now have facilities that permit a sound editor to bring a DAW to the mix and hook it up to the mixing board. Chuck will then have all of the hard drives for each reel available to him, should there be any recutting necessary.

Change Notes/Conformations

As I mentioned in Chapters 11 and 11A, films are often still in a state of flux when they are handed over to the sound house for editing. It is not uncommon to receive Change Notes while the film is being worked on in sound.

These notes will create lesser or greater chaos depending upon what point in the sound editing process you send them to the sound house and how drastic the changes are. You, as the assistant picture editor, will need to convey to Chuck and Liz just where and what the changes are so they can determine just how best to fit them into their work flow. New videotapes need to be created and labeled so Chuck can work with the new material.

When Chuck gets the Change Notes and the new videotapes, he will generally look at the changes to see if there have been any major conformations requiring new effects or a drastic rethinking of the ones already edited. He will then be able to go into his DAW (or have one of his editors do it) and adjust the already edited tracks using the new videotape and the footages on the Change Notes as a guide.

If there is a change at 45'04 then he will be able to go down to that point in the reel. The sound should run out of sync with the new picture from that point on. He will then add or remove the required amount of track on his system. If there is new track to be added, Liz should have digitized it in, at the proper time code so Chuck, or the dialogue editor, can put it on the proper track.

Editing digitally makes this process a lot easier than if Chuck were cutting on film. If a shot needs to be lengthened no one needs to find a trim. The computer remembers the take and will automatically be able to extend either the head or tail of a shot, up to the amount of handle that was digitized. Trimming within shots is also easily accomplished. Since most computer editing systems can display 35mm footages as well as time code, change notes do not have to be converted to time code.

In this case, it will be up to the editor cutting the reel to check off each change note as he or she completes re-editing the tracks to make them conform with the new picture. It will be up to Liz to make sure everyone working on the affected reels (ADR, Foley editors, etc.) gets a new tape and a copy of the Change Notes/Conformation Sheets.

Alternate Versions

There are two other versions of the film that Lone Star should prepare for. One is the foreign version of the film, and the other is the television version.

As we will see in Chapter 15, the mixers will create a mix of the film with all of its dialogue on one set of tracks, all of the music on another, and all of the effects on a third set. Each of these separate sets of tracks is called a *stem*. There will be a dialogue stem, a music stem and an effects stem. When these stems go to a foreign country for the mix in their language, all of the English language dialogue will be dropped from the film.

As we've already discussed in this chapter's section on foley, the problem arises when any sound effects tied in with the dialogue disappear from the film as well. If a character's footsteps or clothes rustling are married to his dialogue, they will be dropped with the dialogue. The same applies for door slams or the sound of a character's hand slamming a table.

All of these effects will need to be recreated, either in the foley sessions or by using a library sound effect, and cut into separate tracks to be held until it is time to mix the foreign version of the film.

The television version of the film will be handled a little differently. First of all, there are liable to be some picture changes to avoid the nudity or excessive violence that may have been in the original version of the film (not, of course, on *Silent Night, Silent Cowboy*; that is nothing but good, wholesome—though thought provoking—entertainment). Wendy will have recut the effected reels of the film and you will have created a new videotape with change notes for anything that has changed. In addition, there will have been a number of television lines recorded in the ADR sessions.

The sound editing for the television version of each reel usually doesn't happen until the domestic version of the full feature has been completed. The three separate dialogue, music, and effects stems (called D-M-E) of the domestic feature are copied onto DA-88s or time-coded DATs and sent to the sound editors. Liz will then digitize each recut reel into the editor's DAW. Using these completed mixed tracks as units, and the change and television ADR notes as guides, Chuck or one of his crew will re-edit the soundtracks wherever a picture or sound change needs to be made. Later on, at the mix, it will be a simple matter to remix the film. Areas with no changes in them will be no more than a simple transfer operation. The only places needing to be remixed will be those with new or cut dialogue. Many of these changes will involve replacing dialogue only, with no change to the picture at all. At areas where picture changes were made, the effects and music stems will probably need to be conformed as well.

Sending It All to the Stage

When all of the material has been completed, checked, cue sheeted, and collected then it should be sent to the mixing stage. Liz should send it over early enough so all of it can be ready to go when the previous reel is completed.

On most films, many of the later reels have not been fully sound edited, even as the earlier ones are being mixed. Liz's responsibilities will also include keeping track of the progress of every reel. A Reel Status Report sheet (*see* Figure 12.5) will help her track the location of everything. The material Liz needs to keep track of for every reel is listed across the top of the chart. Liz will note which version of the reel everyone needs to be working with (this may be a version number or the date of the change notes) in the second column. Then she will enter either a check mark or a date as each task is completed.

It looks very simple laid out on paper. Unfortunately, it rarely ends up being this neat. It will be up to Liz to track down every piece of information necessary to ensure the proper tracks get to the

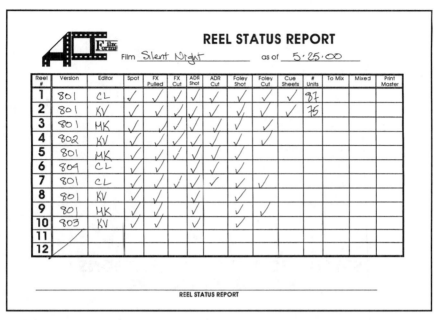

Reel #	Version	Editor	Spot	FX Pulled	FX Cut	ADR Shot	ADR Cut	Foley Shot	Foley Cut	Cue Sheets	# Units	To Mix	Mixed	Print Master
1	801	CL	✓	✓	✓	✓	✓	✓	✓	✓	87			
2	801	KV	✓	✓	✓	✓	✓	✓	✓	✓	75			
3	801	MK	✓		✓	✓	✓	✓	✓					
4	802	KV	✓		✓	✓	✓	✓		✓				
5	801	MK	✓		✓	✓	✓	✓						
6	804	CL	✓	✓		✓	✓	✓						
7	801	CL	✓		✓	✓	✓	✓	✓					
8	801	KV	✓	✓		✓		✓						
9	801	MK	✓		✓		✓	✓						
10	803	KV	✓	✓		✓		✓						
11														
12														

REEL STATUS REPORT

Film Silent Night   as of 5·25·00

REEL STATUS REPORT

FIGURE 12.5 *A Reel Status Report. This sheet will track the status of every reel in the film. If it is created on a computer then updated sheets can be created instantly. The spaces can be filled with either check marks, as each reel is completed, or the date that the box was completed. The Version column can be filled in with either the version number or the date of the version that the sound effects are being edited to. Some sound assistants like to put the dates rather than a check mark in each box.*

363

mix at the proper time. As the pressure builds, all of Liz's organizational skills will be put to good use.

With the time pressure being put on sound editing and mixing today, it is likely that Liz will need to keep tracks of many reels in various stages of completion, being mixed on more than one stage, while the picture department is still editing the film and sending change notes her way. Being able to organize a chaotic work flow and still keep everything moving is what separates the pros from the amateurs.

SPECIAL SOUND CONSIDERATIONS ON A DIGITAL PICTURE

A Difference

Most of the procedures that we've just discussed for the sound editorial department can be applied to digitally edited films just as they are to film edited on film. However, there is one difference, and it normally crops up in the spotting session.

If you've been matching your work print to your edits, you will still be able to screen on a flatbed, with all of the advantages image-wise that offers you. If you have no 35mm film to screen, however, you will need to spot directly from your digital editing machine.

There are many advantages to spotting the movie this way, rather than from a videotape of the output of that machine. For one thing, it is usually possible to spot the movie a bit sooner after your picture lock since you don't have to wait for your output tape to be copied in all of the various formats that are necessary. For another thing, Wendy will have all of her edited tracks at her disposal, from the dialogue tracks to the temp music to the temp sound effects. Though she doesn't have to play them back at the spotting session, they are available if she wants to play a temp effect that Adam really liked as an example for Chuck. When you do an output for the hand over tapes, chances are that you will be dropping all of the temp effects and music so those sounds will not be on the tapes you give the sound department.

The third advantage of this type of spotting session over the videotape screening sessions, is that it is much easier to go backwards and forwards, stopping on a particular frame. This duplicates the advantage of spotting on film on a flatbed.

About the only difficulty in spotting directly from the editing machine, is that on some machines it is difficult to get a large enough burn-in for the person taking notes to see the numbers from across the room.

OMF (Again!)

In the old days, when Wendy cut her sound on 35mm mag track, the sound department received her edited work track and would usually use those exact tracks to split, edit and mix. Today, if you are handing over matched dialogue tracks, the sound editors will rarely work with those tracks. They either recreate them in their DAWs or, at least, reprint those tracks on 35mm mag to get the best quality.

With the advent of digital picture editing, those 35mm tracks were no longer handed over to the sound department. Instead, a series of EDLs representing those tracks is used.

There is, however, a movement to return to the days when the tracks the editor worked on are physically turned over to the sound department. That trend is based on a particular file standard called *OMF*, the Open Media Framework. Using OMFI (Open Media Framework Interchange) files, it is possible for Wendy to edit her sound tracks in her editing machine and to send a copy of them, along with her EDLs (often on a large format hard drive or a Magneto Optical disk), to Chuck. He can then use them with no compatibility problems on his DAW.

365

By the way, this is the same OMF file format we discussed back in Chapter 10A, that allows your editing machines to work with different computers' opticals and CGI.

There are two ways to hand over your digital tracks in OMFI format. In one, you make a copy of the complete takes for every sound take you used in the film. This uses up quite a bit of hard drive space but gives your sound editors a lot more footage to select alternates and room tone.

The second way involves first using the "Consolidate" function on the Avid or the Lightworks. When you consolidate, you are basically instructing your computer to go through all of your footage and save only the material used in the cut. You can also ask for any number of additional frames at the heads and tails of each section to be saved as well. This additional footage should give your sound editors enough extra frames to make segues between tracks possible.

After you've consolidated your footage, you can copy it to an R-Mag or another hard drive in the OMFI format and hand those drives over to your sound department for their work.

Not every digital editing machine can work with sound in the OMF format. Even Avid, the inventor of OMF, has had some problems making the standard viable. However, now that they own the ProTools and the AudioVision DAWs, it is getting easier to take the physical tracks and EDLs from one system and make them work on another. Lightworks is trying hard to get their system to accept OMFI files, with some degree of success.

```
01:02:15:00
01:02:18:05
01:02:21:10
01:02:24:15
01:02:27:20
01:02:30:25
01:02:33:00
01:02:36:05
01:02:38:10
```

366

DIALOG AND LOOPING EDITING

Of course, there is a lot more to preparing for a mix than just dealing with the sound effects. A major sound problem on most films is the condition of the dialogue tracks. Some tracks might have so much extraneous noise that they become completely unusable. Other tracks have sporadic noises on them, making sections of the tracks unacceptable. Still other tracks, while having no generally unacceptable portions on them, have backgrounds that sound slightly different from camera setup to camera setup, making cuts from one to the other noticeable. Each of these problems is handled in the process of dialogue and looping editing.

In editing situations where one sound editor handles multiple functions, it is common for this person to do both the dialogue and effects editing but not the looping editing. However, since both dialogue and looping editing attack the same problems we will deal with them together here.

Dialogue Splitting

In Scene 11 (*see* Figure 4.5) there is a scene between Abby and his neighbor, Bob, in Abby's bedroom. Many different kinds of shots were done of the scene (as we discussed in Chapter 4, this is called *coverage*), including shots of Abby, shots of Bob, and shots of the two of them together. The direction the camera was pointing during each shot affects the sound the microphone picks up. The mike was probably facing towards different portions of the set during each setup, so there will be subtle differences in the sound quality that will become evident when these different takes are cut together. Correcting this is a fairly simple matter for a mixer—he simply uses different *equalization* (the adjustment of the way the everything sounds, i.e., the relative amounts of high, middle and low frequencies), echo, and volume settings on each of the set-ups. To do this, he needs to have each shot's sound on a separate track *element* (or *unit*). To help make the point of the transition less apparent, he will need to *segue* from one to the other. A segue is an audio dissolve in which one sound fades up as a second sound is fading out. You hear musical segues all the time on the radio when the d.j. fades from one song into another.

To accomplish this segue the mixer will need to have a short overlap of the two sounds. That is, he will need a number of frames (anywhere from ten frames to three feet) where both sounds are running simultaneously. This is accomplished by putting *extensions* on each of the tracks.

To understand what extensions are, look at Figure 13.1. You can see that there are two pieces of track, one marked "Abby's track" and the other marked "Bob's track." These correspond to the two slightly different background sounds from the two different setups. If the mixer were to mix the tracks like this, there would be a change in the sound at the point where one ends and the other begins. This change, called a *bump*, would be annoying to the audience.

368

Instead, Chuck or Liz will need to extend the head and tails of each of the shots, by adding a short section of the take where there was no dialogue or noise, only background sound (this means there would only be a general tone, no dialogue or other specific sounds). On film, they would listen to the trims and find a section with only background tone. They would then make multiple transfers of this piece to make it long enough to use in all of the places where the tracks from this take need extensions.

On a DAW the process is much simpler. They could simply listen to the take and look for a short piece of silent tone. It is a simple matter to mark that area and cut it in as many times as necessary to create the handles. In some cases, the wild track recorded on the set may work, in others the wild track will not be usable because it sounds too different from the background of the piece of sound they are attaching the tone to.

After cutting in the extensions, the tracks would look something like Figure 13.2. A little bit before and after the point where the two tracks used to butt up against each other, there are pieces of tone overlapping the original tracks. After the mixer has adjusted all of his settings so the two tracks match as well as they possibly can, he would be able to run both tracks together and one would automatically segue into the other. The mixer might need to do a

Cut between shots

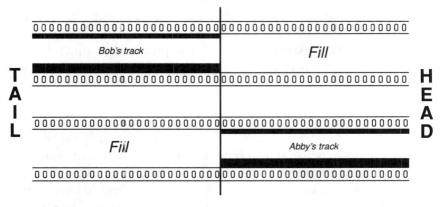

FIGURE 13.1 *A pair of dialogue tracks split onto different tracks, before any extensions have been added (the film portion on the tracks is fill). If the sounds were to be mixed this way the mixer would no capability to ease from Abby's track into Bob's and the difference between the backgrounds would be quite noticeable.*

Cut between shots

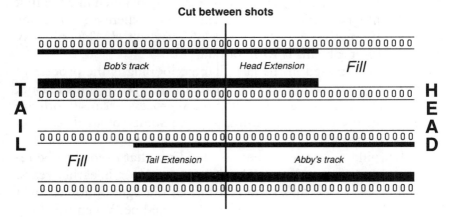

FIGURE 13.2 *After extensions are added, the tracks can be cross-faded in the midst of the overlapping sections.*

short little fade out on Abby's shot while fading in on Bob's track.

In the case of an isolated noise on a track that Chuck wants to get rid of, these sounds can be cut out of the track. This of course produces a *hole*, a section of the track where the sound drops out. This hole is filled by putting tone from the take either on another track with handles (which the mixer will then fade into and out of to cover the hole) or cut directly into the track to replace the fill at the hole. Liz or Chuck must be very careful to make sure that the tone inserted at the hole exactly matches the tone immediately before and after it. If not, they would cut the tone onto another track so the mixer could treat it by equalization and segueing. This is why nearly all sound editors work using a pair of headphones. It is much harder to hear the fine points of the tracks if they're listening on speakers.

Looping

There are cases where these unwanted noises come directly on top of a line of dialogue. When this happens, there is no way to remove the noise without also removing part of the line of dialogue. The first thing the sound editor should do in this case is examine all of the alternate takes containing that word or line (except those where the actor's reading is off-mic, that is, not spoken directly into the microphone) to see if the actor's words can be replaced with the same words from another take without changing the performance. Sometimes, replacing one syllable of the word with an alternate reading is all that is necessary. There are times when even this will not be possible. In that case, the problem is treated very much like the first case of dialogue editing I was talking about—where an entire line or series of lines is unusable because of lousy sound. The only way to cure these problems is with looping.

370

As I mentioned in the last chapter, looping is the process of re–recording words or lines that are unacceptable for some reason. The way this is done resembles the foley process because both are attempting to do the same thing—record some sound directly in sync to a picture.

Looping got its name because the lines that needed to be re-placed were cut into a loop of 35mm mag track (or, in earlier years, optical track) made up of the bad line of dialogue followed by a piece of fill of exactly the same length as the line. When this loop was played back, the actor or actress would hear his or her line followed by a gap. Then the line would repeat, then the space. And on and on. This would enable the actor or actress to repeat the line immediately after hearing it. Each of the actor's repetitions would be recorded until the director was happy with the performance. There are some people who lament the passing of this system, but today, looping is no longer done with loops but in a process known either as *ADR* (Automatic Dialogue Replacement) or *EPS* (Electronic Post Sync). Both terms mean exactly the same thing.

In ADR, the actor or actress faces the screen and hears, in a set of headphones, the dialogue immediately leading up to the line to be replaced. As the line approaches, they hear three beeps. They might also see a streamer; a line moving diagonally from the left to the right of the screen. Streamers are usually two seconds long. The moment the streamer hits the right side of the screen, they begin speaking their line. This would happen at the same moment as a fourth imaginary beep. Both the streamer and the beeps give the actors or actresses cues when they should begin speaking their lines.

Looping requires a certain amount of preparation on the part of the looping editor and assistant. The first order of business is obviously deciding what needs to be looped. This is usually done at the spotting session (as described in Chapter 12) with Chuck, Wendy, and Adam. The kinds of things that determine whether a line should be looped are whether there are extraneous noises over it, whether it is audible, whether it is comprehensible, and whether it is a reading the director is happy with. Sometimes the director will want to change the performance of a line or even its wording.

Another reason for looping a line is to obtain a television alternative. This is a different wording of a line that does not contain an objectionable word heard in the original. These television lines will be used in the "soft" or TV mix of the film. These soft version lines are used for the airline version of the film as well.

Sometimes it is necessary to record lines for off-screen or background characters that were not recorded on the set. In a scene where a lead character is talking to someone at a party, the production sound recordist would never want to mike the scene so that the background characters could be heard and disturb the lead's dialogue. In fact, the extras performing the parts of the background party-goers often merely mime their conversation, without actually saying anything. This gives the mixers the cleanest track possible for the lead character's dialogue. Later on, of course, the background chatter must be added, sometimes by a library sound effect of party walla (a group of people murmuring). The same effect can be gotten more precisely by a group of actors in a looping session. Usually this group (typically called a *loop group)* is brought in near the end of all the looping sessions to record these off-screen lines and walla. You should make sure the person who is organizing the loop group receives a videotape copy of the film so they can properly spot the lines and cast the actors who will be needed.

After it has been determined just what lines need to be looped, the actors and actresses involved should be booked for looping sessions. This is usually done by the producer's office since it involves calling agents to determine the actors' and actresses' availability. The looping department should advise the producer's office of just how much time is needed with each actor or actress and give them the approximate dates when they would like to do all the looping. Depending on how good the talent is, it is usually possible to record about 12 looped lines in every hour of looping.

Then, the reels must be prepared for the looping session. I know of nowhere where this is done using film anymore. It is simply easier, cheaper (in terms of labor and looping stage time), and faster to work from a videotape. Even if you have edited your picture on film, you will need to transfer each reel to videotape for the looping editor to work with. This is, in fact, usually where one of the tapes I mentioned in delivery requirements will go.

After checking the videotape for proper code, the looping editor or assistant will take the looping notes made at the spotting session, sit down at a computer that has been hooked up to a videotape deck and begin marking the reels for looping. There are a number of programs on the market, like the Lartec System, to expedite this process.

The looping editor, let's call her Glynis Lowe, will play the videotape in real time. She should listen to every line, thinking about whether it needs to be looped. It will be easier to hear deficiencies in the sound listening to the videotape with headphones, than over the speakers at the spotting session. Lines that need to be looped for television versions are often forgotten at the spotting session. For this reason, Glynis must be very careful not to miss anything now, even if it isn't on her spotting notes.

When she gets to a line or a series of lines that need to be looped she presses a computer key and the time code on the tape is automatically recorded in the program. She presses another key to mark exactly where she wants to stop looping the line. This is not as self-evident as it all sounds. Most of the time you will want to record a number of consecutive lines in a speech without stopping. But some actors and actresses get tired faster than others. It is often difficult to loop long lines and get acceptable sync. On the other hand, it is unwise to break down the lines too much because that can break up the actor's or actress' concentration, creating a stiff, unnatural reading of each line. Some middle ground has to be found. A safe choice would be to break the line down into more individual cues than necessary. The lines can always be combined during the looping session, because Glynis would have provided time code cue numbers for every possible point of combination. If Glynis chose to break down the line into fewer cues, and the actor or actress needed to break it down even further, some time would need to be taken at the looping session to find the time codes of those additional cue points.

A good looping editor will be able to make intelligent choices.

There is another factor that Glynis needs to take into account when programming the reels for looping. It is time-consuming during the mixing process to go back and forth from looped lines to the original production tracks. Therefore, it is often better to loop the lines surrounding a loop line, even if these additional lines don't need to be looped. In a scene with ten lines, it would be silly to program seven of them for looping and not the other three. Later on, during the mix, the mixers will try to preserve as many of the original production track lines as possible; but it will be much simpler, safer, and cheaper in this case if the entire scene is prepared for looping.

Glynis will then type in the exact reading of the line she is replacing, along with the name of the character who speaks the line. It is important that she spell the character's name the same way each time, since the program will later tally the number of lines to be looped based on the spelling of their names. A character typed in as "Abbie" will be counted as a different character than one marked "Abby," even though they might be the same character in the film.

When Glynis is finished going through all of the reels it will be a simple matter to print out two different forms of looping cut sheets. The first kind will break down every looped line in the film by time code (*see* Figure 13.3). This list will give Glynis a view of every line that needs to be looped in the order they appear in the film. She will use this list to keep a record of all of the loops as they are being recorded.

The other cue sheet Glynis will make is actually a series of sheets dividing the looped lines by character (*see* Figure 13.4). This is the sheet she will give each actor or actress when they come to the looping session. Since it will list only *their* lines, there will be no way for them to get confused as to what lines they are recording.

The computer will also print out a detailed list of the looped line numbers, divided by character. It will also total the number of lines that each character has to loop.

As soon as she has finished with the looping cue sheets, Glynis should get copies of them to Adam, Wendy and *Silent Night*'s producers. They will go through the list, making sure that everything they want to loop has been included. They will also be able to book the acting talent, now that they know exactly how many lines each actor or actress will need to record.

A copy of the list should also go to Chuck or Liz. They need to know just what lines are planned for looping. Every looped line will need to have background tone built behind it to make it sound

ADR CUE SHEET

Film: <u>Silent Night, Silent Cowboy</u>   Reel # <u>1</u>

Editor <u>G. Lowe</u> Date <u>5·11·00</u>   Tape # <u>1</u>

CUE#	CHAR	START (m.s.f)	NOTES	CHANNELS 1 2 3 4 5 6 7 8	DIALOGUE
1026	ABBY	6.12.03 6.13.07	Lo prod	3 (4)	EVENING, MR HEMINGWAY
1027	BOB	6.16.11 6.20.02	Big klunks	(55)	WHY DON'T YOU MOVE INTO THE 20TH CENTURY ...
1028	BOB	6.21.00 6.26.12	Big klunks	58 (60)(61)(62)	... AND GET A WORD PROCESSOR ALREADY.
1029	ABBY	6.30.01 6.32.14	Lo prod	8 11 (12) (9)	HOW'D YOU GET INTO MY APARTMENT?
1030	BOB	6.40.00 6.42.09	To match	65 (68)	HOW'D THE FILMING GO MR. DEMILLE?
1031	ABBY	6.43.08 6.45.00	Lo prod	15 16 (20) ✓	PERFECTLY SHITTY
1032 TV	ABBY	6.43.08 6.45.00	TV	(21)	PERFECTLY SHODDY (for TV coverage)

ADR CUE SHEET

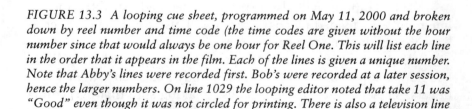

FIGURE 13.3 *A looping cue sheet, programmed on May 11, 2000 and broken down by reel number and time code (the time codes are given without the hour number since that would always be one hour for Reel One. This will list each line in the order that it appears in the film. Each of the lines is given a unique number. Note that Abby's lines were recorded first. Bob's were recorded at a later session, hence the larger numbers. On line 1029 the looping editor noted that take 11 was "Good" even though it was not circled for printing. There is also a television line alternate for line 1031, numbered 1032TV. (Courtesy Westwind Media, Inc.)*

ADR CHARACTER CUE SHEET

Film: <u>Silent Night</u>   Character   <u>ABBY</u>   Reel #   <u>1</u>

Editor <u>G. Lowe</u>   Date <u>5·11·00</u>

CUE#	START (m.s.f)	DIALOGUE	CHANNELS							
			1	2	3	4	5	6	7	8
1026	6.12.03 6.13.07	EVENING, MR HEMINGWAY								
1029	6.30.01 6.32.14	HOW'D YOU GET INTO MY APARTMENT?								
1031	6.43.08 6.45.00	PERFECTLY SHITTY								
1032 TV	6.43.08 6.45.00	PERFECTLY SHODDY (for TV coverage)								
1034	6.46.02 6.50.03	I DON'T EVEN RECOGNIZE WHAT HE'S FILMING								
1036	7.00.13 7.06.12	NO, I STILL RECOGNIZE SOME OF THE PLOT								
1038	7.15.03 7.18.00	HOW'S THE GREAT AMERICAN NOVEL COMING?								
1040	7.23.12 7.29.10	THEN IT'S SITTING IN THAT DUMPSTER WITH MY ORIGINAL SCRIPT.								

ADR CUE SHEET

375

FIGURE 13.4 *In this version of a looping cue sheet all of the loops are divided by character. This is the version of the cue sheet which is given to the talent during the recording of the loops. The looping editor will usually not record notes on this version. (Courtesy Westwind Media, Inc.)*

the same as the lines around it that are not looped. As a result, whoever is cutting the dialogue will need to know which lines are meant to be looped, so they can build tone for them.

As the time for the looping session gets closer, Glynis should call the looping studio and make sure everything has been prepared properly for their session. Generally, the studio will have a video deck for playing back the tape (usually a 3/4" machine) and a number of tape machines for the recording of the ADR lines. The lines are usually recorded onto a 2" 24-track tape machine, with a DAT running to record a backup. Newer studios have started to record the loops directly to a hard drive, with a DAT back up. Glynis should make sure that the stage has pre-striped the 2" tape stock with matching time code so the tape can run in sync with the videotape. For this reason, she should send them a copy of the EOR list so they can precode the tape to the proper reel lengths. Generally, they will precode for ten or twelve minute reels; if any of the reels are too long for the tape they precode, everyone will be in trouble, so it is a good idea to let them know exactly what lengths the reels are. If Glynis has received the picture reels in 20 minute double reels, they will need to precode their tape in those lengths.

In some cases, the studio will be recording the looping using a digitized picture as a guide. If this is the case, Glynis will need to send her set of videotapes to the facility a day or so early, so they can digitize the reels ahead of time.

On the day of the session, Liz should show up a little early with the videotapes to be looped (assuming she hasn't sent them over the day before) and give them to the projectionist and the recordist. She should make sure that any materials she sent over the day before are in the proper studio. Copies of the cue sheets should be given to the recordist, the looping editor, the director, and the actor or actress (called "the talent" in film language). The assistant should also retain a copy for his or her own notes.

The looping process works like this. The videotape is rolled and everyone listens to the dupe track. The engineer recording the lines announces a slate that will sound something like, "Loop 1010, Take 3." The actor playing Abby, in this case, watches the screen while listening to the track in his headphones. He might see a streamer (many sound houses have machines that can automatically put a streamer onto the projected videotape). Then he hears three beeps. At the place where the fourth imaginary beep would be, he begins speaking the line while watching the film, attempting to match his reading to the lip movements of the character on the screen, as well as trying to recreate the feeling of the scene. This is why the ADR/

EPS system is nicer than the old looping system—he gets to see and hear the dialogue in the scene leading up to the line to be looped.

The first take of the loop gets placed on the first of a series of channels the recordist has assigned to this character. If it is unacceptable (either for sync, acting, or because of a mistake) then take two is made on the same channel, wiping out the old one. However, the take is not erased on the backup DAT. This way, if a line doesn't work in the editing room or at the mix, there is always this backup to go to.

Once an acceptable take is done, Adam may want to do another one, either for safety or to get a different reading. He may like the reading on the first track, but the sync is not good (Glynis should be very active in advising the director just what is acceptable, what is passable, and what is not good in terms of sync). In these cases, the take on channel one is saved and another take is made onto channel two.

Glynis will be taking notes on her copy of the master looping cue sheets (*see* Figure 13.3). In this example, Loop #1003 (the third loop on reel l) the first three takes went onto track one, of which the second reading was "not bad" according to Adam. He asked that it be saved, but he wanted to do another take. The next two went onto channel two where the best take was Take 5. Track three was reserved for a television line of which Take 8 was the best.

In addition to these lines, the director may request certain lines from the actor without running the picture. These lines are called *wild lines*, much as track recorded on the set without picture is called wild track. The assistant should make a note as to exactly where these wild lines are. The best way to do this is to keep a separate wild line log listing each take of each wild line recorded, along with the reel number it was recorded on, the date it was recorded, where on the tape it was recorded (e.g., "After 1035"), and any other information (the scene it is for, where it is supposed to go in the scene, comments, etc.). Glynis might want to write some of these notes in the margins of the appropriate looping cue sheet.

Cutting in the Looped Lines

After the day's looping is completed and transferred you will end up with a 2" of all the selected looped lines placed in the proper spot, time code wise, against picture. These lines then need to be digitized into the looping editor's DAW so she can precisely cut them against the picture.

Some sound houses can input directly from the 24 track into their DAWs. Others will need to have the material transferred onto another medium, like DA-88, before they can input it. If this inter-mediate transfer is necessary, be aware that DA-88s, and most other tape mediums, cannot record as many tracks as a 2" 24-track tape can. A series of DA-88s, each labeled for the proper reel and chan-nels, must be created.

Glynis then edits the lines to fit the actor's lips as they move on the picture. She will be concerned with much the same sort of thing that the foley editor is concerned with. Even though the loops were recorded directly to picture, tiny adjustments always need to be made to make the line look *exactly* in sync. She may also need to combine a few takes together to create a line with all of the inflec-tions that Adam wants.

Any words or lines that are to be replaced by looped lines are physically removed from the dialogue tracks by Chuck or the dia-logue editor (where they are replaced by tone). They are shifted over to another set of tracks that are reserved exclusively for dia-logue lines removed from the production tracks for looped lines. These units are generally called the *X and Y tracks*. There, the pieces are cleaned up and sit ready to be used in the event that Adam decides at the mix he does not want to use a looped line and prefers the original. This happens all the time; it is difficult to know whether a line is really superior to the original until the sound editor and mixer have cleaned up the original. For this reason the X and Y tracks should be prepared just as if they were going to be used in the mix. This involves inserting tone in between sections and removing unwanted noises that do not affect the dialogue.

A new program called VocALign, which works with ProTools, is designed to simplify the dialogue and ADR editing process. In essence, it analyzes the guide track that Glynis is going to replace and attempts to adjust the looped (or alternate production dialogue) line using time compression and expansion techniques.

When all these things have been done, the tracks can be built and then output to DA-88s or R-Mags that go to the mix, just as the effects were prepared for mixing. A set of cue sheets is also created, usually automatically, listing every line that was cut into the ADR tracks.

As I mentioned before, some sound houses can record their ADR directly onto the same hard drives Glynis uses for her editing. In these cases, these hard drives are then taken directly to the mix and used as the units that the dialogue mixer will work from. It is a much faster, more efficient way of working, and there will be a time when all mixing is done this way.

13A/DIGITAL

DIALOG AND LOOPING ON A DIGITAL PICTURE

As far as Wendy is concerned, there is almost no difference between the work she does on a digital editing machine and what she would do if she were editing on film.

The only real exception to this statement comes from the ease with which picture digital editing machines allow her to do her own dialogue work. As she is cutting the picture, she may find it so easy for her or you to split tracks and tone out the reels that she will want to hand over the tracks (either on EDL or using the OMFI standard we discussed in Chapter 12A) with those splits and tone already laid out for the dialogue and ADR editor.

On the Lightworks, for instance, there is a function allowing the machine to automatically checkerboard the sound so that every other sound cut is split alternately onto the first or second track, with or without handles. I never use this function since I prefer to split the tracks in my own way. Sometimes it makes sense to split tracks in ways other than a simple A and B on every other cut. However, some editors like this function.

If Wendy has split and toned out her tracks before handing them over, one of the tasks Glynis will have is making sure that the picture editor has made the best selection of tone and, if not, replace it. She will also probably want to split the tracks over more channels then Wendy did, since most picture editing machines are limited to four channels of sound. It will also be up to Glynis to deal with the ADR and to create the X and Y tracks.

Other than that, now that dialogue editing is performed almost exclusively on DAWs, Glynis' job is pretty much the same regardless of how Wendy has edited the film.

MUSIC EDITING

Eventually, when the film's editing is almost complete, Adam's thoughts will turn toward music—in particular, what kind of music would be exactly right for *Silent Night*.

Perhaps Adam will have decided that he wishes to work with the same composer that he's worked with on other films. Perhaps he will have decided that he wants no music, or to use pieces of already recorded music. Or perhaps he will have decided to take a chance on a new composer. But, if there is to be any type of music at all in the film there will have to be a music editor.

On many low budget films, especially if there is to be very little music in the film, the picture editor functions as the music editor, primarily assisting the composer in getting his *timings* and *laying in the tracks* (don't worry, we'll learn about these terms in a short while). But even if this is the case, there will always be someone functioning as a music editor. That is what this chapter is all about.

There is already a good book for the music editor that lays out many of the music editor's tasks. *Music Editing For Motion Pictures*, by Milton Lustig, discusses many of the tasks a music editor must perform and some of the techniques for editing music. Though the book is hampered by being too out–of–date to deal with video, computers and the latest studio techniques, I would still recommend it for those with a further interest in the subject.

The music editor faces three major tasks. The first occurs during the editing of the film when he or she is asked to create a temporary score to be used in previews and other screenings. The second job is to prepare the composer so they can write the music, and the third is to record and edit the music to the film and get it mixed into the film's soundtrack.

Temp Music for Previews

Just as sound editors no longer work on film, it is the rare music editor who doesn't work on a DAW. Music is digitized from any number of sources, the computer is sunk up to a videotape, and the music editor cuts the music tracks to the visuals and the dialog tracks.

The videotape is sunk up to the DAW using SMPTE Time Code, placed either on the second audio channel or in the Vertical Interval Time Code, VITC. Since there are a number of lines where VITC can potentially be located, you should find out which lines your music editor and composer need it to be in to use the tape properly.

Often, the music editor is selected by the composer, with whom they have a long-term relationship. Sometimes, Wendy or the producers will need to do the hiring. Let's say Adam has chosen Lester von Beethoven to write the music for *Silent Night* (he comes from a long line of talented musicians), and Lester has hired Nate High to be your music editor. He may or may not use an assistant at this stage of the film; more often than not, he won't. However, let's assume that he has hired Betty Bound as his assistant. The first thing they will do after they receive the videotapes for a temp mix is to check that the time code is correct. The next thing Betty will do is to create a number of *sessions*, one for each reel. Sessions are, simply, a file with all of the used, edited sounds for that reel cut in sync with the picture. Into this session she will usually digitize the dialogue track for the film, as it was recorded onto the videotape. In some cases, you will have also sent the music department a tape (often a DA-88) of the temp music tracks Wendy used as she was editing the film.

Sometimes these tracks will be given to Betty as a series of OMFI files. In either case, she will take the temp music and put it into the session for that reel.

Nate will then need to replace the music tracks that don't work for Adam and smooth out any music transitions (called *segues*) that don't work. In some cases, he will be called on to create a long music cue out of a number of already recorded smaller ones, or parts of many longer ones.

After all of the tracks have been edited, Betty will output them for the temp mix. The procedure for this is the same as outputting for a final mix, so I will leave the discussion of this for later in the chapter.

Before the Scoring Session

The second task Nate and Betty will have comes when the film is locked and they need to prepare for the recording session. In order to best do this, the first thing they need to do is see the film as many times as they can. Then there must be a spotting session. The spotting session is usually held with the music editor and assistant, the film editor, and the director.

Spotting sessions can be held either in a projection room where the film can be run forward and backward, on a television set with a videotape of the film, or on a flatbed in an editing room. I've occasionally spotted the film with a videotape, while sitting in the composer's home recording studio. There are plusses and minuses to each approach, but I find that it is usually the composer's needs (or the realities of whether film is available) that dictate how and where the spotting session is run.

The composer should certainly view the picture as many times as possible before this spotting session, preferably in a theatre with a preview audience.

Everything else being equal, I prefer to screen the movie on a flatbed in the editing room. This not only gives me the maximum amount of control over the film (videotapes are harder to roll back and forth and stop on an exact frame) but also gives the best picture for the composer.

At the spotting session, Adam will go through the film reel by reel, explaining where he wants the music, what kind of music he wants and where he wants accents in the music. Lester will ask for details so he can better interpret just what it is the director wants musically. Meanwhile, Nate and Betty should be furiously taking notes.

Let's say that we are going to be spotting Scenes 8, 9, 10, and 11 (*see* Figure 4.5). You may remember that these are the scenes where Abby looks on during the shooting of a barroom fight. We then cut to the parking lot that evening as Abby, and the rest of the studio workers, leave work. Abby goes to his car, turns on his engine, and sits watching the cars leave. He then closes his car door and drives off. We cut to Abby as he walks into his apartment, looks around, goes to get a drink and, hearing a typewriter from the other room, exits and goes to his bedroom. There, at a desk, sits Bob, a neighbor. They begin talking.

Adam's idea for scoring this scene is that the music should begin in the barroom set, continue through the parking lot and into the apartment scene where it should go out.

Nate wants to know where in the apartment it will go out.

Lester suggests that it cross–fade (segue) into the sounds of the typewriter as Abby notices them.

They will then begin to give adjectives to the cue. They will discuss whether the music should be wistful (underscoring Abby's sense of isolation from the filmmaking process) or happy (accenting his joy at the shooting of his film). Everybody will talk about at what points in the music cue it should change character to go with Abby's changing mood. This part of the discussion is very important to the composer since, more often than not, the director knows very little about the terminology of music. These adjectives are the best way to describe how he wants the music to sound. This is why I sometimes refer to music spotting sessions as "adjective sessions."

When the spotting session is over, Nate will put together a list of where all the music cues will begin and end in the film, called a *Music Spotting Sheet* (*see* Figure 14.1). Copies of this list should be given to Adam, Wendy, Lester and you. In addition, the sound editors should receive a copy as soon as it is typed up so they know exactly where music is planned for the film. This will help them in their choice and placement of sound effects.

It is then time to do the *music timing sheets* for the composer.

Just like the sound department, the music editorial department will have received a number of videotapes of the film. Most larger recording music studios will need the film transferred onto 3/4" tape because of its professional quality, rather than 1/2". It is likely, however, that Nate and Lester will want to work with 1/2" tapes. You will need to create a complete set of tapes in each format for each need that the music department will have. Betty will be responsible for collecting all of the delivery requirement information and getting it to you before the picture is locked.

383

This list should contain all of the technical specifications that Lester, Nate, and the music recording studio need for their tapes. The spec sheet will look a lot like the lists you saw in Figure 11.4 and 11A.1 for the sound department. On the composer's copy of the videotape, he would normally have the time code superimposed on the picture (sometimes known as *window burn* or *window code*) as well as put onto channel two of the audio channels, channel one being used for the production track of the film. Each reel of the film would be transferred with its own time code—the convention is usually to number each reel with its number in the hour position of the time code and to begin the reel at zero minutes, zero seconds, and zero frames at the picture start mark. Thus, reel five's start mark would be coded 5:00:00:00, and reel eleven's would be 11:00:00:00.

MUSIC SPOTTING NOTES

Film _Silent Night_   Date _3.29.00_

Page _1_ of _12_

Cue #	Title	Start	End	Time	Comments
	Reel One				
1M1	Main Titles	00:08.00	01:21.00	1:13.2	Big, strings
1M2	The Parking Lot	03:59.10	04:13.00	0:18.6	Airy
1M3	Abby Meets Sean	05:40.12	06:53.06	1:12.3	
1M4	Jimmy the Baby	06:56.2	07:41.12	0:45.3	Playback
1M5	The Restaurant	08:11.07	09:33.15	1:22.7	
	Reel Two				
2M1	Roller Coaster	06:08.10	08:04.15	1:56.7	Guide Track
2M2	Can I Be...?	07:57.00	08:32.08	0:35.3	Segue (2M1)
2M3	Out Of It	09:15.05	09:55.05	0:40.0	
	Reel Three				
3M1	Going Home	06:08.10	07:23.12	1:15.2	
3M2	Abby Returns	08:19.06	08:59.6	0:40.6	
3M3	Birthday Party	09:10.3	09:25.5	0:15.2	} will
3M4	The 3 Friends	09:25.5	09:56.1	0:30.6	} transition
		(MORE)			

MUSIC SPOTTING NOTES

FIGURE 14.1 Music spotting notes taken directly from the sit-down spotting session with the director, composer, editor and music editor. This list will give everyone, including the sound editors, a chance to see where the music will fall within the film.

Some film footages are also superimposed on the picture, in their own window. These can be helpful to the editor if he cut finished music on film.

Remember, you may also need to put VITC code on some of the tapes.

When he receives it, Nate will sit down with his videotape of the film as well as his and Betty's notes and go through the film, marking the exact point where the music is to begin at each musical cue. Each cue will be given a number much like the looping numbers. The fifth cue on reel two would be called 2M5 (some editors prefer to call it M205). Each cue will also be given a title for identification and copyright purposes.

Nate will go through the reels marking every potential accent point in every single musical cue. On a timing sheet (*see* Figure 14.2) he would list everything Lester might ever want to accent musically. Normally, composers only use about 10 percent of this information but they rarely know ahead of time *which* 10 percent it will be, so the music editor must detail practically everything. The timing sheet also includes all of the characters' dialogue because it is very important that the composer's music not conflict with the dialogue.

You will also notice that the timing sheet lists the cue points in terms of sequential time from the beginning of each cue. This figure is the only number that Lester will find useful. There is another figure, the time code in the reel, that is important to the editor. Nate will use this footage to prepare the videotape for recording.

There are several computer music programs that music editors use to make their timing sheets. As the editor types in the footage or SMPTE Time Code number of each cue point, the program will automatically create the timings the composer can use to write his music. It will also generate cue sheets of varying types as well as create many other charts and notes that the composer can utilize. If Lester writes with a computer or synthesizer that uses *MIDI codes* (a standard for the synthetic electronic reproduction of music) he can write his music while the videotape is locked to his synthesizer. This means he will be able to hear how his music plays against the dialogue and see how it looks against the picture with a great degree of accuracy. For some composers who write this way, this makes the detailed cue sheets superfluous.

Many composers, however, still work in the old way and require typed timing notes, regardless of how they are generated. As soon as the first few timing notes are done they are sent to Lester. After he receives these detailed notes, he can begin to write the music precisely to sync up with the picture. If Abby shakes his head at

ABS TIME	REL TIME		DESCRIPTION	CLICK #
			Production: <u>Silent Night</u> **Cue: <u>Abby Goes Back Home (5M4)</u>** Record at **click**: _____	
			Adam: "He'd like to join in but he can't. He's an outsider. Not exactly melancholy, but sweetly sad somehow."	
			The DIRECTOR yells "Cut!" and a cheer goes up from the set. ABBY is sitting, staring at the broken bottle on the floor. He looks up.	
08:16:05	00:00		BEGIN cue as ABBY lifts his head up.	
08:17:27	01:22		He wakes up from his reverie.	
08:22:17	06:12	CUT	to what he sees: a MAN is picking up the broken bottle.	
08:35:09	19:04	CUT	back to ABBY as he realizes that everyone is leaving.	
08:41:28	25:23	CUT	to some GRIPS packing away cables.	
08:44:27	28:22	CUT	to ACTORS shaking hands and leaving.	
08:48:20	32:15	CUT	to the DEAD MAN getting up from the floor.	
08:52:08	36.03	CUT	to ABBY as he shakes his head.	
08:54:20	38.15	CUT	to the DEAD MAN getting shot (flashback) from before as ABBY saw it.	
09:06:00	49.25	CUT	to ABBY in a daze.	
09:07:11	51:06	CUT	to a wider shot as he stands up.	
09:13:24	57:19	CUT	to the parking lot, later. ABBY is entering the lot along with a number of other WORKERS on the film.	
09:15:20	59:15		One of the crew waves goodbye to ABBY.	
09:18:15	1:02:10		ABBY waves back.	
09:22:19	1:04:14		... but realizes that the man wasn't waving at him.	
09:23:19	1:05:14	CUT	to Abby's car.	
09:24:16	1:06:11		ABBY enters the frame.	
09:27:02	1:08:27		He begins to open the door to his car.	
09:28:27	1:10.22		He stops and looks out into space.	
09:43:18	1:25:13		**END of CUE** as he shakes off his thought	
09:48:17	1:30:12		He gets into the car.	

TOTAL TIME - 1:25.13

FIGURE 14.2. *A timing sheet. The composer will use these timings to determine exactly where his musical accents should fall. Adam's notes at the top are important as they are a record of what he wanted the music to be like. Once the composer determines the tempo (the click) of the cue, either he or the music editor can determine at which click each cue point falls in the piece. There is a column for this click number at the right of the sheet.*

36:03 into cue 1M4, Lester will be able to write a musical accent to help give additional emotional weight to that moment.

As Lester writes each cue he will determine a tempo (speed) for the piece. Tempi in film are often not given in the metronome settings common in music (120 beats of music per minute, or 120 bpm) but in *clicks*. These are numbers that look something like this: 12/0 or 16/4. The click number represents the number of frames for each beat of music. Each frame is divided into eight parts, each corresponding to one-half of a sprocket. So a 12/0 click would mean that there were twelve and no eighths frames for each beat of music. This is the equivalent of two beats of music each 24 frames (one second) or, for the musicians reading this, 120 beats per minute. A 16/4 click means there are sixteen and one-half frames per beat (four-eighths of a frame is one-half of a frame).

All of this is important because, after Lester determines the click of each cue, Betty will have to prepare each cue with streamersso, during the recording session, the conductor will be able to look at the film and record the music to it.

In the old days, music editors had to physically scratch the streamers onto a dupe of the film. Films are now recorded using video for the visual playback. The music editor need only type in the time code for the start of the cue, the tempo of the cue, and the number of warning clicks Lester wants the conductor to hear (we'll get to this in a minute) and the computer will automatically create the streamers as the video is being played back. Streamers are usually needed at several places within each music cue. The beginning and end of each cue is streamered so the composer knows when to start and finish conducting the music. Any places *inside* the cue that the composer wants to accent may also be streamered. Finally, there will often be streamers *before* the cue, leading up to the first *warning click* before the piece begins.

387

When a cue is to be recorded to a click track (sometimes called an *electric metronome*) the conductor will need to hear some clicks before the cue begins so he can give the rhythm to the musicians (this is called the *count–off*, which is the "and a-one..., and a-two..., and a-three..." that you may hear before pieces of music). These clicks are called *free clicks*. The tempo at which the conductor gives the musicians these counts will determine the tempo at which the song is played. In addition, many of the musicians are fed this *click track* while they are playing so everyone can stay in time with each other, even when the tempo changes during the cue. The click track is a repetitive dull clicking sound that can be set to click at whatever tempo is needed.

In the old days it was necessary for the music editor to determine the distance between the warning streamer and the beginning of the piece. The computer playback systems now do that automatically, but let me give an example of what is involved. Let's say that cue 1M3 ("The Barroom Fight") is the musical cue to be streamered. The composer has written the piece in a 12/4 tempo and has requested eight free clicks. There is a book called Project Tempo (also known as the Click Track Book). This lists, for most tempi, the footages for every beat from the first beat to the six hundredth. For my own use, I have developed a computer program to do the same thing, a page of which is reproduced in Figure 14.3. This sample page lists the data for a 12/4 click. In addition, many computer programs have their own built-in click books.

To find the length of film needed for eight free clicks at 12/4, Betty needs to realize that if the first free click is the first beat then the first beat of the song would be on the ninth beat. She would then look for the length listed for beat number nine, which is eight feet, ten frames. This would be the equivalent of having the streamer begin 4:16 (four seconds and 16 frames) before the start of the cue.

Nate will get the click tempo from Lester, who will have determined this tempo while he was writing the cue. You will also notice on Figure 14.2 that there is a blank column on the right with the header of "Click #." Once Lester determines the click at which the cue will be recorded, it will be a simple matter for him or Nate to find out how many clicks have elapsed from the start of the piece to any particular cue point on the spotting notes.

The music editor programs the computer with the footage or SMPTE Time Code of the end point of the streamer and the tempo that the composer desires. The computer automatically calculates the placement of the streamers and then creates them on the videotape. The beauty of this system is that, in fact, the computer never actually draws the streamer onto the videotape, so it is extremely easy to delete or change them, if necessary.

Once again, computers come to the aid of the editing world.

If Lester has hired an orchestrator, he will send his scores out to this person, who will fully flesh out the music for a full orchestra. Composers without formal training may need this guidance to keep them from writing music that cannot be played by the individual instruments. Many composers, however, orchestrate their own scores.

The score will then be sent to a copyist, who will transcribe the score onto a series of *parts* containing the music for each instrument separately. The violins will receive only the music for the violins, oboes for the oboes, etc.

The click is a 12/4   Metronome setting = 115.2

	0	1	2	3	4	5	6	7	8	9
0	0-00 / 00:00.00	0-0 / 0:0	0-12 / 0:.52	1-9 / 0:1.04	2-5 / 0:1.56	3-2 / 0:2.08	3-14 / 0:2.6	4-11 / 0:3.12	5-7 / 0:3.64	6-4 / 0:4.16
10	7-0 / 0:4.68	7-13 / 0:5.2	8-9 / 0:5.72	9-6 / 0:6.25	10-2 / 0:6.77	10-15 / 0:7.29	11-11 / 0:7.81	12-8 / 0:8.33	13-4 / 0:8.85	14-1 / 0:9.37
20	14-13 / 0:9.89	15-10 / 0:10.41	15-6 / 0:10.93	17-3 / 0:11.45	17-15 / 0:11.97	18-12 / 0:12.5	19-8 / 0:13.02	20-5 / 0:13.54	21-1 / 0:14.06	21-14 / 0:14.58
30	22-10 / 0:15.1	23-7 / 0:15.62	24-3 / 0:16.14	25-0 / 0:16.66	25-12 / 0:17.18	26-9 / 0:17.7	27-5 / 0:18.22	28-2 / 0:18.75	28-14 / 0:19.27	29-11 / 0:19.79
40	30-7 / 0:20.31	31-4 / 0:20.83	32-0 / 0:21.35	32-13 / 0:21.87	33-9 / 0:22.39	34-6 / 0:22.91	35-2 / 0:23.43	35-15 / 0:23.95	36-11 / 0:24.47	37-8 / 0:25
50	38-4 / 0:25.52	39-1 / 0:26.04	39-13 / 0:26.56	40-10 / 0:27.08	41-6 / 0:27.6	42-3 / 0:28.12	42-15 / 0:28.64	43-12 / 0:29.16	44-8 / 0:29.68	45-5 / 0:30.2
60	46-1 / 0:30.72	46-14 / 0:31.25	47-10 / 0:31.77	48-7 / 0:32.29	49-3 / 0:32.81	50-0 / 0:33.33	50-12 / 0:33.85	51-9 / 0:34.37	52-5 / 0:34.89	53-2 / 0:35.41
70	53-14 / 0:35.93	54-11 / 0:36.45	55-7 / 0:36.97	56-4 / 0:37.5	57-0 / 0:38.02	57-13 / 0:38.54	58-9 / 0:39.06	59-6 / 0:39.58	60-2 / 0:40.1	60-15 / 0:40.62
80	61-11 / 0:41.14	62-8 / 0:41.66	63-4 / 0:42.18	64-1 / 0:42.7	64-13 / 0:43.22	65-10 / 0:43.75	66-6 / 0:44.27	67-3 / 0:44.79	67-15 / 0:45.31	68-12 / 0:45.83
90	69-8 / 0:46.35	70-5 / 0:46.87	71-1 / 0:47.39	71-14 / 0:47.91	72-10 / 0:48.43	73-7 / 0:48.95	74-3 / 0:49.47	75-0 / 0:50	75-12 / 0:50.52	76-9 / 0:51.04
100	77-5 / 0:51.56	78-2 / 0:52.08	78-14 / 0:52.6	79-11 / 0:53.12	80-7 / 0:53.64	81-4 / 0:54.16	82-0 / 0:54.68	82-13 / 0:55.2	83-9 / 0:55.72	84-6 / 0:56.25
110	85-2 / 0:56.77	85-15 / 0:57.29	86-11 / 0:57.81	87-8 / 0:58.33	88-4 / 0:58.85	89-1 / 0:59.37	89-13 / 0:59.89	90-10 / 1:.41	91-6 / 1:.93	92-3 / 1:1.45
120	92-15 / 1:1.97	93-12 / 1:2.5	94-8 / 1:3.02	95-5 / 1:3.54	96-1 / 1:4.06	96-14 / 1:4.58	97-10 / 1:5.1	98-7 / 1:5.62	99-3 / 1:6.14	100-0 / 1:6.66
130	100-12 / 1:7.18	101-9 / 1:7.7	102-5 / 1:8.22	103-2 / 1:8.75	103-14 / 1:9.27	104-11 / 1:9.79	105-7 / 1:10.31	106-4 / 1:10.83	107-0 / 1:11.35	107-13 / 1:11.87
140	108-9 / 1:12.39	109-6 / 1:12.91	110-2 / 1:13.43	110-15 / 1:13.95	111-11 / 1:14.47	112-8 / 1:15	113-4 / 1:15.52	114-1 / 1:16.04	114-13 / 1:16.56	115-10 / 1:17.08
150	116-6 / 1:17.6	117-3 / 1:18.12	117-15 / 1:18.64	118-12 / 1:19.16	119-8 / 1:19.68	120-5 / 1:20.2	121-1 / 1:20.72	121-14 / 1:21.25	122-10 / 1:21.77	123-7 / 1:22.29
160	124-3 / 1:22.81	125-0 / 1:23.33	125-12 / 1:23.85	126-9 / 1:24.37	127-5 / 1:24.89	128-2 / 1:25.41	128-14 / 1:25.93	129-11 / 1:26.45	130-7 / 1:26.97	131-4 / 1:27.5
170	132-0 / 1:28.02	132-13 / 1:28.54	133-9 / 1:29.06	134-6 / 1:29.58	135-2 / 1:30.1	135-15 / 1:30.62	136-11 / 1:31.14	137-8 / 1:31.66	138-4 / 1:32.18	139-1 / 1:32.7
180	139-13 / 1:33.22	140-10 / 1:33.75	141-6 / 1:34.27	142-3 / 1:34.79	142-15 / 1:35.31	143-12 / 1:35.83	144-8 / 1:36.35	145-5 / 1:36.87	146-1 / 1:37.39	146-14 / 1:37.91
190	147-10 / 1:38.43	148-7 / 1:38.95	149-3 / 1:39.47	150-0 / 1:40	150-12 / 1:40.52	151-9 / 1:41.04	152-5 / 1:41.56	153-2 / 1:42.08	153-14 / 1:42.6	154-11 / 1:43.12
200	155-7 / 1:43.64	156-4 / 1:44.16	157-0 / 1:44.68	157-13 / 1:45.2	158-9 / 1:45.72	159-6 / 1:46.25	160-2 / 1:46.77	160-15 / 1:47.29	161-11 / 1:47.81	162-8 / 1:48.33
210	163-4 / 1:48.85	164-1 / 1:49.37	164-13 / 1:49.89	165-10 / 1:50.41	166-6 / 1:50.93	167-3 / 1:51.45	167-15 / 1:51.97	168-12 / 1:52.5	169-8 / 1:53.02	170-5 / 1:53.54
220	171-1 / 1:54.06	171-14 / 1:54.58	172-10 / 1:55.1	173-7 / 1:55.62	174-3 / 1:56.14	175-0 / 1:56.66	175-12 / 1:57.18	176-9 / 1:57.7	177-5 / 1:58.22	178-2 / 1:58.75
230	178-14 / 1:59.27	179-11 / 1:59.79	180-7 / 2:.31	181-4 / 2:.83	182-0 / 2:1.35	182-13 / 2:1.87	183-9 / 2:2.39	184-6 / 2:2.91	185-2 / 2:3.43	185-15 / 2:3.95
240	186-11 / 2:4.47	187-8 / 2:5	188-4 / 2:5.52	189-1 / 2:6.04	189-13 / 2:6.56	190-10 / 2:7.08	191-6 / 2:7.6	192-3 / 2:8.12	192-15 / 2:8.64	193-12 / 2:9.16

389

FIGURE 14.3 A page from a click track book. This page is for a 12/4 click. Both the footage and the time from the first click can be found. The length from the first beat to any other beat, say the sixty-fifth, can be found by looking at the numbers at the intersection of the sixties row and the fives column. The top of the two numbers is the number of feet of frames from the first beat (in this case, 50 feet, zero frames). The numbers underneath it give the length in time (33.33 seconds). (Courtesy of the author)

Nate and Betty will not necessarily be involved in any of this; most of the organization for the parts and scores will be handled by a *music contractor*. This is the person who hires the individual musicians, makes sure they file their payment paperwork and that the terms of the musicians' union's contract are upheld during the recording session. They also will generally arrange for the parts to be copied and sent to the recording session.

Nate and Betty will be responsible for making sure that the videotapes and the paperwork for the recording session show up there before the session. I often send the tapes over the day before the session so the studio can check them to make sure that they can play back the tapes.

Betty should make sure everyone at the recording studio has a list of all of the cues that are to be scored (*see* Figure 14.4) in the order Lester wants to record them. Sometimes the contractor will make up this list. Betty should make sure she and Nate have a copy, as well as the studio because this chart gives all the information anyone at the recording sessions might need to set up the mechanics of the recording.

390

At the Recording Session

The day of the scoring session (that is, the recording of the music), Betty should get to the recording studio early. Copies of the scoring cues list should be given to all technical personnel. If she sent anything over the day before, she should also make sure everything has been moved to the correct studio.

Betty should have brought along with her the click track book, all the timing sheets, the continuity for the movie, a stop watch, and plenty of note paper.

From the recording studio Betty can get some *track sheets*. These are preprinted sheets like the one shown in Figure 14.5 listing exactly which instruments are being recorded onto which tracks of the recording tape.

Instrumental sections are generally recorded onto separate tracks, even if they are playing at the same time. Strings are separate from the brass, for instance. This gives the mixer the ability to vary the levels of individual sections against each other in the mix. The aim is to get the music mixed down into sets of stereo pairs. If there is a string section, it is usually recorded separated into pairs of high strings and low strings (each group will have a left channel and a right channel). Sometimes there are three channels. A drum kit, for instance, will often be recorded across three channels: left, center and right.

SCORING CUES LIST

Film _Silent Night_   Date _5/29/00_

Page _1_ of _3_

Cue #	Title	Start	Click	Fr.	Time	Comments
1M1	Main Titles	00:29.0	Free	—	1:13.2	
1M3	Abby Meets	05:40.10	16/2	4	1:12.3	Int at 56.5
10M4	End Titles	04:20.09	12/0	4	3:10.0	
3M1	Going Home	06:08.10	10/6	8	1:56.7	Don't like Guide
3M2	Abby Returns	03:19.06	12/0	8	0:46.6	
5M4	Abby Goes Back	03:16.0	12/4	8	1:25.13	
1M2	Parking Lot	03:54.6	22/2	4	1:57.09	
	— BREAK —					
5M7	Shoot Out	00:26.20	Free	—	0:32.2	2 Alternates
5M7ALT	" "-ALT	00:26.20	12/6	6	0:32.2	
8M3	At The Beach	08:12.13	12/0	8	1:15.06	
6M2	Return to "la Bar"	05:26.02	14/4	4	3:06.02	
4M3	Backstage	04:10.10	12/0	8	3:15.06	
	(MORE)					

SCORING CUES LIST

391

FIGURE 14.4 A page from a scoring cues list. The start are continuous footages within the scoring reels. Note the comment for an internal streamer in cue 1M3. There is also a note that the music recording mixer should not play the guide track for cue 3M1; this is probably because there is a piece of temp music there already which would conflict with the recorded music. Note also that the cue titles are often the same as those on the detailed reel continuity (FIGURE 8.5).

EVERGREEN RECORDING STUDIOS, INC. 4403 W. MAGNOLIA BLVD BURBANK, CA 91505 (818) 841 6800	NAB ☒ 15 IPS ☒ MACHINE # _____ DOLBY ☒ 30 IPS ☐ VSO# _____ FREQ. _ MSTR EDITED BY _____ DATE ___	FILE NUMBER REEL # _____ OF ___

TITLE _Silent Night, Silent Cowboy_ - Q1M1   MASTER # _6_   DATE _5/29/00_

ARTIST _Big Time Film Co._   STUDIO _A_   J.O. # _91.52936_

PRODUCER _L. von Beethoven_   ENGINEER _R. Riccio_   ASST. _TLM_

- TRACK PLACEMENT -

1 Hi-Hat (+ COUNTS)	2 Bs GTR (DIR)	3 Bs DRM	4 SNARE
5 (L) — DRUM	6 KIT — (R)	7 12-STRING GTR	8 6-STRING GTR
9 (L) — PIANO	10 — (R)	11 ELEC. GTR (DIR) O/D - 4/26/91	12 LD. VOC O/D - 4/25/91
13 VOC -DBL O/D - 4/25/91	14 (L) — FLUTES O/D -	15 — (R) 4/27/91	16 HORNS O/D - 4/27/91
17 VLN I O/D - 4/27/91	18 VLN II O/D - 4/27/91	19 VLA O/D - 4/27/91	20 CELLI O/D - 4/27/91
21 Bs O/D - 4/27/91	22	23 SMPTE 01:07:12:10	24 60 HZ

COMMENT: _Q1M1 - Main Titles_

TK 6 ✓ - 2:16

Form 4403-4-79

FIGURE 14.5 A Track sheet for cue 1M1. Two types of sync pulses were laid down — a 60-Hertz sync pulse (on track 24) and a track of SMPTE time code (on track 23). The number in the box for track 23 is the actual time code where the cue begins. The first ten tracks were all recorded at the same time during the original recording session on April 19. The other tracks were added later (overdubbed) on the dates shown. One track has been left open for technical reasons. (Courtesy Evergreen Recording Studios)

Normally, several recordings are made simultaneously. The first is a tape, usually on a piece of 24 or 32 track tape, called the *multi-track master*. Most instrument sounds get recorded separately. At the same time, there is often a recording made of the mix of every instrument onto a separate tape. This mix has the same channel arrangement that Lester will send to the final film mix. If the mix is done onto a DA-88 tape, there is room for eight tracks of information—four stereo pairs. There may be some leakage of one group of instruments onto the channels of other groups because they are all playing at the same time into open microphones. But this separation allows the engineer more control over the sound during the final film mix.

If everything works out fine, then this DA-88 tape is the tape Nate will take back with him to the editing room for preparation for the final film mix. If it isn't, then it will be a relatively easy thing to go back to the multi-track master and remix the cue after the musicians have all gone home.

At most recording sessions there will be at least one assistant, called either an assistant engineer or a tape operator, helping the recording engineer behind the board. One of the things they will do is list the assignment of instruments to individual tracks on the track layout sheet. If most of the cues have the same track assignment it won't be necessary to redo a track sheet for each cue. If the assignments vary, each cue should get its own track sheet.

When the first cue is ready to be recorded the videotape is rolled. The engineer or the music editor will slate the take ("Cue 1M3, Slate 1"—slate numbers run sequentially from the first take until the end of all of the recording sessions; they should not be restarted for new cues, new tape reels, or new recording sessions) and everyone will look for the warning streamer. If the clicks are manually generated, Nate will have his finger poised over the click track generator machine ready for the streamer to hit the right side of the screen. As soon as it does he will press the button, starting the clicks. If a computer is running the session, then it will create the warning clicks and streamers automatically from the numbers Nate has already typed in.

393

As the warning clicks begin, the conductor (who is sometimes the composer) will count out the free clicks and, on the first click after they have finished, will begin conducting the piece while keeping one eye on the projected videotape. It is common to have a large projection of the film on the wall across from the conductor as well as a smaller television monitor at the side of the stand where he or she keeps their scores. Often the conductor will have a clock with a sweep second hand in view during the recording session so they can see how the piece is timing out compared to the timings written on the score, which in turn came from Nate's notes.

During the recording, Nate and Betty should be keeping notes as to the positive and negative aspects of the take. Often chair squeaks or misplayed notes are difficult to hear from inside the recording studio, but are quite noticeable in the control booth where Nate is usually sitting (sometimes, however, he might be out in the studio with the conductor; in this case, the recording engineer and Betty will have to listen for these unwanted noises). A take should not be approved until everyone is sure there are no objectionable sounds or notes on the tape that cannot be mixed out later.

Either Betty or Nate should have also begun a stopwatch at the moment of the first note of music (most recording studios have their own digital stop watches that can be used). At the end of the take Betty should note in a sequential log the length of the piece along with any of the composer's or Nate's comments. The take will usually *not* be erased from the multi-track tape. Though it may not be the preferred take, the conductor or composer (who are often the same person) may want to listen to it later at the music mixing session. In any case, if this was a take Lester liked, he will come into the control booth and listen to a playback. He will then discuss its merits, technically and aesthetically, with the engineer and Adam, as well as Nate and Wendy.

At the end of the playback Lester will decide immediately whether to do another take or to go on to the next cue. If he decides to redo the cue the engineer will send the videotape back to the start of the cue and will resync it to the next open spot on the multi-track. If the take is approved, Nate should let the engineer know where the next cue is that they are going to record. In many cases, this will not be the next cue in the reel, since most composers will want to record all of the cues with similar themes and instrumentations at one time, even if they are spread throughout the film. The list of cues will tell everyone where to go next in the videotape reels.

As more and more takes are recorded, new reels of tape will be necessary. Betty should keep track of exactly what is on each reel of tape. The assistant engineers will also do this, but it is always good to have your own notes to refer to.

There should be something else on the head of the first reel recorded on the first day—a set of *alignment tones*. These tones provide a standard for the relative recording levels on the tape. When the tape is subsequently played back the mixer can set his playback volume and equalization controls so that they make these tones conform to this accepted set of standards. This way, the playback of the tape will sound exactly the same as it did when it was being recorded. In addition, since the tape operators or engineer will set their recording levels by these tones every day, each day's recording sessions will be done at the same standards. There should be a middle, a high, and a low frequency tone recorded (usually 1000–Hertz, 15,000–Hertz and 100–Hertz), about forty-five to sixty seconds of each is the norm. In addition, if the original tape was recorded in *Dolby* (which it can be, regardless of whether the film is to be released in Dolby format), a *Dolby tone* (also called a *Dolby warble*) should be recorded. *Pink noise* is sometimes laid down in the case of Dolby films. These Dolby tones are not necessary if the music is being recorded digitally.

The Mixdown Session

On normal non-musical films it is necessary to come to the film mix with far fewer tracks than the 24 or 32 that were recorded. The DA-88 mixdown, which was recorded simultaneously with the multi-track, should have the proper number of tracks for the final mix. Because of the limits of the DA-88 format (there are only eight tracks) this has become, more or less, the norm for delivery of the music. As mentioned above, Lester will often want to make adjustments to the mixdown, so he and the engineer will return to the multi-track master and remix each cue onto a new piece of the DA-88. This new mixdown will become the mix that goes to the final dub.

Sometimes, the mixdowns are created with time code matching the code in the picture where the music cue will be edited in. This creates a DA-88 with a number of time code jumps, but it makes it much easier to cut the cue in exactly the place Lester intended it.

395

Betty should be keeping thorough notes on all of these mixdowns so she will know exactly which takes of which mixes Lester wants to use in the score of the final film. Quite often Lester will want part of one take edited together with another part of a second take. Nate and Betty should be taking notes so they can recreate Lester's desires back in the editing room.

When I was a music editor, I used to make these notes right on a copy of the score so it would be clear to me just which take would be used for each part of the cue. If Nate doesn't use a score he should make notes telling him to use "Mix 3 of take 24 through the third beat of bar 123; then go to Mix 2 of take 25 to the end of the cue."

Back in the Editing Room

After all of the recording and mixing is over with, Nate and Betty will end up back in their editing room with a number of mixdowns on some sort of tape format, normally a DA-88. Betty will digitize them into Nate's DAW and create a file for every reel in the picture (you may remember that in ProTools, for instance, these files are called *sessions*)

Careful attention must be paid to the way the material is digitized. It must be played back from the DA-88 at the exact level and speed at which it was recorded. There should be a set of tones at the top of the first reel to help Betty determine the sound levels that the music should be played back at off of the DA-88, as well as the levels at which she should record them into the DAW. Betty will also make sure that cues are input with the proper type of time code which will be needed at the final mix—drop frame or non-drop frame.

Nate will then cut the music tracks using the time codes from the DA-88 and his notes. If these codes are not the same as the codes on his videotape, he will be able to refer back to both the Music Timing sheets and any notes he took at the recording session, to ascertain the exact picture sync Lester wants.

In addition to the score, it is quite probable there will be some *source* music that Nate will have to cut in. Source music is music with a definable source in the picture—a radio, a person playing the piano on camera, someone singing on camera, whatever. This material, along with any other cues not created in the recording sessions, will need to be digitized and edited into the DAW tracks against picture. In many cases, the movie will have some popular tunes cut over credits or a montage. These will also need to be cut in and, occasionally, edited to fit the picture a little better.

396

In the case of musicals with playback material, the tracks need to be edited and laid out in a more complex way. In musicals, instruments or vocal tracks that are on screen may need to be heard above the other instruments on the soundtrack. In that case they should be on their own channels in the mix. This usually means there will be many more tracks of music going into the mix on a musical film. There are two rules of thumb that apply to track building here. The first is anything or anybody that is singled out visually should be recorded and mixed separately so their volume can be individually controlled at the film mix.

The second rule for editing musicals is that instruments that were recorded at the same time and may leak into the tracks of other instruments recorded with them should always stay on the same tape as each other. If they aren't then, there is a possibility that you may hear *phasing* of the duplicated instruments when they are played together. We discussed phasing back in Chapter 7 when we wanted to hear this hollow echo in order to know when two similar tracks were in sync with each other. In this case, however, phasing is an unwanted sound.

After all of the music tracks have been built (and they will be built in the same way as sound effects tracks) a set of cue sheets should be prepared. You should not integrate these cue sheets with those for the dialogue or effects, since it is likely that they will be mixed at different times or with different mixers. Betty should then get all of materials they created to the mix.

At the Mix

Nate or Betty should bring with them to the mix all of their units, their cue sheets, their source tapes (the DA-88 mixdowns and original multi-track) their notes, as well as any other materials used in the recording or music mixdown process.

Often a director will reject all or part of a music cue at the dub. Nate will then have to cut a replacement piece of music from cues elsewhere in the film or from alternate takes of the mixdown. If every take has been digitized into the DAW, Nate may want to bring the R-Mags from his editing room to the mix. If not, then Nate better have the DA-88s with all of the mixes on them available.

It is possible, on many mixing stages today, for Nate to bring his DAW to the mix and hook it up to the board. Though the film mixers will rarely use the DAW as their primary source for the music elements, Nate will be able to use it to recut musical cues and to shift them around, without holding up the mixing process. When he is finished recutting the tracks on his DAW it will be very simple for the mixers to mix the cues directly from these new tracks on the DAW.

We will discuss more about the mixing process in the next chapter.

Paperwork and Other Sundries

The music editor has one responsibility that the sound editors do not and that is to provide something called a *music cue sheet* to the legal department of the company making the film. This legal form, shown in Figure 14.6, describes exactly how much of each cue is in the film, who wrote the music, and who owns the copyright. This information is necessary for the musicians' performing rights organizations both in the United States and abroad.

Nate will need to list every cue in the film and describe its use. There are two main categories for this, each with one of two choices. The first is visual/non-visual. A cue is visual if there is something on-screen making the music, either an instrument or a person. Radios and records are not considered visual cues. The second category is Instrumental/Vocal. If there is a voice on the cue, whether it is visual or non-visual, the cue is considered a Vocal. Thus, a cue of a rock and roll tune sung by Elvis Presley coming from a car radio would be considered a Non-Visual, Vocal (and a damned expensive

MUSIC REPORTING CUE SHEET

Film Silent Night, Silent Cowboy   Date 6·26·00

Cue #	Title	Footage	Timing	Voc	Instr.	Non -Vis	Visual	Composer	Publisher
	Reel One								
1M1	Main Titles	12-121½	1:13.2		X	X		L. von Beethoven	BTP Music (ASCAP)
1M2	The Parking Lot	358-380	0:18.6		X	X		"	"
1M3	Abby Meets Sean	510½-619	1:12.3		X	X		"	"
1M4	Jimmy the Baby	625½-703	0:45.2	X			X	M. Kiernan	Lotsa Music (BMI)
1M5	The Restaurant	736-900	1:22.7		X	X		L. von Beethoven	BTP (ASCAP)
	Reel Two								
2M2	Can I Be A Nuisance?	716-769	0:35.3		X	X		"	BTP (ASCAP)
	Reel Three								
3M2	Abby Returns	422-483	0:40.6		X	X		"	BTP (ASCAP)
3M3	Birthday Party	483-650½	1:51.6		X	X		"	"
3M4	The Three Friends	774½-904	1:26.2		X	X		"	"
			(MORE)						

MUSIC REPORTING CUE SHEET

398

FIGURE 14.6 *A page from a Music Reporting Cue Sheet which must be submitted by the music editor to the music or legal department of the distribution company after the mix is finished. The center columns tell whether the cue contained a vocal or whether it was entirely instrumental. When an actor or actress plays an instrument or sings part or all of the cue, the cue is considered visual (see 1M4, our bar song from Scene 19). underscore is entirely non-visual. Note that any cues which may have been recorded but not used in the final mix are not listed on this sheet (cues 2M1 or 3M1 for instance).*

one at that) while a piece of score would normally be considered a Non-Visual, Instrumental (unless there are voices in the cue, in which case it would be considered a Non-Visual, Vocal). A person singing on camera would be considered a Visual, Vocal.

Getting this information is relatively easy if the movie is all scored material. If it is not, there should be someone assigned to the task of researching the rights of the music before it is used. All music must either be out of copyright protection (this is sometimes called "free and clear" or "in the public domain") or it must be purchased for the use of the film. Usually a music supervisor performs this function.

As a music editor, it may not be your job to make sure all the music in the film has been cleared before you go into the mix, but it is certainly in your interest to make sure that it is. For one film I worked on, we found out one week before our final mix that our music supervisor had not adequately cleared the nine Motown songs I had ready to mix. Five days before our mix, I found myself doing music timing notes so our composer could write replacements for all of the songs herself. We went back into the studio five or six days later and recorded nine acceptable but not as good alternatives to the songs that we were unable to buy.

There are two types of rights that need to be purchased if *Silent Night* is to use a piece of already existing music in the soundtrack. First is the underlying copyright to the song, both lyrics and music (these are often owned by two different people). Second is the right to use the particular recording of that song. Thus, even if a song like Beethoven's Ninth Symphony is too old to still be under copyright (this is called *public domain*, because it is owned by the public and not by the original artists), the New York Philharmonic must still be paid if you use their recording of the Ninth.

In the event the film company is purchasing the rights to use an already recorded song, once the rights have been purchased, Nate and Betty must obtain from the record company with the *master tape* (the original tape from which the album was pressed) a copy of the song so they can make a transfer from it into their DAW for use in the mix. Nowadays, if a CD is available with the song on it, the quality of a transfer from the CD will be just as good (if not better). One other advantage of a CD is that if Wendy used the CD as a source for her transfer to 35mm when she was editing *Silent Night*, Nate's transfer of the CD into his DAW will run exactly in sync with Wendy's. This will preserve any edits she made in time with the music.

399

If not, then Nate will need to recut the song to match the cuts.

14A/DIGITAL

MUSIC ON THE DIGITAL FILM

Films that are cut digitally rely on most of the same music editing techniques as film-cut shows. Spotting notes need to be taken, videotapes need to be handed over (though these tapes may be created from a digital output rather than a telecine from the 35mm work print), and so on. There are just a few differences.

The first change is that many editors and directors like to spot the film directly out of their digital editing machines, rather than from a videotape. There are some advantages to this system, the biggest one being that it is possible to play the picture along with the temp music tracks Wendy cut into the lower one or two channels of her edit. On most of the videotapes you created after the lock of picture, the music was deleted. Playing Wendy's original edit will allow her to access all of those tracks should Adam want to make a point in his spotting session.

The second point comes from those edited temp tracks. In some cases, Wendy has used a piece of temp music that Adam has decided to use in the final film (source cues are often like that). How is she going to convey to the music editor how she wants them cut into the film?

Since these tracks were most probably digitized directly from a CD there will be no time code on the original source CD to help Nate line up the tracks with his input track.

The secret is to give Nate a copy of the tracks in some format that will allow him to use them as a guide track. There are two ways to do this; one is to hand over the music tracks in an OMF format. The second is to output the music channels of every reel with the music that Nate needs to mimic to a time-coded DAT or a DA-88 tape. Betty can then digitize these tracks into Nate's DAW. If she does this correctly, these music tracks can be used as a guide track for Nate. If, for some reason, you cannot output a tape to a time coded medium (you may only have a *non*-time coded DAT available) then you should make sure every music track you output has a two pop at six seconds after the start mark. Nate can then use this sound to line all of these new tracks up against his videotape.

If Wendy has edited material from a non-digital and non-time coded source (such as an audio cassette), it is very likely that a new copy of the song, from CD for instance, will not line up in sync with the original music in the temp tracks. On *Sophie's Choice* there was a scene of Kevin Kline conducting Beethoven's Ninth opposite a bank of reflecting windows. The sound recordist had used a nice recording of the Philadelphia Orchestra as a playback for Kline to work with. The problem was, we couldn't afford to buy the Philadelphia recording and no other version of the piece had the same tempo changes as this Eugene Ormandy version.

I found myself methodically removing sprockets (1/96th of a second) in order to bring the version that we actually bought, into sync with the version our editor had cut to. Even with modern technology, it is not an experience I'd ever want to relive.

If the original source material Wendy used to digitize was digital then it should be possible to maintain sync since digital music must be running at an exact speed of either 48 or 44.1 KHz in order to be decoded at all. A transfer from a CD in February will match a transfer from the CD in August.

THE MIX

Everything Arrives

402

Finally, after many weeks of sound and music editing and way too many months of picture editing, *Silent Night, Silent Cowboy* will be ready to mix. Everybody will show up at the dubbing stage (or mixing stage, as it is called in New York). The picture, sound, and music editors, as well as other assorted editorial personnel, will all be there with the mixers—everyone except Adam, who will show up later.

It will be the sound assistant's job to make sure every piece of paperwork and every unit of track arrives at the dub before it is needed. The individual cue sheets are folded up, labeled on their reverse sides with their descriptions ("Reel 1, ADR" or "Reel 7, Background FX," depending upon how the sound editors have split up their tracks), and shoved into large manila envelopes that have been labeled in the same way.

The units will be brought over as well, in whatever format they have been built. In addition to 35mm mag (which is often used as a guide to the cut work track, as Wendy edited it; it runs along with the units to ascertain proper sync) the sound units may be brought over on DA-88s, 2" tape, A-DATs or hard drives.

However they arrive at the mix, they should all be properly labeled, each in their own equally well-marked, box. These labels should list the name of the film, the reel, the type of material on the tape (Dialogue, BG Effects, Hard Effects, Music, Foley, etc.), the type of time code (DF or NDF), and the version number of the edit it was cut to. There should also be a little track sheet inside the box listing each of the tracks that are used and what they are used for (left FX, center FX, right FX, for instance).

And then, finally...

The Mix Begins

When you first walk into your mixing stage, you will see a large room with a big screen at the front. About half to two-thirds of the way back sits a huge electronic console that looks like a stretched out version of the cockpit for a jumbo jet. The board is usually divided up into three sections corresponding to the three mixing categories—dialogue, effects, and music. Sometimes one mixer (or re–recording mixer as they are also called) sits at each position. Often there are only two mixers: one for dialogue and music, and the other for effects. In actuality, if the mixers work well together, they are continually helping each other and the divisions aren't as hard and fast as I've made them sound.

The dialogue mixer also functions as the supervisor of the team. In some situations one mixer handles all three tasks. No matter how many mixers you have, the procedure is pretty much the same. You pre–mix, then you final mix.

Let me explain.

Often, the dialogue tracks will come spread across a dozen units with another two or three for looping, the music will be on at least eight channels, and there might be as many as sixty effects elements as well as eight or ten foley tracks. This gives a total of nearly ninety separate channels of sound to be controlled individually. It not only would be too confusing to mix that many at one time, but there are very few mixing boards in the world able to handle that many tracks.

The solution to this problem is pre-mixing (or pre-dubbing) the individual sections. The dialogue pre-mix, which often comes first, takes all of the original split dialogue tracks and combines them into one easily handled set of units for each reel. All necessary volume and equalization changes needed to smooth out the dialogue tracks are incorporated into this pre–mix. Looped lines are pre-selected and mixed in as well, though the original tracks are kept nearby in case Adam decides he would prefer to use the original production track instead of the loop. Of course, combining seven or more tracks into four isn't really combining all that many tracks, but what the mixers are trying to do is save a lot of time at the final dub by doing all of the smoothing and blending of the dialogue elements now, rather than in the final.

At this stage in the mixing process the re-recording mixers are going to want to accomplish as much of the minute technical detail work as they can while still leaving themselves open to the possibility of change when Adam starts to sit in with them during the final mix (often the director will only come to the dialogue pre–mix to make choices of looped lines). For this reason, they won't mix down the dialogue completely. They are going to want to have the ability to change individual lines of dialogue later on if they need to.

The sound effects are also combined into at least six or twelve tracks (including separate stereo channels for the left, center and right speakers), split in some intelligent way—general effects, specific effects for different characters, foleys, etc. Some effects will not be mixed into the pre–mixes at all but are held out and run as separate elements in the final mix.

Scored music is generally not pre–mixed at all, since it has already been pre–mixed down at the recording studio. Of course, on a musical film there would be plenty of need for a music pre–mix (on *Cotton Club* we pre-mixed music for several weeks), since music functions as importantly as dialogue in such a film (indeed, it often takes the place of dialogue). In cases like this, the music mixer at the dub will make all of the technical and volume adjustments as well as combining a few tracks. He will usually want to keep separate any instruments appearing on screen (the same goes for singers) that may need to have their volumes controlled separately.

404

During the pre–mixes, Liz should be taking thorough notes on anything that is moved, omitted or delayed at the mix. Any track elements not put into the pre-mixes, but needed in the final film mix, should be kept on a list so they are not forgotten when the final mix for that reel is done. Effects built into the tracks but deleted during the pre-mixes should be plainly crossed out on the cue sheets.

Recent advancements in sound board design have allowed the mixers to program all volume, equalization, echo and other settings into a computer that then controls the mix. If the mixers need to correct one little setting it is no longer necessary for them to go through the time consuming task of recreating all of the equalization and volume settings that were used at that point in the mix. This saves tremendous amounts of time.

I should mention something about the picture everyone will be watching. Traditionally, you would mix to a 35mm picture, either a color dupe from the work picture (the splices on the cut work picture would never stand up to the back and forth motion of the projectors) or an early answer print of the film if it is complete. We will discuss answer printing in Chapter 16.

However, it is less common to mix to a 35mm print in today's world of television and digital picture editing. Often, there isn't even a film print to use. In that case, you will probably be mixing to a videotape of the film. If you are doing a television show, you will be mixing to the Final Edited Master (see Chapters 15A and 17A for a more detailed discussion of this).

When all of the pre-mixes have been completed, the director joins the crew on the dubbing stage. Beginning with reel one, all the various sound elements will be combined into one (usually) stereo soundtrack. Adam will be making decisions on the relative volumes of effects, music, and dialogue. He will be deciding if he likes the sound of someone's voice and, if he doesn't, how he wants to change it. He will be making decisions as to the texture of all of the film's sounds and music. The way this is done is to play the various pre–mixes together. The mixer will struggle to get a pleasing sound and then everyone will begin discussing what they've just heard. Adam will ask for a little more door squeak at a certain point and a little less music. The film will be rolled backward until just before that point and the mix redone for that section. This method of repairing the mix at certain sections is called *punching in* and the process by which the sections to be mixed is called *rock and roll projection* (since you move backward and forward in the film finding the areas to correct).

405

The process is a long and tedious one, requiring a lot of concentration on minute details. A ten or twelve reel film might take as long as four to six weeks to pre-mix and mix.

When I said above that the sounds were being mixed down to one soundtrack I was simplifying the process a bit. Actually, all of the sounds are not totally combined. The mix is made onto several pieces of tape or hard drives. All of the mixed dialogue goes onto the first piece, the final mixed stereo music goes onto the second, and the final stereo effects get mixed onto the third. This divided mix is sometimes called the *D-M-E* as a result. Each of the individual parts of this mix is called a *stem*. The dialogue mix is called the dialogue stem, there are also the music and the effects stems, each of which is a stereo mix.

There are several reasons why this is done. First, it helps the re-recordist as he or she finesses the mix. If an effect needs to be redone (for volume, equalization, or any other reason) the mixer can just punch in the change on the effects channel of the mix, without touching the acceptable dialogue and music channels.

A second reason has to do with the creation of alternate versions of the film. As we discussed in Chapter 13, the distributor or whomever has made the contract with the producers, will want to release the movie in foreign countries as well as the United States. In countries where English is not the native language they will be creating a foreign language version of the film with that country's native language dubbed into the film, replacing the English language dialogue. Separating all of the English dialogue onto the first channel of the D-M-E makes it a simple matter to remix the film. The foreign country is supplied with a transfer of this mix, either on 35mm four-track mag or on some tape format. This transfer is called an M&E, or foreign track. Because this mix has the English dialogue separated onto the first channel (or the first *stem*), the foreign distributors can then loop their own dialogue and mix it into a mixed master of their own, without worrying about any English sneaking into it. The English dialogue on channel one is used simply as a guide track.

There are, of course, certain complications to this approach. Naturally, many of the sound effects are part of the original dialogue track of the film (people moving, chair squeaks, etc). When the dialogue channel is omitted from the mix, these effects will also be eliminated. Obviously, someone will have to put them back in, either by effecting them or by foleying them. This can either be done by the company in the foreign country or by the sound editors in the United States after the completion of the regular mix (the domestic version).

406

Most sound editors try to build their elements knowing that this foreign version will eventually be made, creating what is called a *fully-filled M&E* (music and effects track). They split all these production effects off the dialogue track and put them onto the effects tracks (usually on units reserved for production effects, called "PFX"), filling in the resultant holes on the dialogue track with tone. When the main mix (for the domestic version of the picture) is done, these effects will end up on the effects channels of the D-M-E, rather than the dialogue channel. Those effects that are married with the dialogue and, thus, cannot be split off, are foleyed and cut into reels that can later be used in the foreign version mix.

This M&E is usually a part of the film's delivery requirements; those elements of the film that must be handed over to the film's distributor upon its completion (see Chapter 16 for a more thorough discussion of this). Some companies would rather not invest in making a new M&E for the foreign, preferring instead to send the foreign distributors a copy of the domestic M&E, letting the countries they've sold the film to create their own versions. It is a rare case, however, where it is as easy for those in the foreign countries to make a good foreign M&E as cheaply as it can be done when the materials are all around—as they are when the original sound editors are still on the film. Many foreign distributors will refuse to buy a film with an incomplete M&E. In any case, what kind of M&E the producer wants should be ascertained as early as possible.

After each reel of the domestic version is finished being mixed, it should be played back for Adam and everyone. They will take notes on things they would like to change, along with the footage or time code of those areas. After the playback is finished, the reel is rewound to the earliest note and these little changes are discussed and made on a final pass of the reel.

Recent advances in sending data over high speed telephone lines, like ISDN, T-1 or T-3 lines, have made it possible for producers in one part of town to view a mix being played back somewhere else entirely. Lucasfilm developed a system that allows a director in Los Angeles to go into the local Lucasfilm studio to hear and control a mix being played back in their Marin County California facility, more than half a state away. On rushed television series, this can often help a producer listen to mixes without having to drive across the city. I can't begin to tell you the amount of expensive mixing time that I have seen wasted, waiting for busy studio executives to arrive at a mix for a playback. This development, though still imperfect, promises to make the entire process move more smoothly.

Final Mixing Tasks

When you have finished your mix, there are still a few more steps before you can watch your film with its sound married to it. One is creating your *print master*.

Before the print master is transferred to an optical negative for combining with the film, however, there is one very important task that someone will need to attend to—they will have to prepare and cut the *pull-ups* for each reel. To explain just what pull-ups are I will have to back up a second and describe how soundtrack is married to and projected on a picture print.

You'll recall that film is projected one frame at time, each for 1/48 of a second. One frame is shown for that length of time then a shutter falls over the gate, blocking off the light, and in the 1/48 of a second when nothing is being projected, the next frame is pulled down in front of the gate. Then that frame is projected. The shutter is then dropped down again, and the next frame pulled down. And so on.

What we see as a continuously projected picture is actually a stop and go, stop and go, sort of process. This works due to something called the *persistence of vision*, meaning that our eyes retain the image we've just seen for a short time. If we project another image quickly enough (and, after research, 1/48 of a second was determined to be quick enough; silent films were often shot at a slower rate and many of them have a jerky motion that is partially a result of this slower frame rate), the eye will never notice the difference between one frame and the next. We will see continuous motion. But the ear can't be fooled this way. We need to hear one continuously moving soundtrack in order to hear continuous sound. None of this stop and go, stop and go stuff for our ears. So, when the soundtrack is married to the picture print, it wouldn't do to have it being jerked through the sound reader in the same way the picture is pulled through the picture gate.

To get around this problem, a projector is designed so that the picture gate and the sound head are not located in exactly the same spot. The film is run past the sound head using a series of rollers which give it a smooth and continuous motion. It then goes through the picture gate (also called the *hot hole*) where the jerky, stop and start motion is introduced. In 16mm and 70mm projectors, the sound reader actually comes after the hot hole and the process is reversed.

408

This means that the synchronous sound for any given 35mm picture frame is not sitting right next to it on the film, but comes earlier by a certain number of frames (20, to be exact). This type of sync is called "projector sync" as opposed to the sync you have been used to where a picture frame and its synchronous track are exactly lined up. That type of sync is called "editorial sync" or "level sync."

Since the sound is ahead of the picture on the release prints (in "projector sync") there will be twenty picture frames at the end of each reel without track running next to them. There will also be twenty frames of track before the first frame of each reel. When the projection reels are spliced together, or *plattered* (see the section on previews in the next chapter), at the theatres the projectionist will make the splice at the last frame of picture of the outgoing reel (let us say, Reel Two) and the first frame of picture of the incoming reel (let us hope, Reel Three). Since the track is ahead of picture, there will then be 20 frames at the end of Reel Two without sound on them.

This would be a big problem.

Naturally there is a solution, and the solution is called *pull-ups* (we finally get back to them).

Pull-ups, quite simply, are the additional twenty frames of the head of Reel Three's sound mix, spliced onto the end of Reel Two's. This way, the track will run longer than the picture and when the track is pulled-up to get into projector sync, there will be enough sound to run all of the way to the end of the picture reel on Reel

Two when it is spliced together with the release print of Reel Three. There will be no gap in the sound track at all.

Years ago, the sound editors used to take a mag copy of those twenty frames from Reel Three (actually, they usually put thirty or so frames on) and spliced it onto the tail of the preceding reel, in this case Reel Two. Today these pull-ups are created by the mixers. After the head of reel three is mixed, the mixed masters for Reel Two are put up on the recording heads and the first thirty or so frames of Reel Three are transferred onto the tail of Reel Two. This is preferable (though perhaps quite a bit more expensive) since it means there are no physical splices in the full–coat.

In order to do this accurately, the mixers will need to have the exact EOR frame number of Reel Three. They will then line that frame up with the last frame of the Academy head leader of Reel Two. You should make sure that your EOR list is up to date and accurate. If your list reflects 1000 foot editorial reels and you are mixing in 2000 foot reels, you should make an adjusted list reflecting the lengths of the combined reels. Remember, if you do this with addition, there will be no Academy leaders on the even numbered reels, so the combined length of the double reels is actually twelve feet less than the combined EORs of both single reels.

Now you can create your print master.

409

Even though your mixers have been carefully creating your mix so it can be projected in the stereo format you have selected, the mix still isn't in that format yet. This situation exists primarily because the format that is easiest to mix in (the separate dialogue, music and effects; each of which has all of its stereo channels separate) is not the easiest to project. In analog stereo formats, like Dolby or UltraStereo, the four stereo channels must be combined into two tracks in order to fit on the 35mm print (we will discuss the details of these stereo formats in more detail in Chapter 17). Digital stereo formats, like SDDS, Dolby Digital and DTS, have even other requirements to fit onto the limited space around a 35mm frame. Analog and digital stereo formats require their own print masters, so you may find yourself spending as much as a full day or more creating these print masters.

Mixers also use this print master process as time for some final, minor, tweaks in the soundtrack that could not be accomplished during the main mix for one reason or another. At times, a new sound effect is dropped in if it wasn't available during the mix itself. Obviously, there are disadvantages to making changes at this late point in the mix. For one thing, these alterations will not be reflected in the D-M-E itself, meaning that the mixers will need to remember to make these changes in exactly the same way any time they need to create a new print master. In addition, because each of the components of the D-M-E are already mixed together, it will be much more difficult to remix areas that have more than one sound married together.

Because of budget limitations, some feature film mixes are done in smaller television studios. Though this will generally save money, it creates a problem with sound. Films that will be projected in a large theatre won't sound exactly the same in a smaller room. Echo works differently, for one thing.

For that reason, when it is impossible to mix on a large stage, many films insist on print mastering in the larger room. Here, in this crucial last stage, it is possible to make the fine adjustments (particularly in regards to the surround channels) that may be necessary to best make the transition from small mixing stage to large theatre.

After the mix is complete, and all of the pull-ups and print masters have been made, it is wise to make a 35mm mag transfer of your final mix. If your mix was in stereo, then this 35mm mag should also be in stereo, in the print master format. This will be the soundtrack you use for interlock screenings (screenings with separate picture and track), if you ever need to screen one of the silent answer prints.

410

In the case of television movies or shows (or when your feature is transferred to videotape for its videotape release), you also need to make a tape copy of the sound track, with time code. You will use this mixed master during the transfer of the film to videotape. You should make sure that the time code you use is compatible with the video format the tape house is going to be using. Often you will need to make a drop frame encoded tape, rather than the NDF you are used to.

When you have completed creating your print master, it will be time to marry the soundtrack to the final picture answer print (about which we learn more in the next chapter). To do this, you need to transfer the final mix print master onto a piece of film negative that will be printed together with the picture. This *optical track* is actually a piece of 35mm (or 16mm, if that is the gauge of the film you are working in) film with little squiggly lines on the left-hand side of the frame (*see* Figure 16.4). When light is pumped through a print of these lines it lands on a photo-electric cell in patterns that can be decoded to form the sounds that we recognize. This is how almost all films are projected in theatres. This is why filmmakers have problems trying to sneak-preview a film with a magnetic soundtrack. Theatres are not used to projecting anything other than an optical soundtrack.

This optical transfer is done with a special optical camera, which must be precisely set to the standards of the film laboratory that is doing the answer printing for the film. These standards are particular to each lab. To determine exactly what they are, the transfer house making the optical track negative (or *shooting the optical*) will make a *cross-modulation test* which is then developed by that lab and analyzed by the transfer person. Sometimes, your mixing facility will be able to shoot your track negative. If they can't, they can usually recommend a place that will do it.

After the Mix

As I've mentioned, after you have finished with the primary mix of the film, called the *domestic version*, you will need to create at least two other versions of the film. The first is the *foreign M&E* and the second is the *television version* of the film.

Mixing each of these alternate versions will take much less time than the original mix, since most of the artistic and technical work has already been performed on the tracks. To create the foreign version of the film the mixers, along with Charles and, perhaps, Wendy, start at the first reel of the film and play the mix without the dialogue channel. Every sound effect that was audible in the domestic version of the film should exist in this version. Often, effects will be missing because they were tied into the dialogue tracks on the original production tracks. Charles' crew should have prepared clean versions of these missing effects on separate units built specifically for this foreign mix.

411

The television version of the film should have its own videotape reels for every reel of the film affected visually by recutting. As we discussed in Chapter 12, Charles' crew will have already prepared the alternate version of all of the tracks. It should be a relatively simple matter to remix all of the areas of the film that have been re-edited for this soft version. Any places where there have been no changes at all, and that will probably be the bulk of the film, need only to be transferred from the D-M-E units the sound editors have also built.

In the end, if Nate has cut on film, all the sound effect trims and unused sound effects can be thrown away. All that really needs to be saved are the units, the original tapes from the looping sessions, the music mixdown tapes, the original multi-track music recording tapes, and a set of proper cue sheets. There will also be some other elements that you, as the picture assistant, have to supply; we will talk more about that in Chapter 16.

MIXING ON A DIGITAL PICTURE

Like all of the previous chapters about sound preparation for the mix, you will find almost no change in the mixing process whether you've edited on film or digitally. There is one wrinkle, however, and that will only occur if you've been cutting digitally without the benefit of printing and conforming work picture.

412

Let's discuss the picture process once you've locked picture and handed it over to sound. You've created an output directly from your digital editing machine. This output is then copied and given of your sound and music departments, along with your sound EDLs. As a result, they have been editing the sound track, writing and recording the music, to the version of the film Wendy cut on her machine.

If you conform your work picture to match this digital cut, then you can check and make sure every frame is correct before you send the film over to your negative cutter for matching (don't worry, we will discuss this in more detail in the next set of chapters).

However, if you have no film printed and no conformed work print, it is possible that your negative cutter will give you back something that is not precisely what Wendy cut. This is not always the negative cutter's fault. If you haven't checked all of the numbers correctly when you hand over for negative matching, they may be unable to make the exact cut Wendy wanted.

So, it is possible that the version of the film that is negative cut and, therefore, printed may not exactly represent what was on the output tapes Chuck got and you've been mixing to. Unless some changes are made, this will mean that the soundtrack will not exactly match the visual.

This is A Very Bad Thing.

In some cases it may be possible to replace the incorrect shot with the correct one. However, in more cases, it is likely that the incorrect shot will either have to be replaced with a shot different from the one originally planned, or Wendy and Adam will have to live with the miscut shot.

In those cases, it will be necessary to correct the edited tracks and the mix.

For this reason, it is essential to telecine the answer printed reels as soon as they are nearly complete. It would be good if the negative cut was finished, but there may be titles missing or a few opticals that haven't been cut in and answer printed yet. Before the mix is begun (and earlier, if possible) each reel of the answer print should be telecined so Liz can run it against the tracks that Chuck or his crew have built. If there are any differences she should notify you so Adam and Wendy can decide how they want to handle the miscut problem.

By mixing to these telecined answer prints, rather than the copy of the output, you guarantee your mix will sync up with the final print of the film. An added bonus is that the telecine from the timed film will look much better and show detail much more clearly, than the output videocassette.

413

Television and Video Mixing

In the case of projects with no film elements to worry about (television shows or direct-to-video films), you will be mixing in a 30 FPS mode, without worry about matching back to film.

We will learn in Chapter 16A about the finishing process for an all-video project. Let me jump a bit ahead and mention that one of the first things you will do in that finishing process is create an *edited master* tape from the original high-quality tapes made during dailies. This Edited Master will be matched to Wendy's cut using picture EDLs in an *auto-assembly* process. Nearly every optical will be recreated in this on-line assembly, along with every edit. When you are done with this process (it usually takes one day) you will make a set of tape copies to be handed over to the sound and music departments.

It is *this* set of tapes that you will mix to. The good news is, since this is more or less an exact copy of the tape that will go on the air, you will never have to worry about negative miscuts. What you mix to is pretty much what you will see at the end of the video finishing process.

. . . .
TO THE ANSWER PRINT—HO!

Much of what you will be doing to get the film ready for showing to Real People (translate that as "paying audiences") overlaps
and involves what the sound and music editors are doing. Now that
we have seen exactly what the they will be doing during this period
we can get back to what you will be struggling to do—to get the
entire film finished on time.

414

On the Way to the End

There's a toast many picture editing crews use whenever they
are in the final throes of the editing of a picture. By now we've
probably been on the film for up to five or six months. We are
preparing for the sound mix. The end of the film, while actually
quite close, still seems to be very far away. At times like these, when
we are clinking our glasses of wine (or whatever), I usually hear
someone say something like, "To the answer print!" The answer
print is what this chapter is all about.

The workprint you have been cutting for these many months
is, in a sense, nothing more than a blueprint for the actual print of
the film that audiences will see. With the amount of cutting and
recutting that goes on during the editing of a film, it would be impossible to send that actual work picture out to the theatres. It would
be so chopped up that it would be dangerous to run through the
projectors. And, of course, since the sound is on a separate roll
from the picture very few theatres (other than screening rooms)
would be able to handle it. With all of this in mind, you can understand that you are going to have to come up with a way to make

clean, spliceless prints for release to the theatres based on the print you've been cutting for these many months.

The way this is done is quite simple in theory. The workprint you have been working with was struck directly from the original negative that ran through the camera on the set (the OCN, the *original camera negative*, as it is sometimes called). In fact, this workprint is such a faithful copy of the original negative it even includes the key numbers printed through from the negative. Any further prints from this negative will also be identical to your first prints from it.

When the film is locked, someone goes back to the original negative and, using the key numbers, matches, cut for cut, everything Wendy did on the workprint. At the end of this *negative cutting* process you end up with one reel of cut negative for every reel of cut workprint, and the two will be identical. You can then make a positive print from this cut negative that will be a clean, spliceless print of the reel, exactly matching your cut workprint.

You have been splicing film together with pieces of tape during the editing. For negative cutting, however, the splices have to be made with cement if they are to be able to make it through the printing machines at the laboratory without being visible in the prints.

Actually there are three different ways of printing from cut negative in the lab. The first is with the one long strand of cut–together negative, sometimes called *single–strand printing* or *A roll printing*. This is the way 35mm features are usually done. The second way is to make one long optical negative from the uncut camera original, incorporating all the cuts within this optical and printing with that. The third way is called the zero-cut method or *A and B rolling*. It involves printing the film from two (or, sometimes, three) parallel running rolls of film. We discussed this method in the chapter on opticals (Chapter 10). This kind of printing is used primarily for 16mm films.

The reason why A and B roll (or *zero cut*) printing is used in 16mm films can be explained by describing the manner in which negative must be cut. In order to fasten one piece of negative to another, the pieces must be attached using cement. In order to do this, some of the emulsion is scraped off the top part of one frame and the piece of negative that it is being attached to is laid on top of that. In actuality, the way this is done is to cut the outgoing shot a little long (by about one-half of a frame), scraping the first frame of the incoming shot, and overlapping these two frames. In 35mm the amount of frame needed to overlap in order to attain a firm splice is very small (less than one sprocket in length). But in 16mm, nearly one–half of the frame would have to be overlapped in order to make the splice hold. This would be visible when projected. This is why the zero-splice method is used.

One of the obvious problems with cutting the negative is that, unlike cutting the workprint, once the negative is cut (and that one–half frame is scraped off) one frame on either side of the cut is destroyed. You won't be able to use those frames again, they are gone forever. This is the main reason why alternate versions of scenes need to be edited from dupe negative (IP or CRI, about which we will talk more very soon). In the old days, commercials never cut their original negative, but made a long optical negative to print from. They very often had several different versions of the same commercial (ten seconds, twenty seconds, thirty seconds) using differing lengths of the same shots. Though it was vastly more expensive to make an optical negative than it was to cut the original negative, it would have been impossible for them to make all the necessary versions of the commercial without this expense, since by printing everything optically there is never any need to cut the negative. Of course, now that commercials are edited exclusively on video, the need to dupe negative has disappeared.

416

Of course, shots can be (and often are) shortened after the negative has been cut. That is not very difficult since the frame lost in the first negative cutting is not needed to shorten a cut. But this restriction on lengthening shots makes for some sense of finality when the negative is cut.

A and B roll printing (*see* Figure 16.1) is sometimes used on 35mm features because simple opticals can be avoided. The laboratory will be able to accomplish the dissolves and fades (with certain length limitations; you should check first to make sure your lab can handle all of the dissolve lengths that Adam and Wendy want). This means you will not need to make these opticals, and they won't suffer all of the generation loss that every optical does.

So, if you can get much better optical quality from A and B rolling, why don't all 35mm films do their fades and dissolves that way? Well, there are several reasons. First is the fact that, if you wait until you make your answer prints to do your A and B roll opticals, you will never really know just what your fades and dissolves are going to look like during the editing process. Since every shot will fade a little differently, Wendy will never know precisely whether a two or three foot dissolve works better for a particular scene transition, for instance. On films that print their dissolves using A and B rolls it is often necessary to prepare the optical anyway, obviating any cost savings that might be gained.

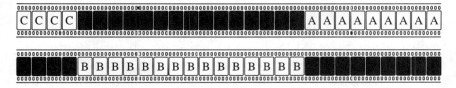

FIGURE 16.1 *In the zero-splice method, cutting from shot A to shot B and then to shot C is accomplished by checkerboarding the negative so that the splices attach the picture to black leader which will not print up in the lab process.*

The second disadvantage to doing dissolves at the lab in this manner is that every time you need to print a reel from the original negative you have a slightly higher cost (in addition to the greater cost of cutting the negative using A and B rolls).

A final disadvantage is that it is impossible to make videotapes from A and B rolls without going to the expense of going into an on-line video editing session to put the two rolls together properly. For shows cutting on digital editing systems not printing film, this makes creating a videotape master much more expensive than creating one from an A roll negative. This also makes the creation of videotapes for the film mix from the original negative, as well as the videotape release master (the master videotape for the videocassette version of the film), more expensive. It will probably be necessary to make an interpositive (or IP) of the cut negative reels first.

417

Previewing

Directors often have a sense of panic when the negative is about to be cut. One director I worked for almost refused to let the negative be cut until I explained to him that not only did every feature work that way but no one was going to be able to see his film if he did not cut his negative. This panic is certainly understandable. Adam, Wendy, Philip, you, and everyone else involved with the creation of *Silent Night, Silent Cowboy* will have been working on this film for half of the year or more. At this point everyone has certainly lost perspective on the film. What works and does not work is a subjective judgment in any case. It is complicated immensely by the fact that all of you know the film backwards and forwards, almost intimately. Things are perfectly clear to you that may not be at all clear to someone seeing the film for the first time.

This is why it is a common practice for the director to screen the film for an audience before cutting the negative. Some directors, like Arthur Penn on *Four Friends*, felt that open previews (previews for the public as opposed to friends and advisors) were not useful. We screened *Four Friends* for several groups of friends and received feedback from them. Milos Forman, however, screened *Hair* many times for people who were given tickets on street corners. On *Trigger Happy*, we had six screenings before we stopped editing. After each screening we handed out questionnaires and re–edited the film based on any comments that seemed important.

Previews are virtually always done with the work print (since you haven't cut negative you couldn't possibly have an answer print yet), and are usually held in screening rooms with double-system projection (separate track and picture). Many films will do a quick mix (a scratch mix) and go to a neighborhood movie theatre for a preview. These sneak previews (or sneaks) are the final acid test of a film's acceptability to a normal audience before its release. These sneaks are often held outside of Los Angeles or New York City, so the reactions of a less movie-hip audience can be ascertained.

But screening in Denver, San Diego, Minneapolis, or such cities can create other problems. For one thing, it is rare that you will be able to find a theatre able to screen double–system (in fact, it is rare to find such theatres in Los Angeles, though they do exist). For another thing, the audiences are made up of people used to seeing only finished films. Scratch mixes, bad prints, visible splice marks, and the like can upset them and taint their reaction to the film.

418

For these reasons, you try to create as professional a movie as possible when you sneak a film. You will only preview a film with a mixed track. If there are any shots in the workprint are scratched, ripped, or missing frames, they must be replaced by reprints. If any shots in the film have a distracting color balance, they are also re–printed with a new color timing. On *Network* we reprinted virtually the entire film in order to get the freshest, cleanest prints for the one preview we ran.

The film itself must be treated with special care. You should have it hand cleaned thoroughly before every screening. In addition, I like to have the film *sonic cleaned* before taking it out on the road. This cleaning, which is usually done at a lab or at a film treatment house, can remove all kinds of ingrained dirt that Ecco cannot. Sonic cleaning can often lighten your code numbers so it is not a good idea to do it more than once, but it does make the film look better than it could otherwise.

The problem of how to accommodate double–system projection is not an easy one to solve. There are two ways to handle this, neither of which is problem-free. The first is to rent a portable double–system projector (many of the big studios own their own), install it at the theatre, and use it instead of their normal projectors. There are many problems with this. The projectors are rarely as good as standard theatre projectors, they tend to break down more often and to be harder on the film. Most of these problems can be ironed out if the people setting up the projectors get there early enough to locate all of the problems and repair them.

A second way of projecting double–system is to bring a separate machine to play back the sound (called a sound dummy), and hook it up to the theatre's projector. This approach has a few problems, primarily that the sync between the two machines might slip, resulting in an out of sync screening. Still, that happens rarely enough to make this the most viable option. The most critical time occurs as the projectors start up, that is, at every reel change.

Fortunately, most theatres nowadays don't even screen from two projectors anymore. They use what is called a *platter system* in which the entire movie is spun onto a very large plate, almost like a phonograph turntable. During projection, the film is then wound off this platter, over a system of wheels that guide the film into the projector, where it is projected and then sent over another system of wheels back onto another platter sitting either below or above the first one. There are no changeovers at all.

What this means to you, as the assistant readying for a preview, is that your film and your track will have to be set up so they can be *plattered* (as the process of putting your editing reels onto these large platters is called). The first thing that you will probably have to do is put your movie onto 2000 foot reels, as opposed to the 1000 foot reels you've been using in the editing room.

The next thing you should do is to have the picture and the mixed track that you will be screening, edge coded in sync with each other (actually, you should do this whether your film is going to be plattered or not). If the film and track ever fall out of sync during a preview, either because of a breakage or a mechanical failure, you are not going to be able to put them quickly back in sync unless you have some new reference code numbers.

One nice thing about the platter system is that it eliminates changeovers. This not only eliminates projectionist error, but also means you don't have to put changeover cue marks on the film. In fact, if there are cues from a previous screening, you will need to remove them.

When you arrive at the theatre each 2000 foot reel of film is placed on an electric table that unspools the film onto one of three large platters sitting next to the projector. You will need to remove the head leader of every reel after the first and hang them in order somewhere where you will be able to easily find them after your preview (when you need to resplice them back onto the print and track). As you attach each reel to the end of the last, you will need to do two things. First, you should remove the tail leader of the outgoing reel and store it with the head leaders. Secondly, after you splice the two reels together, you should draw a large visible line on the outside edges of the film (use a colored grease pencil or marker) bridging the two reels. This will make it much easier to find the reel joins when you are "un-plattering" the film after the screening. Without those marks, it will be much harder to find the LFOAs of every reel.

Taking the film "on the road" is not an easy thing. It is best to carry a mini-editing room with you. A set of rewinds on a board, a splicer, tape, reels, cores, a script, a continuity and a box of supplies so you are prepared for any problem during the screening or any questions after the screening as to potential recutting.

There is no "normal" procedure for going out on these sneaks. There is only an "ideal" that is never reached. The ideal involves having several days before leaving for the sneak city to clean the film, make all reprints necessary (it could actually take a week to reprint, code and cut everything in, if you have a lot of film to re-place), complete as many opticals—including the Main Titles—as feasible, prepare the music and sound and do the temp mix, and to run the film at least once with the film and track you will actually be running at the sneak.

Continuing this ideal scenario, when you were certain that everything was fine, you would fly out to the sneak city the day before the sneak to meet the technician installing your sound dummy in the theatre and to check out the projectors that are already there. Hopefully this technician will have cleared up any of the picture or sound problems that have been found.

Then, preferably the morning of the scheduled sneak, you will have a full run–through at the theatre with the projectionist who will actually be doing the projection work on the night of your sneak. This way you can clear up any potential problems before the sneak.

An hour or two before the sneak you will go into the theatre (which should be closed, rather than on their normal schedule) and run one or two reels of the film. I usually try to pick the reels with the widest range of sound so you can set a good sound level. Check both projectors. You should then be ready to screen. If you've plattered the film, you won't be able to run a reel or two (unless you've brought a test reel of picture and track) since it is impossible to stop a plattered film and rewind it back to the beginning.

That's the ideal. Do you want to take any bets as to how many times it works this way? Fewer than a dozen times. Fewer than half a dozen times. More like never.

Usually, you will not have enough time to prep the picture and track properly because Adam will be tweaking the film up until the last minute, worried about the response from the audience. You will be rushing to cut in the few reprints you were allowed to order, all while you are juggling the sound and music preparations for a rushed temp mix.

You will generally have to arrive at the sneak site the morning of the screening. If there are several sneaks planned in a row, you will be lucky to get even that. You will platter your film and have a run-through the morning or early afternoon of your sneak. You will have very little time to correct any picture or sound problems. If you are lucky, your producers will have bought the theatre for the day and the management will not run their normal feature after your run-through and before your preview. If there has been another film run before your sneak, you need thirty or forty minutes before your preview to run a reel of the film once more to check that the theatre's settings have not been changed. If you're plattering the film you should bring along an extra track print of one reel of the film (with the widest dynamic range) and run a sound-only test. In most cases, most of the settings that might have been tampered with are sound settings, so a track only test will suffice.

421

Preview screenings are a nerve-racking experience; everyone is tense. There is always a lot riding on the sneak, the director's (and the crew's) ego as well as the company's money, so everyone is incredibly nervous. This is why you should try to get everything as perfect as you can. If there are any egregious problems that cannot be resolved you should point them out to Adam before the screening. That may not make him happy but at least he will know what to expect and be able to communicate those problems to the studio executives and the person running the research group organizing the screening.

After the sneak, there will usually be a hurried reading of the audience response cards and all sorts of meetings that you will not be invited to. This will be rather difficult but you have other work to perform. The first thing you need to do is remove the film from the platter and soundtrack from the large reel that you built it in. To do this you will use the same machine that you used to platter the film. The film will generally be tails out, with the final reel's tail leader in view on the outside of the roll. You will thread that leader into a 2000' take-up reel and spin the footage back, looking for the marks you made on the sides of the film, identifying the place where the final reel was joined to the preceding reel. You will also be able to tell where that splice is by looking at the code numbers. At the place where a new reel begins, the code number prefixes change and the footage should be 0012 (the first frame of picture on reel five, for instance, would start at 005S0012). Open the splice at this point, attach the proper head leader to this first frame, and remove the reel from the plattering machine.

You should now put another empty 2000' take-up reel onto the machine, thread the proper tail leader into it, splice it onto the footage on the platter, and repeat the process.

You will continue to unplatter the film until you reach the head of the first reel, which should already have its head leader attached to it. Congratulations! You have finished the picture.

While you are unplattering the picture, Philip should be performing the same tasks on a set of rewinds with the sound.

When both of you have completed all of the reels, you should have used up all of the 2000' take-up reels you brought to the preview (with the exception of any spare empty reels that you brought for safety), and have returned the film to the same state it was in when you arrived at the theatre. When you get everything back to the editing room, you will be able to break the film back down to the editorial 1000' reels.

422

If you are previewing in same town that you are editing in, you will take the film and all of your supplies back to the editing room. If you are out of town then you should give the film a thorough cleaning on your portable rewinds, either at the theatre or in your hotel room. You should have everything packed up and ready to leave as soon after the screening as possible. If Wendy is going to any of the after-sneak talks you should try and provide her with whatever notes she may need (a continuity, script, etc.). Your primary job at this point is to expedite the movement of the film and the portable cutting room.

Negative Cutting

After all of the paranoia has passed, all of the screenings have finished, and all of the recutting has been accomplished, you will find yourself at a point in the film you probably never thought you would reach—the end of the editing. The film is now "locked."

When the film is finally locked you must begin to prepare for the negative cutting. This involves two, possibly three, things. The first task is to make sure all of the negative that your negative cutters will need is in their possession. This is normally a bit more complicated than asking your lab to ship all of your negative over (if you've already selected your negative cutters, they may already have all of the footage). During the course of the editing you will probably have pulled certain pieces of negative to send to your optical house. It will be your responsibility to make sure all of that negative is moved from the optical house to your negative cutters as soon as it is no longer needed. You will need to keep track of where every piece of negative is at all times. On shows with a lot of opticals and CGI, this is a major task. Some films hire an assistant to do not much more than supervise the traffic of negative, and provide him or her with a computer and software for that job (some assistant editors use a program called FileMaker Pro, though any database program will do). This person should also track all the negative for any approved opticals.

In addition to shipping the negative you will also be marking up the film and, perhaps, preparing a negative continuity. Both tasks aim to do the same thing, provide enough information to the negative cutter so they can cut the negative of your film quickly, completely, and correctly. After all, if there are any mistakes in the negative cutting they can't be easily corrected, if they can be corrected at all.

At this stage of the film you should have all pieces of the film cut into your workprint, including as many opticals and titles as are final. Most often, the titles will not be completed in time to make this first negative cut, but you will (hopefully) know where they are going to be in the footage and what their length is so you can slug out the reels to the proper length. Make sure that every piece of film has key numbers on its edges. Occasionally the lab will forget to expose the blue edge of the film with the key numbers on it; if this happens have them reprint that piece properly. In addition, there are times when a shot Wendy has cut in is so short that it has no key number on it at all. In this case, you will have to find the head or tail trim of the piece in the cut. There should be a key number on one of those. After you find it, you should scribe onto the blue edge of the piece in the cut, that key number including the frame number (KI 362783-1286+5)

All marks on the film should be erased with the exception of opticals.

The idea behind marking up the film is to mark every piece of film in the work picture in such a way that your negative cutters will be able to easily see how you want them to match cut your negative. To do this you must mark where every cut in the film should be. You must also tell them where cuts will *not* be if there could be any confusion (such as a place where there is a splice connecting two continuous frames). Write on the film any special notes that might help avoid chaos.

To help to understand why this is necessary, let me briefly explain how a negative cutter works. The first thing that cutters do is determine exactly which takes they need to cut the negative of the film. Then they separate out all these takes and keep them handy. They then take your cut work print, put it in the second gang of a synchronizer, and begin to run it down. On the first gang they will be building the matched negative alongside the workprint. This way they can check key numbers and visual action.

At this point the cutters will cut (with scissors) the negative on each side of the cut, cutting off the part of the next frame that they will need to make the cement join (as discussed earlier in this chapter). They will not actually cement the two takes together. Instead they hook them together with a little cardboard clip that temporarily holds the two pieces of negative together through their overlapped sprocket holes. This keeps the negative and the work print running in sync as well as postponing the messy cement work until later so the negative cutter is not doing two things at one time. The actual splicing/cementing of the negative is done after this matching is all completed, often by another person. When the work is divided up like this, the first stage is usually called *negative matching*, and the second *negative cutting*, though the two terms are often used interchangeably.

424

As you can probably guess, the process of matching the negative is very exacting. Once the scissors cut the negative there is no replacing it, so any help you can give the matcher is that much more safety insurance for you. This is why you must be precise when you mark up your workprint for matching.

Figure 16.2 shows the various notations used in marking up the workprint for the negative cutter. There are notations for places where there are cuts, places where there are splices in the work picture that are actually just extensions of shots, and places where a piece of leader was used to indicate where a shot has been extended but no tail or head trim was cut in. This last notation is rarely used except on lower budget films where a shot is damaged in cutting and there is not enough money to reprint it.

There is also a second kind of negative cutting notation in which the run-through marks are smaller and appear only the track area of the film, and the cut marks are simply lines on the frame lines where the splices occur. The idea behind this style of marking is to keep the projected area of the film clear in case the picture needs to be screened.

Some negative cutters don't like this style of marking, others prefer it; so check with your negative cutter first.

Some negative cutters don't want you to mark the cuts at all, only those places that "might be confusing" to them. Frankly, I would err on safety's side and mark anything even slightly dubious. What might be crystal clear to you may be confusing to them. Don't take any chances. It's the only negative you've got and once a frame of it is gone...it's really gone.

In many cases you will have to start marking up the work picture before all of your opticals have been completed (on *Meet The Applegates* we began cutting our negative while 18 opticals and the main and end titles were still incomplete). If this is the case, you will want to make sure your negative cutter knows there is a piece of negative missing that will come later. The way to do this is to put a piece of paper tape on the head and tail of the shot to be replaced by the optical. You would then write "DO NOT CUT!!! OPTICAL TO COME!!!" on the tape and draw an arrow pointing to the splice mark where the optical will be cut in. The negative cutter should slug cut the missing optical with an equivalent length of leader. This is called "papering."

In addition to marking up the workprint, a few negative

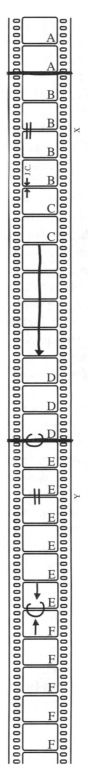

FIGURE 16.2 *A piece of film marked for the negative cutter. Two types of markings are shown. The cut from shot A to shot B is shown with a thick line written in greased pencil. An alternate way of showing cuts is with the large letter "C" which comes between shots D and E. Run-through marks (at the letters X and Y) show where cuts were made in the work picture but are not to be made in the negative. The run-through mark at point X will not show up when the work picture is projected. When a jump cut (as between shots B and C) is made the notation "J.C." is written on the film. An extension of shot C up to the beginning of shot D is shown with the long arrow. Some negative cutters like to have cuts listed as shown between shots E and F.*

matchers request a *negative continuity*. This is, simply, a list of every cut in the film. See Figure 16.3 for an example of just how detailed this list must be. Many negative cutters do not want a negative continuity since they prefer to make their own. If so, it is a job that you can give up very gladly.

Answer Printing—At Last

After the negative has been cut, the reels are sent to the lab where a timer will look at them and decide what color balance each shot should have. The color timer will sit down with the director of photography, the director, and the editor in a screening room and run the work picture one time without the work track. During this running your director of photography (or d.p., as he or she is called) will discuss just how he wants the picture to be timed and Adam will pitch in with a few comments as well. The work picture has probably been processed with a *one–light timing* where all set-ups and takes from any given scene in each day's dailies are timed at the same set of color balances and exposures, regardless of the individual needs of the specific shots. Timing each shot, or even set–up, takes much more time and is therefore more expensive. This means that many of the shots cut into the work picture will not be well timed. No one will want the timer to match the work print's timing exactly in every shot, but the d.p. and Adam can give him an idea of which shots are closer in feel to what they want.

426

It is the timer's job, with the help of the d.p., Adam and Wendy, to correct the color balance of every shot so that each has the appropriate color. The timer will also make sure each shot is perfectly matched to all of the other shots in the same scene, so the characters' faces or clothing, as well the set around them look the same from shot to shot.

Wendy's job at this point, aside from contributing a comment or two, will be to listen hard. It is more than likely the d.p. will not be available to sit with the timer any more than this one time and Wendy will have to supervise the timing of the remaining answer prints. By listening to what the d.p. and Adam want the film to look like at this first session she will be able to guide the timer through all of the subsequent answer prints.

Timing involves determining just what percentages of cyan (blue/green), magenta (red/purple), and yellow should make up each image. This is done by varying the amount of red, blue, or green light that passes through the film negative to the print film. These percentages are given as the number of *points* of each color, ranging from 0 points to 50. Most often the timer will go for what he or she

NEGATIVE CONTINUITY

FILM _Silent Night, Silent Cowboy_   REEL __3__
DATE _3·31·08_   PAGE __1__ of __7__

Shot #	Footage	Key # In	Key # Out	Description
1	12+0	F32X63217+10	228+5	WS-ROOM, MAN #1 in
2	22+11	F32X54098+3	108+2	MS-MAN #1
3	32+10	F32X54115+1	129+6	POV MAN#2 at desk
4	45+7	F32X54075+4	088+1	CU-MAN
5	66+6	F32X63223+3	241+6	MCU-MAN #2
6	74+11	F32X63262+4	261+0	MCU-MAN #1
7	81+7	F48X21112+7	124+3	MCU-MAN#2
8	93+10	F48X22124+5	129+14	MCU-MAN #1
9	99+5	E23X26033+6	041+15	MCU-MAN #2
10	107+6	E23X26052+2	060+12	WS-2 MEN
11	115+3	F32X63291+4	300+15	MS-MAN#2
12	124+6	F32X66119+7	126+11	CU-MAN #1
13	131+2	E17X14108+7	14+11	CU-MAN #2
14	139+2	F32X66136+8	46+10	CU-MAN #1
15	149+1	E17X14122+1	134+13	CU-MAN #2
16	161+4	F32X66160+2	168+3	CU-MAN #1
17	168+10	E17X14152+8	164+15	CU-MAN #2
18	181+6	F32X66310+6	322+14	CU-MAN #1
19	193+5	F32X63899+2	433+5	WS-ROOM w/MEN
20	226+12	H16X11526+6	551+6	Dissolve to beach
21	251+12	F9X76219+7	229+5	CU-MAN #1
22	261+10	E2X66606+7	614+3	his pov beach
23	269+7	F13X03219+6	225+2	MS-GIRL
24	275+6	F13X03620+1	623+1	MCU-GIRL
25	278+6	F13X03811+0	812+12	CU-GIRL
26	280+1	F9X76298+3	309+8	CU-MAN #1
27	291+6	F13X03249+6	278+5	MS-GIRL+MAN
28	320+0	F13X03416+1	422+4	MCU-GIRL
29	326+3	F43X56219+6	280+10	MCU-MAN
30	335+7	F13X03432+10	439+3	MCU-GIRL
31	342+0	F43X56219+6	253+7	MCU-MAN
32	346+1	F13X03493+14	453+6	MCU-GIRL
33	356+7	F43X56312+10	318+15	MCU-MAN
34	362+12	F13X03619+6	624+6	MCU-GIRL

NEGATIVE CONTINUITY LIST

427

FIGURE 16.3 _A sample section of a negative continuity list. Some assistants do not list the descriptions of the scenes. Some negative cutters do not even require a list like, preferring to make their own._

assumes is the best skin tone color and attempt to match the rest of the shots to this.

In any case, after the run–through with the work picture, the timer will go away and, sitting at a color analyzer (called a Hazeltine), will determine exactly what color balance is needed for every piece of cut negative in the film. When this task is completed, the information is put into a computer. At each cut this timing computer adjusts the color balance according to the instructions given to it by the timer. For 16mm films and all other A and B roll printing, items such as fades and other optical effects are also programmed in.

After the timer has made all of his or her adjustments, the lab strikes a print from the cut negative using these timings. This first print is called the *first answer print* (or the *first trial print*). After this first answer print is struck, the editor, the timer, and the d.p. (if he or she is available) all get together and watch it. The director usually does not go to any more answer print screenings except, perhaps, the final one, so he can sign off on the completed job. They will usually screen the film at the laboratory, making comments as each shot appears on screen (a side note here, lab personnel often use the word "scenes" when they are referring to what we would call individual "shots" or cuts). Changes are requested. The timer makes new timing notes and the reel is reprinted. Several days later the second answer print comes out of the lab and is screened.

428

As soon as the color timer has made notes on the first answer print, you should retrieve it from the lab so you can check to make sure that the negative cutting was done properly. To do this, you would take this first answer print and line it up in the synchronizer with your cut work print at the start marks. Then roll down, stopping at every cut to assure that the key numbers match on either side of the cut. Also make sure that no cuts were made where they were not supposed to be made. If there are no miscuts, you can approve the reel for screening.

Occasionally there are some miscuts. This has to be one of the worst kinds of mistakes for a film editor to deal with. At this stage, the film is either being mixed or has already been mixed. Depending upon how bad the error is, parts of the film may have to be recut and remixed.

The problem here obviously stems from the fact that all the sound editing and mixing was done to the videotapes or dupes of the work print. If the negative for a shot of someone talking was cut in one foot later or earlier than it was supposed to be, the mixed dialogue will be out of sync by one foot. Since the negative cutter had to lose one frame of negative at both the head and tail of this shot, it would be impossible to extend it without a jump cut (some editors don't mind the jump cut, depending upon the shot). It may be possible to find another take that can replace the ruined one, though it can never be as good (after all, Wendy and Adam originally chose that take over any other one for a reason—correct?) Normally, some kind of fix in the mix has to be made to accommodate the correction, whether it is a new take or a correction to the already cut–in take.

The worst case that I've ever heard of regarding major laboratory screw-ups began when the lab storing the negative for a feature film accidentally destroyed a few takes of the film before negative cutting began. When the negative matchers went looking for the film they found nothing. As bad luck would have it, there were no alternate takes to be used and no possible way to correct the error with existing material. The editor had to make a duplicate negative directly off the cut workprint and use that negative instead of the camera original. The footage created was, necessarily, of a noticeably different quality than the surrounding material. It was the only solution to an impossible problem.

For one film I worked on, one of our double reels of cut negative was damaged when water got into the can containing the reel. Some of the shots were fixable but many of them, in one rather large section of the cut, were a total loss. We went back and recut the film with alternate takes where we could. We digitally repaired the few shots we could. We reshot what we could. The end result was not what either the director or I had wanted when we had locked the picture two months before.

Horror stories like this are rare (though everyone either has one or knows someone who does; it's kind of like the Six Degrees of Lab Nightmares). Labs and negative cutters have to be extremely meticulous and careful when handling negative since their reputations and livelihoods depend on it. In the few cases where problems occur, they can usually be sorted out through the use of alternate takes. The splices in the negative are carefully pulled apart and the new negative is inserted exactly in place of the old one. If the editor is skillful, the replacement will not be at all noticeable. On *Fame* there were a few problems with the negative cutting, all of which, though annoying, editor Gerry Hambling was able to solve with a minimum of fuss.

After you have approved the negative cutting and the color timer has refined the timing lights, a second answer print is struck and screened for further notes. This screening process is repeated until all the reels are timed to everyone's satisfaction. As the process goes on, reels will be approved. Only the unapproved reels are then retimed and reprinted. It is probable that many reels of your film will be approved after the third answer print, but it is also likely that at least one or two might have to be printed a fourth and fifth time. You will probably want to keep the printing to a minimum since the negative degrades each time it is used. It is not uncommon, however, to go through six or seven answer prints on one or two of your reels before approving them.

At this point a timed interpositive, (also called a *protection IP*, because it will allow the distributor to make prints of the film even if the original negative is damaged) is made of the film. From this IP, an internegative (IN) is made. Prints can then be struck from this dupe negative. As I've discussed before, the actual prints shown in most theatres are not struck from the original cut negative but from a copy of the negative made at the lab. For years, in order to get around the extra generation involved in printing an interpositive and then an internegative, these protection dupe negatives were made on another type of negative stock, called *CRI stock* (Color Reversal Intermediate), which required only one generation to create a positive print. However, the interpositive process is now so good that it is rare that CRIs are struck.

But whether it is the IP/IN or the CRI process that is used, the theory is the same. All of the timer's color balancing instructions are incorporated into the striking of this dupe negative so that when prints are made they can all be made at the same setting, and no adjustment of the color controls will be necessary during the printing process. This considerably brings down the cost of making prints.

430

It is a good idea to screen at least one *check print* made from the dupe negative, since the timings will inevitably change slightly. It may be necessary to make some corrections in the internegative in order to get a print that more closely approximates your original negative prints.

When the laboratory has a track negative in hand (as discussed in the last chapter), they will print the track and the timed picture together. This answer print is called the *married answer print* (*see* Figure 16.4). I never like to marry the picture and the track until I've got the picture timed properly, because that is the only protection you have that an earlier answer print will not get sent out for projection in some theatre somewhere. Labs, however, like to marry the picture and track together as early in the process as they can. If this happens, you will have some unacceptable prints of some of the reels floating around.

As soon as the lab has struck the IP/IN for release printing (the number of IP/INs or CRIs struck will depend on the number of prints needed; distribution companies try and get at least 1000 release prints out of each dupe negative, as IN stock gets better they try to get more), they can begin striking the release prints. At the same time, you will also be able to get a few original negative prints

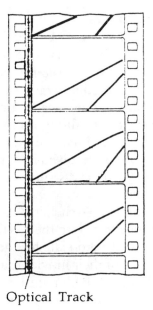

FIGURE 16.4 The optical track is the set of squiggly lines between the left edge of the picture and the sprocket holes.

Optical Track

(sometimes called *EK prints*). Because these prints are made directly from the cut negative, they will be at least one generation closer to the original (second generation as opposed to third or fourth. As a result, they will have less contrast and be sharper in focus than the IP/IN prints. For this reason, a few EK prints are usually struck for the two or three premiere cities. These are the prints the big critics usually see as well as the ones that open at the classy downtown theatres. EK prints, since they degrade the negative, are usually struck only for Los Angeles and New York openings, though sometimes they will be made for London, Chicago, or Boston. In such cases, it is common to make sure that two prints are available per theatre. On *Hair* we opened at the Ziegfeld Theatre in New York City and the Cinerama Dome Theatre in Los Angeles. Both theatres received two prints—an EK print for projection and a dupe negative print for backup. Other major opening theatres, in Chicago, Washington, D.C., San Francisco, and Boston also received two prints, though both of them were made from the dupe neg.

431

When the mix is over you might be responsible for organizing the printing of the movie. You will be organizing the lab screenings for answer prints and making sure the lab personnel have all of the materials they need to make a perfect release print. Once the answer printing of the movie has begun, your tasks begin to get much simpler.

Special Requests

In the months before the premier of a movie, the distribution company is going to be gearing up for the release of *Silent Night, Silent Cowboy*. They are going to want to see the film as soon as possible so they can begin to plan a marketing strategy and an advertising campaign for the film. Usually, their needs come almost simultaneously with the worst crises in the editing room. You will probably be trying to lock the film as well as turning the picture over to the sound department. You will be involved in optical work and many other complicated issues. Then the distribution company will call to ask if they can see the film.

The temptation is to tell them all to go to hell in a hand basket and call back when you've got the time to talk to them—like in two months. Unfortunately, two months will be too late for them. I have heard stories of directors so protective of their movies that they did not let the film companies have a look at the film until it was much too late. As a result, the advertising campaign was rushed and, usually, terrible.

432

Providing for the needs of the distribution company is part of your job as an assistant editor. Though you should never release anything to them without the prior knowledge and consent of Wendy and Adam, you must make it part of your job to do so. It can only help the film.

Early on, after they have seen the film, the distribution company will want a videotape or a film dupe of the entire film so they can begin cutting a trailer. This is the "coming attraction" short you see in the theatres. The best time to give them this dupe is after the film has been turned over to sound since there will be few, if any, changes to the picture after that. The company may need the film earlier, but in normal cases the sound editors begin to come on two or more months or so before the mix and the mix is often three to five weeks. At the absolute worst, this leaves three months between the handover and the release of the film, which is normally enough time for a trailer to be made, printed, and shown in theatres.

As post–production schedules become shorter and shorter, and as publicity gets more and more complex, there are more cases where you will not have the luxury of giving the trailer company a copy of the locked picture. You will need to provide them with a videotape or dupe of whatever cut you are working on when they need it. You should make sure their dupes are marked with the date of the cut so you can keep track of any subsequent changes Adam and Wendy make.

But let's say that *Silent Night* is a normally scheduled film. You can then make an extra dupe or videotape for the trailer department when you make the tapes or dupes for the sound department. When you find out who the trailer people are going to be (they are often an outside service that the distribution company contracts to do the job), ship them all of the material they need. This will often be just the dupe picture and the duped work track, though sometimes they will want a videotape copy of each reel. If you have any music already recorded for the film, they should also receive that. At the least they should be given the name and phone number of your music editor, who can supply them with music materials as they become available.

After the trailer people have finished cutting the trailer, they will do their own mix and make their own release prints of the trailer. To do that, they are going to need a negative. You, of course, cannot give up your own negative since you will need it for the film. Trailers, therefore, are made with dupe negatives—interpositives (IPs). When the trailer company has finished cutting the trailer you will receive a list of code numbers (either the printed through inked numbers from the dupe, or the key numbers) for all of the takes used in the film. Either you, or the assistant at the trailer house, will then order, from a copy of your logbooks, the necessary interpositives, required to create the trailer to be struck from the original negative of the relevant scenes. The trailer house will tell you whether they need normal or registration IPs, (*see* Chapter 10 for more information). In no case is the negative to leave the lab or the optical house that is making the IPs.

433

If your film mix has been completed, it would be helpful to give them a copy of the mix in its D-M-E format. This way they can do their mix from already mixed tracks. This will make for a better and faster trailer mix.

However, it is more often the case that you will not have even begun your film mix when the trailer people want their tracks. If this happens, they may want track reprints of some takes in order to do a reasonable mix. They are not going to be splitting tracks to quite the degree that your sound editors will be. However, they will need to split some of the tracks for overlapping dialogue as well as for some smoothing of backgrounds. You will have to get them a DAT or 1/4" copy of every take they need so they can prepare for and do their own sound mix.

Concurrent to all of these duties, it is important to be sure that the bills for these orders are not charged directly to your production. This makes the accountants crazy. Even though all of the money will ultimately be coming from the same big pot, this pot has a lot of little categories in it. The making of the movie is considered a different thing from the selling of the movie, therefore make sure the bills for the trailer are separated from your own.

After the final answer print has been struck, the distribution company is going to start asking for prints of the film to screen for critics. It is a fact of life that a film with no publicity and no reviews is almost never going to make any money. Film companies, therefore, spend huge sums of money publicizing a film; more, in fact, than the film often costs to make in the first place. Magazine critics must see a film months before it is released because their magazines have long lead times (this means the time between when the writer writes the review and when it is published is often a month or more). The publicity department will be anxious to get as many stories in as many magazines as they can. As soon as a print is available, and often before, they will begin demanding a print to screen for influential critics.

Often these requests can be accommodated quite easily. You will have a print or two at your disposal that can be shown (the first fully approved EK print should stay in the editing room for all your screenings). As soon as another print of the film is made, it should go to the distribution company so they can set up their own screenings without continually bothering you. However, you should always make sure you check the prints before sending them to the company. In their passion to sell the film the publicity people will often be willing to screen inferior prints simply to get the film seen. Make sure that no unacceptable prints go out for screening or, sure as the sun rises, they *will* be used.

Because of the increasingly short post–production schedules, however, you will probably end up breaking this rule more often than you would like. For *Heathers* we needed to start screening the film several months before a final, corrected mix was done. As a result, we ended up showing a print with the incomplete mix just to have something to show. That was the only time that I ever knowingly allowed a bad print to get into the hands of the distribution company, and it was a decision that came back to haunt me when the print kept on showing up, long after we had the corrected prints to screen.

Often, the post-production department of the studio you are making the movie for will handle most of this work. They will order whatever prints they need directly from the lab, leaving you out of the loop.

In most cases, your work on the film will be finished as soon as the final answer print is approved. In those cases, the distribution company will handle all the release printing and screenings.

Video Prints

There may be times when you, or Wendy, will be involved in the preparation of the videotape version of the film. Because of the particularly contrasty nature of television, special prints need to be struck from the cut negative in order to provide a good looking videotape. This print is called a *lo-con print*, short for low contrast print.

This print is exactly what it sounds like. The timing lights that you determined for the EK prints are slightly adjusted (for instance, everything is normally made brighter by anywhere from three to eight points, as measured on the timer's scale of fifty points) to strike a print onto a special stock that is very low in contrast. This print is put onto a *telecine*, a machine that projects a light through your film and converts it into a television signal that can be manipulated and put onto a videotape. In fact, life being what it is, you will generally have to do a week's worth of color manipulation to get the proper color balance on the videotape master. This master will be in a high quality format—DigiBeta and D-1 are very common formats, though some distributors still require 1" tape. In some cases, you will never be able to get the exact colors again (reds, for instance, are particularly troublesome in a videotape transfer). In some cases, you will be able to get better results on video than you were able to get on film. Shots beginning in light and moving to darkness, for instance, are difficult to properly time on film because you can never get both ends of the shot perfect. In videotape, on the other hand, you can program in a special effect called a *dynamic* as you are transferring the film. This makes the color balance gradually change in the middle of the scene.

435

As you transfer your film to video you will also have to be aware of another difference between film and videotape—*aspect ratio*, the ratio between the width and the height of the projected film image. Chances are, your film was shot to be projected in a 1.85:1 ratio. Television, on the other hand, is less rectangular and more square. You will have to accommodate the difference, since you will be showing more of the top and bottom of the frame than you did on film (another alternative is to show less of the two sides). Hopefully, your camera operator framed most of his shots knowing that this video transfer would have to occur sooner or later. In that case, it is a simple matter to reframe those shots. In some cases, however, you will have to blow up, reposition or do some other special visual contortions to get a pleasing frame.

Also, be aware that as you expose more of the top and bottom of the frame you may be exposing the boom microphone or parts of the set that shouldn't be seen.

Another option, though it is rarely used in home VHS video-tapes, is to keep the 1.85:1 ratio by placing a black bar at the top and bottom of the full film frame. This process, called *letterboxing*, blocks out any of the picture area above or below the 1.85 ratio and, effectively, recreates the image seen in a film theatre. Most distributors don't like to do this because it creates a smaller image on the television screen, however on a videodisk or DVD release it is often an option.

Normally, the entire film is programmed into a color correction computer then a copy of the original stereo sound mix master (provided on a time coded DAT or any number of other formats) is put up in sync with it and the transfer is made. A copy of this master videotape is then struck, just in case something were to happen to original tape. If the master tape is made to a digital tape format (such as D-1 or DigiBeta) then this copy, called a *clone*, will be every bit as good as the original, with no generational loss at all.

After the transfer to the master is completed, a few test tapes are made onto either 3/4" or 1/2" for the director and the studio quality control department to examine. Any additional changes that Adam requests are made and, after everything meets with his approval, several corrected tape copies or clones are struck. The videotapes you rent at home are copied from those.

436

After the video print has been completed in the NTSC format, a separate pass is made to create another video master in the PAL format. This is much easier than the first master because you are able to reuse all of the timing numbers again. Some companies try and save a little money by making a copy of the NTSC master, converting it into the PAL format on the transfer. This is rarely completely satisfactory, since the differences in frame rates and scan lines between the two formats create a number of slight visual artifacts in the transfer.

Wrapping Out

Eventually, after all the screenings have been completed and all the prints delivered, it will be time to *wrap out* of the cutting room. That is, it will be time to pack up all of the footage for storage and close out the editing rooms. There are, of course, proper ways to do this.

When the producer originally made the money deal for *Silent Night* he signed a contract with the distributor. That contract, called (not surprisingly) the producer/distributor agreement, specified, among other details, exactly what items the producer had to hand over to the distributor at the end of the filmmaking process. A wording of the section of one such contract follows:

Delivery: Delivery of the Picture shall consist of making physical delivery, at the sole cost and expense of Producer, to the Distributor of the following items, it being agreed that Producer shall include in the Final Production Budget for the Picture, and pay for, as a production cost of the Picture, the cost of each of the items of delivery required hereunder:

1. One positive print,
2. One picture negative,
3. One set of separations (or an interpositive) and two soundtrack negatives,
4. One negative copy of the textless main and end titles,
5. One music and effects track,
6. A multitrack tape of the entire score of the Picture,
7. TV version of the Picture, as below
   - One positive print of each TV reel,
   - One 35mm CRI of each TV reel,
   - One 35mm soundtrack negative for each TV reel,
8. 125 copies of the Picture's dialogue continuity,
9. Twenty copies of the music cue sheets,
10. Such materials as Producer may have on hand at time of the completion of the Picture and also such material as Distributor may require for the making of trailers, TV spots, and teasers, and similar advertising and publicity devices to be used in connection with the distribution of the Picture. In this connection, Producer shall deliver the following:
    - 35mm copy of cut picture,
    - 35mm copy of magnetic work soundtrack,
    - 35mm three-stripe magnetic soundtrack of Picture
    - IP of sections of Picture used in trailer,
11. Three copies of the statement of credits,
12. Three copies of proposed main and end titles, and
13. One copy of the conductor's musical score.

Let's talk about these delivery requirements in order:

One positive print—Simply, the final married EK print which comes from the lab.

One picture negative—This is the cut negative, with all opticals cut in, including main and end titles, that you used to make the EK prints.

One set of separations and two soundtrack negatives—"Separations" is an old term now meant to refer to the IP/INs or CRIs used for release printing the film. This particular contract requires two soundtrack negatives because they tend degrade and get damaged more than the picture negative.

Textless main and end titles—When a copy of the picture negative is delivered to the distributor it will, of course, include the main and end title credits. For certain forms of release (such as television or foreign releases) a different set of titles may be needed rather than the set that you've put on. In that case, the distributor must have a copy of the background scenes used in the title sequences so they can lay new titles on top of it. The easiest way to do this is to have the optical house, while they make your titles, also strike a copy of the title sequence *without* the titles. In the case of our main titles, where they begin in black and then fade into picture, that is exactly what we would see in the textless background negative. The length of the textless background should exactly match the length of the titles. The only exception to this delivery requirement is when the entire set of titles is over a non-pictorial background. There is usually no delivery requirement in this case. You will also have to deliver a textless background for any opticals in the film where you superimposed English words. For *Meet The Applegates* we had to generate textless backgrounds for all of the scenes in which the giant bugs talked with sub-titles.

438

One music and effects track—This is the M & E track discussed in Chapter 15.

Tape of the music score—This is the DAT, DA-88, or other format tape containing the mixdowns of the music discussed in Chapter 14.

TV version requirements—In the next chapter we will discuss the television version of your film. At this point, all I will say about it is that any reel containing dialogue or action that needs to be replaced for a television version must have new positive prints, CRIs (or IP/INs), and soundtrack negative delivered.

Cutting continuity—Though this requirement is sometimes handled by the distributor, then charged to the producer, it is often expedited by the editing room staff. For many reasons the distributor needs to have a detailed script of the film as it was actually cut (rather than as it was scripted). This rather tedious job is handled by a number of specialists who run the completed print of the film (often with a separate soundtrack) on a Moviola or flatbed and list every shot in the film and every piece of dialogue or special sound effect. This list is cued by footage so the location of any shot in the release reels can be exactly pinpointed. There are a few cases where the editing room staff will hire the person to do this task. However, more often than not, the only involvement you will have in this job is to supply whoever is doing the continuity with a separate mixed mag of the film. Please note that even though release reels are double reels (that is, made up of two of your editing reels) I have usually supplied a reel continuity with the reels as they were balanced in the editing room. This is to help the continuity person know where the editing room reels have been joined to form the double release reels. In cases where I have supplied double reels, I have also given the person doing the continuity a list of my LFOAs so he or she could see where the editorial reel changes came. This information will be listed on the cutting continuity because the original cut negative for the film is sometimes maintained on 1000-foot reels, not the double reels that the IP/IN consists of for the release printing. That is also why you will find that prints struck from the original negative usually come to you on single reels and prints struck from the IP/IN come on double reels. In recent years many labs have been mounting their cut negative on 2000 foot reels; some negative cutters even work in these larger reels. In this case, the soundtrack negative must also be provided on 2000 foot reels.

Many people that create cutting continuities now work from a videotape of the final film with feet and frames numbers burned into the picture, as well as time code. This video should reflect the way the film was mixed and printed.

Music cue sheet—See Figure 14.5.

Trailer and other materials—This has already been covered in this chapter except for the "other" item. What the contract means by, "Such material as the Producer may have on hand," is almost all of the material in the editing room. This is explained in more detail below under "Packing Up." You should know, however, that these requirements will vary widely from contract to contract.

Credits lists—These lists should be supplied by the producer.

Conductor's score—Supplied either by the music editor or the music copyist.

Packing Up

These delivery requirements should be conveyed to the address supplied by the distributor. All of the special requirements, like the negative and release printing material, will probably already be in their hands (or at the lab that will be doing the release printing). In addition, certain of the materials may be sent to different addresses. For instance, if there is a music department at the distribution company, the scores, cue sheets, and mixdown tape may be sent to them. The various bits of paperwork will probably go to some office of the company. In the end, you will be left with several editing rooms full of material, some of which the distribution companies do not want.

They will, however, want a large part of that stuff. Among the things they *will* request is: all the original negative not used in the cut negative, all the original production sound tapes, all the work print and work track reels, all the trims and outs, the mixing elements, the wild tracks, the lined script, and the logbooks. The reason for this is quite simple. Often, years after the completion of the editing of the film, changes might need to be made in it. This may be because of a possible re-release of the movie in a different version (such as was the case with *New York, New York, Lawrence of Arabia*, or *Heaven's Gate*) or the creation of a different television version (as was the case with the combined version of the two *Godfather* films for television). All the material needed to recut the movie should be accessible.

440

It is therefore important that you pack the editing room material in as orderly a manner as possible. Thorough lists should be made of exactly what is put in every packing carton. Packing cartons are large cardboard boxes designed to hold a dozen of the two–piece, white trim boxes. The easiest way that I have found of packing is simply to start at the AA (or the 001) trims and begin putting them into one box after another. On a packing list (such as shown in Figure 16.5) I list exactly what is going into each sequentially numbered packing carton. I also list the information on the outside of every packing box. I leave the boxes with the paperwork for last and, when everything is ready (and before packing the last box), make a half dozen copies of the packing list. One copy goes into the last box, along with the logbooks and lined script. It is sealed and marked very plainly as "PAPERWORK—CONTAINS PACKING LIST." It will also have the highest sequential number (every box is marked with its number and the last number; e.g., "Box 45 of 103"). Copies of the list also go to the distributor and to the producer. I also find it helpful to keep one or two copies for myself.

Every box is then sent wherever it is supposed to go. Most of these boxes are sent into storage, never to be seen again. Only the most important paperwork and the release and foreign release printing materials are saved in a more accessible place.

While the boxes are being packed, you should also be returning any equipment you no longer need. I usually hold onto one or two table setups and one Moviola until there is no more film left in the editing room since it is always necessary to check and repair things as you are packing them. Once I've completed packing every

6/29/00

PACKING LIST

Page 1 of 8

Silent Night, Silent Cowboy
(Name of Film)

Box#	Type	Contents
1	Trims/Outs	001-1000 thru 003-2000
2	Trims/Outs	003-3000 thru 009-6000
3	Trims/Outs	010-1000 thru 012-3000
4	Trims/Outs	012-4000 thru 016-4432
5	Trims/Outs	016-4433 thru 022-2000
6	Trims/Outs	022-3000 thru 030-1000
7	Trims/Outs	030-2000 thru 036-2618
8	Trims/Outs	036-2619 thru 042-5000
9	Trims/Outs	043-1000 thru 050-1000
10	Trims/outs	050-2000 thru 061-2000
11	Trims/Outs	061-3000 thru 070-3612
12	Trims/Outs	070-3613 thru 075-6000
13	Trims/Outs	076-1000 thru 083-3000
14	Trims/Outs	083-4000 thru 096-1000
15	Trims/Outs	096-2000 thru 105-3000
16	Trims/Outs	105-4000 thru 113-4000
17	Opticals	Trims + w/Pix Repl. by Opts.

(MORE)

PACKING LIST

FIGURE 16.5 A page from a packing list. Note that when trims with the same code prefix are packed in different boxes the last code number in the box (see box #4, 7 and 11) is listed. Otherwise the code number refers to all trims with that prefix. For instance, box 6 would contain all of the 030-1000 trims whether they are coded 030-1236 or 030-1999.

bit of film away, I no longer have any need for these machines. Every piece of equipment should be accounted for and returned to the lessor. Any supplies that were bought and not used can often be sold back to the supplier or to another film. Sometimes the producer will want them if he or she has another film going into production.

After everything has been packed, shipped out, sold, or thrown out, the editing rooms should look pretty much as they did when you walked into them on the first day of your job—empty and somewhat depressing. I always feel a tinge of sadness at the end of a job, no matter how much I'm looking forward to a long time off. There is something a little naked about an editing room that has no editing being done in it.

I check around the room one last time, close the door behind me, making sure that it locks, march to the front office to turn the keys in, and leave.

Usually for a long vacation.

ANSWER PRINTING DIGITALLY

It should be obvious after going through all of our previous digital chapters that the introduction of computers into the editing process brings great savings in time and work in some things, while introducing another whole series of complications and time-intensive tasks. Moving from the editing process into the finishing process is no different. The digital Lord giveth and the digital Lord taketh away.

Your primary task after the film is locked is very similar to your task in a non-digital editing room—getting the negative cut, color-timed, and printed so release prints can be made for projection in theatres. The computer editing system you have been using will most assuredly give you that ability, through the creation of Film Cut Lists.

We discussed Film Cut Lists back in Chapter 8A when we discussed conforming your work print dailies to your digital cut. The process for creating Cut Lists for your negative cutter is exactly the same. The only difference is that the negative cutter will be cutting and splicing your film's *negative* instead of an easily replaceable work print.

And therein lies the major difference. If you make a mistake matching your work print it is easy to correct. If your negative cutter makes a mistake matching your negative—you and your film are in serious trouble.

This situation is no different than if your negative cutter was matching to the cut work print, as we discussed in Chapter 16. In fact, if you have been conforming your work print all along, you should continue to do that and hand the final cut work print over to the negative cutter for the matching. To do so, you would print out a Change List for the final cut and conform your work picture according to those notes.

Because of the finality of negative cutting, it is a good idea to go through the cut work picture cut by cut, on a flatbed or editing bench sitting near the digital editing machine. You should check each cut, first by eye and then by key number, making sure it correctly represents the cuts Wendy has made.

The value of having completely accurate databases and telecine lists should be more obvious now than ever before. If even so much as one key number frame is off, the negative will be miscut.

The advantages of matching your work print should also be obvious. If there are any errors in the Cut List, you will be able to find them by making those mistakes when you conform your print. This is a correctable error, rather than an irrevocable, never-go-back error made on the negative.

Many films today, however, never have the opportunity to strike filmed dailies because of budgetary restraints. When these films go to cut their negative, the only thing separating them from a irrecoverable negative cut is the accuracy of their databases, logs and cut lists. It will be up to you to make sure that nothing goes wrong.

444

As the cliché goes, an ounce of prevention is worth a pound of cure, and that is truer than ever regarding the creation of cut lists (though I'm sure that this is not what the cliché was invented for). Since you will be under a very tight deadline to hand over the Cut Lists for negative cutting, it is best to make sure during dailies that all of the database numbers are correct. It is also a wise idea to create several Film Cut Lists during the editing of the film to ensure nothing is missing in the process.

If your film is going to be printed in A and B rolls, rather than single strand, make sure that you select "A and B roll" from the Cut List creation tool. The Film Cut Lists that your editing machine generates will be different than usual, but more efficient for your negative cutter's use. You should also make sure that your negative cutter knows you will be working on A and B rolls.

After you create your Film Cut Lists for each reel, look through them cut by cut. You will be looking for any information that looks obviously out of place—key numbers wildly out of sequence with others within the same scene, scene and take numbers that seem to be from the wrong scenes, as well as lengths and footages that appear to be incorrect.

You should step through every edit in every reel on your digital editing machine, checking the key numbers on the Film Cut List against the key numbers burned into the dailies image at that same footage.

Checking for errors is not an exact science, you are looking for things that "smell wrong" to you; your familiarity with the film and its footage will help you here. If you know that a scene is very cutty, you would expect to see a large number of cuts of short duration. If you know a particular shot was used in several places throughout the film, look to make sure it shows up in several places.

You should also be checking to make sure that Wendy hasn't used any frames more than once in the film and that she has left frames for all of her cutbacks (see Chapter 8A for a more detailed discussion of cutbacks). Every 24 FPS editing system should have a command for checking for reused frames, but they are all hampered by the fact that they can only check one reel at a time. If Wendy has reused a shot from one reel in an entirely different one, the software will never catch it. If you have balanced your reels into 2000' double reels your program will be able to catch more reused frames, but you will still be unable to check for frames used in different reels.

The solution to this problem, for just this once, is to build an edit consisting of the entire film. Since this is extremely memory intensive, it is best to clear anything you can off the screen before doing this.

445

The Film Cut Lists will list any reused frames or shots with inadequate cutbacks. As you look over the cut list, you should investigate any frames marked as reused to make sure it is not an error. In some cases you will find that the reused frames are in black, or Academy leaders, or in shots included in opticals. In all of these cases you don't have to worry about dupe frames. In one sense, leaders are just a special kind of optical—they are not made up of original negative, but of copies from the original negative. Since a dupe negative (IP) is made from the original negative for all of your opticals you never have to worry about the original negative being cut and unavailable for reuse.

Before you send your Cut Lists over to your negative cutter you should go through them and highlight where every outstanding optical will be cut in. This is the equivalent of marking "Do Not Cut" at every splice where an optical has not yet been cut into the workprint. I like to highlight them in a bright color and mark "Do Not Cut" on the side of the Cut List.

After you have checked and marked your Cut Lists, you will need to send them along with a tape of your film, to the negative cutter. Often they like to have the feet and frames burned into the picture area; they also will want to see the key numbers, which should be on the burn-in that the original telecine house put on the dailies (it is also possible to burn them in using the BITC function of the Lightworks).

Every negative cutter works a little differently. Some prefer to take your Film Cut List and use it, along with the videotape to match the negative. Others will want a picture EDL and the original logging database (FLEx, Keylog or Evertz file) and will create their own cut list. Eventually, however, nearly all negative cutters today will take the videotape and lock it up to their film synchronizers using a LokBox. This allows the video and film to move together so they can verify the footage of all of their edits.

Along with the tape and Cut Lists, you will need to make sure the negative is safely transported to the negative cutter if it hasn't already been moved. In addition, you will also want to send them the Negative Pull Lists.

If you have not started all of your opticals, make sure any negative that will be used in your opticals is pulled and sent to the optical house before it is cut into by your negative cutter.

446

Once you have handed over these materials then the process begins to look very much like it did in the film mode I discussed in Chapter 16. A *first answer print* (usually silent) is made from the cut negative. Since this will be the first time anyone on the production will have seen a 35mm or 16mm print, it is common practice for the director as well as the director of photography and editor to attend this first answer print screening. Everyone will discuss how close the color and brightness (*density*) of each shot comes to how the director and d.p. envisioned them and the *color timer* will make notes so he or she can go away and create a revised *second answer print* which will, hopefully, more accurately reflect the look everyone wants in the film.

In the cases where you have no matched workprint, you won't have any film to run in sync with this answer print to verify that the negative has been cut perfectly. You will have to check all of the cuts in other ways.

In order to check the cuts, you will need to telecine the answer print and digitize each reel into your editing machine. On most digital editing systems you can lock two edits together and play them in sync. As you play them together you should stop at each cut in Wendy's final edit (or the handover version that you created), and verify that there is a matching cut on the answer print. If your editing machine allows you to view both edits at the same time, you can also look and make sure that the action is the same on both. If you can't play and view both pictures simultaneously then you can find frames on the original edit with good sync points (two objects touching each other, a gun shot with a visible frame, a character's mouth opening or closing, etc.). Another way to check the negative cutting is to play the digitized answer print against the originally edited soundtrack. If a sound or a piece of dialogue looks out of sync then the answer print may be cut incorrectly. This way is not as precise as verifying sync points because audio sync is often hard to check.

A third way to check cuts is to have your sound house lock this new videotape to their dialogue tracks in their DAW. You can then play the two together and check sync without needing an editing machine of your own.

This videotape of the first answer print should also be used on the dubbing stage. It is always better to mix to your answer print (or a video of it) than a digitized output. Not only will everyone be able to see the picture better, but it is your final check that the negative was cut correctly. If there are any problems, they will become apparent if you are mixing to the answer print. It will probably be easier to adjust the sound on the dubbing stage than to recut the negative.

As each succeeding answer print is created, the look of the film will get closer and closer to the final print until it is exactly what the d.p. and Adam want. At that point the soundtrack will be added onto the print, creating the final *married answer print*.

447

Previews

We have already discussed how to prepare for a screening in Chapter 8A. If you are having a preview your procedures will be very similar.

If you are matching back to film then you will need to conform the workprint using a Film Cut List or Change Notes. You will then need to create a good quality audio playout (or Digital Cut, the terminology is different from machine to machine). If you have been editing good quality audio, the output audio will generally be of good enough quality for a preview screening.

What might *not* be of high enough quality is the manipulation of the sound a good sound mix can provide. In most cases you will not be able to create echo, the amount of equalization that you can perform will be limited, and you will generally be unable to manipulate more than four tracks at one time.

If you need higher quality sound than is possible in your editing room, you will need to output your tracks to a DA-88 or A-DAT, keeping them separate. These tracks can then be digitized into a sound editorial workstation and a more professional mix can be prepared. They can then be mixed at a dubbing stage. Another way of handing over the tracks to your sound editors is to convert your sound files to the OMF file format, save them to a disk of some sort (Jaz or removable hard drive) and give them to your sound house.

Regardless of how the tracks are prepared, you will need to end up with a tape (either in mono or stereo, this choice will depend on the requirements of your individual film, your budget, and your preview screening facility) which can be transferred to a piece of 35mm magnetic film. This mag will then be lined up with the picture (using the pop at the nine foot mark) and leadered before it is taken to the screening room.

Make sure that all of your sound tapes and mags are made at film speed. This will be the only way to make sure they sync up with each other.

On some lower budget films, it is common to project the video output from the editing machine, rather than taking the time and considerable expense of matching back to 35mm film. Obviously the quality of the video image will be drastically inferior to 35mm film since it is not only video but it is digitized video from inside the editing machine. You can minimize this effect by digitizing your original dailies at a resolution high enough to cut down on the *digital artifacts* that occur at low resolutions.

You can also create a better videotape image by outputting your film onto Beta-SP tape rather than the inferior 3/4" format. This will also improve your sound quality. There are screening rooms capable of projecting this tape with less of quality loss through a process known as *line doubling*. This technical process can only compensate for image loss due to projection.

You can also redigitize your dailies at a higher resolution than you originally input them. By consolidating your footage first, you can automatically redigitize only the footage you've actually used in your cut (with head and tail handles of whatever length you desire) and then automatically drop the new digitized footage back into the cut in exactly the same sync as the original footage. This is a fairly time consuming process and requires vast amounts of disk space, so it is usually not an option on feature length productions. On a short film, however, the added quality often makes up for the additional cost of added disk storage.

The first thing you will need to do in this process is to create a database of all of the material used in your edit (there is a command for this). This new database can then be used to batch digitize the dailies just as you did during dailies, except you would now digitize at a higher resolution. If you consolidate before redigitizing, you will be able to digitize only the exact frames Wendy has used, omitting all the trims and outs. This will vastly decrease the amount of hard drive space needed.

After you complete the redigitizing you would use a command to rebuild the edit using the new material. This recreates every one of Wendy's original cuts with the new material. When you make a playout of this new edit it will be at the improved resolution.

The quality of this playout will depend on the machine you are using to redigitize. On the Avid, there are several very high resolutions that approach videotape quality. They require tremendous amounts of hard drive storage but the film will look quite good when it is projected.

A third and more complicated way to generate a higher quality viewing tape is to create that tape from the original 3/4" or Beta tapes, rather than using any digitized material. To do this, you would need to create an *EDL* (Edit Decision List) of each reel of the film. This EDL is exactly like a Film Cut List, except it has been converted to a 30 FPS, videotape mode. There are many types of EDLs and each one looks slightly different from another. Sony, Grass Valley and CMX all have their own EDL formats; in fact, each company has several formats. In addition, there are several assembly modes for each type of EDL, which determine how the material will later be assembled. They are called *A-Mode*, *B-Mode*, *C-Mode*, etc.

449

Every editing machine has its own commands for creating and saving EDLs, you will need to consult the manuals for the proper procedure for your machine. In every case, however, you will need to end up with an EDL on a floppy disk for each video reel of your film (there are several formats for these disks) as well as printouts of each EDL.

You will then take these EDLs (as well as an output of your cut for a guide) and all of the 3/4" or Beta dailies tapes to an *on-line editing* facility. There, every edit Wendy made in her off-line machine will be recreated on a master videotape (depending upon the projection system used at your preview theatre, you should try and assemble onto a high quality videotape, like a Beta-SP) using the instructions contained in the EDLs. This process, called an *auto assembly*, will result in a new videotape with all of the edits and dissolves, perfectly matching every edit and dissolve Wendy made on her editing machine. As a guide, some editors like to transfer the video output from the Avid or Lightworks onto the high-quality master tape. You can then cut each shot on top of this video output, erasing the digitized shot as you do. This is an accuracy check because every tape edit should wipe out the entire digitized shot, frame to frame. If it doesn't remove the entire shot or if it goes longer or looks different than the shot on the digitized tape, you know there's been an error somewhere.

Though this will result in a much better picture than the digitized output, there are several potential problems with this approach. For one thing, on-line editing facilities are expensive. Depending upon the length and complexity of your film, it could take more than ten hours to auto assemble. At the prices charged by most on-line editing houses, this is a substantial investment of time and money. Second, the auto assembly will result in a complete video but without final sound unless you output your digitized sound mix onto the master videotape. If you didn't, you will need to take your approved final sound mix and transfer it back onto the audio tracks of this newly created videotape master. This process, known as a *layback* (or an *audio layback*), is usually performed in a separate room at the on-line facility.

When you have completed the auto assembly and the layback you have created the master videotape that you will use for the preview screening.

Films Without a Film Delivery

Many films today no longer need to deliver film as an end product. In some cases these are direct-to-video movies. In other cases, these are television programs, though it is common for television and cable networks to require a 35mm film delivery in addition to a high-quality finished videotape. This film delivery is used either to create better videotape masters for foreign delivery or is held in a vault pending the development of the higher quality digital (or high definition) television. In those cases, and there are already television shows being created in high definition, the hi-def version of the program is created from the 35mm negative, not from the videotape master.

We will discuss the specifics of a video finish in Chapter 17A, but we should briefly note the process here.

If you are working on a film that does not have a film delivery, you will not need to go through the film answer printing process at all. In these cases your finish occurs entirely in the video world, in a manner almost exactly like the auto-assembly described in the preceding section.

You will create a Video EDL for every reel of the film and send that, along with a videotape of Wendy's cut, to your on-line facility where every event from her cut will be matched using the high quality footage from the original telecine session. Next, this Edited Master is color corrected under the director of photography's or the producer's direction, titles and special effects are added, the sound is laid back and the entire show is *formatted* to accommodate any commercial breaks. This process is very analogous to the film finishing process with its color timing, visual opticals and soundtrack optical negative.

Dealing With Opticals

In Chapter 10A, we discussed how to cut opticals into your edit when you are working digitally. Often, there is a complication on lower budgeted movies that is completely driven by money constraints—the editing room is asked to give up their editing machine once the picture is locked and the Cut Lists and EDLs have been prepared.

How, then, can you insert opticals into your movie?

The short answer is that you can't; there is no way to telecine and digitize each of the opticals for editing. In cases like this, it is very important that you have a reliable negative cutter because the negative for the visual opticals will need to be edited into the (usually) already cut negative by eye matching. Your negative cutter will be able to look at the negative and find sync points to line up the optical negative against the playout tape you've given them using their LokBox. Attention must be paid to the fact that, depending on how accurate the telecine was in regards to framing, certain sync points may be unreliable. If the sides of the frames are not absolutely accurate, and there is very little way to tell if it is off a slight amount, then lining up the footage using people or objects entering and exiting the frame may lead to errors of one or two frames. If 1.85 letterbox mattes were put on the dailies, it will be impossible to get sync using objects moving in or out of the top or bottom of the frames. All in all, it is a rather risky situation, but one many low budget films have to face.

451

If a little bit of money can be found to go back into the editing room, you need to prepare yourself for this eventuality before you close up the editing room. In addition to making the normal backups you can try and *consolidate* the footage. As we've already mentioned, this simply means that you instruct the editing machine to save every frame of footage used in the film (along with a *handle*, the number of extra frames at the head and tail of every edit; you can choose how long to make these) and nothing else. If Wendy is not going to be doing any more editing, I would set the handle to one frame. This saves enormous amounts of hard drive space, allowing the production to pay for only a small amount of storage rather than everything that has been digitized.

When you return to the editing room with your telecined opticals, you can digitize them and insert them back into your edit. Then, regenerate the Cut Lists for the reels containing new opticals, highlight the new edits and send the new lists along to your negative cutter who should have already received the opticals negative. It is helpful to call them to let them know where the changes have been made because they will need to retrieve the affected cut negative reels from the lab before they can cut in the new opticals.

Special Requests

Just because you are cutting your film digitally doesn't mean that the requests we talked about in Chapter 16 stop coming. In fact, it is becoming increasingly common for *more* people and studio departments to start asking for special things from you. They reason that, because you're on a computer, everything is easier.

Needless to say, that's never the case.

You will still be responsible, at some point, for supplying a videotape of the cut film (in whatever version of the film is most recent at the time they ask) to the publicity department so they can begin to create trailers and a marketing campaign for *Silent Night*. In some cases, you will be able to make a dub of a version of the film that you've just screened, in a few cases the studio may still want a color dupe of the film. In other cases, you may need to make a video from your matched workprint.

When I have the time, I like to create a separate output of the film with a burnt-in time code (BITC, on the Lightworks) listing the key numbers and the camera roll. When the studio or a trailer company edits the trailer together, they will then have a list of all of the needed key numbers and their original sources so they can order IPs from the lab. They will still want a log book or an EDL for the shot name, but this burn-in gives them an advantage in the ordering process and saves you some of the work of getting the information for them.

You will also need to supply them with a dialogue only track of the film for their use in mixing. Once in a while, they may need to go back to the original production DATs to get better sounding tracks, so they will need an audio EDL of your film as well. In some cases, the trailer company may want to get a DAT tape of your music score if it is ready. For films where I have been cutting with the composer's temp music, I have supplied the temp cues to the trailer house, though they are not usually of high enough quality to be used.

Wrapping Out and Packing Up

Many of the delivery elements you will need to supply will be identical to those we discussed in Chapter 16. The trailer elements in point ten will usually refer to videotape copies rather than film copies.

You will need to pack up a few more pieces of material, however. The computer disks sent from the telecine house during dailies (containing FLEx, Evertz or Keylog files) will need to be packed safely. The final backup, whether it is on magneto-optical, Zip or Jaz disks, will need to be safely stored away. If you are delivering on Zip disks, I like to pack two identical backup disks in case one of them gets damaged. These backups are the only record of all of your material and every saved edit. Once you destroy the digitized material on your hard drive, you will be unable to get back to your edit if you have not saved this material.

Of course, you will need to pack up all of your original dailies tapes, as well as any tapes of intermediate cuts that you output for screenings. The general rule of thumb should be this: any items Wendy might need to recut the picture should be saved.

Some assistants like to make their own copies of the digitized sound effects, leaders and any other pieces of reusable material. If you've gone to some trouble to create countdown leaders or find rare sound effects, you might want to output copies of these items onto a videotape or a Zip or Jaz disk so you can reuse them on another show.

453

After all of your material has been packed up (see Chapter 16 for instructions), you can erase all of the footage from your hard drives. Usually the equipment rental house supplying the editing machine and the hard drives will erase all of the material for you, since they will need to reformat the drives before renting them out again. Some directors and studios insist that you erase all of the material so nobody outside the production can get a copy of the film. This may be a simple task or it may be complex, depending on what type of system you are working on. The higher resolution systems often need to have their drives *striped* rather than simply formatted. Lower resolution systems can be formatted drive-by-drive. You should check with your rental house before you attempt anything. In some cases, it might make more sense to have one of their technicians come out to your editing room on your final day and reformat the drives before they are returned.

When you have completed packing your room, erasing your drives, and returning all rented equipment to its proper owners, then you can walk out the editing room door, locking it behind you for the last time.

ODDS AND SODS

Now that you've been through the lengthy process of doing a film the "normal" way, I should clue you in to a few of the kinks that you may meet along the way. These include 70mm films, Dolby films, television versions of features, and budgeting/accounting systems. This will only skim the surface of the various oddities you may encounter as you work in film editing, but it will be a start.

454

70mm Films

There are several reasons a filmmaker might want to shoot and/or release a film in the 70mm format. First, prevailing wisdom is that saying "in 70mm" on the marquee will bring in a larger audience. As a result some distributors will insist on a 70mm release for certain kinds of films. A second reason you might want to shoot in 70mm is for better picture quality. The picture area of the 70mm frame is about four times the area of a 35mm frame. This means the film needs to be magnified less than a 35mm frame to fill a similar sized screen. In turn, this means that the picture quality of a film shot and released in 70mm will be better than the same film shot and released in 35mm. Certainly, some of the tricky optical work in the *Star Wars* series of films could not have been done as effectively in 35mm. In fact, whether the original negative was shot in 35mm or 70mm, all of the opticals in many of the recent special effects films have been done in the larger format (usually in 65mm, for later integration into the final 70mm and 35mm prints).

A film need not be shot in 70mm in order to be released in 70mm, in fact very few films are still shot in the larger format. An optical *blow-up* can be done to enlarge the 35mm frame to the 70mm

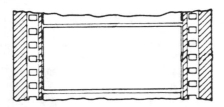

FIGURE 17.1 *70mm film sound consists of six magnetic tracks which are pasted (striped) onto the film. Each of the wider bands on the outside of the film consists of two separate tracks of sound, and there are two thinner bands between the picture area and the sprockets.*

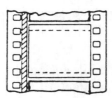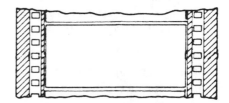

FIGURE 17.2 *Note the difference between the 35mm picture size on the left, and the 70mm on the right. The 1.85 cut–off has been marked on the 35mm film and the 35mm optical track area is shown as a band with slashed lines. Note that the height of the 70mm frame is five sprockets, not four as in 35mm film.*

455

size. Unfortunately, there are two big problems with this. The first is that the quality degrades a little bit as a film goes through the optical process. A blow–up makes every little problem in the film's visuals stand out even more than most opticals since it will be enlarging the film's deficiencies right along with the image. The picture will also become a little grainier. Any shots that are right on the edge of sharpness will likely go out of focus. The second major problem with a blow–up is that 35mm frames are shaped differently than 70mm frames, as you can see in Figures 17.1 and 17.2. The common screen ratio, as I've mentioned, for 35mm film is 1.85 to 1, which is achieved in projection by chopping off the top and bottom of the full 35mm frame as shown. The normal 70mm aspect ratio is about 2.2 to 1.

Since the 70mm frame is far more elongated than the 35mm frame, the 35mm image will not fit properly onto the 70mm blowup negative without some adjustment. There are several ways this can be accomplished. The first, and most problematic, is to blow up each shot in the film in a slightly different manner, attempting to

1.85 image

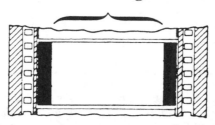

FIGURE 17.3 On Fame we utilized a special 70mm blowup. We took the 1.85 image and placed it as large as we could get onto the 70mm frame. We then blacked out the remaining portion of the 70mm frame. In this way we took advantage of the superior sound of the 70mm format without ruining the picture image (which had been shot for projection in the 35mm 1.85 format).

456

blow up the most important areas of action while losing the least important. In practice this means deciding how much of the top or bottom of your 35mm frame you can afford to lose. This way of blowing up an image is the worst when considered from all sides. It is extremely costly, since each shot must be blown up separately. It also destroys whatever composition the d.p. and camera operator chose for the frame; you are liable to end up with quite a few ugly frames.

The second solution is something that we did on *Fame*. Fame was shot in 35mm but released in 70mm for the Los Angeles and New York premieres to take full advantage of the six–track Dolby soundtrack for the music. Rather than lose anything of the frame we decided to optically place a black matte on either side of the 70mm frame to reduce the screen ratio to more closely approximate 1.85 to 1. This technique is very much like *letterboxing* (as shown in Figure 17.3) and resulted in an image that was smaller than a normal 70mm image. This way, we ended up with a 70mm print that looked very much like our 35mm prints but had a better soundtrack because 70mm films run at a faster speed. 70mm prints are projected at 24 frames per second, as are 35mm. Because 70mm frames are bigger, the film actually moves at a faster inches per second rate. The faster a sound tape moves, the better the sound quality will be.

The third way to shoot in 35mm but release in 70mm is to shoot in what is called an *anamorphic* or *squeezed* format. In this format special camera lenses are used to squeeze the image horizontally to fit it onto a standard 35mm negative, much as the writing on a balloon appears to squeeze together as the balloon deflates. Normally, 35mm anamorphic negative is printed and released on 35mm anamorphic prints. During projection the 35mm film image is unsqueezed (or reinflated, if you will) by the exact amount it was squeezed. This results in an image ratio of approximately 2.3 to 1, the same as the 70mm print ratio. For 70mm prints, the 35mm anamorphic image is unsqueezed as the film is printed onto the 70mm negative. This way, the 70mm print has the wide screen, unsqueezed image and no image is lost. This is definitely the preferred way to go if it is known that the film is going to be blown up to 70mm. The only slight problem with this method is that all of the 35mm prints made for the rest of the theatres in the world (and there will be far more 35mm prints made than 70mm prints) will be in this squeezed format. This will require a special lens to unsqueeze the image at the theatre. Most theatres are equipped to show anamorphic prints but since the alignment of the projector and the frame within the projector gate is more critical than with regular 35mm film, anamorphic 35mm prints are rarely perfectly shown. The edges of the frame tend to be out of focus and frame lines at the top and bottom of the screen are often visible.

Film shot in 70mm (actually the negative is 65mm, since no room needs to be left on the negative for the soundtrack area) is never edited in 70mm. 35mm reduction prints are made of the 70mm negative for dailies and cutting purposes. Opticals are, of course, done in the same manner. When the cutting is finished, the negative cutter matches the 70mm negative to the 35mm workprint.

457

If the film is shot in 35mm squeezed format, the work print will obviously also be in squeezed format. In that case, a large, bulky lens must be mounted on the front of the Moviola to unsqueeze the image. On a flatbed, the adjustment is much easier, there is a dial you can use to switch from a normal lens to an anamorphic. In addition, on KEMs, you can get a special large wide-screen head so you can see a very large image.

Stereo Films

If you have been living anywhere other than Mars for the last ten or twelve years, you are aware of the Dolby phenomenon in motion pictures. The Dolby name seems to pop up on all of the biggest movies. As an assistant film editor you need to be familiar with what Dolby is and what it can do because nearly every film released today uses the Dolby process, or a similar one.

Basically, Dolby does two things for movie sound. To describe just what they are, let me take a short detour into the world of normal film sound. As I briefly mentioned in Chapter 16, sound is placed on the release print in the form of an optical track. The optical track system has been in use in the industry since the introduction of sound (magnetic soundtracks are a more recent development). As a result some standards have been developed that are now very outdated. The most important one of these standards is something called the *Academy roll–off*. This roll–off is a standard way of softening the sound so it will not harm theatre sound systems. More specifically, it removes much of the high frequency sound from your soundtrack. This standard was necessary in the old days of theatre sound when equipment wasn't as good as it is today, and though the roll-off is beginning to die out, it remains a standard in some older theatres and is something of an albatross in terms of cinema sound. It is just not possible to have very good audio when there is no sound above 8000 Hertz (Hz), and decreasing amounts above 2000 Hz.

The first advantage of using Dolby in films is that the Dolby noise reduction system (similar to what you would find on a home cassette deck) puts much of that high frequency range back into the soundtrack. In essence, it sets its own standard, rather than adapting to the Academy standard. Using Dolby you can get sound up to 12,000 Hz. Though this hardly touches the upper range of human hearing (the upper range of an organ scale is almost 20,000 Hz, for instance), and is quite a bit less than good home stereos, it does add much to the fullness of the sound that we can hear from a movie soundtrack. Dolby is, therefore, ideally suited to the soundtrack of a musically oriented film, or a movie with a lot of higher frequency information.

The second use of the Dolby film system is the ability to get stereo sound in theatres. Prior to Dolby the only way to get stereo onto a film was to have separate tracks of magnetic stripes pasted directly onto the film. This is the magnetic format that was described in the section on previewing films in the last chapter. However, it was never a very effective or cheap way of attaining stereo for the reasons discussed there.

The Dolby A system (there are others as we'll see in a minute) takes advantage of the fact that there are two squiggly lines on an optical track. It uses a special matrix to combine (in a process called *encoding*) four channels of sound into two. These two are then put onto the film on an optical track. At the theatre, during projection, these two are then *decoded* (through a similar matrix) back into the original four tracks. This method is often referred to as the *4-2-4 method*, for obvious reasons. Because the Dolby four–track process is an optical process, it costs no more to print (once the optical negative is made) than a normal optical soundtrack print.

For the assistant editor, there is a bit more work involved in the preparation of a Dolby release than for a monaural one (though it is getting very rare for a film to have a mono release; even mono the-atres run Dolby stereo prints since they are compatible). Primarily, this is because the tolerances for a Dolby release are far stricter than for a normal film (you didn't expect there *not* to be a tradeoff, did you?). One of the most frustrating things about making a Dolby film is that the increase in sound quality you hear in the theatres rarely comes close to what you heard in the mixing studio. To ensure that the best possible sound does reach the theatres it is necessary to keep strict controls on the sound during the mixing process and to do more policing of the prints and theatres.

As Dolby has gotten more accepted in theatres and labs, stu-dios now skip most of this policing work. The process has gotten smooth enough so there is rarely a major screw-up from the lab end. Theatres are still often inadequately set up for Dolby screen-ings so the careful producer will check out the major theatres in the major cities before a film's release.

During the finishing process, it is important to make sure that the *equalization curve* (the set of volume and equalization standards) used to mix and transfer the film is maintained throughout. You do this through a series of alignment tones, much the same as I de-scribed in Chapter 14 in regards to recording the music. In this case, however, there are two different kinds of tones used to check align-ment—*pink noise*, and *Dolby tone* (also called *Dolby warble* be-cause it sounds like a regular 1000 cycle tone with a periodic hiccup in it). Pink noise is a combination of *all* frequencies of sound at very specifically set volume levels. It sounds to the ear like a sort of hiss (much like the sound you hear when you are tuned in between stations on the radio). When the pink noise is played back and read through a microphone by an oscilloscope, you can visually see how much volume level of each frequency exists in the sound. If it doesn't match the exact amounts you expect in the Dolby standard (called the *Dolby curve*), you have to adjust the theatre playback system to compensate.

459

As a result, this pink noise and the Dolby tone are important references whenever you are going to play back a Dolby soundtrack (either married to a print or not). Either you or Liz should make sure that you always have a copy of the pink noise and Dolby tone (on loops, most often) when you are projecting your soundtrack, whether it be in a theatre or at the mix.

Because of the tighter tolerances of the Dolby soundtrack, it is essential that better quality control exist at the lab. Many labs offer high–speed printing of release prints at a reduced cost and most distributors take advantage of this savings. However, this increased speed usually results in reduced sound quality, especially if the lab allows their print bath to get dirty. It is important to check on these prints, as much as your budget will allow. Obviously, you can't check every print of a mass release; but you can try to check each print going to a major city or to an important theatre in a major city.

Another important check needs to be done at the theatre showing the print. One of the biggest deficiencies of the Dolby process is that it is incumbent upon the theatres to upgrade and service their equipment so they can play the improved soundtrack. Most theatres, being financially marginal operations, rarely invest the money needed to make sure that this better sound is played back properly. And, even if they do invest in new amplifiers, preamplifiers, and speakers, they rarely keep them in top–notch operating condition. Dolby doesn't have a policing policy for this and, as a result, many theatres with the Dolby playback units still cannot play back proper Dolby sound. There is no point, after all, in having increased high frequencies if you are playing back your sound through a 30-watt amplifier that can't reproduce that better high end.

George Lucas' THX system for theatre sound attempts to deal with the problem by creating a series of standardized equipment specifications that theatres are required to uphold in order to receive the THX logo. It is not a set of recording standards, but a set of requirements for the equipment the theatres are using to playback the sound on films.

On many of the Dolby films I've worked on, I actually went into the theatres where we were going to open the film and tested the sound. To do so, we first played back the Dolby tone loop to determine the playback volume. Then we ran the optical pink noise loop (recorded at the Dolby standard), read the sound coming from the theatre's speakers with an oscilloscope, and finally adjusted the equalization of the theatre's sound system to get closer to the Dolby standard. We then ran a few reels of the film and adjusted the sound again, until I was hearing a sound as close to what I had heard on the dubbing stage as I could. It is axiomatic that no theatre's sound is going to equal the sound you get in a mixing studio. In fact, no two theatres are going to sound alike. Room acoustics are too different. I have even been in theatres where no two *parts* of the theatre sounded alike (this is especially true with domed theatres). It is most important to go for the best sound that the individual theatre can reproduce, even if it is not exactly what you mixed.

Dolby stereo prints on 35mm actually produce four–channel sound. There are three channels fed behind the screen—one each on the left, the center, and the right—and one channel is fed to the surround speakers which can be anywhere that the theatre chooses to put them. Common locations for surround speakers are on the rear wall or down the two side walls. I have been in theatres where they are placed in the ceiling, behind the screen, or all over the theatre. (I was also in one theatre where they placed the surround speakers in the floor, but that's another story.)

You can also get Dolby stereo on 70mm prints but it is of a slightly different type. First, it is a magnetic track, not an optical one. Second, there are six tracks of sound, not four. Dolby uses these two additional channels in a special way. They lead to speakers behind the screen in between the center speaker and the outside ones (for this reason the two additional channels are referred to as left-center and right-center). These channels, called *baby boom channels*, will only reproduce very low frequency information—rumbling sounds or low notes of a score. *Close Encounters of the Third Kind* used these channels extremely effectively during the landing of the spaceship. The low-frequency sound practically rattled the theatre seats.

Dolby SR, is a newer Dolby format. It is, simply, a way of getting even more high and low frequency sounds out of the theatre system. Films mixed in this format sound cleaner, fuller and more like a good home stereo system. In order to preserve the ideal sound quality all the way through the sound process, any of the units (or elements), premixes and mixes that are created in analog sound (we will discuss digital sound shortly) should be done in the Dolby SR format, even if the film is going to be released in the traditional Dolby A format.

By and large, Dolby films are mixed in the same way as mono films though the effects and music need to be recorded on the tracks slightly differently. Effects will have to be panned to go either in the left or right channels (the surround channels are good for certain very general effects—crowd sounds and the like—which come from all around rather than from a specific place).

The major difference between Dolby and mono film mixing involves the rigor with which the tracks need to be monitored. Levels are very important, as is the amount of the stereo separation. As we discussed in the last chapter, you will end up with three stems that need to be combined in the *print master* process to create one combined stereo soundtrack.

Another way in which the Dolby process is different from the monaural is in the creation of the optical track. Because the Dolby stereo format works by collapsing the four tracks into two in a special way, it must be treated differently. The last day of the mix is set aside to create the Dolby two–track *print master*, which is made from the four-track mix master. This two–track then goes to a transfer house (most optical transfer facilities can do Dolby transfers) where a stereo optical track negative is made. This is what then goes to the lab. Care should be taken to listen to the first print from this optical track since Dolby sound is more sensitive than monaural to dirt and printing errors and may not be correct on the first try.

Dolby SR release prints, offer added quality and *split-surround* channels, allowing the mixer to put separate sounds on the left and right surround channels. Nearly every theatre in the United States capable of playing Dolby prints can play Dolby SR.

On lower budget films, a competing stereo system, called Ultra-Stereo, is often used. In order to use the Dolby system on a film, the production company must pay Dolby a license fee—which is not cheap. Ultra-Stereo is appreciably less expensive. This system recreates the Dolby stereo format exactly, but doesn't contain the surround channel information (though you can buy surround for an additional cost).

There is much else to be learned about Dolby sound, enough to fill a small book of its own, but armed with these facts, and a knowledgeable helper, you can control the quality of the picture and sound of your film.

Digital Release Formats

Dolby sound was a leap over mono sound's damaging Academy roll-off, but with the advent of digital recording even those improvements became outmoded. Most films today are mixed using digital sound units (not unlike the digital sound on your home CDs) and many are released in one or more competing digital sound formats.

Digital release printing enables the filmmakers to take advantage of better sound quality and more versatile stereo, just as the first Dolby A prints did. However, there are a number of competing formats that make the creation of digital release prints slightly more complicated.

Dolby Digital puts a six-channel optical soundtrack in between the left sprocket holes. This format, sometimes referred to as *5.1 sound*, gives left, center and right channels in the front of the theatres, separate left and right surround channels, and a sixth channel for bass information, much like the baby boom channel we discussed above. Since Dolby Digital Prints are combined with a separate Dolby SR track (which is the analog format that virtually all theatres can play), this release format is called Dolby SR•D.

DTS (Digital Theatre Systems) sound, developed partly by Universal Studios, is a digital release format that is not printed directly on the film. Instead, the six sound channels are recorded onto a CD, much like the CD-ROMs you use in your home computer. The CD is synchronized to the film using SMPTE code, which is printed onto the release print next to the analog optical track. An interesting extra of this format is that is can control an extra CD-ROM drive that can be played back at the same time as the main CD-ROM. This can be used to play a vocal description of the film's actions for the visually impaired. This audio track can be sent to the audience through wireless headphones in the theatre.

SDDS (Sony Dynamic Digital Sound) is a system set up for eight audio channels, though it has a *fold-down* procedure so it can collapse them down to six, or even one, channel. The tracks are printed outside the sprocket holes along both outer edges of the 35mm release print.

Each of these release formats requires its own *print master* and that can add to your mix time. However, once these print masters are created and their respective optical track negatives are made, it is possible to create a married answer print with a combination of all of these formats, along with the normal analog stereo soundtrack. This makes it possible to have one print that can be played in different theatres with different digital formats, as well as the standard (and still very widespread) analog soundtrack. Prints with more than one sound format on them are called *single inventory* prints, because a single version of the release prints can suffice for the entire inventory of theatres.

Television Versions

It is no secret to the millions of viewers of television, that movies released in the theatres and later broadcast on TV are "edited for television." This is usually due to excessive sex or offensive language in the original version that the television censors will not allow on network television. Six or seven years ago it was not uncommon for the network to re-edit the film for their needs and, in the process, completely butcher it. Recently, however, distributors have taken to insisting that directors shoot alternate versions of potentially objectionable scenes. In *Fame*, for instance, there was a scene where some boys in a school bathroom were looking through a hole in the wall into the girls' room where a number of girls were walking around bare-breasted. The director, Alan Parker, shot an alternate version of the boys' point of view in which none of the girls appeared fully uncovered. This type of *television coverage*, as it is called, is now more the rule than the exception in shooting films. No one is particularly proud of knowingly creating a bowdlerized version of their own film, but the prevailing wisdom is that it is better to do it yourself than let the networks do it. In fact, it is a usually a requirement of the producer-distributor agreement that a television version (often called a *soft version*) needs to be delivered along with the film itself.

Sometime after the completion of the editing of the feature version of *Silent Night* Wendy will have to create a television version of any scenes in the film containing potentially objectionable dialogue or action. On *Fame*, for instance, one of the M-G-M vice–presidential types came down to the editing room and, for a few days, went through the entire film compiling a list of everything that he thought would have to go. The list was actually quite amusing, being topped with a tally sheet counting the number of occurrences of each "dirty" word.

Someone, either the editor or a vice–presidential type, must make up such a list. Then the director and the editor should decide just how to deal with each incident. Some of the objectionable words will be easily replaced by looping them—words like "shit" can be replaced by "shoot," for instance. It is the responsibility of the looping editor to get these replacement lines when he or she is doing the original looping sessions. If some were missed then the actors or actresses must be called back to do these lines.

Lines that can't be replaced by looping (either dialogue or action) must be replaced by recutting. In some cases, a shot of someone saying an objectionable word can be replaced with a shot of another person. The offending word/sentence is either removed or looped.

This recutting is done with a color dupe and a dupe track of the feature version of the film. New shots are cut into this dupe (using the color work picture and original dailies track).

After all the re-editing is done you will have a dupe of the film with the color print changes cut into it, and a soundtrack with additions and deletions made in it. For all the reels that have had changes made in them a mix and a new cut negative must be made. Obviously, you won't want to recut the actual negative made for the theatrical version of the film. You will, instead, want to make an alternate cut with a dupe negative. You will make a dupe negative of all the reels that need to be changed. The negative cutter receives your television recut of those reels (if you've been a good assistant, these TV recuts should be plainly leadered as such) and will match to this new cut. It is also very helpful if you submit a television conformation list—that is, a list of all of the conformations made

464

for the television version (the sound department will get a copy of this conformation list as well so they can create a television soundtrack). The negative cutter can then match the new negative to this print, cutting the new negative into the reel's dupe negative.

In actuality, however, if the negative cutter were to cut the new negative into the dupe negative, any resultant print would look very odd since the difference in quality between the duped portion of the reel and the new portions with original negative in them would be quite extreme. When prints from different generations are cut together it is usually noticeable.

The way to solve this problem is to make a dupe negative (usually an interpositive and then an internegative) of the new material and cut the IN into the new reel. There will then be no difference in generation between the IP/IN of the original film and the IP/IN of the new footage.

You will also have to have a new mix made for the reels where sound changes occurred. You will often find that many more sound changes will be necessary than picture changes. It is your responsibility to make sure that all such changes are communicated to the sound department. When they have had a chance to make the adjustments in all of their reels then they will remix those reels and end up with new mix stems for the television reels.

465

The television version of the film is often the version that is transferred to videotape for distribution to airlines to be viewed on their flights. For this reason, it is a bit of a misnomer to call this version the television version. That is why some people refer to it as the *soft version*.

Money, Money, Money

One of the awesome things about working in films is the incredible amounts of money that are spent every day. Some recent films have cost almost as much to make as the yearly budget of many small countries. It is all a little obscene.

Though no editing room can spend anywhere near the amount of money spent every day during the shooting, you will be spending tens of thousands of dollars every week during the editing. About the only comforting fact in all of this is that it isn't your money you are spending. But the producers, who are responsible for seeing that the money spent is spent wisely, will be very interested in just how you are spending your money. You will be expected, professionally, to treat it as if it *were* your money.

During the shooting of a movie there are usually at least two or three accountants working for the film who are responsible for paying the bills and keeping track of how the money is spent every day. Every week they must send reports to the money people that, in essence, track how much money has been spent the preceding week and estimating if the film is running on budget or not. As part of that process, an elaborate method of billing and payment has been worked out.

Though the system will change slightly from film to film, the basics always stay the same. Every time you commit the production to spending some money you will either have to pay it in cash (and get a receipt for the expense) or write a *purchase order* for the order, listing just what it is that you are ordering and approximately how much it will cost. Each purchase order, or p.o. as it is abbreviated, is given a unique number and completed in triplicate (or more). You will keep one of the copies, one will go to the vendor renting or selling you the item, and the other copy (or copies) will go to the production accounting office.

Later, when the bills come from the vendor, the accountants will send them to you, so you can approve them. You must check the bill against your purchase order (the vendor should write the p.o. number on the bill; if they don't you should *make* them do it) to make sure that the work was properly performed and the quantities and prices are correct. This is why it is helpful to be very specific when you write out these p.o.s. If you've written a p.o. for one and one–half hours of interlock screening time, you will know that there is a problem if you are billed for three hours.

A month or so after the film has finished shooting, the production accountant will probably move on to another film. At this point, either a *post-production supervisor* will come on to the film to keep control of the costs, or Wendy and you will have to keep rein yourselves.

Film budgets are rather complex affairs, dividing every conceivable expense into strictly defined categories. Before the film is approved for shooting, numbers are plugged into all of the necessary categories. Salaries are multiplied by the number of weeks everyone will be working (this is figured out by the producers, the studio, and the production manager). A total for the entire film's production cost is arrived at and that amount of money is approved.

In any case, every bill the production accountants receive has to be coded into one of these catagories. Music transfers will be charged to the music budget, picture reprints will be charged against the reprint category but B-negative prints ordered during the shoot should be charged against the production's laboratory expenses. A portion of one particular budget's post–production

Silent Night, Silent Cowboy							Page 1
Acct#	**Description**	**Amount**	**Units**	**X**	**Rate**	**Subtotal**	**Total**
5300	**Post-Production Sound**						
5302	Dialog						
	Dialog Auto Conforming						
	Dialog Editing		Allow		20,000	20,000	$20,000
5301	Editors						
	Sound Designer	14	Weeks		3,500	49,000	
	Dialogue/ADR Editor	10	Weeks		2,200	22,000	
	Effects Editor	12	Weeks		2,200	26,400	
	Assistant Editor	14	Weeks		1,750	24,500	
	Second Effects Editor	5	Weeks		2,200	11,000	$132,900
5303	ADR						
	ADR Cueing, Spotting and Sup...						
	ADR Stage	5	Hours	8	300	12,000	$12,000
5304	Foleys						
	Stage	7	Hours	8	250	14,000	
	Record Wild Sound FX	1	Day		400	400	
	Foley Walker Package (w/ cue...	7	Days		250	1,750	
	Props Purchased/Rented						
	Foley Package						$16,150
5309	Dubbing						
	Dub Stage - 2 mixers (Pre-Mi...	13	Days	9	700	81,900	
	Dub Stage - 1 mixer (Print M...	2	Days	9	600	10,800	$92,700
5312	TV Version Dubb						
	Mono	0	Hours		750	0	
	Stereo	8	Hours		600	4,800	$4,800
5314	Dolby, DTS, Universal						
	Equipment Fee	0	Day		100	0	
	License Fee Dolby, DTS, UNIV...		Allow		20,000	20,000	$20,000
5318	Mag Stock & Transfers						
	DA-88 Stock (Striped Units)	60	Units		18	1,080	
	Recycled 2" Stock for ADR an...	10	Units		200	2,000	
	Mastering Stock (Striped)						
	Fullcoat w/ Transfer	10,000	Feet		0.9	9,000	
	For Previews						
	Miscellaneous Stock						$12,080
5319	Shoot and Develop Optical Neg...						
	Tests	0	Foot		0.1023	0	
	Optical Negative Shooting and ...	10,000	Feet		0.33	3,300	$3,300
5320	Stage System						
	Stage System - Avid	1			10,000	10,000	
	Stage System - Editor						$10,000

467

FIGURE 17.4 A section of a post-production budget, in this case created on the computer program "Movie Magic." The account numbers on the left-hand side of the page can be broken down even further. When you receive and okay a bill, the production accountant can give credit it to this number. In this way the costs of a film can be tracked and, hopefully, controlled. (Courtesy Screenplay Systems Inc.)

section is shown in Figure 17.4. You can see the complexity of budget's various details.

Almost all budget and accountancy work is now done on computers. Programs, like "Movie Magic," "MacToolkit Budget," and the DISC System are in wide use. Some of the programs are only budget programs, others track all expenses as they are incurred, write checks, and can project how over or under budget the film is.

It is not necessary for you be aware of exactly how the accountants on your film do their job. But the more you know what it is they do, the better you can work with them. At least you will understand why they are asking you for the complicated purchase orders and the bill approvals. There is one other area where you will be required to be money conscious. Quite often, especially on lower budget, non-studio films, you will have to research and select a vendor to supply you with a service. Label printing, copying costs, screening rooms, etc. all have competing prices and qualities. Often it will be up to you to decide what company you should hire to print leader labels or to make overnight video dubs after a screening. It is helpful to know just what things should cost and what the range of quality and prices are so you can tell the production manager or Wendy just where the best place to go for those services really is.

This is one of the advantages of an experienced assistant. You not only know where to go for something, but you have a relationship with the people at that company and can get better and friendlier service as a result. As you build up more contacts you become more valuable to the production. You should, however, beware of always going back to the same suppliers. Sometimes their prices go up or their service slips if they no longer feel they need to perform well for your business. As a result, it is always a good idea to keep your eyes and ears open for competing vendors. Knowledge *and* flexibility make for a very good assistant.

468

DIGITAL ODDS AND SODS

30 FPS Projects

There are a number of projects you might work on that will never need to be finished on film at all. These are films going directly to video, corporate video films, CD-ROM films (about which an entire book could be, and has been, written), or shows made solely for television. Because these projects will never need to return to the 24 FPS world of film, there is no need to edit them in a 24 FPS mode. In the United States these films are edited in a 30 FPS format (in most other countries television and films both operate at 25 FPS). For the Avid, that means editing on a Media Composer, rather than a Film Composer (though they are actually the same program with nearly identical computer code). For the Lightworks, that means editing in a 30 FPS project, rather than in a 24 FPS. For many other systems that means Wendy will edit them in the only mode that they have—video mode.

Television shows are a strange hybrid of this 30 FPS format. As we discussed earlier, even though they are designed for television viewing only, there are often delivery requirements forcing you to work in a 24 FPS mode. Most studios want to prepare their shows for eventual airing on high definition television. Since that format, relatively new as I am writing this, is much higher in quality than present day NTSC video, the only way they can guarantee an acceptable hi-def image is to re-telecine the show from film. For archival purposes only, you will now need to cut negative on the show. Some studios, not wanting to go to the considerable expense of editing and finishing on film, only require you to supply them with a

469

complete Film Cut List, which will be archived in case they need to cut the negative. Regardless of the direction you need to go, this will sometime force you to edit in a 24 FPS mode.

With most other cases, however, you will have no need to edit in a 24 FPS mode.

Editing in a 30 FPS mode is really not much different than editing in film mode, especially if your project has shot on 35mm film. The material is developed in a lab and telecined from the processed negative. Rather than telecining to a 3/4" or Beta tape for your use in the editing room, the transfer is done to a high-quality videotape, usually a D-1 or D-2, two digital tape formats. The reason for this is, unlike on film where the 35mm negative is the master from which all copies will be made, video projects use this D-1 or D-2 master to make all copies. To make the best possible copies, you need to have the best quality Edited Master videotape. The only way to get that, is to start with the best quality dailies.

These sunk-up dailies will be color timed at the telecine session as well as possible, this is why the person doing the synching and telecine operating is often called a *colorist*. This person also creates the computer files (either FLEx, Evertz, or Keylog) that you will use to batch digitize your dailies. Normally, you will have no need for the 35mm information on these files—camera roll and key or inked numbers. You only need the videotape and original sound tape information.

The sunk-up videotapes, and their matching telecine files and logs, are sent to your editing room where you will digitize them, just as we described in Chapter 5A. You will usually arrange the dailies for Wendy just as you would for a 24 FPS project. All of the editorial functions, from machine housekeeping to outputting viewing videotapes, work the same as on a 24 FPS film with the exception of reel balancing.

Since your video project will not have to be negative matched into ten or twenty minute film reels, it will not have to be balanced into sections that small. In fact, the only determining factor for television shows is the length of the final videotape. In most cases, that will mean a maximum of 60 minutes, more than enough for most television shows of one hour or shorter in length (the average one-hour television show actually runs about 48 minutes in length). For longer shows you will need to balance your reels so they are approximately 45 to 50 minutes long.

The reason for this balancing involves another task that you need to perform for television shows, and that is called *formatting*. Though Wendy will not have been cutting the show with commercials in it, everyone knows they will eventually be inserted into the show. All commercial television scripts are written with *act breaks*, which are places where the producers and writers know they will want to stop for a commercial. Each section of program between these commercial breaks is called an *act*. Though the location of these breaks may change during the editing process, you will ultimately need to plan your reel balancing to account for these commercials.

Before the editing process begins (or, certainly, by the time it ends) you should receive a breakdown listing the formatting demands of the television network. Every network and most every time slot has slightly different requirements, but all are rigorously enforced. The sample formatting in Figure 17A.1, for instance, shows that on this two hour television movie, there will be seven acts and a total of eight commercial breaks. Between each of the acts there will be a pre-planned length of commercials. The network gives you these lengths so Wendy can plan the act lengths so the ends of acts don't fall exactly on the hour and half hour.

Between the third and fourth commercial breaks will be the show *bumper* which is, simply, the banner with the show name accompanied by a voice-over saying something like "Silent Night, Silent Cowboy will return in just a minute." The length of this bumper is, like the commercials, fixed. In this case, it is three seconds.

Though the show will eventually be built with the correct length for each commercial break, you will usually deliver a show in the Edited Master with ten second breaks of black in the areas where the commercials will air.

If you are working on a show an hour or less in length, it will fit on one 60 minute videotape. In the case of longer form television, the show should be broken into chunks of approximately an hour in length. The best place for these breaks is at the commercial breaks. The normal procedure is to change reels at the commercial breaks surrounding the bumper, these usually occur at about the hourly point

Both you and Wendy will need to be very concerned about the total running time of your show as well as the approximate running times of each act. Networks don't like to have the commercial breaks come at exactly the half hour or the hour, since they figure that gives the audience an excuse to change channels to the start of a new show on another network (of course, if the material were good enough to prevent channel surfing that would be an entirely different story, but let's not get into that). For similar reasons, they like to have the first act run longer than the later acts. It is never acceptable for the entire show to run longer than the time allotted.

CLASSY TELEVISION NETWORK (CTN)

2 HOUR MOVIE OF THE WEEK FORMAT
for
"Silent Night, Silent Cowboy"

8 Program Segments / 8 Breaks
Program Segments should total 90:10

Any variation to this format must be approved by the CTN Movie Division.

Program Segment 1
The first program segment is Act 1 and should be from 15 to 20 minutes in length. Top of show credits must be supered over program material and include only the credits approved in the Credits Memo. Maximum credit length shall be 1 minute.

Program Segments 2 - 7
These segments will be Acts 2 - 7.

Program Segment 8
The final segment must have the final act. Credits can be no longer or shorter than 50 seconds and **must** be delivered over black. No more than 2 production company logos are allowed and the time for these logos is in addition to the 50 second credit sequence. All credits and logos shall be included in the total program length of 90:10.

In order to insure that a program segment will not break at the top and bottom of the hour, please note the following lengths for each break.

Elements before 1st segment	1:08
Break 1	3:16
Break 2	4:03
Break 3	3:13
Bumper	0:03
Break 4	2:18
Break 5	2:00
Break 6	3:27
Break 7	4:03
Break 8	3:50

FIGURE 17A.1 A Formatting List for a typical television show.

You can imagine how difficult it is to cut a show to run exactly the required number of minutes and seconds (yes, it is that precise), but if a show runs too long or too short it creates problems with the networks' commercial breaks and scheduled programming. For this reason, I usually like to go through my film one last time before locking and adjust a few individual cuts or act break shots in order to force the show to run exactly on time. If this is impossible, the running time can be adjusted in the final on-line to speed it up

FORMAT
for
"Silent Night, Silent Cowboy"
2 Hour Movie of the Week

8 Program segments / 8 breaks
Program segments should total 90:10
(including end credits)

Segment 1	Opening Credits Act 1
Break 1	10 seconds black
Segment 2	Act 2
Break 2	10 seconds black
Segment 3	Act 3
Break 3	10 seconds black
Bumper	3 seconds
Break 4	10 seconds black
Segment 4	Act 4
Break 5	10 seconds black
Segment 5	Act 5
Break 6	10 seconds black
Segment 6	Act 6
Break 7	10 seconds black
Segment 7	Act 7
Break 8	10 seconds black
Segment 8	Act 8 Credits: 50 seconds black Logos: 6 seconds

FIGURE 17A.1 continued

or slow it down using a process called *varispeeding*. This is always a last resort because it can subtly affect the actor's voices and the music pitch, as well as changing the feel of many edited sequences.

After Wendy has finished editing, you will need to go through and make sure the reel balance conforms to the network's formatting needs as well as the lengths of the on-line tapes. You will also need to insert a card that reads "Insert Commercial Here," along with the required amount of black on either side of this banner, wherever a commercial break occurs. Then, You will need to insert a card reading "Insert Bumper Here," along with the required amount of black on either side, where the bumper or bumpers occur.

Also, you will need to fill out a form listing the running time of every act and its start location, by time code, on each reel. These forms will vary depending upon the network. I was surprised on one show by a requirement that specified act lengths were to be rounded up to the nearest five second increment (e.g., 12:10 or 12:35). This pushed the official length of the show over the contracted amount.

The major difference between 24 and 30 FPS projects can be seen when Wendy is finished editing and you are finishing the film. Though you need to create sound EDLs, just as you did for a film project, you do not need a Film Cut List for your negative cutter. Instead, you will generate its video equivalent—a picture EDL (*see* Figure 17A.2), which will be used in your *on-line* editing session.

Creating this picture EDL is very much the same as creating the sound EDLs. You should first determine your on-line video house's requirements. There are several EDL formats (CMX, Grass Valley or Sony), a number of sort modes (A, B, C, D and E modes), and at least three floppy disk formats (RT-11, DOS and Macintosh, though this last is extremely rare). These options can all be set from within your editing machine via the EDL command. Your list will normally include your dialogue audio channels as well (you should make sure nothing is on your audio channels that does not exist on your original dailies videotapes; remove all sound and music that has been transferred from CDs). You then create the list and save it to the correctly formatted floppy disk. These EDLs are small enough that you can put your entire show on one floppy. You should thoroughly look through these EDLs to make sure they don't contain any obvious errors—incorrect reel names or numbers, odd time codes, et al.

You should print out a few copies of the final EDLs. You and several other people will need them.

Within a day or two after Wendy and Adam have finished editing you will go to the *on-line session*. This session is usually at the same video facility that did your telecine and created your dailies videotapes. If not, you should make sure that you send the dailies master tapes to your on-line house. Send a copy of your EDL disk, along with one of the EDL print outs, to the on-line house the day before the session so they can organize the tapes and make sure their machines can read the EDLs. You should also send a copy of the final main and end credit lists, if complete, so they can type all of the credit information into their titling machine.

```
PROJECT:  Silent Night
TITLE:    Act 3 v105
FCM: NON-DROP FRAME


000  A31       A      C    15:01:59:14 15:02:00:17 01:00:00:00 01:00:01:03
* FROM CLIP NAME:   71D-1=
001  044       V      C    21:31:04:15 21:31:15:29 01:00:00:00 01:00:11:14
* FROM CLIP NAME:   71D-1=
002  A31       A      C    15:01:58:04 15:02:00:27 01:00:01:03 01:00:03:26
* FROM CLIP NAME:   71D-1=
C03  A31       A      C    15:02:03:11 15:02:10:06 01:00:03:26 01:00:10:21
* FROM CLIP NAME:   71D-1=
004  A31       A      C    11:44:16:00 11:44:27:24 01:00:10:21 01:00:22:15
* FROM CLIP NAME:   71-3=
005  044       V      C    21:15:35:16 21:15:44:18 01:00:11:14 01:00:20:16
* FROM CLIP NAME:   71-3=
006  044       V      C    21:31:24:00 21:31:26:24 01:00:20:16 01:00:23:10
* FROM CLIP NAME:   71D-1=
037  A31       A      C    11:44:29:28 11:44:34:23 01:00:22:15 01:00:27:10
* FROM CLIP NAME:   71-3=
008  044       V      C    21:15:49:18 21:15:53:21 01:00:23:10 01:00:27:13
* FROM CLIP NAME:   71-3=
009  A31       A      C    15:02:30:29 15:02:34:27 01:00:27:10 01:00:31:08
* FROM CLIP NAME:   71D-1=
010  044       V      C    21:31:36:03 21:31:38:25 01:00:27:13 01:00:30:05
* FROM CLIP NAME:   71D-1=
011  044       V      C    21:15:56:04 21:16:00:19 01:00:30:05 01:00:34:20
* FROM CLIP NAME:   71-3=
012  A31       A      C    11:44:38:12 11:44:43:24 01:00:31:08 01:00:36:20
* FROM CLIP NAME:   71-3=
013  044       V      C    21:25:03:06 21:25:04:12 01:00:34:20 01:00:35:26
* FROM CLIP NAME:   71B-2=
014  A31       A2     C    12:20:26:26 12:20:28:14 01:00:34:20 01:00:36:08
* FROM CLIP NAME:   71B-2=
015  044       V      C    21:31:43:23 21:31:45:17 01:00:35:26 01:00:37:20
* FROM CLIP NAME:   71D-1=
016  A31       A2     C    12:20:28:13 12:20:35:21 01:00:36:08 01:00:43:16
* FROM CLIP NAME:   71B-2=
017  044       V      C    21:25:06:06 21:25:10:26 01:00:37:20 01:00:42:10
* FROM CLIP NAME:   71B-2=
018  A31       A      C    11:44:46:12 11:44:52:20 01:00:41:23 01:00:48:01
* FROM CLIP NAME:   71-3=
019  044       V      C    21:31:45:19 21:31:46:17 01:00:42:10 01:00:43:08
* FROM CLIP NAME:   71D-1=
020  044       V      C    21:16:06:21 21:16:10:09 01:00:43:08 01:00:46:26
* FROM CLIP NAME:   71-3=
021  044       V      C    21:31:47:24 21:31:49:27 01:00:46:26 01:00:48:29
* FROM CLIP NAME:   71D-1=
022  A31       A      C    11:37:26:20 11:37:31:22 01:00:48:01 01:00:53:03
* FROM CLIP NAME:   71-2=
023  044       V      C    21:03:31:11 21:03:34:11 01:00:48:29 01:00:51:29
* FROM CLIP NAME:   71-2=
024  044       V      C    21:31:52:29 21:31:55:10 01:00:51:29 01:00:55:10
* FROM CLIP NAME:   71D-1=
025  A31       A      C    15:02:49:02 15:02:51:09 01:00:53:03 01:00:55:10
* FROM CLIP NAME:   71D-1=
```

FIGURE 17A.2 An Edit Decision List (EDL) for a 30 frame television show. This version contains both picture (v) and sound (A) cuts.

Your on-line session is, in essence, a video version of negative cutting, though this process is much more automated. Basically, it involves recreating every edit Wendy made with her digitized footage, using the high-quality original dailies tapes, called *source tapes*.

A number of these original tapes are put on their own video playback machines (because of the expense, you will rarely do more than three at one time.). Each edit is recreated onto a new high-quality videotape, usually a D-1 or D-2 format, called an Edited Master. Dissolves and other opticals are recreated as well. As the edits from each source reel are completed, new reels are threaded onto the playback machines and the editing continues. This process, called an *auto-assembly,* is quite tedious and can take as long as ten hours for a two hour show, depending upon the complexity of the edits.

There are several different edit sort modes to facilitate this process. Since the most time-consuming part of an auto-assembly is threading and rethreading source reels, it makes the most sense to minimize the number of times the reels have to be put up on the playback machines. One sorting method, called *A-Mode*, in which the edits are made in the order they appear in the show, is the least efficient method for auto-assembling the show. Depending upon your video house, either the B-Mode, C-Mode, D-Mode or E-Mode will work better for you. All these formats work by sorting the edits in the order of the original source tapes first, then by the order those pieces appear in the show.

You will usually be required to attend the on-line session. Not only did you create the EDLs being used, but your familiarity with the show will help the on-line editor get through any of the small problems that inevitably crop up during the session.

The original production audio is usually laid down during the on-line as well, even though it will eventually be replaced by the mixed track. At this stage, it is the only audio you have and it will be used as a guide track for the sound and music editors who will use a copy of the edited master tape to work on the project.

Titles, if they are ready (and they often are not), can be created during this on-line session, unless they are being done elsewhere and dropped in at the on-line as a single edit. If you have sent your titles list over to the on-line house early then they should have typed them all into their titling machine. It is a simple matter to record them onto the edited master in their proper places and at the proper lengths. Often, the titles are not ready by this point, so a separate titling session is set for sometime later in the schedule.

Once the on-line session is finished, slates are added to the top of each reel, identifying it (as an *Edited Master*) and the date it was created. Dubs can then be made of the finished tape. These dubs will go to your sound house, the composer and the music editor, as well as to anyone else needing a tape (the network will usually want to start creating promotional commercials, for instance).

If there are still incomplete CGI effects when this on-line session takes place, it will be necessary to schedule a later session to insert them back into the edited master. It is best to first cut them into the Avid or Lightworks and create a new EDL, but it also may be possible to eye-match the new material into the edited master, using the original telecined shot as a guide.

One side note about CGI shots. It is increasingly common for CGI houses to supply their final work on a large computer disk rather than on videotape. This file will need to be translated into a video image before it can be inserted into the edited master.

At some point, all of the CGI, titling and on-line editing will be finished. It is then time to color correct the edited master. This process is usually done in a different room at the video facility and involves creating a new videotape master using the Edited Master as a source tape. Using the EDL created by the on-line editor, a colorist will go through the film, usually with the director of photography or a producer, and adjust each shot, much as they do with a film color timer. This new videotape, often called a *Final Color Corrected Master*, will supersede the original Edited Master. If the process has been done digitally there will be almost no generational loss. Images on the Final Color Corrected Master will look every bit as good, if not better, than the original dailies telecined tapes.

Once the sound mix has been completed, a tape of that final mix's print master (usually, either a time coded DAT or DA-88) is sent to the videotape facility and it is, under your or Wendy's supervision, laid back on top of the temporary audio tracks that were on-lined. If everyone has done their job properly, the new audio should perfectly line up with the video on this color corrected master. Your job is almost complete. All that remains to be done is to add in the bumpers and the spaces for the commercials.

This process, called *formatting*, involves using the Final Color Corrected Master as a source tape, and creating a new videotape (also a high quality digital tape). This tape will be exactly the same as the final color corrected master, with final mixed audio, except it will have black rather than the "Insert Commercial Here" banners. In addition, the black will be the full length of all of the commercials planned for each commercial break. This *Formatted Color Corrected Master* (sometimes called the *Show Master*) will also have the bumper or bumpers inserted and to length.

Once this formatted master is created then it can be *cloned* (copied digitally) and sent to the network for airing. In reality, this cloned formatted master is often shipped to the network no more than a day or two before the air date, in just enough time for the network's Quality Control (QC) department to screen the master and make sure it is acceptable for airing. Schedules are horribly tight.

Anamorphic Films

There are really no special techniques for anamorphic films except one: the telecine house will need to unsqueeze the image as they make your dailies tapes. You will then have a much smaller picture area to look at (because you'll be losing a lot of the top and bottom of the screen to letterboxing)

You might want to invest in a larger monitor in order to get the picture a bit bigger.

All other facets of editing digitally will still apply. Key numbers are no different, burn-ins should be the same. About the only difficulty will come when you match the film to your digital cut. It will be slightly harder to look at an individual frame to compare it to the image on your video monitor. Everything and everybody will look thinner.

HDTV and the Future of Television

High Definition Television, a television image of vastly superior picture and sound quality than is currently available, is about to become a reality. The technology is here to send these new signals to television sets across the country. All that is needed is a sizable number of people with television sets that can receive HDTV.

That, more than anything, is what is holding up HDTV.

478

Still, television producers and networks are convinced that the future is right around the corner and are insisting their films be finished in a format that can eventually provide high quality image and sound to waiting consumers.

The primary issues affecting editing rooms regarding this new format are image quality and image size. Because of increased number of *scan lines* in a typical HDTV image (and, until one general HDTV standard is agreed upon, it will be hard to say exactly how many scan lines that is) the frame is of much higher resolution and quality than possible with NTSC or PAL images. Therefore, the final edited masters of almost every television program ever made will not measure up to these new standards. The only medium that has the resolution to give us an HDTV quality image, other than HDTV video itself, is film. For this reason, many television producers (looking down the road to further lucrative sales of their product to the HDTV market) are insisting that editing rooms deliver a cut negative or, at least, a Film Cut List with every completed show.

As we discussed in the last section, this leaves Wendy with a choice as to whether to use a 30 FPS project in her editing system for the Video Edited Master, or a 24 FPS film project for the Film Cut Lists. It isn't an easy choice, though many people prefer to cut

on 30 FPS and have the editing software create an admittedly imperfect (but only slightly so) Film Cut List.

The other issue is the aspect ratio difference. All television
today is shot and edited in a 1.33 ratio (also called a 4:3 ratio)—the
size of a full frame on 35mm film. HDTV systems seem to be using
a wider 16x9 (approximately 1.78 to 1) ratio, much closer to the
feature film ratio of 1.85 to 1.

As a result, d.p.s will need to shoot films for television with a
lot more room on the sides of the frames to accommodate this additional width. In the telecine session there will then be a need to
telecine two completely different versions of the show, one in the
standard 4:3 ratio and a second in 16x9.

Recently, a process has been developed allowing the producer
to make only one 16x9 master. The 4:3 NTSC or PAL edited master
is derived directly from this 16x9, without the need to go back to
the original footage. The show is edited in the 16x9 format and
then on-lined that way. This 4x3 derived master is called an *extrac-
tio*n. Deriving the 1.33 master saves a tremendous amount of time
and money in the on-line bay. All that is necessary, beyond making
an extra set of dubs, is to insert new titles on the extraction, to
correct stretching problems.

Alternate and Television Versions

In Chapter 17 we discussed creating *soft versions* of your
film for the television and airplane market. The key to making this
approach work in a film environment is to cut the new sequences
and scenes in a color dupe of the film matching the timed
interpositive created from the cut negative of the film. This way,
you can make it clear to the negative cutter that any areas that
were color dupe material in the re-edit could come directly from
the timed IP, and any areas with new workprint material came from
IP created from original negative.

Because you are not editing with a 35mm print when you are
cutting digitally, you will need to find an analogous way to make it
clear to everyone which areas of the new cut are taken directly from
the cut negative of the film, and which areas are new.

There are several ways to do this. The best way turns out to
be the equivalent of the color dupe process for film. You will make
a videotape of each reel of the answer print of the film and digitize
them into your editing machine, along with the track. This way,
each reel of the original film is put into the machine as one complete
take. You can then create an edit for each reel containing just this
single picture take and its matching audio. Anytime Wendy cuts a

new piece of picture or track into this edit, it will show up as an edit in the Film Cut Lists and EDLs. For the lengths of the recut where she has used the cut negative from the film, there will be no new edits indicated in the new lists. The negative cutter will know to use the timed IP for these lengths.

Another method is to have Wendy re-edit, using a copy of the final edit (much as did as she began to recut the film after each screening). After she has completed the alternate version recut, it may be possible to generate Change Lists to give the negative cutters a good idea about how to proceed. I find this process a little more uncertain because of the iffy nature of Change Lists, especially on audio, though it is dramatically less expensive.

On television projects where a videotape of the on-line session can be cheaply generated, I find it more cost effective to use the first method.

Working With Multiple Editors

Many big budgeted films simultaneously use more than one editor to help complete the editorial process in time for the film's release. When multiple editors first started working on digital editing systems it was nearly impossible for them to work on each other's scenes without much shifting of hard drives and all of the attendant problems of keeping track of the footage as well as the technical issues of swapping hard drives between computers.

In the last year or so, both Avid and Lightworks have developed ways to link multiple editing machines to the same set of hard drives, automatically making every scene available to every editor and assistant. The key to making this work is a bit of computer technology called *networking*. This is a well established set of procedures for linking more than one computer to the same set of files and hard drives. It is used all the time in offices. The real problem with networking digital editing machines is that the sheer amount of data that video images require make it very difficult for multiple machines to share the same hard drives. There is also a limitation on how far away the *server* can be from the individual editing stations that it coordinates.

Still, many of the major digital editing system manufacturers have been working on ways to combat this bottleneck. Using their solutions (Avid calls theirs MediaShare, Lightworks called it Shared Storage; both use *file servers* to store massive amounts of footage) multiple editors can work on the same material, and assistants can also do their jobs using the same footage their editors are working with.

Another way editors are trying to deal with this situation is to use new technology to connect the hard drives and the computers. This magical science, called Fibre Channel, promises to make hard drive access problems a thing of the past. Using software such as StudioBOSS (also called Transoft, after the company that developed the program, the same company that developed MediaShare for the Avid), combined with high speed connecting cables, these systems can permit a large number of editors to quickly retrieve material across a mammoth amount of footage. Speeds of up to ten times faster than server based systems are promised. In fact, recent Avid software has abandoned MediaShare in favor of Fibre Channel technology

There is a huge amount of extra housekeeping work involved in maintaining a system of this complexity. Setting it up is, at present, not a job most assistants can handle. It involves partitioning and striping hard drives, and setting aside small areas for each editor and assistant to work. Each system works differently but the key is understanding that, while everyone is sharing the same media files (the actual picture and sound you've digitized) they are working with their own edits, EDLs and information files.

It may still be advisable, depending upon the complexity of the film, to digitize dailies from the same scene on the same drives. There are also a slew of ever-changing bugs and problems with sharing footage across the network. One assistant runs Norton Disk Doctor, a program that finds and fixes problems on computer hard drives, every night after the editor leaves. Others have reported problems when two editors try to access the exact same shot at the exact same time.

Eventually, when all of these problems are worked out, it should be possible for large crews on large budget movies to operate several editing machines simultaneously with little or no problem. Commercial editing houses will be able to have all of their footage for any commercial currently being edited, instantly available to any editor connected to the network (no more archiving the footage on an R-Mag and shelving it). Editors on television shows will have access to all of that series' stock and second unit footage (the standard exterior shots, cityscapes, etc.) available at all times without needing to redigitize it for each episode.

Assistant editors might actually be able to try their hands at editing sequences at a reasonable hour of the day, while their editors are in their own rooms and the sun is still up in the sky.

Getting Help

Nothing is more frustrating than having a piece of equipment stop working on you just as you're moving into a very intense weekend of time pressure editing. It was always annoying when a Moviola or KEM part decided to give up the ghost. With computers the problems are often more mysterious and nerve-wracking.

Part of the problem comes from the fact that Moviolas and flatbeds were usually fairly trustworthy beasts. They may have looked complicated on the surface, but they were mechanical objects and someone, somewhere, could figure out how to repair anything that wasn't working. Computer programs, on the other hand, are inherently unstable. There are a number of problems in all of the major editing programs that are simply *not your fault,* but the result of programming errors (called *bugs*). As you get more familiar with each of the programs you will learn where these ever-changing pests reside within your system.

There are a large number of problems, however, resulting from "pilot error"—the inability of the assistant to correctly operate this very complex hardware and software combination. When these nasties occur there are a number of sources to help you out.

482

First and foremost are the people at the rental house supplying you with the equipment. Not all of these places will provide service 24/7 (24 hours a day, seven days a week), but it is advisable to rent from a place that will stand behind their equipment, even if they are slightly more expensive. There are a lot of small-time operators who will rent you a Lightworks, Media 100, or an Avid for less than the prevailing rate. You usually, unfortunately, will get what you pay for.

I have found, the support a rental company can offer you is more than worth the additional costs paid.

Most of the digital editing machine manufacturers provide telephone support for their users. In my experience, this support usually leaves something to be desired. Sometimes the person dealing with your question, while well-versed in the programming of your software, will have very little experience using that software in the real world of editing. Sometimes, telephone calls are returned a day later, which is not acceptable on a tight editorial schedule, where one computer problem can mean that your editor won't be able to edit at all.

I find that the best resources for technical support come from friends who have used the machines. It is a good idea for you to keep a list of phone numbers in your address book of other assistant editors. Not only will they be able to help you out in a jam, but they will find that you will sometimes be able to help them. It is important to remember that asking questions is neither embarrassing, nor an admission of incompetence. No one can know everything about how these systems function, the technology moves too fast. One of the characters in *Heathers* remarked that "There are no stupid questions." This quote is truer than ever in regards to seeking help for digital editing computers.

There is also handy, available help on the Internet. All of the popular editing systems have newsgroups usually run by users (not by the company). The Editor's Guild in Los Angeles also maintains a computer bulletin board with sections for most of the picture and sound computer work stations. Once you've signed onto these boards (the Editors' Guild's is available only to members of the local) you can post a question or comment that will be seen by anybody who signs on after you. It is not uncommon for someone with a problem to get three or four solutions posted within 24 hours. Often, these solutions are ones that the editing machine companies don't even know themselves. There is also an archive of postings on an Avid bulletin board. The Internet addresses for these sites are listed in the Bibliography at the back of this book.

Regardless of how you get help, you should make careful records of exactly what you or Wendy were doing on the machine at the moment the problem occurred. If the problem resulted in a *crash* (a problem so severe that the computer stops working, either by freezing, making it impossible to do anything on the machine, or by dropping out of the editing program leaving Wendy on the computer's desktop) then you should note that as well. On some of the higher end systems these notes are automatically created for you, prompting you to retrieve the error log from the computer's hard drive and print it out before you call your support group.

Training

One of the most difficult aspects of working in the digital editing world is making the move from apprentice or college student to working as a capable assistant editor. There is another difficult leap ahead as you try and move from assistant to full editor.

There are a number of courses given by colleges, training facilities, and even the editing machine companies themselves, to train people to become more competent assistant editors. In general, these tend to be introductory courses of greater or lesser depth, but they rarely give the student the real world experience that he or she will need to run an editing room for even a small feature. This is doubly unfortunate because there is a tendency among producers today to keep editing budgets too small to hire a true apprentice. As I've already mentioned, in many editing rooms the assistant is hired only for the digitizing pe.iod then let go, perhaps to be brought back at the end for the creation of cut lists and EDLs. During this time, the assistant may be working evenings, while the editor is cutting during the day, decreasing even further the ability of the editor to teach the assistant through personal contact. It also makes it more difficult to teach the assistant the creative and personal side of editing.

All of these factors make it increasingly more difficult for newcomers to gain real world experiences.

Foreign Systems

Most of the world does not adhere to the 30 FPS, NTSC video standards that the United States lives by. In fact, in addition to the U.S. only Canada, a few countries in the Caribbean, South and Central America, Japan, South Korea, and parts of Yemen use the NTSC standard. Most of the rest of world uses either the PAL or SECAM standards. The biggest difference between those systems and NTSC is that PAL and SECAM images move at 25 FPS, with a field speed rate of 50 fields per second and 525 scan lines per frame. NTSC, you may remember, works at nearly 30 (actually, 29.97) FPS with a field rate of slightly under 60 (59.94) fields per second, with 625 scan lines per frame.

484

The relative merits of each systems have often been debated, but the advantage of having a video frame rate that is the same as the film frame rate (25 FPS in both) means foreign films never have to deal with the 3:2 pulldown problem inherent in film to NTSC tape conversions. This means there are no A-frame issues, no 30 FPS vs. 24 FPS project problems, and, generally, a much smoother ride for the assistant.

Most European films, however, knowing their movies will need to be released in a format suitable for United States consumption, choose to shoot their movies in a 24 FPS format. This means a pulldown will be necessary to get the film to accommodate the 25 FPS video speed, though it will be much less drastic than the 2:3 pulldown necessary in the States.

This *PAL Pulldown Sequence* works by taking the twelfth and twenty-fourth film frames and converting them into three field video frames, rather than the normal two fields. (*see* Figure 17A.3). This successfully converts the 24 frame per second film rate, into a 25 frame per second video rate. It also slightly complicates the telecine regarding the sound, in that most sound will be recorded at the 25 FPS rate with 25 FPS time code. There are various options for

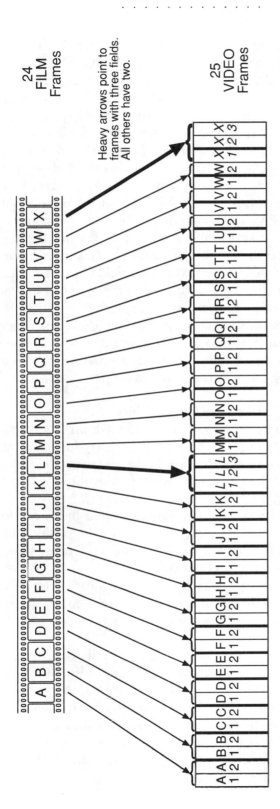

FIGURE 17A.3 *The PAL Pulldown Sequence works by transferring the 12th and 24th film frames (the 'L' and 'X' frames) into three-field video frames, instead of the normal two-field video frames. This means that all of the video frames, from the 14th through the 23rd, are made up of a combination of the last field of one frame with the first field of the succeeding frame.*

correcting for this difference, some of which occur in telecine and some of which occur within the digital editing machine itself.

However you decide to correct this discrepancy, be sure everyone is aware of the changes. Sound recordists, telecine houses, producers, etc. should all be as to notified how they need to perform their jobs in order to give you what you need to input the dailies properly. Never assume everyone knows what they're doing.

Once you have the videotape, it is necessary to digitize them properly. Nearly every digital film editing machine has a PAL 24 setting. This enables a film shot in 24 fps mode to be successfully converted to 25 fps PAL video but still be able to be frame-accurate when converted back to a 24 FPS Film Cut List. If you have had the time code put on the VITC channels it should be simple for many editing machines to determine just which fields have been duplicated. It can then determine how to digitize the material so it accurately reflects the 24 FPS film, frame to frame.

Every international project has its own set of idiosyncrasies, all of which should be dealt with before the first frame is shot. The cost of converting audio recorded in the wrong format, or re-telecining dailies, or converting tapes between formats is prohibitive.

486

Digital Networking

Increasingly, with the growth of small CGI, mixing, and editing houses all over the country, it is often necessary for a director or producer on one coast to need to screen footage created on the other (or even in between). Just a year or two ago, videotapes were made and shipped overnight for viewing.

On higher budgeted films, commercials and industrial films, this transcontinental package shipping is becoming a thing of the past as it becomes possible to screen digital material through phone lines, the Internet and via satellite feeds.

Some systems can provide broadcast quality feeds. In some cases you will need to bring your material to a central office that can take your videotape (or, in some cases, your computer files) and send them over their lines.

One system, called Vyvx, was used to send dailies from a television series shot in Vancouver, Canada to the studio offices in Los Angeles. In another marvel of modern science, phone line hookups between Skywalker Ranch mixing facilities in Marin County, California and a matching mixing facility in Santa Monica, California, created such tightly meshed systems that mixers in Santa Monica could playback and manipulate the sound mix physically located up in the Skywalker Marin mixing stage.

Problems still exist with hardware and software compatibility, so this is not yet a panacea. However, it is increasingly possible for members of the creative team to be split all about the country and still work together as efficiently as if they were in the same room.

Transforms

On both *Trigger Happy* and *MacLintock's Peach*, we had situations where videotaped material needed to be put onto 35mm film. In the first case, we were previewing with large amounts of stock footage (an exploding Big Bang, for instance, representing the beginning of the known universe), much of which would have titles superimposed on it. Since we had received the stock footage for examination on 3/4" tapes, there was no film of the material for us to cut into our matched work picture for preview. In order to create the title sequence we needed to create a 35mm version of our Lightworks edited sequence. This 35mm piece came from a *transform* of a videotape of the sequence. A transform is a transfer from a videotape onto a piece of 35mm negative, which is then printed.

Because the quality of the Lightworks output was not good enough for us to transform and project, we created a picture EDL of the sequence as we had cut it in the Lightworks. My assistant then took it to a video on-line bay, where she did an *auto-assembly* of the material, using the 3/4" tapes we had received from the stock houses as source tapes. Of course, knowing that we were going to have to do the transform, we had placed time code onto track two of each of those tapes (they did not come with any time code). This time code was digitized in to our Lightworks with the footage and provided a match for her in the auto-assembly.

The sequence was recreated (and titles superimposed) onto DigiBeta tape to maintain high quality. This DigiBeta tape was sent to the videotape house for the transform. The resulting 35mm print wasn't lovely, but it was far superior to the Lightworks output, and we were able to get a piece of film for our title sequence to screen at our preview.

On *MacLintock's Peach*, an entire subplot of the film involved intercutting back and forth between the characters involved in the aftermath of a robbery and a series of interviews with people talking about the robbery. Though the robbery and the rest of the main story was shot on 35mm, the interviews were all shot on BetaSP, for artistic, scheduling and budgetary reasons. After we had finished editing the film, all of this material (and there was more than eleven minutes of it) needed to be transformed to 35mm negative so it could be cut into the rest of the negative.

My assistant and I assembled all of the interview material into one long edit and he created a video EDL of this edit. This gave him a list of every BetaSP shot used in the film, complete with the source reel numbers and time code used. This list was then sent to the video house doing the transform along with instructions to add five frames of handle to the top and bottom of each interview section used.

When that material had been transformed we took that negative and telecined it, creating a new reel and FLEx file containing all of the new key numbers that had been generated during the transform. We then digitized this new tape into our editing machine and my assistant eye matched every piece back into the already completed edit, creating a new Cut List incorporating the key numbers for all of the interview transforms. Our negative cutter was then able to use this list to match the negative.

```
01:02:15:00
01:02:18:05
01:02:21:10
01:02:24:15
01:02:27:20
01:02:30:25
01:02:33:00
01:02:36:05
01:02:38:10
```

THE HARDEST JOB OF ALL — FINDING A JOB

Anyone who has ever tried to find a job in the film industry, or any other industry in the known world, has experienced something called the Catch-22 of job hunting. Put simply it goes like this—you can't get a job without experience and you can't get experience without a job. It is a revolving door of missed opportunities. You can't get a job without first having a job. Yet somehow, people still get that first job. It is not impossible, merely absurdly difficult. This chapter will try to give you some hints to help you get that first job.

489

As you may have gathered from the preceding chapters, the job of the assistant has changed tremendously in the last decade. This makes the job of looking for an assistant's position both easier and harder. I will discuss why at the end of the chapter.

You will also notice that there is only one part to Chapter 18. Finding a job is the same rough grind whether you're working on film or digitally. All of the advice that I give here applies equally to assistants looking for jobs in the digital editing world as well as in the film world. In fact, you might say, the assistant able to move freely between both worlds will be the most employable assistant in the modern film editing world.

The Resumé

When people come to me looking for work I always ask them for a resumé. I don't do this just so I can see all of the experience a job applicant has; but for three other reasons as well. First, it gives me an association between a name and a face. Second, it gives me an address and phone number in case I do decide to hire that person. Finally, it gives me a chance to see how well the person has performed the task of writing an intelligible and organized resumé, because both qualities are necessary in a good assistant.

This illustrates something about the problems in looking for work. There are so many people who would like to work in film editing that it is all too easy to forget just who everyone is. Anything to differentiate you from the next job applicant is helpful.

This is advice that I give everyone who asks me how to look for work. Find out what makes you more valuable than the next person—if you speak a foreign language, if you used to work in journalism, if you can read music, etc. List *that* on your resumé. Your differences will be what gets you, as opposed to the next person, hired.

Your resumé need not be an elaborate one. Even in this era of overly word-processed, fancy stationery resumés, most people get by with a simple typed list of their jobs, including short descriptions of the tasks they performed on each. The resumé should, however, be neat and well organized. If a person's resumé is lacking in either, I would think twice about hiring them. There are so many people looking for work that anything indicating you might be unsuitable for the job should be avoided on your resumé.

490

A sample resumé is given in Figure 18.1. Betty has worked in features for her last several jobs. Because she is looking for feature work, that is what she is listing on her resumé, though she has added her other experience at the bottom of the page. She mentions whom she has already worked with and that she is in the editors' union. This is the type of resumé she can give to almost any editor and be guaranteed consideration for an open job.

Most jobs at Betty's level are given to people with whom editors have already worked. A look at Betty's rise in the editing room will show you this. After a year long stint in a sound editing house, she began as an apprentice sound editor on a film Charles Simpson edited. She apparently impressed him enough that when it came time to hire an apprentice editor on his next project, a television movie, he hired Betty. He then hired her on his next feature film. On the basis of this experience, she was asked to be Nate High's assistant music editor on a film. She continued in that function on *Silent Night, Silent Cowboy*. Though Betty's rise is a bit more meteoric than most (many sound apprentices work three or four jobs before being able to move up—either to apprentice picture editor for four or five jobs, or to assistant sound editor) it is illustrative of the way most people move up in the field—through impressing the people with whom they've worked enough to be asked onto other jobs with them.

BETTY BOUND
123 Alphabet Street
New York, NY 10000
212/123-4567 home
212/987-6543 service

FEATURE FILMS

May-June 1999 — **Silent Night, Silent Cowboy** — Assistant Music Editor. Feature film directed by Adam Free. Edited by Wendy Libre. Music Editor — Nate High.
Assisted music editor on spotting session, notes taking, creation of click tracks, liaison with orchestrator and copyist, organized recording session and mixdowns.

January-March 1999 — **Bootleg, Bootleg** — Assistant Music Editor. Feature film directed by Cecil B. DuhMille. Edited by A. Beeg Editor. Music Editor — Nate High.
Assisted music editor on spotting session, notes taking, creation of click tracks, liaison with orchestrator and copyist, organized recording session and mixdowns.

January-October 1998 — **The Escape Of The Monsters From Outer Space With Flashy Cars** — Apprentice Picture Editor. Feature film directed by Eric von Stroheim. Edited by Charles Simpson.
Sunk dailies, digitized footage, worked with CGI and optical houses, organized shipment of negative.

August-November 1997 — **Daddy Weirdest** — Apprentice Sound Editor. Feature film directed by Eric von Stroheim. Edited by Charles Simpson. Supervising Sound Editor — Wallace Foley.
Pulled sound effects, digitized dialogue and effects, created cue sheets, liason with the mixes

TELEVISION AND OTHER EXPERIENCE

November 1997-January 1998 — **Disease Of The Week** (Television MOW) — Apprentice Picture Editor. Edited by Charles Simpson.
Digitized dailies, generated cut lists and EDLs, output cuts, liaison with sound house.

July 1996 - July 1997 — **Sound by Sound** — Assistant/Apprentice Sound Editor at feature and television sound editorial house.
Pulled sound effects, digitized dialogue and effects, created cue sheets, liason with the mixes.

Experienced with AVID, Lightworks, ProTools, and Waveframe editing workstations.

Member, Local 771, IATSE
References Available On Request.

491

FIGURE 18.1 Resumé for an experienced person.

Unless your father happens to own a film studio, when you are first beginning to look for work, you won't have this kind of proximity to those doing the hiring. In this case, the only kind of association you can get with them is to constantly go out on job interviews. A sample of the kind of resumé a newcomer might take around is given in Figure 18.2. Edward Zee, being someone with no contacts in the film industry, has had to stretch his credits a bit. The truth of his career, as opposed to his resumé, is as follows. The trailer company he worked for was a small company run by a friend of his. Ed really didn't do much more than order IPs from the lab and help his friend load the film into his Avid. But he did learn how to do those things. He also came in on weekends to learn how to use the machines. The film *The Apple of Your Eye* was a low budget short that a friend of his directed after he graduated from UCLA. The short, paid for with family money, never went anywhere but Ed's friend does have a print lying around his house somewhere. Ed, though he did not get paid a cent for working on the film, did learn a lot about editing from the woman that cut the film (also, she was working as an assistant editor on a feature during the day while cutting this film at night with Ed).

492

You can see how to subtly stretch the truth in a resumé. The idea is never to misrepresent what you know but to give your experience in the best possible light. What the editor who needs an apprentice is really looking for, is someone who seems enthusiastic about working long and hard hours, someone who knows enough about filmmaking and film editing that it won't be necessary to explain what a frame line or a videocassette is, and someone who gives the impression that they will be easy to work and live with for a long duration of time in a confined area.

Ed also noted near the bottom of his resumé that he has taken two training courses, familiarizing himself with both the Avid and the Media 100 machines. As an editor, I don't put a lot of faith in these training courses, but Ed has also indicated that he has worked with the Avid. That, combined with the determination that he has shown by taking the courses, will lend Ed more credibility.

There are some other items on Ed's resumé that are taking on more importance as computers work their way deeper and deeper into the editing room. While at UCLA, Ed learned a number of visual imaging computer programs and he has listed them on his resumé. Quicktime, Premiere, Photoshop and After Effects are all programs used to manipulate images. Though feature editing rooms don't often use any of these programs now, a job applicant able to use these programs has a much broader resumé than someone who

EDWARD ZEE
987 Sixth Street
Santa Monica, CA 90000
213/765-4321

<u>*Objective*</u>

To work as an Apprentice Editor or anything that will lead to a job in the editing room.

<u>*Work Experience*</u>

1999 — *Sample Trailer Company* — Worked in this trailer editing house in many facets of
the editing process. Ordered IPs from labs, assisted trailer editors in the editing,
prepared tracks for dub, etc. Loaded footage into Avid. Prepared cut lists and
temp mixes.   George L. Tirebiter, Supervisor

1998 — *The Apple of Your Eye* — Worked as an assistant editor helping with dailies and
trims. Sunk dailies, filed trims, digitized dailies.   Phyllis Murphy, Editor

1998 — Edited the following films at UCLA Film School:
        "Cheaper By The Baker's Dozen"
        "Smoked Out"
        "Enough Is Too Much"

1994 - 1998 — UCLA Film School, graduated BFA

Experienced on **AVID**.
Computer-savvy.
Experienced with **Quicktime,** Adobe **Premiere,** Adobe **Photoshop** and Adobe **After-Effects.**
Completed AVID and Media100 Training Courses.

Have edited several films of my own.

<u>*References*</u>
George L. Tirebiter — Editor, Sample Trailer Company — 310/555-1212
Phyllis Murphy — Editor — 213/936-1212

493

FIGURE 18.2 Resumé for an inexperienced person.

doesn't. Having a wide variety of computer skills is a real plus in the
assistant job market. Though I would normally prefer to hire an
assistant with well-developed film skills and teach them digital editing machines, life in an editing room is too hectic and pressured to
make that a cardinal rule. I generally look for people I think I can
work with first, and someone who can handle film and computers
equally second. The job market has now gotten tight enough that

nearly every good assistant looking for work is computer literate (if not downright computer savvy). If you want to get hired in an editing room today you should make yourself comfortable with both computers and film techniques.

Hitting the Pavement

Instead of the connections made by working with other editors, most beginners have only their own personalities to sell themselves. The only way they can be seen is to go out and knock on doors. They should try to visit every editing company or editing room they can find so that they may introduce themselves, drop off a resumé, and make their needs known.

How does one find these editing rooms? Sometimes you can call the phone numbers of production companies listed for television shows and movies being shot in the Thursday and Friday editions of *Daily Variety,* or the very thorough (but sometimes inaccurate) Tuesday edition of *The Hollywood Reporter* and ask them where their movies are being edited. Sometimes they might even tell you. There are several books published listing editorial services, among other things. Motion Picture Enterprises Publications, Inc. publishes a book called *Motion Picture, TV, and Theatre Directory* which is a yellow-covered book listing services for film and television. Called the "yellow book," it is a good place to begin looking for locations of editing rooms either under the "Editing Services," "Cutting Rooms," or "Editing Equipment—Rental" categories. This book is primarily useful for the East Coast, however. On the West Coast there are similar guides published. Three are the *Pacific Coast Studio Directory, Creative Industry Handbook* and *411.*

There are also areas on the Internet listing upcoming productions. Like their print cousins, their reliability varies from site to site and from week to week. Some of the information is hearsay and some of it is prey to the normal erratic process of preparing a movie for production. This means that a film that was originally supposed to go into production in January might end up being postponed several times until it ends up either going in December or being canceled altogether. And, like everything else in this world, the best information is rarely given away for free. However, you can find a list of free sites in the Bibliography.

The best way to reach people is to go to their cutting rooms. This is a minor annoyance to the editorial crews working there, but it is impossible to effectively sell yourself otherwise. And, make no mistake about it, you *will* be selling yourself. You will be in competition with at least twenty or twenty-five other people for every

494

available job. On an average six-month job an editor will accumulate over fifty resumés.

Don't be surprised if you don't get to speak to the editor at all. On most jobs, I have my first assistant talk to all of the job seekers, since I rarely have time to break away from editing. This is not a major problem for you since it is often the assistant editor that recommends personnel to the editor. Get to know the working assistants in town and give them a call every few months or so.

Once again, the best things to try and sell in your door-to-door discussions are your differences. There will be plenty of people looking for work that have worked more than you have. They can sell themselves on the basis of their experience; you cannot. You must sell yourself on the basis of your energy, and your willingness to work hard and learn.

Often it is necessary to work for free while you are looking for a toehold in the industry. Everyone I know in the motion picture business has worked for nothing or next to nothing at the beginning or in transition points of their careers; I did it myself when I was starting out and again when I was making the transition from music to picture editing. It is one way to get experience, it is also a way of meeting people. In the introduction to this book I talked of my first week on the movie *Lenny*, my first paying editorial job. Let me briefly describe what went before that.

495

I went to a public university in New York State, a school much better known for its science and English departments than for its film students. There were about forty students altogether in the Theatre Arts department (that was the department I ended up in; they didn't have a film department). There were, at the time, four film courses, all taught by one professor. One day in my junior year Karl, a Columbia University graduate film student putting together a project near the college, called and asked if there was anyone interested in working on the set of his film for two weeks for no money. My film professor announced this in his class and several people expressed interest. I, however, was the first one to the phone after the class (I remember dashing into the department office so fast that I lost several papers I had been writing; but that is another story).

I got the job and ended up working fourteen hours a day for two straight weeks on a rather charming fiction film about a boy who was an outcast at his school. I ended up working in a crew composed of the director, a cameraman, an assistant camerawoman (who later edited the film), and a soundman. I was the "assistant everything." I learned more in those two weeks than I could have learned in two years in my film classes.

The next year, when Karl was shooting another film, he called me directly to ask if I would like to work on the new film. I did. The summer after I graduated, Karl began directing public service announcements for a small production company. He had been given enough of a budget to hire someone to help out on the set as a production assistant (also known as a "gofer" since they "gofer coffee" and "gofer sandwiches," etc., etc.). Karl hired me. But after having made a few of my own films at college (in lieu of term papers), I had discovered that I liked editing more than any other part of the filmmaking process. I asked to assist him in the editing room. I would do it for free. Karl agreed.

These little jobs did not occur very often. In order to support myself in between these jobs, I worked as a temporary secretary, typing at accounting firms and law offices. In the meantime, I would work for a day or two on the set and several days for free in the editing room with Karl, who was editing his films himself.

Finally, a job came where Karl had enough money to hire an editor—a woman named Kathy. We worked together and liked each other a lot. While we were working together, she was hired to be the supervising sound editor on *Lenny*. She asked me if I would like to work on it as the apprentice sound editor. I thought about it for about two nanoseconds and said "yes."

01:02:18:05
01:02:21:10
01:02:24:15
01:02:27:20
01:02:30:25
01:02:33:00
01:02:36:05

I tell you this story not to bore you, but to show you the difference between being lucky and making your own luck. It was luck that Karl called my college to ask for help, but it was *my* doing that I raced to the phone as soon as I found out about the job. It was Karl's talent that got him paying work at about the time I was graduating from college, but it was *my* work on the earlier films that got him to call me when those paying jobs became available. And while it may have been luck that Kathy was hired to work on the little public service announcement at about the same time she was hired onto *Lenny*, it was *I* who volunteered to work for nothing in the editing room on these films and it was *my* work that Kathy liked enough to prompt her to ask me to work on *Lenny*.

There is no such thing as pure, unadulterated "luck." There is only the ability to put yourself in the position where luck can work for you, and that requires the proper aggressive attitude and need to work in the field. Sometimes, that aggressiveness means you work for free. I don't think it is a bad idea to accept those kinds of jobs, if you can afford it. People get paid in many ways other than money—experience is more valuable than money at the beginning of your career in this field.

When you go around looking for jobs the best thing you have

to sell is yourself, your desire to give the person who will hire you a lot of effort and energy. Everyone starts with no experience. Most editors remember that when it comes time for them to hire someone.

Unions

One of the first stops in looking for work should be the editors' unions in whatever city you are looking for work. In Hollywood and San Francisco it is Local 776 IATSE (the International Alliance of Theatrical and Stage Employees—whew!). In New York, it is Local 771 IATSE. There are other editors' locals in Canada and Chicago and there is a movement afoot to combine at least the United States locals into one large meta-local.

The main job of a union is to serve its membership and, for many, that means keeping the number of people looking for work low so that union members will have more opportunities for the available work. This makes it very difficult to get into the union. There is a federal law saying that any person working on a job for 30 days must not be denied the right to continue working. On a union film, this means you must be allowed to join the union after 30 days. What this law does, however, is introduce another Catch-22 into the work equation—you cannot work on a union job without being in the union and you cannot get into the union without working on a union job. Like all Catch-22s, it is not an easy catch to break through. Like all Catch-22s, however, it is constantly broken by people with the right combination of luck and the ability to generate opportunities for luck.

The Los Angeles working situation is also complicated by something called the Producers' Experience Roster, also called the "Roster." Basically, this is a list of people with experience on union films.

It is only after all of the Roster qualified members are busy that producers and editors are allowed to hire from outside the Roster. Needless to say, this almost never happens. This leaves virtually no chance for the unknown job seeker to break into a union film.

There are ways of getting onto the Roster, and the editor's guild in Hollywood is more open to members now than any other time in recent history (the New York local has always been fairly open). If you are working on a non-union film (or for a non-union company) that becomes union you will be eligible to get on the roster immediately. You can also get in as an editor or an assistant (but not as an apprentice) if you can demonstrate that you have 175 days of work experience within a three year period or 100 days within a two year period. There are some rather steep initiation fees that need to be paid when you apply and the regulations

497

change every now and then, so you should contact the local for current details.

So it isn't easy to get a union job. Yet people do it all the time. How? Some people do it because their parents or their friends are already on the Roster and are willing to hire them, despite the rules. Thirty days later they can join both the union and the Roster. What these people have going for them is their connection into the industry. That is what makes them different from other job seekers, however unfair it may be to those of us who have no one in the business to give us our first step.

How does a normal person break into film and the union? The easiest way is to acknowledge to yourself that this is really two separate tasks, not just one. Your first step should be to try and get into film. Then you can try to break into the unions and the Roster. When you have done enough non–union film work (and there is a lot of it around in Los Angeles and some in New York), you can begin to accumulate the contacts and knowledge to make a break into union work.

In the end looking for your first job boils down to being able to be at the right place and being able to do the right job when you get there.

498

I have always found that good work does not go unrewarded. If you work hard enough and learn well enough, you will be able to move in whatever direction you want. First you must hit the pavements and meet a lot of people; then you will get work (if you are persistent enough without being obnoxious). Then you must be good enough at that work to impress people. Once that happens, you will be able to move toward whatever kind of filmmaking you want to do—whether it be in features, television, documentaries, or anything else. There are too many people in this industry for it to be easy. But it is never impossible.

The Effect of Digital Editing on Job Hunting

Like everything else in editing today, the task of job hunting is made both easier and more difficult by computers. The positive effect of digital editing is that the skills an assistant needs are vastly different than before and many of them can be taught at colleges and universities. With the advent of cheap desktop computer editing software, colleges are now able to provide practical instruction in a way that was prohibitively expensive in the days when they had to process, print and complete on 16mm or 35mm negative (with all of the opticals and answer printing costs). It is now possible to learn the technical aspects of running an editing machine at many small colleges and quick courses, some of them given by small editing facilities that have purchased digital machines and are looking for additional ways to pay them off.

The quality of much of this instruction often leaves something to be desired, however, and you will rarely get the overall knowledge of organization and filmmaking work that a real editing feature or television room can give you, but at the very least, this sort of instruction can give you a level of comfort with the machinery that you can use to great advantage in your interviews and on your resumés.

A final positive effect of digital editing comes once you've gotten your first few jobs. Because it is possible to create many different edited versions of a scene at the same time it is now possible for assistant editors to try their hands at cutting scenes without disturbing their editor's cut. All that is required is the time for the assistant to make the cut. On some films, where there is only one machine, this is easier said than done, but if time can be found for the assistant to try out his or her ideas, the assistant's ability to learn the process of editing (as opposed to the process of running an editing room) can be greatly enhanced.

There is, of course, a downside to this technological manna and it can be summed up in two words—fewer jobs. With more and more films, and all television shows, giving up on printing film, there is much less need for the complex library-style operations that kept assistants busy in the past. Some of the logging and bookkeeping duties that used to be the province of the assistant editor are now being performed by telecine and videotape houses, though I find that it is necessary to verify and correct their work.

499

Therefore, though there may be more films made today than there were five years ago (including cable and made for television movies), there are also fewer entry level jobs on those films. Apprentice editors don't even exist on many films. There certainly are none left in the television world. On many smaller jobs and in smaller companies, the assistant is only hired to digitize at the start of a project and is brought back only at the very end to create EDLs and wrap up the room. The editor works without any assistance for most of the project.

Flexibility and versatility are among the most important traits an assistant editor can have.

It is important for editors and assistants to learn as many systems as they can and to be comfortable with computers and their usage. This includes working on film.

It will be as important for you to learn the technical aspects of your job as it is for someone applying for a job as a welder or a computer programmer. No longer is it good enough to merely love film. The apprentice jobs that used to let people start from scratch are disappearing.

The next challenge you will face is to learn while you are working. The high price of digital editing systems has created situations where the editor is working one shift and the assistant is working another one. It is getting increasingly difficult to learn the techniques of editing room procedures and the more important techniques of navigating the political intrigues in the editing room. How you interact with everyone in the editing room is almost as important as how you sync dailies or digitize footage.

It is a new challenge for job-seekers and it will require that you learn as many new and old skills as you can, present them well, and bring an invigorated sense of fervor to your job hunting. You will have to find many things that set you apart from your competition. In fact, the techniques of job hunting are no different than before, only the intensity has changed. But if you are good and passionate about working in film editing, there is no reason you can't succeed.

500

01:02:15:00
01:02:18:05
01:02:21:10
01:02:24:15
01:02:27:20
01:02:30:25
01:02:33:00
01:02:36:05
01:02:39:10

APPENDIX I

To convert the length of your film, in feet, into time, you can use either a calculator or the following chart.

If you use a calculator it is helpful to have the following conversion chart, which lists the percentage of a second for each number frames in one foot.

	FRAME-TO-SECONDS CONVERSION CHART		
Frames	1/100s of Seconds	Frames	1/100s of Seconds
1	.04	21	.88
2	.08	22	.92
3	.13	23	.96
4	.17	24	1.00
5	.21	25	1.04
6	.25	26	1.08
7	.29	27	1.13
8	.33	28	1.17
9	.38	29	1.21
10	.42	30	1.25
11	.46	31	1.29
12	.50	32	1.33
13	.54	33	1.38
14	.58	34	1.42
15	.62	35	1.46
16	.67	36	1.50
17	.71	37	1.54
18	.75	38	1.58
19	.79	39	1.62
20	.83	40	1.67

Let's find out how long *Silent Night, Silent Cowboy* runs in terms of time. Our film's total footage is 9432'12 (9432 feet and 12 frames)

To convert using this chart and a calculator, first multiply the number of feet in your film (in this case 9432) times 2/3, which is the ratio of seconds to 35mm film feet. This gives you 6288, which is the number of seconds in your film. Dividing by 60 to get the number of minutes gives you 104.8. This is 104 and eight tenths minutes. Eight tenths of a minute is equal to 48 seconds (60 seconds times .8). And, according to the above chart, twelve frames is .50 seconds. The length of *Silent Night, Silent Cowboy* is therefore 104 minutes, 48 and one-half seconds. Put in terms of hours, the film is one hour, 44 minutes, 48.5 seconds.

This may seem a little overwhelming to those of you who are terrible at math and at calculators. For these people I give you my footage-to-time conversion chart. Here's how to use it.

Find your film's length, in feet, in the column marked "feet" in the first chart (forget about the number of frames for now). The time will be directly across from it, in the proper column for you film gauge (each film format runs at a different number of feet per minute). Then use the second chart to find the number of seconds corresponding to the number of frames. Add this to the time obtained from the first chart and you've got it!

Let's figure out our film's length using the chart:

9000	feet	is	1:40:00.0	(1 hour 40 minutes)
400	feet	is	0:04:27.0	
32	feet	is	0:00:21.0	
12	frames	is	0:00:00.5	
TOTAL		is	1:44:48.5	

FOOTAGE-TO-TIME CONVERSION TABLE			
FEET	16mm (Hour: Min:Sec)	35mm (Hour: Min:Sec)	70mm (Hour: Min:Sec)
1	0:00:02	0:00:01	0:00:01
2	0:00:03	0:00:01	0:00:01
3	0:00:05	0:00:02	0:00:02
4	0:00:07	0:00:03	0:00:02
5	0:00:08	0:00:03	0:00:03
6	0:00:10	0:00:04	0:00:03
7	0:00:12	0:00:05	0:00:04
8	0:00:13	0:00:05	0:00:04
9	0:00:15	0:00:06	0:00:05
10	0:00:17	0:00:07	0:00:05
11	0:00:18	0:00:07	0:00:06
12	0:00:20	0:00:08	0:00:06
13	0:00:22	0:00:09	0:00:07
14	0:00:23	0:00:09	0:00:07
15	0:00:25	0:00:10	0:00:08
16	0:00:27	0:00:11	0:00:09
17	0:00:28	0:00:11	0:00:09
18	0:00:30	0:00:12	0:00:10
19	0:00:32	0:00:13	0:00:10
20	0:00:33	0:00:13	0:00:11
21	0:00:35	0:00:14	0:00:11
22	0:00:37	0:00:15	0:00:12
23	0:00:38	0:00:15	0:00:12
24	0:00:40	0:00:16	0:00:13
25	0:00:42	0:00:17	0:00:13
26	0:00:43	0:00:17	0:00:14
27	0:00:45	0:00:18	0:00:14
28	0:00:47	0:00:19	0:00:15
29	0:00:48	0:00:19	0:00:16
30	0:00:50	0:00:20	0:00:16

503

504

	FOOTAGE-TO-TIME CONVERSION TABLE		
FEET	16mm (Hour: Min:Sec)	35mm (Hour: Min:Sec)	70mm (Hour: Min:Sec)
31	0:00:52	0:00:21	0:00:17
32	0:00:53	0:00:21	0:00:17
33	0:00:55	0:00:22	0:00:18
34	0:00:57	0:00:23	0:00:18
35	0:00:58	0:00:23	0:00:19
36	0:01:00	0:00:24	0:00:19
37	0:01:02	0:00:25	0:00:20
38	0:01:03	0:00:25	0:00:20
39	0:01:05	0:00:26	0:00:21
40	0:01:07	0:00:27	0:00:21
41	0:01:08	0:00:27	0:00:22
42	0:01:10	0:00:28	0:00:22
43	0:01:12	0:00:29	0:00:23
44	0:01:13	0:00:29	0:00:24
45	0:01:15	0:00:30	0:00:24
46	0:01:17	0:00:31	0:00:25
47	0:01:18	0:00:31	0:00:25
48	0:01:20	0:00:32	0:00:26
49	0:01:22	0:00:33	0:00:26
50	0:01:23	0:00:33	0:00:27
51	0:01:25	0:00:34	0:00:27
52	0:01:27	0:00:35	0:00:28
53	0:01:28	0:00:35	0:00:28
54	0:01:30	0:00:36	0:00:29
55	0:01:32	0:00:37	0:00:29
56	0:01:33	0:00:37	0:00:30
57	0:01:35	0:00:38	0:00:30
58	0:01:37	0:00:39	0:00:31
59	0:01:38	0:00:39	0:00:32
60	0:01:40	0:00:40	0:00:32

FOOTAGE-TO-TIME CONVERSION TABLE			
FEET	16mm (Hour: Min:Sec)	35mm (Hour: Min:Sec)	70mm (Hour: Min:Sec)
61	0:01:42	0:00:41	0:00:33
62	0:01:43	0:00:41	0:00:33
63	0:01:45	0:00:42	0:00:34
64	0:01:47	0:00:43	0:00:34
65	0:01:48	0:00:43	0:00:35
66	0:01:50	0:00:44	0:00:35
67	0:01:52	0:00:45	0:00:36
68	0:01:53	0:00:45	0:00:36
69	0:01:55	0:00:46	0:00:37
70	0:01:57	0:00:47	0:00:37
71	0:01:58	0:00:47	0:00:38
72	0:02:00	0:00:48	0:00:39
73	0:02:02	0:00:49	0:00:39
74	0:02:03	0:00:49	0:00:40
75	0:02:05	0:00:50	0:00:40
76	0:02:07	0:00:51	0:00:41
77	0:02:08	0:00:51	0:00:41
78	0:02:10	0:00:52	0:00:42
79	0:02:12	0:00:53	0:00:42
80	0:02:13	0:00:53	0:00:43
81	0:02:15	0:00:54	0:00:43
82	0:02:17	0:00:55	0:00:44
83	0:02:18	0:00:55	0:00:44
84	0:02:20	0:00:56	0:00:45
85	0:02:22	0:00:57	0:00:45
86	0:02:23	0:00:57	0:00:46
87	0:02:25	0:00:58	0:00:47
88	0:02:27	0:00:59	0:00:47
89	0:02:28	0:00:59	0:00:48
90	0:02:30	0:01:00	0:00:48

FOOTAGE-TO-TIME CONVERSION TABLE			
FEET	16mm (Hour: Min:Sec)	35mm (Hour: Min:Sec)	70mm (Hour: Min:Sec)
91	0:02:32	0:01:01	0:00:49
92	0:02:33	0:01:01	0:00:49
93	0:02:35	0:01:02	0:00:50
94	0:02:37	0:01:03	0:00:50
95	0:02:38	0:01:03	0:00:51
96	0:02:40	0:01:04	0:00:51
97	0:02:42	0:01:05	0:00:52
98	0:02:43	0:01:05	0:00:52
99	0:02:45	0:01:06	0:00:53
100	0:02:47	0:01:07	0:00:53
200	0:05:33	0:02:13	0:01:47
300	0:08:20	0:03:20	0:02:40
400	0:11:07	0:04:27	0:03:33
500	0:13:53	0:05:33	0:04:27
600	0:16:40	0:06:40	0:05:20
700	0:19:27	0:07:47	0:06:13
800	0:22:13	0:08:53	0:07:07
900	0:25:00	0:10:00	0:08:08
1,000	0:27:47	0:11:07	0:08:53
2,000	0:53:33	0:22:13	0:17:47
3,000	1:23:20	0:33:20	0:26:40
4,000	1:51:07	0:44:27	0:35:33
5,000	2:18:53	0:55:33	0:44:27
6,000	2:46:40	1:06:40	0:53:20
7,000	3:14:27	1:17:47	1:02:13
8,000	3:42:13	1:28:53	1:11:07
9,000	4:10:00	1:40:00	1:20:00
10,000	4:37:47	1:51:07	1:28:53
11,000	5:04:33	2:02:13	1:37:47
12,000	5:32:20	2:13:20	1:46:40
13,000	6:00:47	2:24:57	1:55:33
14,000	6:27:53	2:35:33	2:04:27
15,000	6:55:40	2:46:40	2:13:20

APPENDIX II

To find the length, in feet and frames, for a piece of film of a given length of time, locate the amount of time you want to convert in the "seconds" or "minutes" column (there are two charts: one for "seconds" and one for "minutes.") The length, in feet and frames, will be directly across from it in the proper column for your film gauge.

For example, a 16mm film that lasts 21 minutes and 11 seconds is 762'24.

	TIME-TO-FOOTAGE CONVERSION CHART		
	16mm	35mm	70mm
Secs	Ft'Fr	Ft'Fr	Ft'Fr
1	0'24	1'08	1'11
2	1'08	3'00	3'09
3	1'32	4'08	5'08
4	2'16	6'00	7'06
5	3'00	7'08	9'05
6	3'24	9'00	11'03
7	4'08	10'08	13'02
8	4'32	12'00	15'00
9	5'16	13'08	13'11
10	6'00	15'00	18'09
11	6'24	16'08	20'08
12	7'08	18'00	22'06
13	7'32	19'08	24'05
14	8'16	21'00	26'03
15	9'00	22'08	28'02
16	9'24	24'00	30'00
17	10'08	25'08	31'11
18	10'32	27'00	33'10
19	11'16	28'08	35'08
20	12'00	30'00	37'06

	16mm	35mm	70mm
TIME-TO-FOOTAGE CONVERSION CHART			
Secs	Ft'Fr	Ft'Fr	Ft'Fr
21	12'24	31'08	39'05
22	13'08	33'00	41'03
23	13'32	34'08	43'02
24	14'16	36'00	45'00
25	15'00	37'08	46'11
26	15'24	39'00	48'10
27	16'08	40'08	50'08
28	16'32	42'00	52'06
29	17'16	43'08	54'05
30	18'00	45'00	56'03
31	18'24	46'08	58'02
32	19'08	48'00	60'00
33	19'32	49'08	61'11
34	20'16	51'00	63'10
35	21'00	52'08	65'08
36	21'24	54'00	67'06
37	22'08	55'08	69'05
38	22'32	57'00	71'03
39	23'16	58'08	73'02
40	24'00	60'00	75'00
41	24'24	61'08	76'11
42	25'08	63'00	78'10
43	25'32	64'08	80'08
44	26'16	66'00	82'06
45	27'00	67'08	84'05
46	27'24	69'00	86'03
47	28'08	70'08	88'02
48	28'32	72'00	90'00
49	29'16	73'08	91'11
50	30'00	75'00	93'10
51	30'24	76'08	95'08
52	31'08	78'00	97'06
53	31'32	79'08	99'05
54	32'16	81'00	101'03
55	33'00	82'08	103'02
56	33'24	84'00	105'00
57	34'08	85'08	106'11
58	34'32	87'00	108'10
59	35'16	88'08	110'08
60	36'00	90'00	112'06

508

The chart below gives the footages for time in minutes:

	TIME-TO-FOOTAGE CONVERSION CHART		
	16mm	35mm	70mm
Mins	Feet	Feet	Ft'Fr
1	36	90	112'06
2	72	180	225'00
3	108	270	337'06
4	144	360	450'00
5	180	450	562'06
6	216	540	675'00
7	252	630	787'06
8	288	720	900'00
9	324	810	1,012'06
10	360	900	1,125'00
11	396	990	1,237'06
12	432	1,080	1,350'00
13	468	1,170	1,462'06
14	504	1,260	1,575'00
15	540	1,350	1,687'06
16	576	1,440	1,800'00
17	612	1,530	1,912'06
18	648	1,620	2,025'00
19	684	1,710	2,137'06
20	720	1,800	2,250'00
21	756	1,890	2,362'06
22	792	1,980	2,475'00
23	828	2,070	2,587'06
24	864	2,160	2,700'00
25	900	2,250	2,812'06
26	936	2,340	2,925'00
27	972	2,430	3,037'06
28	1,008	2,520	3,150'00
29	1,044	2,610	3,262'06
30	1,080	2,700	3,375'00

TIME-TO-FOOTAGE CONVERSION CHART			
	16mm	35mm	70mm
Mins	Feet	Feet	Ft'Fr
31	1,116	2,790	3,487'00
32	1,152	2,880	3,600'00
33	1,188	2,970	3,712'06
34	1,224	3,060	3,825'00
35	1,260	3,150	3,937'06
36	1,296	3,240	4,050'00
37	1,332	3,330	4,162'06
38	1,368	3,420	4,275'00
39	1,404	3,510	4,387'06
40	1,440	3,600	4,500'00
41	1,476	3,690	4,612'06
42	1,512	3,780	4,725'00
43	1,548	3,870	4,837'06
44	1,584	3,960	4,950'00
45	1,620	4,050	5,062'06
46	1,656	4,140	5,175'00
47	1,692	4,230	5,287'06
48	1,728	4,320	5,400'00
49	1,764	4,410	5,512'06
50	1,800	4,500	5,625'00
51	1,836	4,590	5,737'06
52	1,872	4,680	5,850'00
53	1,908	4,570	5,962'06
54	1,944	4,860	6,075'00
55	1,980	4,950	6,187'06
56	2,016	5,040	6,300'00
57	2,052	5,130	6,412'06
58	2,088	5,220	6,525'00
59	2,124	5,310	6,637'06
60	2,160	5,400	6,750'00

510

APPENDIX III

This chart converts footage to both non-drop frame (NDF) and drop frame (DF) timecode for 35mm film. You'll notice that the NDF code is the same as the running time of the footage. This is only the case for 35mm film which has been converted in telecine with a pulldown and which is digitized into a 24 frame project. In the case of a 30 frame project, the DF code will accurately represent running time. In that case, this chart will provide a handy conversion from NDF code (if you are editing in that format) to running time. Note that every ten minutes the drop frame time code does not add two frames compared to the non drop frame.

FOOTAGE/TIME CODE CONVERSION

35m	NDF Code	DF Code	35m	NDF Code	DF Code	35m	NDF Code	DF Code
5	00:00:03.10	00:00:03.10	95	00:01:03.10	00:01:03.12	185	00:02:03.10	00:02:03.14
10	00:00:06.20	00:00:06.20	100	00:01:06.20	00:01:06.22	190	00:02:06.20	00:02:06.24
15	00:00:10.00	00:00:10.00	105	00:01:10.00	00:01:10.02	195	00:02:10.00	00:02:10.04
20	00:00:13.10	00:00:13.10	110	00:01:13.10	00:01:13.12	200	00:02:13.10	00:02:13.14
25	00:00:16.20	00:00:16.20	115	00:01:16.20	00:01:16.22	205	00:02:16.20	00:02:16.24
30	00:00:20.00	00:00:20.00	120	00:01:20.00	00:01:20.02	210	00:02:20.00	00:02:20.04
35	00:00:23.10	00:00:23.10	125	00:01:23.10	00:01:23.12	215	00:02:23.10	00:02:23.14
40	00:00:26.20	00:00:26.20	130	00:01:26.20	00:01:26.22	220	00:02:26.20	00:02:26.24
45	00:00:30.00	00:00:30.00	135	00:01:30.00	00:01:30.02	225	00:02:30.00	00:02:30.04
50	00:00:33.10	00:00:33.10	140	00:01:33.10	00:01:33.12	230	00:02:33.10	00:02:33.14
55	00:00:36.20	00:00:36.20	145	00:01:36.20	00:01:36.22	235	00:02:36.20	00:02:36.24
60	00:00:40.00	00:00:40.00	150	00:01:40.00	00:01:40.02	240	00:02:40.00	00:02:40.04
65	00:00:43.10	00:00:43.10	155	00:01:43.10	00:01:43.12	245	00:02:43.10	00:02:43.14
70	00:00:46.20	00:00:46.20	160	00:01:46.20	00:01:46.22	250	00:02:46.20	00:02:46.24
75	00:00:50.00	00:00:50.00	165	00:01:50.00	00:01:50.02	255	00:02:50.00	00:02:50.04
80	00:00:53.10	00:00:53.10	170	00:01:53.10	00:01:53.12	260	00:02:53.10	00:02:53.14
85	00:00:56.20	00:00:56.20	175	00:01:56.20	00:01:56.22	265	00:02:56.20	00:02:56.24
90	00:01:00:00	00:01:00:02	180	00:02:00:00	00:02:00:04	270	00:03:00:00	00:03:00:06
360	00:04:00:00	00:04:00:08	810	00:09:00:00	00:09:00:18	1260	00:14:00:00	00:14:00:26
450	00:05:00:00	00:05:00:10	900	00:10:00:00	00:10:00:18	1350	00:15:00:00	00:15:00:28
540	00:06:00:00	00:06:00:12	990	00:11:00:00	00:11:00:20	1540	00:16:00:00	00:16:01:00
630	00:07:00:00	00:07:00:14	1080	00:12:00:00	00:12:00:22	1630	00:17:00:00	00:17:01:02
720	00:08:00:00	00:08:00:16	1170	00:13:00:00	00:13:00:24	1720	00:18:00:00	00:18:01:04

GLOSSARY

A

A & B Roll Printing The process of cutting negative, and assembling it so alternating shots are placed on two strands of film running parallel to each other. All the odd cuts are placed on one strand (cuts one, three, five, seven, etc.) and the even cuts on the other (two, four, six, eight, etc.). Because of the alternating nature of this layout, this process is also called *checkerboarding*. Black opaque leader is cut in between these shots. When the negative is printed, both strands are run, printing all the shots together onto one piece of print film. This method is more expensive than regular *single strand printing* (also called *A-roll printing* since all cuts are placed on one single roll) but is used on some films to create the fades and dissolves without going to a second generation optical. It is also the only method used in cutting negative for 16mm films.

A Camera See *B Camera*.

A-Frame Because of the difference in frame projection rate between film and *NTSC* video, a *3:2 pulldown* is used when transferring film to video. In this system, only the first frame of each five frame video sequence is exactly the same as its matching film frame (the first in the four frame film sequence). That frame is called the A-frame. The significance of knowing which frame is the A-frame in any roll of video dailies is that the computer editing machine can easily determine which film frames were duplicated in the pulldown process to create the videotape. When it *digitizes* the videotape into the digital editing system at 24 FPS it then knows to drop the video fields with these duplicated frames. As a result, the editor will be cutting from video that exactly matches the film, frame for frame.

A-Mode A method of sorting an *EDL* in which all of the *events* are organized then recorded in the order they appear in the edit.

A-Roll Printing A method of negative cutting in which all negative is cut onto one continuous strand, as opposed to *A & B Roll Printing*. This is the most common method of answer printing 35mm films. Also called *single strand printing*.

A-Side The first part of an *optical* dissolve, the take which leads into the dissolve.

A-Wind Used to describe the position of the emulsion of film negative relative to the center of the wound–up film. A-wind film has its emulsion facing down to the center. A-wind film is common for projected film (work picture, release prints, etc.). See also *B-wind*.

Academy Leader Leader placed at the head of each reel of film and conforming to the standards set by the Academy of Motion Picture Arts and Sciences (AMPAS). From the projection start mark on this leader, it is exactly eight seconds (12 feet in 35mm, four feet and 32 frames in 16mm) until the first frame of the picture.

Academy Roll-Off A standard for monaural movie theatre sound established by the Academy of Motion Picture Arts and Sciences. It involves decreasing much of the high-frequency sound. This roll-off is what the newer film sound systems (such as *Dolby*, *DTS* and *SDDS*) try to avoid.

Access Time The speed of a hard drive or other storage device, i.e. how long it takes to locate a particular bit of information on a computer's hard drive.

A.C.E. The Association of Cinema Editors, an honorary society of editors.

Acmade Coding Machine A coding machine that uses a heating element to emboss eight–digit code numbers onto the edge of the film from a roll of colored tape.

Act Break In television, that time in the running of the show where the action is stopped to allow for a commercial. Television networks put time constraints on the placement of act breaks so the commercials do not come too close together. The assistant editor will generally insert a *banner* at this point reading "Insert Commercial Here."

Add-A-Plate See *Console*.

Address Track Time Code See *LTC*.

ADO Ampex Digital Optics. A digital effects system sold by Ampex. In some cases this term has become a generic one referring to any machine in an *on-line* editing bay that creates optical effects using video.

ADR Automatic Dialogue Replacement. See *Looping*.

AES/EBU A standard for digital audio and video set by the Audio Engineering Society and the European Broadcast Union. It is used by most media, including CDs and D1 videotape.

AIFF One of several standardized formats for digital sound.

Alignment Tones In sound, a set of tones conforming to industry-established standards for recording sound. They are specific frequencies laid down at a specific volume, so when the tape they are recorded onto is played back aligned to these tones it will have the same volume and equalization properties it did when it was originally recorded. In video, these tones are often accompanied by a set of color bars allowing the color settings to be properly adjusted for playback.

Alpha Channel In video editing, a separate channel containing only the processing information used to determine how to show the other three channels of color (red, green and blue) such as luminance or chroma. It is often used for the overlaying of titles or other *keying* information. It is also called a *matte channel* since it is used for *matting* two images, especially if one is a title, together.

Ambiance (1) Low level sounds that play behind specific sound effects to set a mood or suggest the character of a particular location. Distant water or traffic suggest a different feel than a distant train horn or a throbbing, factory sound. (2) Another name for *room tone.*

Analog Soundtrack The most common soundtrack format. It consists of recorded electrical waves which are then converted into sound signals. Technically, it is a signal that varies continuously rather than in discrete steps like the more recent *digital soundtrack* format.

Anamorphic A method of getting wide-screen images onto normal 35mm film. While shooting, a special lens is put on the camera to squeeze the image. A matching lens reverses the process during projection. If you were to look at a frame of anamorphic film without "unsqueezing" it (such images would be called "squeezed") it would look like the writing on a balloon after the air has been let out of it. The normal *aspect ratio* for an anamorphic image is 2.35:1.

Answer Print A timed (color-corrected) print of a film. It may or may not have a soundtrack *married* to it.

Anti-Aliased Fonts Computer generated typefaces (or *fonts*) programmed to be more rounded on their edges. This gives them more pleasing, smoother lines.

Artifact An artificial defect or distortion in a visual image created when it is being *digitized*. Artifacts generally show up as ragged edges or added dots of color in places they don't belong.

ASCII American Standard Code for Information Interchange. A commonly used format for exchanging information between computers. (Pronounced "ask-key.")

Aspect Ratio The ratio of a image's screen width to its screen height. Most movies today are projected at a ratio of 1.85:1, that is, the image is 1.85 times wider than it is high. A second, less-used feature ratio is the slightly taller 1.66:1. Wide-screen *anamorphic* films have a 2.35:1 ratio. Television is shot at a 1.33:1 (also written as 4:3) ratio. The newer wide screen televisions have a ratio of about 1.78:1 (they are usually called *16x9*). A full frame of 35mm film has a 1.33:1 ratio, this is why the television set was developed with that ratio.

Assemble Editing A method of on-line tape editing. The control track, time code, the sound and picture are all recorded at the same time and joined to the end of the previous edit. This method is not as good as *insert editing* because it can lead to jumps in the recorded time code and control track.

Assembly (1) A rough piecing-together of the cut, sometimes called a "rough cut." The assembly consists of all of the scenes and virtually all of the dialogue shot, and usually runs quite a bit longer than the finished film. (2) In video, the process of editing the videotape in an *on-line* session to match the edits the film's editor made on the digital editing workstation in the editing room, called the *off-line* session. This assembly, comparable to *negative cutting* on film, is done from the high-quality *video master* tapes created from the original camera *negative*.

Assembly List See *Negative Cut List*.

ATV Advanced Television. One of the many systems for the new digital television standards. See also *DTV* and *HDTV*.

Audio The sound portion of a film or videotape.

Audio Layback The process of recording the final sound *mix* onto the completed *video master* videotape.

Auto Assembly An on-line tape editing session in which an *Edit Decision List* is used to automatically recreate the *off-line* edit made in the editing room.

516   **Avid** A brand name for a digital editing machine.

B

B Camera A second camera running simultaneously with the main camera during a shot. Footage shot with the B Camera is often referred to as *B Camera footage* regardless of whether the main, or A, camera was running.

B-Mode A method of sorting an *EDL* in which all of the events are organized then recorded, one *source tape* at a time, in the order they appear in the edit. This requires fewer changes of the source reels resulting in a faster edit session.

B-Negative Takes shot and developed but not printed. These are the takes remaining after the director's *circled takes* have been separated out of the processed negative and printed.

B-Side The second part of an *optical* dissolve; the take coming after the dissolve. See also *A-Side*.

B & W Black and White. Also written as *B/W*.

B-Wind Used to describe the position of the emulsion of film negative relative to the center of the wound–up film. B-wind film has its emulsion facing away from the center (an easy mnemonic is to say it has its base wound down). B-wind film is common to camera original and film used as a printing element. See also *A-wind*.

Balance Stripe See *Stripe*.

Balancing See *Reel Balancing*.

Backup A copy of the computer files containing all of the logs and edit lists for a film edited digitally. If something is lost through technical error or natural catastrophe, the information can be restored with minimal loss of data and time. Backups can be made onto any number of formats. The most common are floppy computer disks, magneto-optical (MO) disks, or large capacity computer disks like the Zip or Jaz drives.

Banner The titles announcing when a scene or a shot is missing. Equivalent to Scene Missing Leader. Another often seen banner says "Insert Commercial Here."

Bars and Tone The combination of *Color Bars* and a 1000Hz *Alignment Tone* appearing at the beginning of videotapes. They are used to properly set video and sound levels during playback.

Base The bottom side of 35mm film. It is shiny, as opposed to the top part of the film—the *emulsion*—which is dull. Technically, the base is a plastic material onto which the three layers of color film stock (or the one layer of black and white) are glued. 16mm reversal film projects properly when its base is on top. Also called the *Cel* side of the film.

Batch Digitizing The process of *digitizing* footage from a source tape using a database so the computer editing machine controls the source tape machine, stopping and starting at the code numbers included in that database.

517

Beep A one frame long tone used to mark a specific location on a soundtrack. Commonly used at the beginning of reel (where it is called a *head beep*), two seconds before the first frame of the picture (nine feet after the start mark in 35mm, three feet and 24 frames in 16mm). It is also used in the tail leader, two seconds after the last frame of picture (where it is called a *tail beep*). Also called a *pop*.

Bench An editing table. The term usually refers to the entire editing set-up on the bench, including the synchronizer, splicer, sound box and rewinds.

Betamax Also called "Beta." A videotape format that uses 1/2" tapes. Though this format is almost never seen in the home today, it has extensive use in professional editing because of its superior quality to the more common VHS format. Professionals use two different brands of Beta tape (*Beta-SP* and *Digital Beta*) for high quality recordings.

Beta-SP A very high-quality tape format that uses Beta tapes.

Blacking The process of recording nothing more than the *control track* onto a videotape. When tapes are used that have already been blacked, they are called *pre-blacked tapes*. See also *striping*.

Blanking As a video image is created or projected an electronic gun traces a path on the television screen one line at a time, from left to right.

In the brief time as the gun is moving from the right edge of one line to the left edge of the next, that gun is turned off. This off-time is called *horizontal blanking*. The time in which the gun is off while it goes from the bottom of one field to the top of the next field is called *vertical blanking*. The amount of permissible blanking is set by the *Quality Control* engineers at each individual network or studio.

Blow-Up An *optical* in which a portion of the frame has been enlarged to fill the whole frame. Often used when some unwanted object (such as a microphone) appears in the frame. The image is then blown up so the unwanted object is pushed outside of the frame and disappears. When a film is shot in 35mm but released in 70mm (or shot in 16mm and released in 35mm) the entire film is optically blown-up. This larger format print is then called the *blow-up*.

Blue Screen A device used on set to combine two images created separately. In this process, a foreground image (say, a person) is photographed against a solid blue or green screen. Later, either *optically* or using *CGI*, the colored background is replaced with another image (say, a Parisian street or a floating space ship) that was photographed separately. In video this process is called a *Chroma Key*, and the color being replaced by the background scene is called the *key*.

Boot Up To start your computer.

Broadcast Quality A video show of professional enough technical quality to be aired by a television station. Final determination as to whether a tape is technically good enough to be broadcast quality is done by the QC (Quality control) divisions of the studios and networks.

Bump When two sounds are cut together it is possible that the background sounds will not match exactly. The effect of the different sounds cutting together is called a bump. The tasks of *Dialogue Splitting* and *Mixing* are designed to smooth out these bumps and result in one seamless soundtrack.

Bumpers The short piece of video seen during commercial breaks of television shows identifying the program and telling the audience that the show will return shortly.

Burn-in (1) Superimposing something (usually titles or some other wording) over already shot action. (2) A *window dub* videotape, in which time code or other numbers are superimposed onto the visible picture area.

Burning a CD The process of taking digital information, usually sound or music, and recording it onto a recordable CD. The machine that writes onto the CD is called a *burner*.

Butt Splicer A splicer joining picture or track with a vertical splice. See also *Diagonal Splicer*.

C

C-Mode A method of sorting an *EDL* in which all of the events are organized then recorded in order of ascending reel numbers and time code within each source reel. This means all the edits from one reel are recorded before the recorder moves on to another reel. This ends up saving a tremendous amount of time in the *Assembly* since the same tapes don't have to be loaded, unloaded and reloaded again.

Camera Original The actual film that went through the camera during shooting. See *Negative, Original Camera Negative* and *Reversal.*

Camera Report The form filled out by the camera department listing all of the takes shot on any particular roll of negative and their cumulative footage. Takes the director liked are circled for printing. All other takes are processed but not printed (see *B-negative*).

Caption A title that runs on the lower third of the screen identifying a character on the screen, a location or time, or translates a line of foreign dialogue.

CARA Classification and Ratings Administration. The ratings division of the MPAA responsible for assigning the G, PG, PG-13, R or NC-17 rating to a film.

Card A credit that remains stationary on screen, usually fading in and out. A card with only one name is called a *Single Card* a card with more than one name is called a *shared card*. A list of credits that move up or down the screen is called a *Crawl* or a *Roll-Up*.

519

CCIR The Committee Consultative International Radio. This predominately European organization, much like SMPTE, was responsible for setting standards for video and audio production and broadcast. It has since been replaced by the ITU.

Cel See *Base.*

CGI Computer Generated Imagery. The process of using computers to manipulate film to create special visual effects. See also *Optical.*

Change List A list of change notes that helps the assistant make the conformations between two versions of the same edit.

Change Notes See *Conformation Notes.*

Changeover Cue The second projectionist cue. When the projectionist sees it, he or she should switch the projection from one projector to another.

Changeovers The marks placed in the upper right hand corner of the frame to cue the projectionist to change from one reel to another. The first set of marks is called the *Motor Cue* and the second is called the *Changeover Cue*.

Changeover Tails The amount of footage added to the end of reel (usually 24 frames, but sometimes less) that ensures the projectionist does not make the changeover too early in the action.

Cheated Track A piece of track cut into the edited work track purposely out of sync with the picture.

Checkerboarding The process of placing successive pieces of cut negative or sound on alternating tracks so all odd cuts are on one strand and all even cuts are on a second. Also called *A & B Roll Printing*.

China Girl A standardized image of a white woman's face used by labs and optical houses as a reference to determine proper color balance.

Chroma A term, short for *chrominance*, referring to the amount of color in a video image. See also *luminance*.

Chroma Key The video process of combining two separately created images using a *key* color (usually blue or green). An image is shot against a screen made up of the pre-selected key color and a second image is then inserted everywhere the key color exists in the first image. Also called *keying*. See also *Blue Screen*.

Chrominance The amount of color in a video image. Black, gray and white have no chrominance. Often referred to as *Chroma*.

Cinch Marks A series of scratches, usually horizontal, found on the film if it has been wound too tightly or twisted too hard while being wound.

Cinetabs Small cardboard tabs which are slid into rolled-up film and used for the identification of rolls of picture and track. Also called *Trim Tabs*.

Cinex See *Wedge*.

Circled Takes Takes of picture or sound selected by the director for printing or transferring. These selected takes are circled on the *camera report*. Also called *kept takes*.

520　**Clapper** Also, clapsticks. See *Slate*.

Click Track A musical rhythm. Each click represents the length of film for one musical beat. A click of 12/0 denotes one beat of music for every 12 frames.

Clipping When an electronic signal, either video or audio, is recorded at too high a level the recording equipment will simply quit at its maximum level. When there is more sound volume or color intensity in the original than in the recording, the recorded image is said to have been "clipped."

Clone A copy of a digital tape, such as D-1 or D-2, to another digital tape. Because the process is completely digital there is no loss of picture quality, the copy is identical to the original.

Close-captioned An electronic signal imbedded into the video signal of a broadcast that, when played back through a special decoder, superimposes subtitles on the screen containing the dialogue in the show.

Code Number A number physically printed onto the edge of the film, in ink. It is used to identify pieces of film and track in the editing room and to keep the picture and track in sync. These numbers usually run one every 16 frames (one 35mm foot). Also called an *Edge Number*. Not to be confused with a *Key* Number, or a *Latent Edge Number*.

Coding Machine A machine, such as the *Acmade* or *Moy*, that inks *code numbers* onto the edge of the film and track. Also called a *numbering machine* or a *numbering block*.

Color Balancing See *Timing*.

Color Bars The standardized set of graduated vertical colors recorded to a precise standard onto a videotape. On playback, the monitors can be set to match this standard. Color bars are usually accompanied by a matching length of sound *alignment tone*. When combined they are often referred to as *Bars and Tone*.

Color Card A standardized card containing a scale of colors. When photographed and developed, it is easy to tell just how far the printed colors deviate from the actual colors. Such cards facilitate the color correction (or *Timing*) of the dailies at the lab. see also *Grey Card*.

Color Correction See *Timing*.

Colorist The telecine operator who makes the original sunk transfer from the original negative. He or she will be color timing each shot as closely as possible to final quality.

Color Video Analyzer See *Hazeltine*.

Complimentary Angle See *Reverse*.

Component Video A video signal in which the various Red, Green and Blue *Chrominance* signals (as well as the *Luminance* signals) are kept separate from one another. It makes for a much better quality picture than *Composite Video*. See also *R-G-B*.

Composite Shot Another term for *Blue Screen*.

Composite Video A video signal in which the Red, Green and Blue *Chrominance* signals (as well as the *Luminance* signals) are combined using one of the coding standards—PAL, NTSC and SECAM. It makes for an inferior quality picture to *Component Video*.

521

Compression A computer process, usually performed during *digitizing*, that attempts to throw away redundant computer numbers and conserve space on the computer's *hard drive*. The more compression (that is, the higher the *compression rate*) is used, the more degraded the image will appear. Most of the digital editing machines use their own compression formats. Some more standardized formats are JPEG, MPEG, LZW and *Quicktime*.

Compression Rate The amount of *compression* performed on a particular image. On Avid, for instance, those are assigned "AVR numbers" such as AVR65 or 77.

Conform (1) A 35mm negative made from a videotape master. (2) For other uses see *Conformation*.

Conformation (1) A change made to a reel after it has been *locked*. (2) The process of negative matching, i.e. *negative conforming*. (3) In video editing, the process of matching the edits made in video to the 35mm film so there is a complete 35mm cut work picture and track, matching the video cut in every way. Usually done with a computer generated *Cut List*.

Conformation Notes A list minutely and accurately documenting any conformations made to a reel. Also called *Change Notes*.

Console A Moviola with one picture head and two sound heads. Often a second sound head is attached onto a regular Moviola. This attachment is called an *Add-a-plate*.

Consolidation 1) As a computer's *hard drive* begins to fill up, the files on the drive become *fragmented*. This will often slow down the movement of data on and off the drive. To fix this, you need to clear enough space on the disk so you can retransfer the fragmented file to this new continuous space. This process is called consolidation or *defragmentation*. 2) On a digital editing machine, the process of removing from the hard drive any material not used in an edit.

Contact Print A print from a piece of negative made by physically pressing the negative against another piece of undeveloped film and shooting light through the two. This exposes the second piece of film, creating an image the reverse in color and light (black becomes white and vice versa) from the negative. *Dailies* are one example of contact prints.

Continuity (1) A list of all of the scenes in a version of a film, with scene numbers and short scene descriptions. Also called a *Reel Continuity*. (2) The practice of matching action or some other aspect of a scene—wardrobe, make-up and hair, props, etc.—so the two shots appear continuous when cut together.

Contrast Ratio The ratio of the brightest area in an image to the darkest area. Film has, inherently, a larger contrast ratio than video.

522 **Control Track** A signal on a videotape used to control speed and synchronization during playback. Think of it as video's version of sprocket holes. When you *stripe* a blank tape you are essentially adding a control track to it.

Conversion The process of converting an image from a system with one frame-rate to one with another. Standardized frame rates in film and are 24, 25, 29.97 and 30.

Core A two– or three–inch diameter plastic disk, exactly the width of the film you are using. The film, or track, is wound onto the cores for editing or projection, instead of winding it onto *take–up reels*.

Coverage The various angles a director shoots for a scene.

Crash A computer malfunction so drastic that the machine stops working completely. This is a Very Bad Thing.

Crawl A particular kind of credit optical in which the names move up (or, in rare cases, down) the screen. Also called a *roll–up*.

CRI Color Reversal Intermediate. A particular kind of film that can be *contact printed* directly from the negative, resulting in another negative image, without going through an *interpositive* stage. CRIs were more common when interpositive (IP) stock was inferior to what is used today. Then it was preferable to avoid the extra generation that going to an interpositive and then an internegative would require. Improved IP stock has made CRIs virtually obsolete.

CRI Print A release print from a CRI, rather than from an internegative (IN) or original (EK) print.

Cross-Modulation Test Also called a *cross-mod*. A test done by the sound house making the sound optical transfer to ascertain the exact specifications required to shoot the *soundtrack optical* for the individual lab that will be printing the *married answer print*.

CRT Cathode Ray Tube. The picture tube onto which video images or computer information are projected. Think of it as the television set.

Cut (1) The cut-together work picture and work track. The term is used for picture and track, both together or singly. (2) The place in the film where the editor goes from one take to another.

Cutback Frames When a negative cutter splices the film together, the frame right next to the one being cut away from or into is destroyed. If the editor cuts away from a shot and returns to it at a later point, it is necessary to cut back *after* the frame that will be lost in negative cutting. These frames that cannot be used are called cutback frames. For safety's sake, I like to leave two frames between cutbacks: one for the frame immediately after the frame I cut away from, and a second one for the frame immediately before the piece I am cutting back into.

Cut List See *Negative Cut List*.

Cut Picture See *Work Picture*.

Cutter Moviola A type of upright Moviola without takeup arms. It is easier to thread and gentler on the film than a regular take-up Moviola, making it better as a cutting machine. Some editors work with two cutters, others use one cutter and one take-up.

Cutting Copy The work picture.

Cutting Room Floor According to many actors, actresses and writers, the place where the best parts of their performances or writing usually end up.

523

D

D-1, D-2, D-3, D-5 Four types of digital tape formats used for high-quality recording of videotape *masters*. D-1 is, at present, the highest quality digital videotape available. The biggest difference is that D-1 and D-5 are *component* formats, while D-2 and D-3 are *composite* formats. D-1 and D-2 tapes are housed in different sized cassette shells than D-3 and D-5 tapes. Just to confuse you a bit, there is no D-4 format.

DA-88 A small cassette tape (8mm wide; in fact it uses the popular *Hi-8* home videotape cassette format), able to record up to eight tracks of digital audio. It is now common for a series of DA-88 tapes to be used in the film *mix* rather than 35mm *mag* units. A newer, but similar, tape format is the DA-98 cassette tape.

D-Mode A method of sorting an *EDL* in which all of the events are organized then recorded, one source tape at a time, in the order they appear in the edit with all of the effects performed last.

Dailies Every day during the shooting of a film, the director and some members of the cast and crew view the footage shot the preceding day to verify that everything is proceeding satisfactorily. If it is not, some of the footage may have to be reshot. These screenings are called "dailies screenings" or "rushes." Also used to refer the material screened at the rushes.

DAT Digital Audio Tape. A very small cassette tape onto which two tracks of audio can be recorded. The digital nature of the recording means the tape can be copied countless times (as is often the case in dialog or sound effects editing and mixing) without any loss of quality.

DAW See *Digital Audio Workstation*.

Daylight When it is important that dailies (usually from opticals or reprints) be delivered to the editing room faster than overnight; you can have the laboratory *daylight* the processing. Essentially this means they expedite its processing and printing so you receive it the same day, rather than overnight.

dB An abbreviation for *Decibel*.

Decibel A measure of how loud a sound signal is. Also referred to as *dB*.

Definition A term referring to how sharp, clear or distinct an image is. You can usually see how good or bad an image's definition is by looking at the edges of any object in the image. Hair and other thin objects are the hardest to maintain good definition in a digital environment.

Defragment See *fragmentation*.

Degaussing The process of erasing all sound from a piece of magnetic stock or tape. "Degaussers" are also used to make sure that all of the editing equipment coming into contact with the soundtrack is demagnetized.

Demagnetizing See *degaussing*.

Density The degree of darkness in an image. A dark image is denser than one that is light. Changes in density are achieved by changing all three *timing lights*.

Depth of Field The range of distance away from a lens in which an image is in sharp focus. In general, a well-lit image will have greater depth of field (that is, more area in focus). In close-up shots, for instance, it is good to have enough depth of field that the distance from the front of a person's face (the nose, for instance) to the back of that person's head, is completely in focus.

Desktop The look of the computer screen. On a Macintosh the term is also used to denote the computer screen showing all the hard drives and their contents, as opposed to any screen inside of a program.

Diagonal Splicer A splicer used to join two pieces of track diagonally instead of vertically. Often used in sound and music editing since diagonal splices often smoothes out the differences between the sounds at the cut. See also *butt splicer*.

Dialogue Splitting The process of separating work track pieces that *bump* when played together, onto separate *units* or *elements* so each may be treated separately at the mix.

Digital Audio Workstation (DAW) A computer editing system designed for editing sound or music only.

Digital Beta A high quality Beta tape for recording digital images. Also called *Digibeta* or *DigiBeta*.

Digital Cut The process of outputting a digitally edited sequence or scene onto a tape. Also called a *playout*.

Digital Editing The process of using *Non-Linear Editing* systems, with a digitized picture and sound, to edit film, television shows or other programs.

Digital Soundtrack A recent soundtrack format (like Dolby•D, Sony's SDDS, and Universal's DTS) that records computer numbers which are then converted into sound signals. It is in contrast to the older *analog soundtrack*.

Digital Video Effects (DVE) Computer generated effects, usually performed in an *on-line* session but also possible using some computer non-linear effects packages. Common DVE effects include flipping or flopping the picture, shrinking or spinning it, or placing it inside another image and letting that play within the second picture.

Digitizing The act of taking a visual image on film or videotape and converting it into computer numbers for storage on a computer *hard drive*. In order to save room on the drive some *compression* is usually necessary.

525

Digitizer A separate machine used for *digitizing*. Also called a digitizing station or a Digistation.

Direct A setting on a video deck that essentially passes the signal through the machine without sending it through its electronics. This is a good alternative to the *E to E* setting.

Director The person responsible for creatively piloting all phases of making a film.

Director of Photography The person who, along with the *director*, determines the lighting and camera work on a film. Usually abbreviated as *d.p.*

Director's Cut The edited version of a film presented by the director and editor to the producers and/or studio. It supposedly represents the director's vision of how he or she would like the film to be edited.

Dirty Dupe See *Dupe*.

Dissolve An *optical* in which one image slowly changes into another.

Distributor Usually, the company financing and organizing the publicity and distribution of a film to theatres.

D-M-E Track An *M & E* (music and effects) full-coat track including, usually on channel one, the mixed dialogue, to be used as a reference for foreign looping.

DNU Abbreviation for Do Not Use.

Dolby A soundtrack format, introduced in the mid 1970s, to replace 35mm mono optical sound tracks. Dolby's analog formats use the *4-2-4* encoding system to get four stereo tracks optically married on the print. They also increase the amount of high and low frequencies when compared to the historic Academy mono track. Dolby's recent developments include Dolby *SR*, an analog format with even better sound than the original Dolby format, *Dolby Digital* (a digital sound system), and *SR•D* (a combined analog and digital format).

Domestic Version The major, usually first, release of a film, in the United States and English speaking countries.

DOS Disk Operating System. A series of rather arcane commands telling the computer how to get information on and off the disk drives attached to the system, usually an IBM or compatible computer. The Lightworks system, since it is based on an IBM compatible computer chip, occasionally demands that the assistant manipulate data through its operating system. This is a task most assistants compare to the experience of sitting in a dentist's chair, having root canal work.

Double IP A special process for creating less grainy *opticals* in which two interpositives are made from the original negative rather than one. When the optical is created each IP will offset the grain of the other, resulting in an optical that looks closer to the original take. Because it requires twice as much interpositive and twice and much time to shoot the optical, this is a more expensive path to take.

526 **Double Print** (1) An *optical* in which each frame is printed twice. This is done to slow down the action. An optical in which each frame of the original shot was printed twice would appear to move twice as slowly (at half speed). To slow the action down by one third, you would print each image three times. This is called a *triple print*. (2) On rare occasions, two identical sets of dailies are made, one for the editing room and another for the studio.

Double Reel When the film is ready to be distributed, the 1000 foot editing reels are combined into 2000 foot reels for theatres. This is accomplished by combining editing reels one and two into Double Reel One, editing reels three and four into Double Reel Two, and so on. The original single reels are then referred to as Reel 1A and 1B, Reel 2A and 2B, etc. It is now common practice for labs to mount the cut negative in double reels and print from them. It is also possible to have your *negative cutter* build the reels in this larger size.

Double System A projection system in which the sound and picture are on two separate pieces of film, locked together in projection. This maintains sync as if the two elements were *married* together. You will almost always be screening your film in this manner until the final *married print*.

Drop Frame Time Code A *time code* in which certain numbers are periodically skipped (two frame numbers at every minute except the tenth) in order to make the numbers exactly match real (clock) time. The actual picture frames are not dropped, only numbers are skipped. Because PAL time code runs at real time, this is only necessary on NTSC projects. See also *Non-Drop Frame Time Code*.

Drop Shadow A design for titles in which the letters of the titles have a dark shadow superimposed, slightly below and to the right of them. This makes the letters more readable against background action.

DTS Digital Theater Systems. A digital sound release format in which the sound is not printed directly on the film. The digital track is stored on a special CD-ROM. The *time code* controlling the CD-ROM player is placed on the film next to the stereo *optical* analog track.

DTV Digital Television. One of the many names for a number of new television standards. See also *ATV* and *HDTV*.

Dub 1) For sound, see *Mix* or *looping*. 2) In video, a copy of a videotape. With each copy you introduce some *generation* loss. Digital video formats, like *D-1* or *Digital Beta* drastically reduce these distortions.

Dubbing (1) Mixing the film. (2) Looping. (3) The process of making a copy of a tape, either audio or video.

Dummy A machine able to play back 35mm or 16mm magnetic track interlocked with the pictured and other sound dummies. Typically used at a film *mix*.

Dupe (1) A copy of the picture or track. Picture is often duped onto a piece of cheaper color film. Such dupes are called *slop dupes* or *slop prints*. When track is duped, it is normal to ask for a *one-to-one copy*, which is a sound dupe made at the same volume and equalization as the original. (2) An optical in which a piece of negative is exactly copied to another piece of negative, (usually by making an *interpositive* first). This is done when it is necessary to use the same action more than once in a film.

Dupe Negative A piece of negative created indirectly from another piece of negative (usually by making an intermediate piece of positive or *interpositive* first). Most opticals are dupe negatives.

DVC Digital Video Cassette.

DVE See *Digital Video Effects*.

D/Vision A brand name for a digital editing machine.

Dynamic In a video color correction session it is possible to gradually change settings from one portion of a shot to another. This smooth change is called a *dynamic*.

Dynamic Range (1) In audio, the range between the loudest and softest sounds that a soundtrack can reproduce. The greater the dynamic range the fuller the sound will appear. (2) In video, the range between the picture overload level and the minimum acceptable signal strength that a projection system can handle. See also *Contrast Ratio*.

527

E

ECU An abbreviation for an Extreme Close-Up shot.

E-Mode A method of sorting an *EDL* in which all of the events are organized then recorded, one source tape at a time, in the order they appear on the source tape with all of the effects *events* performed last.

Edge Number See *Code Number.*

Edit Decision List (EDL) A list generated by the computer on which an *off-line* video edit has been made. It lists all of the cuts (called *events*), titles and transitions, the type of cut (e.g. picture only, track only, both), and all of the pertinent time code information from the footage. An equivalent list, giving the matching cuts in terms of the original film numbers, is called a *Film Cut List.*

Edited Master The final edited, though not yet fully color timed, videotape created at the *on-line* editing session. The term is sometimes used for fully color timed tapes as well, which are then used to strike the final copies for air or mass distribution.

Editing Bench A wide table on which most of the editorial equipment sits. As a result, most of the physical cutting of the film, as well as a bulk of the assistant's work, is done on the bench. Both the rewinds and the synchronizer are on this table, as well as the splicers and a host of other equipment. Editors preferring to cut their films on flatbeds do not generally use editing benches as much as editors who cut on uprights since the flatbed itself functions as the bench for most of their work. Sometimes referred to as the *Editing Table.*

Editorial Sync Also called *level sync.* When the location of a picture frame and its synchronous frame of sound pass the picture and sound heads at the same time it is called editorial sync. This is opposed to the sync when a married print runs through a projector and the sound is advanced from the picture, called *projector sync.*

EDL See *Edit Decision List.*

Effect (1) In picture editing, an optical or special photographic manipulation of the film. (2) In sound editing, a specific sound, such as a tire squeal or water dripping. (3) A special manipulation of elements during the shooting of the film, such as the creation of rain or snow.

EK Print A release print from the *camera original* as opposed to an *IP Print* or a *CRI Print.* The abbreviation EK is used because, until recently, most feature films were shot on original negative made by Eastman Kodak.

Electronic Slate A slate with a running time code display on its front surface. As the clapper sticks are struck together the time code number freezes. This makes it obvious to whoever is synching the dailies that this is the frame where the clapper sound should start. Also called an *electronic clapper.*

Electronic Pin Register See *EPR.*

528

Element (1) An individual sound track at the mix. Also called a *unit*. (2) An individual layer of an *optical* which composites more than one layer of film. On a film like *Starship Troopers* a single shot might contain over 250 layers or elements.

Emulsion The light-sensitive side of 35mm film. It is dull, as opposed to the base which is shiny. Your lips will leave a mark when pressed to the emulsion side of the film. In 16mm reversal film, the emulsion side is the down side of the film.

EOR End of Reel. See *LFOA*.

EPR Electronic Pin Register. A device that steadies film as it goes through a telecine. This reduces any horizontal or vertical shifting. Also called a *Steady Gate*.

EPS Electronic Post-Sync. The same thing as *ADR*. See *Looping*.

EQ See *Equalization*.

Equalization The process of adjusting the volume level of individual frequencies of a sound so as to change its tone. Also called *EQ*.

E to E Electronics to electronics. This is a setting on a video deck that essentially passes the signal through the machine when it is idle. This may add some distortion or color changes. Signals should normally be used *direct* and not via E to E settings.

Event In video editing, a visual or sound change. The most common examples of events are cuts or optical effects.

Exposure Wedge See *Wedge*.

Extension In sound or picture editing, a trim added to a piece already used in the film.

529

Eye Sync The process of synching up the picture and track when slates do not exist. It involves finding points in the sound that can also be easily located on the picture, such as door slams. Certain letters of the alphabet also provide good sync points. Words beginning with the letters *b, d, k, p,* or *t,* are likely to be easier to locate pictorially and sound-wise than others.

F

Fades 1) Opticals in which in image gradually goes to black (fade-out) or emerges from black (fade-in). It is also possible to have images fade in from or out to colors other than black. 2) Similarly, you can have a sound fade in which the sound signal fades down to or up from silence

Field Each video frame is actually made up of two intermeshed (called *interlaced*) fields. The first field contains all of the odd scan lines. The gun projecting the lines of picture then shuts off for a brief moment (called the Vertical *Blanking*), moves back up to the top of the image, and begins projecting the second field, containing the even scan lines. Together they make up a full video frame. Thus a field is one-half of a video frame.

Fill (1) Waste film used to space out soundtracks within a reel to preserve synchronization with the picture. It is also called *slug* or *spacing*. (2) In sound editing, background ambiance or tone used to replace any unwanted sounds on the soundtrack. Also called *room tone*.

Film Cut List A list generated by a digital editing system listing all of the cuts, the type of cut (e.g. picture only, track only, both), and all of the pertinent edge code information from the footage needed to help *conform* the printed dailies or cut work print and track to the video edits.

Film Scanner See *Telecine*.

FireWire A new, high-speed method of sending computer data from one place to another. Based on the IEEE1394 standard (don't ask) FireWire promises to raise the level of digital editing to higher standards because it will make it possible to get much more data from the hard drives at a much faster rate. This will also make it easier to *network* multiple editors together more successfully.

First-Generation See *Generation*.

5.1 A standard for audio, used primarily in home videotapes, that includes five channels of sound and a separate low frequency channel.

Flange A platter with a small core at its center. It is used to wind up the film.

Flash Frames As the camera is slowing down at the end of a take it lets more light in. This shows up as a frame or two on the film where the image is very bright. Flash frames, as they are called, are handy for locating the ends of takes.

Flash-to-Flash When *negative* is pulled to create an *optical* or to make a *reprint,* it is always pulled from the flash frame at the beginning of the take to the flash frame at the end. This is called flash-to-flash. This minimizes the possible damage since usable portion of the take is usually not at the very start or end. Also called *Paper-to-Paper*.

Flatbed A type of editing machine. The separate film and soundtrack are run horizontally across this table-like device in sync with each other.

Flipped Track Track that has been turned upside-down, so it cannot be read by the sound head. Track is flipped so it will be in sync and ready to be used in case it is needed. All that has to be done is to unflip the track. Because this places the backside of the *balance stripe* under the sound head, no sound can be recorded on that stripe. This is also why it is not a good idea to flip *full-coat* track.

Flop An optical effect in which the frame is turned around so that what was the left side of the frame becomes the right and vice versa.

Floppy Disk A computer disk, usually about 3-1/2" square. At present they come in two capacities—double density and high density. Make sure you use the right kind—each has its own uses.

Foleys In sound editing, sound effects, often body movement of some sort (such as footsteps or clothes rustle) recorded in sync with picture.

Foley Walker One of the group of people hired specifically to create the foley for a film.

Font The computer term for a typeface. Different style typefaces have different names and can be used in a digital computer editing machine for titles.

Foreigns Another name for the *M & E tracks*, so called because these are the tracks supplied to foreign countries for *mixing*.

Formatting (1) To prepare a computer disk for use, it needs to have certain directory information placed onto it. The process of doing this is called formatting or *initializing*. On large disks, such as magneto optical (MO) disks, there are two degrees of formatting, high-level and low-level. (2) In television, before you hand over a show for finishing, you need to insert leader where commercials, *bumpers*, black, or other programming will be inserted.

Four-Stripe See *Full Coat*.

Four-Track See *Full Coat*.

4-2-4 The method of recording and playing back analog Dolby Stereo sound for film. The tracks are mixed down from their four-track format to a two-track form (called a *Print Master*). It is this two-track version that is transferred to optical track and married to the picture. At the theatres, the Dolby equipment expands the two tracks back into four.

4:2:2 The sampling ratio used in *D1* digital video. For every 4 samples of *luminance* there are 2 samples of each of the combined *chrominance* channels.

4:4:4 A sampling ratio with equal amounts of the *luminance* and both *chrominance* channels.

531

FPS Frames per Second. A rate of speed for projection of a film or video image. Film is normally projected at 24 fps in the United States. Video is projected at approximately 30 fps in the United States and 25 fps in Europe.

Fragmentation As information is erased from and recorded to a computer, the data for any one particular file becomes broken up across different areas of the disk. In other words, it is not saved continuously on the disk. This can slow down the operation of the computer. Periodically it is a good idea to *defragment* the disk to speed it up. There are a number of programs designed to do this; Norton Disk Doctor's Speedisk is one very popular program.

Frame An individual picture on film. Each frame is exposed for 1/48th of a second. The camera shutter is then closed for another 1/48th of a second while the film is pulled down to the next film frame, where it is then exposed for 1/48th of a second. The rapid projection of these succeeding still picture frames, in which the position of the elements within the picture changes slightly from frame to frame, gives the audience the illusion of motion. See also *Persistence of Vision*. In video, a frame is made up of two video *fields* and is projected for approximately 1/30th of a second in the United States and all other countries using the *NTSC* standard.

Frame Line The thin horizontal line between two consecutive frames of film.

Frame Store A digital device designed to store and display a single video frame as a freeze frame. It is often used as a reference in color timing to help the colorist match shots and scenes from later in the film to the stored (already color corrected) frame from earlier in the film. Also called a *Still Store*.

Free Clicks Extra click tracks before a musical piece giving the conductor the tempo for the cue. If there are eight free clicks, for instance, the cue would begin on the ninth click.

Freeze Frame An optical in which a single frame is held for any desired length.

Full Coat 35mm track completely covered with oxide. As many as six tracks of sound can be recorded onto its surface. Other configurations are four and three tracks. For that reason, full coat is also known as *three track*, four track, or six track.

G

Gang One of the wheels of a synchronizer through which film or track is run. Most synchronizers have four gangs.

Gauge The size of film. The most typical sizes are 16mm, 35mm and 70mm.

Generation A stage in the duplication of film, track or video. A copy of a *first-generation* recording (that is, an original recording—either original *negative*, the production sound tapes or the video master) is called *second-generation*. Thus, an interpositive is a second generation piece of film, as is the work print struck from the original negative. Each time a new generation of analog material is made, the quality of the image or sound degrades from the original material. Digital audio or video copies, on the other hand, have almost no perceptible loss of image quality.

Generation Loss As film or video is copied, there is a natural loss in image quality from one generation to the next. One of the advantages of digital video is that there is very little generation loss, allowing copies to be made that are every bit as good as the original.

GIF Graphic Interchange Format. One of several standardized formats for computer pictures. Some others are *Targa* and *TIFF* files.

GIGO Garbage In, Garbage Out. A computer term meaning that the results of any computer operation are only as good as the information you put into it. In other words, if the data you put into your editing machine isn't accurate, any lists using that data will also be inaccurate.

Goodies Sound effects, usually on 35mm track, that have been cut but not built into the units. They are brought to the mix, boxed and ready for insertion into a unit if they are needed. With digital sound editing the need for goodies has all but disappeared.

Grading An English term for *timing*.

Gray Card A standardized card that works exactly like a color card except it shows graduated black-to-white rather than colors. Also called a "gray scale."

Green Screen See *Blue Screen*.

Guillotine Splicer A type of splicer, commonly used in Europe and in 16mm films, using an unperforated roll of clear splicing tape, with the cutting blade to the right side of the block rather than in the center. In fact, there are usually two blades on a Guillotine—one is for straight cuts, the second is for diagonal cuts.

H

Handle (1) An extra number of frames attached to the head and tail of an optical. (2) An extra number of frames at the head and tail of each cut that are saved on the hard drives when the material is *consolidated*. Everything not used in the edit or in these handles is erased from the drives.

Hand Over To give all of the necessary footage and paperwork to the sound and music departments for the beginning of their work. When you hand over your film, you are (in essence) beginning the sound job.

Hard Drive A device that attaches to a computer editing system (or any computer, come to think of it) capable of storing the massive amounts of data necessary to show each frame's image. Usually a series of large capacity hard drives are needed for any production. Other, less roomy, storage devices are *Floppy Disks*, and *Removable Drives*.

Harry A very high-end digital effects system manufactured by Quantel. These are found in *on-line* editing houses only; they are simply too expensive to be used off-line.

Hazeltine The machine the color timer at the lab (or at the optical house) uses to determine how to time the negative. The footage is run through the machine and the timer adjusts the amount of red, blue and green that will be used to print the film while looking at a television monitor showing him what the projected film should look like at those values. Also called a *color video analyzer*.

HDTV High Definition Television. A higher quality, *component video*, television playback format which has better *resolution* image quality and is capable of using wider *16x9* images. There are actually several HDTV standards.

Head Pop See *Beep*.

Head Trim See *Trim*.

Hi-Con Short for "high contrast." A high quality black and white film stock usually used for titles or special effects. It reduces all elements to shades of black and white, thus giving you the maximum contrast between the light and dark elements in the frame. This gives the

533

necessary sharp edges to *superimpose* one element (such as the titles) onto another (such as the background images).

Hi-8 A tape format, 8mm wide, used in amateur videotape cameras. It is also used professionally for the *DA-88* and DA-98 sound tape formats.

High Definition Television See *HDTV*.

Hole A portion of a soundtrack with no sound. Holes should be filled in with *room tone* before screening.

Horizontal Blanking See *Blanking*.

Hot Hole The gate of the film projector where the frame of film being projected sits.

Hybrid editing A style of editing, usually in an *on-line* editing suite, where both *linear* and *non-linear* editing systems are integrated.

I

IATSE The International Alliance of Theatrical Stage Employees. The chief union for most of the technical crafts in filmmaking in the United States and Canada, including editors.

Import To take a computer file created on a different computer or in a different file format and bring it into your own editing program on your own computer.

In point The frame on a source take from which video and/or audio will be inserted into the edit. Often, the editor will select an in point, an *out point*, (these two are the boundaries of the total amount of the source take that will be put into the edit) and a frame to insert the material into.

IN Print See *IP Print*.

Inching Knob A knob on a flatbed that moves the film one frame at a time.

Initializing See *Formatting*.

Ink Number See *Code Number*.

Insert edit In videotape editing, a cut where picture or sound is edited on top of an already recorded time code and control track. This is in contrast to *assemble editing* where the time code and control track are recorded simultaneously with picture or sound.

Insert Shot A close shot of a particular object (such as a newspaper headline) or an action (such as a person turning a key in a lock).

Interlace The process by which two video *fields* are meshed together to make one video frame. First, all of the odd *scan lines* are shown by a video gun, the gun is turned off for a brief period while it repositions itself back up at the top of the frame, then the even scan lines are shown.

Interlock Screening A screening in which the picture and track are on separate elements and are run locked together in sync. Also called *double system*.

Internegative (IN) A duplicate negative struck from an *interpositive*, by *contact printing*.

Interpositive (IP) A piece of negative film stock with a positive image printed on it (having been struck by contact printing directly from a piece of, usually, original negative).

IP/IN The process of making a new negative of a film by striking an interpositive, and from that striking a new negative—the internegative. A few years ago this two-step process was replaced by the CRI process, which eliminated one extra generation of duplication. But advances in the IP/IN stocks now make this the preferable method for release printing and preparing new negatives for opticals.

IP Print A release print from an IP, as opposed to an EK Print. In actuality, the release print is struck from the internegative, which is why the print is also called an *IN Print*.

IPS Inches per Second. A measure of tape speed, usually used to describe audio tape speed.

ITU See *CCIR*.

J

Jam Sync The process of adding time code onto a videotape with time code already on it. A frame is selected and a time code is chosen to start on that frame. When the time code is recorded there might be a jump in the time code between that frame and the previous frame, but the new code will run continuously after that.

Jog A mode of playing a video or sound image slowly back and forth, where the material will follow the movement of a control, e.g. a jog wheel or a key on a keyboard. See also *scrub*.

JPEG The Joint Photographic Experts Group, a group that has developed standards for image *compression*. Because their standard for still picture images is so well known, digital pictures are often referred to as JPEGs. Their standard for moving images is abbreviated as MPEG. Others computer graphic formats are *GIF, Targa* and *TIFF*.

Jump cut A cut where the out and in footage are both from the same take but there is footage in between that is missing.

K

KEM A brand name for a common flatbed editing machine.

KEM Rolls After the rolls of dailies come back to you after the dailies screening, they need to be rearranged for optimum editing. This process involves putting shots the editor will cut away *to* on a separate roll from the shots the editor will cut away *from*.

Kept Takes See *Circled Takes*.

Key Code Electronically readable bar codes imprinted by the film manufacturer onto the edge of the film negative representing the *key numbers* already imprinted there. This number is readable by the machines in a *telecine* session and put onto a computer disk in a format that a digital editing machine can read. Using the Key Code numbers, the machine can create a completely accurate *Film Cut List* to guide in *conforming* the *work print* or the *negative* to the digitally editing scene. Also called *Keykode*.

Key Frame A particular frame of footage to which the editor has assigned a set of parameters that he or she is going to change. For example, a key frame may define a position of a title within a picture. A later key frame will define a different position of the same title and the computer will figure out the speed and position changes that the title will need to go through in order to move from the first to the second key frame. Any effect will have a minimum of two key frames, a start and finish, more complex effects will use more.

Key Number A number imprinted into the edge of the film negative. This number is then exposed onto the print film, giving a unique record of every piece of film used in the movie. Also called a *latent edge number*.

Keying See *Chroma Key* or *Blue Screen*.

Kinescope A film recording of a video image. Also called *kine*. A similar process of transferring video images to film is sometimes called a *transform*.

L

Lab Report The report sent from the laboratory with the picture dailies listing all the takes printed, along with their timing lights.

Lab Roll At the lab, the selected takes from the developed original camera rolls are pulled out and built into rolls of selected takes called Lab Rolls which are then printed to make the picture dailies.

Lap Dissolve An old-fashioned term for *Dissolve*.

Lartec System A computer program a looping editor can use to program a film's loops. It will automatically read the time code from a tape hooked up to it, allowing the editor to easily type in the wording for every loop, and organize all of the loops by character or reel for printing out cue sheets. There are other competing systems that are able to do the same thing.

Latent Edge Number See *Key Number*

Layback See *Audio Layback*.

L-Cut A term used in video editing to denote an edit where the audio and video are cut at different places. See also *Straight cut*.

Leader Film with no image on it, generally a solid color (white, black, green, red and yellow are the most common colors), used for a myriad of purposes. It is used most often at the head and tails of reels to protect the film when it is being wound and rewound. Since the leader is wound on the outside of the reels, the leader will take the typical abuse, rather than the valuable picture. It also provides the thread-up necessary for projection. Because it can be easily written on, it is also used for identification purposes.

Letterbox The black bars at the top and bottom of a video frame blacking off all of the picture area not in the 1.85:1 (or any wide-screen image) *aspect ratio*. This shows the viewer the exact frame that will be projected in the theatre.

Level Sync See *Editorial Sync*.

LFOA Last Frame of Action. The last frame on a reel of film or track before the tail leader begins. Also called LFOP (Last Frame of Picture) and *EOR* (End of Reel).

Lift A series of cut picture and/or track pieces that have been removed from the edited movie and stored intact, rather than being broken apart and stored as *trims*.

Lightworks A brand name for a digital editing machine.

Line Doubling A process of video projection in which the image is projected at a higher video quality than normal. It is often used for projecting large video images with less distortion and color imbalance than on normal projection systems. A more advanced system, called *line quadrupling*, creates an image even better than line doubling. Unfortunately, this process can only correct for projection problems; it cannot repair a video image that is poor to begin with.

Line Quadrupling See *Line Doubling*.

Linear Editing A style of editing on tape in which edits are laid down one after another. When one edit is changed in length, all later edits on the tape need to be remade. See also *Non-linear editing*.

Lined Script The shooting script of the film onto which the script supervisor has noted all of the set–ups shot and what lines of dialogue and action each of the set–ups covered. The term is also used to denote the combination of the lined script and the script supervisor's notes pages, usually facing the pertinent lined script pages and contain information on every take shot including camera and sound roll numbers, length of the action, selected takes, a description of each set-up, and notes given on set for each take.

Lock That point in the editing of the film when the picture editing is completed. The cut is then "locked." This rarely happens until the very end of the film, so it is common parlance in my editing room to say that a film is "latched" instead (locked, but liable to be opened at any time)

LokBox A machine negative cutters use to accurately synchronize the picture image on a video monitor and the negative they are matching on their synchronizers.

Loop (1) An individual line of dialogue created in looping. (2) A short piece of 35mm or 16mm track which has been joined at its ends to form a continuous band. When played, it will go around in a circle, providing a smooth, continuous sound with no clear start or finish. (3) A similar continuous repetition of sound can be achieved using digital workstations by marking a section and repeating it.

Looping Dialogue replacement. Sometimes called *dubbing*, *ADR* or *EPS*. The actor watches the film and hears the dialogue to be replaced in a set of headphones, while speaking the line into a microphone.

LTC Longitudinal, or Linear, Time Code. One of two types of time code that can be placed on a tape. LTC is the analog time code recorded onto an unused audio channel or on a track specifically reserved for time code, sometimes called an *Address Track*. As a result, LTC is sometimes called *Address Track Time Code*. The distinguishing feature of LTC is that it is necessary for the tape to be moving in order to be read. The other type of code is called *VITC*, Vertical Interval Time Code.

Luminance A term referring to the brightness of an image as opposed to how colorful it is (the *chrominance* or *chroma*).

M

538

M & E Track A mixed full-coat with the music on one channel (usually channel two), the mixed effects on another channel (usually track three, or tracks three and four), and no dialogue. This track is sent to foreign countries to create versions of the film in their language. There, they lay their own dialogue onto the empty first channel of a copy of this M & E track. In practice, the English dialogue is generally put onto channel one as a reference for the foreign looping editors, creating a *D-M-E* track.

Mag Soundtrack stock. If the track is wound so the oxide part of the track is facing up, the reel is said to be wound *mag up* or *mag out*. If the track is wound so the oxide is facing into the reel, the reel is said to be wound *mag down* or *mag in*.

Magneto Optical Disk (MO Disk) See *Optical Disk*.

Main Titles All of the titles appearing at or near the beginning of a film. The card with the name of the film is also called the Main Title.

Marking-Up Tracks See *Popping Tracks*.

Married Print At no time during the shooting or editing of a film are the sound and picture on the same piece of film. It is not until the film is ready to go into the theatres that the two are combined, or "married" to each other. The resulting print is called a married print or a married *answer print*. See also *Optical Track*.

Master (1) A shot, usually the widest, containing most or all of the action for a given scene. (2) The *internegative* from which all *release prints* of a film are made. (3) The original video transfer, sometimes called a *video master*, from which all videotape copies are made. If this master is of an edited show it is referred to as the *Edited Master*.

Matte Channel See *Alpha Channel*.

Matte Shot An optical in which part of one shot is combined with part of another to create a third shot not previously existing. An example would be taking a shot of an astronaut shot in a studio, combining it with a shot of a lunar landscape, resulting in a final shot in which the astronaut appears to be on the moon. See *Blue Screen*.

Media 100 A brand name for a digital editing machine.

Mix The combination of all of the many sound elements—dialogue, music, and sound effects—into one cohesive and balanced soundtrack. Also called the *dub*.

Mixed Mag A single mono *stripe* of the mono *mix* of a film. Sometimes the mix is put on a piece of *full coat* mag because full coat is more durable. If the mix is in stereo, and thus needs more than one channel, it must be put on full coat.

Mixing Board An electronic console with separate volume and equalization controls for each of a large number of sounds. The mixer (or recordist) adjusts each of the sounds and then is able to combine them into the final soundtrack. Also called a *Mixing Console*.

MO Disk (Magneto Optical Disk) See *Optical Disk*.

Monitor A television screen designed solely to accept signals from a video playback machine, such as a videotape player. The best monitors do not pick up standard television signals from the air.

MOS A picture take for which no sound was shot. The rumor is that this term comes from the old German filmmakers who used to say that a shot was done "mit out sound." (I'm not kidding here).

Motor Cue The first changeover cue. When the projectionist sees it, he or she should start up the motor on the next projector without turning on its picture or sound. See also *Changeover Cue*.

MOW A Movie Of the Week. A feature length film shot specifically for television. Typically, MOWs will have longer editing schedules than episodic television shows but far shorter schedules than features.

Moviola A brand name for a common upright editing machine. The separate film and soundtrack are run vertically from the feeding reels below onto the takeup reels above in sync with each other. Also called an "upright Moviola" to differentiate it from a Moviola flatbed.

MPAA Motion Picture Association of America. The trade organization of most of the film *distributors*. They administer the film ratings though their *CARA* division.

MPEG Moving Pictures Experts Group. See *JPEG*.

Multi-Track Tape Any audio tape that can record more than one channel. It is typically used to refer to tapes able to record 24 or more channels.

Mute Print See *Silent Answer Print*.

N

Nagra A professional brand of audio recorder. There are mono, stereo and time coded Nagras in the field today.

Negative Sometimes abbreviated as *neg*. Original film exposed in the camera, in which the polarity of the image is reversed—black becomes white, white becomes black. Also called *camera original*. Original camera film that records an image without reversing the polarity is called, paradoxically, *reversal* original.

Negative Assembly The process of stringing together all of the processed, selected dailies takes, for printing.

Negative Cut List A computer generated list containing all of the details necessary to *conform* the original *negative* or *work print* to a digitally edited sequence. Also called an *Assembly List*.

Negative Cutter The person who takes the *camera original* and cuts it to exactly match the cuts the editor has made on his or her work picture or digital cut (using a *Negative Cut List*). Also called a negative matcher.

Negative Pull List A computer generated list of all of the takes necessary to *conform* a video cut or execute an optical. These lists will typically have the key numbers, negative roll numbers, or Acmade code numbers (if they have been entered into the machine) of the entire take used, from its first to its last frame.

Network (1) On higher budget films there might be several electronic editing machines connected together so multiple editors and assistants can work on all of the footage without swapping hard drives from machine to machine. When these machines are electronically connected to each other, we say they are *networked*. (2) One of the television networks such as ABC, CBS, Fox, or NBC.

NG Takes Takes that are No Good.

Noise Video garbage that interferes with the picture.

Non-Drop Frame Time Code *Time code* in which each frame is given a continuous and successive *time code* number. As a result, the code does not exactly represent real time. The mismatch amounts to an 18 frame overrun every 10 minutes. See also *Drop Frame Time Code*.

Non-linear Editing A style of editing on computer in which edits do not need to be laid down one after another. When one edit is changed in length, all later edits are automatically recalibrated. Another feature of non-linear editing is that source material is quickly accessed. This removes the need to thread tapes, wind down to the proper time code of the source material so it greatly speeds up the editing process.

NTSC The National Television Standards Committee. Responsible for developing a set of standards for composite video in the United States and some other countries. Its distinctive features are that its color image has 525 *scan lines* per *frame* transmitted at 59.94 Hertz (Hz). Not compatible with either *PAL* or *SECAM* standards.

Numbering Machine A machine, such as the *Acmade* that inks *code numbers* onto the edge of the film and track. Also called a *numbering block* or *coding machine*.

O

OCN See *Original Camera Negative.*

Off–Line Editing The process of editing video, usually on digital editing *workstations*, at a *resolution* that is not *broadcast quality*. The edit will later be matched, using an *EDL*, with higher quality images in an *on-line editing* room. The process is analogous to editing work print which will later be matched to the original *negative.*

Off–Line Editing System A video editing system not capable of much color correction and not able to do much special manipulation of the image. It is cheaper and more efficient at assembling all of the material into an edit than an *on-line editing machine*. Off-line editing machines usually work at lower *resolutions* than on-line editing machines. The edits are not of a high enough standard for broadcast by a television station (called *broadcast quality*).

Offset The difference in time codes between two different pieces of material.

One-Light Dailies Dailies not individually timed at the lab, but printed at only one set of *timing lights*.

One-to-One Copy A sound transfer at exactly the same level and equalization as the original sound.

On–Line Editing The process of editing the original *master* videotapes into the final viewing tape at a high enough *resolution* to be *broadcast quality*. The final tape is called the final *edited master.*

On–Line Editing System An expensive video editing system which generates cuts and opticals, as well as color balancing the image. The resulting *Edited Master* is of professional enough quality to be aired by a television station (called *broadcast quality*).

Optical A piece of film that has been manipulated in some way, after it has already been shot, to create some special effect. If the film is manipulated in a computer then the process is typically called *CGI*. See also *dissolve, fades, flip, matte, reposition,* and *reverse.*

Optical Disk A computer disk storing information using optical techniques rather than the normal magnetic techniques. Once the data has been written to the disk it cannot be changed. The data on a *magneto optical disk (MO disk)* can be changed and, as a result, it is sometimes used as a medium for *back-up.*

Optical Recorder A machine that transfers a completed mix on magnetic tape or a mixer's hard drive onto an *Optical Track*. It creates a negative filmed image of the track which is then printed, simultaneously with the cut negative or a dupe negative, to create the final *married print*.

Optical Track The soundtrack on a married print. It appears as a set of squiggly lines at the left side of the picture. When light is projected through the optical track (which is a piece of *film*, not a piece of oxide layered track), the light coming through is read by a photocell behind the film. This photocell decodes the patterns of light into sounds—providing us with the dialogue, music and sound effects that we hear on a film's soundtrack.

Original Camera Negative (OCN) The *negative* run through the camera on the set.

O/S Over the Shoulder. Used to denote a shot in which one character is visible over the shoulder (or another body part) of another character. As an example, a shot in which Abby is visible over Bob's shoulder would be described as ABBY—o/s BOB.

Out A take, no part of which has been used in the film. Also called an *outtake*.

Out point See *in point*.

Output (1) The process of transferring a cut shot, scene, or an entire film from a non-linear editing machine to a videotape for viewing. (2) The process of transferring a completed digital optical from the computer that created it onto a piece of 35mm negative.

Overcranked Shot A shot made at a faster than normal camera speed. When projected, the action will appear to be moving more slowly than normal.

542

P

PAL Phase Alternate Line. A set of standards for composite video in Europe and some other countries. Its distinctive features are that its color image has 625 *scan lines* per *frame* transmitted at 50 Hertz (Hz), or 25 frames per second. Not compatible with either *NTSC* or *SECAM* standards.

Pan A camera move in which the image moves horizontally from one side to the other. A *tilt* moves up and down.

Pan and Scan A videotape transfer of a film in which the filmed image is shifted in order to make the 1.85:1 *aspect ratio* of film fit into to video's much squarer 1.33:1 ratio.

Papering When a negative cutter is putting together the cut reels of a film, often a shot or an optical may be missing. To ensure that the first print off of the cut negative still runs the proper length the cutter will cut in the equivalent amount of leader in place of the shot. This is called "papering."

Paper-to-Paper See *Flash-to-Flash*.

Patch Bay A panel with a series of holes into which a number of video or audio cables can be plugged. This directs their signals from one machine to another (the 3/4" deck to the Avid, for instance).

Perfs The sprocket holes in film. There is one perf per frame in 16mm film, and four per 35mm frame.

Persistence of Vision The human eye can only differentiate movement down to as short a time span as approximately 1/20th of a second. The very foundation of filmmaking is based on this biological fact, since projected film tricks the eye into thinking a series of still frames (projected 1/48th of a second apart) are actually one continuously running image. Though each frame is slightly different from the preceding one, the eye merges them, and your brain retains each image until it is superseded by the next. See also *Frame*.

Phasing The hollow sound occurring when two identical tracks are run in near-perfect sync.

Pick–Up Shot (1) After a shot has been made on the set, the director sometimes wishes to re-do part of the take. This re–do is called a pick–up shot since the director "picks up" the filming part way into the previous set–up. Some script supervisors slate it with a new set–up letter, others use the same letter as the original shot and add the letters "pu" after the shot number. For instance, a pick-up to shot 11A could be called 11B or 11Apu. (2) A shot done at a later date than the bulk of the scene for which it is intended. Often, *insert shots* are picked up near the end of principal photography. Pick-up shots are sometimes made by the *second unit*.

Pixel A single dot of visual picture. Enormous numbers of pixels, strung together in *scan lines*, create video frames. *NTSC* images are 640 pixels wide by 480 pixels high. *D-1* images are 720 pixels by 486.

Platter System The most common form of projection in movie theatres today. The entire film, shipped to the theatres on 2000 foot *double reels*, is rolled heads-in onto one huge horizontal metal platter, much like a record turntable. The film is then threaded over a series of guides through the air, into the projector, then out of the projector and over another series of guides where it winds back (heads in) onto another huge platter. This way, the film can be projected without changeovers. All that is necessary is for someone to re-thread the film before each show. As a result, in multiple cinema operations, one projectionist can take the place of four or five. One potential drawback: a scratch or other problem beginning to occur in reel two (let us say) will go all the way through the film until the end.

Playback A musical recording played back to the actors and actresses on the set to maintain the same musical performance or dancing sync from take to take.

Playback Session A meeting in which completely edited sound effects or music tracks are played back for the director or editor so they can

543

make comments. This way, any fixes can be made before the tracks go to the much more expensive mixing stage.

Playout The process of outputting the digitally edited sequence or scene onto a tape. Also called a *digital cut.*

Plug-In An add-on computer software module, which when plugged into the Avid (or similar machine) gives additional capabilities in picture or sound.

Pop See *Beep.*

Popping Tracks The process of marking up the slates on a roll of dailies track. When this is done, you can sync them up with an already marked set of picture takes. Also called *marking up tracks.*

Post-Roll When a source or record videotape is rolled forward to make an edit, it needs a certain amount of time after the event to ensure all of the playback and record machines have properly completed playing back the tapes. This extra amount of time is called the post-roll.

Pre–Blacked Tape A tape with a *control track* already recorded onto it, but no picture or sound. Also called a *Striped Tape.*

Pre–Dub When many *units* (or *elements*) are involved in a dub it is difficult, if not impossible, to play them all at one time. In this case, similar elements are mixed together onto four channels of a *full-coat* or *DA-88* tape (all of the dialogue on one full coat or DA-88, all of the looping on another, all of the foley, all of the effects, for instance) and this new dub (also called a *pre-mix*) will replace those many elements at the mix. This premixing is called a *pre-dub.*

544

Pre-Roll When a source or record videotape is rolled forward to make an edit, it needs a certain amount of time before the event to ensure all of the playback and record machines have properly gotten up to speed before making the edit. This extra amount of time is called the *pre-roll.*

Preview 1) A screening for a non-film industry audience during which the filmmakers attempt to gauge how well their movie is playing to a general audience. 2) In linear editing, the act of going through all the actions of the edit, without recording the result, to check for accuracy.

Principal Photography The primary shooting period, beginning from the first day of shooting and ending on the wrap day.

Print After the film negative has been processed, it is pressed up against another piece of film and light is shot through it. This second piece of film will have a positive image (black will read as black, white as white, etc.) and is called the print.

Print Master After the sound *mix* is completed it needs to be encoded into whatever format the soundtrack will take on the release prints. This encoded soundtrack is called the Print Master. See also *4–2–4.*

Protection IP An *interpositive* copy of the cut *negative* (though sometimes protection IPs are made from individual takes) struck for the purpose of providing a usable negative of the film in case anything should happen to the original negative. Protection IPs are often ordered when you are going to be shipping the negative to another place, or when you have finished cutting the negative and are about to start color *timing* the film.

Projector Sync When a married print runs through the projector, the location of a picture frame and its synchronous frame of sound are not directly next to each other on the married film. This is opposed to the sync when the picture and sound are on different elements, called *editorial sync* or *level sync.*

Pull-Down (1) In telecine, see *3:2 Pulldown.* (2) In film, an additional amount of track added onto the head of each mixed reel, identical to the track ending the preceding reel. This is used to prevent a sound drop-out when successive reels of married release print are cut together in movie theatres. It is necessary because the optical sound track and the picture are offset from one another.

Pull-Up An additional amount of track added onto the end of each mixed reel, identical to the track beginning the next incoming reel. This is used to prevent a sound drop-out when successive reels of married release print are cut together in movie theatres. It is necessary because the optical sound track and the picture are offset from one another.

Pulling Station A computer attached to both a massive CD player and a videotape machine. The sound editor or the assistant sound editor can go through the videotape of the film and audition sound effects against picture for selection. The selected, or pulled, effects are then transferred to a hard drive used by the sound editor on his or her *Digital Audio Workstation* (DAW) to cut the effects in sync with the picture.

545

Q

Quality Control The department at each network or studio that determines whether a finished film or videotape is technically suitable for release or airing.

1/4" Tape A standard width magnetic tape used in recording original production sound. As a result, the original tapes (recorded on the set) are often called "the quarter-inch." A more recent digital standard is the *DAT* tape.

QuickTime A program written by the Apple Computer company giving Macs and PC computers the ability to compress, edit and play back movies (with both picture and sound). Some of the non-linear digital editing systems are designed to use or create QuickTime movies.

R

RAID Redundant Array of Independent Disks. A group of computer hard drives hooked up together with a RAID controller. These combined drives act as one massive disk to provide performance beyond that available from individual drives.

Rank Properly called a "Rank-Cinetel Flying Spot Scanner." This is a brand name for a very common *telecine* machine that takes film and transfers it to videotape. As a result, the process of making a videotape from a negative is often called "ranking."

Raster The actual scanned area of a television tube.

Ratings Usually referring to the G, PG, PG-13, R and NC-17 classifications determined by *CARA*. They refer to the appropriateness of a film for children, as determined by one of a series of ratings boards.

Real-time Optical An *optical* on a digital editing system that does not need to be *rendered* in order to be played back. No new digitized material is created with a real-time optical. Normally, dissolves, fades and wipes are the only effects that can be real-time.

Reconstitution The act of taking the KEM rolls after the editor has removed the footage needed in the cut and adding leader to the picture or track to bring the rolls back into sync from head to tail.

Reel A spool of film. The term usually refers to the approximately 1000 feet 35mm spools.

Reel Balancing The act of apportioning the cut footage in a film between all the 1000 foot reels so no reel has too little or too much film on it. This way, changeovers can be made in theatres without disturbing the sound or music in a way the audience would notice.

Reel Breakdown A list of all of the reel numbers in a version of a film, with the scene numbers contained on each reel. The breakdown usually includes the length of each reel and the total running time of the film.

Reel Continuity A list of all of the scenes in a version of a film, with scenes numbers, short scene descriptions and an indication of where the breaks are in between reels. Also called a *continuity*.

Reel ID The individual reel number assigned by either the assistant or the telecine house to a roll of video dailies. This reel ID is input into the editing computer so any frame of footage can be identified for EDLs.

Reference Tones At the head of every roll of video or audio tape, or roll of sound *mag,* a series of sound tones are laid down at very specific levels. When the tape is played back, these reference tones can be used as a guide to determine just how loud the signal needs to be to precisely match the original recording. The equivalent references for picture are *Gray Cards* and *Color Cards* in film, and *Color Bars* in video.

Registration IP A special type of *interpositive* stock used so the image on the IP will be as rock–steady as possible. This type of IP is often made of the backgrounds behind titles because superimposing the two things would cause any slight jiggle in the backgrounds to be very visible.

Release Print The *married* print that is sent to theatres for showing. Normally, it is not made directly from the *original camera negative* but is struck from a dupe negative, usually an *internegative.*

Removable Drives Computer storage disks that can be inserted or removed from their operating mechanisms. Examples are *Floppy Disks*, and the larger capacity drives like Zip or Jaz drives. See also *R-Mags* and *Hard Drives.*

Render The act of taking a piece or pieces of digitized material and manipulating them to create a new piece of digitized material. A rendered effect is an optical on a digital editing system that needs to be rendered into new material. *Real-time opticals*, on the other hand, don't need to be rendered to be played back.

Reposition An optical in which the image has been reframed or moved in some way. Most every reposition will require the image to be resized as well.

Resolution The amount of detail in a digital picture image. The more *compression* done on an image, the lower the resolution, i.e. the worse the picture.

Reversal An *original camera* stock with a positive image rather than a negative one.

Reverse (1) A piece of *coverage* showing the reverse of the scene from another set–up. For example, if Scene 18A is a shot of John over George's shoulder, then the reverse shot (sometimes known as the *complementary angle*) would be a shot of George over John's shoulder. (2) An optical in which the action is reversed. For example, if Paul was shown giving a dollar bill to Ringo, the reverse optical would show Paul taking the money from Ringo.

547

Rewinds Two high posts, found standing up on the edge of the *editing bench*. Shafts, which stick out of the rewinds, are used to hold the reels of film. These reels are fed off the left rewind onto the right one, usually through a *synchronizer*, set on the bench in between the two rewinds.

R-G-B (1) The three colors of the film printing process, corresponding to the three layers of emulsion on a strip of film—red, green and blue. The process is often called *Y-C-M*, named after R-G-B's complementary colors—yellow, cyan and magenta. See also *timing lights.* (2) Also refers to the three colors used in both the *component* and *composite* formats of color television.

Rippling After an editor has changed the length of a cut in video, all the subsequent edits will need to be readjusted in the edit lists. This process is called "rippling the list." In videotape editing this requires running the new EDL through a separate computer program. In digital editing programs this act is more or less automatically.

R-Mag A large capacity *hard drive* mounted in a removable crate so it can be pulled out of the drive's operating mechanics.

Roll-Off See *Academy Roll-Off.*

Roll-Up See *Crawl.*

Room Tone Background sound, usually just general ambiance, made at the scene when the footage was originally shot. The general idea behind room tone is that it is the sound behind all of the dialogue and other sounds recorded in that location. This is useful to have for filling *holes* or fixing *bumps.*

Rough Cut The first assemblage of all the edited footage.

Rough Mix See *Scratch Mix.*

Run-out The 30 or more seconds of excess leader or fill put onto the ends of any 16mm or 35mm picture reels or sound units so they will not run off the projector or sound *dummies* during the back-and-forth mixing process.

Running Another term for the screening of a film.

Rushes See *Dailies.*

S

Safe Action The area on a film or video image that will certainly be visible on projection. Anything outside of this area might not be visible on all televisions or theatre screens. Also called *Safe Area*. See also *Title Safe*.

548 **Save** To store computer information on a disk or a hard drive. If stored on a disk, this can be used as a back up. If the power to the computer goes out you will be able to restore all of your work from the back up disk. Normally, most computer editing systems will automatically save your data at regular intervals.

Scan In The process of taking film negative and running it through a machine, converting the image into digital information. This term is typically used to describe the process of taking a piece of negative to be manipulated in an optical and putting it into the digital optical house's computers before doing *CGI* work on it.

Scan Line One line of video traced from left to right across the video screen. It takes a large number of scan lines to make each video frame or *field* (there are two fields in each video frame). In typical NTSC video there are 525 lines in each frame. In PAL and SECAM video there are 625 lines.

Scene (1) A division of the script usually taking place in one location at one time. (2) In the laboratory, an individual cut; from one splice mark to the next. Outside of the lab, these are usually referred to as "shots."

Script Supervisor The person who works on the set to determine continuity. He or she also provides a number of pieces of paperwork to the production and the editing room, including the *Lined Script* and a series of notes about every take shot on the film.

Scoring Session The music recording session.

Scratch (1) An abrasive mark on the film, which actually removes one or more of the layers of emulsion. Scratches on the negative generally appear as white on the print, scratches on the print usually appear as colored or black. Some negative scratches can be removed, others cannot. (2) A term for something to be used only temporarily, such as "scratch music" or a "scratch mix."

Screening Viewing the film in a projection room.

Scribe An instrument with a sharp metal point used to write on the emulsion of the film. It is normally used to etch *code numbers* or *key numbers* onto the edge of the film when a piece of film in the cut is too short to have either.

Script Notes The notes that the script supervisor provides the editing room. Typically, they contain a list of every shot made on the film, whether it was printed or not, what lens sizes were used in the shot, the camera and sound rolls, the date shot as well as a short description of each shot.

Scrub To *jog* a piece of audio very slowly so you can hear each modulation very clearly.

SCSI Small Computer System Interface. A computer cabling system used to hook up disk drives to your main computer. It is designed for moving very large amounts of information as quickly as possible. Pronounced "scuzzy." Each disk drive on your system is assigned a unique SCSI number, or address. A number of drives can be daisy-chained to each other. One of the drives will be connected into the back of the editing machine computer through a *SCSI port*. At the other end of the chain, the final drive must have a *SCSI terminator* plugged in so every drive can be read properly. A faster system is now called SCSI-2.

SDDS Sony Dynamic Digital Sound. A digital release sound format, with a simultaneously running analog track. The digital tracks are printed outside the sprocket holes along both outer edges of 35mm film. SDDS can play up to eight channels of sound.

SECAM Séquential Couleur a Mémoire or Systeme Electronique Pour Colour Avec Memorie. A set of standards for composite video in France, the Near East and some other countries. Its distinctive features are that its color image has 625 *scan lines* per *frame* transmitted at 50 Hertz (Hz) or 25 frames per second. Not compatible with either *NTSC* or *PAL* standards.

Second Generation See *Generation*.

Second Sticks When the second assistant cameraperson claps the sticks, there may be times when they accidentally were not recorded on either the film or audio. In that case, he or she needs to clap them a second time. This is called the second sticks and the assistant editor needs to be sure he or she lines the correct audio sticks against the picture slate.

549

Second Unit A separate shooting crew used to get shots not involving the principal actors. The second unit crew usually gets scenery/location shots, action shots, *insert shots* and some *pick-up shots*.

Segue To dissolve from one piece of sound gradually into another.

Server A storage system enabling multiple computer users to access the same material, often simultaneously. This simplifies the task of having more than one editor work on a film since the drives containing the actual material don't have to be moved from one editor's machine to another's.

Set–Up (1) An individual camera position. A given scene will usually be covered with several different camera angles and lens sizes. Each of these is a different set-up. In American notation, each set-up for a given scene (say, Scene 11) will be given a different set-up letter (11, for the master, and 11A, 11B, 11C, etc. for each succeeding angle shot). In English notation each set-up, from the first day of shooting until the last, regardless of what scene it is meant for, is given a sequential set-up number, beginning with Scene 1, Take 1 on the first day. (2) The *editing bench* equipment package—synchronizer, rewinds, splicing block, et al.

Shared Card A title card with two or more credits appearing at the same time.

Shuttle See *jog*.

Signal to Noise (S/N) Ratio The ratio of good picture or audio information (signal) to the interference and distortion called *noise*. The higher the number, the better the sound or image. Second generation videotapes usually have a lower S/N then first generation tapes, so this is a way of measuring generation loss. Digital tapes generally have very good S/N.

Silent Answer Print Also called a *Mute Print*. An *answer print* not yet married to the soundtrack. Typically, anywhere from two to six answer prints are made before the sound is ready to be attached to the print. When they finally are put together the print is known as a *Married Answer Print*.

Simo Cassette An additional videotape created simultaneously with the *Master* (or *Video Master*) at the telecine session. This simo cassette is usually used by the editing room for digitizing.

Single Card A card in which only one name appears on the screen.

Single Inventory A release printing process in which more than one sound format is printed onto the same release print so the distribution company will not need to maintain separate inventories of films for each format. Also called *Single Print Inventory*.

Single Strand Printing See *A Roll Printing*

Single Stripe See *Stripe*.

Single System Projection The process of screening a film with its sound and picture married onto one piece of film. Unless you *sound* your work picture for previews, you will never screen single system until you have your *married print*.

16x9 A wide screen television format in which the aspect ratio is 16 units in width by nine units in height, as opposed to the normal television ratio of 4:3.

Skip Print An *optical* in which frames of the original shot are eliminated. Normally this is used to speed up a shot. If every other frame were skipped then the action would appear to move twice as fast. Also called a "skip frame" optical.

Slate (1) The black-and-white board struck together at the beginning of every take. It is used to provide a visible and audible sync point for synching, as well as providing a visual record of the set-up and take numbers. Also called a "clapper" or the "sticks." (2) In video, an identification card which is run at the head of every roll of video.

Slider An individual volume control, usually a tab-like piece of plastic slid up or down to raise or lower the volume of a track of sound.

Slop Dupe See *Dupe.*

Slop Mix See *Scratch Mix.*

Slop Print See *Dupe.*

Slow Motion Shot A piece of film shot at a faster than normal frame rate (*FPS*). When projected, this shot will appear to be moving in slow motion.

Slug See *Fill.*

SMPTE The Society of Motion Picture and Television Engineers. The organization responsible for establishing and maintaining technical standards for film, video and audio production and broadcast. This is the organization that developed the *SMPTE Code.* The equivalent European organization is the CCIR, or ITU.

SMPTE Code Also called SMPTE Time Code. See *Time Code.*

Sneak A preview of a film, at which audience response is gauged for the purpose of re–editing or determining an advertising campaign for the film.

Soft Version A version of the final film, recut to eliminate offensive material. This version is usually played on airlines and television.

Sort Mode *EDLs* can be sorted in several different ways, with the events being listed in order of record tape or source tape time. The designations *A-Mode, B-Mode, C-Mode, D-Mode* and *E-Mode* all describe different sort modes.

Sound Reader An amplifier. Sound from the mag film is picked up from the sound heads on the *synchronizer* and fed into this reader, where it is translated into audible sound. It is also called a "squawk box."

Sound Report The list submitted by the sound department on the set cataloguing all of the takes recorded on each 1/4" or DAT sound roll. Takes that have been selected to be transferred are circled.

Sounding The process of transferring sound from the mix full-coat onto the already *striped* magnetic tracks of a 70mm or, more rarely, a 35mm release print of a film.

Source Tape The original telecined dailies tape used as the source for editing during an *on-line* session.

551

Spacing See *Fill*.

Split Edit An edit where the picture and sound cuts do not happen at exactly the same frame. See also *L-cut*.

Split Reel A *take-up reel* that can be unscrewed into its two sides. A core is placed inside and, after the sides have been screwed back together again, it can be used as a regular take-up reel. Since flatbed editing machines use film wound onto cores rather than on reels, being able to put these cores into split reels allows the film to be shown easily in places that would normally take film only on take-ups (like projectors).

Split Screen An *optical* in which the screen is divided into any number of sections, in which different images are placed.

Spotting Session (1) A meeting at which the director, composer, editor and music editor determine exactly what music will be used for the film and where it will fall. Called a "music spotting session." (2) A similar meeting to determine all of the sound elements (effects, looping, etc.) held with the director, film editor, supervising sound editor, and looping editor. Called an "effects spotting session," a "looping spotting session," or, more generally, a "sound spotting session."

Sprockets The teeth on the film-driving mechanisms. These teeth link up with *sprocket holes* on the film and transport the film forward at a standard rate. Standard 35mm film has four sprocket holes for each frame, 16mm has one, standard 70mm has five.

552 **Sprocket Holes** The holes in the side of the film that fit over the sprockets, allowing the film or track to be moved at a predetermined rate. Also called *perfs*.

Squawk Box See *Sound Reader*.

Squeezed Image See *Anamorphic*.

SR•D A Dolby release format combining a digital sound track (Dolby D) and the normal Dolby analog optical track (Dolby SR). The digital track is an optically printed six channel soundtrack running between the sprocket holes on 35mm film. The normal analog stereo track runs parallel to it, between the sprockets holes and the image area on the film.

Start Mark A particular frame of picture or track marked near the head of the reel to give an easily seen reference point for threading up in an editing machine, projector or coding machine.

Steady Gate A pin-registered machine used for precise, stable telecine transfers. It is used primarily for the telecine of material that will be used in certain *CGI* effects requiring rock-steady backgrounds. Unlike the *EPR*, it does not run in real time.

Steenbeck A brand name for a common flatbed editing machine.

Sticks See *Slate*.

Still Store See *Frame Store*.

Stock Shot Also called *stock footage*. Often, a production will need a shot that they cannot shoot themselves—an establishing shot of a city on another continent, or an airplane flying, for instance. These shots can be usually purchased from a library that sells hard-to-obtain shots.

Storage Hard drive space. The amount of hard drive space used for digitizing picture and sound is called the Storage Capacity.

Straight Cut A term used in video editing to denote an edit where the audio and video are cut at the same place. See also *L-cut*.

Streamer A long line, usually three feet in length, drawn on the film. It is used to cue someone to perform an action—either an actor or actress to let them know that a line to be looped is coming up, or a conductor to let him or her know that a musical cue is upcoming.

Stripe A piece of clear 35mm film with one strip of oxide glued onto it for the recording of sound. In order for the track to take up correctly on reels, another, thinner, stripe is glued to the top of the film. This is called the *balance stripe* and is not usually used for recording. Also called *Mag Stripe*.

Striped Tape See *Pre-blacked tape*.

Striping (1) The act of gluing a thin layer of oxide onto a 70mm (or, occasionally, a 35mm) release print. Later, sound will be transferred onto it in a process called *sounding*. (2) Pre-recording a time code and a control track onto a videotape. See also *Blacking*.

Stutter. When playing back a digital image on a computer editing machine, occasionally the picture image will appear to momentarily freeze and then pick up playing back a second or two later. This *stuttering* effect occurs when too much digital information needs to be retrieved from the hard drives. This tends to occur more frequently at higher *resolutions* than at lower ones

553

Subtitle Writing that appears at the bottom of the screen. Usually used to translate foreign dialogue on the soundtrack.

Superimposition Also called a *super*. An optical in which one image is seen on top of another.

Surge Suppresser A power strip with circuits designed to reduce the effects of surges in electrical power. See also *UPS*.

Sweetening The term in videotape editing for all audio post-production including sound editing and mixing.

Switcher A row of switches or push buttons that works like a *patch bay*, directing audio and video signals from one machine to another.

Sync The exact alignment of picture and track so they are lined up in the order the events actually occurred during the shooting. Actors' words seem to be properly coming from their lips, door slams are heard at the exact moment when we see them, etc.

Synchronizer A machine that has several rotating wheels (locked together) with *sprockets* on them. By placing pieces of film or soundtrack on these wheels these pieces can be run in perfect sync with each other. Also called a "sync block."

Sync Point Any visual or aural place in the film that can facilitate the finding of the proper *sync* between the picture and sound. A common sync point is the *slate*.

Sync Pop A beep, usually placed at a point exactly three feet before the first frame of action and three feet after the last frame of action on each reel. Since there is no sound for a distance before and after these pops, they will be quite visible on the optical soundtrack and are useful for correctly lining up the optical track negative with the picture negative for printing *married prints*.

T

Tab Short for *Cinetab* or *Trim Tab*.

Tail Pop See *Beep*.

Tail Trim See *Trim*.

Take When the director shoots a particular set-up he or she will shoot it as many times as necessary to get the exact combination of acting, camera and sound desired. Each time the scene is shot, from the clapping of the *slate* through the director's scream of "Cut!," we call it a take. If take one is not satisfactory, the director will do take two, then take three, until he or she is happy. The next *set-up* will start with take one again.

Take-Up Moviola An upright Moviola that uses reels to pull the film vertically through the picture and sound heads.

Take-Up Reel A metal or plastic reel on which film can be wound.

Targa File A particular computer file format used for computer images on the PC platform. Targa files usually have the designation ".TGA" at the end of their names. See also *TIFF File,* and *JPEG*.

Telecine A device that takes a film image and converts it into a video image. It normally uses the *3:2 pulldown* process. It is sometimes referred to as a *film scanner.*

Television Version See *Soft Version*.

Textless A copy of a titles optical recreated *without* the original titles. It is identical in length and background image to the original and is used as the background onto which foreign language titles can be superimposed.

Three-Stripe See *Full Coat*.

Three-Track A strip of 35 mag soundtrack containing three separate channels of sound. A common usage in dailies is to put the sound of the lower track and its matching *time code* on the top or center track. *See Full Coat.*

3:2 Pulldown Because film is shot at 24 frames per second and video at 30 frames per second (in the United States) a special formula is needed to add the frames needed to properly convert the film images to video images. The 3:2 Pulldown is the formula used to do this. Every other film frame is held for three video *fields* rather than the normal two. The first video frame is two fields, the next is three, the next is two, and so on. To be accurate this should be called a *2:3*

Pulldown since the first frame is made up of two fields. In most of Europe, video is projected at 25 frames per second. If the film was shot at 24 frames, a much smaller pulldown is needed. If the film was shot at 25 frames then no pulldown is needed.

THX A trademarked sound standard developed by Lucasfilm for commercial and home theatres. Unlike the Dolby, SDDS and DTS standards, which are for film sound, THX sound is for the theatre playback environment.

TIFF File A particular computer file format used for computer images on the PC and Macintosh platforms. TIFF files usually have the designation ".TIF" at the end of their names. See also *Targa File* and *JPEG*.

Tilt A camera move in which the image moves vertically, up and down. A *pan* moves left or right.

Time Code Electronic code numbers, also called *SMPTE Code*, used on videotape and digital editing *workstations* for identification, much as edge *code numbers* are used on film. It is also used to sync tapes to each other or to another machine. It comes in two forms: *Drop Frame* and *Non-Drop Frame*.

Timing The act of correcting the color balance from the negative so prints made from it look the way the director of photography wants them. After the negative has been cut, each shot has to be timed individually so they match each other, and the naturally occurring slight differences between them can be evened out. Also called *color correction, color balancing* or *grading*.

Timing Lights The numbers, on a scale from one to 50, representing the amounts of red, green and blue (or yellow, cyan and magenta) used in the timing of a shot. Timing lights are generally listed like this: 32-47-36.

Title Words projected on the screen either with or without a picture behind them. The titles may be the credits, an identification line of type (e.g. "The Next Day" or "Manhattan, 1952"), or translated lines of dialogue. See also *Main Titles*.

Title Safe The area of a projected television or film image considered safe to put titles into. The assumption is that some television sets or film screens will not be able to screen outside of this area. See also *Safe Action*.

Tones See *Reference Tones*.

Tracking (1) Editing pre-recorded music not recorded specifically for the film. This is normally the way music is prepared for a temp dub. (2) The movement of the camera during the shooting of a take. (3) A control knob for many videotape machines controlling the precise position of the video playback head over the videotape.

Trailer The "coming attractions" we see in theaters for films soon to arrive.

Transfer (1) A sound copy. The sound recorded on the set has been laid on 1/4" or DAT tape. It must be transferred onto mag stock for use in editing. See also *One-to-One Copy*. (2) A video copy.

555

Transfer House A facility that makes sound or videotape copies.

Transform See *Kinescope.*

Trim A piece of a take left over after a portion of that take has been cut out and used in the film. A piece coming *before* the section used in the film is called a *head trim*, a piece *after* the section used is called a *tail trim.*

Trim Bin A large barrel into which takes of film are hung from a bar of pins. They are usually rectangular and lined with a felt-like material to prevent the film from scratching as it hangs down into the bin. Also called a "trim barrel."

Trim Boxes Cardboard boxes, usually about one foot square, used to store the *trims, outs* and cut work picture and track.

Trim Tabs See *Cinetabs.*

Triple Print See *Double Print.*

TRT Total Running Time. This is the length (in minutes and seconds) of the footage on a videotape. It is usually listed on the outside of the tape box as well as on the tape label.

TV Safe The portion of the filmed image generally considered safe for projection on a normal, home television set. Nearly the full 35mm frame is used on television, but many home television sets have a tendency to show less image than they receive.

24 Frame Software Computer editing machines enabling you to edit at film speed, where there are 24 frames per second, rather than the video standard of 30 frames (in the United States). Without this software, many picture and sound edits will not fall on exact film frames and the *EDL* would need to have adjustments made to it as film is conformed.

2:3 Pulldown See *3:2 Pulldown.*

U

Ultrasonic Cleaner A device, usually found in film labs, used to clean film. You can very often remove dirt that will not come off in any other way, though it does tend to remove inked code numbers as well.

U-Matic Another name for the 3/4-inch video cassette system originally developed by Sony.

Ultimatte The trade name for a high-quality special effects system similar to a *Chroma Key* system. It is used for the compositing of two shots. This is one of *plug-ins* available on the Avid system.

Undercranked Shot A shot made at a slower than normal (24fps) camera speed. When projected, the action will appear to move faster than normal. See also *Overcranked Shot.*

Underscan It is possible on many monitors to flick a switch reducing both the height and width of the frame so the edges can be seen. You would most often use the underscan position on your

556

monitor when you want to see burn-ins placed outside of the normal picture safe area.

Unit An individual sound track at the mix. Also called an *element*.

UPS Uninterruptible Power Source. A constantly charging battery pack for all of your hard drives and your computer. In the event that you suffer a power failure, the battery inside the UPS will keep your system running long enough for you or your editor to save your work and safely shut down the system.

User Bits Portions of the *VITC* and *LTC* set aside for the recording of additional information. Normally, you would request information like Keykode numbers, footage count, sound and camera roll numbers be placed in the user bits.

V

VCR A Video Cassette Recorder and playback machine. Strictly used to mean a video recorder using closed cassette reel-to-reel formats, as opposed to the VTR reel-to-reel format. Today, most people use the two terms interchangeably.

Vertical Interval Indicates the vertical *blanking* period between each video field during which the beam of picture is shut off while it is repositioned from the bottom of one field to the top of the next field. As a result, there is additional time on the videotape into which non-picture information (captioning, test and control signals, time code) can be recorded.

Vertical Interval Time Code See *VITC*.

VHS A videotape format that uses 1/2" tapes. This is the more common of the two video formats used in the home; the less common is *Betamax*.

Video Assist The process of simultaneously shooting a videotape (usually black and white) of each take through the lens of the camera. This way, performance, framing, camera moves and a host of other factors can be evaluated right on the set, as soon as a take is completed rather than waiting until the next day at *dailies*.

Videocassette A case containing video recording tape. This tape may have any one of a number of widths: 1/2" (as is common to the *VHS* and *Beta* home formats), 8mm (a more recent home format), 3/4" or Beta-SP, D-1 or a number of other digital formats.

Videodisc A form of video recording, using a laser to imprint on and, later, play back images from a shiny, flat disc.

Video Master See *Master*.

Virgin Stock Magnetic soundtrack, audio tape or videotape stock onto which nothing has yet been recorded.

Visual Time Code See *Window Code*.

VITC Vertical Interval Time Code. One of two places where time code can be placed on a tape. In VITC, the time code, in digital format, is inserted in the *Vertical Interval* between the individual fields of video. The other location is called *LTC*, Longitudinal Time Code.

Voice Over Also called *VO*. Dialog that does not come from an on screen character.

VTR Video Tape Recorder. Strictly used to mean a video recorder for reel-to-reel formats, as opposed to the VCR cassette format. Today, most people use the two terms interchangeably.

W

Walla A background sound effect of a crowd murmuring. In England, walla is often called "rhubarb" since a small crowd murmuring "rhubarb, rhubarb, rhubarb" sounds indistinct enough (i.e. no individual voices can be heard) for a murmuring crowd effect.

Wedge Also called an *exposure wedge,* or a *cinex*. A test strip of film in which the same frame of negative is sequentially printed at precisely varying colors and *densities*. This wedge is used to test color and density timing at an optical house. When a preferred color balance and density is selected (by marking the frame that looks the way the director, editor and d.p. would like), the optical is shot at that set of timing lights.

Wet Gate Printing A laboratory printing process in which the film is run through a solution of wet tetrachlorthylene before printing. This chemical fills in many kinds of surface scratches and is therefore used to clean up negative defects before release printing. The process of wet gating takes much longer than a normal printing bath.

Wild Line A line of dialogue recorded, either on the set or on a looping stage, without any picture running.

Wild Sound See *Wild Track*.

Wild Track Sound recorded on the set with no accompanying picture.

Window Dub SMPTE *Time Code* that has been *burned in* to the picture area of a videotape so it is visible. It is normally placed in a little rectangular black box somewhere near the bottom or top of the screen. Other information, such as footage, can also be burned-in. Also called *Visual Time Code* or *Window Code*.

Wipe (1) A particular kind of *optical* in which one image is replaced graphically by another image. There are many different styles of wipes; some common ones are those in which the new image is wiped across the frame horizontally, vertically, from one corner to another, or from a circle starting in the center of the frame. (2) To completely erase a magnetic sound or video tape.

Work Picture The cut-together film. Also called the *cut picture*. Together with the work track, the pair is called the "cut."

Workstation A digital editing machine. See also *Digital Audio Workstation*.

Work Track The cut-together soundtrack. Also called the *cut track*. Together with the work picture, the pair is called the "cut."

X

X-Track Dialogue lines that are going to be looped are usually split off from the original production tracks during dialogue editing. These removed lines are prepared for mixing and put onto a separate track or set of tracks in case the director wants to use them, instead of the looped lines. These tracks of original dialogue are called the X-track and the *Y-track*.

Y

Y-C-M Numbers The timing lights that the negative is printed at, representing the amounts of red, green and blue lights. These colors are also referred to by their complements: yellow, cyan and magenta, and are given on a scale of one to 50. The numbers are written as 32-47-36. See also *timing lights* or *R-G-B Numbers*.

Y-Track See *X-track*.

559

Z

Zero Cutting See *A&B Roll Printing*.

Zeroing Out Setting the footage counter to zero feet and zsero frames (0000'00).

BIBLIOGRAPHY

Books

Arijon, Daniel. *Grammar Of the Film Language*. New York: Hastings House, 1976. A discussion of the most basic of editing concepts—the shot, especially in regard to how one shot will cut with another. Extremely thorough though undeniably dull. Useful for directors, editors, and script supervisors who want to have an encyclopedia (in the smallest detail) of how scenes should be staged so they will cut together.

Baker, Fred, and Firestone, Ross. *Movie People*. New York: Douglas Book Corporation, 1972. Includes a wonderful interview with the late editor Aram Avakian, in which he discusses some of the thought processes behind cutting.

Bayes, Steve. *The Avid Handbook: Basic and Intermediate Techniques for the Media Composer and the Avid Xpress*. Boston: Focal Press, 1998. Bayes has assembled a series of techniques for both the editor and the assistant, but his book shines most when it discusses the technical knowledge that separates the good Avid assistants from the rest of the bunch. Written in an informal style, Bayes gives many tips on organization as well as discussing how to accomplish basic and intermediate tasks on the Avid.

Bazin, Andre. *What Is Cinema, Vols. I and II*. Berkeley and Los Angeles: University of California Press, 1971. Not really a book on editing, though parts of it discuss the theoretical aspects of montage.

Burder, John. *The Technique of Editing 16mm Films*. Boston: Focal Press, 1988. A reissue of an older text on the nuts and bolts of cutting 16mm films. It has a lot of detailed information, though some of it is woefully out of date.

Case, Dominic. *Motion Picture Film Processing*. Boston: Focal Press, 1985. A very good, often technical, discussion of what exactly a lab does to film. It includes a lengthy discussion of the properties of light and how film stock reacts to light, but the last half of the book works as a companion volume to the Happé book listed below.

Chambers, Everett. *Producing TV Movies*. Los Angeles: E.C. Productions, Inc. 1986. Discusses the role of the editor within the television movie process. It is useful for the light it sheds on the shortening of the editorial process in the interests of time and money.

Chell, David. *Moviemakers At Work* Redmond, Washington: Microsoft Press, 1987. An entertaining, but out of print, book containing interviews with cinematographers, editors, sound recordists and mixers, production and costume designers, makeup artists, animators, computer graphics specialists and special effects designers. The interviews with Carol Littleton and Thom Noble both offer some personal stories and advice on how to get started in the editing profession.

Cohen, Steven J. and Pappas, Basil. *Avid Media Composer Techniques and Tips*. Venice, California: Self-published, 1995. A valuable collection of Avid techniques compiled by two of the editors associated with the machine since its earliest days. Though it is primarily directed to editors, there are a number of sections with a lot of advice and tips for assistants, particularly about digitizing, cut and change lists, audio, and titles.

Dmytryk, Edward. *On Film Editing*. Boston: Focal Press, 1984. A rather entertaining and sometimes enlightening look at the process of film editing as told by an accomplished director. Also valuable from the same author are *On Screen Writing*, *On Screen Directing*, and *On Screen Acting* and *On Film*.

Eisenstein, Sergei. *Film Forum* and *Film Sense*. New York: Harcourt, Brace, 1949. Both of these works show the initial stages of an editing philosophy. Eisenstein, perhaps justifiably, is considered the titular father of montage. These works are a careful combination of theory, experiment, and inspired conjecture on the nature of editing.

Happé, Bernard. *Your Film and the Lab*. Boston: Focal Press, 1983. A very easy-to-read and informative book about what happens to your film in the lab, discussing different printing stocks and processes. A bit out of date, but very useful.

Kerner, Marvin M. *The Art of the Sound Effects Editor*. Boston: Focal Press, 1989. A very succinct (sometimes, too much so) and nicely written book focusing on the job of the sound editor. Kerner gives a lot of information about the organization of the sound editing room, as well as a general overview of the entire sound editing process. The biggest problem with the book is that it is wildly out of date, with no mention of DAWs.

Lipton, Lenny. *Independent Film Making*. San Francisco: Random House, 1972. This is one of the many how-to books for the independent or

562

college filmmaker just starting out. It is also one of the best of the lot. It caters largely to the 8mm and 16mm filmmaker, but discusses terminology and procedure that all filmmakers need.

LoBrutto, Vincent. *Selected Takes: Film Editors On Editing.* New York: Praeger Publishers, 1991. A wonderful series of interviews with some of the top editors of the past and present. A great way to learn about the craft of editing.

Lustig, Milton. *Music Editing for Motion Pictures.* New York: Hastings House, 1972. A little reference work on the details of preparing a motion picture for scoring, and dealing with other musical problems in films. Though not particularly thorough or detailed, it does compile many facts all in one place for the first time. It has not been updated since its original release, making it sadly behind the times regarding the music editor's new friends—videotape and digital editing.

McAlister, Michael J. *The Language of Visual Effects.* Los Angeles: Lone Eagle Publishing, 1993. A thorough dictionary of most of the terms you run across in visual effects. Inevitably, some of the more recent advances are not covered here, but it is a vast compilation of words often encountered in dealing with optical and CGI houses.

McBride, Joseph. *Filmmakers On Filmmaking, Volumes One and Two.* Los Angeles: J.P. Tarcher, Inc., 1983. Two books offering a collection of many of the American Film Institute's interviews with working filmmakers. Some of the directors discuss the editing process and one editor, the late Verna Fields, is interviewed. Among other things, she discusses the flow of work in the editing from the editor's point of view.

Miller, Pat P. *Script Supervising and Film Continuity.* Boston: Focal Press, 1990. A good overview of a script supervisor's duties. Much of what Miller says impacts on what the editor and assistant editor must do.

Murch, Walter. *In The Blink of an Eye, A Perspective on Film Editing.* Los Angeles: Silman-James Press, 1995. An examination of the thought processes of one of the most accomplished and artistic film editors in the field (he exquisitely edited the film THE ENGLISH PATIENT). More theoretical than most books on the subject; he also discusses how digital editing is changing the way editors work.

Nizhny, Vladimir. *Lessons with Eisenstein.* New York: Da Capo, 1979. Notes from Eisenstein's teachings. Largely concerned with the purposeful choice of camera angles and blocking. There is much to be learned from all of this as it applies to editing, though not necessarily assistant editing.

Oakey, Virginia. *Dictionary of Film and Television Terms.* New York: Barnes & Noble Books, 1983. A very thorough dictionary of most of the technical terms involved in filmmaking.

Ohanian, Thomas. *Digital Nonlinear Editing: New Approaches to Editing Film and Video.* Stoneham, MA: Butterworth-Heinemann, 1993.

A detailed and very technical, though somewhat outdated, guide to the techniques, evolution and machinery of digital editing. Slanted towards the Avid but much of the book can be applied to digital editing in general.

Pudovkin, V. I. *Film Technique and Film Acting*. London: Vision Press Ltd. Possibly the seminal work on film editing. Though a bit dated by developments in other branches of film (notably writing, sound, and acting) his theories stand up today as among the most basic and important.

Reisz, Karel, and Millar, Gavin. *The Technique of Film Editing*. New York: Hastings House, 1968. A down-to-earth discussion of editing principles that never gets too theoretical and nearly always has a valid point to make with pertinent examples.

Rosenblum, Ralph, and Karen, Robert. *When The Shooting Stops....* New York: Viking, 1979. Basically an anecdotal look at the editing process. Some amusing incidents are recounted.

Rowlands, Avril. *Script Continuity and the Production Secretary in Film & TV*. New York: Hastings House, 1977. A short book describing many of the duties of the script continuity person. Much of the discussion is valuable regarding the paperwork as well as the aspects of continuity.

Rubin, Michael. *Nonlinear: a Guide To Electronic Film and Video Editing*, Second Edition. Gainesville, FL: Triad Publishing, 1992. A short but interesting overview on the evolution of digital editing with a brief guide to many of the systems available today and in the past.

564

Schneider, Arthur. *Electronic Post-Production and Videotape Editing*. Boston: Focal Press, 1989. A good, thorough discussion of methods for various forms of video (not digital) editing.

Sherman, Eric. *Directing The Film: Film Directors On Their Art*. Los Angeles: Acrobat Books, 1976. More interviews with directors who've spoken at the American Film Institute, this time grouped by subject matter. The chapter on editing is fun to read, though not particularly illuminating for an assistant editor. There is a lot of discussion about the director/editor relationship.

Solomons, Tony. *The Digital Editing Room Handbook: An Assistant Editor's Guide To The Avid*. Sherman Oaks, CA: Hazeldean House Publishing, 1997. How could I not like a book whose title is a take-off of my own? This is a nuts and bolts look at the Avid from an assistant's point of view. It gives good advice on ways of organizing your editing. In some areas it is detailed, in others it is too brief. This is a book that will hopefully get more valuable with every new edition.

Walter, Ernest. *The Technique Of the Film Cutting Room*. New York: Hastings House, 2nd edition, 1982. An excellent and thorough work on the editing process from the technical point of view. It primarily covers the English system and is, at present, quite a bit out of date. But it remains a readable and reliable guide to the editing room.

Magazines

Many of these magazines have associated web sites, publishing some of the articles found in the print editions.

DV. The low end digital editing machines are getting better and better. This magazine, designed for the professional or semi-professional doing digital filmmaking for CD-ROMs, the Internet and the low end market, is beginning to be of more use to film professionals. Every so often they compare all of the nonlinear editing software and hardware systems available, an article fascinating for a look at what might be coming in the future of professional filmmaking.

Film + Television UPDATE. A quarterly magazine from Avid, spotlighting people and trends on their system. Usually there are several good tips and techniques.

Film & Video. This monthly magazine is an interesting blend of technical information and aesthetic discussions of films. They often have one or more well-researched interviews with directors and members of their crew. There are also sections devoted to sound and new technology. They cover features, television, music videos and commercials equally. Usually a good read.

Filmmaker. A monthly magazine for the independent filmmaker. Though they are primarily interested in the directing and writing facets of filmmaking, they occasionally discuss editing as it applies to low budget filmmaking.

Millimeter. This magazine deals with features, television, commercials and more. Less technical than *Post* it looks more like *Film and Video* but has been around quite a bit longer. There are a lot of pieces about gadgets mixed in with filmmaker interviews.

New Media. Much like DV Magazine, this monthly concentrates on reviews of new hardware and software, as well as publishing articles offering advice on digital techniques.

Post. Though primarily designed for people working in the commercial industry there is a wealth of information in this thick magazine for everyone interested in the more technical side of editing.

565

Internet Sites

Internet locations, like everything else in this fast-changing world of computers, rarely stay the same. It is not only possible, but quite likely, that some of the sites listed below will not be active when you go and type in their exceedingly long addresses. Internet search engines like Yahoo, Lycos and HotBot can help you locate any new sites or new addresses.

In the interest of saving space, I am not listing the increasing number of personal Web home pages put up by a series of capable and entertaining editors. Some of the sites listed below may offer connections (called "links" in Internet parlance) to them. I am also omitting the mandatory "http://" preceding each address.

Hardware Related Sites
Avid—**www.avid.com**
Avid-L—an archive of many discussions about the Avid, from the Avid-L Newsgroup can be found on these two sites: **www.texvideo.com/ dslazyk/avid/andybavid.htm** or **vizlab.beckman.uiuc.edu/avid/mail- archive.**
Kodak—**www.kodak.com**
Lightworks—**www.tek.com/VND/Products/Lightworks**
Media100—**www.media100.com**
Media100 Users Group—**www.wwug.com**
Postforum (contains articles, software and user forums about Media 100, Avid, animation and other Macintosh-centered topics)— **www.postforum.pair.com.**
Stock Footage Libraries
   www.archivefilms.com
   www.bbcfootage.com (the BBC television network)
   www.footagelibrary.com
   www.stocklibrary.net

Industry Related Sites
All Movie Guide—A large site devoted to reviewing films and listing their credits. Its credit listings are not as thorough as the Internet Movie Database listed below, but it is still a good way of getting credit lists for people with whom you will be interviewing.—**www.allmovie.com.**
Australian Screen Editors—**www.ozemail.com.au/~aseweb**
Cinematography Mailing List—**www.cinematography.net.**
Daily Variety—Articles from this newspaper bible of the entertainment in- dustry are available in two places: Yahoo's entertainment site and Variety's own web site. Much of the information on the latter site is not free but there are still a number of news articles daily.— **dailynews.yahoo.com/headlines/entertainment** is the Yahoo site, Variety's site is **www.variety.com.**

Digital Video—www.well.com/user/rid/vidpage

Filmmaker.com—A collection of articles and resources for the small film-maker. Some of the Web pages at this site discuss editing. There is also a good collection of links to other sites.—**www.filmmaker.com**.

Hollywood Reporter—Like its competitor's (Variety's) site, much of the information here is for a fee. Still, it is a well organized and news-worthy site.—**www.hollywoodreporter.com**.

IATSE—The web site for the grandaddy of all film unions. They maintain a long list of films and television shows scheduled for production.—**www.iatse.lm.com**

Indiewire—A site devoted to independent film. They will also, for a small fee, send you the news everyday in your e-mail. You might find some interesting job search possibilities here.—**www.indiewire.com**.

Internet Movie Database—This is an excellent source of credits for most films released worldwide in the last fifty years. You can use it to find an editor's or director's credits when you send in a resumé.—**www.imdb.com**

Los Angeles Editor's Guild—www.editorsguild.com

Telecine Interest Group—This is a collection of papers, contacts, and in-formation related to telecine facilities and operators.—**www.alegria.com/tig3**

<u>Newsgroups</u>

Newsgroups, sometimes called mailing lists or listservs, are like large electronic bulletin boards. People post notes asking for help or information, or comment on something that interests them. All of these postings are collected and sent out to the mailing list for the newsgroup. The people who receive these postings send back their own notes, often answering the posted questions or comment-ing about what they have read. Newsgroups are excellent alterna-tive sources for technical support because the answers come from people who actually use the machines.

Avid-L. Send mail requesting information to:
majordomo@udomo.calvin.edu.

Editing-L. Send mail requesting information to:
editing-l-request@lists1.best.com

Lightworks-users. Sign onto the list at:
www.tek.com/VND/Support/User_Groups/lightusg.html

INDEX

569

575

581

Unit. *See* Sound editing, unit
Upcut 163, 174
Upright. *See* Moviola, upright
UPS. *See* Universal Power Supply

V

Varispeeding
 video 473
Velvet 28
Version numbers
 in digital editing 168
Vertical Interval. *See* VITC
VHS
 cleaning tape 177
Video
 creation of 435
 dynamic 435
 lo-con 435
 release of theatrical film 436
  changes to film 435
Video Master 297
Video reel
 number
  checking 138
Videotape
 1" tape 435
 3/4" 42, 112
  sound editing, in 306
 A&B rolls, from 417
 ADR, for 372
 Beta-SP 43
  previews 448
 copies of screening cuts 219
 cost of editing on 99
 D-1 60, 101, 435, 470
 D-2 60
 dailies 111
 DigiBeta 60, 101, 435
 Editing cassettes 112
 final color corrected master 477
 foley, for 356
 formatted color corrected master
  477
 handover to sound 305
 labeling 177
 length
  television delivery 470
 machines
  cleaning 177
 mix, at 404, 413
 music 383
 pre-black 175
 S-VHS 42, 112
  sound editing, in 306
 scoring session, at 390

show master 477
sound editing, in 311, 326, 335
source 475
speed reference 335
spotting music from 400
storage 47
trailer, for 432
transform 487
varispeeding 473
VHS 44
 sound editing, in 306
 viewing cassettes 114, 159
Virgin stock 28
Virus 171
VITC 107, 110, 142, 313, 328, 335,
 381, 385
 definition 313
 stock footage 203
VocALign 378

W

WAV 202
Waveframe 353. *See* DAW
Wild track 84
 ADR 377
 coding 134
 dailies 133-134
 delivery requirements 440
 filing 157
 trim tab 134
 trims 155
Work print 414
 conforming 227
 delivery requirements 440
 negative matching, in 424
 replaced by opticals 281
 reprints for 245
Wrap out 436
 digital editing room 453

X

X and Y tracks 378, 379

Y

Y-C-M numbers 65

Z

Zero cut 415
Zero out 90, 160, 248, 264, 347
 optical counts 276

OTHER FILM & ENTERTAINMENT BOOKS FROM LONE EAGLE PUBLISHING. . .

■ PRODUCTION ■

FILM SCHEDULING
Or, How Long Will It Take To Shoot
Your Movie? (Second Edition)
by Ralph S. Singleton

*"Detailing step-by-step how one creates a produc-
tion board, shot-by-shot, day-by-day, set-by-set to
turn a shooting schedule into a workable production schedule...For every film production student
and most professionals."*

– Los Angeles Times

FILM SCHEDULING contains a new section on
computerized film scheduling. This section not
only analyzes and compares the various computer programs which are currently on the market
but also instructs the reader on how to maintain
personal control over the schedule while taking
advantage of the incredible speed a computer
offers.

$22.95 ISBN 0-943728-39-8. original trade paper, 6 x 9, 240 pp.

Used by
ALL
leading film
schools

FILM BUDGETING
Or, How Much Will It Cost
to Shoot Your Movie?
by Ralph S. Singleton

The companion book to the best-selling
Film Scheduling and its workbook (*The Film
Scheduling/Film Budgeting Workbook*), FILM
BUDGETING takes the reader through the steps
of converting a motion picture schedule to a
professional motion picture budget.

Using Francis Coppola's Academy Award
nominated screenplay, *The Conversation,* as the
basis for the examples, Singleton explains the
philosophy as well as the mechanics behind
motion picture budgeting. Readers do not have
to be computer-literate to use this text, although
computer budgeting is discussed.

Included are a complete motion picture
budget to *The Conversation,* footnotes, glossary
and index. When used in conjunction with its
companion workbook, *The Film Scheduling/Film
Budgeting Workbook,* FILM BUDGETING can
comprise a do-it-yourself course on motion
picture budgeting.

$22.95 ISBN 0-943728-65-7, original trade paper, 6 x 9,
300 pp, illustrated.

RALPH S. SINGLETON produced *SUPER NOVA,
MURDER AT 1600, LAST MAN STANDING, CLEAR AND
PRESENT DANGER, LEAP OF FAITH,* and *ANOTHER 48
HRS.* He also won an Emmy award for producing the
critically acclaimed television series, *Cagney & Lacey.*
Former head of production for Francis Coppola's
Zoetrope Studios, Singleton has earned his
reputation as "one of the best in the business."

FILM SCHEDULING/ FILM BUDGETING WORKBOOK
Do-It-Yourself Guide
by Ralph S. Singleton

Complete DO-IT-YOURSELF workbook companion to *Film Scheduling* and *Film Budgeting.*
Contains the entire screenplay to Francis
Coppola's Academy Award nominated screenplay, *The Conversation,* as well as sample
production and budget forms to be completed
by the reader. All sheets perforated.

$19.95 ISBN 0-943728-07-X, original trade paper,
9 x 11, 296 pp.

To order or for more information,
call 1-800-FILMBKS (345-6257) or go to www.loneeagle.com